Practical Data Science with Python

Learn tools and techniques from hands-on examples
to extract insights from data

Nathan George

BIRMINGHAM — MUMBAI

Practical Data Science with Python

Copyright © 2021 Packt Publishing

All rights reserved. No part of this book may be reproduced, stored in a retrieval system, or transmitted in any form or by any means, without the prior written permission of the publisher, except in the case of brief quotations embedded in critical articles or reviews.

Every effort has been made in the preparation of this book to ensure the accuracy of the information presented. However, the information contained in this book is sold without warranty, either express or implied. Neither the author, nor Packt Publishing or its dealers and distributors, will be held liable for any damages caused or alleged to have been caused directly or indirectly by this book.

Packt Publishing has endeavored to provide trademark information about all of the companies and products mentioned in this book by the appropriate use of capitals. However, Packt Publishing cannot guarantee the accuracy of this information.

Producer: Dr. Shailesh Jain
Acquisition Editor – Peer Reviews: Saby Dsilva
Project Editor: Janice Gonsalves
Content Development Editor: Alex Patterson
Copy Editor: Safis Editing
Technical Editor: Aniket Shetty
Proofreader: Safis Editing
Indexer: Tejal Daruwale Soni
Presentation Designer: Ganesh Bhadwalkar

First published: September 2021

Production reference: 1290921

Published by Packt Publishing Ltd.
Livery Place
35 Livery Street
Birmingham
B3 2PB, UK.

ISBN 978-1-80107-197-0

www.packt.com

Contributors

About the author

Nate George taught data science as a professor for 4 years at Regis University in Denver, Colorado. He has a background in chemical engineering, phosphors for LED lighting, and thin-film solar cells, and leveraged what he learned to become a data scientist. He's created data science courses for Regis, DataCamp, and Manning liveProject. Nate also mentors students for Udacity AI and machine learning nanodegrees. He currently works as a data scientist at a fintech company, Tink, in Stockholm, Sweden.

I'd like to thank my parents and siblings for their support, when writing this book and everything else. Thanks to the reviewers, David Mertz and Saloua Litayem, for their helpful reviews. I'd like to thank my PhD advisor, Ram Seshadri, for continuing to be supportive through the years, and Shailesh Jain for giving me the opportunity to write the book.

About the reviewer

Saloua Litayem is currently driving business value while leading data science teams. She has experience making sense of data via machine learning models and delivering mature automated systems, streamlining all of the model's life cycle steps (MLOps). For several years, she has worked in the Internet industry, creating and refining search engines using text (NLP) and images (content-based image retrieval). She believes that learning is a lifelong journey and has a big passion for leveraging best practices to deliver efficient and highly effective ML products.

Table of Contents

Preface

"Better than any statistician at computer science and better at statistics than any computer scientist" – this is a phrase I've heard said about data scientists since I started my official data science training. It might be true, but data science has grown to incorporate so many different fields and technologies that it might not be able to be captured with such a simple statement anymore. Not to mention that statistics, and especially computer science, cover a lot of ground, too. But as a quick-and-dirty way to describe data science in three words, "statistics + computer science" works.

Many people learn data science to improve their lives. For me, I wanted to transition out of the physical sciences, which are bound by physical locations, and have more freedom to travel around the world. Working in a digital space like data science allows for that, while high-tech manufacturing doesn't. For others, the increase in pay is alluring. For many of us, we see the stories about data scientists being happy and highly paid and are immediately interested in learning more. Some people learn data science due to their intellectual curiosity and the fun of it. In any case, if you want to be a data scientist, you'd better enjoy working with computers and data!

I wrote this book for a few reasons, and one good reason to create teaching materials or even teach courses is you will learn the materials better by teaching it. So, one thing I'd recommend doing if you want to really learn is to create some teaching materials. An easy way to do this is to write a blog post about using data science to solve a problem. It could be any dataset from Kaggle, for example, or some data you've got access to and are allowed to share.

In the book, we use Python to carry out data science. However, there are a plethora of tools for doing data science, so don't feel like Python is the only way. There is a debate among data scientists whether or not a data scientist *must* be able to program. On the one hand, being able to code enables us to use cutting-edge tools and integrate into other software products more easily.

On the other hand, not all data science work is the same, and some doesn't have to be done with code. Many people doing data science use R and other tools (such as GUIs) to carry out their work. However, Python seems to be the top choice and integrates nicely into software stacks at companies. Python, like any other skill, requires practice and dedication to master. This book is here to get you started, and I hope you have fun learning Python and data science and are excited to continue your data science journey well beyond this book.

Who this book is for

This book is for people who want to get into data science, perhaps from a different career or background (even non-technical backgrounds). The book is intended for beginner to intermediate levels of Python and data science. Some examples of people who might find this book useful are:

- Students starting or about to start a data science, analytics, or related program (for example, a Bachelor's, Master's, bootcamp, or online courses)
- Recent college graduates or college students (all levels) who want to learn something to set them apart in the job market
- Employees of companies who need or want to learn data science and machine learning techniques with Python
- People who want to shift their career toward data science and are just beginning their transition into data science

What this book covers

Part I, An Introduction and the Basics

Chapter 1, Introduction to Data Science, gives an overview of data science, including the history, top skills and tools used in the field, specializations and related fields, and best practices for data science projects.

Chapter 2, Getting Started with Python, explains installing Python and Python distributions (specifically, Anaconda), editing and running code with code editors, IPython, Jupyter Notebooks, basic use of the command line, installing Python packages and using virtual environments, Python programming basics, how to deal with errors and use documentation, and software engineering best practices (including Git and GitHub).

Part II, Dealing with Data

Chapter 3, SQL and Built-In File Handling Modules in Python, covers loading data from ordinary text files using built-in Python capabilities, using Python's built-in sqlite3 module for databases, basic SQL commands, and the SQLAlchemy package in Python.

Chapter 4, Loading and Wrangling Data with Pandas and NumPy, explains how to use the pandas and NumPy packages in Python. Using pandas, we learn how to load and save data with several different data source types (CSV, Excel files, and so on), how to carry out some basic **exploratory data analysis (EDA)**, how to prepare and clean data for later use, and some essential data wrangling tools with pandas and NumPy. We also learn how pandas uses NumPy and a few NumPy basics.

Chapter 5, Exploratory Data Analysis and Visualization, covers EDA and visualization packages in Python, such as pandas-profiling, seaborn, plotly, and more. We also cover visualization best practices.

Chapter 6, Data Wrangling Documents and Spreadsheets, shows how to use Python packages to load data from Microsoft Word and PDF documents, along with some basic preparation, cleaning, and analysis of text data. We also cover reading, writing, and extracting data from Microsoft Excel files.

Chapter 7, Web Scraping, demonstrates the basics of web scraping with base Python and Python packages. We learn about the basic structure of the internet and web pages, and how to parse web pages. Use of web **application programming interfaces (APIs)** is also covered. Finally, we wrap up with the ethics and legality of web scraping.

Part III, Statistics for Data Science

Chapter 8, Probability, Distributions, and Sampling, explains foundational probability concepts, common probability distributions in data science, and useful sampling techniques for data science.

Chapter 9, Statistical Testing for Data Science, covers some useful statistical tests, such as t- and z-tests, ANOVA and post-hoc tests, distribution testing, outlier testing, and testing for relationships between variables.

Part IV, Machine Learning

Chapter 10, Preparing Data for Machine Learning: Feature Selection, Feature Engineering, and Dimensionality Reduction, explains feature selection methods, including univariate statistical methods, such as correlation, mutual information score, chi-squared, and other feature selection methods.

We also cover feature engineering methods for categorical, datetime, and outlier data. Mathematical transformations for feature transformation such as Yeo-Johnson are covered as well. Finally, dimensionality reduction using **principal component analysis (PCA)** is covered, and other options for dimensionality reduction are presented.

Chapter 11, Machine Learning for Classification, covers using Python for machine learning classification algorithms, including binary, multi-class, and multi-label classification. The algorithms covered include logistic regression, Naïve Bayes, and **k-nearest neighbors (KNN)**.

Chapter 12, Evaluating Machine Learning Classification Models and Sampling for Classification, is about performance metrics for classification, such as accuracy, Cohen's Kappa, confusion matrices, and more. We also cover sampling imbalanced data to improve machine learning classification performance.

Chapter 13, Machine Learning with Regression, covers implementing and interpreting linear regression with the scikit-learn and statsmodels Python packages, as well as regularization of linear regression models. KNN and other models are also covered. Evaluation of regression models with metrics such as the coefficient of determination (R^2) and information criteria (such as the Akaike information criterion, AIC) is covered as well.

Chapter 14, Optimizing Models and Using AutoML, demonstrates hyperparameter optimization for ML models using random, grid, and Bayesian searches. The various packages in Python for optimizing models are discussed. We learn how to use learning curves to optimize the amount of data for an ML model. Optimizing the number of features using recursive feature selection is covered. Finally, we cover some different options for AutoML in Python and learn how to use the pycaret AutoML package.

Chapter 15, Tree-Based Machine Learning Models, explains how trees work in ML algorithms, and we learn how to use some of the most advanced tree-based ML models, including random forests, XGBoost, LightGBM, and CatBoost. We also cover feature importances from tree-based methods.

Chapter 16, Support Vector Machine (SVM) Machine Learning Models, covers the basic theory behind SVMs and how to use them for classification and regression in Python as well as tuning SVM hyperparameters.

Part V, Text Analysis and Reporting

Chapter 17, Clustering with Machine Learning, explains the theory and use of some common clustering algorithms for unsupervised learning: *k*-means clustering, DBSCAN, and hierarchical clustering. We also look at what other options exist for clustering.

Chapter 18, Working with Text, covers the basics of text analysis and **natural language processing** (**NLP**). We start with pre-processing and cleaning of text, then cover basic analysis and statistical methods for text. Then we cover unsupervised learning for text, including topic modeling. We also cover supervised learning for classification with text, and finally, sentiment analysis.

Part VI, Wrapping Up

Chapter 19, Data Storytelling and Automated Reporting/Dashboarding, explains how to string together our analysis and data into a captivating story, and best practices for communicating data and results of data science work. We also learn about dashboarding to display our analysis for monitoring results and how to use the streamlit package in Python to create a dashboard.

Chapter 20, Ethics and Privacy, covers the ethical and privacy concerns in data science, including bias in machine learning algorithms, data privacy concerns in data preparation and analysis, data privacy laws and regulations, and using data science for the common good. We cover *k*-anonymity, *l*-diversity, and *t*-closeness to measure the level of privacy in datasets along with an example.

Chapter 21, Staying Up to Date and the Future of Data Science, discusses ways to keep on top of the ever-changing field of data science, and suggests some resources for staying up to date. We also briefly discuss some of the topics we didn't cover in the book and talk about where the future of data science might be going.

To get the most out of this book

- Readers should be interested in computing, using Python, and doing data science

- This book is intended for beginners and intermediates to Python and data science, though more advanced practitioners can benefit by reading it as well (for example, to review and maybe learn some new things)

- Readers should have some basic knowledge of how to use a computer and the internet

- Installation of Python is required, but is covered in the book

Download the example code files

The code bundle for the book is hosted on GitHub at `https://github.com/PacktPublishing/Practical-Data-Science-with-Python`. We also have other code bundles from our rich catalog of books and videos available at `https://github.com/PacktPublishing/`. Check them out!

Download the color images

We also provide a PDF file that has color images of the screenshots/diagrams used in this book. You can download it here: https://static.packt-cdn.com/downloads/9781801071970_ColorImages.pdf.

Conventions used

There are a number of text conventions used throughout this book.

CodeInText: Indicates code words in text, database table names, folder names, filenames, file extensions, pathnames, dummy URLs, user input, and Twitter handles. For example: "Lists or sets can be converted to tuples with the tuple() function."

A block of code is set as follows:

```
def test_function(doPrint, printAdd='more'):
    """
    A demo function.
    """
    if doPrint:
        print('test' + printAdd)
        return printAdd
```

Any command-line input or output is written as follows:

```
SELECT * FROM artists LIMIT 5;
```

Bold: Indicates a new term, an important word, or words that you see on the screen, for example, in menus or dialog boxes. For example: "We can create a new notebook by choosing **New** and then **Python 3**."

> Warnings or important notes appear like this.

> Tips and tricks appear like this.

Get in touch

Feedback from our readers is always welcome.

General feedback: Email feedback@packtpub.com, and mention the book's title in the subject of your message. If you have questions about any aspect of this book, please email us at questions@packtpub.com.

Errata: Although we have taken every care to ensure the accuracy of our content, mistakes do happen. If you have found a mistake in this book we would be grateful if you would report this to us. Please visit, http://www.packtpub.com/submit-errata, selecting your book, clicking on the Errata Submission Form link, and entering the details.

Piracy: If you come across any illegal copies of our works in any form on the Internet, we would be grateful if you would provide us with the location address or website name. Please contact us at copyright@packtpub.com with a link to the material.

If you are interested in becoming an author: If there is a topic that you have expertise in and you are interested in either writing or contributing to a book, please visit http://authors.packtpub.com.

Share your thoughts

Once you've read *Practical Data Science with Python*, we'd love to hear your thoughts! Scan the QR code below to go straight to the Amazon review page for this book and share your feedback.

https://packt.link/r/1801071977

Your review is important to us and the tech community and will help us make sure we're delivering excellent quality content.

Part I

An Introduction and the Basics

1

Introduction to Data Science

Data science is a thriving and rapidly expanding field, as you probably already know. People are starting to come to a consensus that everyone should have some basic data science skills, sometimes called "**data literacy**." This book is intended to get you up to speed with the basics of data science using the most popular programming language for doing data science today: Python. In this first chapter, we will cover:

- The history of data science
- The top tools and skills used in data science, and why these are used
- Specializations within and related to data science
- Best practices for managing a data science project

Data science is used in a variety of ways. Some data scientists focus on the analytics side of things, pulling out hidden patterns and insights from data, then communicating these results with visualizations and statistics. Others work on creating predictive models in order to predict future events, such as predicting whether someone will put solar panels on their house. Yet others work on models for classification; for example, classifying the make and model of a car in an image. One thing ties all applications of data science together: the data. Anywhere you have enough data, you can use data science to accomplish things that seem like magic to the casual observer.

The data science origin story

There's a saying in the data science community that's been around for a while, and it goes: "*A data scientist is better than any computer scientist at statistics, and better than any statistician at computer programming.*" This encapsulates the general skills of most data scientists, as well as the history of the field.

Data science combines computer programming with statistics, and some even call data science applied statistics. Conversely, some statisticians think data science is *only* statistics. So, while we might say data science dates back to the roots of statistics in the 19th century, the roots of modern data science actually begin around the year 2000. At this time, the internet was beginning to bloom, and with it, the advent of big data. The amount of data generated from the web resulted in the new field of data science being born.

A brief timeline of key historical data science events is as follows:

- **1962**: John Tukey writes *The Future of Data Analysis*, where he envisions a new field for learning insights from data

- **1977**: Tukey publishes the book *Exploratory Data Analysis*, which is a key part of data science today

- **1991**: Guido Van Rossum publishes the Python programming language online for the first time, which goes on to become the top data science language used at the time of writing

- **1993**: The R programming language is publicly released, which goes on to become the second most-used data science general-purpose language

- **1996**: The International Federation of Classification Societies holds a conference titled "*Data Science, Classification and Related Methods*" – possibly the first time "data science" was used to refer to something similar to modern data science

- **1997**: Jeff Wu proposes renaming statistics "data science" in an inauguration lecture at the University of Michigan

- **2001**: William Cleveland publishes a paper describing a new field, "data science," which expands on data analysis

- **2008**: Jeff Hammerbacher and DJ Patil use the term "data scientist" in job postings after trying to come up with a good job title for their work

- **2010**: Kaggle.com launches as an online data science community and data science competition website

- **2010s**: Universities begin offering masters and bachelor's degrees in data science; data science job postings explode to new heights year after year; big breakthroughs are made in deep learning; the number of data science software libraries and publications burgeons.

- **2012**: Harvard Business Review publishes the notorious article entitled *Data Scientist: The Sexiest Job of the 21st Century*, which adds fuel to the data science fire.

- **2015**: DJ Patil becomes the chief data scientist of the US for two years.

- **2015**: TensorFlow (a deep learning and machine learning library) is released.

- **2018**: Google releases cloud AutoML, democratizing a new automatic technique for machine learning and data science.

- **2020**: Amazon SageMaker Studio is released, which is a cloud tool for building, training, deploying, and analyzing machine learning models.

We can make a few observations from this timeline. For one, the idea of data science was around for several decades before it became wildly popular. People foresaw that future society would need something like data science, but it wasn't until the amount of digital data became so widespread and easily accessible that data science could actually be used productively. We also note that the two most widely used programming languages in data science, Python and R, existed for 15 years before the field of data science existed in earnest, after which they rapidly took off in use as data science languages.

There is another trend happening in data science, which is the rise of data science competitions. The first online data science competition organization was Kaggle.com in 2010. Since then, they have been acquired by Google and continue to grow. Kaggle offers cash prizes for machine learning competitions (often 10k USD or more), and also has a large community of data science practitioners and learners. Several other websites have appeared and run data science competitions, often with cash prizes as well. Looking at other people's code (especially the winners' code if available) can be a good way to learn new data science techniques and tricks. Here are most of the current websites with data science competitions:

- Kaggle
- Analytics Vidhya
- HackerRank
- DrivenData (focused on social justice)
- AIcrowd
- CodaLab

- Topcoder
- Zindi
- Tianchi
- Several other specialized competitions, like Microsoft's COCO

> A couple of websites that list data science competitions are:
>
> ods.ai
>
> www.mlcontests.com

Shortly after Kaggle was launched in 2010, universities started offering master's and then bachelor's degrees in data science. At the same time, a plethora of online resources and books have been released, teaching data science in a variety of ways.

As we can see, in the late 2010s and early 2020s, some aspects of data science started to become automated. This scares people who think data science might become fully automated soon. While some aspects of data science can be automated, it is still necessary to have someone with the data science know-how in order to properly use automated data science systems. It's also useful to have the skills to do data science from scratch by writing code, which offers ultimate flexibility. A data scientist is also still needed for a data science project in order to understand business requirements, implement data science products in production, and communicate the results of data science work to others.

Automated data science tools include **automatic machine learning** (**AutoML**) through Google Cloud, Amazon's AWS, Azure, H2O, and more. With AutoML, we can screen several machine learning models quickly in order to optimize predictive performance. Automated data cleaning is also being developed. At the same time that this automation is happening, we are also seeing a desire by companies to build "data literacy" among their employees. This "data literacy" means understanding some basic statistics and data science techniques, such as utilizing modern digital data and tools to benefit the organization by converting data into information. Practically speaking, this means we can take data from an Excel spreadsheet or database and create statistical visualizations and machine learning models to extract meaning from the data. In more advanced cases, this can mean creating predictive machine learning models that are used to guide decision making or can be sold to customers.

As we move into the future with data science, we will likely see an expansion of the toolsets available and automation of mundane work. We also anticipate organizations will increasingly expect their employees to have "data literacy" skills, including basic data science knowledge and techniques.

This should help organizations make better data-driven decisions, improve their bottom lines, and be able to utilize their data more effectively.

 If you're interested in reading further on the history, composition, and others' thoughts of data science, David Donoho's paper *50 Years of Data Science* is a great resource. The paper can be found here:

```
http://courses.csail.mit.edu/18.337/2016/
docs/50YearsDataScience.pdf
```

The top data science tools and skills

Drew Conway is famous for his data science Venn diagram from 2010, postulating that data science is a combination of hacking skills (programming/coding), math and statistics, and domain expertise. I'd also add business acumen and communications skills to the mix, and state that sometimes, domain expertise isn't really required upfront. To utilize data science effectively, we should know how to program, know some math/statistics, know how to solve business problems with data science, and know how to communicate results.

Python

In the field of data science, Python is king. It's the main programming language and tool for carrying out data science. This is in large part due to network effects, meaning that the more people that use Python, the better a tool Python becomes. As the Python network and technology grows, it snowballs and becomes self-reinforcing. The network effects arise due to the large number of libraries and packages, related uses of Python (for example, DevOps, cloud services, and serving websites), the large and growing community around Python, and Python's ease of use. Python and the Python-based data science libraries and packages are free and open source, unlike many GUI solutions (like Excel or RapidMiner).

Python is a very easy-to-learn language and is easy to use. This is in large part due to the syntax of Python – there aren't a lot of brackets to keep track of (like in Java), and the overall style is clean and simple. The core Python team also published an official style guide, PEP 8, which states that Python is meant to be easy to read (and hence, easy to write). The ease of learning and using Python means more people can join the Python community faster, growing the network.

Since Python has been around a while, there has been sufficient time for people to build up convenient libraries to take care of tasks that used to be tedious and involve lots of work. An example is the Seaborn package for plotting, which we will cover in *Chapter 5*, *Exploratory Data Analysis and Visualization*. In the early 2000s, the primary way to make plots in Python was with the Matplotlib package, which can be a bit painstaking to use at times. Seaborn was created around 2013 and abstracts several lines of Matplotlib code into single commands. This has been the case across the board for Python in data science. We now have packages and libraries to do all sorts of things, like AutoML (H2O, AutoKeras), plotting (Seaborn, Plotly), interacting with the cloud via software development kits or SDKs (Boto3 for AWS, Microsoft's Azure SDKs), and more. Contrast this with another top data science language, R, which does not have quite as strong network effects. AWS does not offer an official R SDK, for example, although there is an unofficial R SDK.

Similar to the variety of packages and libraries are all the ways to use Python. This includes the many distributions for installing Python, like Anaconda (which we'll use in this book). These Python distributions make installing and managing Python libraries easy and convenient, even across a wide variety of operating systems. After installing Python, there are several ways to write and interact with Python code in order to do data science. This includes the notorious Jupyter Notebook, which was first created exclusively for Python (but now can be used with a plethora of programming languages). There are many choices for **integrated development environments (IDEs)** for writing code; in fact, we can even use the RStudio IDE to write Python code. Many cloud services also make it easy to use Python within their platforms.

Lastly, the large community makes learning Python and writing Python code much easier. There is a huge number of Python tutorials on the web, thousands of books involving Python, and you can easily get help from the community on Stack Overflow and other specialized online support communities. We can see from the 2020 Kaggle data scientist survey results below in *Figure 1.1* that Python was found to be the most-used language for machine learning and data science. In fact, I've used it to create most of the figures in this chapter! Although Python has some shortcomings, it has enormous momentum as the main data science programming language, and this doesn't appear to be changing any time soon.

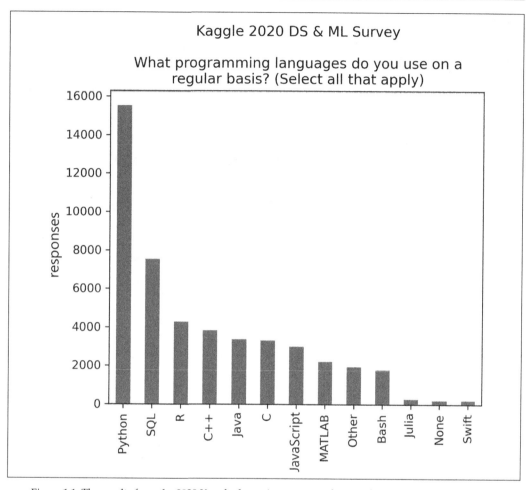

Figure 1.1: The results from the 2020 Kaggle data science survey show Python is the top programming language used for data science, followed by SQL, then R, then a host of other languages.

Other programming languages

Many other programming languages for data science exist, and sometimes they are best to use for certain applications. Much like choosing the right tool to repair a car or bicycle, choosing the correct programming tool can make life much easier. One thing to keep in mind is that programming languages can often be intermixed. For example, we can run R code from within Python, or vice versa.

Speaking of R, it's the next-biggest general-purpose programming language for data science after Python. The R language has been around for about as long as Python, but originated as a statistics-focused language rather than a general-purpose programming language like Python. This means with R, it is often easier to implement classic statistical methods, like t-tests, ANOVA, and other statistical tests. The R community is very welcoming and also large, and any data scientist should really know the basics of how to use R. However, we can see that the Python community is larger than R's community from the number of Stack Overflow posts shown below in *Figure 1.2* – Python has about 10 times more posts than R. Programming in R is enjoyable, and there are several libraries that make common data science tasks easy.

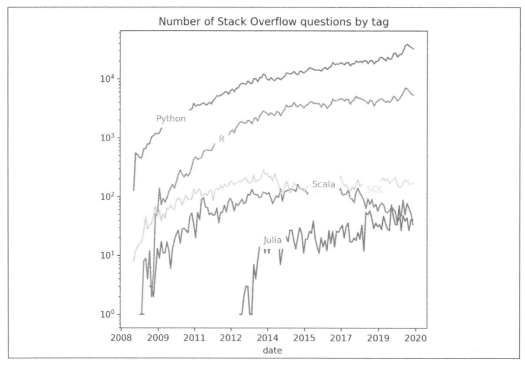

Figure 1.2: The number of Stack Overflow questions by programming language over time. The y-axis is a log scale since the number of posts is so different between less popular languages like Julia and more popular languages like Python and R.

Another key programming language in data science is SQL. We can see from the Kaggle machine learning and data science survey results (*Figure 1.1*) that SQL is actually the second most-used language after Python. SQL has been around for decades and is necessary for retrieving data from SQL databases in many situations. However, SQL is specialized for use with databases, and can't be used for more general-purpose tasks like Python and R can. For example, you can't easily serve a website with SQL or scrape data from the web with SQL, but you can with R and Python.

Scala is another programming language sometimes used for data science and is most often used in conjunction with Spark, which is a big data processing and analytics engine. Another language to keep on your radar is Julia. This is a relatively new language but is gaining popularity rapidly. The goal of Julia is to overcome Python's shortcomings while still making it an easy-to-learn and easy-to-use language. Even if Julia does eventually replace Python as the top data science language, it probably won't be for several years or decades. Julia runs calculations faster than Python, runs in parallel by default, and is useful for large-scale simulations such as global climate simulations. However, Julia lacks the robust infrastructure, network, and community that Python has.

Several other languages can be used for data science as well, like JavaScript, Go, Haskell, and others. All of these programming languages are free and open source, like Python. However, all of these other languages lack the large data science ecosystems that Python and R have, and some of them are difficult to learn. For certain specialized tasks, these other languages can be great. But in general, it's best to keep it simple at first and stick with Python.

GUIs and platforms

There are a plethora of **graphical user interfaces (GUIs)** and data science or analytics platforms. In my opinion, the biggest GUI used for data science is Microsoft Excel. It's been around for decades and makes analyzing data simple. However, as with all GUIs, Excel lacks flexibility. For example, you can't create a boxplot in Excel with a log scale on the y-axis (we will cover boxplots and log scales in *Chapter 5, Exploratory Data Analysis and Visualization*). This is always the trade-off between GUIs and programming languages – with programming languages, you have ultimate flexibility, but this usually requires more work. With GUIs, it can be easier to accomplish the same thing as with a programming language, but one often lacks the flexibility to customize techniques and results. Some GUIs like Excel also have limits to the amount of data they can handle – for example, Excel can currently only handle about 1 million rows per worksheet.

Excel is essentially a general-purpose data analytics GUI. Others have created similar GUIs, but more focused on data science or analytics tasks. For example, Alteryx, RapidMiner, and SAS are a few. These aim to incorporate statistical and/or data science processes within a GUI in order to make these tasks easier and faster to accomplish. However, we again trade customizability for ease of use. Most of these GUI solutions also cost money on a subscription basis, which is another drawback.

The last types of GUIs related to data science are visualization GUIs. These include tools like Tableau and QlikView. Although these GUIs can do a few other analytics and data science tasks, they are focused on creating interactive visualizations.

Many of the GUI tools have capabilities to interface with Python or R scripts, which enhances their flexibility. There is even a Python-based data science GUI called "Orange," which allows one to create data science workflows with a GUI.

Cloud tools

As with many things in technology today, some parts of data science are moving to the cloud. The cloud is most useful when we are working with big datasets or need to be able to rapidly scale up. Some of the major cloud providers for data science include:

- **Amazon Web Services (AWS)** (general purpose)
- **Google Cloud Platform (GCP)** (general purpose)
- Microsoft Azure (general purpose)
- IBM (general purpose)
- Databricks (data science and AI platform)
- Snowflake (data warehousing)

We can see from Kaggle's 2020 machine learning and data science survey results in *Figure 1.3* that AWS, GCP, and Azure seem to be the top cloud resources used by data scientists.

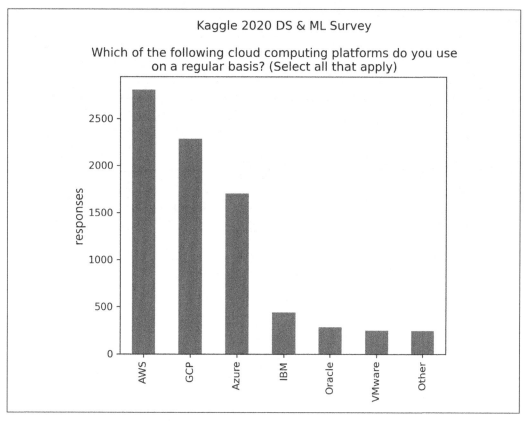

Figure 1.3: The results from the 2020 Kaggle data science survey showing the most-used cloud services

Many of these cloud services have **software development kits (SDKs)** that allow one to write code to control cloud resources. Almost all cloud services have a Python SDK, as well as SDKs in other languages. This makes it easy to leverage huge computing resources in a reproducible way. We can write Python code to provision cloud resources (called infrastructure as code, or IaC), run big data calculations, assemble a report, and integrate machine learning models into a production product. Interacting with cloud resources via SDKs is an advanced topic, and one should ideally learn the basics of Python and data science before trying to leverage the cloud to run data science workflows. Even when using the cloud, it's best to prototype and test Python code locally (if possible) before deploying it to the cloud and spending resources.

Cloud tools can also be used with GUIs, such as Microsoft's Azure Machine Learning Studio and AWS's SageMaker Studio. This makes it easy to use the cloud with big data for data science. However, one must still understand data science concepts, such as data cleaning caveats and hyperparameter tuning, in order to properly use data science cloud resources for data science. Not only that, but data science GUI platforms on the cloud can suffer from the same problems as running a local GUI on your machine – sometimes GUIs lack the flexibility to do exactly what you want.

Statistical methods and math

As we learned, data science was born out of statistics and computer science. A good understanding of some core statistical methods is a must for doing data science. Some of these essential statistical skills include:

- Exploratory analysis statistics (exploratory data analysis, or EDA), like statistical plotting and aggregate calculations such as quantiles
- Statistical tests and their principles, like p-values, chi-squared tests, t-tests, and ANOVA
- Machine learning modeling, including regression, classification, and clustering methods
- Probability and statistical distributions, like Gaussian and Poisson distributions

With statistical methods and models, we can do amazing things like predict future events and uncover hidden patterns in data. Uncovering these patterns can lead to valuable insights that can change the way businesses operate and improve the bottom line, or improve medical diagnoses among other things..

Although an extensive mathematics background is not required, it's helpful to have an analytical mindset. A data scientist's capabilities can be improved by understanding mathematical techniques such as:

- Geometry (for example, distance calculations like Euclidean distance)
- Discrete math (for calculating probabilities)
- Linear algebra (for neural networks and other machine learning methods)
- Calculus (for training/optimizing some models, especially neural networks)

Many of the more difficult aspects of these mathematical techniques are not required for doing the majority of data science. For example, knowing linear algebra and calculus is most useful for deep learning (neural networks) and computer vision, but not required for most data science work.

Collecting, organizing, and preparing data

Most data scientists spend somewhere between 25% and 75% of their time cleaning and preparing data, according to a 2016 Crowdflower survey and a 2018 Kaggle survey. However, anecdotal evidence suggests many data scientists spend 90% or more of their time cleaning and preparing data. This varies depending on how messy and disorganized the data is, but the fact of the matter is that most data is messy. For example, working with thousands of Excel spreadsheets with different formats and lots of quirks takes a long time to clean up. But loading a CSV file that's already been cleaned is nearly instantaneous. Data loading, cleaning, and organizing are sometimes called data munging or data wrangling (also sometimes referred to as data janitor work). This is often done with the pandas package in Python, which we'll learn about in *Chapter 4, Loading and Wrangling Data with Pandas and NumPy*.

Software development

Programming skills like Python are encompassed by software development, but there is another set of software development skills that are useful to have. This includes code versioning with tools like Git and GitHub, creating reproducible and scalable software products with technologies such as Docker and Kubernetes, and advanced programming techniques. Some people say data science is becoming more like software engineering, since it has started to involve more programming and deployment of machine learning models at scale in the cloud. Software development skills are always good to have as a data scientist, and some of these skills are required for many data science jobs, like knowing how to use Git and GitHub.

Business understanding and communication

Lastly, our data science products and results are useless if we can't communicate them to others. Communication often starts with understanding the problem and audience, which involves business acumen. If you know what risks and opportunities businesses face, then you can frame your data science work through that lens. Communication of results can then be accomplished with classic business tools like Microsoft PowerPoint, although other new tools such as Jupyter Notebook (with add-ons such as reveal.js) can be used to create more interactive presentations as well. Using a Jupyter Notebook to create a presentation allows one to actively demo Python or other code during the presentation, unlike classic presentation software.

Specializations in and around data science

Although many people desire a job with the title "data scientist," there are several other jobs and functions out there that are related and sometimes almost the same as data science. An ideal data scientist would be a "unicorn" and encompass all of these skills and more.

Machine learning

Machine learning is a major part of data science, and there are even job titles for people specializing in machine learning called "machine learning engineer" or similar. Machine learning engineers will still use other data science techniques like data munging but will have extensive knowledge of machine learning methods. The machine learning field is also moving toward "deployment," meaning the ability to deploy machine learning models at scale. This most often uses the cloud with **application programming interfaces** (**APIs**), which allows software engineers or others to access machine learning models, as is often called **MLOps**. However, one cannot deploy machine learning models well without knowing the basics of machine learning first. A data scientist should have machine learning knowledge and skills as part of their core skillset.

Business intelligence

The **business intelligence** (**BI**) field is closely related to data science and shares many of the same techniques. BI is often less technical than other data science specializations. While a machine learning specialist might get into the nitty-gritty details of hyperparameter tuning and model optimization, a BI specialist will be able to utilize data science techniques like analytics and visualization, then communicate to an organization what business decisions should be made. BI specialists may use GUI tools in order to accomplish data science tasks faster and will utilize code with Python or SQL when more customization is needed. Many aspects of BI are included in the data science skillset.

Deep learning

Deep learning and neural networks are almost synonymous; "deep learning" simply means using large neural networks. For almost all applications of neural networks in the modern world, the size of the network is large and deep. These models are often used for image recognition, speech recognition, language translation, and modeling other complex data.

The boom in deep learning took off in the 2000s and 2010s when GPUs rapidly increased in computing power, following Moore's Law. This enabled more powerful software applications to harness GPUs, like computer vision, image recognition, and language translation. The software developed for GPUs took off exponentially, such that in the 2020s, we have a plethora of Python and other libraries for running neural networks.

The field of deep learning has academic roots, and people spend four years or longer studying deep learning during their PhDs. Becoming an expert in deep learning takes a lot of work and a long time. However, one can also learn how to harness neural networks and deploy them using cloud resources, which is a very valuable skill. Many start-ups and companies need people who can create neural network models for image recognition applications. Basic knowledge of deep learning is necessary as a data scientist, although deep expertise is rarely required. Simpler models, like linear regression or boosted tree models, can often be better than deep learning models for reasons including computational efficiency and explainability.

Data engineering

Data engineers are like data plumbers, but if that sounds boring, don't let that fool you – data engineering is actually an enjoyable and fun job. Data engineering encompasses skills often used in the first steps of the data science process. These are tasks like collecting, organizing, cleaning, and storing data in databases, and are the sorts of things that data scientists spend a large fraction of their time on. Data engineers have skills in Linux and the command line, similar to DevOps folks. Data engineers are also able to deploy machine learning models at scale like machine learning engineers, but a data engineer usually doesn't have as much extensive knowledge of ML models as an ML engineer or general data scientist. As a data scientist, one should know basic data engineering skills, such as how to interact with different databases through Python and how to manipulate and clean data.

Big data

Big data and data engineering overlap somewhat. Both specializations need to know about databases and how to interact with them and use them, as well as how to use various cloud technologies for working with big data. However, a big data specialist should be an expert in the Hadoop ecosystem, Apache Spark, and cloud solutions for big data analytics and storage. These are the top tools used for big data. Spark began to overtake Hadoop in the late 2010s, as Spark is better suited for the cloud technologies of today.

However, Hadoop is still used in many organizations, and aspects of Hadoop, like the **Hadoop Distributed File System** (HDFS), live on and are used in conjunction with Spark. In the end, a big data specialist and data engineer tend to do very similar work.

Statistical methods

Statistical methods, like the ones we will learn about in *Chapters 8* and *9*, can be a focus area for data scientists. As we already mentioned, statistics is one of the fields from which data science evolved. A specialization in statistics will likely utilize other software such as SPSS, SAS, and the R programming language to run statistical analyses.

Natural Language Processing (NLP)

Natural language processing (NLP) involves using programming languages to understand human language as writing and speech. Usually, this involves processing and modeling text data, often from social media or large amounts of text data. In fact, one subspecialization within NLP is chatbots. Other aspects of NLP include sentiment analysis and topic modeling. Modern NLP also has overlaps with deep learning, since many NLP methods now use neural networks.

Artificial Intelligence (AI)

Artificial intelligence (AI) encompasses machine learning and deep learning, and often cloud technologies for deployment. Jobs related to AI have titles like "artificial intelligence engineer" and "artificial intelligence architect." This specialization overlaps with machine learning, deep learning, and NLP quite a lot. However, there are some specific AI methods, such as pathfinding, that are useful for fields such as robotics.

Choosing how to specialize

First, realize that you don't need to choose a specialization – you can stick with the general data science track. However, having a specialization can make it easier to land a job in that field. For example, you'd have an easier time getting a job as a big data engineer if you spent a lot of time working on Hadoop, Spark, and cloud big data projects. In order to choose a specialization, it helps to first learn more about what the specialization entails, and then practice it by carrying out a project that uses that specialization.

It's a good idea to try out some of the tools and technologies in the different specializations, and if you like a specialization, you might stick with it. We will learn some of the tools and techniques for the specializations above except for deep learning and big data. So, if you find yourself enjoying the machine learning topic quite a bit, you might explore that specialization more by completing some projects within machine learning. For example, a Kaggle competition can be a good way to try out a machine learning focus within data science. You might also look into a specialized book on the topic to learn more, such as *Interpretable Machine Learning with Python* by Serg Masis from Packt. Additionally, you might read about and learn some MLOps.

If you know you like communicating with others and have experience and enjoy using GUI tools such as Alteryx and Tableau, you might consider the BI specialization. To practice this specialization, you might take some public data from Kaggle or a government website (such as data.gov) and carry out a BI project. Again, you might look into a book on the subject or a tool within BI, such as *Mastering Microsoft Power BI* by Brett Powell from Packt. Deep learning is a specialization that many enjoy but is very difficult. Specializing in neural networks takes years of practice and study, although start-ups will hire people with less experience. Even within deep learning there are sub-specializations – image recognition, computer vision, sound recognition, recurrent neural networks, and more. To learn more about this specialization and see if you like it, you might start with some short online courses such as Kaggle's courses at https://www.kaggle.com/learn/. You might then look into further reading materials such as *Deep Learning for Beginners* by Pablo Rivas from Packt. Other learning and reading materials on deep learning exist for the specialized libraries, including TensorFlow/Keras, PyTorch, and MXNet.

Data engineering is a great specialization because it is expected to experience rapid growth in the near future, and people tend to enjoy the work. We will get a taste of data engineering when we deal with data in *Chapters 4, 6*, and *7*, but you might want to learn more about the subject if you're interested from other materials such as *Data Engineering with Python* by Paul Crickard from Packt.

With big data specialization, you might look into more learning materials such as the many books within Packt that cover Apache Spark and Hadoop, as well as cloud data warehousing. As mentioned earlier, the big data and data engineering specializations have significant overlap. However, specialization in data engineering would likely be better for landing a job in the near future. Statistics as a specialization is a little trickier to try out, because it can rely on using specialized software such as SPSS and SAS. However, you can try out several of the statistics methods available in R for free, and can learn more about that specialization to see if you like it with one of the many R statistics books by Packt.

NLP is a fun specialization, but like deep learning, it takes a long time to learn. We will get a taste of NLP in *Chapter 17*, but you can also try the spaCy course here: `https://course.spacy.io/en/`. The book *Hands-On Natural Language Processing with Python* by Rajesh Arumugam and Rajalingappaa Shanmugamani is also a good resource to learn more about the subject.

Finally, AI is an interesting specialization that you might consider. However, it can be a broad specialization, since it can include aspects of machine learning, deep learning, NLP, cloud technologies, and more. If you enjoy machine learning and deep learning, you might look into learning more about AI to see if you'd be interested in specializing in it. Packt has several books on AI, and there is also the book *Artificial Intelligence: Foundations of Computational Agents* by David L. Poole and Alan K. Mackworth, which is free online at `https://artint.info/2e/html/ArtInt2e.html`.

If you choose to specialize in a field, realize that you can peel off into a parallel specialization. For example, data engineering and big data are highly related, and you could easily switch from one to another. On the other hand, machine learning, AI, and deep learning are rather related and could be combined or switched between. Remember that to try out a specialization, it helps to first learn about it from a course or book, and then try it out by carrying out a project in that field.

Data science project methodologies

When working on a large data science project, it's good to organize it into a process of steps. This especially helps when working as a team. We'll discuss a few data science project management strategies here. If you're working on a project by yourself, you don't necessarily need to exactly follow every detail of these processes. However, seeing the general process will help you think about what steps you need to take when undertaking any data science task.

Using data science in other fields

Instead of focusing primarily on data science and specializing there, one can also use these skills for their current career path. One example is using machine learning to search for new materials with exceptional properties, such as superhard materials (`https://par.nsf.gov/servlets/purl/10094086`) or using machine learning for materials science in general (`https://escholarship.org/uc/item/0r27j85x`). Again, anywhere we have data, we can use data science and related methods.

CRISP-DM

CRISP-DM stands for **Cross-Industry Standard Process for Data Mining** and has been around since the late 1990s. It's a six-step process, illustrated in the diagram below.

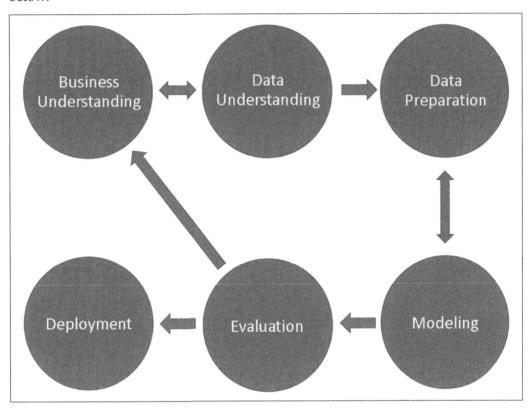

Figure 1.4: A reproduction of the CRISP-DM process flow diagram

This was created before data science existed as its own field, although it's still used for data science projects. It's easy to roughly implement, although the official implementation requires lots of documentation. The official publication outlining the method is also 60 pages of reading. However, it's at least worth knowing about and considering if you are undertaking a data science project.

TDSP

TDSP, or the **Team Data Science Process**, was developed by Microsoft and launched in 2016. It's obviously much more modern than CRISP-DM, and so is almost certainly a better choice for running a data science project today.

The five steps of the process are similar to CRISP-DM, as shown in the figure below.

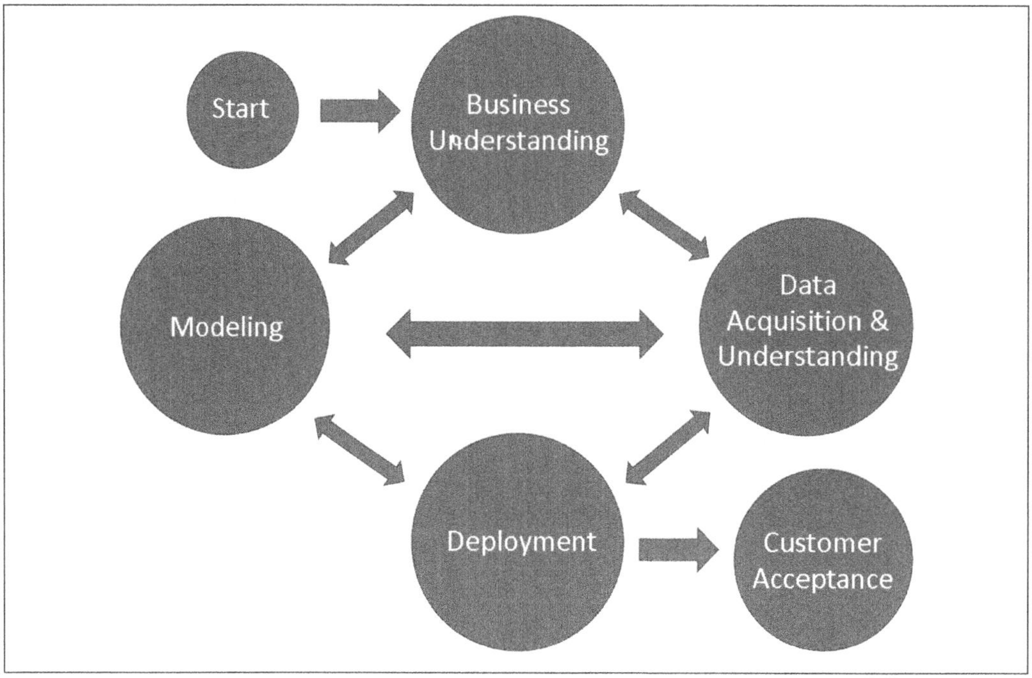

Figure 1.5: A reproduction of the TDSP process flow diagram

TDSP improves upon CRISP-DM in several ways, including defining roles for people within the process. It also has modern amenities, such as a GitHub repository with a project template and more interactive web-based documentation. Additionally, it allows more iteration between steps with incremental deliverables and uses modern software approaches to project management.

Further reading on data science project management strategies

There are other data science project management strategies out there as well. You can read about them at `https://www.datascience-pm.com/`.

You can find the official guide for CRISP-DM here:

`https://www.the-modeling-agency.com/crisp-dm.pdf`

And the guide for TDSP is here:

`https://docs.microsoft.com/en-us/azure/machine-learning/team-data-science-process/overview`

Other tools

Other tools used by data scientists include Kanban boards, Scrum, and the Agile software development framework. Since data scientists often work with software engineers to implement data science products, many of the organizational processes from software engineering have been adopted by data scientists.

Test your knowledge

To help you remember what you just learned, try answering the following questions. Try to answer the questions without looking back at the answers in the chapter at first. The answer key is included in the GitHub repository for this book (`https://github.com/PacktPublishing/Practical-Data-Science-with-Python`).

1. What are the top three data science programming languages, in order, according to the 2020 Kaggle data science and machine learning survey?

2. What is the trade-off between using a GUI versus using a programming language for data science? What are some of the GUIs for data science that we mentioned?

3. What are the top three cloud providers for data science and machine learning according to the Kaggle 2020 survey?

4. What percentage of time do data scientists spend cleaning and preparing data?

5. What specializations in and around data science did we discuss?

6. What data science project management strategies did we discuss, and which one is the most recent? What are their acronyms and what do the acronyms stand for?

7. What are the steps in the two data science project management strategies we discussed? Try to draw the diagrams of the strategies from memory.

Summary

You should now have a basic understanding of how data science came to be, what tools and techniques are used in the field, specializations in data science, and some strategies for managing data science projects. We saw how the ideas behind data science have been around for decades, but data science didn't take off until the 2010s. It was in the 2000s and 2010s that the deluge of data from the internet coupled with high-powered computers enabled us to carry out useful analysis on large datasets.

We've also seen some of the skills we'll need to learn to do data science, many of which we will tackle throughout this book. Among those skills are Python and general programming skills, software development skills, statistics and mathematics for data science, business knowledge and communication skills, cloud tools, machine learning, and GUIs.

We've seen some specializations in data science as well, like machine learning and data engineering. Lastly, we looked at some data science project management strategies that can help organize a team data science project.

Now that we know a bit about data science, we can learn about the lingua franca of data science: Python.

2

Getting Started with Python

As we already discovered in *Chapter 1, Introduction to Data Science*, Python is the most commonly used language for data science, and so we will be using it exclusively in this book. In this chapter, we'll go through a crash course in Python. This should get you up to speed with the basics, although to learn Python in more depth, you should seek more resources. For example, Fabrizio Roman's *Learning Python* from Packt may be a resource you might want to check out in order to learn Python more deeply.

In this chapter, we'll cover the following topics:

- Installing Python with a Python distribution (Anaconda)
- Editing Python code with code text editors and Jupyter Notebooks
- Running code with Jupyter Notebooks, IPython, and the command line
- Installing Python packages and creating virtual environments
- The basics of Python programming, including strings, numbers, loops, data structures, functions, and classes
- Debugging errors and using documentation
- Software engineering best practices, such as Git for version control

Let's get started with installing Python!

Installing Python with Anaconda and getting started

There are several ways to install Python, but the one we will use here is the Anaconda Python distribution. A distribution is a way of installing Python along with several Python packages/libraries, and possibly some other software. This saves us some time when installing and can give us additional functionalities, such as the ability to easily install complex packages with software dependencies. If you are unable to install Anaconda for whatever reason (for example, system administrative permission restrictions), you can try to instead install Python from other sources such as the official Python website (`www.python.org/downloads/`) or from the Microsoft store. In that case, you will need to exclusively use the pip package manager, and not conda.

Installing Anaconda

Our reasons for using Anaconda are severalfold. For one, Anaconda is widely used in the Python community, meaning the network effects are strong. This means a large community is available to help us with problems (for example, through Stack Overflow). It also means more people are contributing to the project. Another advantage of Anaconda is that it makes installing Python packages with complex dependencies much easier. For example, neural network packages such as TensorFlow and PyTorch require CUDA and cuDNN software to be installed, and H2O (a machine learning and AI software package) requires Java to be installed properly. Anaconda takes care of these dependencies for us when it installs these packages, saving us huge headaches and time. Anaconda comes with a GUI (Anaconda Navigator) and some other bells and whistles. It also allows us to create virtual environments with different versions of Python, which we will get to soon.

Installing Anaconda should be relatively easy. We simply query an internet search engine for "`download Anaconda`" and install it with the installer (currently, the download page is located at `www.anaconda.com/products/individual`). When installing Anaconda on Mac, there shouldn't be any options that change things drastically – going with the defaults should be fine. On Linux, be sure to select **yes** when asked **Do you wish the installer to initialize Anaconda3 by running conda init?**. The recommended settings from Anaconda's documentation should work well for installation (`docs.anaconda.com/anaconda/install/`). For Windows, I usually check the box for **Add Anaconda3 to my PATH environment variable**, even though this is not recommended. This will allow us to run Python and conda from any terminal or shell on our system.

You could also manually add conda and Anaconda Python to your PATH environment variable, but checking the box upon installation is easier (even though Anaconda doesn't recommend doing it). In my experience, I haven't had problems when checking the **Add to PATH** box on Windows Anaconda installations.

Once Anaconda is installed, you should be able to open a terminal or Command Prompt and run the command python to get to a basic Python shell, which we will cover in the next section. Now on to the next step – actually running Python code!

Running Python code

We will cover several options for running code here: the base Python shell, IPython, and Jupyter Notebooks. Some text editors and IDEs also allow us to run Python code from within the editor or IDE, although we will not cover that here.

The Python shell

There are several ways to run Python code, but let's start with the simplest – running code through a simple Python shell. Python is what's called an "interpreted" language, meaning code can be run on-the-fly (it's not converted into machine code). Compiling code means translating the human-readable code to machine code, which is a string of 1s and 0s that are given as instructions to a CPU. Interpreting code means running it by translating Python code on-the-fly to instructions the computer can run more directly. Compiled code usually runs faster than interpreted code, but we have the extra steps of compiling the program and then running it. This means we cannot run code interactively one bit at a time. So, interpreted code has the advantage of being able to run code interactively and one line at a time, while compiled code typically runs faster.

To try out Python's interpreted code execution, we should first open a terminal on Mac or Linux, or an Anaconda PowerShell Prompt from the Start menu on Windows (PowerShell has more commands available than a plain Command Prompt on Windows). With our command line ready, we then simply type python, et voilà! We have access to the Python shell. You can try some basic commands, such as 2 + 2 and print('hello').

This allows us to run Python commands as we want and see the results in real time. This is called a **REPL** – a **read-eval-print loop**:

```
Anaconda Powershell Prompt                                                      —  □  ×
(base) PS C:\Users\words> python
Python 3.7.9 (default, Aug 31 2020, 17:10:11) [MSC v.1916 64 bit (AMD64)] :: Anaconda, Inc. on win32
Type "help", "copyright", "credits" or "license" for more information.
>>> 2+2
4
>>> print('hello')
hello
>>>
```

Figure 2.1: An example of running Python code interactively

To exit the Python shell, we can hit *Ctrl* + *d*, or type `exit()`.

Windows also has a terminal application called "Windows Terminal", which is similar to the terminals in Mac and Linux. Currently, I prefer to use Windows Terminal over other PowerShell or Command Prompt options in Windows. You can download it from `www.aka.ms/terminal`.

For Mac, iTerm2 provides a different (some would say better) shell than the default terminal.

The Python shell is good for quick-and-dirty tasks, such as running a single line of code, but has many shortcomings. The IPython shell is much better, which we will cover next.

The IPython shell

While the basic Python shell is great for quick results, it is severely lacking. An improvement is the IPython shell, or interactive Python shell. This has lots of features that the basic Python shell does not have:

- Introspection (getting information about objects in the shell)
- Interactive tab completion
- Command history
- Syntax highlighting
- "Magic" functions

To open an IPython shell, we simply type `ipython` from the command line. We can try the same commands as before (`2 + 2` and `print('hello')`), but notice the syntax is highlighted (for example, the color of the string/text `'hello'` is different from other text):

```
IPython: C:\Users\words                                    —    □    ×
(base) PS C:\Users\words> ipython
Python 3.8.3 (default, Jul  2 2020, 17:30:36) [MSC v.1916 64
 bit (AMD64)]
Type 'copyright', 'credits' or 'license' for more informatio
n
IPython 7.18.1 -- An enhanced Interactive Python. Type '?' f
or help.

In [1]: 2+2
Out[1]: 4

In [2]: print('hello')
hello

In [3]:
```

Figure 2.2: An example of running Python code with IPython

If we press the up arrow on the keyboard, we can see it brings back our previous commands, which we can edit. This is the "history" feature of IPython. We can also bring up the documentation on functions or objects by adding a question mark next to the command, such as `?print` or `print?`:

```
IPython: C:\Users\words                                    —    □    ×
In [3]: ?print
Docstring:
print(value, ..., sep=' ', end='\n', file=sys.stdout, flush=
False)

Prints the values to a stream, or to sys.stdout by default.
Optional keyword arguments:
file:  a file-like object (stream); defaults to the current
sys.stdout.
sep:   string inserted between values, default a space.
end:   string appended after the last value, default a newli
ne.
flush: whether to forcibly flush the stream.
Type:       builtin_function_or_method

In [4]:
```

Figure 2.3: Documentation for functions or objects can be brought up in IPython by using a question mark before or after a command or object

Within the Python or IPython shells, we can also use `help(print)` to bring up documentation for objects.

IPython also has several magic commands. These are prefixed with one or two percent signs (%) and entail special functionality. For example, we can copy some text on our computer (such as `print('this is pasted test')`) and paste it into IPython with the magic command `%paste`. Some of these magic functions can be run without the percent sign as well, such as `paste` – we simply type `paste` in the IPython shell and our pasted text is run once we press *Enter*. This command is very handy for pasting multiple lines of code into IPython at once:

```
IPython: C:Users/words                              –   □   ×
In [5]: paste
print('this is a paste test')

## -- End pasted text --
this is a paste test

In [6]: pas
        pass          %paste
        pasted_block  %pastebin
```

Figure 2.4: The paste magic command pastes text from the clipboard to IPython and runs it as code. It can also be autocompleted by typing some letters of "paste" and then pressing the Tab key

The IPython documentation is comprehensive and covers all of the magic commands here: `ipython.readthedocs.io/en/stable/interactive/magics.html`.

Lastly, IPython, like many other shells, has tab completion. This means we can start typing something, such as `pas`, hit the `Tab` key, and the shell will either autocomplete what we are typing (if there is only one option) or it gives us choices for the autocompletion. If we have choices, a drop-down menu will appear. The arrow keys can be used to select a choice from the drop-down menu, or the tab key will cycle through the options. Although the Python shell also has tab completion, it only works once we have typed enough of an object's name to be unambiguous (for example, `tr` will autocomplete to `try:`, but `t` will show multiple options).

To exit the IPython shell, we can press *Ctrl* + *d* twice or type `exit()`. In Windows, you must enter *y* and then press the *Enter* key after hitting *Ctrl* + *d*, and cannot send *Ctrl* + *d* again until the shell exits. With Mac and Linux, we can press *Ctrl* + *d* multiple times and exit the shell.

Jupyter

The Jupyter ecosystem encompasses a few different open source software packages. These enable the REPL code execution we saw in the Python and IPython shells, but in a way that can be saved and shared easily. The basic Jupyter tool is the Jupyter Notebook. We can open this from the Anaconda Navigator GUI, or from the command line (like a terminal). Within the GUI, there is a Jupyter Notebook panel on which we can click Launch. From the command line, we type `jupyter notebook`. Either method opens our default web browser to the Jupyter Notebook home page. From here, we can create a new notebook by choosing **New** and then **Python 3**. Other kernels besides Python 3 can be installed, including R, Julia, and many more.

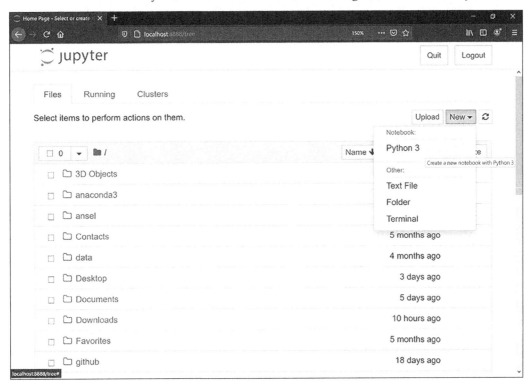

Figure 2.5: The 'New' button in the upper-right corner of a Jupyter notebook page
can create a new Jupyter notebook

Once we have a notebook open, we can run Python code in the cells. For example, try the commands we ran before (`2 + 2` and `print('hello')`) in separate cells (the results are shown in *Figure 2.6*). To run the code in a cell, we have options:

- Click the "**Run**" button on the top menu bar (it contains a **play** button icon)
- *Shift + Enter*

- *Ctrl + Enter* (or *Cmd + Enter* on Mac)
- *Alt + Enter* (or *Option + Enter* on Mac)

Shift + Enter will run the code in the current cell and move to the next one, creating a new cell at the end of the notebook if we are on the last cell. The **Run** button is the same as *Shift + Enter*. *Ctrl + Enter* runs the current cell and stays on the selected cell. *Alt + Enter* runs the current cell and inserts a new cell below.

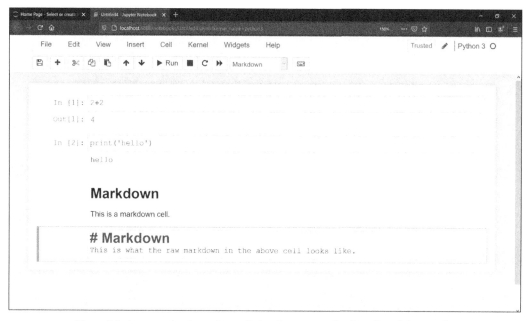

Figure 2.6: An example of running code in a Jupyter notebook and markdown cells

When we have clicked on a cell, we can enter **editing mode** by pressing *Enter*, meaning we can type things in the cell. If we press the *Esc* key, we enter **command mode**, where we are able to use hotkeys.

By default, all new cells are **code cells**, meaning they will run Python code. We can also change them to **markdown cells** for writing notes or analysis. Cell types can be switched from the menu bar by choosing **Cell → Cell Type**, or by using the drop-down menu item that has code in it by default.

Besides code and markdown, the other cell options available in the menu aren't typically used. Markdown cells use markdown syntax, for which there are many online guides. From **command mode** (after pressing the *Esc* key), we can change a cell to markdown with the hotkey *m* and back to a code cell with *y*.

Searching the internet for "markdown guide" or "markdown cheat sheet" brings up several results. One that I like is www.markdownguide.org/cheat-sheet/.

The documentation for Jupyter Notebooks is also quite good and can be found at jupyter-notebook.readthedocs.io.

Since many of the Jupyter notebooks in this book's GitHub repository are large, it's helpful to use a Jupyter notebook extension for collapsible headings. This allows us to collapse sections of the notebook so that it's easier to read. To install this plugin, we need to first install a Python package. We can run these two commands from the command line:

```
conda install -c conda-forge jupyter_contrib_nbextensions
```

Then we need to complete one other installation step:

```
jupyter contrib nbextension install --user
```

Lastly, we restart Jupyter Notebook and then select the **Nbextensions** tab along the top menu of the main Jupyter Notebooks page. From here, we check the box for the **Collapsible Headings** plugin. We may also need to deselect the option **Disable configuration for nbextensions without explicit compatibility**. These instructions are also available in the documentation for the package: https://jupyter-contrib-nbextensions.readthedocs.io/en/latest/.

Jeremy Howard of fast.ai has a great presentation on Jupyter Notebooks, showing useful tools and best practices: https://www.youtube.com/watch?v=9Q6sLbz37gk.

The Jupyter ecosystem also includes Jupyter Lab, which can run Jupyter notebooks, terminals, and edit text files in one browser window. Jupyter Lab can be started from the command line with the command jupyter lab, or from the Anaconda Navigator GUI.

Why the command line?

Although we can use the Anaconda GUI and get by just fine, it can sometimes be better to use the command line. This is because it gives us better control over our environment, helps us to understand the filesystem better, and prepares us to work with cloud resources and other **CLIs (command-line interfaces)**.

As you become more advanced with data science and programming, you may end up using the command line more and more.

Command line basics

In order to use the command line, it helps to know a few basic commands. As with IPython, when we are using a shell (such as PowerShell or a terminal), we have a command history available with up/down arrow keys. We also have tab autocompletion available by typing something and hitting the *Tab* button to autocomplete it.

> What we are learning here are the absolute minimum basics for the command line. These resources may be helpful to learn more about the command line:
>
> - https://linuxjourney.com/
> - https://www.datacamp.com/courses/introduction-to-shell
> - https://www.cfa.harvard.edu/rtdc/shell_cmds/basic/

When using PowerShell in Windows, we essentially have all the same commands as we do with a terminal in Linux or Mac. This is not true if we open a basic Command Prompt in Windows, so it's usually better to stick with PowerShell, Windows Terminal, or Anaconda PowerShell Prompt.

cd

The cd command stands for *change directory*. Note that you may be more familiar with the more common word for directory: "folder". We use cd to navigate the filesystem. For example, when we open Anaconda PowerShell in Windows, we are in our home directory (C:\Users\<your_username>\). We can move to the desktop with cd Desktop. Note that we have tab autocompletion available here too, so if we type cd Des and then hit the *Tab* key, this will complete Desktop for us. We can cycle through the autocomplete options with the *Tab* key in Windows. If in Mac or Linux, we hit the Tab key multiple times to show our options for autocompletion and can use the arrow keys to select from the options in some shells.

If we want to move up one directory (for example, from the desktop back to our home folder), we can use the command cd .. (change directory, followed by two periods). To move up two directories at once, cd ../.. is the command we can use. A single period (.) stands for the current directory, and two periods (..) stands for the directory above our current directory.

ls

The ls command lists out files and folders. If we are using a PowerShell in our Windows home directory (C:\Users\<your_username>\) and type ls, we will see our files and folders listed. ls works in most shells and terminals. If we are using a plain Windows Command Prompt (not a PowerShell), we can use dir instead of ls (and ls will not work). It's best to stick to PowerShell in Windows if possible so that ls and some other POSIX/Linux commands are available to us. In Mac and Linux, POSIX commands are already available in terminals.

Ctrl + c and Ctrl + d

If we have a process running in a terminal (for example, a Jupyter notebook) and want to cancel or stop it, we can usually hit *Ctrl + c*. Sometimes we can speed up cancelling the process by pressing *Ctrl + c* several times, and other times we only need to press *Ctrl + c* once or a few times to get the process to stop. We can also hit *Ctrl + d* to exit shells and terminals, such as the Python or IPython shell. The *Ctrl + d* combination works on Linux and Mac but doesn't always work in all situations in Windows for exiting terminals or shells.

Installing and using a code text editor – VS Code

Visual Studio Code (VS Code) is a text editor from Microsoft specifically for writing code. Their fully fledged **integrated development environment (IDE)** is Visual Studio. IDEs are software that allow us to write code, and then compile, run, and debug it from within the IDE, whereas text editors such as VS Code don't always have all the compiling and debugging tools available. When working with Python data science code, we won't always need an IDE, and a code editor is easier to start with. These code editors are an essential tool for a data scientist, since writing code is often part of the job. IDEs and code editors have lots of useful tools and extensions we can install, such as autocomplete extensions (for example, Tabnine and GitHub Copilot), which can suggest completions to partial code blocks or words. Most IDEs and code editors already come with autocomplete extensions for several common programming languages.

VS Code and Visual Studio are top choices among software engineers and data scientists. Again, this creates a network effect where more people create features for the software and more people in the community are available for support. Visual Studio and VS Code were reported as the second-most used IDE or code editor by data scientists from the 2019 and 2020 Kaggle data science surveys, coming in after Jupyter Notebooks and Jupyter Lab.

To install VS Code, we can use Anaconda Navigator (the GUI from Anaconda), or simply install it from Microsoft. Searching online for "vs code install" should get us there (at the time of writing, it is located at `code.visualstudio.com/download`). The default options when installing work well. Once installed, we should be able to open it from our program list (for example, the Start menu in Windows) or from a terminal. Note that we can also open a terminal in VS Code from the menu (**Terminal** → **New Terminal**) and run `Python` or `IPython` there.

Editing Python code with VS Code

There are two common ways to use VS Code: from the applications menu or the command line. If we open VS Code from the application menu, we can then choose **File** → **Open File** or **Open Folder**. If we open a folder, we can see all the files available in that folder on the left side of the VS Code window. Another method for opening VS Code directly from a folder is from the command line (like an Anaconda PowerShell Prompt). To do this, we open our terminal, navigate to the proper folder via the command line (with `cd`), and then type `code .` to open VS Code. No, that's not a typo – it should be `code`, a space, then a period. Recall that the period means the current directory, so the command is telling our computer to open VS Code within the current directory. The files we have open in that directory will be opened next time we run `code .` from the same directory, which is handy when working on projects over a long period of time.

Running a Python file

We will find ourselves wanting to run entire Python files at times. Python files can be run from the command line with `python file.py`, where `file.py` contains our Python code. Python files should have the extension `.py`. Try opening a PowerShell or terminal and then navigating to your desktop with `cd Desktop`. Then, open VS Code with `code .` and create a new file. Write `print('hello')` in the file and save it as `test.py`. Then, run `python test.py` from the command line (making sure you are in your Desktop directory) and you should see the output `hello` in your terminal.

Another way to run a Python file is from IPython. If we enter the IPython shell with `ipython` from the command line, we can use the magic command `run` or `%run` with our filename to run it within IPython: `run test.py`. This is convenient because it runs the file but keeps our Python shell open. This allows us to inspect variables and the results of the code within IPython, which is useful for developing and debugging code.

Note that you may see the line `if __name__ == "__main__":` in many Python files. The special variable `__name__` will be equal to `"__main__"` if we are running the file, so any code that is indented by four spaces after that will be run when we run the file.

For example, the following code will print `hello` in our terminal if we save this code in a file and run it with Python:

```
if __name__ == "__main__":
    print("hello")
```

This code is contained in the file `name_main_demo.py` in the `Chapter 2` code files on this book's GitHub repository. Note that if we import the file with `import name_main_demo`, it will not print out `"hello"`. We will cover importing packages shortly.

Installing Python packages and creating virtual environments

Part of what makes Python the *de facto* data science programming language is the ecosystem of developers and packages. Packages extend functionality and make certain tasks easier, such as running machine learning models. There are a few primary ways to install and manage packages – `conda` and `pip`.

Pip

Pip is the package installer for Python and is the classic way to manage packages in Python. The command to install packages with pip is `pip install <packagename>`. For example, a common package used in data science is pandas, which we could install with `pip install pandas`. This will install the latest version of the package by default. If our installed package is a little old and we want to upgrade it, we can upgrade with `pip --upgrade pandas`. Sometimes we need to downgrade packages for compatibility or other issues. We can install specific versions of packages, such as `pip install pandas==1.1.4`. The `--force-reinstall` flag can be added to the command to force installation of a particular version (for example, for downgrading or upgrading if the usual `pip install` is not working).

 We have only covered the basics, but pip has a comprehensive usage guide here: `https://pip.pypa.io/en/stable/user_guide/`.

Pip works for installing almost any package in Python, and can be used if other alternatives, such as conda, don't work. By default, pip installs the latest version of packages from PyPI, the Python package index at `www.pypi.org`. PyPI can be searched for packages to see which packages and what versions are available. Pip can also install packages from downloaded files or GitHub. You can find the version history of packages and much more information about almost any Python package on PyPI.

Conda

Conda is the package manager that comes with the Anaconda Python distribution. One advantage of using conda over pip is that conda will install other requirements for software to work. For example, some packages, such as H2O, require specific versions of Java to be installed. This can be difficult if we are using pip – we need to install the package and a specific version of Java separately, but conda takes care of installing Java or other software dependencies for us. Neural network packages, such as TensorFlow and PyTorch for GPUs, have complex dependencies such as CUDA and CuDNN, which can be difficult and time-consuming to install on your own. Conda takes care of these problems for us.

Installing a package with conda is similar to pip. We simply run `conda install <packagename>`. Instead of sourcing packages from PyPI, conda sources them from Anaconda's channels. It can be helpful to add the conda-forge channel, which has most of the recent versions of major packaged, with `conda config --add channels conda-forge`. The available packages can be searched at `www.anaconda.org`. Similar to pip, we can install specific versions with `conda install pandas=1.1.4`.

Anaconda's packages are organized into different channels. People can create their own channels for packages, but oftentimes the most recent versions of packages are in the conda-forge channel. We can specify a channel to install from as follows: `conda install -c conda-forge pandas`. This will install the latest version of pandas from the conda-forge channel.

One drawback of conda is that it can be slow, especially once we have many packages installed or if our computer is not very powerful. We sometimes see conda sitting at a step where it says "`solving environment`" for a long time.

Solving the environment means checking which other packages are installed and making sure that any new packages that are installed are compatible. If we are getting impatient with a conda install, we can press *Ctrl* + *c* (sometimes this needs to be pressed more than once) to cancel the install, and then use pip instead. Another option for faster installs is the `mamba` package. This is an alternative to conda that is intended to "solve the environment" for installing packages faster. It can be installed with `conda install -c conda-forge mamba`.

 There is a comprehensive guide to using conda here: `https:// docs.conda.io/projects/conda/en/latest/user-guide/ getting-started.html`.

Conda can be used to upgrade packages, including itself. After installing Anaconda, it can be a good idea to update conda and Anaconda with `conda update conda anaconda -y`. This command will update both the conda and Anaconda packages. The `-y` flag/option skips the prompt asking us to confirm the install.

Virtual environments

Virtual environments give us a separate Python installation that doesn't overlap with our base Python installation. This is useful because we can use different versions of Python (for example, 3.9 and 3.8) and we can have different virtual environments with certain packages (even pinned to certain versions, such as pandas 1.1.4) for different projects. This means that we can make our work more reproducible so that it runs in the same way no matter who runs it on which computer.

There are many ways in which to run virtual environments with Python: `virtualenv`, `venv`, `pipenv`, `conda`, and more. We will use the conda virtual environment strategy here because it uses the conda package manager. By default, we are in the "base" virtual environment when we open a terminal. We should see (`base`) on the left of our terminal line, which indicates we are in that virtual environment. To create a conda virtual environment, we type `conda create -n datasci python=3.9 -y` in a terminal. This creates a new Anaconda virtual environment called "datasci" with Python 3.9. The `-y` flag skips the step where we are asked to confirm installation of the virtual environment. You can of course name the environment whatever you want, and there are many other commands available for managing conda environments described in the documentation (`https://conda.io/projects/ conda/en/latest/user-guide/tasks/manage-environments.html`). To activate this environment, we simply type `conda activate datasci` in a terminal.

Since the dependencies of some of the packages used later in the book (like pycaret) are complex and can conflict with other packages, it's best to create a conda environment now and install packages as you need. If conda is having trouble installing packages (such as pycaret), it may be best to create a new environment specifically for pycaret.

On the left of the terminal prompt, we should see (`base`) change to (`datasci`) after typing `conda activate datasci`. We can see our available environments with `conda env list`, which should show us **base** and **datasci**. This should also show an asterisk next to the environment we are currently in. Once we are in our virtual environment, we can install packages with conda and pip.

Lastly, we can export our environment to a YAML file so that we can share our environment with others or move it to another machine. This is useful so that others can run our code, or so that we can move code from our machine on to the cloud or another production environment.

To export our environment, we can run this command in a terminal: `conda env export --from-history > datasci.yml`. The option `--from-history` only includes the names of packages we asked to be installed. It's usually good to remove the last line of the `.yml` file, which specifies the file path for the environment. Sometimes, we also need to add conda-forge to our channel list in the `.yml` file if it was not added. Note that this does not include packages installed with pip if we use the `--from-history` option, so we would need to manually add these as well. Exporting environments for cross-platform use from conda is definitely a weak point. Other more complex commands can be used to more easily export a better `.yml` environment file, like the examples shown on Stack Overflow posts on the subject (such as this one: `stackoverflow.com/questions/41274007/anaconda-export-environment-file`). However, most of those commands won't work in a Windows PowerShell.

Another way to export an environment is with `pip freeze > requirements.txt`, which can then be installed in another environment with `pip install -r requirements.txt`.

Once we have our Python virtual environment ready, we can start learning Python basics in the next section.

Python basics

Python is designed to be an easy-to-use and easy-to-read programming language. Consequently, it's also relatively easy to learn, which is part of why it's so popular.

To follow along and run the examples in this and other chapters, I recommend you use one of the following methods:

- Type or copy and paste the code into IPython, a `.py` file, or Jupyter Notebooks.
- Run the Jupyter notebook from this book's GitHub repository.

Be careful when copy-pasting code from the book, however, since sometimes lines of code can spill over on multiple lines in the book. This means when copy-pasted, additional newlines may be added that you will need to look out for (and manually remove). We can infer the intended format from syntax highlighting and formatting, or take a look at the code in the Jupyter Notebooks on the book's GitHub repository.

As you are working through examples in this book, I recommend making modifications to the code to see what happens when you change things. If you are copy-pasting or running the code from the existing notebooks, you should stop to read through and think about each chunk of code you run.

Comments will be used throughout the code, which can be included in a line after the # character like this: # this is a comment. We can also create multi-line comments with three quotation marks, like so:

```
"""
multi-line
comments
can be done like this
"""
```

These multi-line comments are actually multi-line strings that we simply don't assign to a variable.

Numbers

When we think of what to use programming for, one of the first things that comes to mind is math. A lot of what we do with Python for data science is math, so understanding how to use numbers in Python is crucial. Most of the time, we only care about two types of numbers in Python: integers and floats. Integers are whole numbers without a decimal place, such as 2. Floats have a decimal place, such as 2.0. We can check the type of an object in Python with the function type(), such as type(2), which outputs int.

With numbers, we can perform the usual math operations: addition, subtraction, multiplication, and division, as shown here:

```
2 + 2   # addition
2 - 2   # subtraction
2 * 2   # multiplication
2 / 2   # division
2 // 2  # integer division
```

The last line shows the integer division operator, //. This rounds the division result down to the nearest integer, also known as floor division. The division operator, /, is a "float" division, which returns a number as a float (with a decimal value).

We can exponentiate numbers, such as 2^3, which means 2 * 2 * 2. For example, to raise 2 to the 3rd power as we just showed, we do:

```
2 ** 3
```

If we wanted to take a square root of a number, one way is to raise the number to 0.5 as an exponent, such as 2 ** 0.5.

There is also a special operator, %, called the **modulo operator**. This returns the remainder of integer division. For example, if we integer divide 5 by 2, we get an answer of 2 but have a remainder of 1. We can perform modulo calculations like so:

```
5 % 2  # this outputs 1
```

Lastly, we can round a number in a few ways. One easy way is simply to convert a number to an integer with int(). For example, int(5.1) returns 5. This will always return the value rounded down to the nearest integer. If we wanted, we can also convert integers to floats with float().

There is a round() function, which rounds a number to the nearest integer by default. This function also has an argument, ndigits, which allows us to round a number out to a certain number of decimal digits. We will cover arguments shortly, but know that for now, these are parameters we specify when calling a function such as round(). For example, to round 2.11 to 2, we can use the built-in function round, such as round(2.11), while to round 2.11 to 2.1, we can use round(2.11, ndigits=1). We will cover the use of functions in more depth soon.

Within Python, there are several built-in modules and packages that add functionality. One that relates to numbers is the math module, which has various mathematical functions and constants. For example, if we want to get the value for the constant pi, we can use the math module:

```
import math
math.pi
```

The line import math loads the math module, and the math.pi line returns the value of pi (roughly 3.14) from that module. We will cover importing packages and modules shortly in this chapter.

A few new features of the math module were added in Python 3.9, such as math.lcm() for the least common multiple of numbers; for example:

```
math.lcm(2, 3, 5)  # least common multiple
```

This returns 30, since that is the least common multiple of 2, 3, and 5.

> The documentation for the math module in Python can be found here:
>
> docs.python.org/3/library/math.html.
>
> New features in the math module in Python 3.9 are described here:
>
> docs.python.org/3/whatsnew/3.9.html#math.
>
> We will cover documentation in more depth shortly in this chapter.

We can do a lot more with `math` in Python, but that covers the basics.

Strings

In programming, strings are text. We can create a string in Python with either single or double quotes:

```
'a string'
"a string"
```

We can also create multi-line strings with triple quotes, using three double or single quotes on each end of the string. These can also be used as multi-line comments in code, as we saw previously:

```
print("""multi-
line
string""")
```

Certain characters are special in Python strings. The most important is the backslash, \, which is the "escape" character. This tells Python that the character(s) after the backslash are to be interpreted differently. For example, the string '\n' means newline, which moves the output to the next line, and '\t' creates a "tab" character. We can also tell Python to ignore these special characters and treat them literally by creating a raw string.

This is useful for specifying file paths to data on Windows; for example:

```
print(r'C:\Users\Me\Desktop\test.csv')
```

This will print out the string 'C:\Users\Me\Desktop\test.csv'. The r in front of the string instructs Python to treat it as a raw string. Without the r, Python will throw an error. One quirk with raw strings is that a backslash at the end of the string must be escaped. So, if we are specifying a file path with a backslash at the end, we must escape it like so: `print(r'C:\Users\Me\Desktop\\')`.

Some of the operators we used for numbers can also be used for strings. The + operator joins (concatenates) strings, and the * operator can be used to repeat a string:

```
'a' + 'string'  # concatenate strings
'a' * 2  # repeat strings
```

Similar to how we convert a number to an integer or float with `int()` or `float()`, we can convert other objects (such as numbers) to strings with `str()`.

Python strings can be thought of as a series of characters and can be indexed. Indexing means selecting a subset, or part, of the string. In Python, indexing starts at 0, and is done with square brackets after a string. That is, the first element of a string can be selected with the 0th index, like 'a string'[0], which would return a. The second character in the string can be selected with 'a string'[1] (returning the space character), and so on. If we want the last character in a string, we can specify -1 as our index, such as 'a string'[-1], which would give us g. We can also select a subset of a string with indexing by providing start and stop points, such as 'a string'[0:4], which gives us the first four characters: a st. Lastly, we can choose a 'step' for our indexing as the third part of our indexing format. For example, if we want every other letter, we can index a string like this: 'a string'[::2], giving us asrn. If we want to reverse a string, we can provide -1 as the step: 'a string'[::-1], yielding gnirts a. These three parts of the Python indexing system can be thought of as a start, stop, and step, separated by colons: [start:stop:step]. If we do not specify any of start, stop, or step, the default values are taken, [0:None:1], meaning the entire string one character at a time, going forward. Tying it together, if we wanted every other character from the first five characters of a string, we could index it as [:5:2] or [0:5:2]. We will revisit Python indexing again soon when we learn about lists.

```python
'a string'[0]   # first character of a string
'a string'[-1]  # last character of a string
'a string'[0:4]  # index a string to get first 4 characters
'a string'[:4]  # index a string to get first 4 characters
'a string'[::2]  # get every other letter
'a string'[::-1]  # reverse the string
'a string'[:5:2]  # every other letter in the first 5 characters
```

Python has many built-in functions for strings. A few useful ones are .join(), .split(), .lstrip()/.rstrip(), and .removeprefix()/.removesuffix(). The join and split methods are similar but opposite in functionality. join combines a list together with a string. We will cover lists in more depth soon, but a brief explanation is that they are composed of individual elements within square brackets. For example, this line of code combines the strings 'this', 'is', 'a', and 'test' into one string joined with dashes as 'this-is-a-test':

```python
'-'.join(['this', 'is', 'a', 'test'])
```

The strings in square brackets are a list and are passed to the join() function. This function is one of Python's built-in methods for strings, and is used by putting a period after the string, and then the join() function after that. Finally, a list of values (often strings or numbers) is provided inside the parentheses of the join() function. The full line of code then returns the string 'this-is-a-test'.

Similarly, `split` takes a string and splits it into pieces. By default, it splits on white space, including spaces, tabs, and newlines. This line breaks up the string into the list of strings `['this', 'is', 'a', 'test']`:

```
'this is a test'.split()
```

Notice that this is also a function that can be used with strings, and we follow the same pattern: a string followed by a period, then the function, and then a pair of parentheses.

A few other useful methods include the stripping and removal of suffixes and prefixes. The `lstrip` and `rstrip` methods have been in Python for a while. These remove any number of characters from the beginning or end of a string. For example, this line:

```
'testtest - remove left'.lstrip('tes')
```

removes any number of consecutive characters within the set `'t'`, `'e'`, and `'s'` from the left of the string. In the preceding example, `lstrip` removes the entire `testtest` part of the string, returning a string `' - remove left'`. `rstrip` is the same, but removes characters from the end of the string.

In Python 3.9, a few new methods (functions) were added. This includes `removesuffix` and `removeprefix`. Instead of removing a set of characters from the beginning or end of strings, these remove exact matches. For example, to remove the `'testte'` string from the beginning of a string, we can do the following:

```
'testtest - remove left'.removeprefix('testte')
```

This results in the string `'st - remove left'` since it only removes the exact match of the string we provide to `removeprefix`.

 Other built-in string methods (functions) in Python are well documented in the official documentation here: `https://docs.python.org/3/library/stdtypes.html#string-methods`.

Lastly, let's cover string formatting. We can insert dynamic values from variables or calculations into strings with string formatting. We will cover variables in the next subsection – they simply hold a value for us. String formatting can be useful for printing out information from running code. For example, if we are calculating some performance metrics based on updated data that we are loading, we might want to print that out.

There are a few ways to do this, but for the majority of cases, f-string formatting is best. This works as follows:

```
f'string formatting {2 + 2}'
```

We can put any dynamic code we want in the curly brackets. This is useful for printing out metrics or other information as we're running code. We will see some other examples of f-string formatting soon. We have some of the basic variable types in Python covered, so now let's look at how to store them as variables.

Variables

Variables in programming are used to hold values. For example, say we want to keep track of how many books we've read. Here, we could use a variable. In this case, our variable would be an integer:

```
books = 1
```

Variables are set in Python with the equals sign. If we updated the variable, such as adding 1 to books, we can overwrite the old variable with books = books + 1. There is a shortcut for math operations such as this in Python too: books += 1. This works with multiplication (*=), division (/=), addition (+=), subtraction (-=), exponentiation (**=), and even the modulo operator (%=).

Once we have data in variables, we can use the normal operations above for strings and numbers. For example, to concatenate two string variables a and b into one string, we can do the following:

```
a = 'string 1'
b = 'another string'
a + b
```

The expression a + b would then return 'string 1another string'.

It's useful to know what type of object a variable is. To check this, we can use type(). For example, the following code will tell us that the type of variable a is a string (str):

```
a = 'string 1'
type(a)
```

Names for variables can only contain certain characters – numbers, letters, and underscores. Variables must also start with a letter and not numbers. It's also best to avoid variable names, which are the same as built-in functions and keywords.

If you name a variable type, for example, the type function no longer works. But don't worry – overwriting a built-in function with a variable is only temporary within the Python session you are running. You can simply exit the Python or IPython session and then start a new Python or IPython session to get back to normal. Built-in functions such as type() and built-in keywords such as None are often highlighted as different colors in code editors, IDEs, IPython, and Jupyter Notebooks. So, if you are naming a variable and it changes color to green or bold green in Jupyter Notebooks, you shouldn't use that variable name.

Speaking of None, this is a special value in Python that is similar to null in other programming languages. If a variable's value is None, this means the variable is empty. We will see some ways to use this soon. Now, on to data structures in Python.

Lists, tuples, sets, and dictionaries

In most programming languages, we have data structures that can store a sequence of values. In Python, we have lists, tuples, sets and dictionaries; let's go through them each in turn.

Lists

One of the core data structures in Python is a list. Lists are contained in square brackets and can contain several values of differing data types. Lists can even contain lists themselves. We already saw a list of strings earlier when we covered the join() method of strings. Here is another example – a list of integers:

```
[1, 2, 3]
```

Lists have several useful methods available in Python. We will cover the basics here:

- Concatenation
- Repetition
- Length
- Appending
- Sorting
- Indexing

Concatenating lists is simple; we use the plus sign. The following returns a single list of [1, 2, 3, 4, 5]:

```
[1, 2, 3] + [4, 5]
```

The other mathematical operator that works with lists is multiplication. We can use this to repeat lists. For example, we can get the sequence 1, 2, 3 twice in a row like this:

```
[1, 2, 3] * 2
```

A method we sometimes use with lists is length, or `len` for short. This is a function that gives us the number of elements in a list. For our list `[1, 2, 3]`, this tells us it has three elements:

```
len([1, 2, 3])
```

We'll see how this can be useful with loops shortly. Another useful method used in loops is appending. The following example adds the number 1 to the end of an empty list. We create an empty list with two square brackets:

```
a_list = []
a_list.append(1)
```

It can also be useful to sort lists. This can be done with the functions `sort()` and `sorted()`. These work as follows:

```
a_list = [1, 3, 2]
a_list.sort()
sorted(a_list)
```

`sort()` is a method of lists, meaning we use it by putting a period after a list, followed by `sort()`, and it sorts the list in place (meaning it returns nothing). We can run `a_list.sort()`, but then we need to print out `a_list` to see that it has been sorted. On the other hand, `sorted()` is a standalone function and returns a new list that is sorted. By default, these functions sort from least to greatest, but with the `reverse` keyword argument, they can sort from greatest to least:

```
a_list.sort(reverse=True)
```

In the preceding line of code, we are providing the `sort()` function with the `reverse` argument set to `True`, meaning we are telling the function to reverse its sorting. Note that `True` is a Boolean value, which we will talk about more soon.

Lastly, let's revisit indexing. As described in the preceding string section, Python indexing works as follows: we use square brackets to index, with the pattern `[start:stop:step]`. The default values are `[0:None:1]`, meaning we get the entire list (start to finish) and go one element at a time. The values for `start`, `stop`, and `step` must be integers or `None`. Our first element of a list is indexed at 0, so to get the first element of a list, we do the following:

```
a_list[0]
```

To get the last element of a list, we could use the length of the list minus 1, or -1:

```
a_list[len(a_list) - 1]
a_list[-1]
```

The negative number syntax works by counting backward from the last element of a list. -1 denotes the last element, -2 the second-to-last element, and so on.

If we want to select a range of elements, say the first three elements of a list, we can use indexing as follows:

```
a_list[0:3]
a_list[:3]
```

The `start` index is inclusive, meaning its value is included in the values we get back. The `stop` index is exclusive, meaning we get everything up to that element, but not including it. Since Python is 0-indexed, with the first element at an index value of 0, the index 3 means the fourth element. So, indexing a list with `[:3]` gives us the first three elements of the list. Another way to put it is that we get everything up to the fourth element in the list.

The final element of indexing is `step`. This is how many elements we step by when going through the list. To get every other element in a list, we do the following:

```
a_list[::2]
```

Since the default values for `start` and `stop` in `[start:stop:step]` are 0 and `None`, this gives us every other element of the entire list, and would be the same as `a_list[0:None:2]`. We can also reverse lists with the handy trick of using -1 as our step:

```
a_list[::-1]
```

Lists are an essential data structure in Python and are used frequently. Now that we understand lists, we can look at tuples.

Tuples

A tuple is similar to a list, but it cannot be changed once it is created – this is also called immutability. Tuples have parentheses instead of square brackets, like this:

```
a_tuple = (2, 3)
```

Tuples are called "**immutable**" objects because they cannot be changed. These are sometimes used as data structures in various Python packages. Lists or sets can be converted to tuples with the `tuple()` function:

```
tuple(a_list)
```

Note that we can similarly convert a tuple to a list with `list(a_tuple)`.

Sets

Sets follow the mathematical definition, which is a group of unique values. Sets can be created with curly brackets or the `set()` function. For example, if we want to get the unique numbers from a list, we can convert it to a set:

```
set(a_list)
```

We can also create a set from scratch with curly brackets:

```
a_set = {1, 2, 3, 3}
```

This set would have the elements 1, 2, and 3. The duplicate 3's are condensed into one element in the set since sets don't contain duplicate values.

Sets have a few useful functions that stem from mathematical concepts. Two of these functions are `union` and `difference`. If we want to combine two sets, we can use `union`:

```
set_1 = {1, 2, 3}
set_2 = {2, 3, 4}
set_1.union(set_2)
set_1 | set_2
```

The vertical pipe character (|) is an operator that performs a union of sets. In the preceding example, we would get a set with the values 1, 2, 3, and 4, since these are the unique values from the two sets we combined.

There are other operators for sets listed in the documentation: `https://docs.python.org/3/library/stdtypes.html#set-types-set-frozenset`.

For example, we can get the non-overlapping elements of sets with `.difference()`, or the dash character (minus sign): -.

Sets find uses in natural language processing, examining unique values present in datasets, and more.

Dictionaries

Dictionaries are similar to sets because they have a unique set of keys, but they also contain elements with key-value pairs. Here is an example of a dictionary:

```
a_dict = {'books': 1, 'magazines': 2, 'articles': 7}
```

The elements to the left of the colons are the keys, and to the right are values. The keys are usually strings or numbers, and the values can be almost anything. With a dictionary, we can get a value from a key like so:

```
a_dict['books']
```

The preceding line would return the value 1. Another element can be added to a dictionary in this way:

```
a_dict['shows'] = 12
```

We can also use the update method of dictionaries, like a_dict.update({'shows': 12}), to add another dictionary to a_dict. Finally, a new feature in Python 3.9 are dictionary unions, where we join two dictionaries:

```
another_dict = {'movies': 4}
joined_dict = a_dict | another_dict
```

 The union operation for dictionaries is new in Python as of version 3.9. You can read more about it here: www.python.org/dev/peps/pep-0584/.

Now that we understand the basics of lists and dictionaries, we can look at how to loop through them.

Loops and comprehensions

Loops are fundamental to programming because we can step through lists or other data structures methodically, one element at a time. In Python, a for loop can be used to loop through a list or dictionary:

```
a_list = [1, 2, 3]
for element in a_list:
    print(element)
```

This prints the elements of a_list one at a time. The for loop syntax takes the keyword for first and then a variable name (we used element in the preceding example), which stores each element as we loop through our iterable object (like a list). Then we use the keyword in, and lastly provide our list or iterable object (a_list in the preceding example, although it could be something else, such as a tuple). This is finished up with a colon character (:), a newline, and then an indentation (or four spaces). Most code editors and Jupyter Notebooks will automatically convert a tab to four spaces, so it's easy to use the *Tab* key. If you have the incorrect number of spaces, Jupyter and other syntax highlighters may highlight the under- or over-indented line's words with the color red.

A few special keywords are available with loops: continue and break. The break keyword will end a loop, while the continue keyword will immediately move on to the next iteration in the loop, skipping any code left below it. If we wanted to run only one iteration of our loop for testing, for example, we could use break:

```python
for element in a_list:
    print(element)
    break
```

Some commonly used functions with loops are range() and len(). For example, if we want to loop through a list and get the index of that list, we can do that with range and len:

```python
for i in range(len(a_list)):
    print(i)
```

The range() function takes at least one argument (the size of the range from 0 to our size), but can also take up to three arguments, start, stop, and step, which is the same idea as indexing lists and strings. For example, if we want to get a range of numbers starting at 1 and going to 6 in steps of 2, our function call to range is range(1, 7, 2). Just like indexing, the upper boundary to the range is non-inclusive, so the value 7 means our range stops at 6.

A similar approach to this is to use the built-in enumerate() function:

```python
a_list = [1, 2, 3]
for index, element in enumerate(a_list):
    print(index, element)
```

Both of these approaches would print out the numbers 0, 1, and 2, although the enumerate example also prints out the list elements 1, 2, and 3. The enumerate function returns a tuple of a counter that starts at 0, along with the elements of the list or other iterable object.

So, our output from the preceding example looks like this:

```
0 1
1 2
2 3
```

Loops through lists can also be accomplished with list comprehensions. These are handy because they can make code shorter and sometimes run slightly faster than for loops.

Here is an example of a for loop and the same thing accomplished with a list comprehension:

```
a_list = []
for i in range(3):
    a_list.append(i)

# a list comprehension for the same end-result as the loop above
a_list = [i for i in range(3)]
```

We can also loop through dictionaries. To loop through a dictionary, we can use the .items() method/function:

```
a_dict = {'books': 1, 'magazines': 2, 'articles': 7}
for key, value in a_dict.items():
    print(f'{key}:{value}')
```

The idea is the same as looping through a list, but the .items() method of dictionaries gives us tuples of keys and values from the dictionary, one pair at a time.

Notice that we are using f-string formatting here to dynamically print out the keys and values as we loop through our dictionary.

We can also use dictionary comprehensions, which are very similar to list comprehensions. The following code creates a dictionary where the keys are the values 1, 2, 3, and the values are their squares (1, 4, 9):

```
a_dict = {i: i ** 2 for i in range(1, 4)}
```

That's enough on loops to get you started, although there are other more advanced concepts and tools in Python, such as generators, that you can look forward to in your Python progression. With loops, we often incorporate conditionals and control flow techniques, which we'll cover next.

Booleans and conditionals

The last variable type we'll cover in Python are Booleans. These can take the binary values of True (1) or False (0). As implied in the parentheses, we can also use the values of 1 for True and 0 for False. We can use Booleans to test for a condition. Say we want to see whether the number of books we've read is greater than 10 – we can test it in Python like so:

```
books_read = 11
books_read > 10
```

The second line above returns the value True – a Boolean – since 11 is greater than 10. We often use these Boolean values in if/else statements. An if/else statement in Python gives us options for what to do with our code if certain conditions are met. For example, if our value of books_read falls in certain ranges, we can print out different messages:

```
books_read = 12
if books_read < 10:
    print("You have only read a few books.")
elif books_read >= 12:
    print("You've read lots of books!")
else:
    print("You've read 10 or 11 books.")
```

We use the if keyword and then provide a statement to test. This will yield a Boolean value. Next, we end the line with a colon character. Then, the next line is indented by four spaces. We can also use elif after the if statement to check for another condition and can finish up with a catch-all keyword, else. We can have as many elif sections as we want in between the if and else blocks. Notice that the format is similar to our for loops – we have a colon at the end of the line, and then an indented line after that.

For numbers, we can check whether something is greater than a specified number (books_read > 10), less than a number (books_read < 10), and can add in an equals sign for greater than or equal to (>=), or less than or equal to (<=). We can also check for exact equality (==) and inequality (!=).

A few other keywords come in handy for comparisons and conditionals. For example, we can check whether something is equal with the is keyword and negate something with the not keyword. For example:

```
a = 'test'
type(a) is str
```

This returns `True`, since a is indeed a string. To negate this, we can use `not`:

```
type(a) is not str
```

and this returns `False`.

The keyword `is` comes in handy for checking whether a variable is `None`. Sometimes we may expect a variable to have a value, but it could be `None`, and this is an easy way to check. For example:

```
a_var = None
a_var is None
```

The second line above returns `True`, since we set a_var to be `None`.

Lastly, we can use the `in` keyword to see whether some variable is in another variable. This works for checking whether a substring is in a string, or if an item is in a list, set, tuple, or dictionary. An example of checking for a substring is as follows:

```
'st' in 'a string'
```

This returns `True`, since `st` is contained within a `string`.

To check whether an element is in a list, a set, tuple, or the keys of a dictionary, we can also use the keyword `in`:

```
a_set = {1, 2, 3}
1 in a_set
```

The preceding returns `True` since 1 is in the set. Note that checking whether a value is in a set or dictionary is much faster than checking whether something is in a list. This is because Python looks through the list one element at a time. However, with sets or dictionaries, we can instantly know whether something is in there due to a mathematical and computer science technique called **hashing**.

Using the `in` keyword with a dictionary checks whether the item is in the dictionary's keys. The following also returns `True`:

```
a_dict = {1: 'val1', 2: 'val2', 3: 'val3'}
1 in a_dict
```

Boolean can be combined, such as `True and False`. Using and, we arrive at `False` if any of the individual Booleans are `False`. We can also use or, like `True or False`. If any of the statements joined by or are `True`, it will return `True`, otherwise, it returns `False`. This can be extended and other more complex Boolean operators can be used.

These basics on Booleans and conditionals will be sufficient for our purposes. We will now move on to importing and using packages and modules.

Packages and modules

Libraries, also called **packages**, are much of what makes Python so powerful for data science. Each package adds new functionality that wasn't there before, such as installing new apps on our smartphones. Python has a host of built-in modules and packages providing basic functionality, but the real power comes from community packages on GitHub and PyPI.

In most cases, a package and library are synonymous, although it seems the Python community prefers to use the label "package" (for example, "the pandas package"). These are collections of Python files with functionality – for instance, the pandas package provides functionality for loading and preparing data with Python code.

We also have modules, which are individual Python files with functionality – for example, the math module, which we looked at earlier. Combining modules makes up a library or package. One example is the standard Python library, which is made up of Python's core modules. An example of a commonly used Python module is the `time` module. Whether using a module or package in our code, we can import it in the same way. For example, the `time` module can be included in our code like so:

```
import time
```

The built-in `time` module has utilities for timing (by built-in, I mean it comes installed with Python). One function in this module is `time.time()`, which gets us the current time in seconds since the epoch (since January 1, 1970). We can change a package or module name with an alias, like so:

```
import time as t
t.time()
```

Above, we change the name of our imported time module to `t`, and then use the same `time.time()` function. But instead of `time.time()`, it's now `t.time()` with the new alias.

Sometimes, packages have sub-packages or sub-modules in order to organize them more effectively. For example, the built-in `urllib` package has a `request` module, which we can import like so:

```
import urllib.request
```

Then, if we want to open a URL with this package, we can use a function from that module:

```
urllib.request.urlopen('https://www.pypi.org')
```

Such a long string of text for a function is somewhat unwieldy. One way to shorten this is to import the specific function(s) that we want:

```
from urllib.request import urlopen
urlopen('https://www.pypi.org')
```

We can even shorten the name of the imported function with an alias, like `from urllib.request import urlopen as uo`. If we wanted to import multiple functions and/or variables from a module or package, we separate them with a comma, like this:

```
from urllib.request import urlopen, pathname2url
```

Personally, I like to import packages with their full name (such as `import util`) or with an alias if they have a long name (such as `import util_for_numbers as ufn`). Then objects from the imported package or module can be used like `ufn.some_function()`, and it's clear where the object is coming from.

While we can technically import all functions from a package or module with something like `from time import *`, this is bad practice in Python and should be avoided. It makes identifying the parent package of functions difficult when reading our code and can cause other issues if variables or functions from multiple packages overlap. The general rule for Python coding is that anything that makes the code harder to read is not preferred. Over time, you will find out that making your code easier to read helps anyone that reads your code. Most of the time, this ends up being you some months in the future.

You can view the built-in Python packages and modules here: `https://docs.python.org/3/library/`.

Searching `GitHub.com` is one good place to look for Python packages. Another is `pypi.org`. I also find out about new Python data science packages by browsing `Kaggle.com`.

Installing new packages can be done with `conda install packagename` or `pip install packagename`, as well as other methods. For example, you can install the pandas package with `conda install pandas`. Sometimes we have errors with our packages, and we need to check the version of the package to help us understand and fix the error.

We can view the versions of our installed packages with `conda list` and `pip list`, which both print out all our installed packages and version numbers. The `conda list` command is a bit more useful, since it shows us which packages were installed with conda and those with pip – packages installed with pip have `pypi` under the `Channel` column in the output. If a package is giving us errors, we can search the internet for the errors as well as check our package version, and compare it with the latest versions for the package listed on `pypi.org` and `anaconda.org`. If our version is old, we might try to upgrade it with `conda update packagename` or `pip install packagename --upgrade`. We may have to try forcing the version number to a specific version, such as `conda install pandas=1.1.3`. However, note that sometimes packages will be downgraded due to dependency requirements of other packages, and upgrading a package can break the functionality of another package you have installed.

When looking at Python packages, it can be helpful to understand if the package is actively maintained. One way to do this is to check the *"Release History"* section on a package page on PyPI (for example, the pandas page here: `https://pypi.org/project/pandas/`). If there have been frequent updates, the package is likely healthy. We can see that pandas is actively maintained and healthy because it has many version updates per year, and usually at least one per month. We can also view the source code on GitHub, which is where most open source Python packages' code is stored. If we click on "**Insights**" on one of the top menu bars, and then "**Contributors**" along the left menu bar, we can see statistics on the code updates to the package. If there are lots of code updates and at least a few people who help to maintain the code, it is likely a healthy package. If you are using a package that isn't very healthy, it may not be the best idea since it could become outdated and break your code later on.

Now that we have packages and modules down, let's look at how to use their functions in more detail.

Functions

Functions in Python always use parentheses after their function name. We place arguments within the parentheses, like this:

```
a_list = [2, 4, 1]
sorted(a_list, reverse=True)
```

In this case, we are using the `sorted` function to sort our list from greatest to least. We also provides the `reverse` argument as `True`, so it sorts from greatest to least instead of from least to greatest.

If a function has arguments with names, such as reverse, we can provide these as named keyword arguments, as we did above.

We can define and create our own functions like this:

```
def test_function(doPrint, printAdd='more'):
    """
    A demo function.
    """
    if doPrint:
        print('test' + printAdd)
        return printAdd
```

To create a function, we use the def keyword, and then give the function name. The function name can be composed of letters, numbers, underscores, and cannot start with a number, just like variables. Then we give any arguments between the parentheses, although we can also specify no arguments if we choose. If we want to supply a default value to an argument, we set it to the default value with an equals sign, as with printAdd above (printAdd='more'). Then we put a colon character after the closing parenthesis, and the function starts on the next line after an indentation of four spaces. Often, we write some documentation about the function below the function definition as a multi-line comment. If we want to return something from the function, we can add a return statement, which will give us printAdd in this case. The return statement will exit the function.

If we were to call the function as test_function(False), it would not print anything and not return anything, since the if statement would evaluate as False. When we run the preceding function with test_function(True), it prints testmore, and returns the string 'more'. We can supply arguments by their name, such as test_function(doPrint=True).

If we look at a built-in function, sorted, by using a question mark in IPython or Jupyter Notebooks (?sorted), we can see that the documentation looks like this:

```
sorted(iterable, /, *, key=None, reverse=False)
```

The sorted function will sort a list (or another iterable object, like a tuple) from least to greatest, and return the sorted version of that object as a list. We can see that the first argument is iterable, which should be an object of a type like a list, set, or dictionary. The forward slash in the next argument space means the iterable argument (and any arguments before or to the left of the /) are positional only, meaning we cannot provide them by name. The arguments after or to the right of the * are keyword only, meaning we can only supply these arguments by naming them, such as sorted(a_list, reverse=True).

Usually, we don't have the forward slash and asterisk in the function definition. Instead we have arguments that can optionally be specified by name, just like in our example function, `test_function`.

One key concept with functions is scoping. If we create a variable inside a function, we can only access that variable within the function. For example, if we try and access the `func_var` variable outside `test_function`, we cannot:

```
def test_function():
    """
    A demo function.
    """
    func_var = 'testing'
    print(func_var)


print(func_var)  # returns NameError; variable not defined
```

If we run the preceding code, we will define the `test_function` function. Then, when we try to print out `func_var` outside of the function, we get an error: `NameError: name 'func_var' is not defined`. The `func_var` variable can only be accessed from within the function. There are ways around this, such as declaring variables as global variables. However, using global variables is not considered best practice and should be avoided.

Another way to create functions is to use lambda functions, which are so-called "**anonymous**" functions. This means that we don't give the function a name, and it runs as we need it. For example, we can create a function to take 2 arguments and add 10 like so:

```
add10 = lambda x, y: x + y + 10
add10(10, 3)
```

We store the function in the variable `add10`, and then call it with the arguments `10` and `3`. This will return the value 23. Lambda functions have a syntax that starts with the keyword `lambda`. It is followed by a list of arguments separated by commas, then a colon character, and then the actual function. Whatever happens in the function (after the colon) is returned. In this case, we add the two arguments plus 10, and return that value. Lambda functions are often used within other functions, as we will see in later chapters.

We've covered the basics of Python functions, but be aware that there are lots of other more advanced handy tools for Python functions, such as decorators and generators. As our last bit of Python fundamentals, let's talk about classes.

Classes

Python is an object-oriented language, which is a category of programming languages. It means that the Python language is fundamentally based on objects. Objects are a collection of data/variables and functions/methods. Objects can be defined with classes using the `class` keyword. For example, a simple object can be created like so:

```
class testObject:
    def __init__(self, attr=10):
        self.test_attribute = attr

    def test_function(self):
        print('testing123')
        print(self.test_attribute)
```

This creates a `testObject` class on the first line. The `__init__` function is run when we create a new instance of the class and is a standard feature of classes in Python. For example, if we create an instance of the class with `t_o = testObject(123)`, we create a new `testObject` object in the variable t_o, and set the attribute `t_o.test_attribute` equal to 10. Setting the attribute `test_attribute` equal to 10 is done in the `__init__` function, which runs when we initialize the t_o variable as a `testObject` class. We can access attributes from classes such as `t_o.test_attribute`. Functions can be included with classes, such as the `test_function` function above. Note that all function definitions in classes require the `self` keyword as the first argument, which allows us to refer to the instance of the class in the functions. This enables us to set attributes of the object and use them throughout the methods (functions) that the object has.

We can run the `testFunction` method with `t_o.testFunction()` after creating the to object with `to = testObject(123)`. This will print out the string `testing123`, and then print out the value of `test_attribute` for the class.

Classes are used pervasively throughout Python, and we'll see them in this book. Armed with this basic understanding of classes, you should now be ready to use them. Now we'll briefly talk about concurrency and parallelization in Python.

Multithreading and multiprocessing

Modern CPUs have several CPU cores, which can all run calculations simultaneously. However, Python is not parallelized by default, meaning it can only run on one core at a time. Instead, it has the **global interpreter lock**, or **GIL**, which restricts the running Python process to one thread (virtual CPU core) at a time.

There are often two threads per CPU core these days, so a lot of CPU power goes unused by Python by default. This limitation of Python is considered a weakness. Even though Python has the infamous GIL, we can still parallelize code with a few lines of Python.

The `multiprocessing` and `multithreading` modules in Python allow for multiprocessing and multithreading, but it's easier to use the functions from the `concurrent.futures` package. You can check out the `multithreading_demo.py` file in the book's GitHub repository, which briefly shows how to use multiprocessing and multithreading.

Note that multiprocessing is useful for improving performance, but often we can use tools others have built and avoid handcoding it ourselves with the `concurrent.futures` module. For example, we'll see in a future chapter that we can use the `swifter` package for parallelizing data processing, and it's much easier than using `concurrent.futures` ourselves.

Software engineering best practices

Data science is tending to incorporate more software engineering these days, so it helps to understand some software engineering best practices.

Debugging errors and utilizing documentation

When running Python code (or any code from any language), we will inevitably run into problems. This usually manifests as errors that show up when we run the code, as in the following screenshot:

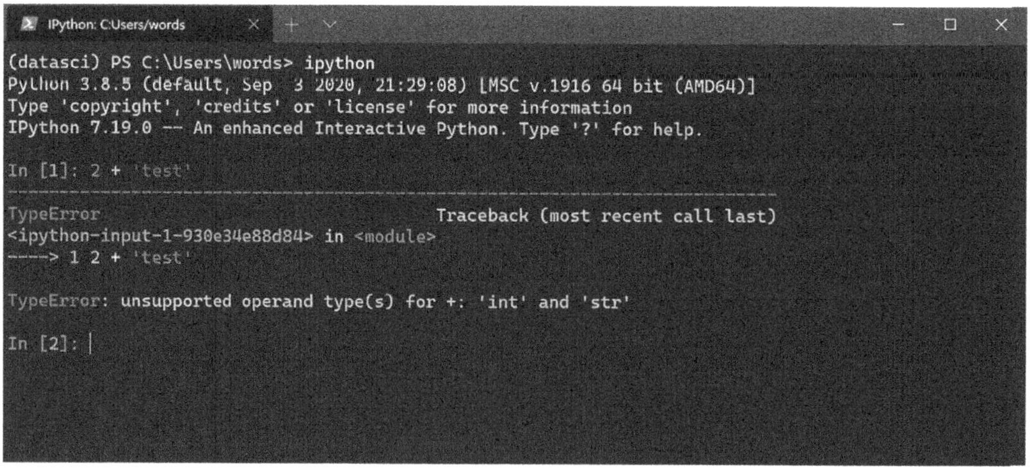

```
IPython: C:Users/words

(datasci) PS C:\Users\words> ipython
Python 3.8.5 (default, Sep  3 2020, 21:29:08) [MSC v.1916 64 bit (AMD64)]
Type 'copyright', 'credits' or 'license' for more information
IPython 7.19.0 -- An enhanced Interactive Python. Type '?' for help.

In [1]: 2 + 'test'

TypeError                                 Traceback (most recent call last)
<ipython-input-1-930e34e88d84> in <module>
----> 1 2 + 'test'

TypeError: unsupported operand type(s) for +: 'int' and 'str'

In [2]:
```

Figure 2.7: An example of an error in IPython. A number cannot be added to a string

In this case, we tried to add a number to text (a string). This is not allowed and gives us the error TypeError: unsupported operand type(s) for +: 'int' and 'str'. If you can tell what the error is from the output, then you can try to fix it straight away. Otherwise, the most important part of the error is usually at the end/bottom of the output and is followed by something with an error, such as TypeError: <error message here>, and will have syntax highlighting similar to TypeError above. Copy this text by selecting it and then right-clicking in Windows, using *cmd* + *c* in Mac, or using *Ctrl* + *Shift* + *c* in Linux. Then, search your favorite internet search engine for the error. Often, this will lead us to Stack Overflow, which has a collection of common errors and their fixes for almost all programming languages. So be on the lookout for stack overflow links when searching for errors.

Debugging

Python comes with a module for debugging code called pdb. To use it, we insert the line import pdb; pdb.set_trace() in our code. Then, when we run our code, the execution stops on that line and allows us to type in Python codes to examine the variables there. For example, try running the following code (or running the pdb_demo.py file from this book's GitHub repository):

```
test_str = 'a test string'
a = 2
b = 2
import pdb; pdb.set_trace()
c = a + b
```

We are creating a few variables, a and b, then initializing the debugger, and finally running one more calculation at the end of the code. When you run this, you'll see that the execution of the code stops, and we're presented with a line with (Pdb) on the far left. This allows us to run Python code one line at a time as if we're in a Python shell. We can inspect the variables we've created so far (test_str, a, and b), but the variable c is not available yet because we haven't yet run that line. To exit the debugger, we can type exit or use *Ctrl* + *d*.

There is also another package, ipdb, which is the interactive Python debugger. This must be installed with pip or conda. The ipdb debugger is like IPython, which has features such as autocomplete.

Documentation

Using documentation is extremely important when coding. For any major programming language or package, there is documentation explaining how its components work.

For example, the official Python documentation has been referenced throughout the chapter so far and is useful for built-in Python functions and Python fundamentals.

Documentation for other packages can be found by searching an internet search engine for "<package name> documentation" or "<package name> docs", since documentation is often abbreviated as "docs". Searching for a specific function in a package can also be helpful in getting to the information you need faster.

Lastly, we can access documentation within IPython or Jupyter Notebooks with a question mark next to any object or using the help() command. For example, to bring up the documentation for the range function, we could use ?range or range?.

Version control with Git

Since data science tends to consist of Python code, we need a way to save and keep track of our code. The best practice for saving code, collaborating, and tracking changes is to use version control. There are several version control systems and software solutions out there, but Git is the most frequently used version control software for now, with GitHub being one of the most frequently used code-hosting platform utilizing Git.

Git is a protocol for keeping track of changes in code, and GitHub allows us to use Git with a web service. GitHub lets us create accounts, store our code on their servers, and share it with the world. We can also easily collaborate with other people using GitHub. A Git/GitHub crash course is beyond the scope of this book, but if you are interested in a book on the subject, we can recommend *Version Control with Git and GitHub*, by Alex Magana from Packt.

 GitHub has a quick-start guide here: docs.github.com/en/free-pro-team@latest/github/getting-started-with-github/quickstart.

Starting out, you might find the easiest way to use GitHub is with the GUI, which is available as an official version on Windows and Mac, and as an unofficial version on Linux. The GitHub GUI can be downloaded from https://desktop.github.com/. However, there is also a **command-line interface (CLI)** tool for GitHub that you may find you prefer. The CLI is more advanced and requires managing your GitHub repositories through a terminal.

Code style

Python has a code style guide described in the **Python Enhancement Proposal 8 (PEP8)**. This covers all sorts of details of Python code best practices. For example, when using math operators, it's best to leave a space between the operators and the numbers, such as 2 * 2. When providing arguments to a function, we should not have spaces between the argument name, the equals sign, and the argument, such as sorted(a_list, reverse=True). These standards help to make Python code more easily readable and searchable, especially as code is shared between large groups of people.

 We can easily format our code to PEP8 standards with a Python package, autopep8.

One other thing to mention with regard to code style is naming conventions. For variables, functions, and classes in Python, we can use letters, underscores, and numbers. We almost always want to start our names with a letter, although there can be some special cases for starting with an underscore. We can also name variables with different patterns, such as camelCase and snake_case. Camel case has a combination of lowercase and uppercase letters, with the start of words being uppercase. Optionally, the first word can be uppercase. Snake case is all lowercase, with an underscore separating words. PEP8 specifies that we should use lowercase variable and function names in the style of snake case.

 PEP8 has an entire section on naming conventions that includes variables that hold constant values, class names, and more: https://www.python.org/dev/peps/pep-0008/#prescriptive-naming-conventions.

Another place you can learn more about good coding style is the book *Clean Code in Python 2nd Edition* by Mariano Anaya.

Whichever naming convention you choose to use, stick with one for each project and be consistent.

Productivity tips

There are a few productivity hacks that can help you code faster. One big trick that we have already touched on is tab autocompletion. Tab autocompletion is available within many command consoles (terminals), IPython, Jupyter Notebooks, IDEs, and code editors. We can simply start typing a word, hit the *Tab* button, and the word can be autocompleted, or possible completions can be suggested.

A similar trick is using the up arrow in a terminal and/or IPython session. This will cycle through your recent commands, so you don't need to re-type the same exact thing more than once.

Another useful trick is using the control key (command or option keys on Mac) on your keyboard to navigate by word chunks. While holding down the *Ctrl* key, we can press the *left* and *right* arrow key to move one word at a time. This can also be used with the *delete* and *backspace* keys to delete whole words at a time. Related to this is the use of the *Ctrl* key to select words by chunks, or even entire lines at a time by using the "*home*" and "*end*" keys on your keyboard. Combining this with *Ctrl* + *c* or *Ctrl* + *x* for copy or cut commands allows you to duplicate or move lines of code around quickly.

Also related to the *Ctrl* + *arrows* trick is adding brackets and quotes around a chunk of text. For example, if we type a word without quotes in Python, but want to make it a string, we can use the *Ctrl* key and the left arrow key to select the entire word and then type a quotation mark (either " or '). In most IDEs, text editors, and Jupyter Notebooks, this will add quotations on both sides of the word. We can also quickly add brackets or parentheses around text in this same way.

In general, learning keyboard shortcuts can dramatically improve your performance. Jupyter Notebooks, VS Code, GitHub's GUI, and other software have several hotkey combinations available that can make you more productive. For example, from the GitHub GUI in Windows, we can open a Command Prompt in the current folder of the repository we're viewing by pressing *Ctrl* + ` (that's the backtick character, which is the button just below the *Esc* key). Another example is creating new tabs, switching between them, and closing them with hotkeys in browsers and terminals. In the terminal for Windows, we can create a new tab with *Ctrl* + *Shift* + *t*, and switch tabs with *Ctrl* + *Tab* and *Ctrl* + *Shift* + *Tab*. Closing tabs can be done with *Ctrl* + *Shift* + *w*. For most applications with tabs, some combination of *Ctrl*/*cmd* with either the *Tab* key or page up/page down can be used to switch between tabs, while *Ctrl* + *t* and *Ctrl* + *w* are often used to open/close tabs. One other trick for switching rapidly between applications is *Alt* + *Tab*. With these keyboard shortcuts, you often barely need to touch the mouse, which can boost your productivity and efficiency. If you are interested in efficiency, you might take a look at the Colemak keyboard layout as well. This is designed to be more efficient than the QWERTY keyboard layout, while keeping the same hotkey locations for copy, paste, and cut.

One trick for running commands from IPython or Jupyter Notebooks as if you are running them in the terminal is to preface the command with an exclamation point. For example, to install a package with pip from Jupyter Notebooks, we can do something like this: `!pip install pandas`. This usually doesn't work for commands that require interaction, so for conda installs, we should add the `-y` flag to skip confirmation, like so: `!conda install pandas -y`.

If you find yourself typing some common commands from the terminal, you might consider adding an alias for it. For example, I set the alias for `jupyter notebook` to simply `jn`. To do this in Windows with a PowerShell (like Terminal from `www.aka.ms/terminal`), first open your profile with `notepad $profile`, and then add the line `Set-Alias -Name jn -Value jupyter-notebook`. When you open new terminals, you can now type `jn` to start Jupyter Notebooks.

In Mac, you can edit a similar profile file with `nano ~/.zshrc` from the command line and then add a line with `alias jn="jupyter notebook"`. The hotkeys for saving and exiting nano are shown on the bottom of the terminal – this is a text editor available in most Linux and Mac terminals by default. In most variants of Linux, the profile file is `~/.bashrc`. Again, when you open a new terminal, you will be able to simply type `jn` to start Jupyter Notebooks.

Lastly, if we are running some code in a terminal or Command Prompt, we can use the *Ctrl* + *c* key combination to cancel running processes, and the *Ctrl* + *d* key combination to exit terminals. With Windows command consoles, we need to type `exit` instead of *Ctrl* + *d*, but in other terminals (Mac, Linux) we can press *Ctrl* + *d* to exit. We already touched on these concepts and commands earlier, but they are worth restating.

Test your knowledge

Work through the `test_your_knowledge.ipynb` file in the GitHub repository for the book, under the *Chapter 2* folder. This will help you practice some of the Python concepts and skills we learned here.

Summary

Well, that certainly was a lot of information in this chapter, but now you have the tools to really dig in and get started on data science. Much like a cook cannot do much without the proper tools, such as sharp knives and specialized utensils, we cannot do proper data science without having the proper tools. Our tools consist of programming languages (mainly Python for data science), code editors and IDEs (such as VS Code), and ways to develop, test, and run our code (such as terminals, IPython, and Jupyter Notebooks).

Although we got started on the basics of Python, there is a lot more to learn, and continuous practice is key to becoming a Python master. There are many other good resources out there for learning Python in more depth, such as *Learning Python* and *Learn Python Programming*, by Fabrizio Romano, from Packt. Remember that if you get stuck with errors in your code or don't know how to do something, internet search engines, Stack Overflow, and the documentation for Python and packages are your friends.

Now that we've gotten our tools prepared for data science, we can start on some of the first steps of learning data science – actually ingesting data into Python.

Part II

Dealing with Data

3

SQL and Built-in File Handling Modules in Python

Introduction

The first step in data science always involves getting a hold of data, since it's a little difficult to do data science without data. The canonical data operations package in Python is pandas, but before we can even get to that, we need to learn some other basic **input/output (I/O)** functions and methods in base Python. In this chapter, we'll cover the following topics:

- How to load data from common text files with built-in Python functions
- How to use the built-in sqlite3 module to save and load data
- How to use basic SQL commands
- How to use the SQLAlchemy package in Python

Let's get started by using base Python to load plain text files.

Loading, reading, and writing files with base Python

When we talk about "base" Python, we are talking about built-in components of the Python software. We already saw one of these components with the math module in *Chapter 2, Getting Started with Python*. Here, we'll first cover using the built-in open() function and the methods of file objects to read and write basic text files.

Opening a file and reading its contents

We will sometimes find ourselves wanting to read a plain text file, or maybe another type of text file, such as an HTML file. We can do this with the built-in open function:

```
file = open(file='textfile.txt', mode='r')
text = file.readlines()
print(text)
```

In the preceding example, we first open a file called textfile.txt in "read" mode. The file argument provides the path to the file. We have given a "relative" path in the preceding snippet, meaning it looks for textfile.txt in the current directory in which we are running this Python code. We can also provide an "absolute" path with the full file path, with the syntax file=r'C:\Users\username\Documents\ textfile.txt'. Notice we prefix the absolute path string with r, just like we saw in the previous chapter. The r instructs Python to interpret the strings as a "raw" string, and means all characters are interpreted literally. Without the r, the backslash is part of special characters, like the \n newline character sequence.

The second argument we provide to the open() function, mode, specifies whether we are reading and writing, among other things. The simplest way to use it is with mode='r' for reading mode and mode='w' for writing mode. The open() function can take several arguments (use introspection with ?open to look at the documentation from IPython or Jupyter Notebook, or take a look at the official documentation here: https://docs.python.org/3/library/functions.html#open).

The second line in the preceding example uses the readlines method of a Python file object. This reads the file into a list, where each element of the list is a line of the file. Our example textfile.txt file looks like this:

```
This is a text file.
Now you can read it!
```

So when we use `file.readlines()` and print out the result (text), we see the following:

```
['This is a text file.\n', 'Now you can read it!']
```

The \n character is a newline or linefeed character, meaning it starts a new line there.

Once we've opened a file and read or written its contents, we should close it like this:

```
file.close()
```

However, a better way to do this is using a `with` statement, like so:

```
with open(file='textfile.txt', mode='r') as f:
    text = f.readlines()

print(text)
```

The first line of the preceding code example opens the file with the `open()` function, and assigns it to the f variable. We can use the opened file within the indented lines after the `with` statement, like on the second line where we read all lines from the file.

 The `with` statement, along with `if` and `for` statements, are called compound statements in Python. These invoke a so-called context manager, which handles the code within the `with` statement itself and the "suite," which is the indented code after the with statement. This can be read about in more detail in the documentation: https://docs.python.org/3/reference/compound_stmts.html#the-with-statement

The `with` statement is like `if` statements or loops in terms of formatting; all lines that are indented by four spaces after the `with` ...: line will be run within the `with` statement. Also, don't forget the colon character (:) at the end of the line – without it, you'll see an error: `SyntaxError: invalid syntax`. We end the `with` block by no longer indenting lines, meaning when we reach `print(text)` in our preceding example, the `with` statement has ended. At that point, the file object is automatically closed for us, and we don't need to call `f.close()`. The result of `print(text)` is the same as in our first example.

Let's look at a few other ways to use file objects: reading the entire file object at once and writing to a file. To read the entire file at once, we use the `read` method instead of `readlines`, like so:

```
with open(file='textfile.txt', mode='r') as f:
    text = f.read()

print(text)
```

This is nearly identical to our previous example, but we use `f.read()`. The `print(text)` line now outputs the entire `textfile.txt` file's contents:

```
This is a text file.
Now you can read it!
```

There are several ways to write to files with `open()`: we can simply write to a file (`mode='w'`), read and write at the same time (`mode='r+'`, if the file already exists), or append (`mode='a'`), among other methods. More methods are described in the documentation, which you can see by executing the `?open` command in IPython or Jupyter. For example, to write content to a file called `writetest.txt` in our current directory, we can do the following:

```
with open(file='writetest.txt', mode='w') as f:
    f.write('testing writing out')
```

Note that this will overwrite anything that exists in the `writetest.txt` file if it exists. If we don't want to overwrite everything, we can use `mode='a'` instead, which adds text to the end of the file. Note that the written content will not be viewable in the file until we close it (which automatically happens upon exiting the `with` statement).

I sometimes find myself writing things to a file if I need a quick and simple solution to save something. An example is web scraping, which we will cover in *Chapter 7, Web Scraping*. When web scraping, it can be helpful to write the results of a web scrape to a `.html` text file, which can be done with the `open()` function as we just covered. Reading files can come in handy for several uses, including reading credentials and reading JSON files, which we will cover next.

Using the built-in JSON module

JavaScript Object Notation (JSON) is a text-based format for representing and storing data and is mostly used for web applications. We can use JSON to save data to a text file or to transfer data to and from an **Application Programming Interface (API)**.

APIs allow us to send a request to a web service to accomplish various tasks. An example is sending some text (such as an email message, for example) to an API and getting the sentiment (positive, negative, or neutral) returned to us. JSON looks very much like a dictionary in Python. For example, here is an example dictionary in Python that stores data regarding how many books and articles we've read, and what their subjects include:

```
data_dictionary = {
    'books': 12,
    'articles': 100,
    'subjects': ['math',
                 'programming',
                 'data science']}
```

We can convert this to a JSON-format string in Python by first importing the built-in json module, then using `json.dumps()`:

```
import json
json_string = json.dumps(data_dictionary)
print(json_string)
```

The preceding `json_string` will look like this:

```
'{"books": 12, "articles": 100, "subjects": ["math", "programming", "data
science"]}'
```

If we want to convert that string back to a dictionary, we can do so with `json.loads()`:

```
data_dict = json.loads(json_string)
print(data_dict)
```

This will print out the Python dictionary we started with:

```
{'books': 12,
 'articles': 100,
 'subjects': ['math', 'programming', 'data science']}
```

If we are sending some data to an API with Python, `json.dumps()` may come in handy. On the other hand, if we want to save JSON data to a text file, we can use `json.dump()`:

```
with open('reading.json', 'w') as f:
    json.dump(data_dictionary, f)
```

In the preceding example, we first open the file using a `with` statement, and the file object is stored in the `f` variable. Then we use `json.dump()`, giving it two arguments: the dictionary (`data_dictionary`) and the file object that has been opened for writing (`f`).

To read JSON data from a file, we can use `json.load()`:

```
with open('reading.json') as f:
    loaded_data = json.load(f)

print(loaded_data)
```

Note that in the preceding `open()` function, we do not supply the second argument (the `mode` argument). This is because the default `mode` is r for reading mode. The `json.load()` function simply takes the opened file object as its first argument, and returns a dictionary. When we print out our data, it looks like this:

```
{'books': 12,
 'articles': 100,
 'subjects': ['math', 'programming', 'data science']}
```

Sometimes downloaded data from websites can be in JSON format, and `json.load()` is one way to load it into Python. There are also other packages in Python that can be used for reading, writing, and parsing JSON, such as the `simplejson` and `ujson` packages. However, for ordinary work with JSON, the built-in `json` module works just fine.

Saving credentials or data in a Python file

Sometimes we will want to save credentials or other data in a `.py` file. This can be useful for saving authentication credentials for an API, for example. We can do this by creating a `.py` file with some variables, such as the `credentials.py` file in this book's GitHub repository, which looks like this:

```
username = 'datasci'
password = 'iscool'
```

Loading these saved credentials is easy: we import the module (a Python `.py` file, named `credentials.py` here) and then we can access the variables:

```
import credentials as creds
print(f'username: {creds.username}\npassword: {creds.password}')
```

We first import the file/module with the `import` statement, and alias it as `creds`. Then we print out a formatted string (using f-string formatting), which displays the `username` and `password` variables from the file.

Recall that f-strings can incorporate variables into a string by putting Python code within curly brackets. Notice that we access these variables with the syntax `creds.username` – first the module name, followed by a period, and then the variable. We also include a line break character (\n) so the username and password print on separate lines.

Of course, we can use this method to save any arbitrary data that can be stored in a Python object in a Python file, but it's not typically used beyond a few small variables such as a username and password. For bigger Python objects (such as a dictionary with millions of elements), we can use other packages and modules such as the `pickle` module.

Saving Python objects with pickle

Sometimes we'll find ourselves wanting to directly save a Python object, such as a dictionary or some other Python object. This can happen if we are running Python code for data processing or collection and want to store the results for later analysis. An easy way to do this is using the built-in `pickle` module. As with many things in Python, `pickle` is a little humorous – it's like pickling vegetables, but we are pickling data instead. For example, using the same data dictionary we used earlier (with data on books and articles we've read), we can save this dictionary object to a `pickle` file like so:

```
import pickle as pk

data_dictionary = {
    'books': 12,
    'articles': 100,
    'subjects': ['math',
                 'programming',
                 'data science']}

with open('readings.pk', 'wb') as f:
    pk.dump(data_dictionary, f)
```

We first import the `pickle` module, and alias it as `pk`. Then we create our `data_dictionary` object containing our data. Finally, we open a file called `readings.pk`, and write the `data_dictionary` to the file with the `pickle.dump()` function (which is `pk.dump()` since we aliased `pickle` as `pk`). In our `open()` function, we are setting the `mode` argument to the value `'wb'`. This stands for "write binary," meaning we are writing data to the file in binary format (0s and 1s, which are actually represented in hexadecimal format with `pickle`). Since `pickle` saves data in binary format, we must use this `'wb'` argument to write data to a `pickle` file.

Once we have data in a `pickle` file, we can load it into Python like so:

```
with open('readings.pk', 'rb') as f:
    data = pk.load(f)
```

Note that we are using `'rb'` now for our `mode` argument, meaning "read binary." Since the file is in binary format, we must specify this when opening the file. Once we open the file, we then load the contents of the file into the `data` variable with `pickle.load(f)` (which is `pk.load(f)` in the preceding code since we aliased `pickle` as `pk`). Pickle is a great way to save almost any Python object quickly and easily. However, for specific, organized data, it can be better to store it in a SQL database, which we'll cover now.

Using SQLite and SQL

SQL, or **Structured Query Language**, is a programming language for interacting with data in relational databases (sometimes called **RDBMS**, meaning **Relational Database Management System**). SQL has been around since the 1970s and continues to be used widely today. You will likely interact with a SQL database or use SQL queries sooner or later at your workplace if you haven't already. Its advantages in speed and momentum from decades of use sustain its widespread utilization today.

SQL is the standard programming language for interfacing with relational databases, and a large fraction of data and databases use relational models today. In fact, SQL has even been approved as an international standard by the **International Organization for Standardization (ISO)**, and the SQL standard is continually updated every few years. This standard language makes it easier for more people to use these databases, adding to the network effects. NoSQL databases are an alternative to SQL databases, and are used in situations where we might prefer to have more flexibility in our data model, or a different model completely (such as a graph database). For example, if we aren't sure of all the columns or fields we might collect with our data (and they could change frequently over time), a NoSQL document database such as MongoDB may be better than SQL. For big data, NoSQL used to have an advantage over SQL because NoSQL could scale horizontally (that is, adding more nodes to a cluster). Now, SQL databases have been developed to scale easily, and we can also use cloud services such as AWS Redshift and Google's BigQuery to scale SQL databases easily.

Much of the world's data is stored in relational databases using SQL. It's important to understand the basics of SQL so we can retrieve our own data for our data science work. We can interact directly with SQL databases through the command line or GUI tools and through Python packages such as pandas and SQLAlchemy. But first, we will practice SQL with SQLite databases, since SQLite3 comes installed with Python. SQLite is what it sounds like – a lightweight version of SQL. It lacks the richer functionality of other SQL databases such as MySQL, but is faster and easier to use. However, it can still hold a lot of data, with a maximum potential database size of around 281 TB for SQLite databases.

For our next examples, we'll be using the chinook database. This is a dataset of songs and purchases from customers and is similar to a dataset of iTunes songs and purchases. We will refer to this dataset as "the iTunes database" from time to time. The chinook.db file is included in the *Chapter 3* folder of this book's GitHub repository, but its source code and data can be found at https://github.com/lerocha/chinook-database. Let's first load the database from the command line and take a look. First, open a terminal or shell and navigate to the directory containing the chinook.db file. Then run the following command to open the database within a SQLite shell:

```
sqlite3 chinook.db
```

Once we are in the SQLite shell, our prompt on the left should look like sqlite>. Let's try our first command: .tables. This prints out the tables in the database, which hold the data. Our result should look like the following:

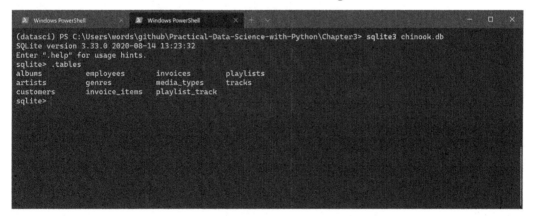

Figure 3.1: The SQLite shell looks like this, and the .tables command lists the tables in the database

SQL databases are organized into tables that can be combined together to extract more information. We can draw an **Entity Relationship Diagram** (ERD) of the database, which shows the tables and their relationships with one another:

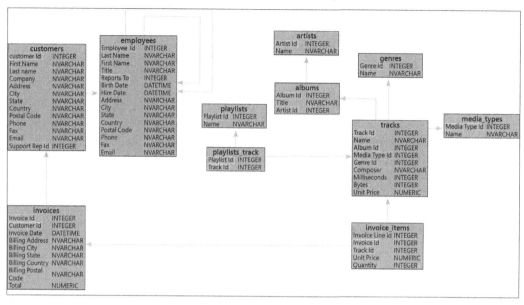

Figure 3.2: This is an ERD of the chinook database and was created with the DbVisualizer software

The preceding ERD shows the tables we listed from the chinook database. The arrows show which tables connect to other tables, and the highlighted/boxed column names show the common columns that can connect them. These connecting columns having matching values that can be paired up to combine rows from the different tables.

Let's try a simple command in our SQLite shell. To retrieve data from a SQL database, we can use the SELECT command. Let's look at some data from the artists table:

```
SELECT * FROM artists LIMIT 5;
```

By convention, SQL commands are typed in uppercase, although they don't have to be, and none of the text in SQL commands is case-sensitive. So, the SELECT, FROM, and LIMIT commands shown in the preceding snippet are the specific SQL commands we've used. SELECT tells the SQL shell which columns to select. With *, we select all columns. Note that from the ERD, we can see that our available columns in the artists table are ArtistId and Name. Next, we choose the table to select our data from – FROM artists. Lastly, we limit our results to 5 with LIMIT 5 so it doesn't print out all the results (which could be massive).

Importantly, notice that we end the line with a semicolon. Without the semicolon, the SQL shell keeps looking for more code to run. We should see printed out results like the following:

```
1|AC/DC
2|Accept
3|Aerosmith
4|Alanis Morissette
5|Alice In Chains
```

The returned results are minimally formatted within the SQLite shell. Not even the column names are shown, but we know them from the ERD or from looking at the table's list of columns. We can look at the list of columns with the PRAGMA table_info(artists); command. To exit the SQLite shell, hit *Ctrl + C* or *Command + C*.

Although there is no official style guide for SQL's code style like there is for Python in the form of PEP8, there are a few style guides out there that are generally consistent with each other:

https://www.sqlstyle.guide/

https://about.gitlab.com/handbook/business-ops/data-team/platform/sql-style-guide/

If we have a SQLite file, we can interact with it via the command line or other software such as SQLiteStudio (currently at https://sqlitestudio.pl/). However, we can also use it with Python using the built-in sqlite3 module. To get started with this method, we import sqlite3, then connect to the database file, and create a cursor:

```
import sqlite3
connection = sqlite3.connect('chinook.db')
cursor = connection.cursor()
```

The string argument to sqlite3.connect() should be either the relative or absolute path to the database file. The relative path means it is relative to our current working directory (where we are running the Python code from). If we want to use an absolute path, we could supply something like the following:

```
connection = sqlite3.connect(r'C:\Users\my_username\github\Practical-Data-Science-with-Python\Chapter3\chinook.db')
```

Notice that the string has the r character before it. As we mentioned earlier, this stands for **raw string** and means it treats special characters (such as the backslash, \) as literal characters. With raw strings, the backslash is simply a backslash, and this allows us to copy and paste file paths from the Windows File Explorer to Python.

The preceding cursor is what allows us to run SQL commands. For example, to run the SELECT command that we already tried in the SQLite shell, we can use the cursor:

```
cursor.execute('SELECT * FROM artists LIMIT 5;')
cursor.fetchall()
```

We use the fetchall function to retrieve all the results from the query. There are also fetchone and fetchmany functions we could use instead, which are described in Python's sqlite3 documentation. These functions retrieve one record (fetchone) and several records (fetchmany, which retrieves a number of records we specify).

When we start executing bigger SQL queries, it helps to format them differently. We can break up a SQL command into multiple lines like so:

```
query = """
SELECT *
FROM artists
LIMIT 5;
"""
cursor.execute(query)
cursor.fetchall()
```

We are using a multi-line string for the query variable with the triple quotes and putting each SQL command on a separate line. Then we give this string variable, query, to the cursor.execute() function. Finally, we retrieve the results with fetchall.

When selecting data, it can be useful to sort it by one of the columns. Let's look at the invoices table and get the biggest invoices:

```
cursor.execute(
    """SELECT Total, InvoiceDate
    FROM invoices
    ORDER BY Total DESC
    LIMIT 5;"""
)
cursor.fetchall()
```

Here, we are using the same connection and cursor as previously. We are selecting a few columns from invoices: Total and the InvoiceDate. We then use the ORDER BY SQL command and sort by the Total column, with the addition of DESC for descending order.

If we use ORDER BY without the DESC keyword, the **DBMS (Database Management System)** sorts by the specified data column in ascending order (from least to greatest) by default. We can also sort text and date columns too – text columns are sorted alphabetically, and dates are sorted from earliest to latest by default.

Another useful SQL command is WHERE, which allows us to filter data. It's similar to an if statement in Python. We can filter with Boolean conditions, such as equality (==), inequality (!=), or other comparisons (including less than, <, and greater than, >). Here is an example of getting invoices from Canada:

```
cursor.execute(
    """SELECT Total, BillingCountry
    FROM invoices
    WHERE BillingCountry == "Canada"
    LIMIT 5;"""
)
cursor.fetchall()
```

We have a similar SELECT statement as in the previous examples, except we are filtering by BillingCountry equal to Canada using the WHERE command. Notice we provide Canada as a string in double quotes – since the entire query string is in single quotes, we can use double quotes within the string. When we fetch all of the results, we see they are only from Canada:

```
[(8.91, 'Canada'),
 (8.91, 'Canada'),
 (0.99, 'Canada'),
 (1.98, 'Canada'),
 (13.86, 'Canada')]
```

As a part of WHERE, we can filter by pattern matching using LIKE. This is similar to regular expressions, which we will cover in *Chapter 18, Working with Text*. We can find any country strings that contain the letters c, a, and n like so:

```
cursor.execute(
    """SELECT Total, BillingCountry
    FROM invoices
    WHERE BillingCountry LIKE "%can%"
    LIMIT 5;"""
)
cursor.fetchall()
```

The LIKE "%can%" section enables our filtering when combined with the WHERE statement. The percent signs (%) mean any number of characters can be at the beginning or end of the string. It is also not case-sensitive, meaning the characters can match lower- or uppercase letters.

At the time of writing, SQLite's documentation isn't thorough or comprehensive (although it may improve in the future). Other SQL variants have better documentation. For example, Microsoft's SQL documentation on `LIKE` describes more of what the command can do: `https://docs.microsoft.com/en-us/sql/t-sql/language-elements/like-transact-sql?view=sql-server-ver15`. And since SQL is a standard, most SQL variants share many of the same commands and features (but not everything).

It can be useful to group data and get summary statistics. For example, maybe we want to know the total amount of sales by country, and see which countries are bringing in the most revenue. We could accomplish this like so:

```
cursor.execute(
    """SELECT SUM(Total), BillingCountry
    FROM invoices
    GROUP BY BillingCountry
    ORDER BY SUM(Total) DESC
    LIMIT 5;"""
)
cursor.fetchall()
```

We are using the `SUM()` command on the `Total` column from the `invoices` table here. This sums the `Total` column based on the column we group by. Looking at the `GROUP BY` clause, we can see we are specifying `BillingCountry` to group our data. This means all entries with the same value for `BillingCountry` are grouped together, and the sum of the `Total` column is then calculated for each group. We are also using `ORDER BY` with `DESC` to arrange the sum of the `Total` column from greatest to least. We can see the USA has the largest total amount of sales:

```
[(523.0600000000003, 'USA'),
 (303.9599999999999, 'Canada'),
 (195.09999999999994, 'France'),
 (190.09999999999997, 'Brazil'),
 (156.48, 'Germany')]
```

The SUM function is called an aggregate function. There are others, including `MIN`, `COUNT`, and so on. SQLite's documentation on these functions can be found at `https://sqlite.org/lang_aggfunc.html`.

Other SQL variants (such as Microsoft SQL Server which uses the T-SQL extension) have more aggregate functions, such as standard deviation.

As we've seen from the ERD of the chinook database, the data is split into several tables. This is called database normalization, which we do to minimize the space used by the database and to minimize any errors upon changing data. This means we need to combine tables in order to extract the data we want. For example, say we want to investigate which tracks were purchased by which countries. Let's start with a simple example, where we look at individual tracks purchased and combine this with the country from the invoice.

```
query = """
SELECT invoices.BillingCountry, invoice_items.TrackId
FROM invoices
JOIN invoice_items
ON invoices.InvoiceId = invoice_items.InvoiceId
LIMIT 5;
"""
cursor.execute(query)
cursor.fetchall()
```

We can see in our query that we are selecting TrackId and BillingCountry, but we are also specifying the tables these are coming from. Since the invoices table has the country, but the invoice_items table has the track ID, we need to combine these two tables. We do this with the JOIN clause on the third line of the preceding query. After our SELECT … FROM segment, we then specify the table we want to join with using JOIN invoice_items. Then, after the ON keyword, we specify the columns we will use to join the tables. Just like with the SELECT statement, we need to first specify the table, then use a period, and finally specify the column, in the form of invoices.InvoiceId here. We also use a single equals sign between the two columns we want to match. By default, this is an INNER JOIN statement, meaning it only returns rows where there is a match in both tables. This is the most common join used, although there are others including left, right, and outer joins. These other joins include more results, but the vast majority of the time we will use an inner join. So, in this example, each row returned has an exact match between InvoiceId in the two tables. When using joins, we need to be careful which columns we choose. Almost always, we want to use a "primary key" column from one of the tables. This means the values will be unique in the table that has that column as a primary key. In the ERD from *Figure 3.2*, the primary and foreign key columns are highlighted in each table. We can also see the primary key by examining a table's information. We can use the PRAGMA command with table_info() on the invoices table to retrieve information on each of the columns:

```
cursor.execute('PRAGMA table_info(invoices);')
cursor.fetchall()
```

This query returns the following:

```
[(0, 'InvoiceId', 'INTEGER', 1, None, 1),
 (1, 'CustomerId', 'INTEGER', 1, None, 0),
 (2, 'InvoiceDate', 'DATETIME', 1, None, 0),
 (3, 'BillingAddress', 'NVARCHAR(70)', 0, None, 0),
 (4, 'BillingCity', 'NVARCHAR(40)', 0, None, 0),
 (5, 'BillingState', 'NVARCHAR(40)', 0, None, 0),
 (6, 'BillingCountry', 'NVARCHAR(40)', 0, None, 0),
 (7, 'BillingPostalCode', 'NVARCHAR(10)', 0, None, 0),
 (8, 'Total', 'NUMERIC(10,2)', 1, None, 0)]
```

The last column of the results is the pk field, meaning "primary key." If the value is a 1, it is a primary key. We can see from the results that InvoiceId is the primary key column in the invoices table. Let's expand on our earlier example and get the number of times each track is purchased across countries, as well as sort it from greatest to least:

```
query = """
SELECT
    invoice_items.TrackId,
    COUNT(invoice_items.TrackId),
    invoices.BillingCountry
FROM invoices
JOIN invoice_items
ON invoices.InvoiceId = invoice_items.InvoiceId
GROUP BY invoices.BillingCountry
ORDER BY COUNT(invoice_items.TrackId) DESC
LIMIT 5;
"""
cursor.execute(query)
cursor.fetchall()
```

Here, we are combining the invoices and invoice_items tables again with an inner join, and once again using the InvoiceId column to join the tables. We are also grouping by country. Finally, we get the track ID and the count of each track ID for each country. The COUNT function is another aggregate function, which returns the count of items in each group. Finally, we are sorting it by the count of the track ID for each country from greatest to least using ORDER BY with the DESC keyword. Our results look like this:

```
[(99, 494, 'USA'),
 (42, 304, 'Canada'),
 (234, 190, 'France'),
 (738, 190, 'Brazil'),
 (2, 152, 'Germany')]
```

We can see that the US has the top number of purchases (494) of the track with ID 99, but we don't know what song that is. In order to get results with the song titles, we need to combine our `invoice` and `invoice_items` tables with one more table – the `tracks` table, which has the song titles. We can do this with multiple `JOIN` clauses:

```
query = """
SELECT tracks.Name, COUNT(invoice_items.TrackId), invoices.BillingCountry
FROM invoices
JOIN invoice_items
ON invoices.InvoiceId = invoice_items.InvoiceId
JOIN tracks
ON tracks.TrackId = invoice_items.TrackId
GROUP BY invoices.BillingCountry
ORDER BY COUNT(invoice_items.TrackId) DESC
LIMIT 5;
"""
cursor.execute(query)
cursor.fetchall()
```

Here, we are combining the `invoices`, `invoice_items`, and `tracks` tables to get the track name, the number of purchases, and the country, and then group the results by country. We can see we first select our columns, specifying which table each of the columns comes from, such as `tracks.Name`, to get each song's title from the `tracks` table. Then we specify our first table: `invoices`. Next, we join with `invoice_items` as we did before on the `InvoiceId` column. Then we join the `tracks` table, which shares a `TrackId` column with the `invoice_items` table. Finally, we group by country and sort by the count of `TrackId` as we did before and limit our results to the top five. The results look like this:

```
[('Your Time Has Come', 494, 'USA'),
 ('Right Through You', 304, 'Canada'),
 ('Morena De Angola', 190, 'France'),
 ('Admirável Gado Novo', 190, 'Brazil'),
 ('Balls to the Wall', 152, 'Germany')]
```

Now we can see the top-selling song by country is `Your Time Has Come`, which sold 494 times in the US. We might want to get the artist names next, which would require two more joins: the `tracks` table with the `albums` table, and the `albums` table with the `artist` table. This is left as a challenge to the reader.

 We could also get the results of the track names and counts of purchases grouped by country if we used temporary tables or subqueries.

Once we are finished with a SQLite database in Python, it's usually a good idea to close it like this:

```
connection.close()
```

Closing the connection is not necessarily required, but will make our code more explicit (following the PEP8 style guidelines) and thorough. This will ensure the connection closes when we expect it to, and can prevent problems if our code becomes involved in a larger project.

There are a lot of other SQL commands we have not covered here. In fact, there are entire books focused on learning SQL. If you're interested in learning more beyond these basics we covered, you might look into *Learn SQL Database Programming* by Josephine Bush from Packt. Another resource is Kaggle's SQL courses at `https://www.kaggle.com/learn/overview`.

Having a basic grasp of SQL commands will help you greatly in your data science journey. You'll be able to retrieve data from many of the databases out there. We can also use SQLite to store our own data, which we'll cover next.

Creating a SQLite database and storing data

As we saw earlier, we can store data in text or `pickle` files. However, as data becomes larger, it can be slow to retrieve our data from a text or `pickle` file. We can improve the performance (speed, primarily) of reading and writing data by using SQL databases instead, like a SQLite database. For example, we might use a SQL database to store data we collect from an API or web scraping. SQLite is nice for this, since it saves the data to a `.sql` file, which can be shared a little more easily than exporting data from other SQL database management systems. Let's take a hypothetical example of storing book sales data. We have the dates of sales, the book titles, prices, and quantities:

```
book_data = [
    ('12-1-2020', 'Practical Data Science With Python', 19.99, 1),
    ('12-15-2020', 'Python Machine Learning', 27.99, 1),
    ('12-17-2020', 'Machine Learning For Algorithmic Trading', 34.99, 1)
]
```

We can see the data is stored in a list since the outer brackets are square brackets. Each element in the list is a tuple since it is surrounded by parentheses. We have the data in the order of date, book title, price, and quantity. We use a tuple for each data row because that is implicitly recommended by Python's `sqlite` documentation (`https://docs.python.org/3/library/sqlite3.html`), although we can also use a list. Tuples are a good idea to use when inserting data into a SQL database because they are immutable, meaning they can't be changed.

This means our data can't be inadvertently changed by a mistake in our code before we enter it into the database or purposefully changed by a hacker (once it's a tuple - it could be changed earlier if it was a list). We can convert a list to a tuple with `tuple()`, in the form of `tuple([1, 2, 3])`.

To create our database, we simply connect to a filename and create a cursor:

```
connection = sqlite3.connect('book_sales.db')
cursor = connection.cursor()
```

The `book_sales.db` file will be created if it does not exist. Then we execute the SQL command for creating a table:

```
cursor.execute('''CREATE TABLE IF NOT EXISTS book_sales
            (date text, book_title text, price real, quantity real)''')
```

Our query uses a multi-line string with triple single quotes surrounding it. We title our table `book_sales` and provide the column names and datatypes for each column next to them, separated by commas. For example, the first column is `date` with a `text` datatype. We also surround the set of column names and datatypes with parentheses. Once we have created the table, we cannot create it again in the same database, or it throws an error. However, adding the `IF NOT EXISTS` statement enables us to run the `CREATE TABLE` command, and it will not return an error if the table already exists. If we needed to delete the table to start over, we could use the `DROP TABLE book_sales;` command.

Once the table is created, we can insert data with the `INSERT INTO` command:

```
cursor.execute("INSERT INTO book_sales VALUES (?, ?, ?, ?)", book_data[0])
connection.commit()
```

We specify the table name after the `INSERT INTO` command, then use the `VALUES` keyword, followed by our data to insert into each of the columns. Here, we are using question mark placeholders, which derive their values from the second argument we give to `cursor.execute()`. We should have one value or placeholder for each column. Next, we supply `book_data` as the second argument to `cursor.execute()`, but we only supply the first element of the list with `book_data[0]`. The question mark placeholders are then replaced by each value in the tuple from `book_data[0]` when the query is executed. We can also use string formatting to place our values into the query, but this is not recommended. String formatting of SQL queries is a little less safe because we can suffer from a SQL injection attack. For example, if a hacker was able to put an arbitrary string into our SQL query, they could insert something like ; `DROP TABLE book_sales;`, which would delete the data in the `book_sales` table.

After inserting the data, we need to call `connection.commit()` to save the changes. Otherwise, the data will not persist in the database. We now have the first row of our data in the database. We can check that it's there with a simple `SELECT` statement:

```
cursor.execute('SELECT * FROM book_sales;')
cursor.fetchall()
```

We can also use the `executemany()` method to insert several data records at once, like so:

```
cursor.executemany('INSERT INTO book_sales VALUES (?, ?, ?, ?)', book_data[1:])
connection.commit()
connection.close()
```

This inserts the rest of our book sales data (the second element through the end of the `book_data` list) into our table and saves the changes with `commit`. Finally, we close our connection since we are done adding data.

SQLite is a great tool available in Python for saving data. For interacting with data from other SQL database systems, such as Microsoft SQL Server and more, we can use another tool in Python – SQLAlchemy.

Using the SQLAlchemy package in Python

SQLAlchemy is a top package in Python for interacting with SQL databases. It supports connecting to a wide range of SQL databases, including all the major SQL variants. Here, we will demonstrate connecting to the SQLite database we just created (`book_sales.db`). First, let's import SQLAlchemy and connect to the database. If you don't have it installed, use conda (or pip): `conda install -c conda-forge sqlalchemy -y`. Let's import SQLAlchemy and connect to the database like so:

```
from sqlalchemy import create_engine
engine = create_engine('sqlite:///book_sales.db')
connection = engine.connect()
```

In the preceding example, we first import the `create_engine` function from the SQLAlchemy package, then connect to our database file with that function. We are using the relative path to the database file here, but absolute paths are allowed as well. The database type, a colon character, then three forward slashes (`///`) is the typical pattern for the beginning of a SQLAlchemy connection string. We then initiate a connection to the database with `engine.connect()`.

The SQLAlchemy documentation covers connecting to SQLite databases with absolute paths in different operating systems, and is available at `https://docs.sqlalchemy.org/en/13/core/engines.html#sqlite`.

We can retrieve data from the database with the `execute` method, similar to the `sqlite3` package:

```
result = connection.execute("select * from book_sales")
```

Note that we can include the semicolon at the end of our query, but we don't have to.

The result that is returned is a SQLAlchemy class (you can verify this using the `type(result)` command). We can access the data by converting it to a list, like this: `list(result)`. We can also loop through the data, and access each column by name:

```
for row in result:
    print(row['date'])
```

The preceding example goes through each row in the data we retrieved and prints out the `date` column. Just like with `sqlite3`, we should close the connection when finished:

```
connection.close()
```

With SQLAlchemy, we can also use a `with` statement to automatically close the database connection when we're out of the `with` block:

```
with engine.connect() as connection:
    result = connection.execute("select * from book_sales")
    for row in result:
        print(row)
```

This creates a connection in the first line in the `with` statement, and all the indented lines after it can use that connection. Remember that we have a colon character at the end of the `with` statement. After we stop indenting lines, the connection is automatically closed.

It's also possible to insert data into SQL tables with SQLAlchemy. We can use the same method we used with `sqlite3`, which is demonstrated in the documentation at `https://docs.sqlalchemy.org/en/13/core/connections.html#sqlalchemy.engine.Connection.execute`.

Another more advanced paradigm for inserting data is possible in SQLAlchemy as well, which is demonstrated in the tutorial in the documentation at `https://docs.sqlalchemy.org/en/14/core/tutorial.html`.

This more advanced paradigm allows us to insert a row of data without specifying data for all the columns, and looks like this:

```
from sqlalchemy import MetaData, Table
from sqlalchemy.sql import select

metadata = MetaData(engine)
book_sales = Table('book_sales',
                   metadata,
                   autoload=True)
conn = engine.connect()

ins = book_sales.insert().values(
    book_title='machine learning',
    price='10.99')
conn.execute(ins)
```

Using the method above, we can load an existing table as a Python object, then use commands like `insert` and `select` as methods of the object. Then we execute the resulting variable with a SQLAlchemy cursor.

Now we've seen a few key ways to store and retrieve data in Python. I recommend practicing some of these skills to help cement your knowledge of the things you learned.

Test your knowledge

We've learned how to retrieve and store data in Python, and it's a good idea to practice what you learned to lock in the knowledge. In the GitHub repository for this book, the *Chapter 3* folder contains a folder called `test_your_knowledge`. Create a Jupyter notebook in this folder, and complete the following:

1. Load the `bitcoin_price.json` data file by opening the file using the built-in `json` module.

2. Save this data to a SQLite database.

3. Query the database using `sqlite3` for the following:

    • The earliest and latest dates (hint: the `MAX` and `MIN` aggregate functions will help)

    • The maximum price for each year (grouped by year) and sorted by year

4. Connect to the `chinook.db sqlite3` database with SQLAlchemy.

5. Find the genre names with the longest average song length. (Hint: join the tables with the genre name and song length and use the SQLite aggregate function for the average along with a `GROUP BY` clause.)

Summary

As we talked about at the beginning of the chapter, accessing and storing data are foundational for data science. In this chapter, we learned how to open plain text files, deal with JSON data, and read and store data with SQL through the `sqlite3` module and SQLAlchemy package in Python. There are many other ways to interact with data stores in Python as well, including packages in Python for interacting with big data and cloud resources, packages for interacting with NoSQL databases such as MongoDB, and the `pandas` package. In fact, we're going to learn how to utilize `pandas` for handling data in the next chapter.

4

Loading and Wrangling Data with Pandas and NumPy

Data sources come in many formats: plain text files, CSVs, SQL databases, Excel files, and many more. We saw how to deal with some of these data sources in the last chapter, but there is one library in Python that takes the cake when it comes to data preparation: pandas. The pandas library is a core tool for a data scientist, and we will learn how to use it effectively in this chapter. We will learn about:

- Loading data from and saving data to several different data source types
- Some basic **exploratory data analysis (EDA)** and plotting with pandas
- Preparing and cleaning data for later use, including the imputation of missing data (filling in missing values) and outlier detection
- Essential data wrangling tools such as filtering, groupby, and replace

Overall, this chapter will be another foundational chapter in your data science journey, giving you the tools necessary to get started working with data. We will go through a couple of examples to learn the basics of working with data in pandas and NumPy. In the first example, we will be using the chinook music data to clean and prepare data, then run an analysis on song purchases. In the second example, we'll clean and prepare bitcoin price data, then analyze it.

Data wrangling and analyzing iTunes data

The terms "data wrangling" and "data munging" have become common phrases in data science, and generally mean to clean and prepare data for downstream uses such as analytics and modeling. Let's dive into data wrangling with the chinook iTunes dataset.

Loading and saving data with Pandas

In this first example, we're working for Apple in the iTunes analytics department. Our first task is to find any useful information from a set of music sales data that could improve the iTunes business. We'll be using the chinook dataset again, which is a sampling of iTunes data that we used in *Chapter 3, SQL and Built-in File Handling Modules in Python.*

The first step to wrangling data is, of course, loading it. Pandas provides several functions to load data for a variety of file types. A co-worker in the iTunes department gave us CSV, Excel, and SQLite database files that we need to load into Python for analysis. We'll start with the simplest file – the CSV. The acronym **CSV** stands for **comma-separated values** and is a plain text file. The format of a CSV is like this:

```
Track,Composer,Milliseconds,Bytes,UnitPrice,Name,Album,Artist
All the Best Cowboys Have Daddy Issues,,2555492,211743651,1.99,TV
Shows,"Lost, Season 1",Lost
Beira Mar,Gilberto Gil,295444,9597994,0.99,Latin,Unplugged,Eric Clapton
```

We can see that there are values separated by commas. The first line is the headers, which are the column labels in a spreadsheet. Lines after that are data, with each value separated by commas. We can load it to a DataFrame like so:

```
import pandas as pd
csv_df = pd.read_csv('data/itunes_data.csv')
csv_df.head()
```

If you don't have pandas installed, you can install it with `conda install -c conda-forge pandas -y` (or install it with `pip install pandas`). When most people use pandas, they import it with the alias `pd` as we did in the first line above. We won't be importing the pandas library in the rest of the examples in this chapter, so whenever you see `pd`, it is the pandas library. After loading pandas, we load the data with `read_csv()`, and finally, look at the first 5 rows with `df.head()`.

Notice in the output of the `head()` function, shown in *Figure 4.1*, that Jupyter Notebook does some nice formatting for us.

We can see DataFrames have a structure with an index column along the left (0 through 4 here), and column labels along the top. Then each row-column intersection has a value. It's very much like an Excel or Google Sheets spreadsheet. The results of the head() command look like this:

	Track	Composer	Milliseconds	Bytes	UnitPrice	Genre	Album	Artist
0	All the Best Cowboys Have Daddy Issues	NaN	2555492	211743651	1.99	TV Shows	Lost, Season 1	Lost
1	Beira Mar	Gilberto Gil	295444	9597994	0.99	Latin	Unplugged	Eric Clapton
2	Brasil	Milton Nascimento, Fernando Brant	155428	5252560	0.99	Latin	Milton Nascimento Ao Vivo	Milton Nascimento
3	Ben Franklin	NaN	1271938	264168080	1.99	Comedy	The Office, Season 3	The Office
4	O Último Romântico (Ao Vivo)	NaN	231993	7692697	0.99	Latin	Lulu Santos - RCA 100 Anos De Música - Álbum 02	Lulu Santos

Figure 4.1: The result of looking at the first 5 rows of the CSV data in a DataFrame in Jupyter Notebook using the head() function

 Note that big data can indeed be handled in pandas. One method is using the chunksize argument in read_csv to read a chunk of the data at a time. A few Python packages that can also help with reading big data in pandas are dask and modin, which can utilize clusters of computers (for example, on AWS or GCP cloud resources).

Another common file format is Excel. We have a few more song additions in an Excel file. We can load it as a DataFrame like this:

```
excel_df = pd.read_excel('data/itunes_data.xlsx', engine='openpyxl')
excel_df.head()
```

The function call to read_excel is similar to read_csv, except we are providing an engine (library) to read the data with. By default, pandas uses the xlrd library to read Excel files. Unfortunately, there is a bug with xlrd at the time of writing, and we are specifying the openpyxl library to be used instead. The xlrd or openpyxl libraries need to be installed with conda or pip in order to read Excel files with pandas.

Lastly, let's get the full data from the chinook SQLite database. Pandas has a few methods for loading from SQL, but we'll use the pd.read_sql_query() function. First, we need to create our engine that will connect to our database with SQLAlchemy, as we did in *Chapter 3, SQL and Built-in File Handling Modules in Python*:

```
from sqlalchemy import create_engine
engine = create_engine('sqlite:///data/chinook.db')
```

Then we create our SQL query as a multi-line string:

```
query = """SELECT tracks.name as Track,
tracks.composer,
tracks.milliseconds,
tracks.bytes,
tracks.unitprice,
genres.name as Genre,
albums.title as Album,
artists.name as Artist
FROM tracks
JOIN genres ON tracks.genreid = genres.genreid
JOIN albums ON tracks.albumid = albums.albumid
JOIN artists ON albums.artistid = artists.artistid;
"""
```

In this query, we are getting the data from the tracks table in the database, and joining it on the genres, albums, and artists tables to get the names of the genres, albums, and artists. We are also selecting only the non-ID columns from each table. Notice we are aliasing some of the columns, such as `tracks.name as Track`. This makes it easier to understand the data when it is in the pandas DataFrame, since the column names will be changed to these aliases. Now we can use the pandas `read` command for SQL queries:

```
with engine.connect() as connection:
    sql_df = pd.read_sql_query(query, connection)
```

We start by using a `with` block, where we create the connection. This structure will automatically close the connection once the `with` block is completed (when we are no longer indented within the `with` block), just like `with open file("filename")` as `f`: from *Chapter 3, SQL and Built-in File Handling Modules in Python*. As we can see, we simply give the `read sql_query` function our query string and SQLAlchemy connection as the two required arguments. We can specify more parameters if needed, which are detailed in the online documentation for the `read_sql_query` function. Now we can look at the top few rows of the data. We use the `head()` method of DataFrames with the first and only argument of `n` as 2 to print out two rows, and then transpose it with `T`, which switches the rows and columns. This is useful for DataFrames that have a lot of columns:

```
sql_df.head(2).T
```

When running in Jupyter Notebook, this prints out:

	0	1
Track	For Those About To Rock (We Salute You)	Put The Finger On You
Composer	Angus Young, Malcolm Young, Brian Johnson	Angus Young, Malcolm Young, Brian Johnson
Milliseconds	343719	205662
Bytes	11170334	6713451
UnitPrice	0.99	0.99
Genre	Rock	Rock
Album	For Those About To Rock We Salute You	For Those About To Rock We Salute You
Artist	AC/DC	AC/DC

Figure 4.2: The result of looking at the first few rows of the SQL-fetched data in pandas

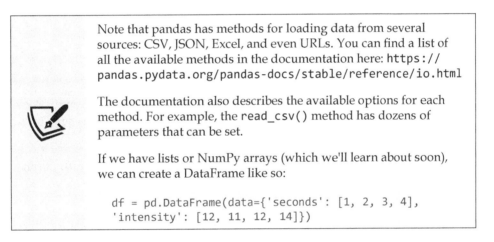

Note that pandas has methods for loading data from several sources: CSV, JSON, Excel, and even URLs. You can find a list of all the available methods in the documentation here: `https://pandas.pydata.org/pandas-docs/stable/reference/io.html`

The documentation also describes the available options for each method. For example, the `read_csv()` method has dozens of parameters that can be set.

If we have lists or NumPy arrays (which we'll learn about soon), we can create a DataFrame like so:

```
df = pd.DataFrame(data={'seconds': [1, 2, 3, 4],
'intensity': [12, 11, 12, 14]})
```

Now that we have our three DataFrames, let's join them together to make one large DataFrame.

Understanding the DataFrame structure and combining/concatenating multiple DataFrames

DataFrames have a certain structure: a number of columns storing data, and an index. This index can be used as one method to access the data. We can access the index like so:

```
sql_df.index
```

This prints out:

```
RangeIndex(start=0, stop=3503, step=1)
```

This is an autogenerated index that is created when we load the DataFrame. We can also specify an index with the `index` argument in any of the pandas `read` commands, such as `read_csv('filename', index='index_col_name')`. We can view the columns we have with this:

```
sql_df.columns
```

Which gives us a list of columns as a pandas index (a list-like structure):

```
Index(['Track', 'Composer', 'Milliseconds', 'Bytes', 'UnitPrice', 'Name',
       'Album', 'Artist'],
dtype='object')
```

Another key data structure in pandas is the Series. Whereas DataFrames can have several columns, a Series only has one column. We can check the type of a variable to see if it is a DataFrame or Series:

```
type(sql_df)
```

This prints out `pandas.core.frame.DataFrame`, since we have a DataFrame. Recall from *Chapter 2, Getting Started with Python,* that the built-in function `type()` tells us the type of an object.

To combine our three DataFrames into one, we'll use the `pd.concat()` function:

```
itunes_df = pd.concat([csv_df, excel_df, sql_df])
```

As we did above, we give the function a list of DataFrames, and then store this in a new variable. By default, this stacks the DataFrames on top of each other, row-wise.

The `pd.concat()` function can also be used to merge DataFrames like a SQL join:

```
itunes_df = pd.concat([csv_df, excel_df, sql_df],
axis=1, join=inner)
```

Here, we set `axis=1` to tell the function to join along the columns, not rows. We also set the `join` parameter to `inner` so that only rows with a matching index are joined.

`pd.merge()` is another function that can be used to merge data, such as a SQL join. With `merge()`, we can join on any column rather than just the index. The official online pandas documentation on `merge` details the available arguments and shows examples: `https://pandas.pydata.org/pandas-docs/stable/reference/api/pandas.DataFrame.merge.html`. Other merging methods are described in the documentation here: `https://pandas.pydata.org/pandas-docs/stable/user_guide/merging.html`

We now have a full DataFrame, and we can explore the data to see what we've got.

Exploratory Data Analysis (EDA) and basic data cleaning with Pandas

Whenever we have some data loaded, it's a good idea to take a look at what we have. In general, we can follow a general EDA checklist:

- Examine the top and bottom of the data
- Examine the data's dimensions
- Examine the datatypes and missing values
- Investigate statistical properties of the data
- Create plots of the data

Some of this EDA can provide a starting point for any further analysis that we do.

Examining the top and bottom of the data

We already know how to look at the top of the data: `itunes_df.head()`. For looking at the bottom of the data, we use `tail()`:

```
itunes_df.tail()
```

This should show the following:

	Track	Composer	Milliseconds	Bytes	UnitPrice	Genre	Album	Artist
3498	Pini Di Roma (Pinien Von Rom) \ I Pini Della V...	None	286741	4718950	0.99	Classical	Respighi:Pines of Rome	Eugene Ormandy
3499	String Quartet No. 12 in C Minor, D. 703 "Quar...	Franz Schubert	139200	2283131	0.99	Classical	Schubert: The Late String Quartets & String Qu...	Emerson String Quartet
3500	L'orfeo, Act, Sinfonia (Orchestra)	Claudio Monteverdi	66639	1189062	0.99	Classical	Monteverdi: L'Orfeo	C. Monteverdi, Nigel Rogers - Chiaroscuro; Lon...
3501	Quintet for Horn, Violin, 2 Violas, and Cello ...	Wolfgang Amadeus Mozart	221331	3665114	0.99	Classical	Mozart: Chamber Music	Nash Ensemble
3502	Koyaanisqatsi	Philip Glass	206005	3305164	0.99	Soundtrack	Koyaanisqatsi (Soundtrack from the Motion Pict...	Philip Glass Ensemble

Figure 4.3: The result of looking at the last five rows of the iTunes DataFrame in Jupyter Notebook

Remember that if we have many columns, we can transpose the printout with `itunes_df.tail().T`, which transposes columns and rows. In this case, it's about the same with or without the transpose.

Another way to look at some lines of data is using indexing. There are two ways to index in pandas: by row number or by index value.

To index by row number, we use `iloc`. This is helpful if we want to look at the first or last row. For example, this is how we look at the first row (the 0th index) and the last row (the -1 index):

```
print(itunes_df.iloc[0])
print(itunes_df.iloc[-1])
```

This looks like this:

```
Track           All the Best Cowboys Have Daddy Issues
Composer                                           NaN
Milliseconds                                   2555492
Bytes                                        211743651
UnitPrice                                         1.99
Genre                                         TV Shows
Album                                    Lost, Season 1
Artist                                            Lost
Name: 0, dtype: object
```

```
Track                                       Koyaanisqatsi
Composer                                     Philip Glass
Milliseconds                                       206005
Bytes                                             3305164
UnitPrice                                            0.99
Genre                                          Soundtrack
Album   Koyaanisqatsi (Soundtrack from the Motion Pict...
Artist                             Philip Glass Ensemble
Name: 3502, dtype: object
```

We see that each column is printed out on a separate row, with the name of the column on the left and the value on the right. We can also see something at the bottom, Name with dtype. This is the index value of the row, with its datatype. The Object datatype means it is a string or mixed values of strings and numbers.

With iloc, we can also choose a single column. For example, the following commands print out the value of the first row and first column (an index of [0, 0]) and the last row and last column (and an index of [-1, -1]):

```
print(itunes_df.iloc[0, 0])
print(itunes_df.iloc[-1, -1])
```

Additionally, indexing can be done by index value. From our use of tail(), we saw our last index value is 3502 (the Name value from tail() above). So, let's print that out using loc indexing with,

```
print(itunes_df.loc[3502])
```

which takes an index value instead of a row number. This will print out all rows with the index value of 3502:

```
Track                                       Koyaanisqatsi
Composer                                     Philip Glass
Milliseconds                                       206005
Bytes                                             3305164
UnitPrice                                            0.99
Genre                                          Soundtrack
Album   Koyaanisqatsi (Soundtrack from the Motion Pict...
Artist                             Philip Glass Ensemble
Name: 3502, dtype: object
```

We can see it's the same as the last row we got from `iloc`. Note that DataFrame indexes don't have to be unique – they can have repeated values. For example, let's create another DataFrame, append a copy of the last row, and use `loc` again:

```
test_df = itunes_df.copy()
test_df = test_df.append(itunes_df.loc[3502])
test_df.loc[3502]
```

On the first line, we make a copy of the existing `itunes_df` so that we won't be altering our original DataFrame. Then we add on the last row with `append`. Now the `loc` indexing returns the two rows with 3502 as the index.

If we do have a situation with duplicate index values, we can change our index to be unique, sequential numbers like so:

```
test_df.reset_index(inplace=True, drop=True)
```

This resets our index for `test_df` to a sequential `RangeIndex`. Note that if we don't use `drop=True`, then the current index is inserted as a new column in the DataFrame.

> Sometimes our data has something at the beginning or end that shouldn't be there, like a disclaimer or extra information at the end. In that case, we can use parameters in our `read` functions to ignore these lines. For example, we could use the `skiprows` parameter in `pd.read_csv()` to skip the first 5 rows if these have extra header information:
>
> ```
> df = pd.read_csv('csvfile.csv', skiprows=5)
> ```
>
> If we wanted to get rid of the last 5 rows, we could use `iloc` indexing:
>
> ```
> df = df.iloc[:-5]
> ```
>
> This will index the `df` DataFrame up to the last 5 rows. Then it overwrites the `df` variable with the result, removing the last 5 rows.

While we're looking at indexing, let's look at selecting columns of data. We can select a column of data like so:

```
itunes_df['Milliseconds']
```

If we want to select multiple columns, we can use a list of strings:

```
itunes_df[['Milliseconds', 'Bytes']]
```

If we are selecting a column, we can type part of the name and then press *Tab* to autocomplete it. For example, if we were in the middle of typing "Milliseconds" here:

```
itunes_df['Mill']
```

With our cursor just after "Mill," we could press *Tab* and it will fill in the full column name for us. This works in Jupyter Notebook and IPython, and potentially some text editors and IDEs.

Examining the data's dimensions, datatypes, and missing values

Next, we want to look at some more characteristics of the data as we have it. We can examine the rows and columns with the shape parameter:

```
print(itunes_df.shape)
```

This shows us:

```
(4021, 8)
```

This means the data has 4,021 rows and 8 columns. It is a tuple, so if we want to get just the number of rows, we can use `itunes_df.shape[0]`. I like to use this after concatenating/merging DataFrames or removing rows/columns to make sure the shape is what I expect.

Looking at the datatypes and missing values can be done with `info`:

```
itunes_df.info()
```

This shows us:

```
<class 'pandas.core.frame.DataFrame'>
Int64Index: 4021 entries, 0 to 3502
Data columns (total 8 columns):
 #   Column        Non-Null Count  Dtype
---  ------        --------------  -----
 0   Track         4021 non-null   object
 1   Composer      2908 non-null   object
 2   Milliseconds  4021 non-null   int64
 3   Bytes         4021 non-null   int64
 4   UnitPrice     4021 non-null   float64
 5   Genre         4021 non-null   object
 6   Album         4021 non-null   object
 7   Artist        4021 non-null   object
```

```
dtypes: float64(1), int64(2), object(5)
memory usage: 442.7+ KB
```

We can see the data has a few types: `object`, `int64`, and `float64`. It's worth sanity-checking that these types are correct. In our case, these all look correct – numeric values are integer or float datatypes, and strings are objects.

The `info` method also shows us the non-null values. As long as this matches the number of rows, it means there are no missing values. However, it's easier to look at the number of missing values with this:

```
itunes_df.isna().sum()
```

This gives us the counts of missing values (stored as `NaN` for not a number, but also called NA for not available). The first part, `itunes_df.isna()`, returns a DataFrame full of `True` and `False` values for each cell in the original DataFrame – `True` if the value is NA, `False` if the value is not NA. Then `.sum()` sums this up along each column. We get this result:

```
Track             0
Composer       1113
Milliseconds      0
Bytes             0
UnitPrice         0
Genre             0
Album             0
Artist            0
dtype: int64
```

Soon we will figure out what to do with the missing values. For now, we simply know that there are some missing values in the `Composer` column.

> There are some more details to how **isna** matches missing values for different datatypes; see the documentation for details: `https://pandas.pydata.org/pandas-docs/stable/reference/api/pandas.isna.html`
>
> There are also other related functions, such as `df.notna()`, `df.notnull()`, and `df.isnull()`.

Once we have an understanding of some of the basic properties of our data, we can look at the statistics of the data.

Investigating statistical properties of the data

The easiest first step to examine the statistics of a dataset is to use a pandas command:

```
itunes_df.describe()
```

For our iTunes dataset, we see this result:

	Milliseconds	Bytes	UnitPrice
count	4.021000e+03	4.021000e+03	4021.000000
mean	3.927276e+05	3.311048e+07	1.050184
std	5.337745e+05	1.042268e+08	0.237857
min	1.071000e+03	3.874700e+04	0.990000
25%	2.069680e+05	6.372433e+06	0.990000
50%	2.554770e+05	8.102839e+06	0.990000
75%	3.217240e+05	1.025143e+07	0.990000
max	5.286953e+06	1.059546e+09	1.990000

Figure 4.4: The result of itunes_df.describe() in Jupyter Notebook

This shows a summary of a few statistics, including the number of non-missing (non-NA) values (count), the average (mean), the standard deviation (std), the minimum and maximum, and a few percentiles. Note that these statistics can also be found with functions, like df.std() for standard deviation. The 25% row means the 25th percentile. What this tells us is that 25% of the data lies at or below the value of 0.99 for the UnitPrice column, for example. We have 25% of the data contained between each of the breakpoints from min through max (including the 25th, 50th, and 75th percentiles). The term we use for these sections of data are quantiles – equal sizes of chunks of data, sorted from least to greatest. If we break up the data into fourths like we did here, the quantiles are called quartiles.

For non-numeric columns, we can look at the mode (most frequent value). For example:

```
itunes_df['Genre'].mode()
```

This returns the following:

```
0    Rock
dtype: object
```

This shows us Rock is the most common genre in the data. We can get more specific and look at how many times each unique value appears:

```
itunes_df['Genre'].value_counts()
```

The first few rows of the results show this:

```
Rock            1498
Latin            656
Metal            420
```

From this, we can see Rock clearly makes up a majority of the songs in our data. If we have many unique values, we can look at only a few with indexing:

```
itunes_df['Genre'].value_counts()[:5]
```

This would show only the top 5 genres by counts.

If we want to investigate how many unique items there are, the `unique` function is helpful:

```
itunes_df['Artist'].unique().shape
```

The `unique()` function will return an array of all unique values. We then use the shape attribute to see how many values there are. In this case, we find there are 204 unique artists in the data.

Lastly, let's look at correlations between our data columns. The `corr` function in pandas calculates correlations:

```
itunes_df.corr()
```

This returns a DataFrame of correlation results:

	Milliseconds	Bytes	UnitPrice
Milliseconds	1.000000	0.957791	0.934829
Bytes	0.957791	1.000000	0.938734
UnitPrice	0.934829	0.938734	1.000000

Figure 4.5: The result of itunes_df.corr() in Jupyter Notebook

This calculation is Pearson correlation, which measures how linearly correlated two datasets are. It ranges from -1 (inverse correlation; variable 1 increases proportionally when variable 2 decreases) to 0 (no correlation) to 1 (perfectly linear correlation; variable 1 increases proportionally when variable 2 increases). So, the correlation between a single numeric data column and itself is 1 by definition – if we plotted a dataset against itself, it would be a straight, diagonal line. We can see from our data that all of our numeric data is strongly linearly correlated, which makes sense. Longer songs are larger in data storage size (bytes) and cost more. Roughly speaking, we can break up correlation strengths into sections of 0.2. So, 0-0.2 is very weakly correlated, 0.2-0.4 is weak, 0.4-0.6 signifies medium correlation, 0.6-0.8 is strong, and 0.8-1 is very strongly correlated. This is only for data with linear relationships. In other words, a scatter plot of two variables should resemble a straight line. If your data has non-linear relationships, then Pearson correlations are not the best method to use. We will learn other correlation methods for non-linear relationships later, such as Phik correlation.

Plotting with DataFrames

Plotting is part of any EDA process, and fortunately, pandas makes it easy to plot data from DataFrames. A few common plots you might use from pandas are bar, histogram, and scatter plots.

 There are more plots available through pandas, which are detailed in the documentation: https://pandas.pydata.org/pandas-docs/stable/user_guide/visualization.html

Let's look first at a histogram of our song lengths. First, we need to import the standard Python plotting library, `matplotlib`:

```
import matplotlib.pyplot as plt
```

This is the conventional way to import the plotting library in Python. Next, we can plot our data:

```
itunes_df['Milliseconds'].hist(bins=30)
plt.show()
```

The first line selects the `Milliseconds` column, and uses the `hist()` method of pandas Series objects. We set the option `bins=30` to increase it from the default of 10 – this specifies how many bars the histogram is broken up into. Then we use the `plt.show()` command to display the plot. In Jupyter Notebook, this is not necessary, but in an IPython shell or Python `.py` file, we need to call `plt.show()` to display the plot on the screen. Our result looks like this:

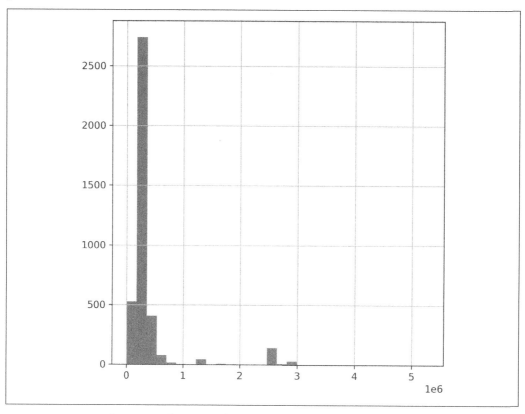

Figure 4.6: A histogram of the Milliseconds column from itunes_df

A histogram shows the distribution of a numeric dataset. On the x-axis, we have values of milliseconds. On the y-axis, we have the number of counts of datapoints within each bar. The number of bars is specified by the `bins` argument in the `hist` function, and I often increase this from the default of 10 to obtain higher resolution.

We see that most of our songs have a shorter song length, but there are some outliers with very long lengths. The x-axis scale has 1e6, meaning the numbers are multiplied by $1*10^6$, or 1 million. From our `describe()` function earlier, we found our 50th percentile of song length (the median) is around 200,000 ms, or 200 s. This seems right, as most songs are around 3 minutes long.

The functions `df.hist()` and `df.plot.hist()` return different results, especially when plotting multiple columns For example, `df[[' Milliseconds' , 'Bytes ']].df.hist()` will plot multiple histograms in separate subplots, while `df.plot.hist()` will plot multiple histograms in a single plot. If we are plotting both histograms within the same plot, the `alpha` parameter can be used to adjust transparency so both histograms are visible, like this: `df.plot.hist(alpha=0.5)`.

We saw that our song length is correlated to other columns, so let's look at a scatter plot of song length and song size in bytes:

```
itunes_df.plot.scatter(x='Milliseconds', y='Bytes')
plt.show()
```

Notice we are using `plot.scatter` here instead of just `scatter`. The `hist` function can also be called with `plot.hist` as we did, but sometimes we are required to put `plot` before the plotting function in pandas as with `scatter`. Our scatter plot looks like this:

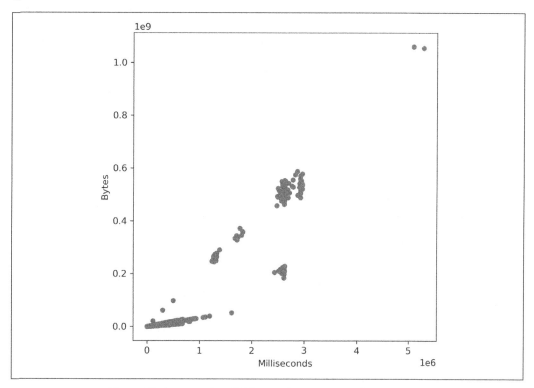

Figure 4.7: A scatter plot of Milliseconds versus Bytes from itunes_df

Notice we have 1e9 on the upper-left side, meaning the Bytes values should be multiplied by 1,000,000,000, and we have 1e6 on the lower-right side, signifying the Milliseconds values should be multiplied by 1,000,000. We can see from the plot there are some groups of data – two groups follow roughly straight lines at different slopes. Within the steeper line, we see at least three groups of data. Then there is another group of data around $2.5*10^6$ ms and 0.2e9 bytes. Finally, one group resides with a long song length and large file size (in the upper-right part of the plot). We will revisit some of these groups soon and examine these groups in more detail.

Lastly, let's look at a bar plot of non-numeric data. We can use `value_counts` again and create a bar plot:

```
itunes_df['Genre'].value_counts().plot.bar()
plt.show()
```

We select the `Genre` column, and then use `value_counts()` as we did before to get the counts of unique values for genres. We need to use `plot` before calling the `bar()` plotting function here. Our resulting plot looks like this:

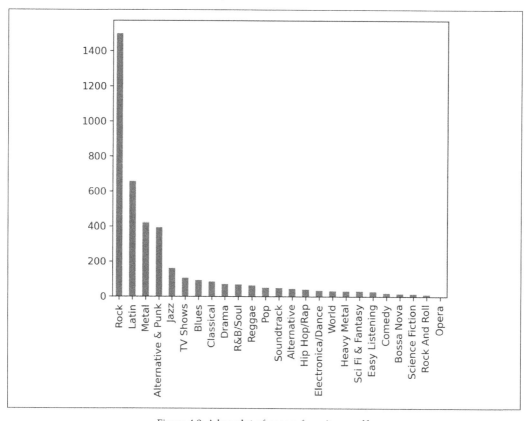

Figure 4.8: A bar plot of genres from itunes_df

It's easier to interpret the data from `value_counts` when looking at a bar plot instead of just the raw numbers, so this method can be quite useful.

Cleaning data

After we've completed some EDA, we can then move on to some other cleaning steps. Some surveys have found data scientists spend anywhere between 25% and 75% of their time cleaning data, as we covered in *Chapter 1, Introduction to Data Science*, although sometimes data scientists spend upward of 90% of their time cleaning data. Quite often, we can carry out most or all of our data cleaning with pandas. Some common data cleaning steps include:

- Removing irrelevant data
- Dealing with missing values (filling in or dropping them)
- Dealing with outliers
- Dealing with duplicate values
- Ensuring datatypes are correct
- Standardizing data formats (e.g. mismatched capitalization, converting units)

Before we get started with the checklist for data cleaning, let's learn how to filter DataFrames for specific values.

Filtering DataFrames

Similar to the SQL commands we used in *Chapter 3, SQL and Built-in File Handling Modules in Python*, we can filter data in pandas DataFrames. For example, let's get the longest songs from our data that we saw in our scatter plot. These have lengths over 4,000,000 ms:

```
itunes_df[itunes_df['Milliseconds'] > 4e6]
```

We use the usual indexing format for DataFrames – the variable name followed by square brackets. Then, we give it a so-called Boolean mask. Try running just the inner part of the indexing:

```
itunes_df['Milliseconds'] > 4e6
```

You will see this returns a pandas Series with `True` or `False` values. This is our Boolean mask. When we provide this as an indexing command to our DataFrame, it only returns rows where our mask is `True`. Notice we are using scientific notation for 4,000,000 as well – 4e6 means $4*10^6$.

From our filtering command above, we get two returned rows. Here, we are only showing `Genre` and `Artist` for clarity:

```
            Genre                 Artist
2833   TV Shows   Battlestar Galactica
2898      Drama                   Lost
```

We can see both of these long "songs" are actually the audio from TV shows. Let's take this one step further and look at the value counts of genres from songs over 2,000,000 ms:

```
itunes_df[itunes_df['Milliseconds'] > 2e6]['Genre'].value_counts()
```

Here, we are using filtering in the same way we did before. Then, we are indexing the result using `['Genre']`. The first part, `itunes_df[itunes_df['Milliseconds'] > 2e6]`, returns a DataFrame, which can be indexed as usual. Then we use `value_counts` to get the following output:

```
Drama                     69
TV Shows                  67
Sci Fi & Fantasy          31
Science Fiction           15
Comedy                     2
Name: Genre, dtype: int64
```

We can see all these long "songs" are not really songs, but shows, possibly e-books, and comedy shows. Recall from our scatter plot of milliseconds versus bytes that there were two clouds of points right around 2.5e6 ms, but with a few different values for bytes. We can get the points with the smaller values of bytes by filtering with multiple conditions:

```
itunes_df[(itunes_df['Milliseconds'] > 2e6) \
          & (itunes_df['Bytes'] < 0.4e9)]['Genre'].value_counts()
```

Notice we now use the same condition for milliseconds as before, but in parentheses. These parentheses are important for combining Boolean masks – without them, the code will return an error. Then we use an ampersand (&), which stands for "**and**." After that, we give another filtering condition for bytes to get the smaller bytes values. We can string together as many conditions with & as we want, and the Boolean mask will require that all conditions are met. Instead of the ampersand, we could use a pipe symbol, |, which means "**or**." This would mean as long as either condition is met, the mask returns `True`.

The results of our filter are as follows:

```
TV Shows     32
Name: Genre, dtype: int64
```

Aha! For some reason, TV Shows has a smaller value for bytes than other genres. Perhaps some sort of difference in audio properties of shows compared with music means the TV show data can be compressed into a smaller size than music.

We can negate conditions in a few ways. For example, if we want to get all genres that are not TV Shows, we could use this filter:

```
itunes_df[itunes_df['Genre'] != 'TV Shows']
```

The same Boolean comparison operators from *Chapter 2, Getting Started with Python,* can be used here: == for "**equals**", != for "**not equals**", >= for greater than or equal to, and so on.

Another way to negate a condition is with the tilde character:

```
itunes_df[~(itunes_df['Genre'] == 'TV Shows')]
```

Again, this returns all genres that are not TV shows.

There are some other methods for filtering that are useful. The first is string methods. We can get genres with 'TV' in them like so:

```
itunes_df[itunes_df['Genre'].str.contains('TV')]
```

 There are more string methods in the documentation: https://pandas.pydata.org/pandas-docs/stable/user_guide/text.html#method-summary

We can also use the isna() and other NA methods we discussed earlier in the chapter for filtering. One more useful filtering tool is the method isin, which we will cover shortly.

Removing irrelevant data

We might already have an idea of which data we want to remove. This involves dropping columns or rows we don't want. For example, with our iTunes data, we may not really need the Composer column. We could drop this column like so:

```
itunes_df.drop('Composer', axis=1, inplace=True)
itunes_df.columns
```

We use the `drop` function of DataFrames, giving the column name as the first argument. We can drop multiple columns at once by supplying a list. The `axis=1` argument specifies to drop a column, not a row, and `inplace=True` changes the DataFrame itself instead of returning a new, modified DataFrame. Then we examine the remaining columns with the `columns` attribute of our DataFrame.

If we have other irrelevant data we want to remove, say any genres that are not music, we could do so with filtering:

```
only_music = itunes_df[~itunes_df['Genre'].isin(['Drama', 'TV Shows', 'Sci Fi
& Fantasy', 'Science Fiction', 'Comedy'])]
```

This uses filtering with the `isin` method. The `isin` method checks if each value is in the list or set provided to the function. In this case, we also negate this condition with the tilde (~) so that any of the non-music genres are excluded, and our `only_music` DataFrame has only genres that are music, just as the variable name suggests.

Dealing with missing values

Missing values arise all the time in datasets. Often, they are represented as `NA` or `NaN` values. Other times, missing values may be represented by certain numbers or values, such as `None` or -999. It helps to examine the data with EDA and check any documentation on the data to see if missing values are represented in a special way. We can fill in missing values, which is also called imputation. In terms of dealing with missing values, we have some options:

- Leave the missing values as-is
- Drop the data
- Fill with a specific value
- Replace with the mean, median, or mode
- Use machine learning to replace missing values

The best option for you depends on the situation and the data itself. For example, we saw that our `Composer` column has several missing values. We can use filtering to see what some of these rows look like:

```
itunes_df[itunes_df['Composer'].isna()].sample(5, random_state=42).head()
```

Here, we take a random sample of 5 datapoints with `sample()`, giving it a `random_state` so the results are the same every time we run it. Then we look at a few rows with `head()`. In this case, we get results from all sorts of genres – TV shows, latin, and so on.

It appears there is no data on some of the composers, for some unknown reason. For EDA, we can leave the values as-is. Some machine learning packages, such as H2O, can handle missing values in their algorithms, so we could leave it as-is for H2O machine learning as well.

Another option is to drop the missing values. We can either drop the entire column, as we did earlier, or we can drop the rows with missing values like this:

```
itunes_df.dropna(inplace=True)
```

The dropna function has several other parameters (options), but we are simply specifying that it should modify the existing DataFrame with inplace=True. By default, this drops any rows with at least one missing value.

If we were trying to do another type of machine learning, like clustering, we might want to fill the missing values with a specific value. Filling with a specific value could be done like so:

```
itunes_df.loc[itunes_df['Composer'].isna(), 'Composer'] = 'Unknown'
```

Here, we use filtering again to get rows where Composer is missing. Then we select the Composer column as the second element of loc. Finally, we set the missing values to Unknown. Another way to accomplish this is using fillna:

```
itunes_df['Composer'].fillna('Unknown', inplace=True)
```

Here, we select the column of interest (Composer) with DataFrame indexing, and then give the value for replacing NAs as our first argument. We use the inplace=True argument to make the changes on the existing DataFrame instead of returning a new DataFrame.

Let's say instead we wanted to fill missing values with the mode, which is the most common value for a series of data. This could make sense if we have a dataset where most of the values are a particular value, such as with the UnitPrice column. In our case, 94% of the values are 0.99 for UnitPrice, so filling with the mode would make sense there. Filling with the mode can be done similarly as we did above, except using the mode function:

```
itunes_df['UnitPrice'].fillna(itunes_df['UnitPrice'].mode(), inplace=True)
```

In other cases, we may want to fill with the mean (average). This makes sense if we have a distribution of values that is somewhat Gaussian or a normal distribution, meaning it follows a bell curve shape. Instead of using mode, we can use mean.

In other cases, it makes more sense to use the median (the 50th percentile), which means using something like df['Column'].median(). The median is best when we have a skewed distribution, as shown in *Figure 4.9*:

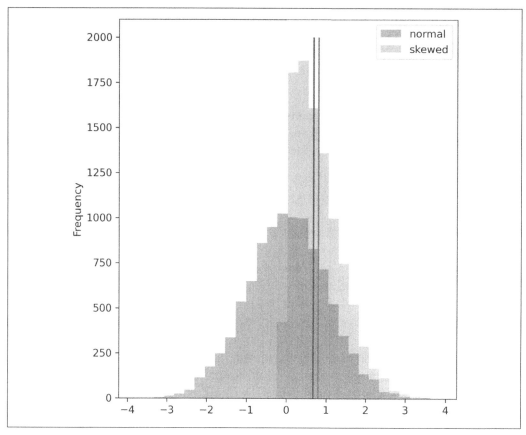

Figure 4.9: A normal/Gaussian distribution and a skewed normal distribution. The vertical line on the left is the median of the skewed distribution; the vertical line on the right is the mean

In the skewed distribution, the median is closer to the peak of the histogram, as shown by the blue (left) line above. The red (right) line is the mean, which is further from the peak of the histogram. This sort of distribution shows up with wages and housing prices, for example. For the normal non-skewed distribution, the median and mean are nearly identical.

The most advanced method of replacing missing values is using machine learning. We can use the machine learning techniques that we will learn later in the book to predict missing values for each row and fill them in. Another option is using a pre-built imputer function, like the `sklearn.impute.KNNImputer` function, which accomplishes the same thing. Usually, replacing with the mean, median, or mode (or even a constant value such as 0) is good enough to start, but **KNN (k-nearest neighbors)** imputation works well (but requires more effort).

An example where KNN imputation can work is demographic data. KNN works by taking a certain number, *n*, of the closest datapoints, and averages them to get new values. It gets the nearest points by Euclidean distance, which is a straight line between two points in space. We will cover this algorithm in more detail in a future chapter.

To see KNN imputation in action, let's create missing values in our `Bytes` column:

```
import numpy as np
itunes_df.loc[0, 'Bytes'] = np.nan
```

We first need to import the NumPy library to be able to create NaN values, and then we get the location where the row index is 0 and the column is `Bytes`, and set the value to `np.nan`. Next, we import the `KNNImputer` function from the `sklearn` (scikit-learn) machine learning library and create an instance of the `imputer` object:

```
from sklearn.impute import KNNImputer
imputer = KNNImputer()
```

We leave the object with its default of the five nearest neighbors for calculations. Then, we use the `fit_transform` method:

```
imputed = imputer.fit_transform(itunes_df [['Milliseconds', 'Bytes', 'UnitPrice']])
```

This takes in data with missing values, fits a KNN model, and then fills in the missing values with predictions from the model. Unfortunately, `sklearn` can only handle numeric data without missing values, so we can't pass it any strings. Then, to replace our missing values, we overwrite the `Bytes` column with our new data:

```
itunes_df['Bytes'] = imputed[:, 1]
```

The imputed variable is a NumPy array, which is like a pandas Series. We are indexing it with [:, 1], which means retrieving all rows and the second column. If we examine the prediction for the missing value compared with the original value, it's close but not perfect. Our predicted value from `KNNImputer` for the first row with an Index value of 0 (there are a few rows with an Index value of 0) is 3.8e8, but the actual original value was 2.1e8 before we set it to `np.nan`. However, the `KNNImputer` prediction is much closer than the mean value for `Bytes` of 3.3e7, which is an order of magnitude smaller than the actual value. So, the `KNNImputer` method does a much better job of filling in missing values compared with using the mean for data that has a very wide distribution or is not close to a Gaussian distribution.

> If you instead used `itunes_df.iloc[0]['Bytes'] = np.nan` to try and set the first row as a missing value, it would give you a warning: A value is trying to be set on a copy of a slice from a DataFrame. It's better to set values with `loc` instead of `iloc`, because it won't work properly with `iloc`. Sometimes when you see this warning, it also means you indexed/sliced the DataFrame and then tried to set the value of a column or entry in the DataFrame. To avoid that, go back to the point where you sliced, indexed, or filtered the DataFrame and use the `copy` function like this:
>
> ```
> new_df = df[df['Column'] == 'Value'].copy()
> ```

The `KNNImputer` method of replacing missing values is the most advanced that we covered here. Don't be worried if it's confusing at this time; we will cover machine learning methods like KNN later in the book.

Dealing with outliers

Outliers are data that are not in the usual range of values. For categorical data, such as the genres, these may be some of the minority classes, like TV shows. We could remove these rows with filtering, or we could also group all minority classes into a class we label as `Other`. Dealing with categorical outliers can help a little with analysis, but often has a minimal impact.

For numeric data, it's easy to quantify an outlier. Typically, we use interquartile range (IQR) or z-score methods. We will cover the IQR method here, since it relates to boxplots, which we will cover in the next chapter.

Recall that we get quartiles (25th, 50th, 75th percentiles) from the `describe()` function in our EDA. These are sometimes called the first, second, and third quartiles, respectively (Q1, Q2, and Q3).

The IQR method uses these quartile levels to detect outliers. The formula is:

$$IQR = 75\_percentile - 25\_percentile$$

For our outlier boundaries:

$$upper\_boundary = 75\_percentile + 1.5 * IQR$$

$$lower\_boundary = 25\_percentile - 1.5 * IQR$$

We can exclude outliers from a DataFrame like so:

```
def remove_outliers(df, column):
    q1 = df[column].quantile(0.25)
    q3 = df[column].quantile(0.75)
    iqr = q3 - q1
    upper_boundary = q3 + 1.5 * iqr
    lower_boundary = q1 - 1.5 * iqr
    new_df = df.loc[(df[column] > lower_boundary) & \
                        (df[column] < upper_boundary)]
    return new_df
```

Here, we have created a function that takes a DataFrame and column name as an argument. The first two lines calculate the 25th and 75th percentile levels with the quantile() method, and store them in the q1 and q3 variables. Then we calculate IQR from the difference between Q1 and Q3. Next, we get the upper and lower boundaries for outliers using the IQR outlier formulas. Then we use DataFrame filtering to only keep the points between the upper and lower boundaries (keeping only the non-outlier points). The result is stored in a new DataFrame, new_df. Finally, we return our DataFrame. We could use this with a numeric column like this:

```
itunes_df_clean = remove_outliers(itunes_df, 'Milliseconds')
```

We can then use the shape attribute, itunes_df_clean.shape, to check that some rows were actually dropped. In this case, we excluded about 400 rows of data by removing the Milliseconds outliers.

Other methods for dropping outliers can be found in this helpful Stack Overflow question and its answers: https://stackoverflow.com/questions/23199796/detect-and-exclude-outliers-in-pandas-data-frame

In fact, the function above was adapted from one of those answers.

Removing outliers can make it easier to visualize data and can improve the performance of machine learning models. Another easy way to remove outliers is to exclude any datapoints that lie outside of extreme percentiles in the data. For example, we could remove any points outside of the 1st and 99th percentiles, meaning we only keep the middle 98% of the data.

Dealing with duplicate values

It's always a good idea to check for duplicate values, since they can creep into data in numerous ways. An easy way to check for duplicates is the duplicated() function:

```
itunes_df.duplicated().sum()
```

This prints out the number of rows that are exact duplicates. In this case, we see that 518 rows are duplicated! There must have been some issue with the data when we loaded and combined it at the beginning of the chapter, or somewhere else upstream. We can drop these duplicated rows like so:

```
itunes_df.drop_duplicates(inplace=True)
```

Once again, we use inplace=True to modify the existing DataFrame. There are other options for drop_duplicates, but the defaults check for exactly duplicated rows.

Ensuring datatypes are correct

Sometimes data will be loaded as an object datatype (string) instead of numeric if there are some non-numbers in that column. We want to use the df.info() function as we did before to check that our columns are the correct datatype, and then convert any columns that need it. For example, we could convert Milliseconds to an integer datatype like so:

```
itunes_df['Milliseconds'] = itunes_df['Milliseconds'].astype('int')
```

Within the astype function, we can use strings such as 'float', 'int', or 'object', Python datatypes like int or float, or NumPy datatypes like np.int. For most work, we only need the datatypes object (for strings), int, and float.

Standardizing data formats

Sometimes we will have string data in several formats. This tends to happen when data is entered by hand. For example, some people may capitalize gender like "Male," "Female," or "Nonbinary," while others may leave it lowercased. Some people may only use a one-letter abbreviation, like "M." Cleaning this sort of data often means using DataFrame filtering, loc indexing, and string methods to replace values. We will cover this in the next section.

Data transformations

Simple data transformations in pandas are easy, such as basic math operations. For example, we can convert milliseconds to seconds like so:

```
itunes_df['Seconds'] = itunes_df['Milliseconds'] / 1000
```

If we wanted to create another column, say, the ratio of song length to bytes, we could do so like this:

```
itunes_df['len_byte_ratio'] = itunes_df['Milliseconds'] / itunes_df['Bytes']
```

Of course, all the other mathematical operators in Python can be used in the same fashion, even exponentiation (**) and the modulo operator (%).

Using replace, map, and apply to clean and transform data

A handy way to replace several values at once is with the map and replace functions. For example, we can replace variations of genres in our iTunes data like so:

```
genre_dict = {'metal': 'Metal', 'met': 'Metal'}
itunes_df['Genre'].replace(genre_dict)
```

First, we create a dictionary, where the keys are the existing values in the DataFrame, and the values are what should replace the existing values. In this case, we replace variations of the Metal genre (metal and met) with Metal. In the second line, we select the Genre column, then use replace with our dictionary of replacement values. This returns a new pandas Series.

The replace function replaces any matching values it finds in the supplied dictionary, and one use case is replacing some (or all) of the values in a Series. Any values that are not in the dictionary passed to replace will be left alone. If we want any non-matching values in our provided conversion dictionary to be replaced with NaN instead, then we can use map. This makes it easy to check if any values were not converted to something new by checking for NaN values in the Series (for example, this can be useful in unit tests). The performance of map and replace are similar.

Another handy tool is the apply function, which is a Swiss army knife function – it can do anything. For example, to lowercase all values in the Genre column, we could use apply after selecting the Genre column:

```
itunes_df['Genre'].apply(lambda x: x.lower())
```

Remember from *Chapter 2, Getting Started with Python*, that a lambda function is an "anonymous" function, created on the fly. It starts with the `lambda` keyword, then is followed by the inputs as variable names, then a colon character, and finally the actual function. The result of putting the inputs through the function is returned. An equivalent way to lowercase the `Genre` column is as follows:

```
def lowercase(x):
    return x.lower()


itunes_df['Genre'].apply(lowercase)
```

Here, we define a function called `lowercase`, which returns the lowercased version of the input. Then we simply give this function to `apply`. However, pandas has a built-in method for lowercasing strings, which makes for cleaner and simpler code:

```
itunes_df['Genre'].str.lower()
```

Often it's better to stick with the built-in pandas solution for simplicity. Exceptions to this rule occur when we are doing something rather complex that's not built-in.

> If we do need to use `apply`, an easy way to potentially speed it up is with `swifter`. This is a package in Python that attempts to automatically parallelize our `apply` code. We can use it like so:
>
> ```
> import swifter
> itunes_df['Genre'].swifter.apply(lambda x: x.lower())
> ```
>
> Another option for parallelization of `apply` is to use the Dask package, which `swifter` will use if it is the best solution.

The various built-in pandas functions include string methods (such as `df['Genre'].str.lower()`), math methods (such as `df['Bytes'].mean()`), and datetime methods (such as `df['date'].dt.month`).

Using GroupBy

One last useful tool we'll cover is groupby. This is just like in SQL – group by unique values in a column. For example, we can look at the average length of songs by genre, and sort them from least to greatest:

```
itunes_df.groupby('Genre').mean()['Seconds'].sort_values().head()
```

First, we take our DataFrame, then use the groupby method. We supply the column name we want to group by, and then take the average, or mean.

This returns a pandas Series. We can then use the `sort_values()` method to sort from least to greatest. Finally, we use `head()` to get only the first five rows:

```
Genre
Rock And Roll      134.643500
Opera              174.813000
Hip Hop/Rap        178.176286
Easy Listening     189.164208
Bossa Nova         219.590000
Name: Seconds, dtype: float64
```

We can see `Rock And Roll` has the shortest average song length.

Writing DataFrames to disk

Lastly, we often want to save our data after preprocessing and cleaning. Pandas offers several ways to save data: CSV, Excel, HDF5, and many others (detailed well in the documentation: `https://pandas.pydata.org/pandas-docs/stable/reference/io.html`). All of the major `read` functions have a corresponding `to` function that saves the data to disk. For example, to save our iTunes data to a CSV:

```
itunes_df.to_csv('data/saved_itunes_data.csv', index=False)
```

We first give the filename as an argument for `to_csv`, and then tell it to not write the index to the file with `index=False`. This filename would save the data as `saved_itunes_data.csv` in the directory named "data" within the same folder/directory where the code is being run.

There are many other ways to save data. Some others I like to use are HDF and feather. HDF and Parquet files offer compression, and HDF allows us to append to files and retrieve only parts of the data at a time (via the index). Feather files are nice because they are very fast, compressed, and were designed for passing data between R and Python. However, feather is not considered a good idea for longer-term storage because the format could change. One last option to consider is writing to an Excel file (`df.to_excel(filename)`) if the data needs to be shared with less technical colleagues.

There is a lot more on the advanced side of the pandas package – aggregations, working with temporal data, and reshaping data. To learn more about advanced pandas usage, consider Packt's *Pandas 1.x Cookbook*, by Matt Harrison and Theodore Petrou, which is highly rated.

Wrangling and analyzing Bitcoin price data

For our second example, we'll use the same bitcoin price data from the *Test your knowledge* section in *Chapter 3, SQL and Built-in File Handling Modules in Python*. We can load the data like so:

```
btc_df = pd.read_csv('data/bitcoin_price.csv')
btc_df.head()
```

The first five rows look like this:

	symbol	time	open	close	high	low	volume
0	btcusd	1364688000000	92.500000	93.033000	93.74999	91.00000	3083.079791
1	btcusd	1364774400000	93.250000	103.999000	105.90000	92.49999	5224.401313
2	btcusd	1364860800000	104.000000	118.229354	118.38670	99.00000	8376.527478
3	btcusd	1364947200000	117.958261	134.700000	146.88000	101.51088	12996.245072
4	btcusd	1365033600000	134.716560	132.899000	143.00000	119.00000	6981.668305

Figure 4.10: The first five rows of our bitcoin price data

The `symbol` column is all `btcusd`. You can verify this by examining unique values:

```
btc_df['symbol'].unique()
```

Let's drop this column since it does not give us any information:

```
btc_df.drop('symbol', axis=1, inplace=True)
```

Next, we are going to convert the `time` column to a pandas `datetime` datatype:

```
btc_df['time'] = pd.to_datetime(btc_df['time'], unit='ms')
```

In this line of code, we use the handy pandas function, `to_datetime`, to convert our `time` column to a `datetime`. Often, this function can auto-detect the format of the datetime data. However, in this case, it fails – it assumes the units are seconds since the epoch instead of milliseconds, so we provide the argument `unit='ms'`. "Seconds since the epoch" means the number of seconds since 1-1-1970 and is used widely in computer science and programming. If you see a datetime column that is a large integer, it's probably the time since the epoch or epoch time.

We can quickly figure out if a timestamp is in seconds, milliseconds, or another unit like nanoseconds by putting your timestamp into https://www.epochconverter.com/ or another online conversion tool for "time since the epoch" to datetime. We can also divide the number by 1e9. If it comes out as a single digit in the ones position (like 1.6), then it is in seconds. Otherwise, if it comes out in the thousands (like 1600), then it is in ms.

We can confirm that the conversion worked by examining btc_df.info(), which should now show datetime64[ns] for the time column's datatype.

Next, we set the time column as the index:

```
btc_df.set_index('time', inplace=True)
```

This allows us to easily plot the data:

```
btc_df['close'].plot(logy=True)
```

Here, we are plotting the daily closing price as a line plot and using a logarithmic scale on the y-axis with logy=True. This means the y-axis has major tick marks equally spaced by powers of 10 (for example, 10, 100, 1,000), and by means of which it is easier to visualize large ranges of data. We can see the results in *Figure 4.11*:

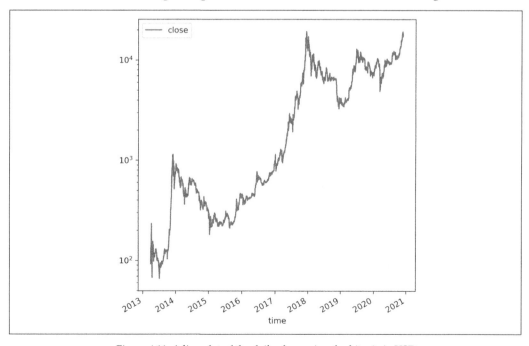

Figure 4.11: A line plot of the daily close prices for bitcoin in USD

That was a few lines of code to get the data preprocessed to a point where we can easily plot it as a time series. If the `time` column was a datetime string, like 12-11-2020, we could load it directly as a datetime index like this:

```
btc_df = pd.read_csv('data/bitcoin_price.csv', index_col='time', parse_
dates=['time'], infer_datetime_format=True)
```

The `index_col` argument tells pandas to set that column as the index. The `parse_dates` argument will parse the provided list of columns as datetimes. Finally, the `infer_datetime_format` argument is a handy trick – it auto-detects the datetime format of the columns that will be parsed to datetimes. Unfortunately, it doesn't work with seconds since the epoch, although we could instead provide a function to the `date_parser` argument like so:

```
date_parser = lambda x: pd.to_datetime(x, unit='ms')
btc_df = pd.read_csv('data/bitcoin_price.csv', index_col='time', parse_
dates=['time'], date_parser=date_parser)
```

Here, we create a function called `date_parser` (the same as the argument name, which is a common practice) which parses dates as milliseconds since the epoch.

Now that we have a datetime index, we can do some other handy things, like easily indexing times. Here is an example of getting the data from 2019 using a date range:

```
btc_df.loc['1-1-2019':'12-31-2019']
```

It's even simpler to provide the year: `btc_df.loc['2019']`.

As always, it's best to run through the additional EDA and data cleaning steps we went through in the last section and didn't cover here. There are also a lot of other analytic steps and methods we can apply with pandas to datetimes that we won't cover here; the *Pandas 1.x Cookbook* mentioned earlier covers much of the rest of the datetime and time series functionality in pandas.

Understanding NumPy basics

Another library that's useful for dealing with data is NumPy (numpy). The name stands for "Numeric Python," and it has many tools for advanced mathematical calculations and the representation of numeric data. NumPy is used by other Python packages for computations, such as the scikit-learn machine learning library. In fact, pandas is built on top of NumPy. With NumPy, we'll learn:

- How data is represented in NumPy

- How to use some of NumPy's mathematical function and features
- How NumPy relates to and works with pandas

The pandas library actually stores its data as NumPy arrays. An array is similar to a list, but has more capabilities and properties. We can extract an array from our DataFrame like so:

```
close_array = btc_df['close'].values
```

This gives us a NumPy array:

```
array([   93.033      ,   103.999     ,    118.22935407, ...,
        17211.69580098, 17171.        ,  17686.840768  ])
```

NumPy arrays can be multidimensional, like DataFrames. They also have similar properties to DataFrames, like the shape parameter (`close_array.shape`) and a datatype (`close_array.dtype`).

Another way to get a NumPy array is by creating it from a list:

```
import numpy as np

close_list = btc_df['close'].to_list()
close_array = np.array(close_list)
```

First, we import the NumPy library with the alias np, which is typical. Then we use the `to_list` method of our DataFrame's `close` column (which is a pandas Series), and finally convert it to a NumPy array with the function `np.array`.

Using NumPy mathematical functions

One reason NumPy arrays are useful is we can execute math operations more easily and in less compute time. This speed boost is due to something called vectorization, where operations are applied to a whole array instead of one element at a time. For example, if we want to scale down our closing bitcoin prices by 1,000 (putting the units in kilodollars), we can do this:

```
kd_close = close_array / 1000
```

Common math operations, including addition, subtraction, and so on, are available. Of course, we could do this with a list comprehension or `for` loop:

```
kd_close_list = [c / 1000 for c in close_list]
```

The advantage of NumPy is that it executes much faster, since NumPy is mostly written in C and is vectorized. We can use the magic command %timeit (or %%timeit for more than one line of code) in Jupyter Notebook or IPython to measure how long the execution is for the two preceding examples:

```
%timeit kd_close = close_array / 1000
```

and

```
%timeit kd_close_list = [c / 1000 for c in close_list]
```

For NumPy, this returns something like this (it will differ depending on the machine this is run on):

```
3.49 µs ± 180 ns per loop (mean ± std. dev. of 7 runs, 100000 loops each)
```

Compare this with the list comprehension:

```
167 µs ± 5.44 µs per loop (mean ± std. dev. of 7 runs, 10000 loops each)
```

That is a massive difference in speed of about 50x! Notice that this is the same way we used simple math operators with pandas – this is because pandas is built on top of NumPy.

NumPy also allows for element-by-element multiplication. If we wanted to get the market cap from our bitcoin data, we would multiply volume and the closing prices:

```
volume_array = btc_df['volume'].values
close_array * volume_array
```

Since pandas uses NumPy under the hood, this actually works with pandas too – we could just as easily use our DataFrame:

```
btc_df['market_cap'] – btc_df['close'] * btc_df['volume']
```

Lastly, let's take a look at NumPy's mathematical functions. These are well-documented in NumPy's documentation (https://numpy.org/doc/stable/reference/routines.math.html). Many of these functions are already included in pandas, but some are not. For example, if we wanted to logarithmically scale our data, like we did when plotting it, we could do this with NumPy:

```
np.log(btc_df['close'])
```

Many other mathematical functions and abilities exist within NumPy, but often these are only needed for more advanced work. If you are interested in taking a deep dive with NumPy, a book from Packt's collection that can help you is *Mastering Numerical Computing with NumPy*, by Umit Mert Cakmak and Mert Cuhadaroglu.

Test your knowledge

You've started a new data science position at a solar cell installation company. They have some solar cell and solar irradiation data in Excel files they want you to load, clean, and analyze, and then deliver your results to the executive team and president. You should deliver a small summary of your EDA work from pandas and save your cleaned and prepared data as a new Excel file. The data files are `solar_data_1.xlsx` and `solar_data_2.xlsx` on the GitHub repository for this book. The `metadata.csv` file describes the different columns.

You can read more about this data and what the different fields mean here: `https://www.kaggle.com/jboysen/google-project-sunroof`

You can also look at the notebooks of existing and aspiring data scientists linked on the Kaggle dataset page for more inspiration.

Summary

This chapter was rather long, but it makes sense – as we've covered a few times, data scientists can spend anywhere between 25% and 75% (sometimes upwards of 90%) of their time cleaning and preparing data. The pandas package is the main package for loading and cleaning data in Python (which is built on top of NumPy), so it's important we have a basic grasp of how to use pandas for data preparation and cleaning. We've seen the core of pandas from beginning to end:

- Loading data
- Examining data with EDA
- Cleaning and preparing data for further analysis
- Saving data to disk

We also took a look at NumPy, but keep in mind that most NumPy functionality can be used directly from pandas. It's only when you need more advanced math that you might have to turn to NumPy.

In our next chapter, we'll take our EDA and visualization skills to a whole new level.

5

Exploratory Data Analysis and Visualization

We already briefly touched on **exploratory data analysis** (**EDA**) and visualization in the previous chapter, and now we will go deeper. EDA is a crucial step in any data science project because we need to understand our data to properly use it. EDA is iterative and happens continually throughout a project. As we learn more about how our data looks from analysis to modeling, we also need to incorporate more EDA to deepen our understanding.

Visualization goes hand in hand with EDA, and other books often show solely visual EDA. In this chapter, our EDA will focus on visualizations as well, since we already touched on numerical EDA in the previous chapter with pandas. However, visualization also involves a lot more – there are loads of best practices for making good visualizations. We will cover the key best practices for visualizations here, so you can make impactful and professional visualizations with Python.

In this chapter, we'll cover:

- EDA and visualization libraries in Python
- Performing EDA with Seaborn and pandas
- Using EDA Python packages
- Using visualization best practices
- Making plots with Plotly

We're going to be using the same iTunes dataset that we used in the last chapter, with the same goal to discover more insights about the data using EDA and present them via outstanding visualizations.

EDA and visualization libraries in Python

Within Python, there are several EDA and visualization packages, and we will cover some of the top packages here. We already saw some of what we can do with pandas. For further EDA, we will look at the `pandas-profiling` Python library, which can automate EDA plots and statistics for us with a few lines of code. However, for better visualizations that we might use in reports or presentations, we should make things a little more polished and precise with custom visualizations.

For more polished plots, we can use one of several plotting packages in Python depending on our use case. The original base-level plotting package in Python is `matplotlib`. It is essentially the most basic way to make plots and visualizations in Python, and although it's simple to use for small tasks, it becomes difficult for complex plots. For example, plotting time series, adding text annotations, and combining multiple subplots can all make `matplotlib` a pain to use. To ease these burdens, people have created other, higher-level packages. Some of these packages are the ones we will cover here: Seaborn and Plotly.

There are other plotting packages, such as HoloViz, Bokeh, Altair, plotnine, and more, that we will not cover. But we will cover some other auxiliary Python packages that are useful for EDA and visualization. Let's start by delving deeper into EDA.

Performing EDA with Seaborn and pandas

We already looked at some of the steps of EDA – mainly numeric analysis, with some plotting. There are many other plots we didn't cover in the previous chapter: boxplots, violin plots, correlograms, missing value plots, and more. Let's look at creating some of these plots.

Making boxplots and letter-value plots

First, we'll take a look at the classic boxplot. This was invented in 1970 by the legendary statistician and mathematician John Tukey. The boxplot helps us to quickly see some information about the distribution of a dataset and enables us to compare subsets of the data easily. Just like histograms and bar plots, boxplots are available in the pandas plotting tools. Before we start examining data, let's first load it and transform some columns:

```
import pandas as pd

df = pd.read_csv('data/itunes_data.csv')
df['Minutes'] = df['Milliseconds'] / (1000 * 60)
df['MB'] = df['Bytes'] / 1000000
df.drop(['Milliseconds', 'Bytes'], axis=1, inplace=True)
```

First, we are loading our iTunes data. Note that this data has no duplicates, but doesn't have missing values filled in. We are then converting ms to minutes by dividing by 1000 ms/s and 60 s/min. Doing these sorts of conversions is easier if you line up all the unit conversions like so:

$$ms * \frac{1\ s}{1000\ ms}\ \frac{1\ min}{60\ s}$$

This is called dimensional analysis. You can then easily see how units cancel out and we are left with minutes transformed from ms. We also convert our bytes column to megabytes. Both of these conversions will make our EDA and plots easier to interpret.

Now we can make the boxplot:

```
df['Minutes'].plot.box()
```

In Jupyter Notebook, the plot shows up automatically. If you are running the code through IPython or from a Python file, you have a few options to show plots. One is to import matplotlib:

```
import matplotlib.pyplot as plt

df['Minutes'].plot.box()
plt.show()
```

The `plt.show()` command at the end instructs your computer to display the plot. This will also work in other settings, like running a Python file, running code in IPython, or in the Python shell. Another option to show the plot is to use IPython magic commands. If our plots aren't showing up automatically in Jupyter Notebook, we can use:

```
%matplotlib inline
```

With IPython, we can use the magic command:

```
%matplotlib
```

This causes our plots to show up automatically from IPython, without calling `plt. show()`. Another benefit of this magic command is that when we plot something, we can still run commands in IPython without closing our plot. Note that these magic commands, like `%matplotlib`, only work in IPython and Jupyter Notebook, and not a basic Python shell.

> There is another part of `matplotlib` called `pylab`. You can load the same plotting capabilities as `matplotlib.pyplot` along with `numpy` by using this import:
>
> ```
> import pylab as plt
> ```
>
> In fact, there is a magic command, `%pylab`, that imports `pylab` and other packages. However, the best practice these days is to use `import matplotlib.pyplot as plt`, since `pylab` also imports `numpy`.

If you run the preceding code to load and plot the iTunes song lengths data in IPython, you'll notice the plot is interactive – you can zoom in and move around in the plot. In Jupyter, this is not the case by default. You can use this magic command to make plots interactive within Jupyter notebooks:

```
%matplotlib widget
```

Another option are the `%matplotlib notebook` or `%matplotlib` magic commands, which create plots in new windows.

Now that we know how to see our boxplot, let's take a look at it.

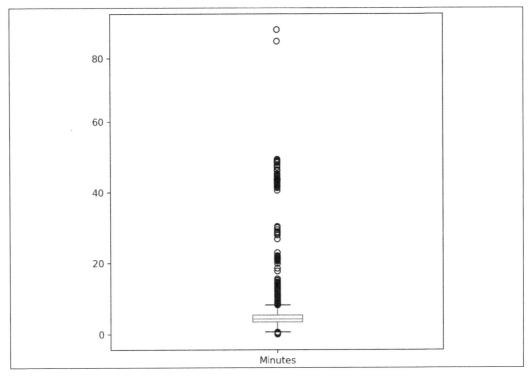

Figure 5.1: A boxplot of the length of songs, in minutes, from the iTunes dataset

A boxplot has a few components. First, the horizontal line in the center of the box is the median, also known as the 50 percentile or 2 quartile (Q2). This is the middle data point in our data series when ordered from smallest to greatest. The bottom and top of the box are the first and third quartiles (Q1 and Q3). These quartiles are formed when we break up a dataset into four equal pieces by ascending or descending values. So, 25% of the data lies at or below Q1, and 25% above Q3. You can also think of Q1 as the middle data point between the minimum and the median. The "whiskers" of the box are the outlier boundaries. Usually, these are calculated in the same way we did in *Chapter 4, Loading and Wrangling Data with Pandas and NumPy*. Recall the formulas are Q1 - 1.5 * IQR and Q3 + 1.5 * IQR, where IQR is Q3 - Q1 (the interquartile range). The points plotted outside the whiskers are the outliers according to the IQR method.

In the case of this dataset, we can see the middle 50% of the data is compressed to a small range somewhere around song lengths of 5 minutes. However, we also see a lot of outliers, especially on the high side. In fact, this is one of the drawbacks of a classic boxplot – it doesn't often do well with bigger datasets and can show too many outliers. It was designed at a time when datasets were small, and even explored via hand-drawn charts. Now, our datasets are so large that some of these older methods don't work well with them, and new methods have been designed.

Enter the letter-value plot. This was invented around 2011 by a trio of statisticians, including the famous Hadley Wickham. Wickham is well-known in data science due to his extensive work in R and statistics – he's authored and maintains several prominent data science libraries in R, and has a number of books published on data science with R. Hadley helped create the letter-value plot to improve on the boxplot's shortcomings. Instead of showing any outliers outside the IQR, one method (out of four possible methods) for plotting outliers with a letter-value plot results in five to eight outliers on the upper and lower extremes. The letter-value plot also shows the distribution better by grouping data into more quantiles. Take a look at the difference between the boxplot and the letter-value plot (which goes by the name "boxenplot" in seaborn):

```
import seaborn as sns

sns.boxenplot(y=df['Minutes'])
```

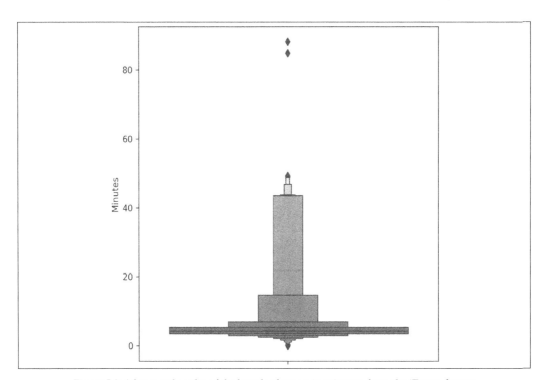

Figure 5.2: A letter-value plot of the length of songs, in minutes, from the iTunes dataset

To produce the plot, we first import the seaborn library with the alias sns, which is the convention. We then give a pandas series (by selecting a column from our DataFrame) as the y argument. We could also use the x argument instead for a horizontal plot. For plotting multiple columns from our DataFrame at once (like Minutes and MB), we use the data argument: sns.boxenplot(data=df[['Minutes', 'MB']]).

We can send the output of the function to the underscore character, `_ like _ = sns.boxenplot(y=df['Minutes'])`. This is a special character in Python that usually holds the last output (for example, if we are running code in a Python or IPython shell). We can also use the underscore character as a throwaway variable if we don't care about saving the data that is output from a function. In the case of plotting, our functions usually return the plot object or something similar. This doesn't show up when running code from a Python file or within IPython, but does print out lines of text in Jupyter Notebook. Using the underscore trick is a handy way to hide the output and make your notebooks cleaner.

Yet another way to do this is simply adding a semicolon at the end of the line, like `sns.boxenplot(y=df['Minutes']);`. This way is quicker and easier in a notebook, although the underscore trick shows up in other people's code sometimes.

Our letter-value plot improves upon the boxplot by adding more quantiles. The median is still shown as a horizontal line within the center and largest box. This middle box, spanning above and below the median, contains half of the data. Each set of boxes beyond it contains a shrinking amount that's cut in half repeatedly: the next set of boxes contains about 25% of the data, the next two boxes contain around 12.5% of the data, and so on, with each set of boxes containing about half the percentage of data as the previous set of boxes. We can also see these boxes have lighter shades and a smaller width as they go out from the median, which signifies fewer points in each box. By default, the boxes end when we have roughly five to eight total points as outliers outside the boxes.

There are three other ways to set the algorithm for the number of outliers with letter-value plots using the k_depth argument. The documentation for the function shows the options here: https://seaborn.pydata.org/generated/seaborn.boxenplot.html.

The difference in algorithms is explained in the original paper discussing letter-value plots: https://vita.had.co.nz/papers/letter-value-plot.html.

Another way to make our plot a little easier to read is to use a log scale. A log scale is organized in powers, or multiples, of 10. Here's how we can change our y axis to a log scale:

```
sns.boxenplot(y=df['Minutes'])
plt.yscale('log')
```

The function plt.yscale('log') is what converts the y axis to a log scale. This works with almost any matplotlib plot and can similarly be done for the x axis with plt.xscale('log'). Our log scale letter-value plot is a little easier to read (at least on the small end of the scale) than the non-log version.

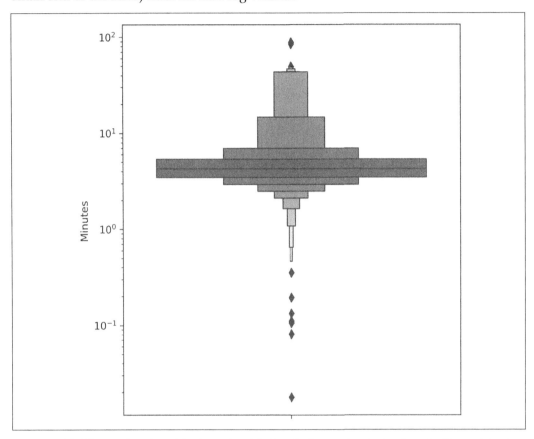

Figure 5.3: A letter-value plot, with a log scale, of the length of songs, in minutes, from the iTunes dataset

Notice each y axis major tick is a power of 10. 10^{-1} is 0.1, 10^0 is 1, and 10^1 is 10. The minor ticks in between powers of 10 are the nine equally spaced values between the powers of 10. So, the first minor tick mark above 10^0 is 2, for example. From this, we can see that the median song length is around 4 to 5 minutes, which is close to what we would expect with common knowledge of music on iTunes. We can also confirm this by using df['Minutes'].describe(), where we see that the median song length is 4.26 minutes.

Next, let's look at the related violin plot.

Making histograms and violin plots

Another way to see the distribution of data is using histograms and **kernel density estimation** (**KDE**). Recall from *Chapter 4*, *Loading and Wrangling Data with Pandas and NumPy*, that histograms group the data into bars (bins) that show the counts of points in each bin. This helps us to see the distribution of the data. The KDE essentially fits a line to the distribution of data and produces something like a smoothed histogram. We can make a histogram with a KDE line with seaborn using `histplot`:

```
sns.histplot(x=df['Minutes'], kde=True)
```

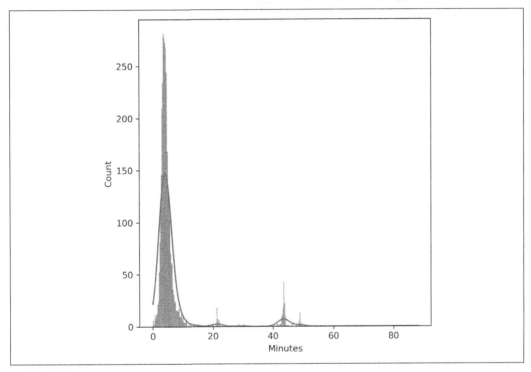

Figure 5.4: A histogram of song length in minutes, with a KDE, from the iTunes dataset

The `histplot` function draws our histogram from the provided data, and the `kde=True` argument results in the KDE line. The resulting plot shows bars that represent the density of the data – bigger bars mean more points. The line is the KDE fit to the data. A violin plot is similar to this, but shows the KDE and a boxplot:

```
sns.violinplot(data=df, x='Minutes')
```

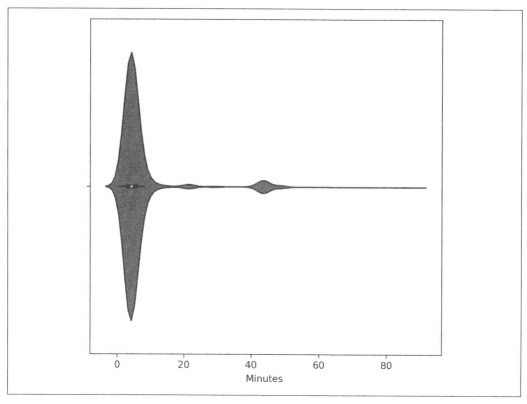

Figure 5.5: A violin plot of the length of songs in minutes from the iTunes dataset

For many seaborn functions, we can provide a data argument, which should be a pandas DataFrame. We can then provide x and y arguments as column names. Here, we are only showing the Minutes data as the x argument. We can see the KDE is the main feature of the plot, and this KDE is mirrored on the x axis. We also see a small boxplot in the middle of the mirrored KDE distribution, with the white point being the median, the box showing the Q1 and Q3 quartiles, and the lines showing the IQR outlier boundaries.

Let's look at a few groups of data at once with a violin plot. Let's first select the top five genres by number of songs and create a separate DataFrame with only this data:

```
top_5_genres = df['Genre'].value_counts().index[:5]
top_5_data = data=df[df['Genre'].isin(top_5_genres)]
```

Then we provide the y argument to the violinplot function: This gives us separate violin plots for each genre:

```
sns.violinplot(data=top_5_data, x='Minutes', y='Genre')
```

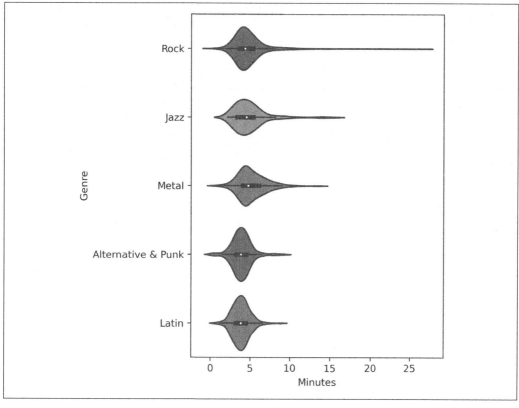

Figure 5.6: Violin plots of the length of songs in minutes, grouped by the top five genres, from the iTunes dataset

This helps us see that rock, jazz, and metal have wide distributions of song lengths, although most lie near the 3- to 5-minute range.

Similar plots can be made with many other functions in seaborn, such as letter-value plots: `sns.boxenplot(data=df, x='Minutes', y='Genre')`.

 Violin plots also have several other options available and are shown in the documentation examples: `https://seaborn. pydata.org/generated/seaborn.violinplot.html`.

Next, let's look at making scatter plots with seaborn.

Making scatter plots with Matplotlib and Seaborn

Scatter plots are an essential EDA plot for continuous, numeric data. Continuous data, of course, is data that can take any value between two bounds, such as length or temperature. Let's take a look at our song length versus size in MB first. So far, we've looked at plotting data with `pandas` and `seaborn`, because it's generally easier. However, the base `matplotlib` library can also be used for any type of plot. In fact, packages like `seaborn` and `pandas` derive their plotting capabilities from `matplotlib`. Here is a simple scatter plot with `matplotlib`:

```
plt.scatter(df['Minutes'], df['MB'])
```

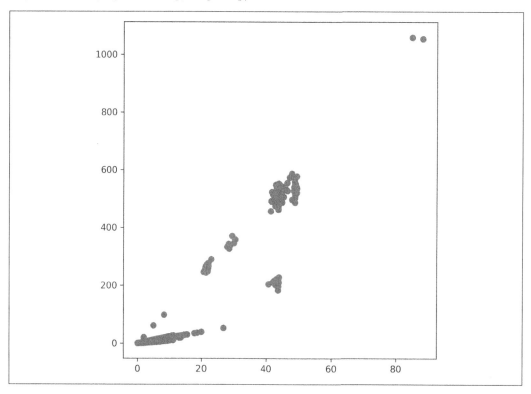

Figure 5.7: A scatter plot of the length of songs in minutes versus size in MB from the iTunes dataset, using matplotlib

We can see the plot is very basic – the points and axes are shown, but there are no axes labels. To add axes labels, we add the lines:

```
plt.xlabel('Minutes')
plt.ylabel('MB')
```

Another option that can improve scatter plots is the transparency of the points. We can use the `alpha` argument in `plt.plot()`, like `alpha=0.1`, to add transparency to the points. The lower the value for `alpha`, the more transparent the points. This `alpha` parameter works for most plotting packages in Python.

Another common plot in `matplotlib` is the line plot, which we can make with `plt.plot(df['Minutes'], df['MB'])`. This works for data that follows some sort of pattern across points, like a time series. In our case, a scatter plot is much better.

 We can create almost any type of chart with `matplotlib`, and most of these are demonstrated in the official gallery: `https://matplotlib.org/stable/gallery/index.html`.

While `matplotlib` can be nice because we can customize every little aspect of our charts, it can also be a pain to figure out how to perfectly tune every bit of a chart. This is why I'm recommending using higher-level packages like Seaborn and Plotly to make your charts instead. For example, here is how we can make a scatter plot in Seaborn:

```
sns.scatterplot(data=df, x='Minutes', y='MB')
```

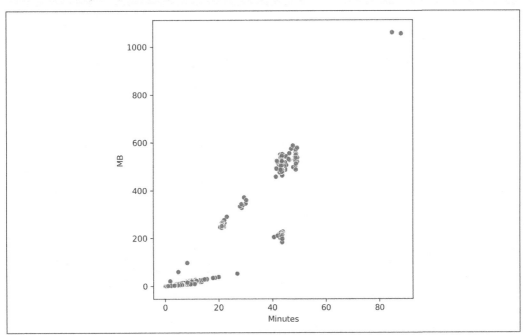

Figure 5.8: A scatter plot of the length of songs in minutes versus size in MB from the iTunes dataset, using Seaborn

Recall we looked at this data in *Chapter 4, Loading and Wrangling Data with Pandas and NumPy*, but using the pandas plotting function. The Seaborn and pandas packages create a decent-looking plot for us by default, with axes labels and some styling to the points that makes them a little easier to read compared with the default `matplotlib` plot.

The `seaborn` package's plots have different styling than `pandas`, and many more options. For example, as with most plots in `seaborn`, we can group by a column using the hue argument:

```
sns.scatterplot(data=top_5_data, x='Minutes', y='MB', hue='Genre')
```

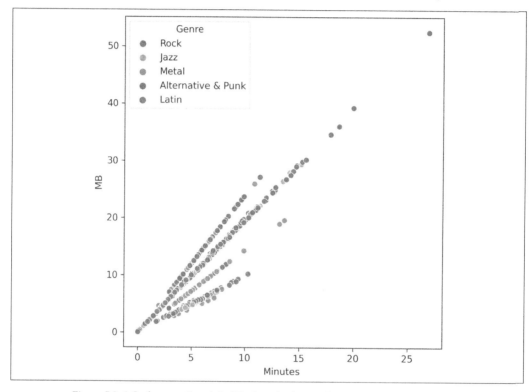

Figure 5.9: A Seaborn scatter plot of the length of songs in minutes versus size in MB, grouped by the top five genres, from the iTunes dataset

Here, we are using only the top five genres by song count to plot instead of the full dataset. We can see that there are a few different slopes of minutes versus MB in the data. This tells us there are some significant differences in the audio properties of these different audio tracks, leading to different relationships between MB and minutes. A steeper slope means more data per minute exists, so the points near the upper left of the plot might be higher resolution audio, or may be songs with more variety in their sounds.

Some other common EDA plots for continuous, numeric data are correlograms and pairplots, which we'll look at next.

Examining correlations and making correlograms

When we have several numeric columns, it can be helpful to plot their relationships with one another. Let's make scatter plots and histograms of our numeric columns with one command in Seaborn:

```
sns.pairplot(data=df)
```

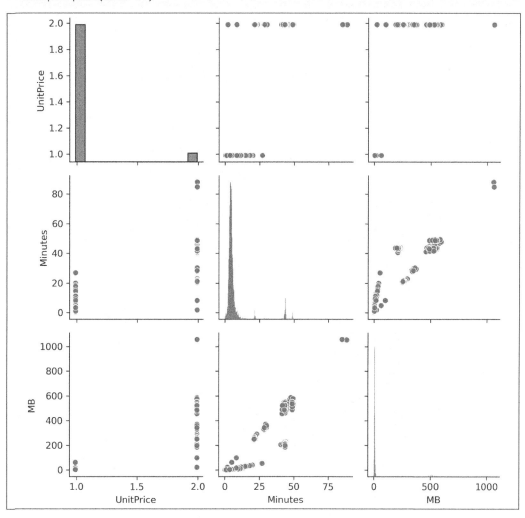

Figure 5.10: A pairplot of the numeric columns from the iTunes dataset

From this plot, we can quickly see the relationships between all the variables. From this, we can see the same song length to MB relationship we saw in our scatter plot – a bigger MB means a longer song in general. However, we also see histograms for each column, showing the one-dimensional distribution of the data. We can see in the upper left that the unit prices are mostly 0.99, with a few 1.99 songs. We can also see the longer, more expensive songs tend to a have higher MB value, meaning a bigger data file.

While pairplots can be helpful for EDA, we often want to see how strongly correlated different numeric columns are. For this, correlations are helpful. Remember we can use `df.corr()` with a `pandas` DataFrame to get correlations. We can simply plot this with `seaborn`'s `heatmap`:

```
sns.heatmap(df.corr(), annot=True)
```

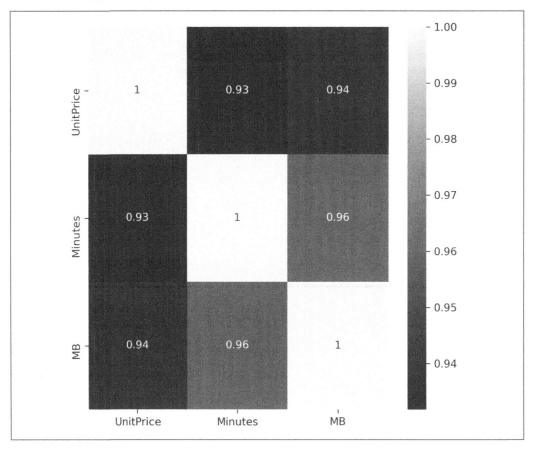

Figure 5.11: A correlogram of the numeric data from the iTunes dataset

The `df.corr()` function calculates the Pearson correlation between numeric columns. This is looking for linear relationships and is like fitting a best-fit line to the scatter plot between two columns of data. If the data is perfectly correlated, it has a correlation of 1. By using `annot=True` in the `sns.heatmap` function, we have the correlation values plotted in each square. We can see each column is perfectly correlated with itself since it has a value of 1. We can also see the minutes and MB of each song are strongly correlated with price – longer and bigger songs have higher prices usually.

We can use other types of correlation calculations by providing arguments to pandas' corr function. The other types of correlations available are Spearman and Kendall. These both use different calculations compared with Pearson and are better suited for non-linear relationships. We can change the correlation type we use by specifying the `method` argument in `df.corr()`:

```
sns.heatmap(df.corr(method='spearman'), annot=True)
```

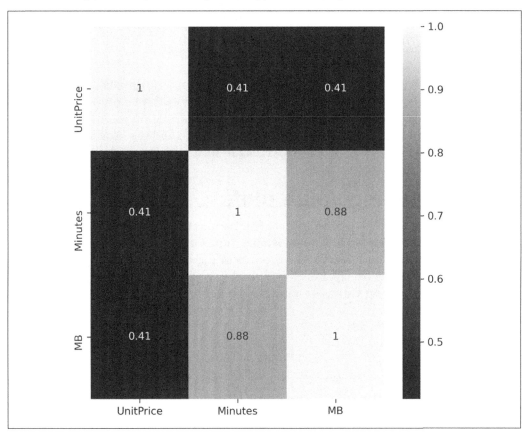

Figure 5.12: A correlogram with Spearman correlation of the numeric data from the iTunes dataset

Here we use Spearman correlation. We can see it returns very different values for some of the correlations. The Spearman and Kendall methods calculate correlations by rank rather than only the raw value. Points are ranked from least to greatest for two columns of data, and if both columns' ranks increase at the same time, the correlation value is high. These methods are good at looking for relationships between non-linear data columns. In general, Spearman runs much faster than Kendall, so you should almost always use either Pearson or Spearman to look for correlations between columns.

> We've looked at several of the Seaborn plots, but not all. Seaborn is an actively developed package and will have new plots added over time. The list of available plots is on their website here: `https://seaborn.pydata.org/api.html`.
>
> The documentation for individual plotting functions shows several examples of how to use each function. You can also draw inspiration from their gallery: `https://seaborn.pydata.org/examples/index.html`.

We only examined correlation metrics that work with numeric data here, but there are also some others that work with categorical data. For example, phi-k with the `phik` package in Python, Cramér's V, and mutual information score are some other methods that can be used with categorical data. We will see how the phi-k correlation is included in the `pandas-profiling` reports soon.

Making missing value plots

Although we can examine missing values with pandas (`df.isna().sum()` or `df.info()`), it can be easier to look at a visualization. One package that makes it easy to do so is `missingno`. This is available via conda or pip and can be installed with `conda install -c conda-forge missingno -y` or `pip install missingno`. We can make a plot of the missing values in our dataset like so:

```
import missingno as msno

msno.matrix(df)
```

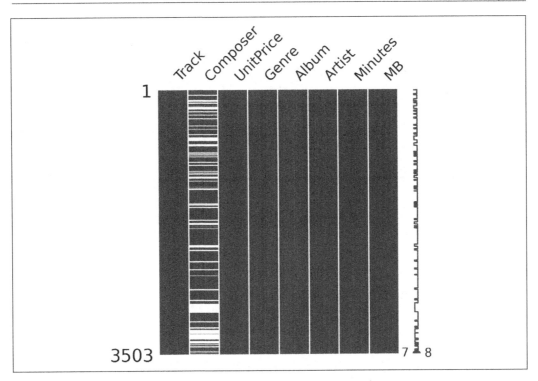

Figure 5.13: A missing values plot of the iTunes dataset

This shows a matrix of non-missing values in gray and missing values in white. Each row is a line across each column. From this, we see that the **Composer** column has several missing values, but none of the other columns are missing any values. The spark line on the right side shows the total missing values across all columns for each row and shows the maximum and minimum number of complete values for the rows. In our case, 7 means the minimum number of non-missing values in a row is 7, and the maximum number of non-missing values in a row is 8.

Almost all modern Python packages have a page on GitHub with more documentation. We can see the documentation (abbreviated as "docs") for `missingno` here: `https://github.com/ResidentMario/missingno`.

We can also search `anaconda.org` and `pypi.org` to see if the package is available to install via `conda` and `pip`. If the documentation is not on GitHub, we can also use a search engine like Google or DuckDuckGo to look for documentation by searching for something like "missingno documentation" or "missingno docs".

We just created a lot of useful plots for EDA. Like many things in Python, someone has created packages to automate a lot of EDA for us, and we'll take a look at that next.

Using EDA Python packages

Sometimes it's helpful to create some specific EDA plots and statistics to investigate features of interest, but often, it's helpful to run an auto-EDA package on our data as one of our first steps. There are a host of different EDA packages in Python (and R), but we'll stick to just covering `pandas-profiling`. This is a convenient package that creates an EDA summary with only a few lines of code from a `pandas` DataFrame. Once we have our data loaded, we load the `ProfileReport` function from `pandas-profiling`:

```
from pandas_profiling import ProfileReport
```

Since dashes are not allowed in module names, we need to use an underscore for the library name, `pandas_profiling`. Once we have this loaded, we can create our report and display it:

```
report = ProfileReport(df)
```

Within Jupyter Notebook, we have a few options for display. We can simply print out the variable in a Jupyter Notebook cell like so:

```
report
```

Or, we can use `report.to_widgets()` or `report.to_notebook_iframe()` (the iframe method is the same as printing out the `report` variable). These each result in a different backend being used for the display, but the information is the same.

You may get an error when trying to run the `pandas-profiling` report, such as `TypeError: concat() got an unexpected keyword argument 'join_axes'`. Many of these errors have to do with using older versions of `pandas` and `pandas-profiling`. We can check our versions with `pip list` or `conda list`. We can also check versions of packages in most cases by importing the package and then checking the `__version__` attribute:

```
import pandas_profiling

pandas_profiling.__version__
```

Additionally, it's always a good idea to copy and paste the error (such as `TypeError: concat() got an unexpected keyword argument 'join_axes'`) into Google, DuckDuckGo, or another internet search engine. Some of the first results for this at the moment of writing are GitHub issues, where people discuss the issue and show that the version of `pandas-profiling` is too old in most cases. If needed, we can specify the version to install with something like `conda install -c conda-forge pandas-profiling=2.9.0`.

Our report looks something like this:

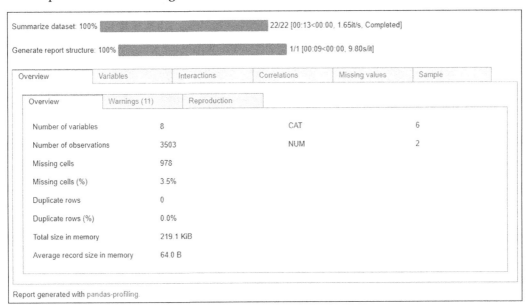

Figure 5.14: The pandas-profiling report of the iTunes dataset using report.to_widget()

The report takes some time to run, as it is calculating several statistics, and progress bars are displayed as it runs. One way to speed this up is by adding the argument `minimal=True` to the `ProfileReport()` function, although this omits some of the statistics in the EDA report. We can see that the report's default page shows us some overall statistics of the data: the number of columns (variables), rows (observations), statistics on missing and duplicate values, and the types of variables (categorical/string and numeric).

The other two subtabs on the overview show **Warnings**, which is geared toward warning us of potential problems with the data for machine learning, and **Reproduction**, which has notes on the date and time the report was run and the `pandas-profiling` version. This allows someone to reproduce the report later. We can see from the warnings below that several columns have many unique values (high cardinality). This makes analysis and machine learning difficult because it's hard to find patterns among data that is composed of mostly unique values. The other warnings are high correlations between columns and some missing values. Missing values are always an issue because it might mean errors in data collection, and we need to decide how to deal with the missing values. High correlations mean we only need one or a few of the highly correlated variables in a predictive model, since they contain redundant information. We'll learn more about that in later chapters. The next figure shows the subtab overviewing the warnings:

Figure 5.15: The "Overview/Warnings" section of the pandas-profiling report of the iTunes dataset

The next major tab is **Variables**, which contains a summary of each of the columns. For string/categorical columns, this looks like the following image for the **Track** column:

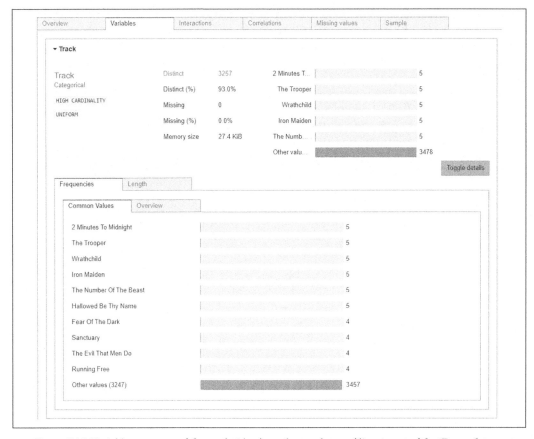

Figure 5.16: Variable summary of the track titles from the pandas-profiling report of the iTunes dataset

Note that we have also clicked the **Toggle details** button shown above on the middle right. We can see this shows a few descriptions/warnings of the data on the upper left – HIGH CARDINALITY (many unique values) and UNIFORM, meaning it is close to a uniform distribution. A uniform distribution is equally distributed across all values. For text/categorical variables, this means almost all the values are unique. We can also see this is likely the case because the unique values are so spread out – each song title seems to show up four or five times at most, and the majority of the song titles in the display are grouped in the **Other values** category. For numeric data, this **unique** warning means the data would be nearly equally distributed across its range. The **Frequencies -> Overview** tab will show a histogram of the value counts – in other words, it shows how often unique values appear. Lastly, the **Length** tab shows some overall stats about the length of the strings in this column (like mean and median length) and shows a histogram of the number of characters in each value. We could generate the same histogram like so:

```
df['Track'].str.len().plot.hist(bins=50)
```

This selects the **Track** column, and then accesses the `str` property of that column (the "string" property). The `str` property allows us to use string methods, such as `len()`, which returns the length of each row's string in the **Track** column. The length is calculated from the number of characters in the row, and can also be calculated like `len(df.iloc[0][ 'Track'])`.

This concludes all of what `pandas-profiling` will show for a string or categorical column. If we simply printed out the `report` variable or used the `report.to_notebook_iframe()` method, the interface is slightly different – we scroll down to the **Variables** section instead of clicking on a tab. The `report.to_notebook_iframe()` method also looks a little more like current internet pages, so you may prefer to use that instead.

Let's next look at a summary of a numeric data column by selecting **Minutes**:

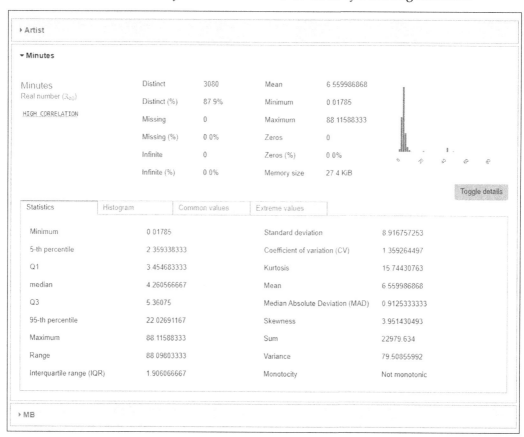

Figure 5.17: Variable summary of the Minutes column from the pandas-profiling report of the iTunes dataset

We can see this view provides warnings under the variable name, just like with the **Tracks** column. Here, we see the HIGH CORRELATION warning, which means that this column has a high correlation with at least one other column. This can be important for machine learning methods, because we may only want to keep one of the highly correlated columns in our model. We'll talk more about that in *Chapter 10, Preparing Data for Machine Learning: Feature Selection, Feature Engineering, and Dimensionality Reduction*.

We also see a summary of statistics in the upper part of the panel. Again, it shows the missing and unique number of values and percentages, but here it also shows the number and percent of values that are infinity. Some other basic statistics are shown there as well, such as the average/mean, minimum, and maximum. We also have a histogram drawn for us in the upper right.

Clicking on the **Toggle details** button shows us many more detailed statistics. We will cover some of these statistics in *Chapter 8, Probability, Distributions, and Sampling*, but we can see the left column of statistics is all related to quantiles (quartiles including Q1 and Q3) like we've seen before. The statistics on the right side are mostly about the shape of the distribution. For example, the skewness shows us how asymmetric the distribution is – the higher the skew, the more asymmetric the distribution. The last statistic in this column, **Monotocity**, describes if the values are monotonic. If the values are monotonic, it means they always increase or always decrease as we move along the data. In this case, it is calculated by looking at how the data changes versus the index. So, our data would need to constantly increase as we move down the rows to be monotonically increasing.

The other subtabs within the details area are **Histogram**, **Common values**, and **Extreme values**. **Histogram** simply shows us a larger version of the histogram in the upper right. The **Common values** section shows the top 10 common values and the percent of the data they make up. If we see a strange value that shows up often, like -999, this could mean we have missing data signified by -999, for example. Lastly, the **Extreme values** section shows the top and bottom five values.

Some of the other main-level tabs available are **Interactions**, **Correlations**, **Missing values**, and **Sample**. The **Interactions** section shows a heatmap of numeric variables. For example, it shows minutes versus MB, and the idea is you see the density of points and how they relate. It's like a scatter plot, but the values are grouped into hex bins.

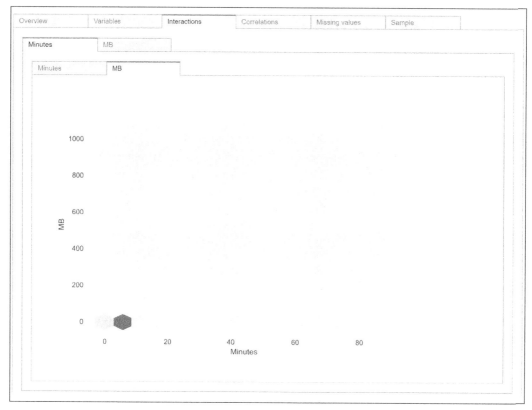

Figure 5.18: Hexplot of minutes versus MB from the pandas-profiling report of the iTunes dataset

Because we have some large outliers, this interaction plot doesn't work very well here. The outliers show up as faint hex bins in the middle and upper right of the plot. Instead, we should transform this into a log-log plot by creating the heatmap ourselves. We can create a similar plot with seaborn:

```
import numpy as np

df_log = df.copy()
df_log['log(Minutes)'] = np.log(df_log['Minutes'])
df_log['log(MB)'] = np.log(df_log['MB'])
sns.jointplot(x="log(Minutes)", y="log(MB)", data=df_log, kind="hex")
```

Our code to create the log-log hexbin plot has become a bit more involved. First, we import the numpy package to be able to use the logarithm calculation. Then, we make a copy of our DataFrame so as not to alter our original data. Next, we create two new columns: log(Minutes) and log(MB) by using np.log() to take the logarithm of the columns' values. Finally, we plot the data with seaborn's jointplot function. These log-log plots are good for visualizing data that spans a wide range on both axes. We can see we have the hexbin plot in the center, with the histograms of each variable across the top and side. Since we named our columns log(Minutes) and log(MB), they are labeled as such, and each value on the axes is a power of 10. For example, most of the data lies around a spot where log(MB) is 2, meaning the actual value for MB would be 10^2, or 100.

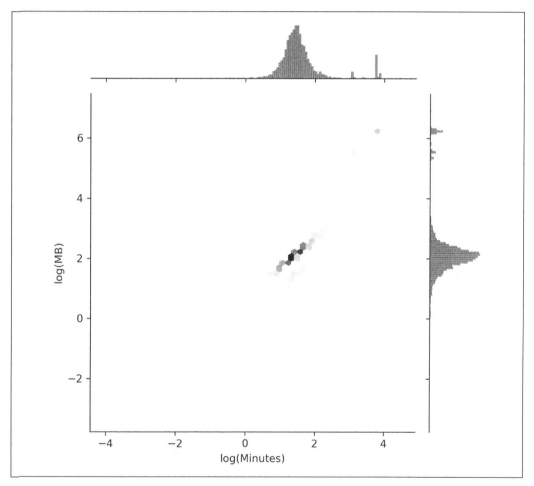

Figure 5.19: A log-log hexbin plot of Minutes versus MB

The next general tab in the pandas-profiling report, the **Correlations** section, shows a correlogram between numeric values just like we created before with sns.heatmap(df.corr()). There are subtabs for different correlation methods, such as Spearman, that we talked about before. Another correlation method, phi-k, is available in a subtab. This is a newer correlation method that also includes the categorical variables that don't have a uniform distribution.

The **Missing values** section shows a few missing value plots. One is the missing value matrix plot we created before with msno.matrix(df), another is a bar plot showing the missing values for each variable, and the last is a dendrogram of missing values:

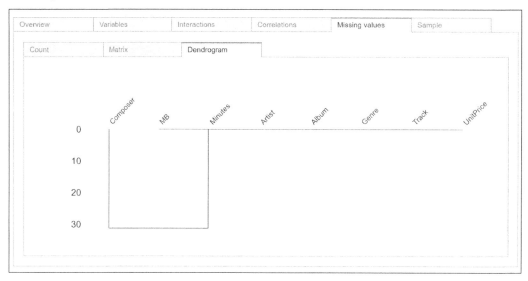

Figure 5.20: Missing value dendrogram from the pandas-profiling report of the iTunes dataset

The dendrogram is a type of clustering algorithm and draws a tree. Here, the tree is only one level deep since only one column is missing values (the **Composer** column). The tree starts out at the top and connects columns with the most similar number of missing values with horizontal lines. Then, these connected values have a vertical line drawn down to the next level, where the groups with the most similar number of missing values are grouped with a horizontal line. At the bottom of the tree, all columns are connected into a single horizontal line. In our case, all of the columns except **Composer** are not missing values, so they are connected together first in the top level of the tree. The **Composer** column is on its own since it is the only column missing values. Then, in the next level down, these two groups are joined, since each time we move down a level in the tree, we are required to join the two groups that have the most similar number of missing values.

The last section is **Sample**, which simply shows some of the first and last rows of the data, just like with `df.head()` and `df.tail()`. So, we can see `pandas-profiling` automates a whole lot of steps for us – it checks correlations between variables, makes missing value plots, and so on. However, sometimes we want to create some extra EDA plots or need to customize plots. Although it's often best to start with `pandas-profiling` if your data is not too big, it also helps to create some additional EDA plots as we did earlier.

We've created a lot of EDA plots, and they look decent, thanks to `seaborn`. However, for production-level charts (like for presentations or reports), we want to hold ourselves to a higher standard. Next, we'll learn about best practices for creating professional visualizations.

Using visualization best practices

Making good visualizations is akin to telling a good story. We need to have a coherent plot, it needs to be interesting, the message should be clear, and it needs to be tailored to our audience. With visualizations, several aspects come into play:

- Data presentation
- Color
- Text
- Axes
- Labels

We will use these components to create some best practice guidelines:

- Avoid chart junk
- Use color sensibly
- Present data properly
- Make charts "redundant" in case they are printed in black and white
- Clearly label axes and datasets, and use a single font size with a sans-serif font
- Tailor your visualizations to the audience

Most of the time, we want to keep our plots as simple as possible, unless we are in a special situation where our message is that the data is complicated. Adding in extra components to charts, such as cheesy graphics or too many annotations, is called "chart junk" or "chartjunk." Common chart junk includes gridlines, color gradients, 3D effects, graphic backgrounds, and ornamental shading.

In almost all cases, you should avoid 3D effects. For example, Microsoft Excel allows all sorts of 3D effects, like turning a bar chart into 3D, but we don't need to do that – it simply isn't necessary. This brings us to the first best practice: **avoid chart junk**.

Microsoft Excel usually adds some chart junk by default: it always adds a border to the plot and gridlines. We usually don't need gridlines and they add clutter. However, if the gridlines help to convey the meaning of the data better, they can be included. The default for a 3D bar plot in Microsoft Excel is shown in the figure below, labeled **(a)**. We are plotting the value counts of the top five genres in our iTunes dataset.

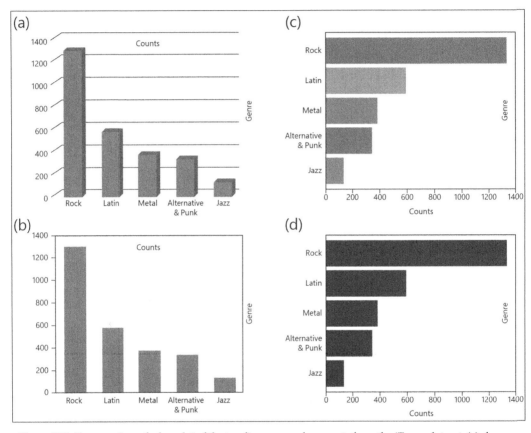

Figure 5.21: Four versions of a bar plot of the top five genre value counts from the iTunes dataset. (a) shows a Microsoft Excel 3D bar plot, (b) shows a pandas bar plot, (c) shows a Seaborn bar plot with default colors, and (d) shows a Seaborn bar plot with a single color

We can see the 3D effect adds nothing to the chart besides making it harder to read. The gridlines can sometimes help if we want to convey specific values to our audience, but are not needed here (or most of the time).

The outlined border of the plot also adds junk. Compare this to **(b)**, where we create a plot with pandas:

```
df['Genre'].value_counts()[:5].plot.bar()
```

We can see that pandas (which uses matplotlib) does not add gridlines or a chart border, but instead adds axes lines that form a border around the plot. It also does not show axes labels, but we can add an x-axis label with plt.xlabel('Genre').

Lastly, in **(c)** and **(d)**, we have a plot made with Seaborn:

```
sns.countplot(y='Genre', data=df, order=df['Genre'].value_counts().index[:5],
color='darkblue')
```

This requires a more-complex function call. We give our DataFrame, df, as the data argument, then select the **Genre** column with the y argument. This causes our bars to be horizontal. Next, we set the order of the bars to be the top five genres by value counts with the order argument. Finally, we set the color argument to 'darkblue' so that all bars are a single color. Without this, each bar is set as a different color by default, as shown in **(c)**. The colors are telling us nothing new here, so we don't need them – we already have the **Genre** labels from the y axis. Out of the above visualizations, the best one is the Seaborn plot at the bottom right, **(d)**.

The comparison of **(c)** and **(d)** above leads us into the second visualization best practice: **use color sensibly**. We can see in **(c)** that the colors are not telling us any new information and become clutter. Another problem here, which is common with default color sets, is that red and green are used together. This is to be avoided due to the 5% to 10% of the population that has some form of color blindness. Red-green color blindness is common, which makes it hard to distinguish red and green color combinations on plots. If red and green must be used, using colors with lighter and darker shades can help. For color gradients, the viridis and cividis color maps can be used.

If we are simply making a bar plot as above, a single color will suffice. Often, dark blue is a good color choice – it's the color choice for many organizations and companies, such as IBM, American Express, Lowes, Intel, GE, PayPal, and many more. Dark blue seems to be a color that gives us the impression of trust and professionalism.

In a case where we do want to use multiple colors, they should be used to convey a new dimension of the data. For example, we could use the color of the bars to display which country purchased that genre most often in our iTunes dataset. However, using color to display a continuous value isn't always a good idea. This is because color is difficult to distinguish in a gradient, which leads us on to our next best practice: **present data properly**.

This principle is a bit broad but means that we should choose the proper methods to present our data. For example, we could show a pie chart of the value counts of genres, but pie and donut charts are generally frowned upon. This is because it is difficult to compare the size of arcs or slices of a pie, and it's much easier to compare the length of bars. We could also present data as circles or bubbles, but again, it's hard to compare circle areas to one another. Most of the time, we can make use of a few charts:

- **Bar plots** – for categorical plots
- **Histograms** – for the distribution of continuous values
- **Line charts** – for time series
- **Scatter plots** – for relationships between two continuous variables
- **Heatmaps** – for relationships between two continuous variables and correlations

The examples for each of the plots above are not all-encompassing but give an idea of some of the types of data these plots are commonly used for. There are, of course, many other plots we could use, such as stacked area charts. Often, these are derived from one of the simpler charts listed above. More technical statistical charts, like boxplots and letter-value, are not often used to present data to non-technical people since we would need to explain how to read the chart and what it means. Simpler charts, like bar, line, and scatter plots, are easy to intuitively understand.

As we saw above, counts of categories work well in a bar chart, and we saw earlier that histograms work well for looking at the overall distribution of numeric data (like the **Minutes** column). Scatter plots are good for looking for relationships between two numeric datasets, and heatmaps are good for the same idea, but with larger datasets where the number of points makes it hard to see what's going on in a scatter plot.

Line charts are typically well suited for time series data. For example, we can collect the cumulative sum of sales from the top three countries in our iTunes dataset. The following steps could also be accomplished with a SQL query, but we'll use pandas here. First, we load the data:

```
from sqlalchemy import create_engine

engine = create_engine('sqlite:///data/chinook.db')

with engine.connect() as connection:
    sql_df = pd.read_sql_table('invoices', connection)
```

Here, we are connecting to our Chinook SQLite3 database, and then reading in the entire invoices table. The next step, getting the cumulative sum of sales for the top three countries, is more complex:

```
top_3_countries = sql_df.groupby('BillingCountry').sum(). \
    sort_values(by='Total', ascending=False)[:3].index.values
```

First, we get the top three countries by total sales values. Here, we group by country and take the sum of all columns. Then we sort the resulting values from greatest to least by the **Total** column. Lastly, to get the country names, we take the first three values, get the index (which holds the country names), and then get the values as a NumPy array. This last step could be done a few different ways, like first getting the index and values, and then indexing to get the first three values. Try breaking down the steps into smaller chunks and running them in Jupyter Notebook to see what is happening at each step. For example, try running `sql_df.groupby('BillingCountry').sum()`, then add on the `sort_values()` function, and then add on the next selection and indexing steps one by one.

Once we have the top three countries by sales, we can then get their cumulative sales over time. This is, again, a little complex:

```
sql_df.set_index('InvoiceDate', inplace=True)
gb = sql_df[sql_df['BillingCountry'].isin(top_3_countries)]. \
        groupby([pd.Grouper(freq='M'), 'BillingCountry']).sum(). \
        groupby(level=-1).cumsum()
gb.reset_index(inplace=True)
```

Note that because the first command is a long line of code, we are breaking up the lines and using a forward slash to continue the same logical line of code, but on the next line of text. First, we need to set the date as our index so that we can group by date. Then we filter the DataFrame so we only have the top three countries with `sql_df[sql_df['BillingCountry'].isin(top_3_countries)]`. Next, we group by the month from the index, and after that, the country. This requires the use of the `pd.Grouper()` function to group a time series by a unit like months. We then get the sum of the columns with `sum()`, so each unique date-country pair has a numeric value. Next, to get the cumulative sum over time for each country, we use `groupby()` again with `level=-1`. The results from the first `groupby()` statement are in a multi-index pandas DataFrame, and `level=-1` instructs `groupby()` to use the second index, which is the country name. Then we take the cumulative sum with `cumsum()`, meaning each value is added to the next one in time, starting at the first date. Again, try breaking down each of the steps and running them to see what is happening more clearly. This ends up giving us a DataFrame where we have a date and country as indexes, and the cumulative sum of the columns as values.

Our **Total** column, which originally was the total for each individual invoice, is now the running sum of total invoice amounts, grouped by month and country. Lastly, we reset the index so that the date and country become columns that we can use in our plot.

Finally, we can plot our data:

```
sns.lineplot(data=gb, x='InvoiceDate', y='Total', hue='BillingCountry')
```

Incidentally, we can see how 90% of the work here was simply collecting and preparing the data, and only one line of code was used to actually plot it! Remember that this relates to surveys of data scientists stating they often spend the majority of their time collecting and preparing data.

Looking at the plot in **(a)** below, we can see colors are automatically chosen, and a legend is placed in the best location (automatically determined by `seaborn`).

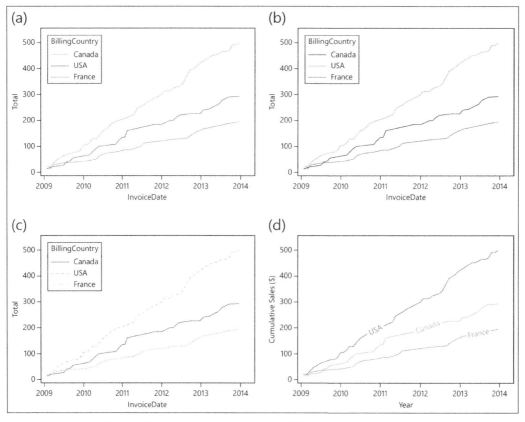

Figure 5.22: Four versions of a line plot of the top three countries with cumulative sales from the iTunes dataset using Seaborn

However, what if the chart is printed in black and white? The result of a grayscale transformation is shown in **(b)**. We can see it's not easy to distinguish between the various lines. There are a few ways to combat this, but this is our next best practice: **make plots "redundant."** This helps for black-and-white printing, as well as for the colorblind. Our solution for making plots redundant is to add another feature to each line. We can either make the lines different textures (like dashed, dotted, and so on) or we can directly label the lines. Here is how we could make the lines dashed, which is shown above in **(c)**:

```
sns.lineplot(data=gb, x='InvoiceDate', y='Total', hue='BillingCountry',
style='BillingCountry')
```

We simply add the argument `style` with the variable we want to have different styles applied to. The line styles are determined automatically, but we can also add another argument, `dashes`, to specify our exact line styles. For example, we could use `dashes=[(2, 1), (5, 2), '']` to specify the first line should have a 2-point line and a 1-point space. A point is a typographical term that is used for measurement in print, like with 12-point font (roughly the size of most fonts we read). The second line style in the `dashes` argument is `(5, 2)`, meaning a 5-point line with a 2-point space, repeating. Lastly, the blank empty, `''`, means the last data series should be a solid line.

Although this styling works for redundancy, an even better solution is to directly label the lines. This is actually a good idea in general, since we can more easily read the information that way – there is less movement of the eye between the legend and the lines. In general, try to make your charts as easy to read as possible. We can directly label the lines using the package `matplotlib-label-lines`:

```
from labellines import labelLines

f = plt.figure()
ax = f.gca()
for country in top_3_countries:
    c_df = gb[gb['BillingCountry'] == country]
    ax.plot(c_df['InvoiceDate'], c_df['Total'], label=country)

labelLines(ax.get_lines())

plt.xlabel('Year')
plt.ylabel('Cumulative Sales ($)')
```

This package must be installed with `pip`, like `pip install matplotlib-label-lines`, and then the imported package name is `labellines`, as shown above. Since it is a minor and recently developed package, it has not been ported to the Anaconda repositories at the time of writing.

We can see we first import the function `labelLines` from the package `labellines`. Then we create an empty figure with `plt.figure()`, and get the axes of that figure with `f.gca()`. The acronym **gca** stands for **get current axes**, which will return us a `matplotlib` axes object. From this, we can then loop through our top three countries, and plot the total sales over time. We first filter the gb DataFrame so we only keep values with the current country in the current cycle of the loop (this is our DataFrame that was grouped by month-year and country). Then we plot the actual data: `Total` (the cumulative sum of total invoice amounts) over the `InvoiceDate` range. We also provide the argument `label` so that our country labels can be drawn on the plot. Alternatively, this would also allow us to use `plt.legend()` to show a legend on the plot with the labels. Notice we are using the ax variable to plot our data with `ax.plot()` so the plots all show up on the same figure. This allows the next line of code, where we use `labelLines()` to work properly. We then get the lines from the axes object with `ax.get_lines()`, and pass that to the `labelLines()` function as our only argument (these line objects hold the raw data that is used to locate and draw the label on the line). This draws the country labels directly on the lines. Finally, we add x and y axis labels, and our plot is complete.

The results are shown in **(d)** in *Figure 5.22*, and this is our best-practice line chart for our time series data here. From the figure, we can see the US is clearly on a sharper trajectory in terms of sales compared with Canada and France, which have nearly equal line slopes. This might mean we should focus our efforts on our US customers, as they look to be providing most of our revenue in the future.

Our second-to-last best practice is to **clearly label axes and datasets, and use a single font size with a sans-serif font**. This is usually done automatically for us with `seaborn` and many Python plotting packages, but with others, axes labels and datasets are not always labeled. With a `pandas` plot, for example, we can add axes labels with `plt.xlabel('your label here')` and `plt.ylabel('label goes here')`. As we saw above, it's also best to directly label datasets if possible with the `labellines` package. We should also minimize the number of different font sizes used and strive for a single font size. Many different font sizes make plots look busy and cluttered. Lastly, be sure to use sans-serif fonts. Serifed fonts have curved edges to the letters, like the writing in this book. It helps us to read lots of text more easily but adds clutter to plots, and the amount of text on plots should be minimized regardless. Stick with simple, sans-serif fonts for charts, and avoid Comic Sans (unless it's appropriate for your audience).

That brings us to our last best practice on our list, which is to **tailor the chart to our audience**. For example, Comic Sans is usually not appropriate as a font style for charts since it looks unprofessional. However, in a more informal setting, like a children's classroom or an online comic like xkcd, it can work. Another example is pie charts. In general, pie charts are frowned upon in visualization communities, but there are cases when we could use them.

For example, teaching fractions to children is aided by pie charts, because they can see the parts of the whole easily, and it relates to pies, which most children like. Other aspects of tailoring the chart can include a title, graphics, colors, and text annotations. For example, if we are creating a chart to share on Twitter, we may want to add a title in case people share the chart without giving context. The title should be short and descriptive of the data, which could be something like "Cumulative iTunes Sales for the Top 3 Countries" for our line charts above. This can be added to `matplotlib`-based plots with `plt.title('Cumulative iTunes Sales for the Top 3 Countries')`. For a more informal setting like Twitter, we may also add a small graphic or logo in the corner of the plot for branding. However, in a professional meeting or report, a cute graphic could be a mistake. We also want to make sure to highlight any interesting phenomena in the data with highlights or text annotations. An example of a highlight would be making one of the lines bolder in our line chart above, which we could accomplish with:

```
sns.lineplot(data=gb, x='InvoiceDate', y='Total', hue='BillingCountry',
size='BillingCountry', sizes=[1, 5, 1])
```

This will make the US line thicker, drawing attention to it. We first give the argument `size='BillingCountry'` to specify that the `country` variable will be used to determine the sizes of the lines. We then provide a list of numbers to the `sizes` argument, which are point sizes for the lines. Since the second data series corresponds to the US, we increase the point size of that line to highlight it. Figuring out how the order of the data series corresponds to the order of the `sizes` argument takes trial and error (or we can see it from the legend). We could also use different textures or colors to draw attention to parts of the data that warrant our interest.

That wraps up our visualization best practices. However, some aspects of visualizations are subjective, and others may have slightly different ideas for what the best visualizations look like. In general, the ideas we talked about here are agreed upon by most: keep plots simple and free of junk, use the right plot for your data, properly label your plots, use color and text properly, and tailor your charts to your audience.

 A few good books for learning more about visualization best practices are *Data Visualization: A Successful Design Process*, by Andy Kirk from Packt, and *Storytelling with Data: A Data Visualization Guide for Business Professionals*, by Cole Nussbaumer Knapflic.

Now that we have some best practices down, let's look at saving plots so that we can share them more easily.

Saving plots for sharing and reports

Creating visualizations is great, but sometimes we want to save them as an image for sharing with others. For example, all the charts in this book were saved to PNG files. To save images from `seaborn`, `pandas`, or any other `matplotlib`-based plot, we simply use the function `plt.savefig()`. Let's use our same line plot from the last section:

```
f = plt.figure(figsize=(5, 5))
sns.lineplot(data=gb, x='InvoiceDate', y='Total', hue='BillingCountry')
plt.tight_layout()
plt.savefig('cumulative_sales_lineplot.png', facecolor='w', dpi=300)
```

Here, we first create a blank figure with `plt.figure()` so that we can set the figure size. The `figsize` argument takes a tuple of numbers, which are the width and height in inches. For applications where your image may be scaled down, square images typically scale well. Next, we create the line plot as before. Then we use `plt.tight_layout()`, which automatically adjusts margins so that everything is contained within the figure, including all text and graphics. Sometimes, bigger axes labels or other text can run outside the figure, and this function is one remedy to that problem. Lastly, we save the figure with `plt.savefig()`, giving it the filename as the first argument. Our figure's file type is set with our extension. Options include .png, .jpg, .svg, .pdf, and more. We can see the available file types with the command `plt.gcf().canvas.get_supported_filetypes()`. We also set the `facecolor` argument to `'w'` for white, which changes the background color behind the axes labels from transparent to white. Transparent backgrounds are the default for the .png image type, but a white background is the default for most other image types. We also set the **DPI**, or **dots per inch**, to 300, which gives us decent resolution for the figure. A higher `dpi` value means a higher resolution, but also a bigger file size.

Now that we've saved our `matplotlib` plots, let's take a brief look at one other popular and useful plotting library: Plotly.

Making plots with Plotly

Plotly is one of several visualization libraries in Python. An advantage of Plotly is that visualizations can be automatically published and saved to Plotly's cloud, meaning you can share visualizations with others easily, and even edit them online. Another key advantage is that these plots can be included in websites and retain their interactivity there. The interactivity within Plotly also has hover-over effects: the value of points is displayed when you hover over them. Plotly is used by several large corporations for visualization, so it can be a helpful skill to know. It can be used in many programming languages, including Python, R, and others.

Plotly also has visualization web dashboard capabilities (named Dash), which means you can create a web page with several interactive plots that can stream live data. Let's take a look at creating some of the same plots we did before, but with Plotly: line charts, scatter plots, and histograms. We'll also look at creating a map chart.

First, let's create the same line plot as before:

```
import plotly.express as px

px.line(gb, x='InvoiceDate', y='Total', color='BillingCountry',
template='simple_white')
```

This gives us the following plot:

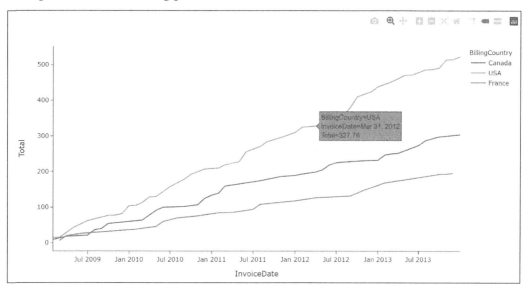

Figure 5.23: A line plot of the top three countries with cumulative sales from the iTunes dataset, using Plotly. We can see our mouse pointer is hovering over a data point, which shows us the raw data from that point

We first import Plotly Express, which is the quick and easy way to create plots with Plotly. Other methods allow much greater customization but are more difficult. As we can see, the `px.line()` function strongly resembles the Seaborn functions – we give it our pandas DataFrame, gb, then the x and y column names, and a `color` argument that states the column name to use for labeling different lines. We also use the `template` argument here to make the plot look a little nicer with `simple_white`. The default `plotly` theme has gridlines and a gray plot background, which unfortunately adds chart junk. There are other themes available of course, which are discussed in the documentation: `https://plotly.com/python/templates/`.

Plotly has a few different ways to create plots, and
`plotly.express` is the simplest. You can read about other ways
to create Plotly charts here: `https://plotly.com/python/`
`creating-and-updating-figures/`.

Next, let's make a scatter plot using Plotly. We'll plot the minutes versus MB as we
did much earlier in the chapter:

```
px.scatter(df, x='Minutes', y='MB')
```

As we can see, this is again very similar to Seaborn – we provide a DataFrame, then
an x and y argument. The advantage of plotting with Plotly versus Seaborn is that
we gain mouse hover interactivity, where the values of each point are shown as we
hover over them.

Creating a histogram is almost the same; we provide a DataFrame and an x or y
argument, depending on if we want the histogram to be horizontal or vertical:

```
px.histogram(df, x='Minutes')
```

Here, we show the histogram in the usual vertical orientation, with the bars running
vertically.

Lastly, let's look at creating a map plot. This is straightforward in Plotly Express but
can be used in much more powerful ways with other Plotly methods if required.
Let's plot the sum total of sales by country on a choropleth map. A choropleth map
plots a numeric value as a color value on areas on a map. Although perceiving
numbers via colors is not ideal if we have other options, it's a good way to visualize
numeric data on a map:

```
gb_countries = sql_df.groupby('BillingCountry').sum()
gb_countries.reset_index(inplace=True)

px.choropleth(gb_countries, locations="BillingCountry",
              locationmode='country names',
              color="Total")
```

First, we need to organize our data in the proper manner. We do this by grouping
our `sql_df` (which is our invoices table from the iTunes database) by the billing
country, then taking the sum of these groups. This gives us the sum total of sales for
each country. We then reset the index so that the country name is a column we can
use when plotting. Next, we use the Plotly Express function `choropleth`, giving it our
DataFrame as the first argument.

We then specify the column name that holds our location labels. We also need to set `locationmode` to `'country names'`, since our countries are labeled by name (and not an alternative label like ISO code). We can see the available location modes by looking at the documentation for choropleth by executing `?px.choropleth` in a Jupyter Notebook cell or IPython. We also specify a column name that holds numeric values, which will be used to color our countries; here, we want to visualize the **Total** column, so we set the argument `color="Total"`. Our plot looks like this:

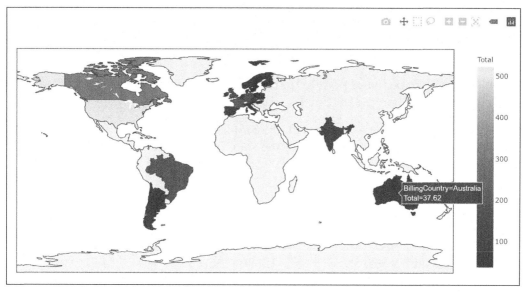

Figure 5.24: A Plotly choropleth of total sales by country from the iTunes dataset. We can see the country name and the Total value is shown when we mouse over a country

As we can see, the countries in our dataset are colored, and others are left a neutral gray color. We can also see when we hover over countries that the **Total** and country name are shown.

Plotly has a lot more mapping capabilities, which are demonstrated and explained in their documentation: `https://plotly.com/python/maps/`.

In fact, Plotly has a huge array of capabilities, and is growing all the time. Check out their Python page for more ideas on what you can do with Plotly: `https://plotly.com/python/`.

That wraps up our brief section on Plotly using Plotly Express, but don't forget to check out what else you can do with Plotly and its dashboard capabilities, Dash.

Test your knowledge

To practice what you've learned, complete the following challenge:

You landed a job as a financial analyst at a hedge fund. Your first task is to gain insights into government-sponsored loans by analyzing the **Paycheck Protection Program** (PPP) loan data, included in the file PPP Data 150k plus 080820.csv in this book's GitHub repository. Perform EDA on the data (using any necessary data wrangling/preparation steps) and create some professional visualizations to share with your team highlighting your key findings. Be sure to add a written analysis with your visualizations, explaining what they mean.

The full dataset can be found here: https://data.sba.gov/dataset/ppp-foia (although this may change over time).

However, we will only be working with the $150k+ loans data, which are large loans. For an extra challenge, you can combine the state-by-state data with the $150k+ loans data to get the full dataset.

Summary

We covered quite a lot in this chapter, starting with EDA and EDA plots, moving through visualizations and best practices for creating charts, and finishing with Plotly for making plots. Recall that for your first EDA step, it's not a bad idea to utilize one of the auto-EDA packages, such as pandas-profiling, that we covered here. With a few lines of code, we have an array of EDA statistics and charts for us to examine. But remember that we often need to create custom EDA figures and statistics, or use pandas filtering, groupby, and other methods to generate custom EDA insights.

EDA overlaps significantly with visualization, and much of EDA ends up being visualization. If our charts move beyond EDA to something we want to share with others, then we need to think more about visualization best practices. Remember in general we want to keep visualizations as simple as possible (avoid chart junk), use color and text properly, use the best methods to convey our data and its key meaning, and tailor our charts to our audience.

Lastly, we looked at using a few of the key visualization packages in Python – seaborn and Plotly. The seaborn package is part of the matplotlib family of plotting libraries, which also includes pandas. This means it is easily customized with matplotlib commands. However, for more advanced plots, interactivity, and web interfaces, Plotly can be much better. Plotly also has a much wider range of plots available and is growing faster than seaborn, but creating some advanced or highly customized plots in Plotly can be difficult.

We now have an idea of what to do with data after loading and preparing it with pandas, which we learned in the previous chapter. In our next chapter, we'll learn about dealing with other sources of data commonly encountered in the wild – documents (like Microsoft Word and PDFs) and spreadsheets.

6
Data Wrangling Documents and Spreadsheets

Now that we have some basic Python and data skills under our belt, let's take a look at how we can work with some common types of data you will see in the wild: documents and spreadsheets. Most organizations use Microsoft Office with Word and Excel, and this generates huge amounts of data. There are also loads of PDF documents out there with valuable information contained within. If our data lies in a pile of Excel and PDF files, then dealing with these types of data becomes necessary when doing data science. Once we have data loaded from these files, it's also useful to have a few basic analysis techniques at the ready. We'll learn data extraction techniques, as well as basic analysis techniques for the text from documents and the data from Excel spreadsheets that we might encounter. Specifically, we'll learn the Python tools and techniques for:

- Loading Word and PDF documents using the `python-docx` and `PyPDF2` packages and some basic data cleaning
- Basic text analytics techniques for analyzing text
- Loading Excel files with the `openpyxl` and `pandas` packages and writing data back to Excel
- Using `openpyxl` to extract data from complex Excel files

Let's begin by wrangling some Word documents and extracting insights from the text.

Parsing and processing Word and PDF documents

As we know, Microsoft Office documents are everywhere, especially Word and Excel documents. Of course, PDF documents are also used widely to share reports and information. In fact, certain fields, such as finance and public service, are absolutely drowning in PDF documents.

Reading text from Word documents

Let's first look at reading text from Word documents. We will assume the role of a data scientist working with a non-profit organization that is trying to reduce gun violence in schools. We have a few Microsoft Word documents from the US Department of Education's Gun-Free Schools Act reports (these are stored as .docx files in the GitHub repository for the book under `https://github.com/PacktPublishing/Practical-Data-Science-with-Python/tree/main/Chapter6/data/gfsr_docs/docx`). As our first step, we want to extract the text from the Word files and look at the most common words and word pairs.

There aren't a whole lot of packages in Python for working with Word files, and most haven't been updated in a few years at the time of this writing. Nevertheless, we can still use these packages to read Word files. Two of the top packages are `python-docx` and `textract`, but another package, `docx2text`, can also be used. Here, we will cover the `textract` package, although code samples for `python-docx` and `docx2text` can be found in the Jupyter notebook for this chapter. The fact that there aren't a lot of packages for working with Word files tells us that the current packages work well enough for people's needs, but also that there may not be that many people extracting data from Word files.

First, we need to install `textract`. The latest version is available through pip, but not conda. So, we can install the package with `pip install textract`.

Note that there are instructions for installing `textract`'s dependencies in full here: `https://textract.readthedocs.io/en/stable/installation.html`

However, there are no official instructions for installing in Windows. There is a set of instructions here: `https://github.com/deanmalmgren/textract/issues/194#issuecomment-506065817`

If you only need to read .docx files, installing `textract` with pip works fine.

Our first step will be to get a list of our files. One easy way to do this is to use the built-in glob module:

```
from glob import glob
word_files = glob('data/gfsr_docs/docx/*.docx')
```

With the glob function, we simply give a file path and usually include an asterisk as a wildcard character – it will match any number of any character at that point in the string. In the case of our string above, we are looking for any file that ends with .docx in the data/gfsr_docs/docx folder.

First, let's extract text from the first file:

```
import textract
text = textract.process(word_files[0])
text = text.decode('utf-8')
text[:200]
```

The textract.process() function extracts text from any number of files, including .docx files. For other file types, we need to follow the installation instructions from textract's documentation to install other software dependencies.

In the preceding example, the text variable returned by textract is a byte string. This is the format in which data is stored on our computers. If you print out the string, it will be prefaced with b, such as b'Report on'. If you check the class with type(text), it will show it is of the bytes class. The next line, text.decode('utf-8'), converts this byte string to a character string, which shows the actual characters we can read. For the English language, this usually isn't too different, but the byte string and characters can differ greatly for other languages. The utf-8 encoding we used is a common one.

If you aren't sure of the encoding of a file, you can use the beautifulsoup4 package. First, make sure it's installed with conda or pip: conda install -c conda-forge beautifulsoup4 -y. Then, the encoding can be detected with UnicodeDammit:

```
from bs4 import UnicodeDammit
with open(word_files[0], 'rb') as f:
    blob = f.read()
    suggestion = UnicodeDammit(blob)
    print(suggestion.original_encoding)
```

I assume the name of the class is due to the frustrating nature of encodings. There are countless encodings and it can be difficult to ascertain which one to use at certain times. Whoever wrote that code must've just dealt with encodings for a frustratingly long while!

We can also find out the encoding for a Word `.docx` file by replacing the `.docx` extension with `.zip`, and then examining the first `.xml` file inside (`.docx` files are actually `.zip` files). When we open the first `.xml` file we see inside the `.zip` (`.docx`) file, it will have a line at the top specifying the encoding.

Once we've converted the preceding text, we then print out the first 200 characters to make sure everything looks OK with `text[:200]`:

```
'Report on State/Territory Implementation of the Gun-Free Schools Act\n\n\
n\n\n\nSchool Year 1999-2000\n\n\n\n\n\n\n\n\n\n\n\n\n\n\n\n\n\n\nFinal
Report\n\nJuly 2002\n\n\n\n\n\n\n\n\n\n\n\n\n\n\n\n\n\n\n\nPrepared under
contract by:\n\n\n\nWestat\n\n\n'
```

By letting Jupyter print out the variable contents, the newlines (\n) are kept. However, if we use the `print()` function, the newlines would be printed as blank lines.

Extracting insights from Word documents: common words and phrases

A simple way to derive some useful insights from text is to look at common words and phrases. But before we do that, we have a few cleaning steps we want to perform first.

Cleaning text often includes the following steps:

- Removing punctuation, numbers, and stopwords
- Lowercasing words

There are more steps for a more thorough text analysis that we will learn in *Chapter 18, Working with Text*. However, these will give us improved results compared with our analysis here.

Let's first remove punctuation and numbers. This can be done with the help of the string module:

```
import string

translator = str.maketrans('', '', string.punctuation + string.digits)
text = text.translate(translator)
```

We need to first import the built-in string module, and then we can access a string of common punctuation and numeric digits with string.punctuation and string.digits. We use the maketrans() method of the built-in str class to remove punctuation and digits. In the case of the maketrans() function, we can provide three arguments, and each character in the third argument will map to None. The first two arguments should be left as empty strings – if these contain characters, each individual character in the first string will be converted to the corresponding character (by index) in the second string.

Once we have our translator from maketrans(), we then use the built-in method of strings in Python translate() with our translator. This maps all the characters in string.punctuation + string.digits to None, removing our punctuation and digits for us.

Next, we will remove stopwords. These are common words without much meaning, like "the". We can use the NLTK (natural language toolkit) package to retrieve a list of stopwords. First, we should install the package with conda install -c conda-forge nltk -y. Then, we can import it and download the stopwords:

```
import nltk
nltk.download('stopwords')
```

This should return True.

> If you are not able to download the stopwords, this may be due to your router or firewall blocking access to raw. githubusercontent.com where the data is stored. You can try accessing the data from the NLTK data page (http://www.nltk. org/nltk_data/) to ensure that you are able to connect and download the stopwords. If you are still unable to download the stopwords, you can use the stopwords from scikit-learn instead (conda install -c conda-forge scikit-learn -y):
>
> ```
> from sklearn.feature_extraction.text import ENGLISH_
> STOP_WORDS as en_stopwords
> ```

Once our stopwords are downloaded, we can then import them and remove the stopwords from our text:

```
from nltk.corpus import stopwords

en_stopwords = stopwords.words('english')
en_stopwords = set(en_stopwords)

words = text.lower().split()
words = [w for w in words if w not in en_stopwords and len(w) > 3]
```

Here, we first load the English stopwords from `nltk` with `stopwords.words('english')`, and then convert this list to a set. We do this because of a performance issue – when we are checking whether a word is in our stopwords, it is much faster to check whether something is in a set rather than a list.

Searching a set is faster than a list because of how Python searches lists versus sets. For lists, we might search from the beginning to the end of the list. If our word is at the end of the list, this will take longer. With sets, our data is hashed, or converted to a number. You can try it out with the built-in `hash()` function in Python: `hash('the')`. Combined with some other computer programming principles, this means we can check whether something is in a **set** much faster than checking whether it's in a **list**.

Next, we lowercase the text with `text.lower()`, and then break up the text into individual words with the built-in `split()` function of strings. Lastly, we use a list comprehension to loop through each of the words and keep it if it's not in the stopwords. We also filter out any short words less than or equal to three characters long – usually these are noise in the data, such as a stray punctuation mark that wasn't in our punctuation set, or a stray letter in the data. The list comprehension removing stopwords and short words is equivalent to the `for` loop below:

```
new_words = []
for w in words:
    if w not in en_stopwords and len(w) > 3:
        new_words.append(w)
```

We now have a list of single words. While we're at it, let's get a list of bigrams, or word pairs as well:

```
bigrams = list([' '.join(bg) for bg in nltk.bigrams(words)])
bigrams[:3]
```

The `nltk.bigrams()` function takes a list of words, and returns pairs of words as tuples. We use the `join()` function of strings with a single space to join each bigram tuple in a single string, and this is done for each bigram with a list comprehension. Something like (`'implementation'`, `'gunfree'`) becomes `'implementation gunfree'`. If we examine the first three bigrams, we see the following:

```
['report stateterritory',
 'stateterritory implementation',
 'implementation gunfree']
```

Now that we've cleaned our data and created bigrams, we can move on to an analysis of our prepared data.

Analyzing words and phrases from the text

The simplest way to analyze words and phrases from our text is to look at count frequencies. The `nltk` package in Python makes this easy for us. We can use the `FreqDist` class of `nltk` to get frequency counts for our words (unigrams) and word pairs (bigrams):

```
ug_fdist = nltk.FreqDist(words)
bg_fdist = nltk.FreqDist(bigrams)
```

Unigrams and bigrams are specific cases of n-grams, which are groups of words of size *n* that occur together.

The `FreqDist` class in `nltk` is handy because we can easily look at the top few n-grams, as well as plot them. For example, this will show the top 20 unigrams and bigrams, along with their number of occurrences:

```
ug_fdist.most_common(20)
bg_fdist.most_common(20)
```

Here are the first few bigrams we see from this:

```
[('state law', 240),
 ('educational services', 177),
 ('services alternative', 132),
 ('students expelled', 126)]
```

We can also plot these quite easily:

```
import matplotlib.pyplot as plt

ug_fdist.plot(20)
```

This returns the following plot:

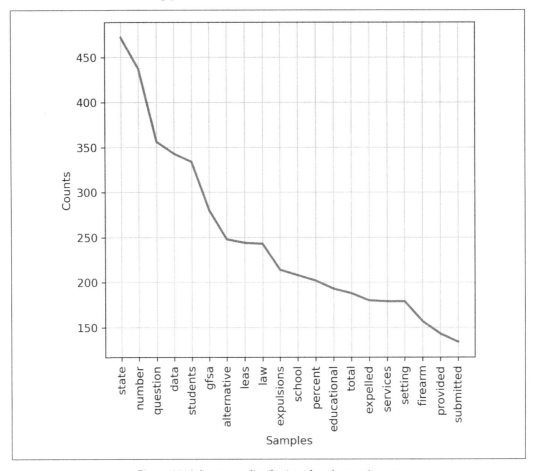

Figure 6.1: A frequency distribution plot of our unigrams

We can see that many of the results of the top few words are what we'd expect, such as "students," "gfsa," and "school." There are some other interesting words in there: "expulsions," "alternative," and "law." We also see "leas," which seems strange. Examining the document shows that this is an acronym for **local educational agencies (LEAs)** and is used a lot in the document.

We can use the argument show in FreqDist.plot() to control whether the plot is displayed or not. If we set show=False, then we can customize the plot further.

These frequency plots are concise, clear ways to plot the word counts. Word clouds are another method you might see being taught or used in the data science community. However, word clouds show the same data as the frequency plots, but less clearly. In general, we should avoid word clouds, but they could be used *occasionally* for something like a graphic on a title slide of a presentation.

To create word clouds in Python, we should make sure we have the wordcloud package installed: conda install -c conda-forge wordcloud. Then, we can import it and create a word cloud from our text:

```
from wordcloud import WordCloud

wordcloud = WordCloud(collocations=False).generate(' '.join(words))
plt.imshow(wordcloud, interpolation='bilinear')
plt.axis("off")
plt.show()
```

By default, this generates a word cloud with collocations, which are word pairs that co-occur (calculated with a few statistical methods, such as pointwise mutual information, or PMI). We set the collocations=False argument to avoid this and only plot single words. We can see that this looks like the following:

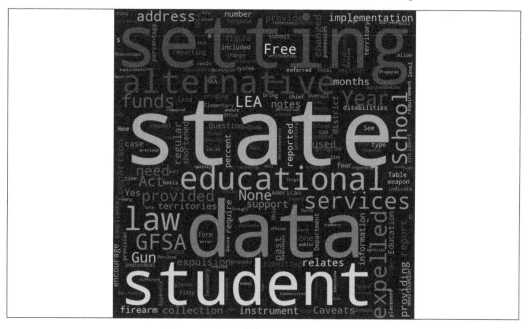

Figure 6.2: A word cloud of our cleaned text

Each word is sized in proportion to the frequency of its occurrence in the text. So, it's another way of looking at the unigram frequency, besides looking at the raw data from the `FreqDist` class of `nltk` or the line plot of the unigram frequencies. But notice how it's impossible to get a quantitative handle on the ranking of word frequencies, and things appear cluttered (like chartjunk, which we discussed in *Chapter 5, Exploratory Data Analysis and Visualization*). Again, word clouds should be used sparingly or not at all, since they are intended to be more artistic and less about extracting useful insights.

> There are lots of options for the format when creating word clouds with the `wordcloud` package in Python, and since word clouds are intended to be artistic and not informative for insights, we should take the time to make it aesthetically appealing.

Now that we have written all the pieces to load and perform a simple analysis of Word document text, let's put it all in a function so that it's easier to use:

```python
import os
from glob import glob
import textract
import nltk
en_stopwords = set(nltk.corpus.stopwords.words('english'))


def create_fdist_visualizations(path):
    """
    Takes a path to a folder with .docx files, reads and cleans text,
    then plots unigram and bigram frequency distributions.
    """
    word_docs = glob(os.path.join(path, '*.docx'))
    text = ' '.join([textract.process(w).decode('utf-8') for w in word_docs])

    # remove punctuation, numbers, stopwords
    translator = str.maketrans('', '', string.punctuation + string.digits)
    text = text.translate(translator)
    words = text.lower().split()
    words = [w for w in words if w not in en_stopwords and len(w) > 3]

    unigram_fd = nltk.FreqDist(words)
    bigrams = list([' '.join(bg) for bg in nltk.bigrams(words)])
    bigram_fd = nltk.FreqDist(bigrams)

    unigram_fd.plot(20)
    bigram_fd.plot(20)
```

The pieces to this function are the same as we used before, and we are including the necessary imports just above the function. The steps for data wrangling are as follows:

- List word files in a directory (folder) with .docx
- Remove punctuation, digits, stopwords, and short words
- Lowercase words

Then, for the basic text analysis of our prepared data, the steps are as follows:

- Create unigrams and bigram frequency distributions with FreqDist
- Plot the frequency distributions of unigrams and bigrams

One small addition to our code is the use of os.path.join() to join the path and the file extension. This function will ensure that the full path to the files is a valid path. For example, if we simply used string concatenation, we could end up with an unintended path if we executed r'data\gfsr_docs\docx' + '*.docx' – this would result in 'data\\gfsr_docs\\docx*.docx' (remember the backslash is a special escape character, so two of them in a row means it will be interpreted as a normal backslash). The os.path.join() function adds slashes between arguments to the function, so the path from os.path.join(r'data\gfsr_docs\docx', '*.docx') would be 'data\\gfsr_docs\\docx*.docx'.

We can run our function like so,

```
create_fdist_visualizations('data/gfsr_docs/docx/')
```

and it plots out our unigrams, bigrams, and plots the uni- and bigram frequency distributions.

Reading text from PDFs

Although we may run into Word files, we will probably see more PDF files in the wild. Luckily, there are several packages for dealing with PDFs in Python. One of them is the same package we used before, textract. There are several others:

- pdfminer.six
- tika
- pymupdf
- pypdf2

One problem with textract at the moment is that it seems to no longer be actively maintained. We can see from the GitHub repository activity (for example, the Contributors page under Insights here: https://github.com/deanmalmgren/textract) at the time of this writing (2021) that it hasn't been updated substantially in about 2 years. There are some bugs with the package that have gone unfixed for a while, including not being able to read text-encoded PDFs well. We will use pdfminer.six to read PDFs here, although there are not huge differences between the three packages. The tika package requires installation of Java on your system, which you can do with conda install -c conda-forge openjdk if you don't have it installed. The tika package does have one advantage over the others: it returns all the metadata about the PDF file when it reads it. This includes things such as when the file was created, who created it, and how it was created.

There are also methods for reading PDFs that are images or scans, and don't have the text encoded in them. These are **Optical Character Recognition (OCR)** methods, and often rely on the tesseract OCR engine. Installation instructions for tesseract can be found here: https://github.com/tesseract-ocr/tessdoc/blob/master/Installation.md

For installation on Windows, you should add the tesseract folder to your PATH environment variable. On Windows 10, the tesseract.exe executable is installed at C:\Program Files\Tesseract-OCR\ and you can add it to your PATH by following these instructions: https://superuser.com/a/143121/435890

Once you have tesseract installed, you can use textract or other packages to read scanned PDFs, like you would a text-encoded PDF. For textract, it's as simple as

```
text = textract.process('filename.pdf',
method='tesseract')
```

Let's begin our PDF data wrangling by listing out the PDF files we have using glob. Our PDF files (included with the GitHub repository for this book) are 10 arXiv.org scientific papers that have "data science" in the title. We are going to get an idea of what people are working on and talking about at the cutting edge of data science at the time of writing. We get a list of our files with glob:

```
pdf_files = glob('data/ds_pdfs/*.pdf')
```

We will need to install pdfminer.six before using it with conda install -c conda-forge pdfminer.six.

Then, we will check out the reading capabilities of `pdfminer` with the first PDF file:

```
from pdfminer.high_level import extract_text
text = extract_text(pdf_files[0])
```

It's easy to use `pdfminer` – it simply returns the text from the PDF. If we need to change the encoding, we can set the `codec` argument to our encoding – by default, it is `'utf-8'`. We can find the encoding of a file using the `UnicodeDammit` class from the `beautifulsoup4` package as described in a note earlier. Taking a look at the PDF files, we can see that they have lots of hyphens connecting words that continue over two lines. Ideally, we want these words without the hyphens. We can accomplish this data cleaning step like so:

```
lines = text.split('\n')
cleaned_lines = []
for ln in lines:
    if len(ln) == 0:
        continue
    if ln[-1] == '-':
        cleaned_lines.append(ln[:-1])
    else:
        cleaned_lines.append(ln + ' ')

cleaned = ''.join(cleaned_lines)
```

Here, we first split up the text into lines by splitting on the newline character, \n. Then we create an empty list to hold the cleaned data and start looping through the existing lines. Some of the lines are blank, so if the length of the characters in the line is 0 (`len(l) == 0`), then we use the Python keyword `continue` to move on to the next line in the loop. If our line ends with a hyphen character, we remove that character by indexing the line up to the last character (`l[:-1]`), and then append this line to the cleaned lines. Otherwise, we append the line plus a space to the cleaned lines.

Lastly, we join together our cleaned lines without any spaces between the lines. In this way, our hyphenated words have the hyphens removed, and other words are unchanged.

As before, we can use the same text cleaning and analysis steps, and put this all in a function:

```
def create_fdist_visualizations(path, extension='docx'):
    """
    Takes a path to a folder with .docx files, reads and cleans text,
    then plots unigram and bigram frequency distributions.
```

```
"""
docs = glob(os.path.join(path, f'*.{extension}'))
if extension in['doc', 'docx']:
    text = ' '.join(textract.process(w).decode('utf-8') for w in docs)
elif extension == 'pdf':
    text = ' '.join(extract_text(w) for w in docs)
    lines = text.split('\n')
    cleaned_lines = []
    for l in lines:
        if len(l) == 0:
            continue
        if l[-1] == '-':
            cleaned_lines.append(l[:-1])
        else:
            cleaned_lines.append(l + ' ')

    text = ''.join(cleaned_lines)

# remove punctuation, numbers, stopwords
translator = str.maketrans('', '', string.punctuation + string.digits)
text = text.translate(translator)
words = text.lower().split()
words = [w for w in words if w not in en_stopwords and len(w) > 3]

unigram_fd = nltk.FreqDist(words)
bigrams = list([' '.join(bg) for bg in nltk.bigrams(words)])
bigram_fd = nltk.FreqDist(bigrams)

unigram_fd.plot(20)
bigram_fd.plot(20)
```

One update to the function is the addition of another argument for the file extension. The extension argument is included in the os.path.join() function with f-string formatting (f'*.{extension}'). If the file extension is .docx or .doc, then we will continue as we did before. If it is .pdf, we will use pdfminer.six to read the text, and then clean the text to remove line-continuation hyphens.

The same unigram and bigram plots are then drawn:

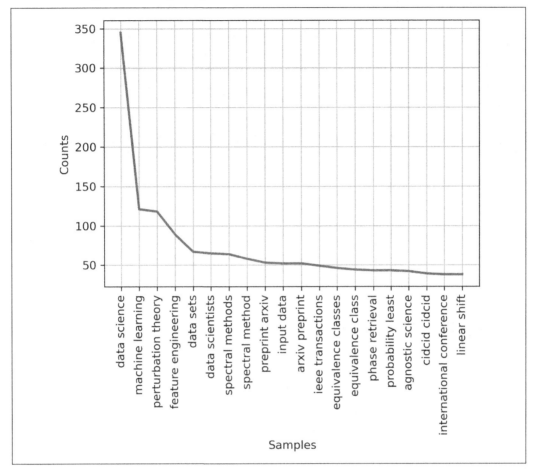

Figure 6.3: A word frequency plot showing bigrams from 10 arXiv data science papers

We can see that some of the subjects in these recent papers include machine learning, feature engineering, spectral methods, and perturbation theory. Of course, "data science" is the top bigram that shows up in the papers. We might think about adding common words such as these to our stopwords list, since they aren't giving us much meaning here.

That wraps up our data wrangling and analysis of PDF and Word files. However, we will learn much more about how to analyze text in *Chapter 18, Working with Text*, with more advanced tools such as topic modeling. Now, we will see how to interface with another common file type that holds loads of data – Excel spreadsheets.

Reading and writing data with Excel files

Excel files seem to be ubiquitous in organizations and knowing how to work with them will help us extract more data for analysis. There are a few packages in Python for working with Excel files:

- `pandas`
- `openpyxl` (for `.xlsx` files, also used by pandas)
- `xlrd` and `xlwt` (for `.xls` files)
- and more

For most Excel data wrangling situations, `pandas` does everything we need.

Using pandas for wrangling Excel files

We need to ensure that `pandas` is installed with conda or pip, and also install `openpyxl` for reading Excel files: `conda install -c conda-forge openpyxl -y`. Then we can open Excel files with the `pd.read_excel()` function.

We will analyze some Excel files from the **Midcontinent Independent System Operator** (**MISO**) organization, which provides electricity to large parts of the US and Canada. In this section, imagine you are working for Dynasty Power Inc. as a junior power analyst analyzing energy markets (this is actually a job Dynasty Power is hiring for at the time of writing). The idea is that we are buying and selling energy futures contracts in order to make a profit, and this may also help to stabilize the price of energy. MISO publishes a lot of data (`https://www.misoenergy.org/markets-and-operations/real-time--market-data/market-reports/`), and our first task is to analyze some aspects of the **Multiday Operating Margin** (**MOM**) forecast report the "Summary" section of MISO's market reports page. We've been tasked with analyzing the wind and energy load forecasts from the reports. Our deliverable is to create an Excel spreadsheet with 5-day forecasts for wind power and electricity load each day in the historical data, as well as perform some analysis on the data.

	1/24/21 HE 20	1/25/21 HE 20**	1/26/21 HE 20**	1/27/21 HE 20**	1/28/21 HE 09**	1/29/21 HE 09**
RESOURCE COMMITTED	72,247	67,592	76,485	77,938	74,684	67,994
RESOURCE UNCOMMITTED	31,091	52,090	42,850	42,447	45,850	53,284
Uncommitted >16 hr	2,384	14,742	10,862	11,007	13,078	18,652
Uncommitted 12-16 hr	3,475	7,555	6,432	5,490	4,923	5,748
Uncommitted 8-12 hr	4,909	6,724	5,819	5,499	6,129	6,453
Uncommitted 4-8 hr	3,467	4,978	3,731	4,155	4,180	4,381
Uncommitted < 4 hr	16,857	18,093	16,007	16,297	17,542	18,051
Renewable Forecast	5,374	14,353	6,351	4,667	7,529	14,354
MISO resources available	108,712	134,034	125,686	125,051	128,063	135,632
NSI (+ export, - import)	-2,362	-2,851	-2,851	-2,851	-3,166	-3,166
Total Resources Available	111,074	136,885	128,537	127,902	131,229	138,798
Projected Load	77,528	81,575	82,841	81,974	82,897	83,236
Operating Reserve Requirement	2,410	2,410	2,410	2,410	2,410	2,410
Obligation	79,938	83,985	85,251	84,384	85,307	85,646
Resource Operating Margin *	31,136	52,900	43,286	43,518	45,922	53,152

Figure 6.4: The MISO worksheet in the first Excel file under
Chapter6/data/excel in the book's GitHub repository

The data we'll use can be found in the GitHub repository for the book under
`Chapter6/data/excel`. Before jumping straight to Python and loading the data, it's
always a good idea to open up one of the Excel files before getting to work on them
– this helps us get familiar with the layout of the data and Excel file. We notice from
the file that it has several sheets, but we can get the data we need from the **MISO**
sheet from the rows **Renewable Forecast** and **Projected Loadl** (shown in *Figure
6.4*). Note that these rows are also in the regional breakdown tabs (for example, the
SOUTH tab), so we could easily extend our Python code to cover the individual
regions. We can see that the first four rows of the sheet don't contain any information
of interest. Putting these things together, we can load the data from the **MISO** tab:

```
from glob import glob
import pandas as pd


excel_files = glob('data/excel/*.xlsx')
df = pd.read_excel(excel_files[0], sheet_name='MISO', skiprows=4, nrows=17,
index_col=0, usecols=range(7))
```

We first list the Excel files ending in .xlsx, as we did with the .pdf and .docx files.
We use pandas' `read_excel()` function, and provide several arguments: the filename,
the worksheet name (`MISO`), how many rows to skip (`skiprows`), how many rows to
parse (`nrows`, which covers the data we want to parse here), which column to use
as the index (we are using the first column, A, with `index_col=0`), and how many
columns to parse (columns 0 through 6 using `usecols=range(7)`).

The code `range(7)` will give us a range from 0 to 6, which includes the row labels and the 6 days of forecasts in the spreadsheet (columns B through G). The DataFrame is small enough that we can print it out in full by executing `df` in a Jupyter notebook cell. We can see a few rows containing only missing values (`NaN`), which we could remove with `df.dropna(inplace=True)`:

	1/24/21 HE 20	1/25/21 HE 20**	1/26/21 HE 20**	1/27/21 HE 20**	1/28/21 HE 09**	1/29/21 HE 09**
RESOURCE COMMITTED	72247.3	67591.5	76485.2	77937.5	74683.8	67994.4
RESOURCE UNCOMMITTED	31091.0	52089.8	42849.8	42446.9	45850.4	53283.5
Uncommitted >16 hr	2383.8	14741.5	10861.6	11006.6	13077.6	18652.0
Uncommitted 12-16 hr	3475.0	7554.5	6432.0	5490.0	4923.0	5748.0
Uncommitted 8-12 hr	4908.9	6723.5	5818.5	5498.5	6128.5	6452.5
Uncommitted 4-8 hr	3466.5	4977.5	3730.5	4154.6	4179.5	4380.5
Uncommitted < 4 hr	16856.8	18092.8	16007.2	16297.2	17541.8	18050.5
Renewable Forecast	5373.7	14352.5	6350.8	4666.5	7529.2	14353.6
MISO resources available	108712.0	134033.8	125685.8	125050.9	128063.4	135631.5
NSI (+ export, - import)	-2362.0	-2851.0	-2851.0	-2851.0	-3166.0	-3166.0
Total Resources Available	111074.0	136884.8	128536.8	127901.9	131229.4	138797.5
NaN	NaN	NaN	NaN	NaN	NaN	NaN
Projected Load	77528.0	81575.0	82841.0	81974.0	82897.0	83236.0
Operating Reserve Requirement	2410.0	2410.0	2410.0	2410.0	2410.0	2410.0
Obligation	79938.0	83985.0	85251.0	84384.0	85307.0	85646.0
NaN	NaN	NaN	NaN	NaN	NaN	NaN
Resource Operating Margin *	31136.0	52899.8	43285.8	43517.9	45922.4	53151.5

Figure 6.5: The pandas DataFrame of the parsed MISO data

Next, we want to convert the projected load and renewable forecast into a DataFrame. The method shown here is one way to do this, although there are certainly many other ways to do it. First, we obtain the data from both the load and renewable rows:

```
loads = df.loc['Projected Load', :].to_list()
wind = df.loc['Renewable Forecast', :].to_list()
```

We use `df.loc[]` to access the DataFrame by index, and use the two index values that match the rows we want. We convert these values to lists so that we can easily concatenate them in the next steps.

The next step is to generate column labels for our DataFrame:

```
load_labels = [f'load_d{d}' for d in range(1, 7)]
wind_labels = [f'wind_d{d}' for d in range(1, 7)]
```

Again, we use lists so we can concatenate them easily. We are using f-string formatting here, so we can easily fill in the value of d in the list comprehensions. This gives us values such as `load_d1` and `wind_d6`. Our final steps entail creating a dictionary to give to `pd.DataFrame()`, and an index:

```
data_dict = {col: val for col, val in zip(load_labels + wind_labels, loads +
wind)}
date = pd.to_datetime(excel_files[0].split('\\')[-1].split('_')[0])
```

We are using a dictionary comprehension in the first line to create a dictionary with values such as `{'wind_d1': 5373.7}`. Notice that we use the `zip()` function, which returns tuples from the two lists we give it. If you wanted to see what this looks like, try printing out `list(zip(load_labels + wind_labels, loads + wind))`. The `zip()` function returns a zip object, so we need to convert it to a list to be able to print it out. This allows us to iterate through the matching column label and value, and store these as `col` and `val` variables in our dictionary comprehension. Notice that we are concatenating the label and value lists here with the plus sign operator (concatenation operator for lists).

Our next step after that is to get the date of the data from the filename. Each filename has the date in a format such as 20210123, which is a 4-digit year, followed by a 2-digit month, and then a 2-digit day. Luckily, the `pd.to_datetime()` function works well at parsing this particular date format. Of course, if that doesn't work, we can always specify the `format` argument in `to_datetime()`, using Python's datetime format codes (the link to the format codes can be found on the pandas `to_datetime()` documentation web page).

Now that our data is ready, we can put it in a DataFrame:

```
df = pd.DataFrame.from_records(data=data_dict, index=[date])
```

Our DataFrame now has 2021-01-23 as the index, column labels `load_d1` through `wind_d6`, and has the data from the spreadsheet in it. We will now create a function that can do this same data parsing for any number of files and creates one large DataFrame. We'll use the `append()` function of DataFrames, which adds another row on to the end. Here is our full function:

```
import os

def extract_miso_forecasts(path):
    """
    Takes a filepath to .xlsx MISO MOM reports and extracts wind and load
    forecasts.
    Saves data to an Excel file - miso_forecasts.xlsx, and returns the
```

```
DataFrame.
    """
    excel_files = glob(os.path.join(path, '*.xlsx'))
    full_forecast_df = None
    for file in excel_files:
        df = pd.read_excel(file, sheet_name='MISO', skiprows=4, \
                            nrows=17, index_col=0, usecols=range(7))

        # get data
        loads = df.loc['Projected Load', :].to_list()
        wind = df.loc['Renewable Forecast', :].to_list()

        # make column labels
        load_labels = [f'load_d{d}' for d in range(1, 7)]
        wind_labels = [f'wind_d{d}' for d in range(1, 7)]

        # create and append dataframe
        data_dict = {col: val for col, val in zip(load_labels + wind_labels, \
                                        loads + wind)}
        date = pd.to_datetime(file.split('\\')[-1].split('_')[0])
        forecast_df = pd.DataFrame.from_records(data=data_dict, index=[date])
        if full_forecast_df is None:
            full_forecast_df = forecast_df.copy()
        else:
            full_forecast_df = full_forecast_df.append(forecast_df)

    full_forecast_df.sort_index(inplace=True)
    full_forecast_df.to_excel('miso_forecasts.xlsx')
    return full_forecast_df
```

We first import the os module so that we can use it for os.path.join() again, as in the previous section. We then create an empty variable, full_forecast_df, with the value None. In this way, we can create our DataFrame from scratch when reading the first file, and then append to it when reading subsequent files. Next, we loop through each Excel file, performing the same data extraction steps we did before. Once we have our DataFrame, we check whether the full_forecast_df variable is None, and if so, we copy our current DataFrame (forecast_df) into that variable.

Otherwise, we use the append() method of DataFrames to add our current DataFrame (forecast_df) to the full_forecast_df one. After we exit the loop and have parsed all the data into full_forecast_df, we sort the index, updating the DataFrame in place. This will ensure that our data is sorted from the earliest to latest date, just in case we read the files out of order. Lastly, we write the data to an Excel file with pandas' DataFrame.to_excel() function, and then return the full DataFrame from the function. We can now use our function like this:

```
df = extract_miso_forecasts('data/excel/')
```

What we've done here is the necessary data wrangling to extract data from an arbitrary number of Excel files, and we now have this data ready for analysis.

Analyzing the data

Now we can do some simple analysis on the data, such as looking at a plot of how the forecasts change over time:

```
df[['wind_d1', 'wind_d2', 'wind_d3']].plot()
```

However, that plot is difficult to read, since the forecasts for the same day in the future are offset by 1 and 2 days for d2 and d3, respectively. Instead, we can shift the d2 forecasts forward by a day and the d3 forecasts forward by 2 days with the shift() method of DataFrames:

```
plot_df = pd.concat([df['wind_d1'], df['wind_d2'].shift(), df['wind_d3'].
shift(2)], axis=1)
plot_df.index += pd.DateOffset(1)
```

This shift() function moves the data in the DataFrame forward, relative to the index, by an offset (default of 1). It can also move data backward relative to the index with a negative value for the argument to shift(). This has the effect of lining up the 1-, 2-, and 3-day predictions in our DataFrame so that they are all predictions for the same date in each row. Then we add one day to the index with a pandas DateOffset of 1 day, so that the index will now be the day the forecast is predicting for. When we plot the data, it is now easy to interpret:

```
plot_df.plot()
```

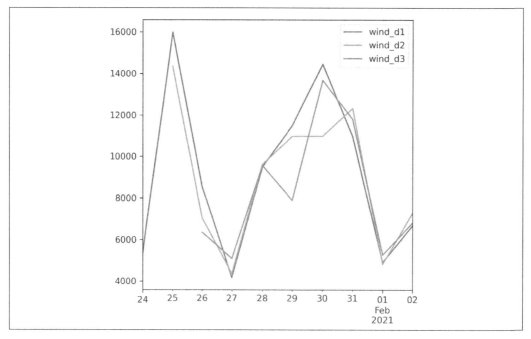

Figure 6.6: A line plot of the wind energy forecasts from the MISO data

We can see that most of the forecasts are remarkably similar for the predictions 1 and 3 days into the future, but there are some days where they change drastically.

Other analysis we might do would draw on things we've already learned from previous chapters – EDA, for example. We might want to look at correlations between the data in a correlogram:

```
import seaborn as sns
```

```
sns.heatmap(df.corr())
```

However, the data we've examined here is small, and we want to examine a much bigger set of data when looking for correlations. In the next chapter, we'll learn how to web scrape MISO for all the historical MOM reports.

Using openpyxl for wrangling Excel files

For most situations, reading and writing Excel files with pandas works just fine. For more intricate situations, we can move down to a lower-level package (which pandas uses for `.xlsx` files): openpyxl. This package has a lot a functionality: we can read data cell by cell from Excel workbooks, we can write data, and write complex data such as Excel formulas, and we can read complex data such as hyperlinks in data cells.

Here, we will look at how we can use openpyxl for handling messy data that may have typos as a result of manual entry. For example, what if the MISO data was created by hand and there were typos in the worksheet names and mistakes in the data labels in the worksheets? One way to deal with this is fuzzy string matching, which is a breeze in Python.

Let's first load our first Excel file from our list of files with openpyxl:

```
from openpyxl import load_workbook

wb = load_workbook(excel_files[0])
print(wb.sheetnames)
```

We simply load the entire Excel file, and then print out the names of the sheets in a list. To do fuzzy string matching, we can use the python-levenshtein package, which we can install with conda: conda install -c conda-forge python-levenshtein -y. Then we use the ratio function:

```
from Levenshtein import ratio

miso_sheetname = [name for name in wb.sheetnames if \
                 (ratio(name.lower(), 'miso') > 0.8)][0]
```

This calculates the Levenshtein distance between two strings, which is essentially the number of characters that need to be edited to make the strings match. The ratio() function returns a number between 0 (no similarity) and 1 (a perfect match). Similar functions are available through the fuzzywuzzy package, which actually uses the python-levenshtein package.

Here, we are using a list comprehension to loop through the worksheet names. Then we use the ratio() function to compare the lowercased version of each worksheet name with the 'miso' string. If this returns a value greater than 0.8, meaning roughly 80% or more of the two strings match, then we keep that string in our list.

Then we simply get the first index of the list of matches as a quick-and-dirty solution. This code would need to be improved to use on real-world data. For example, you might create a dictionary of worksheet names as keys with similarity scores as values, and choose the most similar string to 'miso'.

Once we have the proper worksheet name, we can access that sheet like so:

```
miso = wb[miso_sheetname]
```

Now, let's consider that the data in the Excel workbooks may have been entered by hand, and there may be some typos. This causes the row that should be "Renewable forecast" to sometimes be a slightly different string, such as "Renewwable forecast", which would not work in our `extract_miso_forecasts()` function we created earlier. We can again use fuzzy string matching, along with the ability of `openpyxl` to iterate through rows:

```
for row in miso.iter_rows():
    for cell in row:
        if ratio(str(cell.value).lower(), 'renewable forecast') > 0.8:
            print(cell.value)
            print(f'row, column: {cell.row}, {cell.column}')
```

Here, we first use the `iter_rows()` method of our workbook object to go through each row. The `row` variable contains a list of the cells for each row, and we then check whether the value of that cell has a string 80% or more similar to "renewable forecast". Notice that we are converting `cell.value` to a string – this is because some cell values are `None`, and others are numbers. Without this string conversion, we get an error. Once we find a cell that matches, we print out the value and the row and column numbers. When we run the code, we find our needle in the haystack:

```
Renewable Forecast
row, column: 13, 1
```

These are some clever ways in which we can use `openpyxl` to parse messy data, which we are certain to encounter when doing data science. Keep in mind that `openpyxl` has a lot of other capabilities, including advanced abilities for extracting data from Excel files and writing data or even formulas to Excel files

Test your knowledge

Now that we've learned ways of dealing with documents and Excel files, let's practice what we've learned. For the first task, examine a different set of PDFs of `arXiv.org` papers, and perform an n-gram analysis to understand what some of the common words and phrases are in the papers. Add trigrams (3-word groups) to your analysis. The `ngrams` function from `nltk.utils` might be helpful (you might find Stack Overflow to be helpful, or the official documentation here: `http://www.nltk.org/api/nltk.html?highlight=ngram#nltk.util.ngrams`). In the GitHub repository for this book, there is a collection of PDF files from arXiv with "machine learning" in the title. However, you might go to `arXiv.org` and download some recent papers with "machine learning" or "data science" in the title.

Be sure to write an analysis of your results, explaining what the n-gram frequency distributions are telling us.

For the second task, combine the historical actual load data with our MISO load forecast data we collected. The historical actual load data can be found from MISO and is in the GitHub repository for this book under `https://github.com/PacktPublishing/Practical-Data-Science-with-Python/tree/main/Chapter6/data/excel`. Compare the actual load with the 6-day ahead forecast from our collated data. You might use the following pandas functions – `pd.Dateoffset()`, `pd.Timedelta()`, `DataFrame.shift()`, `merge()`, `groupby()`, and/or `concat()` – in your work. To get the actual load for each day, take the average of the load per hour from the historical data. As always, be sure to write some analysis explaining what the results signify.

Summary

We learned some useful tools for extracting and wrangling data from some common data sources here: documents (MS Word and PDF files) and spreadsheets (MS Excel files). The `textract` package proved useful for extracting data from `.docx` files, and works for `.doc` and many other files as well, including reading scanned PDFs with OCR. We also learned that several other packages can be used to read text-encoded PDFs: `pdfminer.six`, `tika`, `pymupdf`, and `pypdf2` (among others). Recall that `tika` will give us metadata from PDFs, but also requires Java to be properly installed on our system. Once we loaded text from documents, we saw how we can perform some basic analysis on them with n-grams and frequency plots in order to see a summary of the content of the documents.

The other major file type we examined was Excel spreadsheets. We saw how `pandas` works well for simpler tasks, such as reading and writing simple Excel spreadsheets. For more complex tasks, we should use another package such as `openpyxl`, which can perform tasks, including extracting hyperlinks from cells and writing formulas to cells.

Next up is the final chapter in our *Dealing with Data* part – web scraping. This is an exciting topic that opens up a vast amount of data to us and is a topic that many people enjoy. We'll even tie it together with this chapter by scraping the MISO MOM reports to get a fuller picture of how the wind and load forecasts look over time.

7

Web Scraping

In this final chapter of the *Dealing with Data* part of the book, we'll be learning how to collect data from web sources. This includes using Python modules and packages to scrape data straight from webpages and **Application Programming Interfaces (APIs)**. We'll also learn how to use so-called "wrappers" around APIs to collect and store data. Since new, fresh data is being created every day on the internet, web scraping opens up huge opportunities for data collection.

In this chapter, we'll cover the following:

- Understanding the structure of the internet
- Performing simple web scraping
- Parsing HTML from scraped pages
- Using APIs to collect data
- The ethics and legality of web scraping

We'll learn these topics using the following Python packages and modules:

- `urllib`
- `beautifulsoup4`
- `lxml`
- `requests`
- Selenium
- `praw` (a Reddit API wrapper)

Web scraping is a fun subject because it's not too tough to get started, and it's enjoyable to do. It also provides us with fresh data that we can use for a number of tasks, like sentiment analysis, trend monitoring, and marketing optimization. Let's get started with the basics.

Understanding the structure of the internet

Before undertaking web scraping, it's important to have a rudimentary understanding of how the internet works. Most of us simply interact through web browsers and don't see all the details behind webpages, but behind the images and text that we see in our browser, there's a lot of complex code and data exchange happening.

When we visit a webpage, we type in a web address in our browser address bar and ask for a file from a remote server. The file is returned to us and displayed through our browser. The web addresses we use are URLs, or Uniform Resource Locators. An example we'll use here is

```
https://subscription.packtpub.com/book/IoT-and-Hardware/9781789958034
```

which is a page for the book *MicroPython Projects*, by Jacob Beningo. URLs follow a pattern, which we can use when web scraping:

```
[scheme]://[authority][path_to_resource]?[parameters]
```

In our example:

- Scheme – `https`
- Authority – `subscription.packtpub.com`
- Path to resource – `book/IoT-and-Hardware/9781789958034`
- Parameters – no parameters used here

The scheme is usually **http (Hypertext Transfer Protocol)** or **https (HTTP Secure)** for websites, although many other schemes are possible, such as **ftp** for file transfer. Within the authority is the domain name (`subscription.packtpub.com` here). Domain names have a top-level domain on the far right, like com or org, and these domains are broken up into subdomains that are separated by periods. For example, `packtpub` is a subdomain of the `com` top-level domain, and `subscription` is a subdomain of `packtpub`.

After the authority, we then have a path to a resource we want to retrieve. Here, our path is book/IoT-and-Hardware/9781789958034. However, you might also see a simple path like /index.html. This is the resource, or file, we are retrieving from a remote computer somewhere. After the path, we can also include parameters. These follow a question mark and could look like this: ?key=value. They are similar to a dictionary in Python, with a key and value. These get sent to the web server we are requesting the webpage from, and the server can use these parameters when running its code. For example, we could send a search term via parameters.

GET and POST requests, and HTML

When we send our request to the server for a webpage, we are using HTTP. This stands for Hypertext Transfer Protocol, which is an application layer protocol used primarily in client-server communication mode. In other words, HTTP is a standard way of sending and retrieving data between computers on the internet. There are several different methods within HTTP, but we're most concerned with the methods GET and POST. These are ways of asking for a resource, like a webpage. Most of the time we are using a GET request, which simply asks for the resource. Other times we can use a POST request to send data along with our request. An example of sending data may be sending some text to an API for the server to perform sentiment analysis and send back the result.

Along with GET and POST requests, we can send headers. These contain extra information as strings that can be passed between our computer and the server we're getting a website from. A common example is a cookie. Cookies are key-value pairs like a dictionary in Python and are often used for personalization and tracking. Cookies can also keep us logged in on a webpage, which can be useful for web scraping.

Once we send our GET request, we get back a webpage with HTML, or Hypertext Markup Language, which is the instructions that tell our browser how to display the page. Here is an example of simple HTML for a page:

```
<html>
<body>
<h1>This is the title</h1>
<p>Here's some text.</p>
</body>
</html>
```

If you want to see this HTML example working in your browser, you can save the example HTML text above in a file such as `test.html`, then open it in a web browser. We can see the HTML is composed of tags with different keywords like `html` and `body`, and the tags are enclosed with angle brackets (`<>`). Tags should come in pairs, with the opening tag looking like `<p>` and a closing tag with a forward slash, like `</p>`. Tags are also hierarchical – the `html` tag should be the outermost tag, followed by other tags such as `body`. Within the body, we can have heading tags, like `h1`, and paragraph tags (`p`). Tags that are nested inside other tags are called children, and the tags that contain children are called their parents. So, the `html` tag in the example above is the parent of the `body` tag, and the `body` tag is the child of the `html` tag. There are loads of other tags, far too many to cover here. Other references such as W3Schools have tables listing all the HTML tags (`https://www.w3schools.com/tags/default.asp`).

One important tag within HTML is `<script>`, which contains JavaScript code. Much of the web now utilizes JavaScript for dynamic behavior of webpages (like loading more menu items when you scroll down on a page), and we will see how it can make web scraping difficult. JavaScript code looks similar to Python code, although it has its own unique syntax, of course. We now have a basic understanding of the important components for web scraping: URLs, HTTP methods, and HTML. Next, we'll use Python to scrape data from the web.

Performing simple web scraping

There are a few ways to perform GET and POST requests in Python, and we'll execute these with the `urllib` and `requests` libraries here.

Using urllib

The simplest way to web scrape in Python is with built-in modules from `urllib`. With this library, we can easily download the content of a webpage or a file. For example, let's download the Wikipedia page for general-purpose programming languages and print out the first bit:

```
from urllib.request import urlopen

url = 'https://en.wikipedia.org/wiki/General-purpose_programming_language'
page = urlopen(url).read()

print(page[:50])
print(page[:50].decode('utf-8'))
```

We import the `urlopen` function from the `urllib.request` module (which is a Python file in the Python standard library). Then, we use the function by providing a URL as a string. There are other arguments we can provide, like `data`, but those are for usage with POST requests. Notice at the end of the `urlopen()` line we use the `read()` method of the returned object from `urlopen()`. This reads the data by fetching the page. Then we print out the first 50 characters. You'll notice it looks like this:

```
b'<!DOCTYPE html>\n<html class="client-nojs" lang="en'
```

We can see it's a bytes object (or a bytestring). If you remember from *Chapter 6, Data Wrangling Documents and Spreadsheets*, this is how we store data on disk, and it's how we get the data from an HTTP request. We can convert it to a normal character string with the `decode()` method of bytes objects in Python, and we use the common utf-8 encoding. If we wanted to, we could use the `UnicodeDammit()` class from the `beautifulsoup4` package (like we did in *Chapter 6*), which tells us the encoding is utf-8.

Since a GET request with `urlopen` simply returns data, we can also use it to retrieve data files. For example, let's download a MISO **Multiday Operating Margin** (**MOM**) report:

```
datafile = 'https://docs.misoenergy.org/marketreports/20210203_mom.xlsx'
mom_data = urlopen(datafile_url).read()
print(mom_data[:20])
```

If you recall, these are the same spreadsheets we loaded and analyzed in *Chapter 6*. To get this URL, we can visit MISO's market reports page, then click the **Multiday Operating Margin Forecast Report (xlsx)** option in the navigator (the market report page is here: `https://www.misoenergy.org/markets-and-operations/real-time--market-data/market-reports/#nt=/MarketReportType:Summary`). Then we can right-click (*Ctrl + click* on Mac) on a link to a `.xlsx` file and choose **Copy link address** to get the URL to the file.

Notice we use the same `urlopen().read()` function to retrieve the data – this is because HTTP is a general protocol and works for any type of file or data. Again, when we print out the first few characters, we see it is a bytes object. However, we can't use `decode('utf-8')` here because it is not text. Instead, we can directly load it into a pandas DataFrame:

```
import pandas as pd
df = pd.read_excel(mom_data)
df.head()
```

Once this code is run, we'll see the first few rows of the data – it worked! We just downloaded a file through HTTP and Python, then loaded it into a pandas DataFrame. In fact, there's an even easier way to do this – we can directly use `read_excel()` with the URL:

```
df = pd.read_excel(datafile_url)
```

Behind the scenes, pandas is using the same `urlopen().read()` function we did. This works for other pandas `read` functions as well, such as `read_csv()`.

We can check that the entire file downloaded fine by writing to our hard drive and opening it in Excel: `df.to_excel('mom_report.xlsx')`. Doing this, we find the format and images of the Excel file didn't download properly. This makes sense, since pandas isn't made to preserve images and Excel formatting – it's only meant to read the string and numeric data. One way to save the entire Excel file with images and formatting is to use Python's built-in file handling:

```
with open('mom_report.xlsx', 'wb') as f:
    f.write(mom_data)
```

This works fine, but there's also a function from `urllib.request` that downloads and saves a file for us:

```
from urllib.request import urlretrieve

urlretrieve(datafile_url, 'mom_report.xlsx')
```

The two crucial arguments to provide to `urlretrieve` are the URL and the filename where the data should be stored. Remember that here, `datafile_url` is the URL, so we are saving the file to `mom_report.xlsx` in the same directory where the code is being run. Now, when we open the `mom_report.xlsx` file in Excel, we'll see the images and format are preserved.

Using the requests package

The `urllib` library works quite well for simple or even moderately complex tasks. For more advanced tasks, the `requests` package is better. Visiting the documentation's front page, we can see the package boasts advanced capabilities for the modern web, like multipart file uploads and SSL verification. Since it's a third-party package, we need to install it: `conda install -c conda-forge requests -y`. We can scrape HTML content from a webpage like this:

```
import requests as rq

url = 'https://en.wikipedia.org/wiki/General-purpose_programming_language'
```

```
response = rq.get(url)
response.text[:50]
```

First, we import the `requests` library and alias it as `rq`. Then we use a GET request to retrieve the Wikipedia general-purpose programming language page, which returns an object of type `requests.models.Response` (you can verify this with the `type()` function). Finally, we are able to get the text from the response with the attribute text. Looking at this text, we can see it's a character string and not a bytestring.

There are many other attributes and methods of requests `Response` objects. Some of the important ones are `status_code`, `ok`, `content`, and `json()`. The `status_code` attribute (`response.status_code`) stores the server's HTTP response code. For a normal, successful web request, this is 200, or at least in the range 200-299. The 400s mean something went wrong on our end, and the 500s mean an error happened on the server's end. There are also other codes in the 100s for informational responses and in the 300s for redirects. The `ok` attribute is similar and returns `True` if the status code is under 400 (not an error). We can use these attributes (`status_code` and `ok`) if we are looping through webpages and want to check if a request was successful.

The `content` attribute gives us the raw data as a bytestring. We can use this to download a file, like with `urllib`:

```
res = rq.get(datafile_url)
df = pd.read_excel(res.content)
```

Here, we are downloading the same MOM report Excel file as before.

The `json()` method will return a list of dictionaries with data that is sent to us (if there is any). This is useful with API methods, as we will see later in the chapter.

We also have `headers` and `cookies` attributes, which allow us to see the headers and cookies returned from the server. This can be useful for debugging unexpected behavior with more advanced web scraping.

Scraping several files

It can be useful to download a collection of files from a website for data analysis. For example, the MOM reports from MISO span years and hundreds of Excel files. While we could hire an intern to manually download all of them, that's not a very fun job or a good use of human potential. Instead, we can use `urllib` or `requests` to download the files as we saw. Oftentimes, files online will follow patterns.

If we examine the URL of a few files, we can usually deduce the pattern and represent it in our Python code.

Two of the URLs for the Excel files look like this:

- `https://docs.misoenergy.org/marketreports/20210202_mom.xlsx`

- `https://docs.misoenergy.org/marketreports/20210201_mom.xlsx`

The pattern here is easy – the date is used in the filename. The rest of the URL stays constant. In other cases, the URL may increment sequentially. If we want to download all the data, we can view the oldest file available and use that as our starting date. In this case, the oldest date is from 2019, and the newest date is currently 2021. We can create a string that we can format with the dates, and use pandas to create a date range:

```
url = 'https://docs.misoenergy.org/marketreports/{}_mom.xlsx'
dates = pd.date_range(start='20191106', end='20210205')
dates = dates.strftime(date_format='%Y%m%d')
```

We first create the `url` variable with a placeholder for the date string using curly brackets. We can insert a string into these curly brackets with `url.format('20191106')`, as we'll see shortly. Next, we create a date range from the earliest data on MISO to the current date at the time of writing. You can update the end parameter to match the current date when you are reading this. Then, we use the `strftime` method of pandas datetime objects, which stands for "string format time." This converts the datetime objects into strings with the year, month, and day, just like they are in the MISO files. The function takes a `date_format` argument, which uses datetime format codes. We are specifying a 4-digit year with `%Y` and a 2-digit month and day with `%m` and `%d`. Our resulting `dates` object looks like this:

```
Index(['20191106', '20191107', '20191108', '20191109', '20191110', '20191111',
       '20191112', '20191113', '20191114', '20191115',
       ...
       '20210127', '20210128', '20210129', '20210130', '20210131', '20210201',
       '20210202', '20210203', '20210204', '20210205'],
      dtype='object', length=458)
```

We can see it matches the expected MISO file format for dates.

 The Python datetime format codes can be found in the official Python documentation: `https://docs.python.org/3/library/datetime.html#strftime-and-strptime-format-codes`

Next, we can loop through our dates and download the files:

```
import os
from urllib.error import HTTPError

for d in dates:
    filename = f'mom_reports/{d}_mom.xlsx'
    if os.path.exists(filename):
        continue

    try:
        urlretrieve(url.format(d), filename)
    except HTTPError:
        continue
```

We first format the filename with the date string, check if the file exists, then download the file. When we download the file, we are using a try-except block. This is a way of gracefully handling errors in Python and continuing on with our code. Some of the dates are not present in the data. For example, the first date missing is 11-24-2019. When we try to download a file that isn't there, we get a 404 error ("Not Found"). If you want to see the error, you can run this line of code: `urlretrieve(url.format('20191124'), filename)`. To handle this, we can import the `HTTPError` exception from `urllib`. The try-except blocks have the keywords `try` and `except` followed by colons, like an if-else statement. Lines that are indented after `try:` and `except:` are executed in those blocks. The code in `try:` is tried first, and upon an error, we can go to the `except` blocks that follow it (you can have as many as you want). We can provide a specific exception to look for, like `HTTPError` in this case. If we don't provide an exception, it catches all errors. The `continue` keyword in the except block takes us to the next iteration in the loop, though we could also use the keyword `pass`, which does nothing.

Notice in `urlretrieve()` we are formatting the `url` string with the `format()` method. This built-in string method takes any number of arguments and replaces the curly bracket pairs in the string with the arguments provided to the function, and this is how we dynamically generate URLs based on our date range here.

Also note we are using the `os` module to check if the file exists at the beginning of each loop – there is no reason to download it again if we already have it. In fact, most of the files are included with the GitHub repository for this book, so you only need to update it with the latest files at the time when you read the book. If the `os.path.exists(filename)` function returns `True` (the file exists), then the `continue` keyword takes us to the next iteration in the loop.

Extracting the data from the scraped files

Now that we have so much more data, we can use the same function, `extract_miso_forecasts()`, from *Chapter 6, Data Wrangling Documents and Spreadsheets*, to extract data from all the spreadsheets. The only thing we changed in the function is adding a try-except block when loading the data. It turns out the older reports only had one worksheet with a different sheet name. If we are using `xlrd` to load the data, then we can import the proper exception. For another library like `openpyxl`, the error will be slightly different. To find how to import the error, we can query an internet search engine, but we can also search the package's source code for the exception on GitHub if it's available there. This will help us figure out how to properly import the exception. Here is the update to the `extract_miso_forecasts()` function from the last chapter:

```
from xlrd import XLRDError


    try:
        df = pd.read_excel(file, sheet_name='MISO', skiprows=4, nrows=17, \
                        index_col=0, usecols=range(7))
    except (XLRDError, ValueError):
        df = pd.read_excel(file, sheet_name='MOM Report', skiprows=4, \
                        nrows=17, index_col=0, usecols=range(7))
```

Recall that the `extract_miso_forecasts()` function takes a file path to a folder with `.xlsx` files, loads them all, gets the wind and load forecasts, and combines this into one big DataFrame, which is returned from the function. To use it, we simply call the function with the data path:

```
df = extract_miso_forecasts('mom_reports')
```

Just like in last chapter, we can shift the 2-day-out wind load predictions back by a day (so the predicted date is the same for the 1-day-out and 2-day-out predictions), and shift the 3-day-out wind prediction back by 2 days:

```
plot_df = pd.concat([df['wind_d1'], df['wind_d2'].shift(), df['wind_d3'].
shift(2)], axis=1)
plot_df.index += pd.DateOffset(1)
plot_df.plot()
```

The last line plots the data as a line chart. Since there is a lot of data, it helps to make the plot interactive. To make the plot interactive in Jupyter, we can run the magic command `%matplotlib widget`.

If you are running the code in IPython, you may need to run `import matplotlib.pyplot as plt` or run a matplotlib magic command like `%matplotlib` to see the plot. Our results look like this:

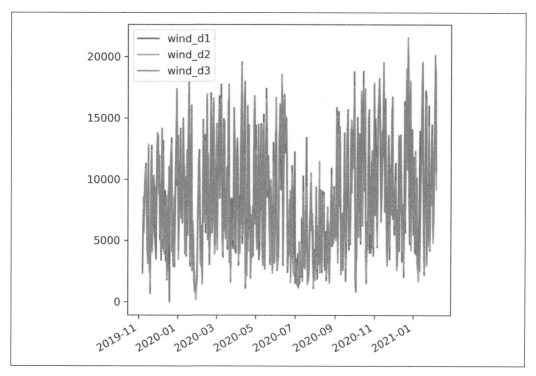

Figure 7.1: A line plot of the predicted wind load from several MISO MOM reports

That's a lot of data, and to really see how the predictions compare, we need to zoom in with our interactive plot. Interestingly, we can see the wind died down in the summer of 2020.

A better way to compare the predictions for this bigger set of data is to use some summary calculations. We can get the mean difference between the 1-day-out and 2-day-out predictions like this:

```
(plot_df['wind_d2'] - plot_df['wind_d1']).abs().mean() / \
plot_df['wind_d1'].mean()
```

This takes the absolute value of the difference between 2-day-out and 1-day-out predictions with `abs()`, then takes the average of those absolute differences. Then we normalize by the average of the 1-day-out predictions. We could also normalize each individual difference by each 1-day-out prediction like so:

```
((plot_df['wind_d2'] - plot_df['wind_d1']) / plot_df['wind_d1']).abs().mean()
```

However, this returns `inf` because some of the `wind_d1` values are 0, and dividing by 0 results in a value of infinity.

We have a general idea of how to download files: find the URLs (finding the pattern in URLs to loop through them), loop through the URLs and use `urlretrieve()` from `urllib` to download the files, and consider adding a try-except block to catch HTTP 404 errors. Next, let's look at parsing HTML content for information.

Parsing HTML from scraped pages

As we already saw, we can easily download a webpage in Python with `urllib` or the `requests` library. One thing to note is these libraries do not work with dynamic JavaScript content. For example, we can download and save the Packt home page:

```
res = rq.get('https://www.packtpub.com/')
with open('packt.html', 'wb') as f:
    f.write(res.content)
```

When we open it, it looks OK, except not all the content displays properly. For example, some of the icons are missing because they load dynamically with JavaScript. For gathering data from pages where JavaScript plays a heavy role, we can instead use other packages, like `requests-html`, Selenium, or the Scrapy package with the `scrapy-splash` plugin. The point is, you may notice some data missing when scraping data from pages. This could be due to JavaScript loading content, meaning you should try one of those other packages for scraping data from that page.

As our first example on parsing HTML, let's use the Wikipedia general-purpose programing languages page again:

```
url = 'https://en.wikipedia.org/wiki/General-purpose_programming_language'
wiki_text = urlopen(url).read().decode('utf-8')
```

We don't need any of the extra functionality of `requests`, so we'll stick with `urllib` for now. Remember that the `read()` method loads the bytestring from the request, and the `decode()` method converts it to a character string.

Once we have the text of the HTML, we can parse it. The two main libraries for parsing and searching HTML are Beautiful Soup and `lxml`. These can be installed with `conda install -c conda-forge beautifulsoup4 lxml -y`. We will call Beautiful Soup by its import name, `bs4`, from now on. Parsing HTML with `bs4` and `lxml` makes it searchable, so that we can find things like lists, links, and other elements within webpages.

The `lxml` package actually does the parsing, and `bs4` provides the framework for easily searching the parsed HTML. Let's import the two libraries:

```
from bs4 import BeautifulSoup as bs
import lxml
```

Notice that the `bs4` import line is a little long, but this is a standard way to import the key class (`BeautifulSoup`) from the library. The `BeautifulSoup` class has a long name, so I like to shorten it to the alias `bs`. Next, we can parse our HTML text:

```
soup = bs(wiki_text)
```

The first argument to the `BeautifulSoup` class initializer is our HTML text. We can also provide a second argument to specify the parser. There are three main parsers available:

- `html.parser` – built-in with Python
- `lxml` – fast
- `html5lib` – best for broken HTML

Most of the time `lxml` works fine, but if the HTML has missing closing tags (for example, a `<p>` tag without a matching `</p>` tag), `html5lib` may work best. Once we have our HTML parsed, we can search it. In this case, we are going to get the links to all the programming languages on the page. First, let's retrieve all the links and print out the 101st link:

```
links = soup.find_all('a')
print(links[102])
```

This prints out:

```
<a href="/wiki/Programming_language" title="Programming
language">programming-language</a>
```

We can see this link has a reference to the programming language page. The text we would see in our browser is the text between the opening and closing link tags (`<a>` and `</a>`), which is "programming-language." We can retrieve this text with `links[100].text`.

The `find_all()` method can take several arguments; the ones we will cover are `name`, `attrs`, and `text`. The `name` argument is the first argument, and can be used to find tags by name, like we did with the tag a for links. The second argument is `attrs`, which we can use to find elements by specific attributes.

For example, the link we printed out above has a `title` attribute of `"Programming Language"`, so we can find all links with that attribute like this:

```
soup.find_all('a', {'title': 'Programming language'})
```

This returns two results, so we know this exact link shows up twice on the page.

We can also search for elements containing text. To search for an exact match of text, we simply provide it to the `text` argument:

```
soup.find_all('a', text='Python')
```

This returns a list with one element:

```
[<a href="/wiki/Python_(programming_language)" title="Python (programming language)">Python</a>]
```

We can see the text in between the a tags is exactly "Python". It is also possible to match a pattern instead of an exact string match. For this, we need to use the `re` module from Python, which enables us to use regular expressions. These are sequences of characters that define a search pattern. For example, if we want to find links that contain "programming" and any other characters, we can use a regex (regular expression):

```
import re

soup.find_all('a', text=re.compile('.*programming.*'))
```

We first need to import the built-in `re` module, then we can use the `compile` function to create a regex. Here, we are using a period for a wildcard to match any character, then an asterisk after the period to signify we should have 0 or more of these matches to any character. We do this at the beginning and end of the string, so that any text in `<a>` tags with "programming" in it will be returned. Regular expressions can be used in the other parts of `bs4` functions as well, like the `name` argument and strings in the `attrs` arguments.

 Google has a nice course on regular expressions in Python here: `https://developers.google.com/edu/python/regular-expressions`

There is also a Packt book, *Mastering Python Regular Expressions*, by Félix López and Víctor Romero, that's much more in-depth.

Now that we have a basic idea of how to parse HTML, let's use it to gather more information from our Wikipedia page.

Using XPath, lxml, and bs4 to extract data from webpages

Next, let's see how we can extract the links to the programming languages under the **List** section. It's usually useful to inspect the page from our browser. We can do this by right-clicking *(Ctrl + click* on Mac) on an area of the page and choosing **Inspect** or **Inspect Element** depending on your browser. This brings up the browser developer tools. You should see a new subdivision of your screen, like this (it may also be a horizontal split):

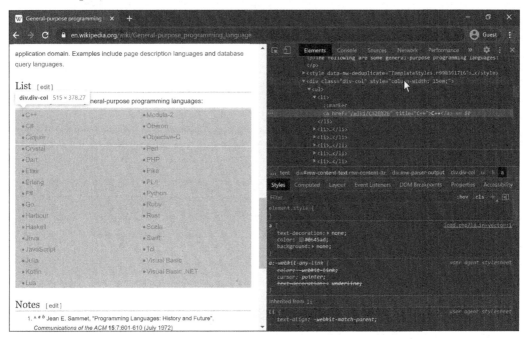

Figure 7.2: Inspecting a Wikipedia page's source

There are lots of useful tools in the browser developer tools pane – the **Console** tab allows us to run JavaScript, and the **Network** tab shows us all the web requests that are happening, along with a half dozen other tabs. For basic web scraping, the **Elements** tab is enough, but the **Console** and **Network** tabs are useful for advanced web scraping.

Here, I clicked on the **C++** link in the list, which is why it's highlighted in the **Elements** section on the right. When we mouse over different elements in the inspector, we see the elements highlighted on the page. In this case, we can see the `<div>` element that holds the programming language links is highlighted because we have the mouse pointer on that element in the inspector. We can see the links are organized in this `<div>` element, then they are in `<ul>` elements (unordered lists) for the two columns, and each link is in a `<li>` element (an individual list element within a `<ul>` tag). There don't seem to be any uniquely identifying attributes for the links or the `div` element, unfortunately. If the `div` had a unique ID, like `<div id="aeuhtn34234">`, then we could use that to find the element, and find the links in that element. We will have to use a different method.

One way to easily find an element after inspecting it is using an XPath, which stands for XML Path Language. It's an expression language, like regex, that allows us to search XML and HTML documents. We can obtain the XPath for an element on a page by right-clicking the element in the inspector, then choosing **Copy**, then **Copy XPath**, as shown in *Figure 7.3*:

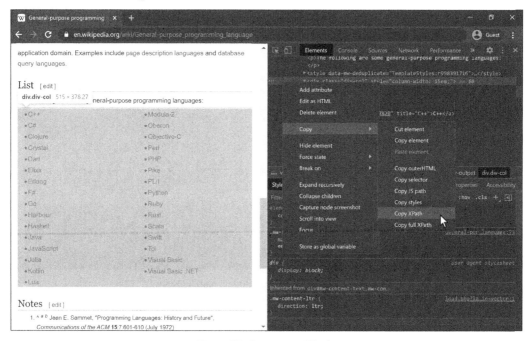

Figure 7.3: Copying an XPath

Once we have the XPath copied, we can use it with `lxml` to find an element:

```
import lxml.html

tree = lxml.html.fromstring(wiki_text)
```

```
link_div = tree.xpath('//*[@id="mw-content-text"]/div[1]/div[3]')
```

First, we import the `lxml.html` module, and use its `fromstring()` function to convert our HTML string into an `lxml` object we can search. Next, we use the `xpath()` method of this object to search for our XPath we copied from the browser. This returns a list of elements that match this XPath. At this point, there are several ways to get all the links within this `div` element, which are shown in the Jupyter Notebook for this chapter on this book's GitHub repository. However, the simplest is to modify the XPath to get all links within this `div` element. Let's first understand how XPath works.

The XPath expression format follows a pattern: the forward slash (`/`) means the root node (the top-most element in our HTML, usually `<html>`), and the asterisk (`*`) is a wildcard to match any element. For example, we can see the root node is `html`, as expected with this line of code, which returns `html`:

```
tree.xpath('/*')[0].tag
```

Two forward slashes specify that the element can be anywhere in the document. So the expression `tree.xpath('//*')` should return all elements from the document. The square brackets with `@id="mw-content-text"` in our XPath signifies an attribute to match. So, with the expression `//*[@id="mw-content-text"]`, we are retrieving any element in the document that has an `id` value of `"mw-content-text"`. This matches a `div` element that holds the main content of the page. Next, we can specify paths to the elements we want. The rest of our XPath is `/div[1]/div[3]`, which means we are getting the first `div` element inside of `id="mw-content-text"` `div` with `div[1]`, then getting the third `div` inside of that with `div[3]`. If we want to find all link elements (`a`) anywhere inside of this path, we simply add `//a` to our XPath like so:

```
wiki_url = 'https://wikipedia.org'

link_elements = tree.xpath('//*[@id="mw-content-text"]/div[1]/div[3]//a')
links = [wiki_url + link.attrib['href'] for link in link_elements]
print(links[:5])
```

The `xpath()` method returns a list, so we can loop through it in a list comprehension, where we get the `href` attribute from each link and append it to our base Wikipedia URL. We use the `attrib` attribute of the `lxml` objects, which is a Python dictionary, to get the `href` URL path. The first five results look like this:

```
['https://wikipedia.org/wiki/C%2B%2B',
 'https://wikipedia.org/wiki/C_Sharp_(programming_language)',
 'https://wikipedia.org/wiki/Clojure',
 'https://wikipedia.org/wiki/Crystal_(programming_language)',
 'https://wikipedia.org/wiki/Dart_(programming_language)']
```

Success! We now have a list of links to general-purpose programming languages from the Wikipedia page, which we can use to collect data from each of the pages.

One of the problems with this method is that the XPath can be brittle – if the structure of the page changes, it could break our XPath. For example, during the writing of this book, the XPath we wanted here changed from `'//*[@id="mw-content-text"]/div[1]/div[2]//a'` to `'//*[@id="mw-content-text"]/div[1]/div[3]//a'` (the last `div` increased by 1). So you may need to modify the example code to get it working properly. However, XPaths are a nice way to quickly extract a particular element from a page by copy-pasting the XPath from the browser element inspector as we saw.

There is another method we could use to find these elements with `bs4`:

```
language_link_elements = soup.find_all('ul')[1].find_all('a')
language_links = [wiki_url + link.attrs['href'] for link in language_link_
elements]
```

Here, we are finding the `ul` elements in the page and taking the second `ul` element we find with index 1 of the returned list. This takes some manual inspection of the results of `soup.find_all('ul')` – printing out the returned elements one at a time like `print(soup.find_all('ul')[0])`, `print(soup.find_all('ul')[1])`, and so on (or looping through them). Just like with XPath, this method is brittle – if another `ul` element gets added at the beginning of the page, we need to change our index to 2 instead of 1: `soup.find_all('ul')[2].find_all('a')`.

One solution to making the code more robust would be to search the `text` attribute of the `ul` elements for some text we expect, such as "C++", and use this to find the correct index for the `ul` elements from `find_all()`. For example:

```
import numpy as np

index = np.where(['C++' in u.text for u in \
                  soup.find_all('ul')])[0][0]
index
```

Here, we use the `where` function from NumPy, which returns a tuple of arrays. By default, it checks where elements are `True` in the provided iterable (a list here) and returns a tuple with an array that holds index values where the list is `True`. Inside `np.where`, we are using a list comprehension to get a list of `True`/`False` values, which are `True` when C++ is in the text of a `<ul>` section. We index the tuple from `np.where` to get the first element with `[0]`, then get the first element of the array with `[0]`. In this case, it returns 1 since the second `ul` element is the only one containing "C++" in the text.

Now that we have our list of links to programming language Wikipedia pages, let's collect the data from them and do some basic text analysis.

Collecting data from several pages

The idea here is to see the top n-grams for the general-purpose programming language pages, to see what's talked about most on the pages. To get the text from each of the pages we have links to, we loop through the pages and collect text from the p tags, and join the text together with the join() method of strings:

```
all_text = []
for link in language_links:
    html = rq.get(link).text
    soup = bs(html)
    paragraph_text = soup.find_all('p')
    all_text.extend([p.text for p in paragraph_text])

text = ' '.join(all_text)
```

For each of our links, we use requests to fetch the page and extract the HTML text from it. Then we convert it to a bs4 object and find all the p elements. These are paragraph elements that hold the text, which we can see by manually examining the page. We then use the extend method of lists to concatenate another list to the end of it. In this case, we concatenate the list containing text from each of the p elements to the all_text list. Once the loop is done, we join the text together with a single space between each element in the all_text list.

Like in the last chapter, we should do some pre-processing before analyzing the text:

```
import string

from nltk import FreqDist, bigrams
from nltk.corpus import stopwords
en_stopwords = set(stopwords.words('english'))

translator = str.maketrans('', '', string.punctuation + string.digits)
cleaned_text = text.translate(translator)
cleaned_words = [w for w in cleaned_text.lower().split() if w not in en_
stopwords and len(w) > 3]
```

We first make the necessary imports for the string module and the nltk library, then remove punctuation, digits, and stopwords like in the previous chapter. Remember that the str.maketrans() function takes three arguments: the third argument maps all characters in that argument to None, and the first two arguments should be left as empty strings for our purposes here.

Then we use this translator object to remove punctuation and digits from the text.

Lastly, we lowercase the text and split it into words (by splitting on any whitespace) using the lower() and split() methods of strings. We only keep words that are not in the en_stopwords set and are longer than three characters long.

Once we have our cleaned words, we can create unigram and bigram frequency distributions from it:

```
unigram_freq = FreqDist(cleaned_words)
bg = [' '.join(bigr) for bigr in bigrams(cleaned_words)]
bg_fd = FreqDist(bg)
list(bg)
```

Just like in the last chapter, we are using the FreqDist class from nltk. The bigrams function returns tuples, so we use ' '.join(bigr) to join these tuples into a single string, with the words separated by a single space.

Using the function bg_fd.plot(20) we can see some of the top phrases from these pages:

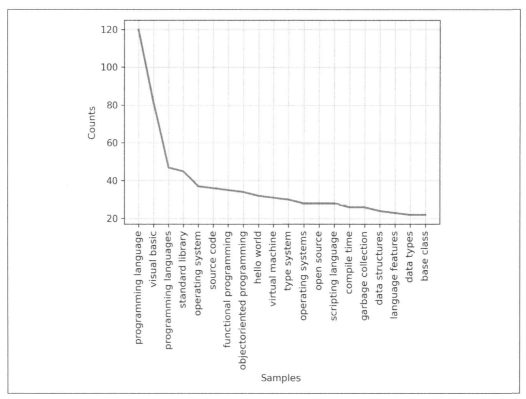

Figure 7.4: The top bigrams from the general-purpose programming language Wikipedia pages

We can see "programming" and "language" are two of the top words – we should add these to our stopwords since they aren't telling us much. We do see a lot of talk about visual basic and the standard library (probably for C languages). We also see that functional and object-oriented programming languages are talked about most out of the types of programming languages, even though there are other types of programming languages, like declarative languages. This clues us in to the type of characteristics that are important for general-purpose programming languages.

A common typo when people try to write "web scraping" is "web scrapping". The word "scrapping" from "scrap" means to discard, unlike the word "scrape" from "web scraping". This concludes our brief tour of basic web scraping; however, there are many more advanced methods within the topic. For example, we can create scraping spiders that will crawl the web or entire websites (manually, or with the Scrapy library). We also may need to deal with JavaScript, for which we can use the `requests-html` package, Scrapy with `scrapy-splash`, or Selenium. Note that Selenium is not intended for web scraping, although it works for the purpose. It is rather slow but also offers the advantage of browser automation. For example, we can easily click different buttons, log in by sending keystrokes to the webpage, and even combine Selenium with the `pyautogui` package to control the mouse and keyboard. For example, some webpages load content dynamically as you scroll down the page. Selenium allows us to send JavaScript commands to scroll down the page, or we can use `pyautogui` to scroll down the page to load more content. However, it is often possible to find the base web requests that are being used from careful sleuthing of the **Network** tab in the browser developer tools; then we can use the `requests` library to collect the data more directly.

 Some other resources that are helpful for learning more advanced web scraping are the book *Web Scraping with Python: Collecting Data from the Modern Web*, by Ryan Mitchell, and *Hands-On Web Scraping with Python*, by Anish Chapagain. One other resource I've found helpful is the Make Data Useful YouTube channel, which demonstrates how to track down web traffic and use a tool called "curl to requests."

Now that we've seen how to scrape data from the webpages and files on the web, let's learn about an even easier way – APIs.

Using APIs to collect data

API stands for Application Programming Interface, and these allow us to interface between two different software applications. For example, we can use Python with `requests` to collect data from MISO directly.

We can also simply use our web browser. MISO's APIs are listed on their site here: `https://www.misoenergy.org/markets-and-operations/RTDataAPIs/`. If we click the link for the **Day Ahead Wind Forecast**, we are taken to another page with JSON data that looks like this:

```
{"MktDay":"02-06-2021","RefId":"06-Feb-2021 - Interval 22:00 EST","Fore
cast":[{"DateTimeEST":"2021-02-06 12:00:00 AM","HourEndingEST":"1","Val
ue":"12764.00"},...DateTimeEST":"2021-02-07 11:00:00 PM","HourEndingEST":"24"
,"Value":"2079.00"}]}
```

The ... in the middle of the JSON data signifies that there is more data we are not showing. This new page has a long URL string:

```
https://api.misoenergy.org/MISORTWDDataBroker/DataBrokerServices.asmx?message
Type=getWindForecast&returnType=json
```

We can see that the subdomain of `misoenergy.org` is `api`, which makes sense (as we are using an API). We then see the path takes us to an `asmx` file. After that, we have some parameters that follow the question mark. We are specifying that we want to get the wind forecast in JSON format with the two parameters specified by `messageType=getWindForecast&returnType=json`. We can see how these parameters have a name, then an equals sign, then the value of the parameter. The parameters are separated by an ampersand (&). Most API calls are going to have some sort of data sent with the request, like options or login credentials. APIs usually have documentation, but because this one is simple, there doesn't seem to be documentation.

To collect this data in Python, we can easily use `requests`:

```
url = 'https://api.misoenergy.org/MISORTWDDataBroker/DataBrokerServices.asmx?
messageType=getWindForecast&returnType=json'
res = rq.get(url)
print(res.json())
```

This prints out:

```
{'MktDay': '02-06-2021',
 'RefId': '06-Feb-2021 - Interval 22:00 EST',
 'Forecast': [{'DateTimeEST': '2021-02-06 12:00:00 AM',
   'HourEndingEST': '1',
   'Value': '12764.00'},
 ...
```

We can see it's the same data as before (the ... once again indicates that not all data is shown). If we look at the JSON data, it's a Python dictionary with keys and values. We can examine these with `res.json().keys()`, and there are three keys we can see above: `'MktDay'`, `'RefId'`, and `'Forecast'`. The forecast wind power is under the `Forecast` key, and we can use a JSON-parsing function from pandas to easily parse this into a DataFrame:

```
df = pd.json_normalize(res.json()['Forecast'])
```

The `json_normalize` function is flexible and can handle most formats of JSON data we provide. Our DataFrame looks like this:

	DateTimeEST	HourEndingEST	Value
0	2021-02-06 12:00:00 AM	1	12764.00
1	2021-02-06 1:00:00 AM	2	12395.00
2	2021-02-06 2:00:00 AM	3	12050.00
3	2021-02-06 3:00:00 AM	4	11679.00
4	2021-02-06 4:00:00 AM	5	11331.00

Figure 7.5: The wind forecast from the MISO API

If we want to take this further and set up some sort of automation that downloads this data daily and stores it as an Excel file, we could use the `MktDay` key to create the filename:

```
df.to_excel('miso_wind_forecast_{}.xlsx'.format(res.json()['MktDay']))
```

Although some APIs are open for anyone to use without any authentication, many other APIs will have an authentication step. This helps API providers verify that you've paid for the service or have agreed to their terms of service and are not requesting too many items from the API. Most APIs will have a rate limit that limits the number of API calls or requests you can make in a unit of time (like 100 calls per minute).

Now that we've looked at a simple API call, let's look at a more complex API with authentication.

Using API wrappers

For more complex APIs, we may need to provide authentication credentials and the URL may become complex. If an API is used frequently or by lots of people, someone has usually written a wrapper for it. An API wrapper is a package in another software that makes it easier for us to use the API.

An example of an API wrapper is the PRAW package in Python, which stands for "Python Reddit API Wrapper." Reddit is a social media website where people discuss a huge range of topics, and we can use this data for data science projects. For example, we can perform sentiment analysis on different topics, we can perform topic modeling to see what people are talking about, or we can monitor social media for public safety. Installing the `praw` package can be done using conda: `conda install -c conda-forge praw -y`. Then, we can create a `praw.Reddit` object, which will allow us to use the API:

```
import praw

reddit = praw.Reddit(
    client_id="_ZKiZks98gi6yQ",
    client_secret="ONbY1wJvXiM2t41O9hVm9weSmfpvxQ",
    user_agent="python_book_demo"
)
```

Notice we are providing some login credentials to this Reddit class. At the time of writing, we can obtain these by creating a Reddit account and then visiting `reddit.com/prefs/apps`. Then we create an app near the bottom of the page, choosing "script" and giving it a name and a redirect URI. The URI can be any URL (such as `https://www.google.com`) and doesn't matter for our purposes here (although it can be used with other aspects of the API):

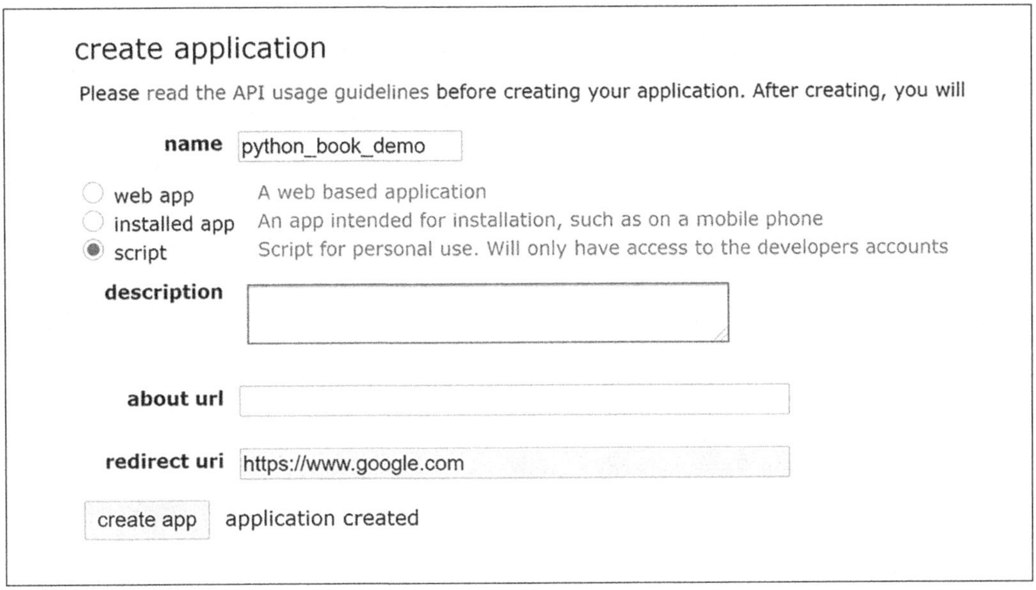

create application
Please read the API usage guidelines before creating your application. After creating, you will
name
python_book_demo
web app
A web based application
installed app
An app intended for installation, such as on a mobile phone
script
Script for personal use. Will only have access to the developers accounts
description
about url
redirect uri
https://www.google.com
create app
application created

Figure 7.6: Creating a Reddit API application

Once we create our application, we are shown the credentials. We can also revisit these credentials by visiting `reddit.com/prefs/apps` and clicking **Edit** for this application. Our credentials look like this:

python_book_demo
user agent
personal use script
_ZKiZks98gi6yQ
client id
change icon
secret
ONbY1wJvXiM2t41O9hVm9weSmfpvxQ
developers
nateFromAccounting (that's you!) remove
add developer:
name
python_book_demo
description
about url
redirect uri
https://www.google.com
update app
delete app

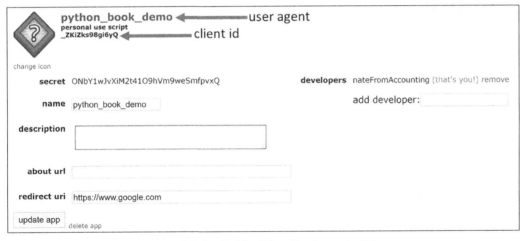

Figure 7.7: Our Reddit API application credentials

These credentials are what we filled in for the `praw.Reddit()` class above. Once we have our `Reddit` object, we can use it to retrieve data. Let's look at some of the top things people are talking about in a subreddit. Reddit is divided into subreddits, kind of like subdomains on the web. Each subreddit is focused on some specific topic. For example, there is a California subreddit where people talk about things going on in the US state of California. Let's collect some data from there:

```
post_text_list = []
comment_text_list = []
for post in reddit.subreddit("california").hot(limit=100):
    post_text_list.append(post.selftext)
    # removes 'show more comments' instances
    post.comments.replace_more(limit=0)
    for c in post.comments.list():
        comment_text_list.append(c.body)

all_text = ' '.join(post_text_list + comment_text_list)
```

First, we create some empty lists to hold the text data from each post and the text data from the comments on the posts. Then we use the `subreddit()` method of our `reddit` object to target a specific subreddit. Within this, we retrieve the top 100 "hot" posts – viewing "hot" posts is one of the options on Reddit, along with "new" and "top" posts. For each post, we get the text with `post.selftext`. Then we get the comments with `post.comments`. The `post.comments.replace_more(limit=0)` line of code removes any instances of "show more," which are links in the comments sections. If we run the code without this line, we end up with an error when trying to loop through the comments. Then we loop through the comments, which we retrieve as a list with `post.comments.list()`, and retrieve the text of each comment with `c.body`, appending it to our overall comment list. Finally, we make one large string of all post and comment text, each separated by a space, using the `join()` method of Python strings.

To figure out how to use an API wrapper like this (for example, to learn about the `replace_more()` method), it's helpful to consult the official documentation. For PRAW and many API wrappers (as well as many Python packages), there is usually a quickstart section that is helpful for learning the first steps. For retrieving and processing comments on Reddit posts, there is a "Comment Extraction and Parsing" page in the PRAW documentation, which demonstrates the use of the `replace_more()` method (`https://praw.readthedocs.io/en/latest/tutorials/comments.html`).

We can also use other documentation examples to get started, then take our Python objects and see what methods they have available. One way to do this is to type the variable name with a period after it, like `post.`, then hit the *Tab* key in Jupyter or IPython. This will suggest autocompletions, showing us the attributes and methods.

We could also use the `dir()` function in Python to list out all attributes and methods, like `dir(post)`. You can try this with the `c` and `post` variables after running the code example above – these variables will hold the value of the comment and post from the last iteration in the loop.

Once we have our text data, we can clean it and look at the top n-grams. Cleaning is similar to what we've done before: removing punctuation, digits, and stopwords. Note that because the stopwords in the NLTK stopword set have punctuation, not all stopwords are properly removed. We could remove stopwords after lowercasing but before removing punctuation to remedy this, or simply add some stopwords without punctuation to our stopwords set. Since the word "don't" showed up in the top bigrams, I added it to the stopwords as "dont" so it is removed from the text after we remove punctuation. We also add "removed" to the stopwords, since this shows up in text for comments or posts that were deleted or taken down by moderators. Our cleaning code looks like this:

```
translator = str.maketrans('', '', string.punctuation + string.digits)
cleaned_text = all_text.translate(translator)

reddit_stopwords = set(['removed', 'dont']) | en_stopwords
cleaned_words = [w for w in cleaned_text.lower().split() if w not in reddit_
stopwords and len(w) > 3]
```

As we did earlier in the web scraping section, we use a translator to remove punctuation and digits. Then we combine the English stopwords set with our new stopwords using a set union (|). Finally, we loop through our lowercased words and keep them if they are not stopwords and are longer than three characters. Then we can look at the top bigrams:

```
bg = [' '.join(bigr) for bigr in bigrams(cleaned_words)]
bg_fd = FreqDist(bg)
bg_fd.most_common(10)
```

This gives us the result:

```
[('middle class', 40),
 ('property taxes', 38),
 ('outdoor dining', 34),
 ('stay home', 33),
 ('climate change', 33),
 ('southern california', 30),
 ('many people', 29),
 ('seems like', 29),
 ('public transit', 27),
 ('santa cruz', 26)]
```

We can see that at the time of data collection, people are talking a lot about socio-economic issues (taxes, income) and the pandemic situation (stay-at-home orders, outdoor dining, and so on).

There are tons of other social media API wrappers out there, for Twitter, Facebook, and others. People have also written social media web scraper wrappers, like the `facebook-scraper` package. These don't use the API and instead use web scraping to collect data but can be used similarly to an API wrapper.

There is a newer type of API technology called a websocket. This is useful for real-time data. For example, most of the cryptocurrency exchanges' APIs use websockets. Some impressive Python packages that use these websocket APIs are the `cryptostore` and `cryptofeed` Python packages by Bryant Moscon, which you can find on GitHub.

An API use we didn't cover, because it could constitute an entire chapter on its own, is using APIs for data processing. There is a plethora of sentiment analysis APIs, where we send text to a server and receive a sentiment score (positive, negative, neutral). For example, Google has a natural language API, with a tutorial on the subject here: `https://cloud.google.com/natural-language/docs/sentiment-tutorial`. Most major cloud providers, and many other providers, offer a huge range of APIs for analyzing text, images, and other data.

APIs are a huge source of data on the web, and there are many of them. If you need data for a project, you might consider seeing if that data can be collected via an API before trying other methods.

The ethics and legality of web scraping

The legality of web scraping has changed over the years. For example, a company called "Bidder's Edge" was scraping eBay in the late 1990s for their auction data. eBay took them to court and Bidder's Edge agreed to pay eBay a settlement in cash and stop scraping their data. However, in more recent times (2019), the company hiQ won a court ruling against LinkedIn, allowing hiQ to scrape LinkedIn's public-facing data. The legal precedent at this point seems to be that if the data is public-facing, it can be scraped. This means if we can access the data without logging in to an account (and without clicking any buttons agreeing to terms of service), then we are *probably* legally allowed to scrape the data. However, big companies have lots of resources and lawyers, so scraping their data and using it to create a business runs the risk of litigation, like in the case of hiQ.

Craigslist is an example of a site that is very aggressive against web scrapers, sending cease-and-desist letters (threatening legal action) to developers who create services based on scraped Craigslist data.

If we do have to log in to an account, like with the job-posting site Glassdoor, then we have agreed to their **terms of service (TOS)**. Most TOS state that web scraping (or even manual web scraping by humans) is not allowed.

Ethically speaking, we should be following TOS and the robots.txt file websites have. This is usually at the main directory of a site, like en.wikipedia.org/robots. txt for the English version of Wikipedia. It will have sections with a user-agent and allow/disallow specifications. For example, here is part of Wikipedia's robots.txt:

```
User-agent: *
Allow: /w/api.php?action=mobileview&
Allow: /w/load.php?
Allow: /api/rest_v1/?doc
Disallow: /w/
Disallow: /api/
Disallow: /trap/
Disallow: /wiki/Special:
Disallow: /wiki/Spezial:
Disallow: /wiki/Spesial:
Disallow: /wiki/Special%3A
Disallow: /wiki/Spezial%3A
Disallow: /wiki/Spesial%3A
```

Our user-agent is what we are using to retrieve the data. For the requests library, we can find this with rq.utils.default_headers(), which shows something like 'python-requests/2.25.1' for our user agent. With a web browser, it's more complex, and looks like this:

```
Mozilla/5.0 (Windows NT 10.0; Win64; x64) AppleWebKit/537.36 (KHTML, like
Gecko) Chrome/88.0.4324.150 Safari/537.36
```

The * for User-agent in the robots.txt file means any user agent, and the allow and disallow sections are self-explanatory – we're not allowed to scrape anything under en.wikipedia.org/w/, for example, but are allowed to scrape things under en.wikipedia.org/w/load.php?. If we see Disallow: /, it means we're not supposed to be scraping anything on the site. Ethically, we should respect the robots.txt instructions and the site's TOS, even if we don't have to agree to the TOS to access data.

Practically speaking, if we are not creating a burden on the server (for example, we only send a few requests and not thousands or millions per second) and we aren't damaging the site's business in any way, our scraping is not hurting them. Legally, the precedent has been set (at the time of writing) that public-facing data is more-or-less OK to scrape. However, each situation is unique, and you will need to consider the ethical, practical, and legal aspects of web scraping before undertaking any large web scraping project.

Test your knowledge

To test your knowledge of what we just learned, download the "Peak Hour Overview" files from MISO, combine them, and explore some of the data within. For example, the "forecasted capacity margin" is something that would be good to examine with a line plot. As an additional challenge, try combining this data with historical regional forecast and actual load data to see how the peak hour energy usage compares with forecasts from the peak hour overview data. The data has already been collected up to 2-7-2021 and is available in the GitHub repository, so be sure to either use that as your start date, or check if the files already exist before downloading them.

For the second challenge, collect the links under the list in the "Libraries" section of the Wikipedia Python page (`https://en.wikipedia.org/wiki/Python_` `(programming_language)#Libraries`). Perform some basic text analysis (for example, n-gram analysis) on the text from these pages and write out an explanation and interpretation of the results.

As your third challenge, collect data from another subreddit of your choice and perform some basic text analysis on it. You might also look at the other available attributes of the posts and comments and perform analysis on them as well (such as the number of upvotes or users who comment the most.

Summary

Web scraping is a great way to gather more data for data science projects. In fact, Wikipedia can be a great source of information and has an API as well. For example, Wikipedia data can be combined with social media and sports data to predict how successful athletes will be (`https://www.kaggle.com/noahgift/social-power-nba`).

We saw how we can use web scraping to collect data files from the web, and how we can use it to collect text and data from webpages. These methods are useful for collecting data that may not otherwise be accessible, but remember to consider the ethics and legality before undertaking a large web scraping project.

We also saw how we can use APIs to collect data, such as with the Reddit API. Again, remember that websites and APIs each have their own TOS that we should follow.

This chapter concludes the *Dealing with Data* part of the book. We've gone from the basics of Python file handling and SQL all the way to collecting and analyzing raw data from the web. Next up, we'll learn how to use statistics for data science, starting with distributions and probability.

Part III

Statistics for Data Science

8

Probability, Distributions, and Sampling

Life is full of uncertainty – we make decisions based on incomplete information all the time. Much of data science has to do with making decisions based on incomplete information. For example, should we show an advertisement for an exercise bike or an iPad to a website visitor? Loans provide another example; deciding on whether to give someone a loan based on their credit history and current income is a decision we might make with a machine learning algorithm. We will examine concepts of probability in this chapter, which lay the foundations for machine learning and statistical methods. Closely related to probability are sampling techniques and probability distributions. In this chapter, we'll cover:

- Foundational probability concepts
- Common probability distributions in data science
- Useful sampling techniques for data science

Once we have these techniques down, it will improve our ability to apply other machine learning models and probabilistic methods, such as those we will learn in the next chapters. Let's get started with the basics of probability.

Probability basics

Probability is all about uncertainty. For example, if we flip a normal coin, we're never sure if it will land on one side or the other (heads or tails). However, we can estimate the probability of the coin landing on heads with a probability function.

The simple frequentist definition of probability and a probability function is that we count the number of times the desired event happens over the total number of outcomes. In the case of a coin toss, we could flip the coin 10 times, count the number of heads, and divide by 10. Most of the time we will have something close to 5/10, or 50%. So, our probability function could be thought of as each coin flip (action, or event) resulting in a 50% chance of landing on heads (our desirable outcome). We can write the equation for our probability function as $P(coin flip == H) = 0.5$ and $P(coin flip == T) = 0.5$. Our total probability across all possible (discrete) events must sum to 1 in probability theory, as it does here.

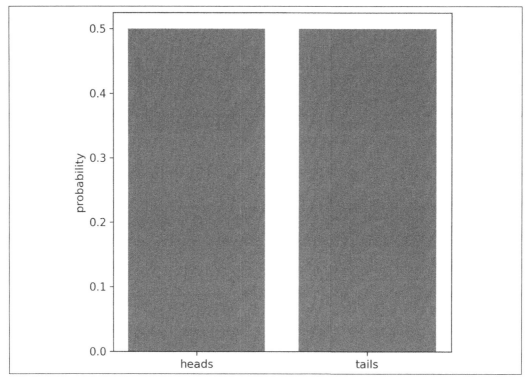

Figure 8.1: The probabilities of getting heads and tails from a coin flip

This coin flip example introduces us to some other probability concepts. One is a random variable, which is a variable with an outcome that depends on randomness. With the coin flip, we might flip it with more or less energy; there could be differing wind resistance, and it could bounce in random ways off the table or floor.

The point is that the value of a random variable is not perfectly predictable. Contrast this with a deterministic event, like a mathematical equation executed in Python. Every time we execute the code 1 + 2 we will get the result of 3, so the outcome of the event 1 + 2 is not a random variable.

Another example of a deterministic variable has to do with macro physics. If we shoot a bullet in the vacuum of space with an exact input force, we can perfectly predict the trajectory of the bullet. The bullet's position in space is a deterministic variable, not a random variable.

In the coin flip example, the random variable is also *discrete*. This means it can only take on certain values, like heads and tails, and not infinite values. Another example of this is the number of help requests a customer makes to an organization.

More complex handling of probability incorporates the concept of infinity and continuous variables. A continuous variable is one that can take any value between two points, like time or length. We can measure the exact time right now, but we can always measure it down to a more precise value (like 1.01 s versus 1.0114 s versus an even more precise 1.0114595 s). We can define probability as a function that maps an event to the relative probability of an occurrence.

For example, say we are measuring the efficiency of solar cells coming off a manufacturing line. Due to random errors in the manufacturing equipment, the efficiencies are not always the same. This sort of process where the outcome has randomness is also called *stochastic*. We can measure the efficiencies of cells and find some empirical probabilities, meaning probabilities we derive from measuring a sample of solar cells. For example, we could find the median efficiency of the cells we measure is 12%. So that means there is a 50% chance our efficiency is greater than 12%, which we could formulate as $P(efficiency > 12\%) = 0.5$. We can formulate these sorts of statistics more easily than the probability for any particular value. Since the solar cell efficiency value can be anything from an array of infinite values, the probability of each particular value is 0 (1 divided by infinity).

Independent and conditional probabilities

These probabilities we've talked about so far are independent probabilities. We aren't considering the effects of other actions on the outcome of the probability. When the outcome of one event affects the probability of another event happening, we describe this as a conditional probability. This is usually illustrated by drawing samples from a bag. Say we have a bag of candy with 3 red, 3 blue, and 3 orange candies, and the red candy is our favorite (so we want to draw that one). The probability of drawing a red candy, P(R), is 3/9 or 1/3. Let's say we draw a red candy for our first sample, and we put the candy in our pocket. Now the probability of getting another red candy, given that we already drew one red candy, is 2/8 or 1/4.

Let's start the experiment over with 3 of each type of candy in the bag and find the probability of getting 2 red candies in a row. To do this, we simply multiply the two probabilities we got above – 1/3 * 1/4 = 1/12, which is roughly 8.3%.

We call this dependent or conditional probability. The probability of getting a red candy on the second draw is *conditional* on what happens on the first draw. We can write this probability of getting red candies in two draws in a row as:

$$P(R1 \text{ and } R2) \ = \ P(R1) \ * \ P(R2 \mid R1)$$

The P() represent probabilities of an event as before. The R1 and R2 notation represents drawing a red candy in our first and second draws, respectively. The P(R2 | R1) notation means the probability of drawing a red candy on the second draw (R2) *given* we drew a red candy on the first draw (R1). The pipe symbol (|) is the mathematical way of representing conditionality or dependence in probability equations like these.

Our probabilities we calculated before are the following:

$$
\begin{aligned}
P(R1) &= 1/3 \\
P(R2 \mid R1) &= 1/4 \\
P(R1 \text{ and } R2) &= 1/12
\end{aligned}
$$

The P(R1 and R2) is called a joint probability, which is the probability of two things happening. The P(R2 | R1) is a conditional probability, which is the probability of an event happening given another event already having happened. A diagram of the situation follows:

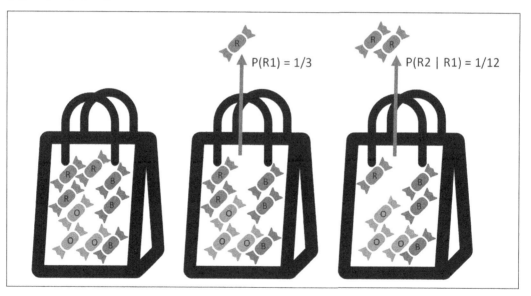

Figure 8.2: A diagram of drawing candy samples from a bag

These sorts of probabilistic methods can be extended to other situations beyond drawing samples as well. For example, we could think about trying to filter spam out of our email inbox with an algorithm or rule.

If we are reasonably certain the message is spam then we automatically move it to our spam folder. For example, if the probability that a message is spam exceeds 90%, we will filter it. We can use our joint probability equation from earlier, and let's focus on seeing the word "Xanax," since this has shown up in spam emails where people try to sell counterfeit Xanax or simply steal people's money. Of course, if we are a doctor and regularly email with people about Xanax and the word "Xanax" is in many non-spam emails, we would not be able to use this exact formulation of the problem here.

One way to formulate our joint probability equation is like this:

$$P(\text{"Xanax" and spam}) = P(\text{"Xanax"}) * P(\text{spam} \mid \text{"Xanax"})$$

However, we will be in a situation where we see a word in an email (such as "Xanax") and want to get the probability of that message being spam. So, we rearrange the equation to get the probability of the email being spam given it contains the word "Xanax":

$$P(\text{spam} \mid \text{"Xanax"}) = P(\text{"Xanax" and spam}) / P(\text{"Xanax"})$$

Here, we have an equation for the probability that a message is spam given the word "Xanax" shows up in the message. On the right side of the equation, we have a term P("Xanax" and spam), which is the joint probability our message contains the word "Xanax" and is spam. This joint probability can be written two ways, actually:

$$P(\text{"Xanax" and spam}) = P(\text{spam}) * P(\text{"Xanax"} \mid \text{spam})$$

$$P(\text{"Xanax" and spam}) = P(\text{"Xanax"}) * P(\text{spam} \mid \text{"Xanax"})$$

 Because the joint probability is not a dependency, we could write it as P("Xanax" and spam) or P(spam and "Xanax") as they are equivalent.

Then we can substitute the first equation above into our equation for P(spam | "Xanax") and arrive at:

$$P(\text{spam} \mid \text{"Xanax"}) = P(\text{spam}) * P(\text{"Xanax"} \mid \text{spam}) / P(\text{"Xanax"})$$

At this point, we have arrived at Bayes' law, which is a statistical theorem (axiom, in fact) that is used in machine learning and data science, and we can use it for our spam classification system.

Bayes' Theorem

Bayes' Theorem (sometimes called Bayes' law or Bayes' rule) is named after a reverend from the 1700s, Thomas Bayes, who partially invented it (it's complicated, but Richard Price sort of co-invented it). The theorem can be written as an equation:

$$P(A|B) = P(A) * P(B|A) / P(B)$$

We can see there are some independent probabilities for two events, A and B, and two conditional probabilities: the probability of A given B, $P(A|B)$, and the probability of B given A, $P(B|A)$.

Another way to write this is with a hypothesis (a condition we can test), H, and evidence, E:

$$P(H|E) = P(H) * P(E|H) / P(E)$$

We can also think of these components as concepts:

$$Posterior = prior * likelihood / evidence$$

To connect this with our spam example, here is our spam equation again in Bayes' law form:

$$P(spam | "Xanax") = P(spam) * P("Xanax" | spam) / P("Xanax")$$

Our hypothesis is that the message is spam, and our evidence is seeing the word "Xanax" in the email. The "prior," P(spam), is our prior belief about the probability of an occurrence; in this case, it's whether any given email is spam. The chance of any given email being spam is estimated to be around 45% or 0.45. The likelihood, or probability of seeing the evidence given the hypothesis, is how compatible our evidence is with the hypothesis. In this case, perhaps roughly 1/3 of our spam messages contain the word "Xanax," so we could set this value to 0.33. This is divided by the *marginal* probability of seeing the word "Xanax," which we will cover shortly. The posterior term on the left is our updated probability for the hypothesis (our hypothesis is the message is spam) given that evidence is present (the evidence is the word "Xanax" is in the email).

It may help to see a diagram of the situation:

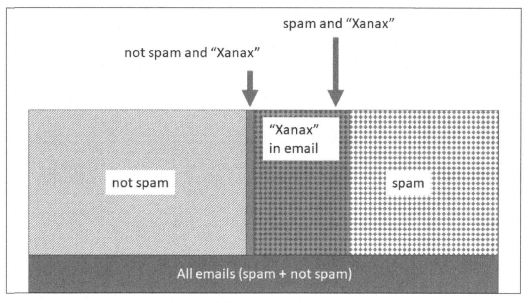

Figure 8.3: A diagram of all our emails including spam and not spam,
and emails with the word "Xanax" in them

We have values for everything but P("Xanax"), or the *marginal* probability of the evidence. This term is the probability of seeing the word "Xanax" in any email message, regardless of whether it's spam or not. To calculate this value, it's easiest to rewrite the equation using another statistical theorem, the law of total probability:

P("Xanax") = P(spam) * P("Xanax" | spam) + P(not spam) * P("Xanax" | not spam)

This is the same as:

$$P(E) = P(H) * P(E \mid H) + P(!H) * P(E \mid !H)$$

where the exclamation point (!) represents a negation; *!H* means the opposite of the hypothesis, *H*. Filling in values for the components, we have:

P("Xanax") = P(spam) * P("Xanax" | spam) + P(not spam) * P("Xanax" | not spam)

$$P(Xanax) = 0.45 * 0.33 + 0.55 * 0.001$$

Since we already know 45% of messages are spam, this means 55% of messages are not spam (since the probabilities of all outcomes in a discrete probability space must sum to 1). We also already specified that 33% of spam messages contain the word "Xanax." The last term, P("Xanax" | not spam), or the probability of seeing the word "Xanax" in a non-spam email, is set to 0.1% or 0.001. In other words, we are saying 1 out of 1,000 emails that are not spam contain the word "Xanax." Of course, if you are a doctor and regularly send emails with the word "Xanax" in them, you might change this to a much higher value.

 Notice the first half of the equation for P(E) is the numerator (top part) for Bayes' law. So, the numerator of Bayes' law must always be smaller than the denominator, and our probabilities from Bayes' law will always be less than or equal to 1, as they should. If you find yourself calculating probabilities with Bayes' law and getting probabilities above 1, you likely made a mistake in the P(E) term.

Our Bayes' law for our spam filtering example is now:

$$P(\text{spam} \mid \text{"Xanax"}) = 0.45 * 0.33 / (0.45 * 0.33 + 0.55 * 0.001)$$
$$= 99.6\%$$

So, we've arrived at the conclusion a message with the word "Xanax" in it is likely spam with 99.6% certainty. We'll send those to the spam folder.

Bayes' law and Bayesian statistics find application in data science in a few ways – machine learning models like Naïve Bayes, and advanced hyperparameter tuning techniques, to name a couple.

Frequentist versus Bayesian

The statistics we have described so far have been what is called "frequentist." This involves measuring past performance over many repetitions and using that to formulate probabilities and statistics. Somewhat confusingly, we can use frequentist methods to calculate probabilities with Bayes' law, by plugging in numbers to Bayes' law based on empirical measurements of past events.

However, we can also use Bayesian methods with Bayes' law. This is done by plugging in some probabilities based on our intuition or beliefs instead of measured probabilities.

For example, we might not measure the exact number of messages that are not spam and also contain the word "Xanax," but simply estimate it based on our intuition. In fact, that's some of what I did here – I estimated that 1 out of 1,000 legitimate emails may contain the word "Xanax."

The probabilities we calculate from the probability equations above can be useful for thinking about problems, implementing algorithms (like our spam classifier), or for describing a situation to others (like when giving a report to stakeholders). However, we can also model probabilities for situations, or even model data, with probability distributions. This allows us to extract descriptive statistical information from our data.

Distributions

Probability distributions are a way of describing all possible outcomes a random variable can take within a sample space. There are lots of probability distributions, With the solar cell manufacturing example, we might expect to see something similar to a normal distribution.

The normal distribution and using scipy to generate distributions

The normal distribution is also called the Gaussian distribution or the bell curve and shows up often. This is something we could see when taking measurements from a biological population (like dimensions of plants) or measurements of a manufacturing process, like the efficiency of solar cells coming off a manufacturing line. We can generate most common distributions in Python with `scipy`. We want to first make sure we have scipy installed: `conda install -c conda-forge scipy -y`. Then we can create and plot a normal distribution:

```
import numpy as np
from scipy.stats import norm

x = np.linspace(-4, 4, 100)
plt.plot(x, norm.pdf(x))
plt.plot(x, norm.cdf(x)
```

First, we import the `norm` class from `scipy.stats`. Then, we create a numpy array with 100 values ranging from -4 to 4, equally spaced with `np.linspace()`. Next, we plot these x-values versus the **probability density function** (PDF) of a normal distribution with `norm.pdf(x)`, and our **cumulative density function** (CDF).

Our plot looks like this:

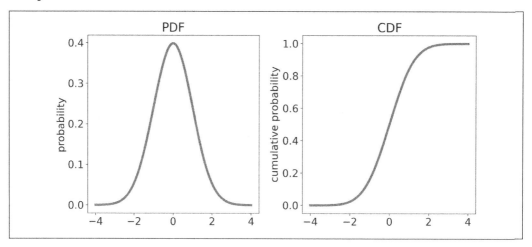

Figure 8.4: A plot of a normal distribution probability distribution function (PDF) and cumulative distribution function (CDF)

The probability density function gives us the relative likelihood of an event at that value *x*. For example, in the plot on the left above, the probability of observing a 0 for the value of *x* is the maximum value on the PDF, so we have the highest chance of observing a value around 0 with this distribution. The CDF is simply the cumulative sum of the PDF. This tells us the probability that our value will be less than or equal to any point on the plot. We can see there is a 50% chance that our value of *x* will be less than or equal to 0 from the CDF.

 Note that the CDF ends at a value approaching 1 and is the cumulative area under the PDF (which sums to 1). Since the sample space for a continuous variable is infinite, the exact probability of any one value occurring is 0 (1 divided by infinity). These PDFs are calculated from mathematical formulas. As the PDF moves toward negative and positive infinity, the relative probabilities approach 0, but never exactly reach 0.

The scipy distribution classes, like norm, have a set of common functions such as pdf() and cdf(). Another common function is rvs(), which is "random variable sampling." We can use this to generate samples of data from a distribution.

For example, we can generate 10,000 datapoints for our normal distribution and plot the data in a histogram like so:

```
data = norm.rvs(size=10000, random_state=42)
plt.hist(data, bins=30)
```

We use the `rvs()` method of the `norm` class, and provide a `size` argument for the number of points, as well as a `random_state` argument. This `random_state` argument sets the "seed" for our randomly generated points, which means our generated points will be the same every time we run this function. Otherwise, we would get slightly different results every time we run it. Our histogram looks like this:

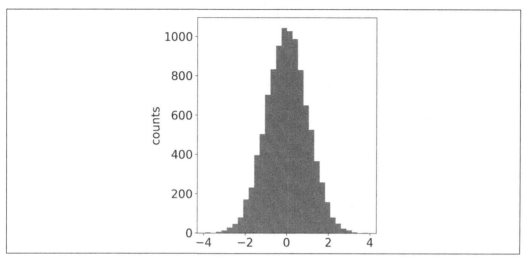

Figure 8.5: A histogram of our data sampled from a normal distribution

We can see this histogram looks almost the same as our PDF, which it is. When we plot distributions of data, it's often as a histogram and represents the empirical PDF (the measured probabilities for each value of *x*) for that data. This is a good start to generating data from distributions, and the next step is to customize our distributions with parameters.

Descriptive statistics of distributions

Distributions are mathematical equations characterized by parameters. For example, the normal distribution's PDF is represented with an equation:

$$f(x|\sigma\mu) = \frac{1}{\sigma\sqrt{2\pi}} e^{-\frac{1}{2}(\frac{x-\mu}{\sigma})^2}$$

This is in fact how `scipy` is calculating the PDF in our Python code above. Here, the function uses the same math notation as we did with conditional probabilities – the PDF function is for a value of *x* given values for the Greek characters sigma (σ) and mu (μ). These values are the standard deviation and mean, respectively.

The standard deviation is how spread out the data is (there is an equation for calculating it from data, not shown here), while the mean is the average of the data (also with a formal equation, not shown here). We also see the constant pi (π, 3.14) in there as well as Euler's number (e, roughly 2.72). Euler's number exponentiated to the value $-\frac{1}{2}(\frac{x - \mu}{\sigma})^2$ is what gives the normal distribution its bell-curve shape. The other part of the equation, $\frac{1}{\sigma\sqrt{2\pi}}$, is just a scaling factor.

 Wikipedia is one place where you can find the PDF and CDF equations for most probability distributions. You'll see that many of the PDF equations use the gamma function, which is a symbol that looks like an upside-down L.

Once we know the parameters in the PDF of a distribution, we can use them to create distributions with different characteristics. For example, if we know from measurements that the average efficiency from a solar cell manufacturing line is 14% and the standard deviation is 0.5%, we can create and plot a normal distribution with those parameters:

```
x = np.linspace(12, 16, 100)
plt.plot(x, norm.pdf(x, loc=14, scale=0.5))
```

We are first creating an array of 100 equally spaced x-values from 12 to 16 with `np.linspace()`, which centers around our mean of 14. We then set the mean and standard deviation parameters (`loc` and `scale`) to the specified values of 14 and 0.5. Our probability distribution function looks like this:

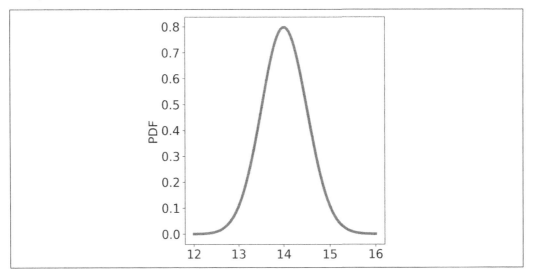

Figure 8.6: A normal distribution PDF with a mean of 14 and a standard deviation of 0.5

The arguments `loc` and `scale` are described in the `scipy` documentation for the `scipy.stats.norm` class. For the other distributions we will cover in this chapter, `scipy` has similar documentation explaining what the argument names are for each distribution's parameters. The `loc` and `scale` arguments show up as parameters in many distributions in `scipy`.

Let's take a sample of 10,000 points from this normal distribution we just created with the `rvs()` function:

```
solar_data = norm.rvs(size=10000, loc=14, scale=0.5, random_state=42)
```

If you like, try plotting it to make sure it looks okay with `plt.hist(solar_data, bins=30)`. Once we have this data (which is a `numpy` array), we can generate some descriptive statistics of the data:

```
solar_data.mean()
solar_data.std()
```

These will calculate the mean and standard deviation of our data, which should be very close to 14 and 0.5. These are a few of the key methods we can describe our data with, especially if it resembles a normal distribution. Another couple of ways we can describe a distribution that may be similar to a normal distribution are *skewness* and *kurtosis*.

The mean, standard deviation, skewness, and kurtosis are called moments, which are quantifications of the data distribution's shape. The mean is called the first raw moment, while the standard deviation is actually the square of the second central moment, variance. Skewness is the third normalized moment, and kurtosis is the fourth normalized moment. The terminology raw, central, and normalized signify slight differences in calculations. "Raw" is as it sounds, simply an equation without normalization or adjustment. "Central" means a moment around the data's mean, and "normalized" means the moment is normalized (divided) by the standard deviation. This results in us being able to compare skewness and kurtosis across distributions of data, even if they have wildly different standard deviations (spread of the data).

An easy way to calculate skew and kurtosis is to put our data in a `pandas` DataFrame:

```
import pandas as pd
df = pd.DataFrame(data={'efficiency': solar_data})
df['efficiency'].skew()
df.kurtosis()
```

As we can see above, the skew and kurtosis are simply functions we can call with a pandas DataFrame or Series. The skew measures the magnitude and direction of the asymmetry of a distribution. In other words, it's which way the tails on a distribution are biased towards (left or right). For a distribution with positive skew, most of the data will be on the left of the center if we plot it, with a tail extending to the right, and vice-versa for a negative skew. The kurtosis measures how much of the data is in the tails of the distribution; a higher kurtosis means more data is in the tails. In other words, we have likely more outliers with more data in the tails. The following chart shows the difference between a normal distribution, a skewed distribution, and a distribution with high kurtosis:

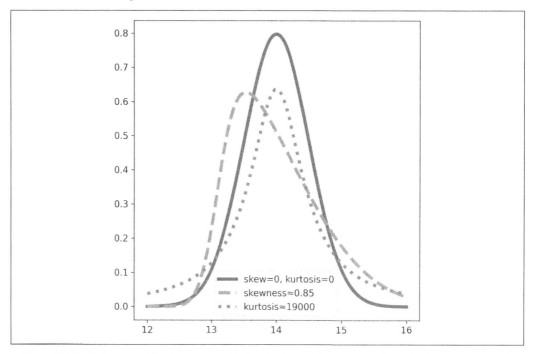

Figure 8.7: PDFs for normal (or close to normal) distributions with mean 14 and standard deviation 0.5 and different skew and kurtosis values. Values for skew and kurtosis are 0 unless otherwise specified.

We can see the high skewness distribution has its center of mass moved to the left and a tail extending to the right, corresponding to a positive skew value. This value scales between -1 and +1, so a value of 0.85 is quite high. The high kurtosis PDF shows fatter tails than the default normal distribution. This measure has no upper bound, but 19,000 is a high value for kurtosis.

These measures of distributions can be used to compare the distributions of data in a quantitative way. The measures can be calculated for any distribution but are most useful when applied to something that may be similar to a normal distribution or one of its variants.

Variants of the normal distribution

Two of the variants of the normal distribution are the skewed normal and lognormal distribution. The skewed normal distributions simply introduces a skew parameter to alter the skewness of the distribution, and we used it in the plot above with the function call `scipy.stats.skewnorm.pdf(x, scale=1.15, loc=13.1, a=5)` after importing scipy with `import scipy`. The lognormal distribution is a distribution where the logarithm of our data is normally distributed ($\log_b(x) = y$, where the logarithm is the inverse of exponentiation, $b^y = x$), and looks like this:

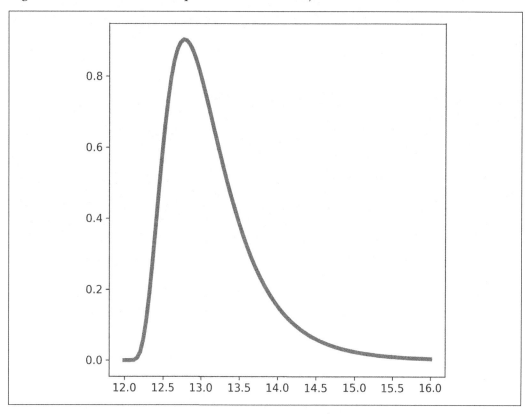

Figure 8.8: A lognormal distribution PDF

The lognormal distribution shows up in many places. For example, it shows up in the length of comments in online forums and the amount of time people spend on web pages for articles. We can access distributions for skewed normal and lognormal distributions through the `scipy.stats` classes `skewnorm` and `lognorm`. Here is the function call for the PDF of the lognormal distribution above:
`plt.plot(x, scipy.stats.lognorm.pdf(x, loc=12, s=0.5))` (where x is from earlier, `x = np.linspace(12, 16, 100)`). The s parameter is the "shape" parameter and moves the peak of the PDF left and flattens the PDF as s increases.

Fitting distributions to data to get parameters

If we have data from measurements, say the efficiency of solar cells from a manufacturing line, we can fit a distribution to that data to extract the distribution's PDF parameters and moments like mean, variance (and standard deviation), skewness, and kurtosis. This is more useful for other distributions that have different parameters that are not simply the mean and standard deviation. As an example, let's load some simulated solar cell efficiency data (available in the GitHub materials for this book under `Chapter8/data/`):

```
df = pd.read_csv('data/solar_cell_efficiencies.csv')
df.describe()
```

The result of `describe()` looks like this:

```
efficiency
count  187196.000000
mean   14.181805
std    0.488751
min    9.691218
25%    13.932445
50%    14.205567
75%    14.482341
max    17.578530
```

We can see the mean near 14 and standard deviation near 0.5. We can also examine the skew and kurtosis with `df['efficiency'].skew()` and `df['efficiency'].kurt()`, which return -0.385 and 1.117. The negative skew tells us our distribution leans to the right, with a tail to the left. The kurtosis tells us we have a few more datapoints in the tails than a usual Gaussian distribution, but barely.

To fit the distribution and extract the PDF parameters, we simply run:

```
scipy.stats.norm.fit(df['efficiency'])
```

This gives us 14.18 for the mean and 0.488 for the standard deviation, the same as we saw in the `describe()` results. Since we can get these parameters from `describe()` or `mean()` and `std()`, it's not that useful. For other distributions in `scipy` with more complex parameters, this is more useful.

The Student's t-distribution

The t-distribution shows up in statistical tests, as we will see in the next chapter. This distribution can be used from the class `scipy.stats.t`. For example, the PDF with high kurtosis in *Figure 8.7* above was generated with `t.pdf(x, loc=14, scale=0.5, df=1)`. The t-distribution has the `loc`, `scale`, and `df` (degrees of freedom) arguments. The `loc` and `scale` arguments act similar to how they do with the normal distribution, and the `df` argument causes fatter tails in the distribution as it gets smaller.

The Bernoulli distribution

The Bernoulli distribution is a discrete distribution, meaning it can only take on a few values. The other distributions we discussed (normal and its variations, and *t*) are continuous distributions. Discrete distributions have a probability mass function (PMF) instead of a probability distribution function (PDF).

The Bernoulli distribution represents binary outcomes: 0 or 1, for example, from a coin flip. Another example of a binary outcome would be a customer conversion – for example, if a customer buys something or not. We can use this distribution through `scipy` to generate a sample of an event using the `rvs()` function:

```
scipy.stats.bernoulli(p=0.7).rvs()
```

First, we are creating a `bernoulli` class from `scipy.stats` with a probability of `0.7` for success (the probability of getting a 1 and not 0). This also demonstrates another way to create distributions with `scipy`: we can provide the parameters to the class name instead of the function. Then we can use functions like `rvs()`, `pmf()`, or `pdf()` from there.

The binomial distribution

The Bernoulli distribution is for a single binary event, and the Binomial distribution is for a collection of Bernoulli events. The binomial distribution represents a number of successes (1s) out of a number of Bernoulli events (binary with a 1 or 0 outcome) with the probability of success *p*. For example, if 10 customers visit our website and we have a 70% chance of them buying a product, our binomial distribution would be:

```
binom_dist = scipy.stats.binom(p=0.7, n=10)
plt.bar(range(11), binom_dist.pmf(k=range(11)))
```

This creates our distribution object in the first line, then plots the PMF (from 0 to 10) as a bar chart on the second line. Since it's a discrete distribution, we should only point to each discrete value of x. Notice for the pmf() function, we provide a range of integers for the argument k. These should span from 0 to our value of n in the binom() class (our number of trials) to get the full PMF. The plot looks like this:

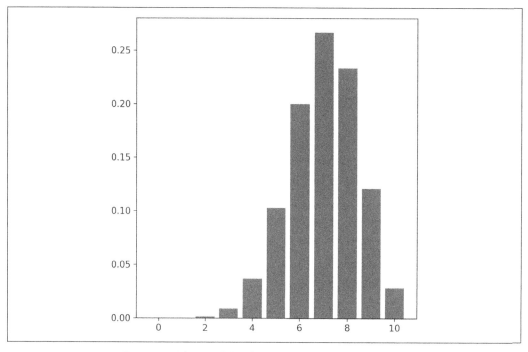

Figure 8.9: A binomial distribution PMF with n=10 and p=0.7

We can see the probabilities of getting 0, 1, 2, or 3 successes are very low, and the probability of getting 7/10 successes is the highest. This is because our probability of success for each trial is 0.7. We can use this distribution to model situations like the customer conversion situation, or anything else where we want to understand how many successes we are likely to get in a trial of binary events.

The uniform distribution

The uniform distribution shows up when we have several events, all with an equal likelihood of occurring. The canonical example is rolling a 6-sided dice. Each value of 1 through 6 has an equal likelihood of occurring. This distribution can also be used for getting random values between a range. It's available in scipy through the scipy.stats.uniform() class. It can also be useful for describing existing datasets, as we saw in *Chapter 5, Exploratory Data Analysis and Visualization*, with pandas-profiling reports.

The exponential and Poisson distributions

The exponential distribution describes the space or time between events that are independent. Some examples are support center calls and radioactive materials emitting particles. These events are assumed to be independent (for example, we assume each support call doesn't affect the next one) and events have some characteristic time by which they tend to be separated. In the exponential distribution, this parameter is called lambda (λ) and appears in the PDF equation as $y = \lambda e^{-\lambda x}$. The e here is again Euler's number and is sometimes written $\exp(-\lambda x)$. We can specify this value of lambda with the `scale` argument in `scipy`:

```
from labellines import labelLines

x = np.linspace(0, 5, 100)
plt.plot(x, scipy.stats.expon.pdf(x, scale=1), label='λ=1')
plt.plot(x, scipy.stats.expon.pdf(x, scale=0.25), label='λ=4')
labelLines(plt.gca().get_lines())
```

Here, we are plotting the exponential distribution from 0 to 5 with a few different values for lambda/scale, as well as drawing a legend. We are also using the package `matplotlib-label-lines` to label the lines directly as we did in *Chapter 5, Exploratory Data Analysis and Visualization*. Alternatively, we could call `plt.legend()` instead of the `labelLines()` function. The results look like this:

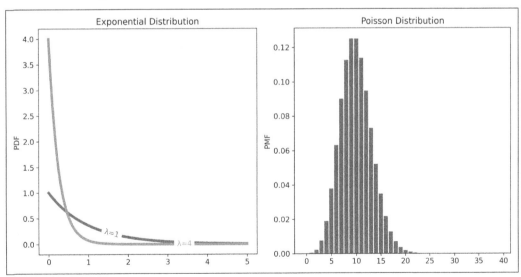

Figure 8.10: Two exponential distribution PDFs with different lambda values, and a Poisson distribution PMF

The `scale` argument in `scipy` is actually 1/lambda. As lambda increases, our average time between events decreases.

Related to the exponential distribution is the Poisson distribution. This is a discrete distribution, so has a PMF instead of PDF. We can plot a Poisson distribution PMF like so:

```
bar(range(40), scipy.stats.poisson.pmf(range(40), mu=10))
```

The results of this plot are shown in *Figure 8.10* above. The Poisson distribution has a lambda parameter like the exponential (the mu argument in the scipy.stats.poisson() functions) and is a generalization of the exponential distribution. The Poisson distribution provides the probability that a number of events will happen within a characteristic time, lambda. This characteristic time is the average time between exponential distribution events occurring. So, if we get a call at a call center on average every 10 minutes, we can set our lambda value to 10 to describe this distribution.

 Although scipy cannot fit data and extract distribution parameters for discrete probability distributions like the Poisson distribution, another package, statsmodels, has a module statsmodels.discrete.discrete_model that can do so.

The Poisson and exponential distributions show up in situations such as call centers, packets arriving at routers, or numbers of mutations on a strand of DNA per unit length, where we have events occurring in space or time with a characteristic frequency.

The Weibull distribution

The Weibull distribution is like an extension of the exponential distribution, where the characteristic time or space between events changes over time. This can be useful for time-to-failure analysis, like with hard drives. It also can be used with wind forecasting for wind speed distributions, which can be used for forecasting with the MISO energy data we examined in the previous chapter. There are two implementations of Weibull in scipy: the max and min versions. The max version is for *x*-values that are negative, and the min version is for positive values. We can plot the PDF like so:

```
x = np.linspace(0, 10, 100)
plt.plot(x, scipy.stats.weibull_min(c=3).pdf(x))
```

The main parameter is c, the shape parameter. There are also scale and loc arguments available. The scale argument changes the spread of the data while the loc argument changes where the distribution begins on the x-axis. The shape parameter, c, determines if the time-to-failure is decreasing over time (c<1), staying constant (c=1, the exponential distribution), or increasing over time (c>1).

The Zipfian distribution

The last distribution we'll touch on is the Zipfian distribution, which comes from Zipf's law. This can be used in text data to model the ranked frequency of words, and we'll learn more about it in *Chapter 18, Working with Text*. The distribution shows up in surprising places, like the ranking of cities by population from greatest to least and the distribution of company sizes. The distribution is available in scipy, and we can plot the PMF (it's a discrete distribution) like so:

```
x = range(1, 50)
plt.plot(x, scipy.stats.zipf(a=1.1).pmf(x), marker='.')
plt.xscale('log')
plt.yscale('log')
```

Since the distribution starts with rank 1 of a series of data, we start our range at 1. Then we provide the shape parameter a to the zipf() class and plot the PMF function. We use a log scale on both the x- and y-axis, since this distribution is best viewed that way. When using a log-log plot like this, the distribution makes a straight line.

This concludes our section on distributions, but there are many more. The scipy package has classes for many of the other distributions as well. However, we visited some of the more useful and common distributions we might encounter here. We already saw how we can sample from these distributions, but let's now look at sampling from raw data.

Sampling from data

Sampling methods and caveats are good to know as a data scientist. For example, we can use sampling to downsize a large dataset for analysis or prototyping code, we can use sampling to estimate confidence intervals, and we can use it to balance imbalanced datasets for machine learning. Let's begin with a few fundamental tenets of sampling.

The law of large numbers

The law of large numbers is a mathematical theorem, and essentially says we will approach the true mean of a random variable's outcome as we increase our number of samples. A few examples are useful here: as we roll a 6-sided dice many times, the average value of the rolls will approach 3.5, which is what we would fundamentally expect given the uniform distribution and average of the values 1-6.

In general, this means we should expect the average value of a measurement to approach an exact value with an increase in sampling, assuming the underlying process is random and follows some distribution. For example, we might expect the value of our solar cell efficiencies from a manufacturing line to tend towards a single average value if the only processes causing variations are random ones. We can observe the average value of measured metrics, taking care to think about if the underlying process is random enough for the law of large numbers to apply. If the average value is still moving as we increase our sample size and we think the underlying process has only random variables, we should collect more data.

The central limit theorem

The central limit theorem is another mathematical theorem fundamental to probability theory. It states that the mean (average) of many samples from a population will tend towards a normal distribution, even if the underlying distribution of data is not normal. An easy example of this is flipping a coin many times. Say we flip the coin 100 times and count the number of heads. Then we do this 100 times. Our plot of the count of heads would be near a normal distribution. We can conduct this experiment in Python with the binomial distribution:

```
binom = scipy.stats.binom(p=0.5, n=100)
heads = binom.rvs(10000)
```

Here, we are creating our binomial distribution with a probability of success of 50%, and 100 Bernoulli trials (coin flips). Then, we take 10,000 samples from this distribution. This simulates flipping a coin 100 times, counting the number of heads, then doing that 10,000 times. We could also create a loop and use the Bernoulli distribution, but that's much less efficient.

Then we can plot a histogram with a KDE (essentially a fit to the histogram) with seaborn. Seaborn automatically chooses the number of bins, so is a little better than `plt.hist()`:

```
import seaborn as sns
sns.histplot(heads, kde=True)
```

This ends up looking just like a normal distribution, demonstrating how the central limit theorem works. Another application is taking a sample of a population, calculating the mean, and doing this many times. The resulting histogram of mean values will approach a normal distribution, even if the underlying distribution isn't Gaussian. We can then use the average of the sample means, which should be the population mean.

Random sampling

The easiest sampling method is randomly sampling from a dataset. Let's use our solar cell efficiency data from before:

```
df = pd.read_csv('data/solar_cell_efficiencies.csv')
```

Taking a random sample is like choosing a random value from a uniform distribution. With pandas, this is as easy as using the `sample()` function:

```
df.sample(100, random_state=42)
```

This will give us a random sample of 100 datapoints. The `random_state` argument shows up in many Python functions and should be set to a value when it's available. Random sampling in programming usually uses something like an element from the computer's clock as a seed for a pseudo-random number generator. The `random_state` argument will set this seed so we get the same sample each time. There are other ways to set random seeds as well, such as `np.random.seed()`, and similar functions for other packages with random processes. We can use random sampling when we are developing code to scale down our data size so code runs faster. However, it's a good idea to use a Boolean variable or function argument to specify you are sampling the data, so you can change this easily when you no longer want to sample your data.

Bootstrap sampling and confidence intervals

Bootstrap sampling is random sampling, but with replacement. The interesting name comes from the phrase "pull oneself up by one's bootstraps," meaning to achieve success without outside help. Bootstrap sampling works like so: every time we take a sample, it's independent and from the entire dataset. With our candy-drawing example in *Figure 8.2*, we could draw a red candy on our first draw. We would record that we drew a red candy, then replace the red candy back in the bag, and draw again. This is also called sampling with replacement.

Bootstrapping simply does this many times on a dataset and can be used to calculate average statistics. Other applications include A/B testing and calculating confidence intervals. One package in Python that makes this easy is `bootstrapped` (although we could code it from scratch), which can be installed with `pip install bootstrapped`. Let's look at using this to calculate confidence intervals of our average efficiency from our solar cell dataset:

```
import bootstrapped.bootstrap as bs
import bootstrapped.stats_functions as bs_stats

bs.bootstrap(df['efficiency'].values, stat_func=bs_stats.mean)
```

The first two lines import a few modules from the package. Then we simply call the `bootstrap()` function with a NumPy array of values and a `stat_func` argument, which is our statistical function to calculate from bootstrapping. Here, we calculate the mean, which gives us our mean and confidence intervals:

```
14.181805365742568     (14.17962009850363, 14.184020814876083)
```

The confidence intervals, presented in parenthesis, tell us the range we can expect our mean to be in. Usually these are 95% or 90%; by default they are 95% for this package. This result tells us we have 95% certainty that the mean is between 14.179 and 14.184 – a pretty tight spread around the mean. Another way to think of this is 95% of the time we measure the mean from a sample, we will lie within this range. Or, some people describe it as 95% of the time we measure these confidence intervals, the true mean will be in the interval. We can change this with the argument `alpha`, which is 0.05 by default for a 95% confidence interval. We could also change the `stat_func` argument to other things, such as `bs_stats.std` for the standard deviation.

To code a bootstrap algorithm by hand, we can simply use numpy's sampling with `np.random.choice(data, sample_size, replace=True)`. This samples a number of points (`sample_size`) from our data array, `data`, and does this with replacement. For example, we could loop through our data 10,000 times and calculate the mean with a bootstrapped sample each time:

```
means = []
for i in range(10000):
    sample = np.random.choice(df['efficiency'], 1000, replace=True)
    means.append(sample.mean())

sns.histplot(means)
```

We then plot the data with `seaborn`, and can see that it resembles a normal distribution:

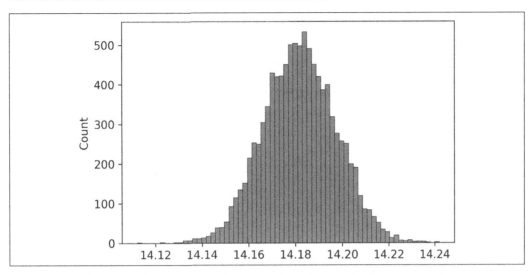

Figure 8.11: The mean of the solar cell efficiency data from bootstrapped samples

These two sampling techniques (random sampling and bootstrapping) are the basics. We will revisit sampling in *Chapter 11, Machine Learning for Classification*, and learn about sampling techniques for balancing datasets.

Test your knowledge

To reinforce what we've learned here, practice it with the following tasks:

- Use Bayes' law to calculate the probability of getting a data science job if you've got an interview for the job. This could be written P(get the DS job | interview). You'll have to use Bayesian probability methods (your intuition or beliefs) to assign values to the different components of Bayes' law.

- Determine the type of distribution and extract the distribution's PDF parameters from the MISO wind power generation data (the MWh column), stored under Chapter8/test_your_knowledge/data/miso_wind_data.csv. Write a short analysis explaining why you chose that distribution and what the parameters mean.

- Apply bootstrap sampling to the MISO wind power generation data and plot the distribution of the mean wind power generation values.

Summary

This chapter introduced us to the basics of probability and some ways it can be used with data science. We started with the absolute basics, like random variables, discrete versus continuous variables, and probability spaces. We saw how Bayes' law can be used to estimate conditional probabilities. We also saw how frequentist statistical methods rely on data, while Bayesian methods rely on intuition or beliefs. Perhaps confusingly, Bayes' law can be used with frequentist and Bayesian statistical methods.

We also examined several common probability distributions that can be used in data science, including the well-known normal or Gaussian distribution. Lastly, we looked at a few tenets of probability theory (the law of large numbers and the central limit theorem) as well as a few sampling techniques (random and bootstrap sampling).

In our next chapter, we'll take some of this knowledge and extend it to statistical testing. We'll see how this can be used for things like A/B testing and other experiments.

9
Statistical Testing for Data Science

In the previous chapter, we laid the groundwork for understanding probability and statistics. Now, we will leverage that understanding to perform statistical tests that we can use to test hypotheses. We will cover the following statistical tests in this chapter:

- The t-test, z-test, and bootstrapping for comparing the means of data (for example, A/B testing)
- The ANOVA test for comparing the means of groups
- Testing if data comes from a distribution (for example, a Gaussian distribution)
- Testing for outliers with the scikit-posthocs package
- Tests for relationships between variables (Pearson and chi-squared tests)

This is only a small number of the total amount of statistical tests out there, but there are some that we can use for practical tasks. Some of these tests are also used in other data science methods, such as linear and logistic regression, which we will cover in *Chapter 11, Machine Learning for Classification*, and *Chapter 12, Evaluating Machine Learning Classification Models and Sampling for Classification*. Let's begin with the basics of statistical testing.

Statistical testing basics and sample comparison tests

Almost all statistical tests center on *hypothesis testing*. A hypothesis in this case is an expected outcome of a situation. For example, we might be measuring efficiencies of solar cells coming off a manufacturing line as we did in the previous chapter. We can choose our hypothesis; for example, we can hypothesize that the average efficiency of the solar cells is 14%. Then, we can use a statistical test to check if the data supports or rejects our hypothesis.

In the parlance of statistics, the base case, or no-effect case, is called the *null hypothesis*. In the example of the solar cell efficiencies, this null hypothesis is that the average efficiency is no different from 14%. The other case is called the alternative hypothesis; in our example, this is the case when the average efficiency is significantly different from 14%. "Significant" is quantified with calculations from mathematical/statistical equations. We can use a classic statistical test that's over 100 years old for this purpose – the t-test.

The t-test and z-test

The t-test has an interesting history, dating back to 1908 when William Gosset invented the method while working at the Guinness brewery in Ireland. Gosset wanted a method for taking a sample of beer and testing that it was within quality control specifications. In our example, we will use the test to first check if our average solar cell efficiency is where we expect it.

The t-test has a few variants:

- One- and two-sided
- One- and two-sample
- Paired

One-sided tests are for determining if a value is greater than or less than a specified value by a statistically significant amount. Two-sided tests determine if a value is either greater or less than a specified value. One-sample t-tests are for a single sample – for example, comparing a batch of solar cells to an expected efficiency. Two-sample t-tests are for comparing two samples – for example, checking if two batches of solar cells have the same average efficiency. Paired t-tests are for comparing the same group before and after a treatment, such as comparing the blood pressure of a group of people before and after taking a medication. Let's start with one of the simpler variants, which is the one-sample, two-sided t-test.

One-sample, two-sided t-test

In our example of testing if the average efficiency is 14%, we are comparing the mean of our sample to an expected value. This is the one-sample t-test. The sample is a portion of the full data, or population. For example, if Gosset took three Guinness beers off the manufacturing line for one day and measured them, the population would be all the beers produced off the line that day and the sample is the three beers.

Our null hypothesis in the one-sample test is that the sample mean is no different from the expected mean of 14%. Our alternative hypothesis is that the mean *is* different from 14%. The two-sided part means that our sample mean could be above or below the expected value of 14% – we are not including a direction (greater than or less than) in our hypothesis. To carry out this test in Python, we can use `scipy` after loading our data:

```python
import pandas as pd
from scipy.stats import ttest_1samp

solar_data = pd.read_csv('data/solar_cell_efficiencies.csv')

ttest_1samp(solar_data['efficiency'], 14, alternative='two-sided')
```

First, we import the one-sample t-test from `scipy.stats`, then use the function by giving it our data as a first argument and the expected mean (14) as a second argument. The actual mean of the data is around 14.18. The `alternative` argument is `'two-sided'` by default, but we are specifying it here to be explicit. This function returns the values:

```
Ttest_1sampResult(statistic=160.9411176293201, pvalue=0.0)
```

The p-value is what we most often use, although the t-statistic can be used with a t-table to look up the p-value. The p-value is the probability of observing a statistic at least as extreme as the observed statistic, assuming the null hypothesis is true. This means our probability of observing a mean of 14.18 is very low (close to 0) assuming the null hypothesis is true. Remember the null hypothesis here is that our mean is no different than the expected value of 14. We compare the p-value to an alpha value (α, our significance level) that we choose. This value for α is commonly 0.1, 0.05, or 0.01. It represents the chance of a false positive, also called a type I error, occurring. A false positive in this case would be finding the average efficiency is statistically significantly different than 14% when in reality, it is not.

If our p-value is below our chosen α value, then we reject the null hypothesis. In the one-sample t-test, this states our sample mean is different from the expected mean of 14. Let's choose α = 0.05, which is the most common choice. We can see our p-value from the function is 0.0, which is less than α, so we can reject the null hypothesis and say our sample mean (which is 14.18) is significantly different from 14. In reality, the p-value is very small, but the precision restrictions of our computer are unable to handle such a small value.

The other type of error would be a false negative, or type II error. This would be if we fail to reject the null hypothesis (in other words, we say the sample mean is the same as the expected mean), but there really is a significant difference between the population mean and the expected mean we failed to detect.

The value of 0.0 seems strange for the p-value; however, the p-value is so small that it cannot be printed out by Python. In fact, the t-test was not originally meant for such large data (there are almost 200,000 data points here). The t-test is intended for sample sizes of 50 or fewer; some people even say 30 samples or fewer. If we sample down our data to a size of 30, we can see a different result (with a sample mean of 14.10):

```
sample = solar_data['efficiency'].sample(30, random_state=1)
print(sample.mean())
ttest_1samp(sample, 14)
```

Our t-test result looks like this:

```
Ttest_1sampResult(statistic=1.2215589926015267, pvalue=0.2317121281215101)
```

We can see our p-value is greater than the significance threshold (α) of 0.05, so we fail to reject the null hypothesis. In other words, the sample mean is the same as the expected mean of 14.

The z-test

The proper test to use for larger sample sizes is the z-test. This ends up being about the same as a t-test, however. We can use this from the `statsmodels` package (which should be installed with `conda install -c conda-forge statsmodels`):

```
from statsmodels.stats.weightstats import ztest

ztest(solar_data['efficiency'], value=14)
```

Just like `scipy`, it gives us a statistic value (the z-statistic) and a p-value:

```
(160.9411176293201, 0.0)
```

We can see this matches our result from the t-test exactly.

One-sided tests

Let's say we want to make sure the average efficiency of our latest batch of solar cells is greater than 14%. The sample we used that was measured from a recent production run is in our solar data we've already loaded. We can formulate our null hypothesis as this: the sample mean is less than or equal to the expected mean of 14%. The alternative hypothesis is then: the sample mean is greater than the expected mean of 14%. We can perform this test with `scipy` like so:

```
Ttest_1samp(solar_data['efficiency'], 14, alternative='greater')
```

The `alternative` argument is set to `'greater'`, meaning the alternative hypothesis is that the sample mean is greater than the expected mean. Our results show the null hypothesis is rejected, and it looks like our sample mean is greater than 14% with statistical significance:

```
Ttest_1sampResult(statistic=160.9411176293201, pvalue=0.0)
```

On the other hand, if we set `alternative='less'`, we get a p-value of 1.0, showing we fail to reject the null hypothesis. In that case, the null hypothesis is that the efficiency level is equal to or greater than 14%.

Two-sample t- and z-tests: A/B testing

Let's say we have a website selling t-shirts and want to experiment with the design to try and drive more sales. We're going to change the layout in a B version of the site and compare our sales rates to the A version. We have data in the file `Chapter9/data/ab_sales_data.csv` in the GitHub repository for this book. We can load the data and take a look:

```
ab_df = pd.read_csv('data/ab_sales_data.csv')
```

We have a column for the A design, and each row is a website visitor. A value of 1 represents a sale, while 0 represents no sale. The B design column is the same, and the samples are not paired up (each sample from A and B is individual and independent). We can look at the mean sales rates easily:

```
ab_df.mean()
```

This shows us B has a slightly higher sales rate:

```
a_sale    0.0474
b_sale    0.0544
dtype: float64
```

To test if B is really better than A, we can first try a two-sample, two-sided t-test. The null hypothesis is that the means of the two groups are the same; the alternative is that they are not the same (for a two-sided test). We'll use the `statsmodels` `ztest` for this, and will assume the usual α value of 0.05:

```
ztest(ab_df['a_sale'], ab_df['b_sale'])
```

This returns:

```
(-2.252171812056176, 0.02431141659730297)
```

Remember that the first value is the z-statistic, and the second value in the tuple is the p-value. In this case, it looks like there is a significant difference in the means, since the p-value of 0.024 is less than our significance threshold of 0.05. We already know from examination that the B sales rate was a little higher, so it appears the B design is better.

To be a little more precise, we can also specify the direction of the test. With `statsmodels`, the options for the `alternative` argument are `two-sided`, `larger`, and `smaller`. Specifying `larger` means the alternative hypothesis is that A's mean is larger than B's. The null hypothesis in that case is that A's mean is less than or equal to B's mean. We'll use `smaller` to carry out our one-sided z-test to see if B's average sales value is greater than A's:

```
ztest(ab_df['a_sale'], ab_df['b_sale'], alternative='smaller')
```

This has a null hypothesis that the A mean is larger than or equal to B's mean. This returns a p-value of 0.012, less than our α of 0.05. So, we reject the null hypothesis and state that A's mean is smaller than B's mean with statistical significance. Something to notice here is the one-sided test's p-values will always be half that of the two-sided test's. One last detail with this function is we can specify an expected difference in means with the `value` argument. So, if we wanted to see at least a 0.01 magnitude difference between the means, we could use the function like this:

```
ztest(ab_df['a_sale'], ab_df['b_sale'], value=-0.01, alternative='smaller')
```

This returns a p-value of 0.83, so we fail to reject the null hypothesis, and A's mean is not at least 0.01 smaller than B's mean (we can see this from the raw mean values of 0.0474 and 0.544). A clearer way to write this might be:

```
ztest(ab_df['b_sale'], ab_df['a_sale'], value=0.01, alternative='larger')
```

where our alternative hypothesis is that B's mean is larger than A's mean by at least 0.01. We get the same p-value of 0.83, failing to reject the null hypothesis. In other words, we don't see any evidence that B's mean is at least 0.01 greater than A's mean.

Paired t- and z-tests

One last type of t- or z-test is the paired test. This is for paired samples, like before-and-after treatments. For example, we could measure the blood pressure of people before and after taking a medication to see if there is an effect. A function that can be used for this is `scipy.stats.ttest_rel`, which can be used like this:

```
scipy.stats.ttest_rel(before, after)
```

This will return a t-statistic and p-value like with other `scipy` t-test functions.

Other A/B testing methods

Some other newer A/B methods are being developed for use with website design and A/B testing. For example, a whitepaper was written in 2015 about Bayesian A/B testing methods (`https://cdn2.hubspot.net/hubfs/310840/VWO_SmartStats_technical_whitepaper.pdf`). This provides some advantages over t-tests, like giving us the probability that B is better than A. However, it's much more complex to implement than a t-test.

Bootstrapping, as we covered in the previous chapter, is another method for A/B testing. With this, we can use sampling with replacement (bootstrapping) to calculate many means of our A and B datasets, then get the confidence intervals of the difference in mean values between A and B. If the confidence interval for the difference in means doesn't pass through 0, we can say with a certain percent confidence that the means are different. For example, we can use the `bootstrapped` package (which you will need to install with `pip install bootstrapped`) to do this:

```
import bootstrapped.bootstrap as bs
import bootstrapped.compare_functions as bs_compare
import bootstrapped.stats_functions as bs_stats

bs.bootstrap_ab(test=ab_df['b_sale'].values,
                ctrl=ab_df['a_sale'].values,
                stat_func=bs_stats.mean,
                compare_func=bs_compare.difference,
                alpha=0.05)
```

Here, we first import the classes and modules of the package we need. Then we use the `bootstrap_ab()` function, providing our test and control datasets first, where the control set is our original design, A.

We need to get the numpy arrays from the pandas Series with the .values attribute. Then we provide a statistic to compare; here, it is the mean. Next, we instruct the function to compare the difference between the values (we could also choose bs_compare.percent_change or others). Lastly, we set our alpha to 0.05 for 95% confidence intervals. This returns:

```
0.006999999999999999     (0.0008000000000000021, 0.013000000000000005)
```

The values are small, but we can see the 95% confidence interval doesn't quite pass through 0, so we can say with 95% confidence B is better than A. However, it could be that B is only better than A by 0.0008 in absolute value, which wouldn't be much of an improvement on A.

Testing one or two samples is useful in many situations, but we can also find ourselves needing to test the means between several groups. We can use multiple t-tests with the Bonferroni correction as one method, but another way is to use ANOVA and post hoc tests.

Testing between several groups with ANOVA

Let's say we want to test more than one design at a time and compare them all to see which is best: A, B, and C designs. For comparing the means of three or more groups, we can use an ANOVA test. There is also a way to compare several groups with t-tests using what's called the Bonferroni correction; this is available in the scikit_posthocs.posthoc_ttest() function from the scikit-posthocs package (you will need to install this package with conda or pip). This would tell us the difference between all the pairs from our groups of data – we will come back to other ways to do this shortly.

However, ANOVA can be first used to see if there is any difference between *any* of the groups. Instead of a t-test, it uses an F-test. Again, this method provides a p-value, which we compare to a significant value we choose (usually 0.05). We have another dataset with three groups, the abc_sales_data.csv file on this book's GitHub repository. Because one assumption for ANOVA is that the data comes from normal distributions, we are using data from binomial distributions. This is chunks of 100 website visitors, with a count of how many visitors made a purchase.

Each row is a number between 0 and 100. As we learned in the previous chapter, sampling data from distributions many times tends toward a normal distribution, so if we structure our data in this way, we can approach a normal distribution instead of a binomial distribution like with our other set of A/B sales data.

In this case, a binomial distribution is based on Bernoulli trials (like coin flips), and a collection of binomial distribution samples tends toward a normal distribution. We can load the data with pandas, then conduct an ANOVA test:

```
from scipy.stats import f_oneway

abc_df = pd.read_csv('data/abc_sales_data.csv')
f_oneway(abc_df['a_sale'], abc_df['b_sale'], abc_df['c_sale'])
```

This returns:

```
F_onewayResult(statistic=186.87190542706728, pvalue=3.2965090243696937e-77)
```

Here, we provide as many datasets as we want to our `f_oneway()` function, which performs an ANOVA test. We get an F-statistic and p-value. As usual, we compare the p-value to our significance level to determine if we can reject the null hypothesis. The null hypothesis here is that the means are all the same; the alternative is that the means are different. Since $p < 0.05$, we can reject the null hypothesis, and our test shows the means to be different. Looking at the means with `abc_df.mean()`, we can see they are 4.9, 5.5, and 6.9 for A, B, and C, which look quite different. However, it would be nice to know which differences between the groups are significant. For this, we can use a post hoc test.

Post-hoc ANOVA tests

There are several post hoc tests, but we will use one common post hoc test: the Tukey test. This is named after John Tukey, the legendary statistician who created boxplots and pioneered EDA, which we discussed in *Chapter 5, Exploratory Data Analysis and Visualization*. Different ANOVA post hoc tests have different subtleties that make them useful in different situations, but Tukey is a decent general test to use as a default. To use this test, we need to first install a new package with conda or pip: `conda install -c conda-forge scikit-posthocs`. Then we can perform the test:

```
from scikit_posthocs import posthoc_tukey

melted_abc = abc_df.melt(var_name='groups', value_name='values')
posthoc_tukey(melted_abc, group_col='groups', val_col='values')
```

Here, we load the Tukey test function from our new package. Then, we reshape the DataFrame with `melt` into two columns: groups and values. The resulting DataFrame is shown on the left below:

	groups	values
0	a_sale	4
1	a_sale	9
2	a_sale	6
3	a_sale	5
4	a_sale	3

	a_sale	b_sale	c_sale
a_sale	1.000	0.001	0.001
b_sale	0.001	1.000	0.001
c_sale	0.001	0.001	1.000

Figure 9.1: The melted DataFrame on the left and Tukey test results on the right

The Tukey test function then returns the results on the right, above. These are p-values for the hypothesis we are testing that the means are not different between pairs. Since the p-values are small between all the pairs (0.001, much less than 0.05) we can say the differences between the means of all the groups are significant. It is possible with the test that some differences between groups may be significant while others may not.

Assumptions for these methods

For t-tests, z-tests, and ANOVA, a few assumptions should be true about the data for best results. For all three tests, the data should be independently and randomly sampled from a population (unless we are doing a paired t-test). For t- and z-tests, the means of the data should be normally distributed. This follows naturally from the central limit theorem as we discussed in the previous chapter, so is usually not something to worry about. For an ANOVA test, the population distributions should be Gaussian.

For t-tests, z-tests, and ANOVA, the variance of the different groups (spread of the data) should be similar. Of course, there is a statistical test that can be carried out to test this assumption, called Levene's test. We can also plot histograms of the data and make sure the distributions look similar. If the variances are not similar, we can use Welch's t-test instead of the t-test. This is done by simply setting the argument `equal_var=False` in `scipy.stats.ttest_ind()`. For post hoc ANOVA tests, the assumptions may differ slightly depending on the test. The Tukey test has the same assumptions as ANOVA, however.

Other statistical tests

The tests we have covered so far were mainly for testing the difference in means between groups. There are a huge number of other tests, and many of them have specific purposes. One set of tests we will not cover here are non-parametric tests, which are for small sample sizes and non-Gaussian distributions. Those tests also return p-values for a hypothesis test like the t- and z-test. Some of the common non-parametric tests are the sign test, the Wilcoxen signed-rank test, and the Mann-Whitney U test. Here, we will cover tests for checking if data comes from a specific distribution, an outlier test, and tests for relationships between variables.

Testing if data belongs to a distribution

The first set of tests we will examine test if data is from a normal distribution. The first way to test this is to simply plot a histogram and "eyeball" it. There are several other tests for checking if something comes from a normal distribution, however, including the Anderson-Darling test, the Shapiro-Wilk test, and the **Kolmogorov-Smirnov (KS)** test. We will use the KS test here because it can also be used for any distribution, not just the Gaussian one.

Let's use our solar cell efficiency data again. We can check if this data comes from a normal distribution like this:

```
from scipy.stats import kstest, norm, skewnorm

kstest(solar_data['efficiency'], norm(loc=14, scale=0.5).cdf)
```

We import a few functions from `scipy.stats` first, including our KS test. Then we give the efficiency data as our first argument, and the distribution we want to test against as the second argument. The second argument should be the `cdf` function (without the parentheses, as above). Notice we also set the mean (`loc`) and variance (`scale`) arguments to match our expected values from the data. The null hypothesis is that there is no difference between the data and distribution. This returns a p-value of 0, rejecting the null hypothesis. It looks like this data is not a normal distribution.

We can also check against other distributions. For example, let's fit the data to a skewed normal distribution and extract parameters:

```
skewnorm.fit(solar_data['efficiency'])
kstest(solar_data['efficiency'], skewnorm(loc=14, scale=0.5, a=-1.5).cdf)
```

The `loc`, `scale`, and a parameters for the `skewnorm` function are returned from the fit to the data on the first line. The KS test on the second line still returns a p-value of 0, so it looks like the distribution isn't quite a skewed normal distribution. In fact, this data was simulated from a combination of a t-distribution and skewed normal distribution. These tests for normality and the KS test for distributions can be quite sensitive, so the data needs to be very close to the exact distribution in most cases for it to fail to reject the null hypothesis.

Generalized ESD outlier test

The generalized **extreme studentized deviate** (ESD) test is available through the scikit-posthocs package (along with a few other tests). This test can check data for an arbitrary number of outliers. We can use it like so:

```
from scikit_posthocs import outliers_gesd

outliers = outliers_gesd(solar_data['efficiency'], outliers=50, hypo=True)
solar_data['efficiency'][outliers]
```

We first import the function from the scikit-posthocs package, then we run it on our pandas Series. We provide a number for the maximum number of outliers to check for. The bigger the number, the longer it will run. Setting `hypo=True` will return a Boolean mask, which can be used to select only the outliers from the pandas DataFrame. From there, these values can be clipped to the non-outlier max/min values or the rows can be dropped.

The Pearson correlation test

The last test we will examine is the Pearson correlation test. This is used to test for linear correlation between variables. If two linear variables increase at the same rate in the same direction, they will have a correlation near 1. If the variables increase at the same rate in opposite directions, the Pearson correlation will be near -1. If there is no correlation, it will be near 0. The following charts illustrate this:

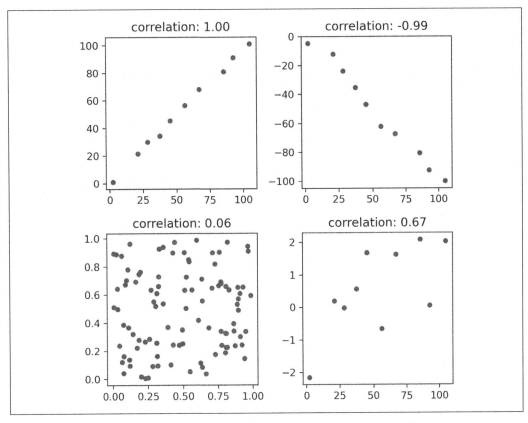

Figure 9.2: Four scatterplots with the Pearson correlation as the titles

We can perform a Pearson correlation test like so:

```
import numpy as np
from scipy.stats import pearsonr

np.random.seed(42)
a = [t + np.random.random()**2*10 for t in np.linspace(1, 100, 10)]
b = [t + np.random.random()**2*10 for t in np.linspace(1, 100, 10)]
c = [np.random.random() for t in range(10)]
print(pearsonr(a, b))
print(pearsonr(a, c))
```

First, we load `numpy` and the `pearsonr` function from `scipy`. Then we set the random seed (for reproducibility) and create a few random datasets. Last, we use `pearsonr()` on these datasets. The first test between a and b results in:

```
(0.9983249247436123, 3.4374952899986435e-11)
```

This gives us the Pearson correlation value first, then the p-value second. The 0.998 value is very high, meaning the data is almost linear like the top left of *Figure 9.2*. The p-value is very small (smaller than the usual alpha of 0.05), so we can conclude the result is statistically significant. The second test between a and c results in:

```
(-0.11783235599746164, 0.7457908412602139)
```

This correlation is -0.118, which is very weak. This result is most similar to the lower-left chart in *Figure 9.2*. We also see the p-value is large (significantly greater than 0.05) so we cannot reject the null hypothesis. The null hypothesis in the case of Pearson is that there is no linear relationship between the two variables.

That wraps up our brief tour of statistical testing. There are many other statistical tests we didn't cover here, such as chi-squared tests, time series tests (tests for autocorrelation and stationarity), and many more. Some books you may find useful for more comprehensive statistical testing references are *Applying and Interpreting Statistics* by Glen McPherson and *Design and Analysis of Experiments* by Douglas C. Montgomery.

Test your knowledge

Use the MISO wind generation data from this book's GitHub repository and see if the mean wind loads for different seasons (summer, fall, winter, spring) are significantly statistically different. You may need to try some different tests. Be sure to write some analysis explaining the results and your methodology.

Summary

Although we covered some of the statistical tests here, there are far too many to cover all of them. Since statistical tests are simply math equations, more can be created. However, we covered the basic tests here for a comparison of means of groups, testing if data belongs to a distribution, testing for outliers, and testing for correlation between variables. We'll see how some of these tests come into play in future chapters, such as *Chapter 12, Evaluating Machine Learning Classification Models and Sampling for Classification*, with linear regression.

This concludes our statistics for the data science section of the book. In the next section, we'll cover machine learning.

Part IV

Machine Learning

10

Preparing Data for Machine Learning: Feature Selection, Feature Engineering, and Dimensionality Reduction

In this section of the book, we'll be coving **machine learning** (**ML**) methods. These methods are used to extract patterns from data, and sometimes predict future events. The data that goes into the algorithms are called *features*, and we can modify our set of features using feature engineering, feature selection, and dimensionality reduction. We can often improve our ML models dramatically with these methods that we cover here. In this chapter, we'll cover the following topics:

- Feature selection methods, including univariate statistical methods, such as correlation, mutual information score, chi-squared, and other feature selection methods
- Feature engineering methods for categorical data, datetime data, and outliers
- Using mathematical transforms for feature engineering
- Dimensionality reduction using PCA

Let's get started with the basics of ML before moving on to feature selection.

Types of machine learning

As we will see in the coming chapters, ML algorithms have inputs that we often call "features." These can be used to extract patterns from the data with ML algorithms in a few different ways. We tend to group ML algorithms into three groups:

- Supervised learning
  - Classification
  - Regression
- Unsupervised learning
- Reinforcement learning

Supervised learning is where we take features and predict a target. In other words, we take inputs and predict an expected output. An example of this is classifying if someone will default on a loan (fail to pay a loan back). For example, we might have someone's credit score, yearly income, age, and job title, and could use that to predict the probability that they default on their loan. Our inputs, or features, would be the credit score, income, age, and job title, and the target (which we could call the output or label) would be if someone will default on their loan.

Within supervised learning, there are two subgroups – classification and regression. Classification is where our outputs are categorical. This can be binary classification, as with the loan default example. In that case, our outputs are default/no default, which can also be represented as 1 and 0 for default and no default. We can have multi-class classification as well, where we have several classes we are trying to predict. For example, we could classify the breed of a dog based on an image. The targets for multi-class classification can also apply to a single data point. For example, we could be predicting which objects are present in an image; this would be a multi-label, multi-class classification, where each data point could have multiple labels or targets. Most of the time, we will have binary classification or multi-class classification where each target has one label. We will learn more about classification in *Chapter 11, Machine Learning for Classification*.

The other subgroup of supervised learning is regression. This is where we are predicting a continuous numeric value, like the temperature outside. Each data point has input features and a single target. We will learn more about regression in *Chapter 13, Machine Learning with Regression*.

Unsupervised learning is used to extract patterns out of data without using a target variable. Most of these techniques include clustering, where we see how data groups together. Some of the dimensionality reduction techniques we will discuss at the end of the chapter can be used for unsupervised learning as well. We will learn more about these techniques in *Chapter 16, Support Vector Machine (SVM) Machine Learning Models*.

There is one other class of ML algorithms that combines unsupervised and supervised learning: semi-supervised learning. This utilizes a combination of labeled and unlabeled data to make target predictions for a dataset. This is not usually mentioned when talking about the main categories of ML algorithms, but is a useful technique we'll talk more about in *Chapter 17, Clustering with Machine Learning*.

Lastly, we have reinforcement learning. This is a complex class of algorithms where an agent uses data from its environment to execute actions in order to achieve goals. For example, DeepMind's AlphaGo algorithm is a reinforcement learning algorithm that was able to beat the world champion in the complex game of Go.

The majority of this chapter focuses on techniques for preparing data for supervised learning, which is what ends up being the bulk of what data scientists do with ML. We'll start with feature selection.

Feature selection

When we are using features to predict a target, some of the features will be more important than others. For example, if we are predicting whether someone will default on a loan, their credit score will be a much better predictor of default than their height and weight. While we can use a large number of features as inputs to ML models, it's much better to minimize the number of features we're using with feature selection methods. ML algorithms take computational power and time to run, and the simpler and more effective we can make the input features, the better. With feature selection, we can screen our inputs for those that have the most promise. These features should have some relationship to the target variable so that we can predict the target with the features. Then we can throw out variables that aren't going to help predict the target.

The curse of dimensionality

Feature selection is related to a concept called "the curse of dimensionality." This idea is that as our number of dimensions (features) increases, a few things happen:

- The volume of the sample space grows exponentially with increased dimensions.
- We need exponentially more data to sufficiently cover the sample space as we increase our dimensions.

- The difference in relative distances between points approaches zero. For example, the distance from point A to B ends up being nearly the same as any other point to B.

- The distance to the center of the data (mean) increases and every point looks like an outlier.

- Any arbitrary grouping of samples becomes linearly separable, also known as Cover's theorem. This leads to model overfitting because we fit to noise in the data instead of the underlying patterns.

One of the biggest problems here is that our models can overfit to the data with too many dimensions.

Overfitting and underfitting, and the bias-variance trade-off

Overfitting usually happens when our model has too much complexity. This will look like the fit to the data on the right side in the following figure:

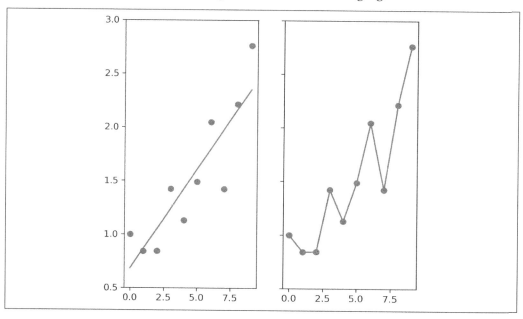

Figure 10.1: An example of a high-bias (left, underfitting) and high-variance model (right, overfitting)

The points in *Figure 10.1* represent some data that we are trying to model. The lines are the fits to the data. On the right side, we are using a high-complexity polynomial fit to the data. We can see that it exactly fits every single point. However, if we were to make a prediction for a new data point, our model would not do very well.

We can also label this model as high variance, meaning the variance of predictions from the model is high.

The other extreme is underfitting. This is demonstrated with the linear fit on the left of *Figure 10.1*. Our fit gets the general trend right, but the error in prediction for each individual point is high. This is also called high bias. Most of the time, we make a trade-off between bias (model errors or underfitting) and variance (overfitting), commonly called the bias-variance trade-off in data science, ML, and statistics. By selecting features and removing some features, we can usually reduce the variance of our models and avoid overfitting.

Methods for feature selection

There are several ways to perform feature selection. Here are some common methods:

- **Variance thresholding**: Remove features with too little or too much variation
- **Univariate statistical selection**: Use statistical tests between features and the target to measure relationship strength
- **Sequential feature selection**:
    - Forward selection: Start with one feature and add features one at a time. ML models are trained and evaluated (checking the accuracy or another metric) to find the best features one at a time.
    - Backward selection: Start with all the features and subtract features one at a time. ML models are used to evaluate feature importance.
- **Recursive feature selection**: Use an ML model with feature importance to remove unimportant features one at a time (we will learn more about this in *Chapter 13, Machine Learning with Regression*)
- **Built-in feature selection**: Some models have built-in methods for feature selection, such as LASSO regularization, which we'll cover in *Chapter 11, Machine Learning for Classification*

Here, we will cover variance thresholding and univariate methods since many of the other methods rely on ML models we will learn in the coming chapters. We will cover some of the other methods, such as aspects of recursive and built-in feature selection, in the next few chapters.

We will use a few Python packages for feature selection here: scikit-learn (`sklearn`) and `phik`. The `sklearn` package has many tools for ML and related methods. The `phik` package is a specialized package for a new correlation method we will use.

To learn feature selection, let's take a look at a loan default dataset, available in the GitHub repository for this book under the `Chapter 10` materials (`Chapter10/data/loan_data.csv`). There is also a `Data Dictionary.xlsx` file available in the GitHub `Chapter 10` materials that explains what the columns in the data are. We first load the data into `pandas` and use pandas profiling to generate an EDA report as we did in *Chapter 5, Exploratory Data Analysis and Visualization*:

```
import pandas as pd
from pandas_profiling import ProfileReport

loan_df = pd.read_csv('data/loan_data.csv',
                      parse_dates=['DATE_OF_BIRTH', 'DISBURSAL_DATE'],
                      infer_datetime_format=True)
report = ProfileReport(loan_df.sample(10000, random_state=42))
report.to_file('loan_df1.html')
```

Notice we are parsing two columns as datetime columns using the `parse_dates` and `infer_datetime_format` arguments. For pandas profiling, we're sampling down our data so it runs faster. There are many columns in the data, which causes the report to run for a while without these tweaks, although we can run it on the full dataset with all pandas profiling calculations if we don't mind waiting. Lastly, we are saving the report to an HTML file so we can open it in another browser window. When there are many columns in the dataset, it helps to do this. Otherwise, the Jupyter notebook can start to run slower because it has so many elements to display.

The target column here is `LOAN_DEFAULT`, which is a 1 or 0 depending on whether the customer couldn't pay the loan (a 1 represents a default, or not being able to pay the loan). With its many columns, the data can take a while to run in some of the examples in this chapter. If you want the examples to run faster in the code samples in this chapter, you can sample down the DataFrame with something like `loan_df = loan_df.sample(10000, random_state=42)`.

Variance thresholding – removing features with too much and too little variance

The simplest way to start with feature selection is to look for variables that have too much or too little variance, or variables with lots of missing values. Let's first look for columns with too much variance. In the pandas-profiling report, these will have warnings such as `UNIQUE`, `HIGH CARDINALITY`, or `UNIFORM`. An example of a few of these warnings is shown in *Figure 10.2*.

We can see right off the bat from our report that the UNIQUEID column is flagged as UNIQUE, as we might expect. This won't be any use for us with ML, so we'll drop that column:

```
loan_df.drop('UNIQUEID', axis=1, inplace=True)
```

Another option would be to set the ID column as our DataFrame index. The other columns flagged as HIGH CARDINALITY appear to be date columns, such as DATE_OF_BIRTH and AVERAGE_ACCT_AGE. We will deal with some of these columns in the next section with feature engineering.

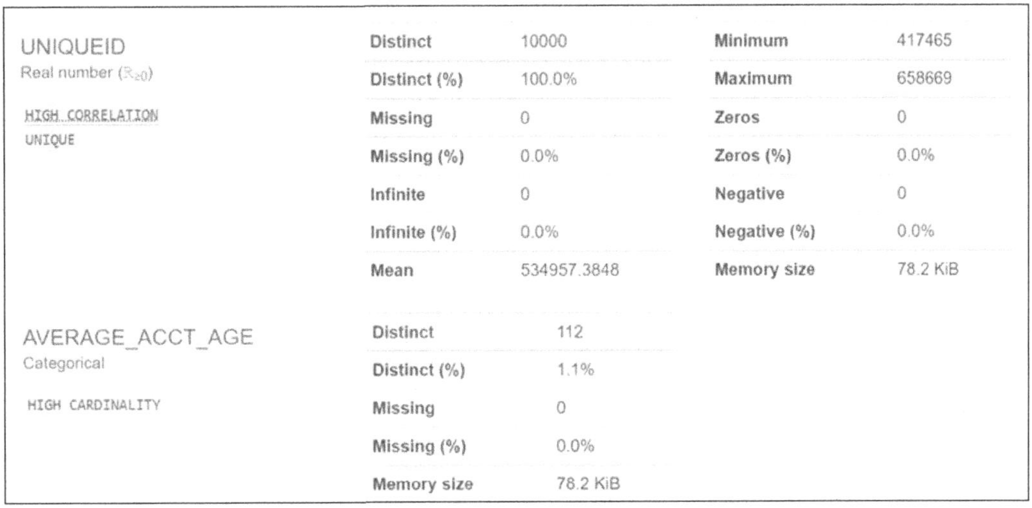

UNIQUEID	Distinct	10000	Minimum	417465
Real number (ℝ≥0)	Distinct (%)	100.0%	Maximum	658669
HIGH CORRELATION	Missing	0	Zeros	0
UNIQUE	Missing (%)	0.0%	Zeros (%)	0.0%
	Infinite	0	Negative	0
	Infinite (%)	0.0%	Negative (%)	0.0%
	Mean	534957.3848	Memory size	78.2 KiB
AVERAGE_ACCT_AGE	Distinct	112		
Categorical	Distinct (%)	1.1%		
HIGH CARDINALITY	Missing	0		
	Missing (%)	0.0%		
	Memory size	78.2 KiB		

Figure 10.2: An example of pandas-profiling warnings for our loans data

If we wanted to screen through our features and list those with high numbers of unique values, we could use a loop:

```
for col in loan_df.columns:
    fraction_unique = loan_df[col].unique().shape[0] / loan_df.shape[0]
    if fraction_unique > 0.5:
        print(col)
```

Here, we are going through the column names from the loan_df DataFrame, and then calculating the fraction of values in that column that are unique. We do this by getting the array of unique values for each column with loan_df[col].unique(), and then get the number of rows with .shape[0]. We then divide this by the total number of rows in the DataFrame. If the fraction is greater than 50%, we print the column. We could also add the columns to a list here and drop them from our DataFrame after the loop. This would allow us to set up more automation in a feature selection pipeline.

Next, let's look for features with too little variance. The extreme example of this is a column with only one unique value – that wouldn't give us any opportunities to learn patterns in our ML algorithms. Within pandas profiling, we can see these columns labeled as CONSTANT, REJECTED, MISSING, or ZEROS. An example of this is MOBILENO_AVL_FLAG, which is a 1 or 0 depending on whether the customer shared their cell number. All values in this column are 1, meaning we have no variance at all. We will drop this column. Most other flags (such as DL_FLAG) are mostly one value, but we will examine these with other feature selection methods. We'll start with a list of columns to drop:

```
drop_cols = ['MOBILENO_AVL_FLAG']
```

The other columns that don't have much variety are mainly the columns starting with PRI and SEC. These are other loans from the customer where the customer is the primary or secondary signer on the loan. These columns have 0s for more than 50% of their values, and some have 0s as 90% or more of their values. It's not clear if these 0s are all truly 0, or if some of them are missing values. We will make it simple here and drop all PRI and SEC columns, although we could keep these and use some of our feature selection techniques to check whether these are related to the target variable. We first create a list of PRI and SEC columns using a list comprehension, and then add it to our existing list using the extend method of lists. This extend function modifies the list in place, so we don't need to assign the output back to the list. Finally, we drop these columns:

```
pri_sec_cols = [c for c in loan_df.columns if c[:3] in ['PRI', 'SEC'] and \
                c not in ['PRI_NO_ACCTS', 'PRI_OVERDUE_ACCTS']]
drop_cols.extend(pri_sec_cols)
loan_df.drop(columns=drop_cols, axis=1, inplace=True)
```

The list comprehension got a little long. We are throwing out any columns where the first three characters (c[:3]) match PRI or SEC, but actually are keeping two PRI columns: the number of accounts and the number of overdue accounts. There are about 11% of borrowers that have overdue PRI accounts, and we would expect that this may relate to loan defaults. The primary number of accounts has 50% of values as 0, so we will see with other methods if this relates strongly enough to the target to keep.

If we examine the shape of the DataFrame before and after dropping columns (with `loan_df.shape`), we can see that we dropped 15 columns.

Lastly, we might look for columns with lots of missing values. If a column is missing most of its values, we should probably throw it out. We can also try replacing the missing values with a constant number (for example, -1 or -999) and try other feature selection methods on it. If we are missing less than 10% of the data in a column, we can usually impute it with methods such as mean, median, or KNN imputation, which we covered in *Chapter 4, Loading and Wrangling Data with Pandas and NumPy*.

Univariate statistics feature selection

The methods we covered so far were mostly by hand and involve some arbitrary choices. For example, if a column is missing 50% of its values, we might not be sure if we want to throw it out. For these borderline cases, we can keep them and check whether the feature is important with other mathematical methods.

Correlation

One simple way to check how strongly features relate to the target is by using correlation, as we saw in *Chapter 5, Exploratory Data Analysis and Visualization*. If we expect a linear relationship between features and the target, we can use Pearson correlation. For a binary target as in our case, we can still use Pearson correlation. However, it is called point biserial correlation for a binary target. For this, we can simply use the pandas `corr` function. If we index to the `LOAN_DEFAULT` row and create a bar plot, we can easily see what our correlations look like:

```
loan_df.corr().loc['LOAN_DEFAULT'][:-1].plot.barh()
```

We are also indexing this row up to, but not including, the last value. The last value is the correlation of `LOAN_DEFAULT` with itself, which is always 1. This throws off the scaling of the bar plot, so we are ignoring that value. We can see that the biggest correlation is the CNS score, which has a correlation of around -0.4 with loan defaults. This means that a higher CNS score is a lower chance of default, which makes sense.

The CNS score is like a credit score, and the better you handle debt (for example, successfully paying back loans), the higher your CNS score:

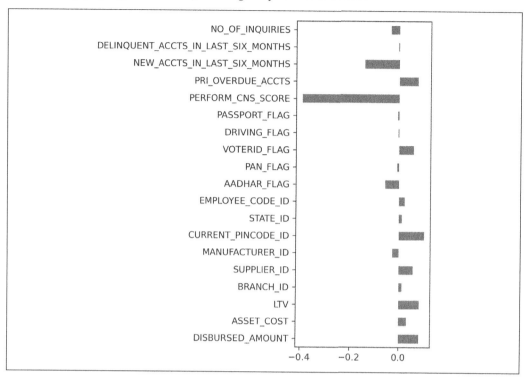

Figure 10.3: A bar plot of Pearson correlation values with the LOAN_DEFAULT column

Recall from *Chapter 5, Exploratory Data Analysis and Visualization* that we can group correlations into five categories: very weak, weak, moderate, strong, and very strong, with groups occurring at absolute values of 0-0.2, 0.2-0.4, 0.4-0.6, 0.6-0.8, and 0.8-1. These ranges are somewhat arbitrary, and others sometimes assign different regimes (such as anything above 0.5 or 0.7 being strong). Regardless, we can see we have several correlations near 0. To see whether these variables are worth further examination, we can look at their p-values from the Pearson correlation using `scipy`:

```
from scipy.stats import pearsonr
from pandas.api.types import is_numeric_dtype


for c in loan_df.columns[:-1]:
    if is_numeric_dtype(loan_df[c]):
        correlation, pvalue = pearsonr(loan_df[c], loan_df['LOAN_DEFAULT'])
        print(f'{c : <40}: {correlation : .4f}, significant: {pvalue <= 0.05}')
```

Here, we first import a few functions from `scipy` and `pandas` for the Pearson correlation and a function for checking if a column has a numeric datatype. We loop through all the columns except the last one (which is `LOAN_DEFAULT`) with a `for` loop. Then we check whether each column is numeric, and if so, we calculate the Pearson correlation. Recall from the previous chapter that this function returns the correlation value and p-value. Conventionally, we set our alpha value (significance level) to 0.05, and if the p-value is smaller than this, we can say that our correlation is significantly different from 0. In the last line, we are using f-string formatting to print out the column (c), the `correlation` value to 4 decimal places, and `True` or `False` if the p-value is less than 0.05. We are using some features of Python string formatting here. First, we are aligning the column to the left and padding it with spaces to reach 40 characters with `c : <40`. Then we are specifying the correlation variable to be printed to four decimal places as a float with `{correlation : .4f}`. These tweaks make the printout easier to read. One of our results with a small correlation and non-significant p-value result looks like this:

```
DRIVING_FLAG                            : -0.0035, significant: False
```

We can see that the correlation is very small, and our p-value is greater than 0.05. We have one other column with a small p-value, and we will drop both these columns now:

```
loan_df.drop(columns=['DRIVING_FLAG', 'DELINQUENT_ACCTS_IN_LAST_SIX_MONTHS'],
axis=1, inplace=True)
```

Note that you may want to use more methods to make sure columns are not useful before dropping them, especially depending on your data. For example, if our target was a continuous value like the loan amount, then we might not have linear relationships between our features and the target. In that case, we might want to look at some other feature selection methods before dropping columns.

We can also use feature-feature correlations to try and trim down our features. For example, from the pandas-profiling report, we can see that the asset cost and disbursed amount are highly correlated. We should consider keeping only one of these columns if they have a high correlation value (this could be above 0.7 or 0.9). This is especially true if two features are perfectly colinear, meaning their Pearson correlation is 1.0. Although more complex ML methods can deal with collinearity, linear and logistic regression typically cannot.

There are other correlation methods you might consider using depending on your data. Spearman and Kendall-tau can be used when the data may not have a linear relationship since these correlation methods look for relationships between the ranked (least to greatest) pairs of the data instead of a linear relationship.

You'll also notice that if you don't use `minimal=True` in the pandas-profiling report, it generates correlation plots. These plots show some other methods: phi-k and Cramer's V. Cramer's V is suitable for measuring the strength of categorical-categorical relationships, but ideally, a corrected version of Cramer's V should be used. The function and example usage for a corrected version of Cramer's V can be found here: `https://stackoverflow.com/a/39266194/4549682`.

The phi-k (also written ϕ_K and here as phik) correlation calculation is a good all-around method that was created in 2018 and can be used for data containing categorical, ordinal, and interval features and targets. It can also capture non-linear relationships between data, unlike Pearson's correlation. Phik uses the chi-squared test as its foundation. The chi-squared test is useful for comparing categorical-categorical relationships, but the phik calculation groups numeric data so it can be used with chi-squared. Because of this, phik can handle any type of data, including ordinal data.

 Ordinal data is where the order of values matters but exact distances between levels are not known, such as university degree levels or a Likert 1-5 rating scale. Interval data is where the order and difference between values are important and known, such as the loan amount. We also called interval data continuous data in the previous few chapters.

To calculate phik correlations, we should make sure we have the package installed first with pip or conda (for example, `conda install -c conda-forge phik`). Once we import `phik`, we can simply use a new method of DataFrames from phik: `phik_matrix()`. Note that this can take a long time to run with a lot of variables, and there are implementations of phik with Spark and other big data software to speed up the calculations. Because the phik method bins interval data into groups and is performing many other calculations, it can take a long time to run even with a small number of data points on a single machine.

We first convert our datetime columns to seconds since the epoch, and take a sample of the data:

```
loan_df_epoch_time = loan_df.copy()
loan_df_epoch_time['DATE_OF_BIRTH'] = \
    (loan_df_epoch_time['DATE_OF_BIRTH'] - \
```

```
      pd.to_datetime('1-1-1970')).dt.total_seconds()
loan_df_epoch_time['DISBURSAL_DATE'] = \
    (loan_df_epoch_time['DISBURSAL_DATE'] - \
    pd.to_datetime('1-1-1970')).dt.total_seconds()

sample = loan_df_epoch_time.sample(10000, random_state=1)
```

We are making a copy of the DataFrame so that we don't alter the original data, and then take the total seconds since 00:00:00 UTC on January 1st, 1970 for our two datetime columns. This is Unix time or time since the Unix epoch, which is a standard way to measure timestamps. Lastly, we sample 10k points and set a random seed (`random_state`) so we get the same sample every time we run the code.

We can then calculate the phik correlation matrix:

```
interval_columns = ['DISBURSED_AMOUNT', 'ASSET_COST', 'LTV',
                    'DATE_OF_BIRTH', 'DISBURSAL_DATE', 'PERFORM_CNS_SCORE',
                    'NEW_ACCTS_IN_LAST_SIX_MONTHS', 'NO_OF_INQUIRIES']
sample.phik_matrix(interval_cols=interval_columns)
```

It helps to set the interval (continuous) columns, although phik will try to autodetect which are interval columns. The phik correlations span 0 to 1, with 1 being perfect correlation and 0 being no correlation. We can also get p-values from phik:

```
sample.significance_matrix(interval_cols=interval_columns)
```

Since it can take a long time to run on the full dataset, we can minimize runtime by only calculating correlations between the target variable and the features. First, we will convert columns to the `category` datatype in pandas for non-interval columns. We could also use the datatype `object` to represent the data as strings. The `category` datatype in pandas has a few extra features beyond the `object` datatype, although we are not using them here. Pandas' documentation explains more about the `category` datatype: https://pandas.pydata.org/pandas-docs/stable/user_guide/categorical.html:

```
for c in loan_df_epoch_time.columns:
    if c not in interval_columns:
        loan_df_epoch_time[c] = loan_df_epoch_time[c].astype('category')
```

Here, we loop through all column names and convert any non-interval columns to a category datatype. Now we can calculate the phik correlations and p-values:

```
phik_correlations = []
phik_significances = []
columns = loan_df_epoch_time.columns
```

```
y = loan_df_epoch_time['LOAN_DEFAULT']

for c in columns:
    x = loan_df_epoch_time[c]
    if c in interval_columns:
        phik_correlations.append(phik.phik_from_array(x, y, [c]))
        phik_significances.append(
            phik.significance.significance_from_array(x, y, [c])[0])
    else:
        phik_correlations.append(phik.phik_from_array(x, y))
        phik_significances.append(
            phik.significance.significance_from_array(x, y)[0])
```

The `phik_from_array()` function can take several arguments (see the documentation for further details: https://phik.readthedocs.io/en/latest/phik.html#phik.phik. phik_from_array), but we only need our two arrays, x and y, and a list with numeric variables that need to be binned. The phik correlation works for interval data by binning values into groups and then using another statistical test (chi-squared) to calculate the relationship between the two variables. For the interval columns, we tell the phik and significance calculation functions to bin our variable by providing the third argument, `[c]` (the argument is named `num_vars`), which is a list of numeric variables that should be binned. If we are looking at the other categorical columns, we do not bin the feature.

The `phik.significance.significance_from_array()` method returns a tuple of a p-value and Z-score (a statistical significance value). We will use the p-value here to check whether correlations are significant, so we only keep the first element of these returned values in our `phik_significances` list.

Once the calculation is finished, we can put the data in a DataFrame and plot it:

```
phik_df = pd.DataFrame({'phik': phik_correlations, \
                        'p-value': phik_significances},
                       index=columns)
phik_df.sort_values(by='phik', ascending=False, inplace=True)
phik_df.iloc[1:].plot.bar(subplots=True)
```

We first create the DataFrame from the correlations and p-values with the original column names as the index. Then we sort the correlation values from greatest to least, and finally plot the correlation and p-values in subplots.

We are indexing the DataFrame from the second row onward, since the first row is the correlation of LOAN_DEFAULT with itself (which is 1). Our result looks like this:

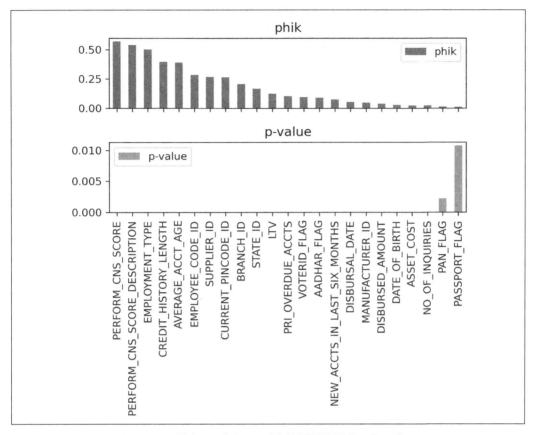

Figure 10.4: Phik correlations to LOAN_DEFAULT and p-values

We can see that the first five features ordered by the phik correlation seem to have a strong correlation. Most of these are actually category datatypes, except for the CNS score (credit score). This strong correlation agrees with the Pearson correlations we saw, where the CNS score was the strongest correlation. Many of the flag features seem to have a weak correlation with the target variable, and the PAN and passport flags have non-zero p-values. However, these p-values are smaller than 0.05 (the usual alpha value), so the correlation still seems significant, although weak. If we were to use this for feature selection (we are not in this example), we might consider throwing out variables with correlations weaker than 0.1 (features starting at the voter ID flag) or correlations less than 0.2 (starting at the state ID feature).

Mutual information score and chi-squared

While phik works as a general correlation measurement between any two types of variables, we can also use other methods to complement phik. Mutual information scores can be used to measure relationships between two variables of any type, although the implementations in the scikit-learn package only allow for certain comparisons:

- Categorical-categorical with `sklearn.metrics` mutual information methods
- Numeric-numeric, numeric-binary, and binary-binary with `sklearn.feature_selection.mutual_info_classif`

We can easily calculate mutual information between categorical-categorical columns as follows:

```
from sklearn.metrics import normalized_mutual_info_score

loan_df.corr(method=normalized_mutual_info_score)
```

We first import the mutual information score from the scikit-learn package. If you do not have this package installed already, it can be installed with `conda install -c conda-forge scikit-learn -y`. This function is intended for measuring agreement between clustering methods (we will learn more about clustering in *Chapter 17, Clustering with Machine Learning*), but we can use it for categorical-categorical relationships as well. This function returns a value between 0 and 1, where 1 is a perfect correlation and 0 is no correlation. From this, we don't see very strong relationships between the loan default target and other variables (most are closer to 0 than 1), but we do see that the PAN and passport flags have a very weak relationship (similar to what we saw with phik).

The other mutual information method in scikit-learn can be used for numeric-numeric relationships, including a binary target such as we have here:

```
from sklearn.feature_selection import mutual_info_classif

numeric_features = loan_df.select_dtypes(include=['number']).copy()
numeric_features.drop('LOAN_DEFAULT', axis=1, inplace=True)
list(zip(numeric_features.columns,
         mutual_info_classif(numeric_features,
                             loan_df['LOAN_DEFAULT'])))
```

Here, we first import the function, then select our numeric columns with the `select_dtypes` pandas function, and drop the target variable from our numeric features DataFrame. We then provide this DataFrame as the first argument in `mutual_info_classif`. The second argument should be the target column.

Lastly, we zip together the column names and mutual information scores so that they are easier to read and deal with (we need to convert them to a list so we can print them out). Our results look like this:

```
[('DISBURSED_AMOUNT', 0.008546445254898227),
 ('ASSET_COST', 0.00827254098601693),
 ('LTV', 0.008548222647203563),
 ('BRANCH_ID', 0.013475308245299633),
 ('SUPPLIER_ID', 0.02222355430615841),
 ('MANUFACTURER_ID', 0.00563919231684018),
 ('CURRENT_PINCODE_ID', 0.020973276540538155),
 ('STATE_ID', 0.01034124631058675),
 ('EMPLOYEE_CODE_ID', 0.02566780585102446),
 ('AADHAR_FLAG', 0.014049992897749775),
 ('PAN_FLAG', 0.0),
 ('VOTERID_FLAG', 0.00134686411350593),
 ('PASSPORT_FLAG', 0.0019906978414252485),
 ('PERFORM_CNS_SCORE', 0.11092887637496096),
 ('PRI_OVERDUE_ACCTS', 0.003229554693775283),
 ('NEW_ACCTS_IN_LAST_SIX_MONTHS', 0.016193752448300902),
 ('NO_OF_INQUIRIES', 0.0)]
```

There is no upper limit to the mutual information score, but the lower limit is 0. We can see the CNS score has the largest value here, which is an order of magnitude above the other values. Although we can use this mutual information method with categorical variables if we undergo some feature engineering (one-hot encoding or label encoding), it's best to use this mutual information method between numeric and binary variables only. Trying to use categorical features here would become too confusing, and we could simply use phik or a different method instead.

The chi-squared test

Another method we can use for some categorical-categorical relationships is the chi-squared test. Although this method (and the mutual information scores from the `sklearn.metrics` module) can deliver results for numeric columns, the current implementation in the scikit-learn package in Python is intended for categorical-categorical relationships. Furthermore, this chi-squared implementation is specifically intended for binary columns or frequency count columns, like word counts. We can use the chi-squared method like so:

```
from sklearn.feature_selection import chi2

chi2(loan_df[['PAN_FLAG', 'STATE_ID']], loan_df['LOAN_DEFAULT'])
```

Here, we first import the chi-squared test from `sklearn`. Then we give our features as the first argument to the function, and the target as the second argument. Our results are as follows:

```
(array([ 8.46807323, 48.3495596 ]), array([3.61434074e-03, 3.56624293e-12]))
```

The function returns two arrays; the first is chi-squared test values, and the second is p-values. We can rank the strength of relationships by the chi-squared values, where bigger means a stronger relationship. We can also check whether the relationship is statistically significant with the p-value by comparing it to a significance threshold (alpha, with the usual value of 0.05). Here, the p-values (the second array of numbers in the returned results) are very small so it looks like the relationships are significant. The stronger relationship to loan default here is with the state ID column.

ANOVA

One more method for measuring feature relationship strength to the target is to use the ANOVA test we learned about in the previous chapter. Again, this can be used as a complement to other methods, such as the phik test. This is useful for comparisons of numeric or binary data to a numeric or binary target variable. We can use it with `sklearn` like so:

```
from sklearn.feature_selection import f_classif

f_classif(loan_df[['PERFORM_CNS_SCORE', 'PAN_FLAG', 'STATE_ID']],
          loan_df['LOAN_DEFAULT'])
```

First, we import the function, and then provide our features as the first argument and the target as the second argument. This results in two arrays; the F-score from the ANOVA test and the p-values:

```
(array([2.41525739e+04, 9.15861992e+00, 1.74974209e+01]),
 array([0.00000000e+00, 2.47596457e-03, 2.87881660e-05]))
```

As with most of the statistical tests we've seen, a higher F-value means a stronger relationship between the variables, and the p-value can be compared with an alpha value (usually 0.05) to check for significance. The p-values signify if the means of the features differ significantly between the different target groups, which would signify that the features may have some predictive power. Here, the p-values are all very small, so it appears the average feature values are different between the two groups of target values. For example, the average PAN flag value is statistically significantly different between the default and no-default groups according to this test.

The F-value is largest for the CNS score, signifying this is the most important of the features we looked at here, agreeing with the other methods we've seen.

Using the univariate statistics for feature selection

To summarize, we have several univariate statistics we can use for feature selection:

- **Variance methods**: Remove features based on too much or too little variance in data

- **Pearson correlation**: Good for linear relationships between numeric and binary data

- **Phi-k correlation**: Good for any relationships between any kind of data

- **Mutual information score**: Can be used for categorical-categorical relationships or numeric-numeric (including binary data) with `sklearn`

- **Chi-squared**: Can be used for binary or frequency count variables in `sklearn`

- **ANOVA**: Can be used with a numeric or binary target column and numeric or binary features

We can often start with the phik correlation, and add other methods to confirm our findings. Then we can combine them with other ML feature importance methods we will start learning about in the next chapter.

We can also simply select the *k* best features based on our univariate stats as a quick way to trim down our feature space. Scikit-learn has a few functions for this from the `sklearn.feature_selection` module: `SelectKBest` and `SelectPercentile`. For example, to select the top five features based on the ANOVA F-values:

```
from sklearn.feature_selection import SelectKBest

k_best = SelectKBest(f_classif, k=5).fit_transform(
    loan_df_epoch_time[interval_columns],
    loan_df_epoch_time['LOAN_DEFAULT']
)
```

Note that we are only using the interval columns here since those are all numeric columns and this method can only handle numeric data. We first import the class, then create a new class using the ANOVA method as our scoring function (`f_classif`), and set k=5 to select the top five features by the largest F-values. Then we use the `fit_transform()` function of this class, giving it our features as the first argument and the target as the second argument. Our new array, `k_best`, has a shape of (133154, 5) since we only have five remaining features. We could then use this trimmed-down array as an input to an ML algorithm.

The other methods for feature selection, such as sequential and recursive feature selection, rely on ML methods. Although we can use these in the same quick way where we specify an arbitrary number of features to select (as with `SelectKBest`), it's better to use the performance of ML algorithms to select features based on these methods. We will learn more about these in the next chapter.

This concludes our section on feature selection. Remember, we can use these methods to trim down our inputs so we can reduce the chance of overfitting due to the curse of dimensionality, and our ML algorithms will run faster with less data. As part of the iterative process of preparing our data for ML, we also perform feature engineering, which we'll cover next.

Feature engineering

The process of preparing data for ML is somewhat iterative. We will be doing EDA, cleaning data, performing feature selection, and feature engineering, but these steps will be mixed together depending on our situation. For example, we might start with some basic EDA (pandas profiling) and then look at univariate statistics for feature selection as the next step in our EDA. Based on the results, we could remove some features. We might also notice some data that needs cleaning along the way (for example, erroneous strings in numeric columns that need cleaning) and may need to repeat some earlier EDA and feature selection steps after cleaning. We might also notice columns that could be used in feature engineering as part of this process.

Feature engineering is creating new features based on existing features. We use this along with data cleaning to prepare our data for ML, so our algorithms perform better (for example, making predictions with higher accuracy). We can do this in several ways:

- Combine multiple columns (example: multiply two numeric columns)
- Transform numeric data (example: take the logarithm of numeric data)
- Extract specific datetime features from a datetime column (example: get the day of the week from a date)
- Bin data, where we group data into categorical bins
- One-hot encoding and label encoding (converting categorical data to numeric values)

Data cleaning and preparation

Before we start feature engineering, we will also look at a few other related tasks with data cleaning and preparation:

- Parsing and converting string values to numeric data (example: convert strings to datetimes or date spans)
- Outlier clipping
- Converting all data to numeric data for `sklearn`

The last item on the list is important – we need to make sure all features and targets are numeric before using any ML algorithms from the `sklearn` package. Other packages, such as H2O, have ML algorithms that can handle categorical values and missing values, but `sklearn` cannot.

Let's start by looking at a few columns that are strings but should be date spans.

Converting strings to dates

The columns that need string-to-date conversion are the `AVERAGE_ACCT_AGE` and `CREDIT_HISTORY_LENGTH` columns. We can see these look like `0yrs 6mon`, with a year and month value. We can parse these with a regular expression. Regular expressions, also called regex, are patterns we use to extract information from strings.

> Google has a nice course on Python regex here: `https://developers.google.com/edu/python/regular-expressions`.
>
> The Python `re` module documentation also has lots of helpful information on regex: `https://docs.python.org/3/library/re.html`.

To parse these two columns and convert them to date spans, we can do the following:

```
import re

re.search(r'(\d+)yrs\s+(\d+)mon', '1yrs 11mon').groups()
```

We are prototyping a regular expression here. First, we import Python's built-in `re` module. Then we use the `search()` function, which takes a few arguments, the pattern, and then the string we will search. It returns a `re` match object, which has several methods available. If there is no match, the function returns `None`. Here, there is a match, so we use the `groups()` function to get the returned matching groups (if there is no match, this would return an error).

The regular expression here is composed of the following parts. The `r` in front of the string signifies a raw string, meaning all characters are interpreted literally. This means the backslash is treated as a backslash and not an escape character.

The \d sequence matches a digit (0-9). The + after \d means it will match one or more digits in a row. The parentheses around the \d+ bits mean it treats these sections as subgroups. The groups() function returns a tuple of the subgroups, so here, it returns ('1', '11') from '1yrs 11mon'. The main "group" is the entire match, which we can retrieve with group(0). After the first digit subgroup (the (\d+) part), we then look for the yrs string. Then we search for \s+, which is one or more spaces. Finally, we have one subgroup to get the number of months, and then match the last part of the string, mon. We can put this in a function so it's easier to use on the entire DataFrame:

```
def convert_date_spans(date_str):
    """
    Parses date spans of the form "1yrs 1mon"
    into the number of months as an integer.
    """
    yrs, mon = re.search(r'(\d+)yrs\s+(\d+)mon', date_str).groups()
    yrs, mon = int(yrs), int(mon)
    months = yrs * 12 + mon
    return months
```

Here, we use the same regular expression we tested, and return the two parts of the tuple to the variables yrs and mon. Then we convert these to integers and add them together to get the total number of months. One small improvement to this function would be error handling – we could first get the result of the re.search() method and check that it's not None before getting the groups. If it was None, we could return 0 or another value, such as -1, to signify the data is missing.

Once we have this function, we can apply it to our DataFrame, creating some new columns and dropping the old ones:

```
import swifter

loan_df['AVERAGE_ACCT_AGE_MONTHS'] = \
    loan_df.swifter.apply(lambda x: \
                          convert_date_spans(x['AVERAGE_ACCT_AGE']),
                          axis=1)
loan_df['CREDIT_HISTORY_LENGTH_MONTHS'] = \
    loan_df.swifter.apply(lambda x: \
                          convert_date_spans(x['CREDIT_HISTORY_LENGTH']),
                          axis=1)
loan_df.drop(['AVERAGE_ACCT_AGE', 'CREDIT_HISTORY_LENGTH'], axis=1,
inplace=True)
```

We are using the swifter package here, which you may need to install with conda or pip. This library automatically parallelizes our use of pandas' apply function, making it run much faster.

Now that we have our string columns parsed to dates, we can look at our next data cleaning and transformation step – outlier cleaning.

Outlier cleaning strategies

Many times, data will have outliers. Sometimes, the outliers are obvious errors, such as when someone's age is well over 100 years in a dataset. Other times, we can use statistical outlier detection methods that we've learned earlier in *Chapter 9, Statistical Testing for Data Science,* to detect outliers. Once we have the outliers detected, we can "clip" these values to the maximum and minimum values we might expect. The values for clipping might be the **IQR (inter-quartile range)** outlier boundaries or a percentile of the data (like the 5th percentile for the minimum, and the 95th percentile for the maximum). We could also use a simple filter where any value above a threshold is clipped to the maximum value below the threshold. Lastly, we could use a statistical test for outliers like the GESD test we learned about in the previous chapter from the scikit-posthocs package. Most of these methods (IQR, GESD, and percentiles) depend on our data being close to a normal distribution. If our data is not a normal distribution, we should consider using a hand-picked threshold for outliers.

To decide if we want to clip outliers, it can be helpful to look at histograms and box plots of the data. We can see whether there are many outliers or if the distribution looks like it is very spread out. If there are only a few outliers (around 1% of the data), we could deal with them by clipping the values. If there are many outliers, it may be a part of the natural distribution for the data, and we may not want to alter it. We should also use common sense when clipping outliers. For example, for something like someone's age, we probably don't need to clip outliers on the low end, but may need to deal with outliers on the high end.

We can create a boxplot of all the data with seaborn:

```
import seaborn as sns

sns.boxplot(data=loan_df, orient='h')
```

However, since many of the scales are different between the features, we may want to drop several of them when plotting a boxplot. For example, the DISBURSED_AMOUNT and ASSET_COST variables are much larger than the others, so we could create a few different boxplots to make them more readable like this:

```
sns.boxplot(data=loan_df.drop(['DISBURSED_AMOUNT', 'ASSET_COST'], axis=1),
orient='h')
sns.boxplot(data=loan_df[['DISBURSED_AMOUNT', 'ASSET_COST']], orient='h')
```

Another option for dealing with data over different scales is to use a logarithmic scale, which we can do with `plt.xscale('log')`. However, this doesn't work too well in this situation, and separating the variables out by their different scales works better.

We can also look at our histograms of data to "eyeball" how normal they are (which we also have in the pandas-profiling report):

```
loan_df['AVERAGE_ACCT_AGE_MONTHS'].plot.hist(bins=30)
loan_df['DISBURSED_AMOUNT'].plot.hist(bins=50)
```

From this, we can see that the account age is highly skewed and more like an exponential distribution. The disbursed amount looks to be more normal with some very large outliers on the high side:

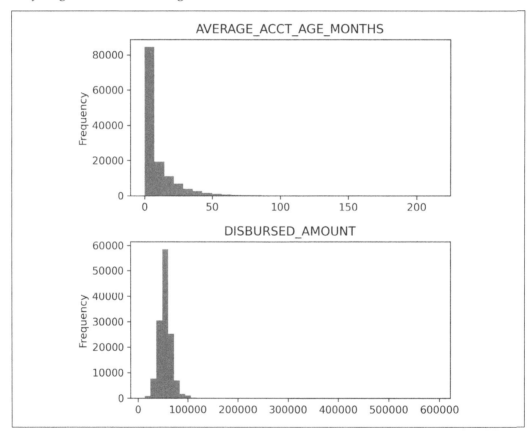

Figure 10.5: Histograms of the AVERAGE_ACCT_AGE_MONTHS and DISBURSED_AMOUNT features

We can detect outliers using the IQR method for the DISBURSED_AMOUNT column and examine where the cut-off is:

```
import numpy as np

q3 = loan_df['DISBURSED_AMOUNT'].quantile(0.75)
q1 = loan_df['DISBURSED_AMOUNT'].quantile(0.25)
iqr = (q3 - q1)
outliers = np.where(loan_df['DISBURSED_AMOUNT'] > (q3 + 1.5 * iqr))[0]
print(1.5 * iqr + q3)
```

First, we get the Q3 and Q1 quartiles (the 75th percentile and 25th percentile of the data), and then calculate the interquartile range as the difference between these two. We use NumPy's where() function to return the indices where the disbursed amount is above 1.5 times the IQR plus the Q3 quartile. The where() function returns a tuple, so we index the first element of the tuple to get the indices of the outliers. When we print the outlier boundary, it is around 80,000, which seems to line up well on the histogram.

We can examine these outliers with loan_df['DISBURSED_AMOUNT'][outliers]. To clip these to our outlier boundary, we can use a pandas function:

```
loan_df['DISBURSED_AMOUNT'].clip(upper=1.5 * iqr + q3, inplace=True)
```

We provide an upper argument to clip() to tell it where to clip the maximum values (we can also use the lower argument to clip values below a threshold). This will change our large outliers to this upper value. If we set the argument inplace=True, we will update the data in the underlying DataFrame. We can see that our outliers have been changed to the upper boundary with loan_df['DISBURSED_AMOUNT'][outliers] after clipping the data.

This clipping to maximum values works, but another way of dealing with outliers we discussed before was to impute these values as we do with missing values. If someone's age is far too high in our dataset and it looks like a data entry or other spontaneous error, we could impute it using the mean, median, or KNN imputation.

Although we only demonstrated cleaning one column here, it would be ideal to use a boxplot or histogram to examine all the data and deal with any problematic columns. It would also be best to clean our data as we learned in *Chapter 4, Loading and Wrangling Data with Pandas and NumPy*, before undergoing feature engineering. Once we have our data sufficiently cleaned to our satisfaction, we can start on our feature engineering. However, it's not a bad idea to come back and check for outliers again after performing feature engineering too.

Combining multiple columns

One simple method for feature engineering is to combine existing columns. We might do this with numeric columns that can be combined, such as height and width, to create an "area" feature (height times width). Another example of where this can be used is creating a time-based feature based on two date columns. In our data here, we can create the customer's age at the time of the loan by combining the DISBURSAL_DATE and DATE_OF_BIRTH columns:

```
loan_df['AGE'] = (loan_df['DISBURSAL_DATE'] - loan_df['DATE_OF_BIRTH']) // 365
```

We are taking the difference between the dates here and dividing by the number of days in a year. The difference in dates is calculated as days by default for pandas. We can also specify days (or another unit of measure) like so:

```
(loan_df['DISBURSAL_DATE'] - loan_df['DATE_OF_BIRTH']).dt.days
```

The dt accessor provides datetime functionality and properties to us, including days and seconds. However, this doesn't take into account leap years (although we could divide by 365.25 to try and account for that). A slightly more accurate solution is to use the actual time delta between the dates:

```
from dateutil import relativedelta

def calculate_age_in_years(x):
    return relativedelta.relativedelta(
        x['DISBURSAL_DATE'],
        x['DATE_OF_BIRTH']
    ).years

loan_df['AGE'] = loan_df.swifter.apply(
    lambda x: calculate_age_in_years(x), axis=1)
```

We first import the relativedelta module from the built-in dateutil library. Then we define a function that will get the difference in years between the disbursal and birth dates, which takes a single argument we've simply called x. Finally, we use swifter with apply to run the calculations over the entire DataFrame. Now we can generate some EDA plots and stats of the new column. For example, we could plot a histogram with loan_df['AGE'].plot.hist(bins=50) as shown below. Again, it is useful to check this new column for outliers:

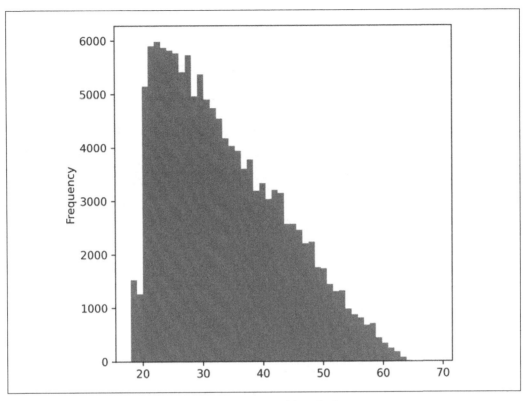

Figure 10.6: Histograms of the AGE feature

We don't see any outliers here from examining the histogram, so we can move forward without cleaning this new column. If we weren't sure from the histogram if there were outliers, we could be more precise by using quantiles (for example, with the pandas `clip` or `quantile` functions).

Transforming numeric data

Another way to engineer features is to pass numeric data through functions to change its values. Some ML algorithms work better on data that is closer to a normal distribution, and others work better when the data has been scaled in particular ways, which can improve performance. These transformations could be any mathematical operation, but we'll look at three useful methods here: standardization, the Yeo-Johnson transformation, and log scaling.

Standardization

Standardization divides each data point by the standard deviation and subtracts the mean. This ensures that the mean is 0 and the standard deviation is 1. This can be useful for certain algorithms such as neural networks to perform optimally (for example, a similar scaling of images for classification problems can improve performance). We can also use standardization (or other similar normalizations, like min-max normalization) to preprocess data for clustering, which we will cover in *Chapter 17, Clustering with Machine Learning*. Any algorithm that uses distance calculations, such as clustering, *k*-nearest neighbors, or **support vector machines** (**SVMs**, which we will cover in *Chapter 16, Support Vector Machine (SVM) Machine Learning Models*), benefits from standardization or feature normalization. We can easily carry this out with the `StandardScaler` class from `sklearn`:

```
from sklearn.preprocessing import StandardScaler
import matplotlib.pyplot as plt

scaler = StandardScaler()
loan_df['standardized_age'] = scaler.\
    fit_transform(loan_df['AGE'].values.reshape(-1, 1))

f, ax = plt.subplots(2, 1)
loan_df['AGE'].plot.hist(ax=ax[0], title='AGE', bins=50)
loan_df['standardized_age'].\
    plot.hist(ax=ax[1], title='standardized_age', bins=50)
plt.tight_layout()
```

We first import the class and then create a new `StandardScaler` class. We use this new class to fit to the `AGE` data, and then transform it (standardizing it). To give data to this function, it needs to have two dimensions, and it will standardize each column if we have more than one. If we only provide a single column, it needs to have the shape (`rows, 1`). We can make our data have this shape by first getting the values as a NumPy array with `.values`, and then using the `reshape()` method of arrays to add another axis, making it so that we have a single column. The `-1` in reshape uses the existing dimension, so it reshapes it into (`loan_df['AGE'].shape[0], 1`).

Next, we plot the `AGE` column before and after standardization in two histograms to compare them. We first use the `plt.subplots` function, which takes arguments for the number of rows and columns. Then we can reference the subplots, such as `ax[0]` and `ax[1]`, for the top and bottom subplots, respectively. We provide these axes objects to the pandas histogram, plotting functions to direct where to plot these histograms.

We then use the `tight_layout()` function from `matplotlib` at the end, which auto-adjusts margins so everything fits well in the figure and doesn't overlap. The result looks like this:

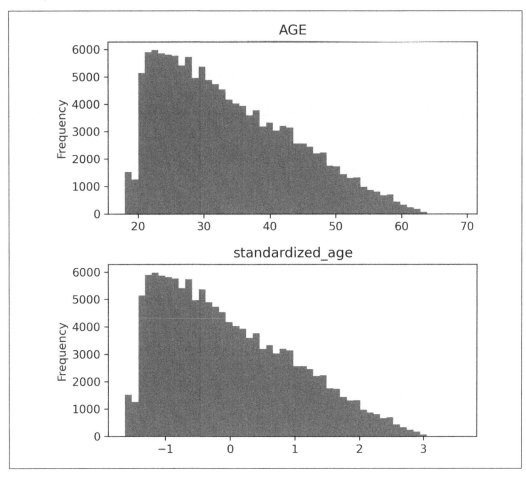

Figure 10.7: Histograms of AGE before and after standardization

We can see that the shape is the same, and only the *x*-axis scale has changed. If we check the mean and standard deviation with `loan_df['standardized_age'].describe()`, we can see that the mean is essentially 0 and the standard deviation is 1.

There are other normalization and transformation classes available in `sklearn` through the `sklearn.preprocessing` module, as we will see with the Yeo-Johnson transform.

Making data more Gaussian with the Yeo-Johnson transform

For some ML algorithms such as **linear discriminant analysis (LDA)**, there is an assumption that the distribution of the data or targets is Gaussian. For example, linear and logistic regression assume this for continuous data used in those algorithms. We can also get small boosts in performance for distance-based algorithms, such as clustering, *k*-nearest neighbors, and SVMs. Although we can manually try different transforms, like squaring our data, taking the square root or logarithm, and so on, it's easier to let an algorithm do the work for us. We can easily transform data to a more Gaussian form with `sklearn`:

```
from sklearn.preprocessing import PowerTransformer

pt = PowerTransformer()

loan_df['xform_age'] = pt.fit_transform(loan_df['AGE'].values.reshape(-1, 1))

f, ax = plt.subplots(2, 1)
loan_df['AGE'].plot.hist(ax=ax[0], title='AGE', bins=50)
loan_df['xform_age'].plot.hist(ax=ax[1], title='xform_age', bins=50)
plt.tight_layout()
```

We can see that this is very similar to `StandardScaler`. We first import the class and then create a new `PowerTransformer` class instance. Then we fit it to the `AGE` data and transform it. Again, we need to reshape our data to have a single column for the transformer. This transformation fits a parameter, lambda, which controls the transformation of the data. This lambda value can be any real number (essentially any number from negative infinity to positive infinity) and produces different transforms of the data. Using some complex math, it optimizes this lambda parameter so that the data most closely resembles a normal distribution.

After we've completed the transform, we can again plot histograms of the before and after data to compare:

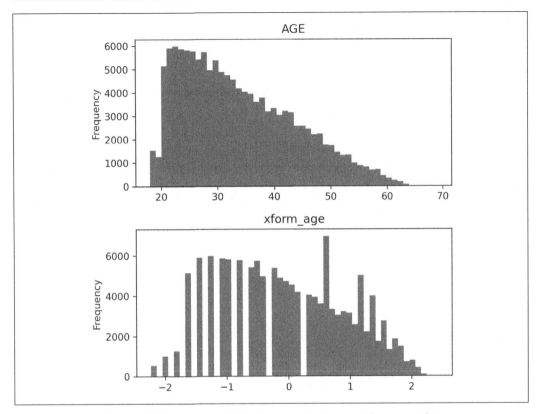

Figure 10.8: Histograms of AGE before and after the Yeo-Johnson transform

We can see that our transformed distribution is a little closer to a normal distribution, although it's not perfect. The `PowerTransformer()` class, by default, uses the Yeo-Johnson transform and standardizes our data. We can change these settings if we want with arguments when we initialize the class. The other option for transforming is the Box-Cox transformation by setting the `method='box-cox'` argument. The problem with Box-Cox is that it only works with positive input values, whereas Yeo-Johnson can work with negative values. We can also turn off standardization with the `standardize=False` argument, although if we are already transforming the data with Yeo-Johnson, we might as well have the transformer standardize the data too.

If we want to transform more data later, we can always do so with the `transform` method of our fitted transformer:

```
pt.transform(loan_df['AGE'].values.reshape(-1, 1))
```

We can, of course, save this object for later use by using `pickle`:

```
import pickle as pk

with open('age_pt.pk', 'wb') as f:
    pk.dump(pt, f)
```

Then, if we want to use it again, we simply load it and apply the transform method to new data.

Extracting datetime features

We have already seen that if we have a difference between dates, we can extract days and seconds from it:

```
loan_df['DISBURSAL_DATE'] - loan_df['DATE_OF_BIRTH']).dt.days
```

We can also extract other useful information from datetimes. For example, we may suspect that the day of the week the loan was disbursed on could be related to default probabilities. We can extract the day of the week like so:

```
loan_df['DISBURSAL_DATE'].dt.dayofweek
```

This returns integers, with 0 representing Monday, and 6 for Sunday. Again, we use the `dt` datetime accessor with our pandas series, and then provide the datetime property we want to access. Among the other properties we can extract are the following:

- `year`
- `month`
- `day`
- `hour`
- `minute`
- `second`
- `microsecond`
- `nanosecond`

- dayofyear
- weekofyear
- quarter

Another strategy for feature engineering datetimes is to calculate date spans, as we did to calculate the age of customers.

Binning

As we learned, a larger dimension of features can be problematic (the curse of dimensionality). One way to reduce the size of our feature space is to bin numeric data. Instead of having a large numeric range, we can group values into bins. The `sklearn` package has a built-in class for doing just that:

```
from sklearn.preprocessing import KBinsDiscretizer

kbd = KBinsDiscretizer(n_bins=10, encode='ordinal')
loan_df['binned_disbursed_amount'] = kbd.fit_transform(
    loan_df['DISBURSED_AMOUNT'].values.reshape(-1, 1)).\
    astype('int')
```

Here, we import the binning class from the `sklearn.preprocessing` module. Then we initialize a new class in the `kbd` variable. We choose to use 10 bins and will encode the output as values from 0 to 9. The default encoding is one-hot encoding, which we will learn about next. This ordinal encoding returns a number for the bins, with the smallest number corresponding to the bin with the smallest values, and the largest number (9, here) corresponding to the largest values, and this is returned as a single feature. As with other preprocessors, we use the `fit_transform()` method and need to reshape our data to be 2D. We also convert the datatype to an integer, since it returns a float. Float datatypes take up a little extra memory, so this is a minor optimization.

The default method to break up data into bins is to use quantiles, set by the argument `strategy='quantile'` in the `KBinsDiscretizer` class initialization. This means the data is split into equal fractions by counts of data points from the least to the greatest. There are a few other options (`uniform` and `kmeans`), but `quantile` is often going to be the best choice.

This `ordinal` encoding method gives us only one new feature that we can use to replace our continuous values with. If we use one-hot encoding, we will end up with a new feature or column for each unique bin. This would defeat the purpose of reducing dimensionality, although for a small number of bins, it can work. Next, we'll look at how label encoding and one-hot encoding work in more depth.

One-hot encoding and label encoding

Let's first look at label encoding. This is where we transform categorical values into numbers. The simplest example is mapping a binary variable onto the numbers 0 and 1. We can see from our EDA that the EMPLOYMENT_TYPE feature is only "Salaried," "Self employed," and missing values. We'll fill the missing values with the mode (Self employed), and then convert these to a 1 for "Self employed" and 0 for "Salaried":

```
loan_df['EMPLOYMENT_TYPE'].fillna('Self employed', inplace=True)
loan_df['EMPLOYMENT_TYPE'] = \
    loan_df['EMPLOYMENT_TYPE'].\
    map(lambda x: 1 if x == 'Self employed' else 0)
loan_df['EMPLOYMENT_TYPE'] = loan_df['EMPLOYMENT_TYPE'].astype('int')
```

The first line simply fills in missing values with the mode (the most common value). Then we use the map() function of pandas series and DataFrames with a lambda function to return 1 if the EMPLOYMENT_TYPE is "Self employed" and 0 otherwise. Finally, we convert this column to an integer datatype since it is still an object datatype that takes up much more memory (and will be treated differently by ML algorithms). By checking the unique values before and after conversion with loan_df['EMPLOYMENT_TYPE'].unique(), we can see that we've converted from strings to integers.

When we have more than two unique values, we can instead assign a number for each value. Again, sklearn has a convenient class for this:

```
from sklearn.preprocessing import LabelEncoder

le = LabelEncoder()
loan_df['le_branch_id'] = le.fit_transform(loan_df['BRANCH_ID'])
```

Like other preprocessors, we import it and create a new instance of the class. We then use the fit_transform method, which assigns a unique integer for each unique item or category in our data. Notice that we don't need to reshape the data here. This returns a NumPy array that looks like this:

```
array([ 2, 34,  4, ...,  2, 24,  1], dtype=int64)
```

We can see the maximum number of categories by looking at the shape of the unique value from the original data, with loan_df['BRANCH_ID'].unique().shape (which is 82). Or, we can look at the maximum value of the encoded data, which shows 81, since the label encoder starts at 0 (since Python is 0-indexed). If we want to get back the original values from encoded values, we can use the inverse_transform method of our encoder.

Simplifying categorical columns

When we have several values for a categorical column, we can reduce the feature space size by grouping the minority values into an "other" column. For example, let's take a look at the top categories for the MANUFACTURER_ID feature and decide which to keep, and which to put in the "other" category:

```
loan_df['MANUFACTURER_ID'].value_counts()
```

This shows us:

```
86      62507
45      32389
51      15395
48       9641
49       5831
120      5512
67       1416
145       450
153         9
152         4
Name: MANUFACTURER_ID, dtype: int64
```

We can see that the top few groups contain the majority of the data. Let's plot it to see whether we can decide on how many groups to keep:

```
(loan_df['MANUFACTURER_ID'].value_counts().cumsum() / \
    loan_df.shape[0]).reset_index(drop=True).\
    plot(marker='.', figsize=(5.5, 5.5))
plt.xlabel('MANUFACTURER_ID')
plt.ylabel('cumulative percent of values')
plt.xticks(range(loan_df['MANUFACTURER_ID'].unique().shape[0]), \
            loan_df['MANUFACTURER_ID'].value_counts().index)
```

We are combining several commands in the first line. We first get the value counts, and then take the cumulative sum of them. Then we divide this by the number of rows to get the cumulative percentage of the data for each unique value. We then reset the index so that the plotting will work properly (otherwise the index values are the actual IDs), and drop the ID index column resulting from this with drop=True. Finally, we plot it and display points with the marker='.' argument.

We also add *x*- and *y*-axis labels for readability and set the *x* tick labels to be the actual manufacturer IDs for better readability. Our plot looks like this:

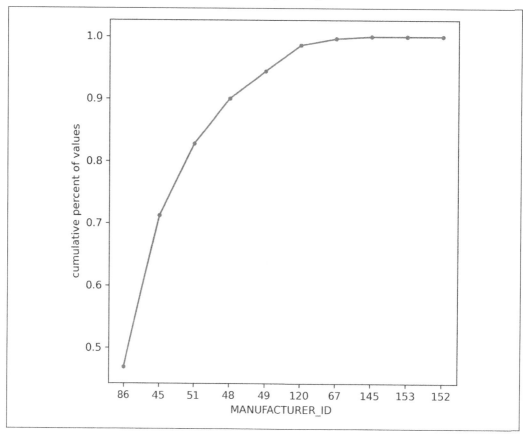

Figure 10.9: Cumulate percentage of MANUFACTURER_ID unique values, from the most prevalent to the least

With a plot like this, we are looking for an "elbow," where the increase in cumulative percent starts to flatten out. We can see at the fourth unique ID with the most value counts (48), we have captured 90% of the values and the slope of the line begins to decrease. We also see at the ID of 120 that we are near 99% of all values and the slope decreases drastically. This ID==120 elbow is the better choice for a flattening of the slope, although the more categories we keep, the bigger our feature space will be. We will choose ID==120 as our elbow in the plot and put the other IDs into the "other" category. This can be accomplished in a few ways. One is to filter by excluding the top categories:

```
loan_df.loc[~loan_df['MANUFACTURER_ID'].isin([86, 45, 51, 48, 49, 120]), \
            'MANUFACTURER_ID'] = 'other'
```

We use the tilde character (~) at the beginning of the filter clause in our `.loc[]` indexer to negate the condition. So, this line will filter the `MANUFACTURER_ID` column of `loan_df` where the values are *not* in the list provided. The other way would be to choose the IDs we want to set to `other`:

```
loan_df.loc[loan_df['MANUFACTURER_ID'].isin([67, 145, 153, 152]), \
            'MANUFACTURER_ID'] = 'other'
```

Both achieve the same outcome. The `loc` indexer allows us to select rows by filtering for those rows where the manufacturer ID is in the top four we identified by value counts. Then we select `MANUFACTURER_ID` as the column in `loc[]`. This allows us to set these values to a new value, which we provide as `'other'`.

Although we could have one-hot encoded our manufacturer IDs without doing this step, this will help to keep our dimensions smaller. Next, we will look at how to one-hot encode our manufacturer IDs.

One-hot encoding

One-hot encoding takes a categorical variable and creates a new column for each unique value. Each new column is composed of binary values (1s or 0s), signifying whether that row has that categorical value. For example, our first row has 51 for the manufacturer ID, so we could create a one-hot encoding column called `manu_ID=51`. This column would be 1 for the first row. Other manufacturer ID one-hot-encoded columns, such as `manu_ID=45`, would be 0. Although there is a one-hot-encoder class in `sklearn.preprocessing`, the pandas function `get_dummies()` is much easier to use. One-hot encoded variables are also called dummy variables, which is where the name for the function comes from. We can use it to get a one-hot-encoded DataFrame like so:

```
manufacturer_ohe = pd.get_dummies(
    loan_df['MANUFACTURER_ID'],
    prefix='MANU_ID',
    prefix_sep='='
).drop(['MANU_ID=other'], axis=1)
```

We provide the data we want to dummy or one-hot encode as the first argument and provide a prefix and separator between the prefix and the category labels (`prefix_sep`) to use for column names. This results in patterns for column names such as `MANU_ID=45` here. Lastly, we drop the `other` column. If all the other one-hot-encoded columns are 0, we can infer it is the `other` category. We could drop one of the one-hot-encoded columns for this reason.

However, sometimes it can be helpful to keep all one-hot-encoded variables so that we can get information from ML algorithms about each one. The `manufacturer_ohe` DataFrame we have now looks like this:

	MANU_ID=45	MANU_ID=48	MANU_ID=49	MANU_ID=51	MANU_ID=86	MANU_ID=120
0	0	0	0	1	0	0
1	1	0	0	0	0	0
2	0	0	0	1	0	0
3	0	0	0	0	1	0
4	1	0	0	0	0	0
...	...	...	...	...	...	...
133149	1	0	0	0	0	0
133150	0	0	1	0	0	0
133151	0	0	0	1	0	0
133152	1	0	0	0	0	0
133153	0	0	0	1	0	0

Figure 10.10: A one-hot-encoded DataFrame from the MANUFACTURER_ID top unique values

We can see it's simply a set of binary values for our unique manufacturer IDs. We can then combine it with our original data like so:

```
loan_df_ohe = pd.concat([loan_df, manufacturer_ohe], axis=1)
```

We can use one-hot encoding to prepare categorical data so that it can be used in `sklearn`. However, we should be cautious to not increase our feature size too much (recall the curse of dimensionality). One-hot encoding is a useful tool, but be careful not to overuse it.

Dimensionality reduction

One last subject we'll examine is dimensionality reduction. Another way to combat the curse of dimensionality is to reduce the size of our dimensions with mathematical techniques. There are several:

- **Principle Component Analysis (PCA)**
- **Singular Value Decomposition (SVD**, sometimes also called LSA)
- **Independent Component Analysis (ICA)**

- **Non-Negative Matrix Factorization** (NMF)

- t-SNE and UMAP (better for non-linear structures, like natural language and images)

- Autoencoders (a neural network technique that ends up being similar to PCA)

Covering all these methods is beyond the scope of this book, and we will only explore PCA. However, many other ML and feature engineering books cover these methods, such as *Building Machine Learning Systems with Python – Third Edition*, by Luis Pedro Coelho, Willi Richert, and Matthieu Brucher from Packt (which has an entire chapter on dimensionality reduction). Let's take a look at PCA.

Principle Component Analysis (PCA)

PCA is a common and easy-to-use dimension reduction technique. It finds dimensions among our feature space that capture the most variance and breaks our data up into those components. The components are made of linear combinations of our features, so it's easy to apply the transformation to new data or to take the inverse transform of PCA-transformed data. Some people consider PCA to be an unsupervised learning technique, but it is often used for dimensionality reduction. We can easily use it with `sklearn` like so:

```
from sklearn.decomposition import PCA

ss = StandardScaler()
scaled = ss.fit_transform(loan_df_epoch_time[interval_columns])

pca = PCA(random_state=42)
loan_pca = pca.fit_transform(scaled)
```

The dimensionality reduction classes and techniques are found in the `sklearn.decomposition` module. Before we use PCA, we should usually standardize our data to have mean 0 and variance 1 (unit variance) as we did here with `StandardScaler`. This should be done when we have features that are in different units, such as here where we have costs, datetimes (in seconds), credit scores, and more. If we have data where all the features are in the same units, we might leave the data as is.

Once we have our data standardized, we first initialize a new instance of the class, setting the `random_state` argument. When this `random_state` argument is available in functions, it's a good idea to set it for reproducible results. Then we use the `fit_transform` method we've seen before, providing it with a NumPy array of data (which is how pandas stores its data).

This function can only take numeric data, so we select our scaled interval (continuous) columns from earlier in the chapter from our DataFrame where the datetimes have been converted to seconds since the epoch. From this, we can then plot the explained variance ratio and feature importance for the most important PCA component:

```
idx = pca.explained_variance_ratio_.argsort()[::-1]
ticks = range(pca.n_components_)

f, ax = plt.subplots(1, 2)

ax[0].barh(ticks, pca.explained_variance_ratio_[idx])
ax[0].set_title('explained variance ratio')
ax[0].set_ylabel('pca component')
ax[0].set_yticks(ticks)

comp_idx = abs(pca.components_[0]).argsort()[::-1]
ax[1].barh(ticks, abs(pca.components_[0, comp_idx]))
plt.yticks(ticks, np.array(interval_columns)[comp_idx])
ax[1].set_title('PCA dim-0 components')

plt.tight_layout()
```

The first line uses NumPy's array `argsort` method to get the indices of the sorted array (from least to greatest). We reverse this so that we have the indices from greatest to least with indexing: `[::-1]`.

The `explained_variance_ratio_` property of our `pca` object holds the percentages of explained variance for each PCA component, and sums to 1. The next line simply creates *x*-axis ticks for our bar plots based on the number of features.

Then we create our plot using `plt.subplots`. The first two arguments are the number of rows and columns for our subplots. It returns the `figure` object, which we store in `f`, and the axes objects, stored in `ax`. We can then get the first row's subplot with `ax[0]`. We create the bar plot of explained variance ratios using our greatest-to-least sorted index variable, `idx`. We can index NumPy arrays with a list of values or an array like this (but not Python lists). Then we set the title and *x* axis label for better readability.

Next, we get the absolute value (with the built-in `abs()` function) of the coefficients for each of the features for the first PCA dimension. This is the PCA dimension that explains the biggest amount of variance in the data, so it is the most important to examine first. We again use `argsort` and reverse this with `[::-1]` indexing. This gives us the index values for the first PCA component's feature importances, sorted from greatest to least. We then use that to index the `components_` property of our `pca` object for our bar plot on the second subplot (which is on the second, or bottom, row), `ax[1]`.

> To create subplots in a grid, we can use `f, ax = plt.subplots(2, 2)`. This creates two rows and two columns. We then access the axes with `ax[0][0]` for the upper-left (first row, first column) subplot. We could use this to plot feature importances for the first three PCA dimensions along with the explained variance ratio.

Next, we set the *x*-axis tick labels with `plt.xticks` so that the labels will be the feature names. This `xticks` function takes the tick locations as the first argument and the new labels as the second argument. We convert our `interval_columns` list to a NumPy array so we can index it with our sorted index, `comp_idx`.

Then we also rotate the labels by 90 degrees so that they are readable. Finally, we set the title for this second subplot and use `tight_layout()` to make sure all the figure components are visible and not overlapping. Our result looks like this:

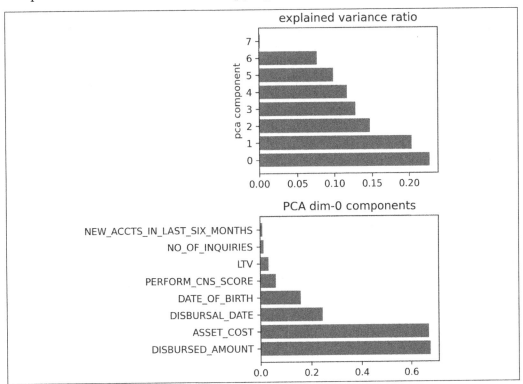

Figure 10.11: Explained variance ratio of the PCA components and feature weights for PCA component 0

From this, we can see the first PCA dimension makes up a little over 20% of the variance in the data, closely followed by the second PCA dimension with around 20% explained variance. We see that this first PCA dimension is mainly composed of the disbursed amount and asset cost. Looking back at our initial EDA, we can see that these two columns are actually strongly correlated. As mentioned earlier, we may only want to keep one of these columns since they are strongly correlated. Beyond these first two important features, we see that the rest of the features have much smaller coefficients, meaning they are less important in this first PCA dimension.

Once we have our transformed PCA data (`loan_pca`), we can access the PCA components with the column indexer. For example, if we wanted to select only the first two PCA components, we would use `loan_pca[:, :2]`.

This selects all rows with the first colon, and then selects the first column up to the second column (an index of 1) with `:2`. We can use PCA to reduce our dimension size, but choosing the number of PCA dimensions to keep depends on your application. For ML, we can try increasing numbers of PCA dimensions and see how it affects the performance of our algorithms (for example, we could examine the accuracy of predictions from an ML algorithm). Once our accuracy reaches a plateau, we might stop adding PCA dimensions. There are other methods for determining the number of important PCA components, which are heuristics and should not be blindly relied upon. Many of these are described in a paper by Cangelosi and Goriely here: `https://biologydirect.biomedcentral.com/articles/10.1186/1745-6150-2-2`. In our case above, the only PCA component we might not use would be the last one, since the explained variance is very low. So, we could reduce our dimensionality by one.

This wraps up our feature engineering part of the book. There are even more ways to do feature engineering and several books on the subject. One you may enjoy is *Python Feature Engineering Cookbook,* by Soledad Galli, from Packt. Although we looked at basic feature selection and engineering here, we will also look at how to do feature selection using ML algorithms in the coming chapters.

Test your knowledge

We learned a lot of feature selection and engineering techniques here. To practice some of these, use the same loans dataset with the LOAN_DEFAULT column as the target variable, and perform the following:

- Plot the ANOVA F-scores and p-values for the numeric features.

- Evaluate the STATE_ID feature and decide on the number of top state IDs to keep. Put all other state IDs in an other column, and then one-hot encode this feature. Finally, join it together with your original loan DataFrame.

- Extract the day of week from the DISBURSAL_DATE feature and check the phi-k correlation. Comment on the strength of the correlation and if this new feature should be used.

As always, write some analysis explaining and interpreting the results.

Using another loan default dataset (the "default of credit card clients.xls" file in the GitHub repository for the book under Chapter10/test_your_knowledge/data), perform PCA and examine the explained variance ratio of the PCA components. Decide on how many PCA components you might keep for further analysis, such as ML. Don't use the default payment next month column, which is the target.

This data comes from the UCI ML repository: https://archive.ics.uci.edu/ml/datasets/default+of+credit+card+clients.

Summary

In this chapter, we covered the basics of feature selection and feature engineering. We also covered some basic feature cleaning and preparation steps, such as converting strings to dates and checking for and cleaning outliers. We ended with a dimensionality reduction technique known as **Principal Component Analysis (PCA)**, which can be used to linearly combine features into PCA dimensions we can use for later analysis.

The chapter began by introducing the three main types of ML: supervised, unsupervised, and reinforcement learning. Then we learned why it's important to prune down our features: the curse of dimensionality and overfitting. When we have a lot of features, this can lead to problems, including ML model overfitting (with supervised learning), where the model fits to noise in the data. Feature selection can be used to remove some features and reduce this chance for overfitting, as well as making our models run faster. We saw several ways to undergo feature selection and focused on variance-based methods (removing features with too much or too little variance) and univariate statistics screening methods. Of these statistics methods, phi-k correlation is a good choice, although it can take a while to run on larger datasets.

Within feature engineering, we covered combining columns (like taking the difference between two datetime columns), numeric transforms, such as standardization, and the Yeo-Johnson transform, extracting features from datetime columns, such as the day of the week, and encoding categorical values as numbers with label encoding and one-hot encoding. These techniques can be used to create new features that we can use in ML models to try and improve performance.

Now that we have an idea of how and why to select and engineer features, let's look at actually using them in supervised ML algorithms for classification in the next chapter.

11

Machine Learning for Classification

Once our data has been prepared with some cleaning, feature selection, and feature engineering, we can begin using machine learning algorithms. As we saw in the previous chapter, machine learning falls into three broad categories: supervised, unsupervised, and reinforcement learning. Classification falls under supervised learning, since we have targets or labels in our data. For example, we will look at a credit card loan default dataset here first. This dataset has labels for each data point, indicating whether someone defaulted on a credit card payment.

We will learn the basics of classification with machine learning in this chapter using the `sklearn` and `statsmodels` packages. In this chapter, we'll cover the following topics:

- Machine learning classification algorithms for binary and multi-class classification
- Using machine learning classification algorithms for feature selection

Let's begin by covering some of the basic machine learning classification algorithms.

Machine learning classification algorithms

There are many machine learning algorithms, and new algorithms are being created all the time. Machine learning algorithms take input data and learn, fit, or train during a training phase. Then we use the statistical patterns learned from the data to make predictions during what is called "inference." We will cover some of the basic and simple classification algorithms here:

- Logistic regression
- Naïve Bayes
- *k*-nearest neighbors (KNN)

The idea with these algorithms is that we give them labeled training data. This means that we have our features (inputs) and a target or label (output). The target should be a class, which could be binary (1 or 0) or multiclass (0 through the number of classes). The numbers 0 and 1 (and others for multiclass classification) for the target correspond to our different classes. For binary classification, this can be something like a payment default, approval to take a loan, whether someone will click an ad online, or whether someone has a disease. For multiclass classification, this might be something like a budget category for payments from your bank account, the breed of a dog, or the emotion classification from a social media post (for example, sad, happy, angry, or scared). Our inputs, or features, should have some relationship with the target. For example, we might be interested in someone's annual income and length of tenure at their current job if we are predicting if they will default on a loan. Although there are many classification algorithms, we'll begin with logistic regression.

Logistic regression for binary classification

Logistic regression has been around for a while – since 1958. But don't let its age fool you; sometimes the simplest algorithms can outperform more complex algorithms, such as neural networks. Logistic regression is primarily used for binary classification, although it can be used for multi-class classification as well. It's part of a group of models called generalized linear models (GLMs), that also includes linear regression, which we'll talk about in *Chapter 13, Machine Learning with Regression*. In some Python packages, such as statsmodels, logistic regression can be implemented through a GLM class.

We will learn logistic regression by using it with a credit card defaults dataset (from here: `https://www.kaggle.com/uciml/default-of-credit-card-clients-dataset`, also available in the GitHub repository for the book). The Kaggle data page for the dataset provides descriptions of the different columns in the dataset. There are features for 6 months of data from April to August in 2005. The PAY columns (like PAY_0) contain data on whether the payment was late for that month. The PAY_0 column is for payment for August 2005, the latest month in the dataset. Other columns, such as BILL_AMT and PAY_AMT, contain the amount of the bill and payment for the 6 months in the dataset. Other columns should be self-explanatory from the column title. Let's start by loading the data and running pandas profiling for EDA:

```
import pandas as pd
from pandas_profiling import ProfileReport

df = pd.read_excel('data/default of credit card clients.xls',
                   skiprows=1,
                   index_col=0)
report = ProfileReport(df, interactions=None)
report.to_file('cc_defaults.html')
```

As in the previous chapter, you might sample down the data (`df = df.sample(10000, random_state=42)`) in order to get the code running faster or if your computer is not very powerful. We set `interactions=None` in `ProfileReport` because that part of the EDA report takes a long time to run.

Our target variable that we will be predicting is the "default payment next month" column, and all other columns will be features. We can see from looking at the correlations (for example, with `df.corr().loc['default payment next month']`) that some of the features have a relationship to the target – the Pearson correlation is around 0.1-0.3 for a handful of features, and the PAY features have a phik correlation around 0.5 with the target. We won't do any data cleaning, feature selection, or feature engineering yet. We can see from `df.info()` that there aren't any missing values. Both the `sklearn` and `statsmodels` implementations of logistic regression cannot handle missing values, so missing values need to be dealt with before using the model.

To fit the logistic regression model, we need a set of training data broken down into features and targets. We can create our features and targets like so:

```
train_features = df.drop('default payment next month', axis=1)
train_targets = df['default payment next month']
```

The first line drops the target column, keeping all other columns as features, and the second column only keeps the target column in the `train_targets` variable. Let's use the `sklearn` logistic regression implementation first:

```
from sklearn.linear_model import LogisticRegression

lr_sklearn = LogisticRegression(random_state=42)
lr_sklearn.fit(train_features, train_targets)
```

All `sklearn` models work similarly. We first import the model class (`LogisticRegression` here), and then instantiate it (the second line of code here). When we create the model object, we can provide arguments to the class. For many models, there is a `random_state` argument, which sets the random seed for random processes. This will make our results reproducible if there are any random processes in the algorithm. We have other arguments we can set, although we aren't doing that yet. Once we have our initialized model object, we can train it on our data using the `fit()` method. This is where the "machine learning" part comes in – the model (machine) is learning from the data we give it. You will see that there is a warning emitted when we run this code, talking about iterations reaching their limit. We will explain more about what this means soon.

Once the model has fit to our training data, we can evaluate its performance on the same data easily:

```
lr_sklearn.score(train_features, train_targets)
```

The `score()` method of trained models calculates a default scoring metric. For classification algorithms such as logistic regression, this is usually accuracy, which is the number of correct predictions divided by the total number of data points. The `score()` method returns 0.7788 here, so our accuracy is around 78%. To understand if that's any good, it helps to compare it to the majority class fraction, which we can find from `train targets.value_counts(normalize=True)`. This shows us that the class of 0 is 0.7788, so our model is doing no better than guessing that everything is a "no default" label.

Getting predictions from our model

With our trained model, we can also predict values for our target from input data. For example, we can predict the last value in the training set like so:

```
predictions = lr_sklearn.predict(train_features)
```

The data we give the `predict()` method must be a 2D array, so if we only predict a single data point, we reshape it to be a 2D array with a single row:

```
lr_sklearn.predict(train_features.iloc[-1].values.reshape(1, -1))
```

The `predict` function returns a NumPy array of values for class labels. For binary classification, this consists of 0s and 1s. If there are more than two classes, we will have 0 through n-1 for the number of classes.

Instead of getting the exact class predictions, we can get probabilities for all the predictions with `predict_proba`:

```
lr_sklearn.predict_proba(train_features)
```

This returns a NumPy array with c columns (for c classes) and n rows for n data points. With our data, it looks like this:

```
array([[0.54130993, 0.45869007],
       [0.65880948, 0.34119052],
       [0.65864275, 0.34135725],
       ...,
       [0.59329928, 0.40670072],
       [0.97733622, 0.02266378],
       [0.6078195, 0.3921805 ]])
```

The first row shows the probability of class 0 is 0.54 (54%), and for class 1 is 0.46. These probabilities sum to one for each row. We can use the probabilities to choose a threshold for rounding our predictions. For example, the default threshold is `>=0.5`. In other words, we are selecting the probabilities that each data point is 1 (the second column), and then rounding it like so:

```
proba_predictions = lr_sklearn.predict_proba(train_features)[:, 1]
proba_predictions = (proba_predictions >= 0.5).astype('int')
```

The `proba_predictions >= 0.5` statement creates a Boolean array, so we convert it back to an integer with `astype('int')`. Then we can check if this is equal to the `predict` method with:

```
predictions = lr_sklearn.predict(train_features)
np.array_equal(predictions, np.round(proba_predictions))
```

which returns `True` from the second line.

How logistic regression works

Let's take a look at how the logistic regression algorithm works. The algorithm is defined by the equation:

$$p(y = 1) = \frac{1}{1 + e^{-(b_0 + b_1 x_1 + \cdots + b_n x_n)}}$$

We are calculating the probability that y is 1 ($p(y=1)$), using our different features (x_1 through x_n) to carry out this calculation. We have Euler's number (e) in the equation, as well as coefficients b_0 through b_n. This equation is also called a sigmoid function or sigmoid curve, because it makes a characteristic s shape, as we can see in the following figure:

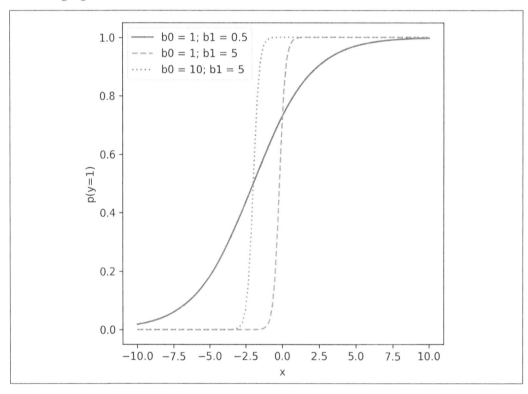

Figure 11.1: Three examples of the sigmoid curve with different parameters

In the first curve (the solid line), our y-intercept (b_0) is 1 and our first feature coefficient (b_1) is 0.5. The intercept term controls the value of y when it crosses the x axis. A larger intercept value means the sigmoid curve shifts left, as we can see in the figure with the dotted line where b_0=10. When the feature coefficient changes from b_1=0.5 to b_1=5, we can see that the sigmoid curve steepens. We can access these coefficients from the `sklearn` model with the `intercept_` and `coef_` attributes:

```
lr_sklearn.intercept_
lr_sklearn.coef_
```

These show us the intercept from our fit is -2E-5 (-2 * 10^{-5}, the E here represents multiplication by 10 exponentiated to a power, not Euler's number) and the coefficients range from 4E-7 to 7E-4. To understand more about how these coefficients relate to the target variable, let's look at the odds ratio and log-odds ratio.

Odds ratio and the logit

The odds ratio is the ratio of the probability of a class divided by 1 minus that probability:

$$odds\ ratio = \frac{p}{1-p}$$

For our situation here, the target of 1 means a payment default. If we then take the natural logarithm (log base e) of this equation, we have the log-odds, or logit:

$$logit = \ln\left(\frac{p}{1-p}\right)$$

This is defined as equal to the coefficients term in logistic regression:

$$\ln\left(\frac{p}{1-p}\right) = b_0 + b_1 x_1 \ldots$$

This logit equation can be rearranged to the logistic regression equation we saw earlier. We can use this logit equation to describe what the coefficients mean. For example, we saw from the coef_ attribute of our logistic regression equation that the PAY_0 column had a coefficient of 5E-5. We can say that with all other variables held constant, a unit increase in PAY_0 means an increase of the log-odds of default risk of 5E-5. A more helpful way to think of this is with the odds ratio, which is Euler's number exponentiated to the coefficients ($e^{b_0 + b_1 x_1 + \cdots}$). When we exponentiate our coefficients with np.exp(lr_sklearn.coef_), we find the coefficient for the PAY_0 feature to be 1.00005073. We compare these exponentiated coefficients to the value of 1 as our baseline. A value of 1 means the feature and target have no relationship. Values greater than 1 mean the odds increase multiplicatively by e^{b1} for each unit increase in our feature, while values less than 1 mean the odds decrease multiplicatively for each unit increase in our feature. For PAY_0, this is the number of months someone was late on a payment for the most recent month in the dataset. Higher values of PAY_0 (later payments) mean a slightly higher odds ratio for default in the next month, which makes intuitive sense.

However, we can see that the coefficients are very small, and the odds ratios of the coefficients are all close to 1. To ascertain whether these coefficients are statistically significantly different from 0, we can use a statistical test that gives us p-values. To do that, we can use the `statsmodels` package. Before we go there, let's look at the feature importances with `sklearn` to understand which features seem most important for predicting the target.

Examining feature importances with sklearn

We can roughly estimate the importance of features by comparing the absolute value of the coefficients we find. We do need to scale our inputs before fitting the data with our model (if they are in different units), for example, with `StandardScaler`. A bigger coefficient means the feature is more "important" because it more strongly affects the prediction. It's important to scale the features prior to doing this so they are comparable (unless the features are all in the same units). We can scale our features, fit the logistic regression model, and plot the feature importances like so:

```
from sklearn.preprocessing import StandardScaler
import matplotlib.pyplot as plt

scaler = StandardScaler()
scaled_features = scaler.fit_transform(train_features)
scaled_lr_model = LogisticRegression(random_state=42)
scaled_lr_model.fit(scaled_features, train_targets)

logit_coef = np.exp(scaled_lr_model.coef_[0]) - 1
idx = abs(logit_coef).argsort()[::-1]
plt.bar(range(len(idx)), logit_coef[idx])
plt.xticks(range(len(idx)), train_features.columns[idx], rotation=90)
```

First, we import the scaler for standardizing the data and `matplotlib` for plotting. Then we scale the features and fit a logistic regression model to this data. We use the `coef_` attribute of the model, indexing the first row with `[0]`. The `coef_` array has rows containing coefficients for each target variable and columns for each feature. Since we only have one target variable, we only have one row. We exponentiate Euler's number (e) to the coefficient values with `np.exp()` in order to get the odds relationship to the target variable. We then subtract 1 from this value, since a value of 1 for the exponentiated coefficient means there is no relationship to the target. Values close to 0 in the `logit_coef` array then mean that there is little relationship between that feature and the target, and the farther away from 0 the values are, the more important the features to predicting the target.

Next, we use `argsort()` on the absolute values of our coefficients to get the index values, and then reverse this array with `[::-1]` so that our coefficient values will be greatest to least. Finally, we plot the odds coefficients and label them with the column names. Our resulting feature importances look like this:

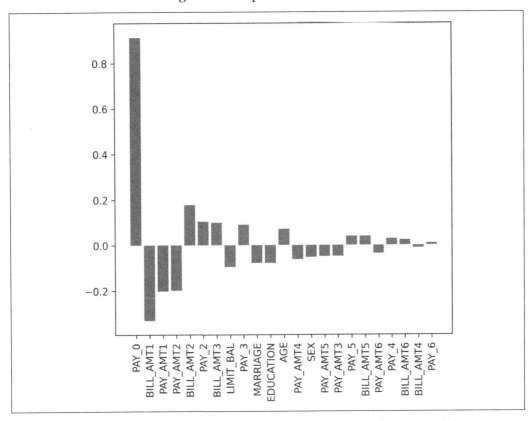

Figure 11.2: The feature importances from logistic regression of the credit card default dataset

We can see that the most important feature is PAY_0, which is the number of months late for the most recent month's payment in the dataset, with a positive relationship to the target. Some other features from recent months have a negative relationship to the target, meaning the larger the value, the smaller the chance of default. For PAY_0, this makes intuitive sense – if a customer is late on their most recent payment, they probably have a higher chance of not paying their bill next month. As we get beyond the LIMIT_BAL feature, our odds ratios for features become very close to 1 (0 in the plot above) for the most part. We can use these feature importances to prune away some features by removing those with small coefficients or low relative importance. Here, we might try removing everything from PAY_2 and smaller on the feature importance plot, since the coefficient for PAY_2 has a large jump down in importance from the BILL_AMT_2 feature.

This feature importance method can be useful for better understanding the data and performing feature selection, and we'll see how it relates to other algorithms as well. Another way to examine the significance of our coefficients is with a statistical test that gives us p-values.

Using statmodels for logistic regression

The `sklearn` package does not give us p-values, but the `statsmodels` implementation of logistic regression does. It uses a likelihood ratio test to calculate these p-values. Just like in *Chapter 9, Statistical Testing for Data Science*, we can compare these p-values to an alpha value (usually 0.05) to test for the significance of the result. If the p-value is less than 0.05, we can say that our null hypothesis is rejected. For logistic and linear regression, the null hypothesis is that the coefficients are no different from 0. So, if our p-values are less than 0.05 for coefficients, we can consider keeping those coefficients and throwing out other coefficients with large p-values. The `statsmodels` approach to modeling is slightly different, and works like so:

```
import statsmodels.api as sm
import numpy as np

np.random.seed(42)
lr_model = sm.Logit(train_targets, train_features)
lr_results = lr_model.fit()
lr_results.summary()
```

We first import the `statsmodels` package's `api` module with the alias `sm` – this is the convention and how it is demonstrated in the `statsmodels` documentation. Then we set a random seed with NumPy. We will see shortly how random processes are used with logistic regression, but remember we also set a random seed with the `sklearn` implementation. Next, we instantiate the `Logit` class from `statsmodels`, giving it the targets as a first argument, and features second. Then we call the `fit()` method of this object (`lr_model`), which is where the machine learning part happens. This returns a new object with the results of the training, or fitting, process. We can then examine the results with the `summary()` method of this new object, which looks like this:

Logit Regression Results

Dep. Variable:	default payment next month	No. Observations:	30000
Model:	Logit	Df Residuals:	29977
Method:	MLE	Df Model:	22
Date:	Sun, 21 Mar 2021	Pseudo R-squ.:	0.1197
Time:	20:06:29	Log-Likelihood:	-13955.
converged:	True	LL-Null:	-15853.
Covariance Type:	nonrobust	LLR p-value:	0.000

	coef	std err	z	P>|z|	[0.025	0.975]
LIMIT_BAL	-9.196e-07	1.55e-07	-5.927	0.000	-1.22e-06	-6.16e-07
SEX	-0.1963	0.027	-7.391	0.000	-0.248	-0.144
EDUCATION	-0.1383	0.020	-6.869	0.000	-0.178	-0.099
MARRIAGE	-0.2827	0.023	-12.438	0.000	-0.327	-0.238
AGE	0.0005	0.001	0.394	0.693	-0.002	0.003
PAY_0	0.5733	0.018	32.431	0.000	0.539	0.608
PAY_2	0.0801	0.020	3.971	0.000	0.041	0.120
PAY_3	0.0702	0.023	3.109	0.002	0.026	0.114
PAY_4	0.0243	0.025	0.972	0.331	-0.025	0.073
PAY_5	0.0337	0.027	1.255	0.209	-0.019	0.086
PAY_6	0.0096	0.022	0.436	0.663	-0.034	0.053

Figure 11.3: The results of summary() from a statsmodels logistic regression fit
(not all columns are shown since the report is long)

We are showing the top portion of the report here, and there are more rows displayed in the full report. At the top of the report are several details about the model and some diagnostics. On the left column at the top, we have our target variable listed as the dependent variable, the model type is shown (Logit), our method for finding the parameters is shown (MLE, or maximum likelihood estimation), the date and time of the fit, if our model converged (more on that shortly), and lastly, the covariance type used to calculate the other values for each coefficient, such as std err and z.

This covariance type can be changed with the argument `cov_type` in the `.fit()` method; for example, we can use `cov_type='HC0'` (other values for `cov_type` are listed in the documentation here: `https://www.statsmodels.org/stable/generated/statsmodels.regression.linear_model.OLSResults.get_robustcov_results.html`). It's fine to leave this as the default for most cases, and changing this setting is an advanced topic. It usually only slightly effects the standard error and confidence intervals for coefficients.

In the upper-right column of the results, we have the number of observations, the degrees of freedom for the residuals (difference between predictions and actual values), the degrees of freedom for the model (number of coefficients minus 1), and some metrics for the model. The first metric, pseudo R-squared, approaches 1.0 for a perfect model (that perfectly predicts the data) and approaches 0 for a model that does not have any predictive power (cannot predict better than always guessing the majority class). Often, this value will be small and can be used to compare multiple models. The next three metrics have to do with log-likelihood, which is an equation we will cover shortly. It measures how well our model fits the data, and bigger is better. The LL-Null term is the log-likelihood of the "null" model. The null model is where we only use an intercept term (constant) in our logistic regression. Lastly, the LLR p-value is the log-likelihood ratio statistical test. If our p-value is smaller than a chosen alpha value (again, we usually compare this to an alpha value of 0.05), then the LLR test tells us that our model is statistically significantly better than the null model.

There is also another summary function, `summary2()`. This shows most of the same information, but also includes AIC and BIC. These are **information criteria** (**IC**). AIC is the Akaike Information Criterion, and BIC is the Bayesian Information Criterion. Both are better when smaller and can be used to compare models on the same dataset. Smaller is always better for IC – IC have an additive penalty term for the number of features, so the same accuracy with fewer predictors will have smaller IC values.

Next, we have rows for each of our features (also called exogenous variables, independent variables, or covariates). The `coef` column shows the coefficient value for the logistic regression equation, followed by the standard error (an estimate of the standard deviation), a z-value from a Wald test, a p-value from the same test, and 95% confidence intervals (we expect the `coef` value to lie within these bounds 95% of the time when fitting to samples of the data). We can use the p-values to select features by only keeping features where $p < 0.05$:

```
selected_features = sm.add_constant(
    train_features).loc[:, lr_results.pvalues < 0.05]
lr_model_trimmed = sm.Logit(train_targets, selected_features)
lr_trimmed_results = lr_model_trimmed.fit()
lr_trimmed_results.summary()
```

First, we generate a pandas DataFrame for our `statsmodels`-ready features with `sm.add_constant(train_features)`. Then we select all rows and columns where the p-values are less than 0.05 with `loc`. We can fit the model and evaluate metrics with `summary()` and `summary2()`. From this, we see the performance of the model is nearly the same as the model with all features. So, we can use our model on fewer features (12 plus a constant term) instead of the model on the full set of features. If model performance is nearly the same with fewer features, it's better to choose the simpler model to minimize overfitting concerns and to minimize required resources.

With `statsmodels`, we have a `predict` function just like with `sklearn`. This can be used from our `results` object:

```
lr_trimmed_results.predict(selected_features)
```

It returns a pandas series of predicted probabilities that the class is 1. We can round this up based on a threshold like so:

```
predictions = (lr_trimmed_results.predict(
    selected_features) > 0.5).astype('int')
```

This will give us a pandas series of binary values that can be compared directly to the 0 and 1 targets. We can use this with metrics such as accuracy:

```
from sklearn.metrics import accuracy_score

accuracy_score(predictions, train_targets)
```

With many `sklearn` metrics like this one, we provide the true values as the first argument and predicted values as the second argument. However, it's always best to check the documentation to be sure. We find our accuracy is around 81% (0.8091), which is a little better than the `sklearn` model.

You may have noticed that the coefficients, as well as the accuracy score from the `sklearn` and `statsmodels` logistic regression models, are different. This primarily has to do with two settings: the optimization algorithm and regularization. To understand the optimization algorithm, let's look at how logistic regression finds its parameters.

Maximum likelihood estimation, optimizers, and the logistic regression algorithm

Logistic regression uses an iterative optimization process to calculate the coefficients for each feature and intercept. As we saw from `statsmodels`, it is also using something called maximum likelihood estimation, or MLE. This MLE process relies on a likelihood function, which we are trying to maximize. The likelihood function is the conditional probability of seeing the data given our parameters: $P(X|\theta)$, where X is an array of data and theta (θ) are our parameters (our coefficients, b_0, b_1, and so on). The logistic regression log-likelihood function is:

$$P(X|\theta) = \sum_{i=1}^{N} \log\left(\hat{y}_i\right) * (y_i) + \log\left(1 - \hat{y}_i\right) * (1 - y_i)$$

All this equation requires is the actual target values (y_i) and the predicted probability values (between 0 and 1) for y ($\hat{y}_i$, called y-hat). When a value is an estimate, often the "hat" is put on top of the symbol. Sometimes, y-hat will be written as t or p in the same equation. The big "E" symbol is a sum – we take the values of the equation for each data point (i=1 to N) and add them all up. This equation reaches a maximum (near 0) when the predictions are very close to the actual values and is always negative. Sometimes, the entire equation has a negative sign put in front of it so that the function is minimized at its optimum value. Minimizing a cost function is a common practice is mathematical optimization, which is why the log-likelihood is sometimes converted to **negative log-likelihood (NLL)**, which, somewhat confusingly, makes the NLL values positive. The "negative" in NLL is because we put a negative sign in front of the entire equation.

This equation is also called binary cross-entropy or log-loss, and is implemented in `sklearn` as `sklearn.metrics.log_loss()`. The `sklearn` documentation also has a short explanation of this concept here: `https://scikit-learn.org/stable/modules/model_evaluation.html#log-loss`. This loss function heavily penalizes confident (high predicted probability of an outcome) and wrong answers. It also penalizes predictions that are correct, but that have low confidence. So, if the true value of y is 1 and we predict a low probability near 0, we will get a large negative value for $\log(\hat{y}_i)$, making the value of our likelihood large. The log function is non-linear, so as our $\hat{y}_i$ value gets closer to 0, the $\log(\hat{y}_i)$ value approaches negative infinity in an exponential manner. We can visualize this using NumPy and matplotlib:

```
x = np.linspace(0.01, 1, 100)
y = np.log(x)
plt.plot(x, y)
plt.xlabel('x')
plt.ylabel('log(x)')
```

From this, we get the following plot:

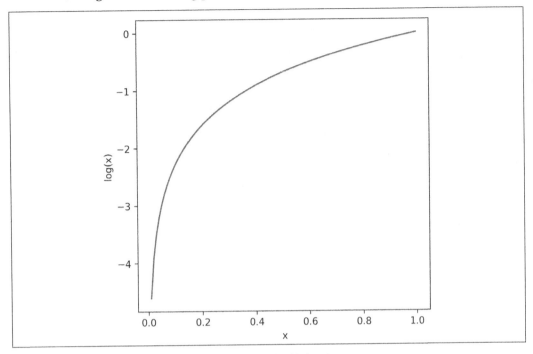

Figure 11.4. The log(x) function

Now that we have our log-likelihood or loss function, we can use it to fit our model with the logistic regression algorithm. To get the parameters (coefficients) for our logistic regression, we first initialize them to a value (for example, coefficients are initialized to 0 by default in `statsmodels`). Then we calculate predictions for our targets from the logistic regression equation and calculate the value of the likelihood function. Next, we change the parameters so that the likelihood function moves toward 0. We can do this with various optimizers. One that you will see with other algorithms (such as neural networks) is gradient descent. However, several other optimizers can be used. All of them change the parameters (coefficients) so that the log-likelihood function is optimized (maximized in our case, moving the log-likelihood value toward 0). Maximizing the log-likelihood function by changing parameters is like letting a balloon rise to the center of a dome if the balloon is our model and the dome is the likelihood surface over all possible parameters. The mathematics of the optimizers gets complex and we will not delve into it, but we can change these optimizers as a parameter of our `sklearn` and `statsmodels` functions. To recap, the logistic regression algorithm is:

- Initialize coefficients
- Predict target values (y-hat values for each data point)

- Compute the log-likelihood or loss function
- Use an optimizer to update the coefficients so that the loss function is optimized
- Repeat until the change in loss function is sufficiently small

With the `statsmodels` logistic regression `fit` method, the argument for the optimizer is `method`. By default, it's `newton` for the Newton-Raphson optimizer. We can also set a `maxiter` argument for the maximum number of iterations the optimizer will undergo. If we see a warning with `ConvergenceWarning: Maximum Likelihood optimization failed to converge.`, we can try other optimizers and/or increase the `maxiter` argument to see whether we can get the model to converge. These arguments should be set in the `fit()` method of `statsmodels` models like this:

```
lr_results = lr_model.fit(method='newton', maxiter=10)
```

With `sklearn` we can use the `newton-cg` method, which we specify with the `solver` argument. This is not exactly the same as the default Newton-Raphson method used in `statsmodels`, but is close. We also need to increase the `max_iter` argument so that the algorithm can converge:

```
lr_sklearn = LogisticRegression(solver='newton-cg', max_iter=1000)
lr_sklearn.fit(train_features, train_targets)
```

However, we still get warnings here about the line search algorithm (our optimizer) not converging. The coefficients are more similar to the `statsmodels` results, so it seems it came close to converging and there may be a bug or peculiarity in the `sklearn` code, causing these warnings to show up with `newton-cg`. We can see from `lr_sklearn.n_iter_` that 185 iterations were undertaken, less than our limit of 1000 – so it seems it should've converged. Interestingly, the `statsmodels` `newton` solver only takes 7 iterations to converge.

Another difference between the default logistic regression settings in `sklearn` and `statsmodels` is regularization.

Regularization

Regularization adds a penalty term to the log-likelihood function (also called our loss function). This penalty term moves the log-likelihood values further from 0 as coefficients get larger. There are three primary ways of enacting regularization with logistic regression: L1 (also called Lasso), L2 (also called Ridge), and Elastic Net (L1 + L2) regularization. Regularization prevents overfitting and gives us a dial to tune the bias-variance trade-off for our model.

For usual log-likelihood, L1 regularization subtracts the term $\lambda \sum |b|$, where $|b|$ is the absolute value of a coefficient and gamma (λ) is a constant value we choose. Some implementations use negative log-likelihood, and we flip all the signs (so the regularization term would be added instead of subtracted). As we saw earlier, bigger coefficients mean a feature has a bigger influence on the target. If we have a lot of big coefficients, we may be fitting to noise in the data rather than the actual patterns. With L1 regularization, some coefficients can be regularized down to 0, providing some feature selection for us.

L2 regularization uses the penalty term $\lambda \sum b^2$, which results in shrinking coefficients but not reducing them to 0. Elastic Net combines the two. When using regularization, it's important to scale our features since the penalty terms penalize the raw magnitude of the coefficients. The only exception to this, as with PCA and logistic regression feature importances, is if our features are in the same units – then we might consider not scaling them.

In `sklearn`, the `penalty` argument specifies the regularization method. By default, it uses L2 regularization. There is also a `C` argument, which is the inverse of the regularization strength – so a larger `C` value means less regulation. The documentation for the `LogisticRegression` class describes these parameters, and also states which solvers (optimizers) can be used with the different penalty terms (there are restrictions). If we set the value of `C` to a smaller number than the default of 1 and use L1 regularization, we can force some coefficients to be 0:

```
scaler = StandardScaler()
scaled_features = scaler.fit_transform(train_features)

lr_sklearn = LogisticRegression(penalty='l1', solver='liblinear', C=0.01)
lr_sklearn.fit(scaled_features, train_targets)
lr_sklearn.coef_
```

We first standardize the data in preparation with `StandardScaler` as we've done before, and then set the value of `C` to 0.01 for a strong regularization effect. After fitting the model, we can see that the `BILL_AMT` features 2-6 have been regularized to 0. We could consider dropping these features going forward, especially since they also had large p-values from the `statsmodels` results.

To use regularization with `statsmodels`, we use the `fit_regularized()` method of `Logit` objects:

```
scaled_features_df = pd.DataFrame(
    scaled_features,
    columns=train_features.columns,
    index=train_features.index
)
```

```
lr_model = sm.Logit(train_targets, sm.add_constant(scaled_features_df))
reg_results = lr_model.fit_regularized(alpha=100)
reg_results.summary()
```

First, we create a pandas DataFrame from our NumPy array of scaled data. We also need to set the column names when creating the DataFrame as well as the index. This is so that we will have the column names from our DataFrame in our summary report. The targets and features must have the same index if they are DataFrames or Series.

Once we create our model object, we fit it and specify the regularization strength with the `alpha` parameter. Larger values mean more regularization, and this is the same as 1/C from the `sklearn` model. These values may be somewhere around 0.001 to 100. Once we fit the model and examine the report, we can see that the same five features have been regularized to 0 – `BILL_AMT` features 2-6.

Regularization is a handy tool to prevent overfitting, but choosing the optimal `C` requires some iteration. We could do this with a `for` loop, but an easier way is to use pre-built cross-validation tools.

Hyperparameters and cross-validation

The `C` parameter in the `sklearn` logistic regression and the `alpha` value in the `statsmodels` implementation are called hyperparameters. These are settings for the model that we choose. By contrast, parameters are the coefficients that the model learns. This gets confusing because in Python programming, a parameter is also a setting we provide to a function or class, also called an argument. So, the `C` value is a parameter in Python programming parlance and a hyperparameter in machine learning terminology.

A major part of machine learning is optimizing hyperparameters, which we will learn about in more depth in *Chapter 14, Optimizing Models and Using AutoML*. For now, we can easily perform a hyperparameter search for the `C` parameter with the `LogisticRegressionCV` class in `sklearn`. This uses cross-validation, which breaks the data up into train and validation (or test) sets. For example, we could use 75% of our data for our model training and keep 25% as a validation set. We fit the model to the training set, and then calculate the accuracy or other metrics on the validation set. **Cross-validation** (**CV**) does this several times so that we train on and evaluate every part of the dataset as train and test. For example, we can use 3-fold cross-validation, which divides the data into thirds. We first fit to the first two-thirds of the data and evaluate the last third. Then we fit the model from scratch on the last two-thirds of the data and evaluate on the first third.

Finally, we train on the first and last thirds, and evaluate on the middle third. Then we average the scores obtained on the three validation sections to get our score for that hyperparameter setting. We can change the hyperparameter settings and repeat the CV process and keep the hyperparameter settings with the highest score. A diagram of the CV process is shown here:

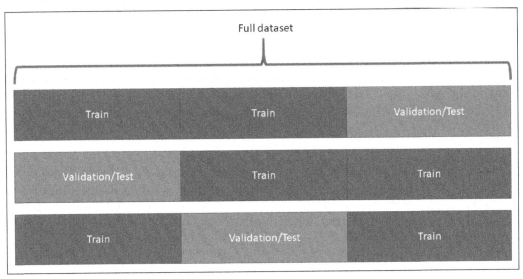

Figure 11.5: A diagram of cross-validation

As shown in the preceding diagram, we will obtain three validation scores, which we then average to get an overall cross-validation score on the dataset for one algorithm with one set of hyperparameters. We can perform this for a range of hyperparameters (for example, C values) and choose the hyperparameters with the best validation score.

For some models in sklearn such as logistic regression, this is made easy with a CV class. We can perform cross-validation on our data to find the optimal C value like so:

```
from sklearn.linear_model import LogisticRegressionCV

lr_cv = LogisticRegressionCV(Cs=[0.001, 0.01, 0.1, 1, 10, 100],
                             solver='liblinear',
                             penalty='l1',
                             n_jobs=-1,
                             random_state=42)
lr_cv.fit(scaled_features, train_targets)
```

First, we import the `LogisticRegressionCV` class. Then, we initialize it with several parameters: the list of C values we want to try (`Cs`), along with the `solver` and `penalty` arguments. We are using the L1 penalty here so that we may be able to remove some features. Since only the `liblinear` and `saga` solvers work with L1 (as described in the documentation for the `LogisticRegressionCV` class), we are specifying the `liblinear` solver. We also set the `n_jobs` parameter to -1, which tells `sklearn` to use all available CPU cores in parallel to run the cross-validation process. This is a common argument we will see in other `sklearn` functions. Lastly, we set `random_state`, which affects how the `liblinear` solver works and will provide more reproducible results. From this search, we find from the attribute `lr_cv.C_` that the best C value is 1. We can also look at the cross-validation scores with `lr_cv.scores_`. To get the average validation set score for each value of C, we can do the following:

```
lr_cv.scores_[1].mean(axis=0)
```

This returns an array the same length as our number of C values and shows us the score was around 81% (0.81) for the value of C=1. With CV, we could also optimize other hyperparameters and settings such as the regularization type (L1, L2, Elastic Net), but that requires a more advanced implementation of hyperparameter search, which we'll cover in *Chapter 14, Optimizing Models and Using AutoML*.

Logistic regression (and other models) with big data

Often, we'll find that we may encounter big data in our work and need a way to deal with it. Both `sklearn` and `statsmodels` can be adapted to work with big data. For example, `statsmodels` has a `DistributedModel` class that could be used, though examples of how to use it are lacking. For `sklearn`, the `dask` Python package can be used (with an example here: `https://examples.dask.org/machine-learning/incremental.html`). However, one simple and quick fix (although not ideal) to dealing with big data is to sample the data down to something that can be handled on a single machine. But for actually using all the data, there are several other Python packages available that can perform logistic regression on big datasets:

- Vowpal Wabbit
- H2O
- TensorFlow
- Dask
- Spark (`pyspark`)

Of these packages, TensorFlow has the best documentation and most examples, but Dask has sufficient documentation as well. Vowpal Wabbit is the only package of the five listed above that doesn't have as many examples for deploying on the cloud.

H2O can also be used for logistic regression on a single machine or scale up to a cluster. A small example is shown in the code for this chapter on this book's GitHub repository. Some advantages of H2O for ML are that it can handle missing values and non-numeric values (for example, strings) gracefully. It also has convenience methods for plotting the feature importances from ML models (which H2O calls "variable importances").

Logistic regression has a page in H2O's documentation here, with examples in Python: `https://docs.h2o.ai/h2o/latest-stable/h2o-docs/data-science/glm.html#examples`.

However, the R documentation tends to be more organized and easier to read: `https://docs.h2o.ai/h2o/latest-stable/h2o-r/docs/reference/h2o.glm.html`.

Most, if not all, of the R and Python function names and arguments are the same with H2O.

Logistic regression is a good first model to use and learn because how the model works and its results are relatively easy to understand (compared with some other machine learning models). However, there are many other models for binary classification, and we'll look at a few more within `sklearn` now.

Naïve Bayes for binary classification

The Naïve Bayes classifier is an extension of Bayes' Law, which we saw in *Chapter 8, Probability, Distributions, and Sampling*. With the Naïve Bayes model, we predict the probability of a class by multiplying conditional probabilities along with the prior probability of each class, $P(y)$. The class is 0 or 1 in binary classification as we've been doing thus far, and our distributions of the class are around $P(0)=0.78$ and $P(1)=0.22$. The conditional probabilities the model learns are $P(x_i|y)$, where x_i is the ith feature and y is the class. For example, we could look at the conditional probability that someone has paid the most recent month's bill in full and did not default on next month's bill:

```
df[(df['default payment next month'] == 0) & \
    (df['PAY_0'] == -1)].shape[0] / df.shape[0]
```

This turns out to be around 16%, and this fraction (0.16) is multiplied by the other conditional probabilities for the other features for a sample with `PAY_0=1`. We would also multiply this by the $P(0)=0.78$ value to get our prediction probability for $y=0$. The `sklearn` documentation provides a more detailed explanation of this with equations here: `https://scikit-learn.org/stable/modules/naive_bayes.html`.

There are a few different Naïve Bayes classifiers in `sklearn`. All are used for classification, but take different types of features:

- `BernoulliNB` – binary features (1s and 0s)
- `CategoricalNB` – discrete, non-negative categorical features (for example, one feature could contain 0s, 1s, and 2s)
- `ComplementNB` – takes non-negative categorical and numeric features; similar to `MultinomialNB`, but better for imbalanced datasets where the distribution of targets is not uniform
- `GaussianNB` – takes any numeric features; assumes the likelihood of features (the $P(x_i|y)$ terms) is Gaussian
- `MultinomialNB` – takes non-negative categorical and numeric features

With our data, we can try using `GaussianNB`. However, we can easily see our features and target are not normally distributed, so we could guess this algorithm won't do too well. We can fit it and check the score like so:

```
from sklearn.naive_bayes import GaussianNB

gnb = GaussianNB()
gnb.fit(train_features, train_targets)
gnb.score(train_features, train_targets)
```

As with all `sklearn` algorithms, we first import it, and then initialize the model object. Then we fit the model to the training features and targets and can evaluate the score. Our score is only 37.8% accuracy, which is not great – far worse than guessing the majority class.

These Naïve Bayes models have the `predict()` and `predict_proba()` functions that work the same as with the logistic regression class (we simply provide the features to the prediction functions). The Naïve Bayes models also have a `partial_fit()` method, where we can provide part of the data at a time for the model to update its parameters. In this way, we can handle bigger data or streaming data by fitting it a little bit at a time.

One way to use the Naïve Bayes models is for text classification. For example, if we want to categorize text as positive or negative, we could use the multinomial Naïve Bayes classifier with word counts. We will look more at that in *Chapter 18, Working with Text*, on text data.

k-nearest neighbors (KNN)

One last model we'll look at is the ***k*-nearest neighbors** (**KNN**) algorithm. This is a distance-based algorithm. If we want to predict the class of a data point, we take the nearest *k* points to our data point (measured by distances between features of the points) and take a weighted average of the classes of the nearest points to make our prediction. KNN is different from other ML algorithms because there is no training – we only store our data, and then calculate the distances upon evaluation to make predictions. We can easily use KNN in `sklearn`, but we want to make sure to scale our features before using it:

```
numeric_columns = ['LIMIT_BAL', 'AGE'] + \
    [f'BILL_AMT{i}' for i in range(1, 7)] + \
    [f'PAY_AMT{i}' for i in range(1, 7)]
categorical_columns = ['SEX', 'EDUCATION', 'MARRIAGE'] + \
    ['PAY_0'] + [f'PAY_{i}' for i in range(2, 6)]

scaler = StandardScaler()
scaled_numeric_features = scaler.fit_transform(
    train_features[numeric_columns]
)

scaled_features = pd.concat(
    [pd.DataFrame(data=scaled_numeric_features,
                  columns=numeric_columns,
                  index=df.index),
     train_features[categorical_columns]],
    axis=1
)
```

First, we create lists of our numeric and categorical features. Then we use `StandardScaler` to scale the numeric features. Finally, we join the two sets of features back together using `pd.concat()`. We create a DataFrame out of our scaled features, providing the column names and the index from the original DataFrame so that our DataFrame merges properly. Then we can fit the KNN model:

```
from sklearn.neighbors import KNeighborsClassifier

knn = KNeighborsClassifier(n_jobs=-1)
knn.fit(scaled_features, train_targets)
knn.score(scaled_features, train_targets)
```

First, we import the class as usual with `sklearn` models and then instantiate it. The `n_jobs=-1` argument specifies that we should use all available processers for calculating distances, which speeds up the runtime. There are other arguments available for the distance calculations. By default, it uses the Euclidean distance, which is the straight-line distance between points. We can set the argument `p=1` in `KNeighborsClassifier()` to use the Manhattan or city block distance, which tends to work better for higher-dimensional data (with many features).

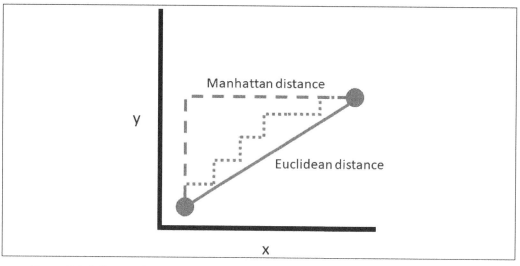

Figure 11.6: A diagram demonstrating the Manhattan and Euclidean distances between two points. Two examples of the Manhattan distance are shown as the dashed lines.

Instead of a straight-line distance between points, the Manhattan distance is the distance between two points measured along axes at right angles (orthogonal). It looks like traversing through the downtown area of a city (for example, Manhattan in New York City) via car. An example of Manhattan distance is shown in *Figure 11.6*. The Manhattan distance will be a larger value than the Euclidean distance.

 Both the Euclidean and Manhattan distances are derived from the Minkowski distance (https://en.wikipedia.org/wiki/Minkowski_distance).

KNN is very easy to understand and implement. The main hyperparameters we can tune are the number of neighbors (the `n_neighbors` argument), the weighting of nearby points for calculating the predicted class (`weights`), and the distance calculation (`p` and `metric`). The easiest way to search these is to simply optimize the `n_neighbors` argument.

We will look at this in more detail in *Chapter 14, Optimizing Models and Using AutoML*, since there is not a specific KNN cross-validation class in sklearn. Our accuracy on the training set for this model is 0.8463 (84%), which is not bad for such a simple model, and actually looks better than our logistic regression models so far. In fact, our accuracy improves a little after scaling/standardizing all the features with sklearn's StandardScaler. Without scaling, our accuracy on the training dataset is 81.7%. However, we do need to be careful when evaluating accuracy on the same data we trained on. If our model is overfitting to the data (fitting to noise in the data), we may see a very high accuracy on the training data, but low accuracy on new data. We will revisit this soon in the next chapter.

The sklearn documentation has explanations and examples for its functionality. For example, the KNN examples and explanation can be found here: https://scikit-learn.org/stable/modules/neighbors.html#nearest-neighbors-classification. To recap, the KNN algorithm works like so:

- Store our training data in memory
- To make a prediction, compute distances using a distance metric between the new data point and existing data points (there are multiple ways of doing this; the brute-force method is to compute all distances)
- Take the *k* nearest points and take an average or weighted average to arrive at our $\hat{y}$ value

So far, we've looked at binary classification – predicting 0s and 1s as our targets. However, many problems are multiclass classifications, which we'll cover next.

Multiclass classification

In multiclass classification, we have three or more classes in our target. This is also called multinomial classification. All classifiers in sklearn can perform multiclass classification, and there are a few other multiclass classification tools in sklearn.

Logistic regression

Let's use the same logistic regression model as before, but using PAY_0 as our target:

```
pay_0_target = df['PAY_0'].replace({i: 1 for i in range(1, 9)})
pay_0_features = df.drop(['PAY_0', 'default payment next month'], axis=1)

lr_multi = LogisticRegression(max_iter=1000)
lr_multi.fit(pay_0_features, pay_0_target)
```

First, we create a pandas series with the PAY_0 column as a target. This has values -2 through 8 for different categories of payments (-2 is "no consumption", -1 is paid on time, 0 is the use of revolving credit, and 1-8 is the number of months late on payment). We convert any value from 1 through 8 to the value 1 to simplify the classes – with this change, 1 signifies a late payment. Then we create a set of features without our target column and without the binary default column. We can use the sklearn LogisticRegression class on this with no modifications, although we increased the max_iter argument so that our model can fully fit the data (it takes 228 iterations to converge, greater than the default max_iter of 100). With other classification models in sklearn, we can also simply give it a multi-class target and use the classifier as usual.

The multinomial logistic regression algorithm carries out the same logistic regression equation as before, but on k classes. There are multiple ways to formulate the equations for solving for the coefficients and predictions for class probabilities, but we end up with the same result – a probability for each class, where the sum of probabilities for each prediction sums to 1. For example, we might end up with a vector of probability predictions that looks like [0.25, 0.25, 0,5] for the probability of 3 different classes from multinomial logistic regression. With sklearn, the logistic regression coefficients are an array of shape (n_classes, n_features + 1). The +1 is for the intercept term.

 The loss function used for multi-class logistic regression is the same as the binary case (cross-entropy) but is generalized to multiple classes. The sklearn documentation shows the exact equation for this: https://scikit-learn.org/stable/modules/model_evaluation.html#log-loss.

We can also use the MNLogit class from statsmodels, which gives us the coefficients for k-1 of the classes:

```
multi_sm = sm.MNLogit(pay_0_target, sm.add_constant(pay_0_features))
multi_sm_results = multi_sm.fit()
multi_sm_results.summary()
```

We can get predictions from this model with multi_sm_results.predict(sm.add_constant(pay_0_features)), which again are probabilities for each class, and sum to 1 for each data point.

This multinomial logistic regression technique relies on an assumption of **independence of irrelevant attributes** (**IIA**), which says the probability of preferring one class over a second class shouldn't depend on another "irrelevant" class.

In our case, this assumption holds, but an example where this does not hold is if we have a perfect substitute for another class. For example, if our 0 value of `PAY_0` (using revolving credit) had a perfect substitute, such as another class with a value of -3 that involved using nearly identical revolving credit, this IIA assumption would not hold, and our logistic regression results may not be reliable.

This implementations of multinomial logistic regression can be thought of as fitting k-1 binary logistic regression models against each class versus the last class, which is why `statsmodels` returns *k*-1 sets of coefficients for *k* classes. However, there are a few other multiclass modeling strategies: one-versus-rest and one-versus-one.

One-versus-rest and one-versus-one formulations

The **one-versus-rest (OVR)** and **one-versus-one (OVO)** formulations of multinomial classification are slightly different. OVR formulates the problem so each class is fit against all other classes in a binary classification problem, giving us *k* models for *k* classes. An advantage of OVR is that it's easy to interpret – each model has the coefficients or parameters for that single class versus all others. The OVO implementation creates a model for each pair of classes, and results in `k * (k - 1) / 2` models. These models are not as easy to interpret as OVR or the default implementation from `sklearn` models, but OVO can provide an advantage for algorithms that don't scale well with the number of samples (for example, KNN when using the brute-force distance calculation approach). We will discuss the runtime scaling of algorithms as related to the size of the data in the computational complexity section later in this chapter. The OVO gets predictions by taking the majority vote for the predicted class from all its classifiers.

To use OVR with logistic regression, we can set the `multi_class` argument to `'ovr'`:

```
lr_multi_ovr = LogisticRegression(max_iter=1000, multi_class='ovr')
```

This keeps the same logistic regression object and interface that we've used before. Another method that is general to any model is to use other classes from `sklearn`:

```
from sklearn.multiclass import OneVsOneClassifier, OneVsRestClassifier

lr_ovr = OneVsRestClassifier(LogisticRegression(max_iter=1000), n_jobs=-1)
lr_ovo = OneVsOneClassifier(LogisticRegression(max_iter=1000), n_jobs=-1)

lr_ovr.fit(pay_0_features, pay_0_target)
lr_ovo.fit(pay_0_features, pay_0_target)
```

Here, we import the OVO and OVR classes from `sklearn` and simply wrap our logistic regression algorithm with these classes. We can then use the same `fit`, `predict`, and some other methods that we used before. The `predict_proba` is not available to the OVO model, however. We are setting the `n_jobs` argument to -1 in order to use all available processors. We can also get each individual model like so:

```
lr_ovo.estimators_[0]
```

This gives us the first logistic regression model out of 6 models. There are 4 classes (-2, -1, 0, 1) and the pairs of targets for the models follow a pattern: the first class is paired with the next classes in a row, then the second class is paired with the following classes in a row, and so on. This gives us the pairs: (-2, -1), (-2, 0), (-2, 1), (-1, 0), (-1, 1), and 1, and (0, 1). With the individual models, we can access any of the models' attributes and methods, such as `predict_proba`.

Models in `sklearn` will tend to use the best implementation for each algorithm, OVR, or OVO. However, we can always try the different implementations for algorithms and see which works best.

Multi-label classification

Some classification problems can have multiple labels for each target. For example, if we are classifying the topic of a news story, it might fall under several categories at the same time (a news story could be about both economics and politics, for example). Classifiers for multilabel problems (which we could also call multitarget) are multi-output classifiers by definition. We can use the PAY columns in our default dataset to create a multilabel classification problem:

```
import swifter

mo_targets = df[['PAY_0'] + [f'PAY_{i}' for i in range(2, 7)]].copy()
mo_targets = mo_targets.swifter.apply(lambda x: (x > 0).astype(int), axis=1)
```

Here, we retrieve the PAY columns from our original DataFrame and make a copy (so as not to alter the original DataFrame or have any `SettingwithCopyWarning` warnings from pandas). We then apply the function across rows (with `axis=1`), which returns 1 if the value is greater than 0, and 0 otherwise. This gives us 1s for each of the PAY columns where there was a late payment, and 0 otherwise. We use the `swifter` package to parallelize the `apply` function.

Some `sklearn` models can handle multi-label data out of the box – for example, tree-based models such as `DecisionTreeClassifier`, as well as KNN. However, many other models cannot handle this, and we must use another `sklearn` class:

```
from sklearn.multioutput import MultiOutputClassifier

mo_clf = MultiOutputClassifier(LogisticRegression(max_iter=1000), n_jobs=-1)
mo_clf.fit(mo_features, mo_targets)
```

Here, we import and use the `MultiOutputClassifier` class, which behaves nearly identically to the OVO and OVR classes. We give it an estimator as the first argument and tell it to use all available processors with the n_jobs=-1 argument. Then we can use similar methods as before, such as `predict`, `predict_proba`, and `score`. This class fits an individual model for each target, and stores the models in the `estimators_` attribute of our `mo_clf` variable.

Another similar method is the `ClassifierChain` class from `sklearn`. This fits individual models for each class, but fits them sequentially. It first fits a model to the first target value, and then sequentially fits models for the other target values using the actual value (in training) or predicted value (during inference or prediction) of the class from the previous model. We can use this model like so:

```
from sklearn.multioutput import ClassifierChain

cc_clf = ClassifierChain(LogisticRegression(max_iter=1000))
cc_clf.fit(mo_features, mo_targets)
```

This can be useful if there are correlations between the target values. In this case, the score on the training data for the multi-output and chain models is about the same at 67% accuracy, so it does not appear to make a difference.

Choosing a model to use

Once we've learned about several models, it can be difficult to know which one to choose. There are some guidelines provided here you can use to help, and we will cover using metrics to compare models in the next chapter.

The "no free lunch" theorem

The "no free lunch" theorem applies to mathematics and machine learning. In machine learning, it states that no model is necessarily the best for a given task. Therefore, it makes sense to try several models and compare the scores on a metric or metrics of choice, choosing the model with the best performance.

There are many more classification models available in `sklearn`, which are described in the documentation: `https://scikit-learn.org/stable/supervised_learning.html`.

The `sklearn` documentation also has a comparison of some of the different classification models here: `https://scikit-learn.org/stable/auto_examples/classification/plot_classifier_comparison.html`.

We can use cross-validation to score models, or split data into a train and validation set, comparing the scores on the validation set. We will look at this in more detail in the next chapter.

Computational complexity of models

Another consideration for choosing models is the computational complexity, or big O runtime. We can consider the time it takes a model to run (both in training and inference) and the space it takes to run the model (again, both in training and inference). These considerations only matter for big data, since we can run into problems where we run out of resources (computer memory or time) if our data is large.

In computer science and related fields, big O notation describes the behavior of an algorithm as the number of inputs or iterations become large values – this is usually called computational complexity, and we usually think about time and memory complexity. For example, if an algorithm's runtime only depended linearly on the size of the input data, n, its computational runtime (or time complexity) would have big O notation $O(n)$. For logistic regression, the big O runtime is roughly the size of the data multiplied by the number of steps the optimizer has to take: $O(ns)$, where s is the number of steps from the optimizer. During inference (predictions), the runtime is $O(n)$ where n is the size of the data on which we're predicting, as we simply multiply the logistic regression coefficients by the data. The space complexity is $O(ns + n + s)$ during training and $O(n)$ during inference.

By contrast, KNN has a drastically different big O runtime – $O(1)$ (instant) during training (we simply store the data in memory), and $O(nd)$ for the best-case time complexity during inference, where n is the number of samples in our training data and d is the number of features. Space or memory complexity is $O(nd)$ for both training and testing. As we can see (and already found out from practical experience), the inference step for KNN is much slower than for logistic regression. Understanding the big O runtime and space complexities for algorithms can help you understand why a particular model may be running very slowly.

It can also help you understand how to make it run faster or take less memory. For example, we can trim down the dimensions with feature selection or PCA to shrink our time and space complexity for KNN. For most algorithms, the time and space complexities can be found in various places in books or online, including computer science books, Stack Overflow, course lecture materials, and elsewhere. For example, KNN complexity is discussed in the following link on Stack Overflow: `https://stats.stackexchange.com/questions/219655/k-nn-computational-complexity`. One resource for learning more about big O notation is the book *Hands-On Data Structures and Algorithms with Python – Second Edition*, by Dr. Basant Agarwal and Benjamin Baka. Of course, we can also derive computational time and space complexities from the mathematical equations for the algorithms of ML algorithms.

Test your knowledge

To test your knowledge, use the `loan_data.csv` dataset in the `Chapter11/test_your_knowledge/data` folder in this book's GitHub repository to fit ML classification models to the data to predict the `TARGET` column. You will need to do some cleaning of the columns (for example, converting strings to numbers) before using it with ML algorithms. The value of 1 for the target means a default or late payment on the loan, while 0 means no late payments or defaults. Examine p-values from a logistic regression fit and see whether any features could potentially be thrown out. Check your accuracy of the models you try and compare it to the majority class fraction. Write a short analysis of the results and process.

Summary

In this chapter, we covered machine learning classification algorithms. We saw how they fall into a few categories: binary classification, multiclass single-label classification, and multiclass multi-label classification. We learned about one of the foundational classification algorithms – logistic regression. Logistic regression is easier to interpret than many other models, as we can get rough feature importances from the coefficient sizes. It can also be used for feature selection by throwing out features whose coefficients have small p-values. We also touched on cross-validation and how it can be used to optimize hyperparameters such as the regularization hyperparameter `C`. Many Python packages can be used for logistic regression (even with big data), but here, we used the `sklearn` and `statsmodels` packages, and saw how `statsmodels` can provide p-values while `sklearn` cannot.

Besides logistic regression, we also saw how to use Naïve Bayes models and *k*-nearest neighbors (KNN). The Naïve Bayes models are often used for text classification problems, where we have word counts as our features. KNN is a simple model but can be slow to make predictions for big data (if we have not scaled it up using something like pyspark). It's not a bad idea to be aware of the big O runtime and space complexity for algorithms, which determines how the algorithms scale with bigger data.

Now that we've seen some classification ML algorithms, let's look at metrics for measuring their performance and sampling strategies for dealing with unbalanced data.

12

Evaluating Machine Learning Classification Models and Sampling for Classification

Once we have some classification models trained to predict our target variable, we need a way to compare them and choose the best one. One way to compare models is to use metrics such as accuracy and others. In classification, we can often find that our classes or targets are imbalanced. We can improve the performance of ML classification algorithms by means of sampling techniques, such as oversampling and undersampling. In this chapter, we will learn about ways to evaluate our classification models and sampling methods:

- How to evaluate the performance of our algorithms (performance metrics)
- Sampling imbalanced data for classification

Let's start with metrics for comparing ML classification algorithms.

Evaluating classification algorithm performance with metrics

There are several metrics available for comparing classification ML algorithms, each with their strengths and weaknesses. We'll look at some of the more common metrics for classification here.

Train-validation-test splits

When evaluating the performance of an algorithm, it's important to look at performance on data that was not used for training. The model has already learned all the ins and outs of the training data, and may have even overfit to the training data, learning patterns related to noise in the data. Instead, we want to evaluate performance on a hold-out set, which we may call a validation or test set. For some algorithms, such as neural networks, we train the model on a training set, monitor performance during training on a validation set, and then evaluate final performance on a test set. For most other ML algorithms, we simply use a training and test set If our test or validation sets contain information from the training data, this is called data leakage. Data leakage leads to high validation or tests scores which are not representative of the true performance of our model. It's like having the answers before a test and scoring well, even though you don't really know the material on the test.

We will use the same data as in the previous chapter – the binary classification of credit card default payments. We first load the data and create our features and targets data frames and series:

```
import pandas as pd

df = pd.read_excel('data/default of credit card clients.xls',
                   skiprows=1,
                   index_col=0)
target_col = 'default payment next month'
features = df.drop(target_col, axis=1)
targets = df[target_col]
```

Next, we can split our dataset into training and test sets quite easily with `sklearn`:

```
from sklearn.model_selection import train_test_split

x_train, x_test, y_train, y_test = train_test_split(features,
                                                    targets,
                                                    train_size=0.75,
                                                    stratify=targets)
```

The `model_selection` module from `sklearn` contains the `train_test_split` function, which takes arguments of features, targets, and more. With binary or multi-class classification, it's always a good idea to use the `stratify` argument with our class labels so that the proportion of classes stays the same across the training and test sets. This ensures that we don't have biases due to class imbalances between training and test sets. We also choose a training size of 75% of the data here, which is typical. Somewhere between 60% and 90% of the data used as the training set is common.

We can then fit our model to the training data:

```
from sklearn.linear_model import LogisticRegression
lr_model = LogisticRegression(max_iter=1000)
lr_model.fit(x_train, y_train)
```

Now, we are able to assess performance on the test set.

Accuracy

One of the simplest classification metrics is accuracy, and is the default for most (if not all) `sklearn score()` methods for classifiers. We can assess the performance on the training and test sets like so:

```
print(lr_model.score(x_train, y_train))
print(lr_model.score(x_test, y_test))
```

This shows that both accuracies are around 78% (or 0.78 as returned from the `score` function). Since the training and test scores are quite similar, we don't see evidence of overfitting to the data. If the train score was much higher (for example, 90% accuracy on training and 60% accuracy on test), we should be concerned that our model is likely overfitting to the data. We should then use strategies to reduce overfitting, such as feature selection and pruning, regularization, or using a simpler model.

The accuracy value seems high, but we should compare it to the "no information rate." This is the accuracy we could expect with no information about the target (no features). We can approximate this with the majority class fraction, and our "no information" model could guess that all samples are this majority class. We can calculate the class fractions like so:

```
df['default payment next month'].value_counts() / df.shape[0]
```

This shows us that the majority class (0, no default) composes around 78% of the data, so our model is no better than guessing the majority class for every prediction. We could also find this result using `sklearn.dummy.DummyClassifier` (using the `strategy='most_frequent'` argument), but the preceding method is faster and easier:

There is also an `sklearn.metrics.accuracy_score()` function that can be used, which takes an array of true labels and an array of predicted values.

Another way to estimate the performance of a classifier is cross-validation, as we discussed earlier. We can get a more reliable accuracy score using cross-validation. First, we need to load the classification models we used in the previous chapter, as well as create our scaled (standardized) features:

```
from sklearn.naive_bayes import GaussianNB
from sklearn.linear_model import LogisticRegressionCV
from sklearn.neighbors import KNeighborsClassifier
from sklearn.preprocessing import StandardScaler

scaler = StandardScaler()
scaled_features = scaler.fit_transform(features)

gnb = GaussianNB()
lr_cv = LogisticRegressionCV()
lr_cv.fit(features, targets)
lr_best_c = LogisticRegression(C=lr_cv.C_[0])
knn = KNeighborsClassifier()
```

Then we can perform cross-validation on these models to assess performance:

```
from sklearn.model_selection import cross_val_score


print(cross_val_score(gnb, features, targets, n_jobs=-1).mean())
print(cross_val_score(lr_best_c, features, targets, n_jobs=-1).mean())
print(cross_val_score(knn, features, targets, n_jobs=-1).mean())
print(cross_val_score(knn, scaled_features, targets, n_jobs=-1).mean())
```

The drawback of cross-validation is that it trains and evaluates several models (5 with the default settings), so is slower to run than a single training/test split. However, it gives us a more robust measure of the performance of the algorithms. cross_val_score also uses stratified training/validation splits by default, so we don't need to worry about class imbalances in the training and validation sets. In the preceding code, we import the cross_val_score function from sklearn, and then use it with our models we created in the previous sections. The cross_val_score function returns a NumPy array of scores on the validation sets with 5-fold cross-validation (so we have a 5-element NumPy array, although this can be changed with the cv argument). We then take the average of this with mean(). We try it with the Naïve Bayes model, our logistic regression model with the C hyperparameter optimized, and KNN with the scaled and unscaled features. Our results are as follows:

```
0.37909999999999994
0.7788
```

```
0.7553333333333334
0.7916333333333333
```

We can see that the KNN model on scaled features performs best. We also see that scaling also improves the performance of the KNN model (79.2% accuracy versus 75.5% with unscaled data). If we train these models and evaluate them on the same training data, the scores on the training data alone were a little different (usually better) than these cross-validation scores. It's always best to evaluate metrics on a validation or test set or to use cross-validation to get an accurate reading in terms of which model is best.

Cohen's Kappa

Although we can compare accuracy to the "no information" rate, one way to automatically incorporate this into an accuracy-like metric is Cohen's Kappa. This metric takes into account a random model and gives us a value between -1 and +1. A value of 0 means that our model is no better than random guessing. A value of 1 means we have perfect accuracy, while negative values mean we have a model that's worse than random guessing (or using a "no information" model, such as guessing the majority class for every prediction). Cohen's Kappa does, however, have a drawback where it tends to return lower values when our classes are more imbalanced. But it can still be useful for comparing models without having to consider the no information rate. We can use it with sklearn like this:

```
from sklearn.metrics import cohen_kappa_score

cohen_kappa_score(y_test, lr_model.predict(x_test))
```

This function works like most metrics in sklearn – we provide an array of true values and predicted values (although the order doesn't matter for this particular metric). For our default logistic regression model, which had an accuracy near the "no information" rate of 78%, our Cohen's Kappa score is very close to 0.

We can also use any arbitrary scoring metric with the cross_val_score function, like Cohen's Kappa:

```
from sklearn.metrics import make_scorer

print(cross_val_score(lr_model,
                      features,
                      targets,
                      scoring=make_scorer(cohen_kappa_score),
                      n_jobs=-1).mean())
```

We provide the `scoring` argument and need to use the `make_scorer` function to convert the metric to a scoring function. Again, the result here is a Cohen's Kappa score near 0.

Confusion matrix

Another common set of metrics for classification can be examined with a confusion matrix. A confusion matrix contains a table of metric values with rows as actual values and columns as predicted values. For binary classification, this contains true positives (TP, where predictions for positive cases, or values of 1, were correct), true negatives (TN, correct negative cases), false positives (FP, where predictions for negative cases were 1 but should've been 0), and false negatives (FN, where the prediction was 0 but should've been 1). There is a function in `sklearn` for this, `sklearn.metrics.confusion_matrix`, which generates a text-based version, and another function to plot confusion matrices:

```
from sklearn.metrics import plot_confusion_matrix

plot_confusion_matrix(lr_model,
                      x_test,
                      y_test,
                      cmap=plt.cm.Blues,
                      display_labels=['not defaulted', 'defaulted'],
                      colorbar=False)
```

We import the `plot_confusion_matrix` function and set several arguments for it. We first provide the model, followed by the features and targets (using the test set), and then change some options for aesthetics. We change the colormap to a set of blue colors (which is better than the default colors), provide labels for the targets and predictions on the plot with `display_labels`, and turn off the colorbar since it is extraneous (the values are already printed on the cells).

 If gridlines show up in your plot, you may be able to turn them off with `plt.grid(b=None)` or `ax.grid(False)`. To remove the colorbar without the `colorbar=False` argument, you can use `f.delaxes(f.axes[1])`, where f is a figure created with `f, ax = plt.subplots(1, 1, figsize=(5.5, 5.5))`.

A few other packages contain convenient methods for plotting confusion matrices that are almost the same: `yellowbrick` and `mlxtend`. These packages also have other functionality. We can install these with conda: `conda install -c conda-forge yellowbrick mlxtend`.

With packages that depend on sklearn, such as yellowbrick, you may run into versioning issues (for example, conda may downgrade your sklearn version or you may run into errors that occur because sklearn needs to be downgraded for compatibility issues). You can try installing with pip if conda cannot "solve the environment," which may fix the issue. The other option is to create a separate conda environment for yellowbrick so that another version of sklearn that is not the latest can be used. Examples of plotting confusion matrices with these packages can be found in the Jupyter notebook for this chapter in this book's GitHub repository. Our results of the sklearn plot_confusion_matrix function are shown below:

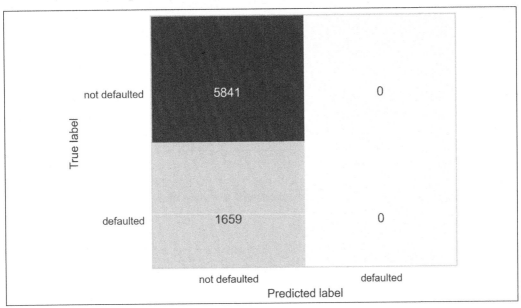

Figure 12.1: The confusion matrix of our binary default data using sklearn

Right away, we can see we have a problem – we haven't got any true positives (the value of 0 in the bottom right of the confusion matrix) or positive predictions at all. Our model is having trouble with predicting defaults based on our data.

The confusion matrix can also be used for multi-class classification. First, we need to create our multi-label features and targets and fit the logistic regression model to the data:

```
pay_0_target = df['PAY_0'].replace({i: 1 for i in range(1, 9)})
pay_0_features = df.drop(['PAY_0', 'default payment next month'],
                         axis=1)

lr_multi = LogisticRegression(max_iter=1000)
lr_multi.fit(pay_0_features, pay_0_target)
```

Here, we are predicting the multi-class PAY_0 column after replacing all the values greater than 0 with 1 (which are late payments) – this has 4 unique classes. Then, we can plot our confusion matrix:

```
plot_confusion_matrix(lr_multi,
                      pay_0_features,
                      pay_0_target,
                      display_labels=['no consumption',
                                      'paid on time',
                                      'revolving credit',
                                      'late'],
                      cmap=plt.cm.Blues,
                      colorbar=False)
ax.grid(False)
```

The function call to `plot_confusion_matrix` is essentially the same as before, although we've added labels to correspond to the 4 unique classes (sorted numerically from least to greatest). We can see that our confusion matrix looks like this:

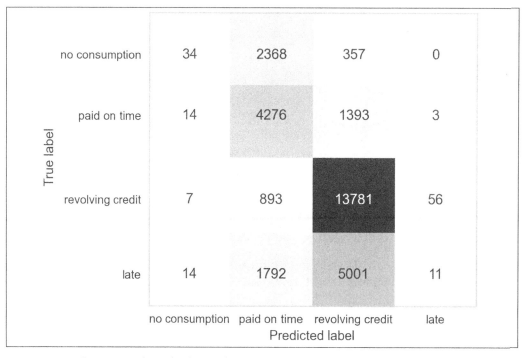

Figure 12.2: The multi-class confusion matrix for our default data using sklearn

Lastly, we can also look at plotting confusion matrices from our multi-class, multi-label problem, where we predicted the values of 0 or 1 for each of the `PAY_i` values in the previous chapter. First, we create the multi-class, multi-label data again:

```
import swifter

pay_cols = ['PAY_0'] + [f'PAY_{i}' for i in range(2, 7)]
mo_targets = df[pay_cols].copy()
mo_targets = mo_targets.swifter.apply(lambda x: (x > 0).astype(int), axis=1)

mo_features = df[[c for c in df.columns if c not in pay_cols +
                 ['default payment next month']]]
```

Then, we fit our multi-label classifier to the data:

```
from sklearn.multioutput import MultiOutputClassifier

mo_clf = MultiOutputClassifier(LogisticRegression(max_iter=1000), n_jobs=-1)
mo_clf.fit(mo_features, mo_targets)
```

Finally, we use another `sklearn` function to get confusion matrices for each class, loop through them, and plot each one:

```
from sklearn.metrics import multilabel_confusion_matrix,
ConfusionMatrixDisplay

ml_cm = multilabel_confusion_matrix(mo_targets, mo_clf.predict(mo_features))

for i, cl in enumerate(mo_targets.columns):
    f = ConfusionMatrixDisplay(ml_cm[i], display_labels=['on-time', 'late'])
    f.plot(cmap=plt.cm.Blues, colorbar=False)
    plt.title(cl)
    plt.grid(b=None)
```

We first get all the confusion matrices with the `multilabel_confusion_matrix` function, which takes the same arguments as the `confusion_matrix` function. Then we loop through our class names from our `mo_targets` data frame, and use the `enumerate()` built-in function. This function returns a tuple of a counter (starting at 0 by default) and our object (each `mo_target` column name).

We use this index (i) to get the confusion matrix for each class and plot it with the `ConfusionMatrixDisplay` function. This function does not require a model and only needs the confusion matrix, which suits our purposes here. We provide the display labels to this function as well. It returns an object which has a `plot` method, where we can change the color and remove the colorbar. Finally, we set the title as the class name (`cl`) and turn off the gridlines.

It is also possible to get a confusion matrix, as we saw in Figure 12.2, although there is no convenient method for this in `sklearn` or related packages. We would need to manually rearrange and plot the data.

Precision, recall, and F1 score

Closely related to TP, FP, FN, and TN from the confusion matrix are precision, recall, and the F1 score. Precision can be thought of as the correctly predicted positives divided by all the predicted positives. This is TP / (TP + FP). Recall can be thought of as the correctly predicted positives divided by all the actual positives, which is TP / (TP + FN). As you can see, the one thing directly missing from precision and recall is the true negative values. The F1 score is the harmonic mean of these two measures, which is:

$$2 * Precision * Recall / (Precision + Recall)$$

The F1 score can also be weighted so that precision or recall has more weight in the equation, which is usually a parameter called "beta." We can easily calculate F1, precision, and recall with the `classification_report` function from `sklearn`:

```
from sklearn.metrics import classification_report

print(classification_report(y_test,
                            lr_model.predict(x_test),
                            target_names=['no default', 'default']))
```

It's important to print the report since the resulting string has some formatting, such as newlines. The function takes the true target values first and predicted values second. We also set the class names in the report with the `target_names` argument. This gives us the following:

	precision	recall	f1-score	support
no default	0.78	1.00	0.88	5841
default	0.00	0.00	0.00	1659
accuracy			0.78	7500
macro avg	0.39	0.50	0.44	7500
weighted avg	0.61	0.78	0.68	7500

Figure 12.3: The results of the sklearn classification report on our binary default data

We can see that the precision, recall, and F1 score are present for each unique class. We also have support, which is the number of samples in the dataset we are evaluating for each row. The overall accuracy is shown, as well as a macro-weighted average. The macro average is unweighted, meaning all classes are treated equally (it's the simple average of the precision values, for example). The weighted average is sometimes called the micro average and aggregates the TP and other values to calculate the precision, recall, and F1 scores.

We can easily plot this report with `yellowbrick`:

```
from yellowbrick.classifier import ClassificationReport

f, ax = plt.subplots(1, 1)
viz = ClassificationReport(lr_model,
                           support=True,
                           classes=['no default', 'default'],
                           cmap='Blues')
viz.score(x_test, y_test)
plt.gcf().delaxes(f.axes[1])
viz.show()
```

First, we import the `ClassificationReport` function from `yellowbrick`, and then give this function our model and a few arguments. We tell the function to include the support with `support=True` (the number of samples from our evaluation), we give it labels for the classes with the `classes` argument, and change the colormap to be shades of blue. Then we use the `score` method of the returned object (`viz.score()`) on our test data.

The yellowbrick ClassificationReport function returns an object that can perform modeling, so we can use other methods such as fit() on data. Near the top of the code block, we also created a new figure and axis object with plt.subplots. This allows us to remove the colorbar by getting the current figure with plt.gcf() and deleting the second axis object where the colorbar is stored. This is a little hacky, but it works, and removing the colorbar may be added as an argument in future versions of yellowbrick. You may also need to try different values for indexing f.axes in the delaxes function, such as 0. This results in the following plot:

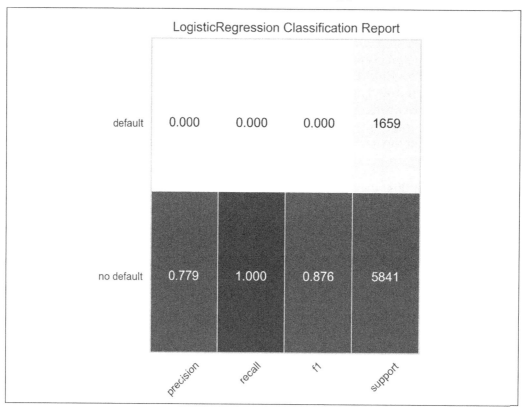

Figure 12.4: The classification report plot from yellowbrick

We can see that it's the same information as the sklearn report, minus the accuracy, as well as macro and micro averages. Of course, this easily extends to multi-class models (single-label, not multi-label). For example, with sklearn, we can do this:

```
print(classification_report(pay_0_target,
                            lr_multi.predict(pay_0_features),
                            target_names=['no consumption',
                                          'on time',
```

```
                    'credit',
                    'late']
            )
    )
```

The `yellowbrick` report plotting can be used with the same data and classifier above for multi-class analysis.

AUC score and the ROC curve

Another useful metric for classification is the area under the curve score (AUC) from the receiver operating characteristic (ROC) curve. To get the AUC, we first calculate the ROC, and can plot it as follows:

```
from yellowbrick.classifier.rocauc import roc_auc

roc = roc_auc(lr_model,
              x_train,
              y_train,
              x_test,
              y_test,
              classes=['no default', 'default'],
              macro=False,
              micro=False)
```

The `yellowbrick` package provides a convenient way to do this, although there is a function in `sklearn` that can do the same thing (`sklearn.metrics.plot_roc_curve`). The advantage of `yellowbrick` at the moment of writing is that it can plot multiple classes whereas `sklearn` cannot. For example, we can use:

```
roc = roc_auc(lr_multi,
              pay_0_features,
              pay_0_target,
              macro=False,
              micro=False)
```

To plot ROC curves from our multi-class, single-label classification problem. In our above example here, we simply use the `roc_auc` function from `yellowbrick` similarly to the classification report, giving it our model, x and y values for training and test sets, and a list of class names for better labeling. We also turn off the macro and micro averages since these don't make much sense for ROC curves and AUC.

If we leave the `macro` and `micro` averages on by leaving the macro and micro arguments as their default of `True`:

```
roc = roc_auc(lr_model,
              x_train,
              y_train,
              x_test,
              y_test,
              classes=['no default', 'default'])
```

Then our plot looks like the following:

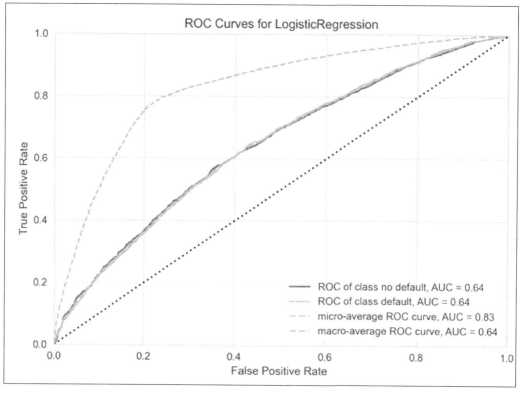

Figure 12.5: The ROC curve of our binary classification results from yellowbrick with macro and micro averages

We can see the dashed lines are difficult to read in the plot, and the significance of the macro and micro averages is not clear. The micro average sits in the same spot as the two ROC curves for the two classes as well. Using `sklearn` to plot the ROC curve instead results in a simpler plot, and only shows the ROC curve for our positive class (1, if a customer defaulted on their payment):

```
from sklearn.metrics import plot_roc_curve

roc = plot_roc_curve(lr_model, x_test, y_test)
plt.plot([0, 1], [0, 1], c='k', linestyle='dotted', label='random model')
plt.plot([0, 0, 1],
         [0, 1, 1],
         c='k',
         linestyle='dashed',
         label='perfect model')
plt.legend()
```

We first import the sklearn plot_roc_curve function and give it our model, *x*, and *y* data. We also plot a diagonal dashed line with a black color (c='k'), which represents a random-guessing or "no information" model, and call plt.legend() so that all our labels show up. Finally, we plot a dashed line that represents a perfectly accurate model passing through the upper left of the plot. The resulting plot looks like this:

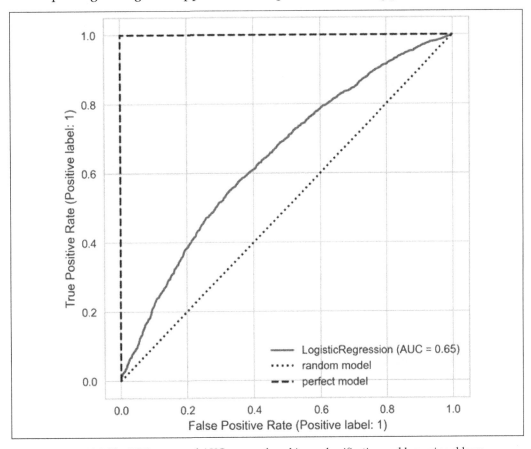

Figure 12.6: The ROC curve and AUC scores of our binary classification problem using sklearn

We can see this is much simpler and easier to interpret than the default yellowbrick ROC curve plot. The plot shows the false positive rate (FPR) on the *x* axis, which is FP / (FP + TN). The *y* axis has the true positive rate (TPR), which is TP / (TP + FN). We can see that the ROC curve is to the left and above the dashed line, which means we are doing better than random guessing. We also see that the area under the curve (AUC) score in the bottom right is 0.65, which is the integral (sum) of the area under the ROC curve. We can get this metric with `roc.roc_auc` from the returned object from `plot_roc_curve()`. A perfect model with 100% accuracy would have an AUC score of 1, and the ROC curve creates the dashed line that goes through the upper left of the plot shown in the preceding figure.

The AUC score gives us a way to compare models that takes into account all the different rounding thresholds for our probability predictions that we may use. Since most models can produce a probability estimate for each class, we can choose what the rounding threshold is for rounding up or down. When we have a rounding threshold of 1 or higher, so that all predictions are rounded down to 0, we have no FP and no TP, and we are at the bottom left of the ROC curve. On the other hand, a threshold of 0 means all cases are predicted as positive (1), and we have an FPR of 1 and a TPR of 1 (the upper right of the plot). All other thresholds are in between and form the ROC curve. There are a few different methods for choosing the optimal threshold, and some involve the ROC curve.

Choosing the optimal cutoff threshold

By default, our threshold for rounding is 0.5 – any probability prediction greater than 0.5 is rounded up to 1, otherwise we round down to 0. We can change this threshold to optimize different metrics. For example, we can maximize the F1 score, giving us a balance between precision and recall, or we can manually change the threshold to achieve a desired precision, recall, or other metric value. A few ways we'll look at here are as follows:

- Youden's J (maximum TPR – FPR)
- Upper-left distance (minimum distance from ROC curve to the point [0, 1])
- F1 maximum

These three approaches are slightly different. Youden's J maximizes the "discrimination" of the model between true positives and false positives, while the upper-left method maximizes the TPR while maintaining a good FPR, and the F1 score balances precision and recall. We can find the optimal threshold with Youden's J like so:

```
import numpy as np
```

```
roc = plot_roc_curve(lr_model, x_test, y_test, drop_intermediate=False)
youdens_idx = np.argmax(roc.tpr - roc.fpr)
thresholds = np.unique(lr_model.predict_proba(x_test)[:, 1])
thresholds.sort()
thresholds = [1] + list(thresholds[::-1])
y_thresh = thresholds[youdens_idx]
```

First, we calculate the ROC curve again using the `sklearn` function and set the `drop_intermediate=False` argument, which keeps all threshold values used in the calculation of the curve. The threshold values are the unique values from `predict_proba` for the "positive" class (1, here). Then we take the difference between TPR and FPR and get the index of the maximum value with `np.argmax()`. Next, we get the unique probability values from the predictions for class 1, which are used in the ROC calculation. We sort these with NumPy (which sorts from least to greatest), reverse the order with `[::-1]`, and add a 1 to the beginning of the threshold list (since the ROC curve calculation uses a high value for the first threshold, and this will make the size of our threshold and TPR/FPR arrays match). Finally, we can get the threshold by indexing our threshold list with the index from `np.argmax()`. Our threshold turns out to be around 0.27. To get the nearest point on the curve to the top left of the ROC curve plot, we can do the following:

```
upper_left_array = np.vstack((np.zeros(roc.tpr.shape[0]),
                              np.ones(roc.tpr.shape[0]))).T
roc_curve_points = np.vstack((roc.fpr, roc.tpr)).T
topleft_idx = np.argmin(np.linalg.norm(upper_left_array - roc_curve_points,
                                       axis=1))
tl_thresh = thresholds[topleft_idx]
```

We first create an array of 0s and 1s that is the same size as our TPR and FPR arrays. The `np.vstack()` function is used to vertically stack these two arrays so that they have two rows. Then we transpose them with `.T` (switching rows and columns) so that each row is a data point. That array represents the upper left of the plot (coordinates [0, 1]). We then do something similar with the FPR and TPR using `np.vstack` and the transpose so that we can take the difference between these two arrays. We take the difference between `upper_left_array` and `roc_curve_points`, and use `np.linalg.norm` with the `axis=1` argument to get an array of Euclidean distances (straight-line distances) between the upper-left corner of the plot and the ROC curve. The `axis=1` argument is necessary so that it takes differences between each of the rows and doesn't calculate the distance between the two arrays as a single value. We get the index of the minimum value of that array with `np.argmin`, which is the shortest distance from the curve to the upper left of the plot. Finally, we store this threshold (which is 0.264) in the `tl_thresh` variable.

Lastly, we can get the optimal threshold via the F1 value using `yellowbrick`:

```
from yellowbrick.classifier.threshold import discrimination_threshold

dt = discrimination_threshold(lr_model, x_train, y_train)
f_idx = dt.cv_scores_['fscore'].argmax()
f_thresh = dt.thresholds_[f_idx]
```

The `discrimination_threshold` function plots the F1 score and other metrics and returns an object with F1 scores along with other metrics. We use this `dt` object to retrieve the F1 scores with `dt.cv_scores_['fscore']` and get the index of the maximum value with `argmax`. This `yellowbrick` method performs cross-validation on the provided data to get error bars for the plotted metrics (so it is fitting the model to the data we provided), and the `cv_scores_` attribute is a dictionary holding the values of the plotted metrics. We provided the `x_train` and `y_train` data, meaning the data in the plot looks a little smoother, since the training data has more data than the test set. The threshold from this method is 0.223 and we store it in the `f_thresh` variable. The plot from the `yellowbrick` function looks like this:

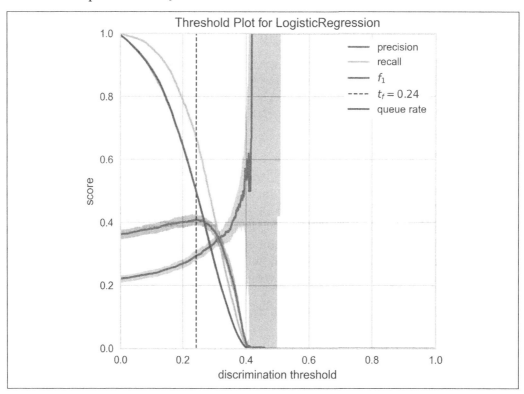

Figure 12.7: The threshold plot from yellowbrick

We can see that the plot contains some metrics with the dashed line showing the ideal threshold based on the F1 score. It contains a "queue rate" line, which is simply the FPR. This is intended to show what percent of samples would benefit from a review in a business setting. For example, if our procedure is to manually screen any loan application where our algorithm predicted the customer would default, the FPR or queue rate can be used to optimize a threshold to meet our review capabilities. We could take the number of reviews our company can do per week, the number of applications per week, and combine this with the FPR and TPR to find out what our threshold should be so we can review all applications with a prediction of a default. We can access the queue rate values from `dt.cv_scores_['queue_rate']`.

Now that we have a few different thresholds, we can examine the accuracies of these methods like so, using the `sklearn.metrics.accuracy_score` function:

```
from sklearn.metrics import accuracy_score

for t in [y_thresh, tl_thresh, f_thresh]:
    print(accuracy_score(y_test, lr_model.predict_proba(x_test)[:, 1] >= t))
```

From this, we see that the accuracy for Youden's J, top left, and the F1 methods are 64%, 62%, and 54%. These accuracies are lower than our default threshold of 0.5, which gave us an accuracy of around 78%. However, these thresholds give us more true positives on the test set, whereas the 0.5 threshold gave us none. We can plot the confusion matrix for our Youden's J threshold with `mlxtend`:

```
from mlxtend.plotting import plot_confusion_matrix as mlx_plot_cm

predictions = lr_model.predict_proba(x_test)[:, 1] >= y_thresh
mlx_plot_cm(confusion_matrix(y_test, predictions))
```

We're using `mlxtend` because the `yellowbrick` and `sklearn` plotting functions require us to provide our model, and don't let us set the rounding threshold for predictions (they use the 0.5 default). By contrast, the `mlxetend` version simply takes the confusion matrix returned from the `sklearn.metrics.confusion_matrix` function.

Our result looks like the following:

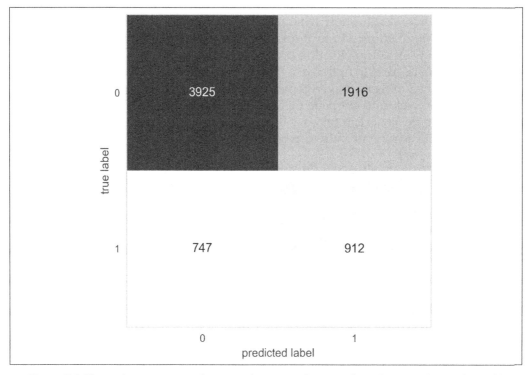

Figure 12.8: The confusion matrix on the test set from using the optimal Youden's J prediction threshold

If you recall from earlier, the confusion matrix with the 0.5 threshold predicted all test set default values (1s) to be 0s, or non-defaults, and we had 0 true positives in the bottom right of the confusion matrix. With the lower threshold, we can actually get some true positives, which could be useful in a business setting.

These optimal threshold methods could also be applied to multi-class, multi-label classification problems, where we get an optimal threshold for each class. For a multi-class, single-label problem, we already take the maximum probability from our predictions as the predicted class and don't need to do threshold optimization.

With the metrics we've seen here, we can compare models and choose the best model depending on our situation. For example, we may care about precision, recall, or accuracy the most depending on our application, or we can use the AUC score as a more general performance metric. Another option would be to combine multiple metrics into a meta-metric by means of averaging or weighted averaging.

We did not exhaustively cover all the classification metrics here, and there are more of them for classification. Some of the other metrics are listed in the sklearn documentation: `https://scikit-learn.org/stable/modules/classes.html#classification-metrics`. Another place that has many other classification metrics is the Wikipedia page for the confusion matrix here: `https://en.wikipedia.org/wiki/Confusion_matrix#Table_of_confusion`.

Something else we've learned about our data is that it's imbalanced, with far fewer defaults than non-defaults. We saw that we should consider this imbalance with certain metrics such as accuracy, and that other metrics are not as sensitive to class imbalance, such as the ROC curve and AUC. Another way of dealing with imbalanced data is with sampling techniques.

Sampling and balancing classification data

Sampling data can be used to shrink the data size for code development or to balance the classes between the dataset. We can also use synthetic sampling techniques, such as SMOTE and ADASYN. We'll start with the simplest methods, which are downsampling and naive upsampling.

Downsampling

To simply shrink the size of our dataset while preserving the class balance, we can use `train_test_split`:

```
_, x_sample, _, y_sample = train_test_split(features,
                                            targets,
                                            test_size=0.1,
                                            stratify=targets,
                                            random_state=42)
```

The `stratify` argument is key here so that our targets retain the same balance. We can confirm that the class balance has been retained with `np.bincount(y_sample) / y_sample.shape[0]` and `train_targets.value_counts(normalize=True)`, which calculate the fraction of 0s and 1s in the features and sample. We are not keeping the first and third returned values from the function, sending them instead to the underscore character (_). This means that we aren't going to use those variables in the future, although the _ variable will hold the third value returned from the preceding function.

We also specify the `test_size` argument to 0.1, which means that our `x_sample` and `y_sample` will have 10% of the original data. Lastly, we set the `random_state` so our results are reproducible. For sampling down data to a smaller amount for prototyping or developing code, this works great. However, it doesn't solve the issue of class imbalance.

We can instead use a Python package entirely focused on sampling: `imblearn`. This can be installed with `conda install -c conda-forge imbalanced-learn`. The documentation is extensive; for example, undersampling is covered here: `https://imbalanced-learn.org/stable/under_sampling.html`.

The `imblearn` interface is simple to use, although it is highly customizable and has c undersampling, we can do the following:

```
from imblearn.under_sampling import RandomUnderSampler

rus = RandomUnderSampler(random_state=0)
x_resampled, y_resampled = rus.fit_resample(features, targets)
```

The interface is similar to `sklearn`, where we create a class (with the same `random_state` argument as in `sklearn`), and then use methods such as `fit`. Instead of using `fit_transform`, as we did in the scalers in `sklearn`, we use `fit_resample` here, providing our features and targets. This returns pandas DataFrames and Series and works with multi-class as well as single-class targets. Multi-label targets are not supported currently since it is much more complex to deal with. Perhaps in the future, `imblearn` will support multi-label targets, but for now, we would need to code something by hand to downsample multi-label targets (where each datapoint can have multiple target classes).

From our preceding resample, we can verify that the data was resampled with `y_resampled.value_counts()` and `train_targets.value_counts()`, which show that our resampled data has 6,636 of each class, and the `y_train` data has 6,636 of the minority class (1). There are other, more complex undersampling techniques in `imblearn` described in the documentation that we won't cover here.

Oversampling

Another way to sample data for balancing classes is to use oversampling techniques, such as bootstrapping (sampling with replacement) to sample existing data so that the classes become balanced. We will use our same training/test split data as before, and can perform random bootstrap oversampling with `imblearn`:

```
from sklearn.metrics import roc_auc_score
from imblearn.over_sampling import RandomOverSampler

ros = RandomOverSampler(random_state=0)
x_resampled, y_resampled = ros.fit_resample(x_train, y_train)

lr_model = LogisticRegressionCV(max_iter=1000)
lr_model.fit(x_train, y_train)
print('unmodified:',
      roc_auc_score(y_test,
                    lr_model.predict_proba(x_test)[:, 1])
     )

lr_model_rs = LogisticRegressionCV(max_iter=1000)
lr_model_rs.fit(x_resampled, y_resampled)
print('resampled:',
      roc_auc_score(y_test,
                    lr_model_rs.predict_proba(x_test)[:, 1])
     )
```

This `RandomOverSampler` class bootstraps all minority classes to be up to the same number of samples as the majority class by default, although this is customizable with the `sampling_strategy` argument described in the documentation. We will have repeats of our data in the dataset, but at least the classes will be balanced. We are using the CV logistic regression class for our model, which automatically tries 10 different values of `C` (L2 regularization strength). We then get the AUC score from the `roc_auc_score` function of `sklearn`, which is 0.651 for the unmodified data and 0.658 for the resampled data. It looks like this resampling helped a little bit, but not significantly.

SMOTE and other synthetic sampling methods

Bootstrapping improves our models a small amount, but there are other synthetic sampling techniques that generate new samples based on existing data that can help too. These interpolate new data based on existing data – essentially, they draw a line connecting some of the data points and generate some new data along that line. SMOTE (synthetic minority oversampling technique) is one of the classic methods but has some problems. It generates samples randomly without consideration for which samples might be best to generate. Usually, generating new samples in the feature space where classes are overlapping or nearby is ideal, so that the classifier can learn to separate the data better.

Another method is ADASYN (adaptive synthetic) sampling, which incorporates consideration for where new data should be generated. SMOTE also has several variants that generate samples on the boundaries of classes, and the newest and potentially best SMOTE variant (at the time of writing) is *k*-means SMOTE, which was invented around 2017. We can use this method to oversample our data like so:

```
from imblearn.over_sampling import KMeansSMOTE

kmSMOTE = KMeansSMOTE(k_neighbors=5,
                      cluster_balance_threshold=0.2,
                      random_state=42,
                      n_jobs=-1)
x_resampled, y_resampled = kmSMOTE.fit_resample(x_train, y_train)

lr_model_rs = LogisticRegressionCV(max_iter=1000)
lr_model_rs.fit(x_resampled, y_resampled)
print('resampled:',
      roc_auc_score(y_test,
                    lr_model_rs.predict_proba(x_test)[:, 1])
     )
```

The *k*-means SMOTE method has some parameters we need to set, such as `cluster_balance_threshold`, in order for it to work properly. For our data, this needs to be a smaller value than the default of 0.1 or 0.2. The `k_neighbors` parameter is also adjustable and could be tuned as a hyperparameter in the pipeline of oversampling and then fitting a model. With this model, we get an AUC score of 0.643, which is not an improvement beyond random oversampling.

There are several other oversamplers in `imblearn`, most of them variants of SMOTE. The `imblearn.combine` module also contains more oversamplers, which oversample and then prune the data according to certain algorithms. We can try all these other oversamplers to see how they affect the AUC score:

```
from imblearn.over_sampling import SMOTE, BorderlineSMOTE, SVMSMOTE, ADASYN
from imblearn.combine import SMOTEENN, SMOTETomek

samplers = [
    SMOTE(random_state=42),
    BorderlineSMOTE(random_state=42, kind="borderline-1"),
    BorderlineSMOTE(random_state=42, kind="borderline-2"),
    SVMSMOTE(random_state=42),
    ADASYN(random_state=42),
    SMOTEENN(random_state=42),
    SMOTETomek(random_state=42)
```

```
    ]

    for s in samplers:
        x_resampled, y_resampled = s.fit_resample(x_train, y_train)
        lr_model_rs = LogisticRegressionCV(max_iter=1000)
        lr_model_rs.fit(x_resampled, y_resampled)
        ra_score = roc_auc_score(y_test,
                                 lr_model_rs.predict_proba(x_test)[:, 1])
        print(f'{str(s):<55} {ra_score}')
```

We first import all the other oversamplers and then put them in a list. Next, we loop through the oversamplers, resampling data, fitting our model, and then printing out the oversampler and the AUC score. We use f-string formatting so we can left-justify the oversampler name within a 55-character space with the {str(s):<55} part of the string. Our results are the following:

```
SMOTE(random_state=42)                                  0.6616400000866853
BorderlineSMOTE(random_state=42)                        0.6636431539885734
BorderlineSMOTE(kind='borderline-2', random_state=42)   0.6611377410562134
SVMSMOTE(random_state=42)                               0.6679814460333662
ADASYN(random_state=42)                                 0.6596417996332178
SMOTEENN(random_state=42)                               0.6541560619011809
SMOTETomek(random_state=42)                             0.6616288548277391
```

From this, we see that the SVMSMOTE method appears to have a slightly higher AUC score than the rest of the methods, but not by much. In this case, it doesn't hurt to oversample the data for training as long as it doesn't take too long to run, but it doesn't help that much either. The improvement here of a few percent with synthetic oversampling is typical. Most of the time, we can't expect dramatic improvements with oversampling and should be careful to compare the metrics between models on the same level. For example, we trained the models on the training split of the data and evaluated all the models on the unmodified test set. If we were to evaluate models on the resampling data, for example, we would get much higher accuracies and AUC scores, but it would not be an accurate representation of the situation. Although not a magic bullet, oversampling can be helpful in squeezing out some extra performance from our classifiers.

Test your knowledge

To test your knowledge, use the same loan_data.csv dataset from the previous chapter (also available in the Chapter12/test_your_knowledge/data folder in this book's GitHub repository) and our ML classification models from the *Test your knowledge* section in the previous chapter trained to predict the TARGET column.

Compare the models using metrics and select the best one. Try balancing the classes in the data and see whether this improves performance. Finally, select the ideal threshold for rounding probability predictions and plot the confusion matrix with this ideal threshold. Write a short analysis of the results and process.

Summary

In this chapter, we covered metrics as well as sampling techniques for classification ML algorithms. Once we have a few models that we've tried fitting to the data, we can compare them with metrics. For evaluating metrics, we want to split our data into training/validation or training/test splits or use cross-validation to compare models, using the test or validation set to compute our metrics. Common classification metrics include accuracy, precision, recall, F1 score, and the AUC score from the ROC curve, and we can also use Cohen's Kappa as a metric. Additionally, we can optimize the rounding threshold for probability predictions from models using a few different methods with Youden's J, using the ROC curve or maximizing the F1 score. Visualizations for many of these metrics as well as confusion matrices can be created with the `sklearn`, `mlxtend`, and `yellowbrick` packages.

Lastly, we looked at undersampling and oversampling data to achieve a balance between classes in our dataset. Many of the oversampling methods use synthetic sampling, which generates new samples based on existing data, such as SMOTE. We saw how these can add a small boost to our performance.

Now that we've seen one side of supervised learning (classification), let's turn to the other – regression, which we can use for continuous values such as stock prices or the weather.

13
Machine Learning with Regression

In situations where we want to predict continuous values, such as temperature, housing prices, or salary, we can use regression models. These are another type of supervised learning besides the classification that we learned about in the last chapter. In this chapter, we'll cover some of the basics around regression models, including:

- Linear regression using sklearn and statsmodels
- Regularization with linear regression
- KNN and other sklearn models for regression
- Evaluating regression model performance

Let's get started by learning how linear regression works.

Linear regression

Linear regression has been around since the 1800s but is still used today. It is an easy-to-use and -interpret method that generally works for many datasets as long as we have relationships between our features and target that are somewhat linear and a few other assumptions are met.

With linear regression, we predict continuous values based on our features, and our results may look something like this:

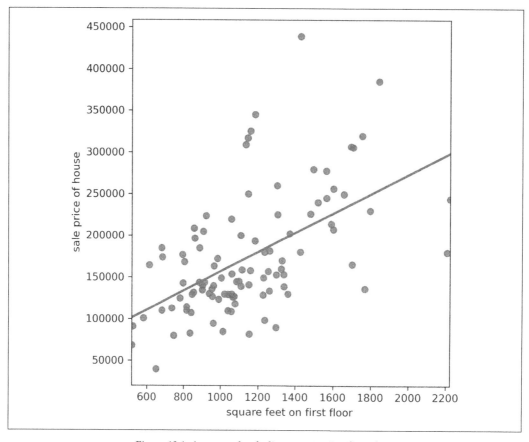

Figure 13.1: An example of a linear regression fit to data

Here, we have a scatter plot of square feet of the first floor of a house on the x-axis and the sale price on the y-axis. We can see a generally linear relationship holds, with higher prices corresponding to bigger square footage. The line shows a linear fit to the data.

To fit a simple 1-D linear model as shown above, we use the equation:

$$y = mx + b$$

Where m is the coefficient for our input feature and b is the value at which the line intersects the y-axis (the y-intercept). We can generalize this to multidimensional data (with n features) like so:

$$\hat{y} = \beta_1 x_1 + \beta_2 x_2 + \cdots + \beta_n x_n$$

For a y-intercept, we can add one more feature that is a constant (a column of all 1s) and our corresponding coefficient for that feature will be our y-intercept.

 Sometimes you will see the equation written with $+\epsilon$ at the end and $\hat{y}$ without the hat (y). The epsilon (ϵ) is the error term that represents the errors for each datapoint. Assuming epsilon captures all other errors in the system, we then can predict or model exact values for the y-values. You may also see the equation written in matrix notation like $\mathbf{Y} = \mathbf{X}\beta$.

For a normal implementation like this (with no regularization) we can exactly solve the equation for the coefficients (beta values, β). Adding regularization will add a penalty for coefficients becoming large, which prevents overfitting. If we use regularization, the coefficients are found by iterating in the same way as we did for logistic regression in the previous chapter. In that case, we initialize the variables and make predictions, then change the coefficients so our predictions become closer to the targets. We do this with mathematical optimizers and can use gradient descent where we change the coefficients in the way that should decrease the difference between predictions and actual values the most.

Using linear regression with `sklearn` and `statsmodels` is straightforward, even when adding regression. We will use a housing price dataset to learn linear regression. The dataset comes from Ames, IA, and was compiled by Dean De Cock in 2011 (`http://jse.amstat.org/v19n3/decock.pdf`). Other copies of the dataset can be found in Kaggle's datasets. For our demonstrations, only a few of the features were retained, which are all numeric.

Before doing linear regression, it's not a bad idea to look at the Pearson correlation between our features and the target. Let's first load our data:

```
import pandas as pd

df = pd.read_csv('data/housing_data_sample.csv', index_col='Id')
```

We are setting the `Id` column as the index since it is a unique identifier for each datapoint. Examining the data with some EDA is not a bad idea, such as using `pandas-profiling` and `df.head()`. The first few rows look like this:

Id	LotArea	YearBuilt	FullBath	TotRmsAbvGrd	GarageArea	1stFlrSF	2ndFlrSF	SalePrice
1	8450	2003	2	8	548	856	854	208500
2	9600	1976	2	6	460	1262	0	181500
3	11250	2001	2	6	608	920	866	223500
4	9550	1915	1	7	642	961	756	140000
5	14260	2000	2	9	836	1145	1053	250000

Figure 13.2: The first 5 rows of our housing price dataset

We have a target column, SalePrice, which is the price at which a house is sold between the years 2006 and 2010. The other columns are features that describe the house, such as the area of the land the house is on (LotArea) and the number of rooms above ground (TotRmsAbvGrd). The Garage and SF columns describe the square footage of different parts of the house.

Let's then look at the Pearson correlation between features and our target:

```
df.corr()['SalePrice']
```

This shows us:

```
LotArea          0.263843
YearBuilt        0.522897
FullBath         0.560664
TotRmsAbvGrd     0.533723
GarageArea       0.623431
1stFlrSF         0.605852
2ndFlrSF         0.319334
SalePrice        1.000000
Name: SalePrice, dtype: float64
```

We can see all the features seem to have at least a moderate-strength Pearson correlation with the target variable, SalePrice. Remember that the Pearson correlation is the default method used by the pandas corr function. It measures the strength of linear correlations between variables, with a +1 being a perfect positive correlation (both variables always increase together by proportional amounts), -1 being a perfect negative or inverse correlation, and 0 being no linear correlation at all. Since we have several correlations that are well above 0, we can expect linear regression to work for this problem. Let's first take a look at how to model the sale price with linear regression.

Linear regression with sklearn

First, we'll use scikit-learn to fit a linear model to data. As with all `sklearn` models, our data needs to be fully numeric before we fit a model, so we need to convert any string or categorical columns into numeric types with methods we covered in *Chapter 10, Preparing Data for Machine Learning: Feature Selection, Feature Engineering, and Dimensionality Reduction*. Our data is already fully numeric here, however.

Before we fit a model to the data, let's break our data into train and test sets as we did in the previous chapter. Remember that we want to evaluate the performance of our models on an unseen test set to get an idea of how well the model will perform on new data. We use `sklearn` to break up the data into train and tests sets as before:

```
from sklearn.model_selection import train_test_split

x_train, x_test, y_train, y_test = train_test_split(df.drop('SalePrice',
                                                    axis=1),
                                        df['SalePrice'],
                                        random_state=42)
```

We give the `train_test_split` function our features first (by dropping the target column from the DataFrame), then our targets (by selecting only the target column). We also set the random state for reproducible results (so we get the same results every time).

For data with a time series aspect to it, it's much better to break up the data into continuous chunks by time. For example, if we will use the model to predict future home prices, we might want to use the earlier data as training and the latest data as a test set. We can do this by sorting the DataFrame by its time column (`YrSold` in the full dataset) then indexing the DataFrame to get something like 75% of the first part of the data as train and the rest as test.

Now we can fit a linear regression model from `sklearn` to the data and use the built-in evaluation function:

```
from sklearn.linear_model import LinearRegression

lr = LinearRegression()
lr.fit(x_train, y_train)
print(lr.score(x_train, y_train))
print(lr.score(x_test, y_test))
```

This works just the same as we saw for classification models in `sklearn`. First, we import the class for the model, then initialize it. There are some options we can set for the `LinearRegression` class but we don't need to do it for now (for example, it fits a y-intercept term by default).

We then train the model by using the `fit` method with the train features (*x*) and targets (*y*) and use the built-in `score` method to evaluate performance. This returns:

```
0.6922037863468924
0.7335111149578266
```

The built-in score method is R^2, or the coefficient of determination. We will explore this in more detail in the evaluation section in this chapter. For now, all we need to know is R^2 is 1.0 when we have a perfect model (that exactly gets all y values correct) and 0 when we use the average value of the target variable as our prediction for all datapoints. We can see our R^2 values are not too bad – at least they are closer to 1 than 0. We also don't see evidence of overfitting since the test score is not significantly lower than the train score.

Once our model is trained, we can examine the coefficients and y-intercept:

```
print(lr.coef_)
print(lr.intercept_)
```

This shows us:

```
array([ 4.69748692e-01,  8.27939635e+02, -3.57322963e+03, -2.59678130e+01,
        6.46264545e+01,  9.74383176e+01,  7.18384417e+01])
-1619889.0110532893
```

The way to interpret these coefficients is that the value is the increase in the home price with a unit increase in the feature. For example, there is (on average) an increase of 0.47 in the home price for each unit increase in lot area (the first coefficient and feature). The coefficients are lined up with the column names in x_train, so we can create a bar plot that's a little easier to interpret:

```
import seaborn as sns

sns.barplot(x=lr.coef_, y=x_train.columns, color='darkblue')
```

Our plot looks like this:

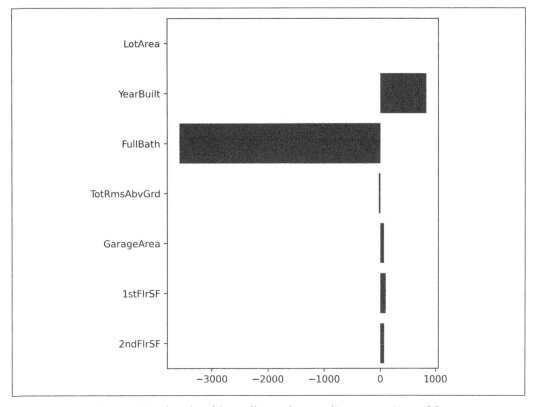

Figure 13.3: A bar plot of the coefficients from our linear regression model

Something seems off with these coefficients. The Pearson correlation was positive for all features with relation to the target variable, so we would expect the coefficients to be positive. We can also create scatter plots of the features with the targets to observe their relationships - for example, with:

```
sns.scatterplot(x=df['FullBath'], y=df['SalePrice'])
```

which looks like the coefficients should all be positive. Intuitively, we know that more bedrooms and bathrooms in a house tend to increase the price as well, so losing around $3,000 in home value for each bathroom added makes no sense. In order to understand what's going on, it helps to use `statsmodels` to get the statistical significance of our coefficients.

Linear regression with statsmodels

Just like with logistic regression from the previous chapter, we can get the p-values and standard error of our coefficients with `statsmodels`. Let's train another linear regression model with `statsmodels` and examine the results:

```
import statsmodels.api as sm

sm_lr = sm.OLS(y_train, sm.add_constant(x_train))
res = sm_lr.fit()
res.summary()
```

First, we import the `statsmodels` package as `sm`, then initialize our linear model with the `sm.OLS` class (OLS stands for ordinary least squares, which is the method we are using for our linear regressions here). Remember that with `statsmodels` we give the data to the model class when we initialize it, giving it the target as the first argument and features as the second argument. We need to add a constant to our features with `sm.add_constant` if we want to get a y-intercept term. Then we train the model with `fit`, and finally look at the results with the `summary()` method of the returned object from the fit. Our results look like this:

OLS Regression Results

Dep. Variable:	SalePrice	R-squared:	0.692
Model:	OLS	Adj. R-squared:	0.690
Method:	Least Squares	F-statistic:	349.2
Date:	Wed, 21 Apr 2021	Prob (F-statistic):	6.20e-273
Time:	21:50:35	Log-Likelihood:	-13242.
No. Observations:	1095	AIC:	2.650e+04
Df Residuals:	1087	BIC:	2.654e+04
Df Model:	7		
Covariance Type:	nonrobust		

	coef	std err	t	P>|t|	[0.025	0.975]
const	-1.62e+06	1.07e+05	-15.165	0.000	-1.83e+06	-1.41e+06
LotArea	0.4697	0.126	3.729	0.000	0.223	0.717
YearBuilt	827.9396	55.108	15.024	0.000	719.810	936.069
FullBath	-3573.2296	3523.070	-1.014	0.311	-1.05e+04	3339.558
TotRmsAbvGrd	-25.9678	1451.611	-0.018	0.986	-2874.245	2822.309
GarageArea	64.6265	8.145	7.934	0.000	48.645	80.608
1stFlrSF	97.4383	5.722	17.029	0.000	86.211	108.665
2ndFlrSF	71.8384	5.337	13.461	0.000	61.367	82.310

Figure 13.4: The results of the statsmodels linear regression on our housing data. Note that there are some more results and notes that are output from the summary() function we are not showing here

We can look at the two features with negative coefficients, `FullBath` and `TotRmsAbvGrd`. They both have large p-values, signifying that their values are not significantly different from 0. We can also see their standard errors are larger than or about as large as the coefficients themselves and the 95% confidence interval for these coefficients passes through 0. This means these coefficients are not useful and we could drop these two columns from our dataset in this model. It appears the other features are more important or better predictors of the home price. Note that the `FullBath` and `TotRmsAbvGrd` features are still related to the target since they have moderate Pearson correlations to `SalePrice` – if we fit a model using only one or both of these, the coefficients will be positive and the p-values small.

By dropping these two features, we can perform some feature selection. We can also use regularization to perform feature selection or at least prevent overfitting from our model.

Regularized linear regression

Regularization in linear regression works the same way as we saw in the previous chapter with logistic regression. With logistic regression, we had a loss function we optimized that captured the difference between predictions and actual values. With linear regression, we use the same idea, and are minimizing the difference between predictions and actual values. We minimize the sum of the squared differences between predictions and actual values, which we can write in matrix notation as: $||Y - X\beta||^2$. With regularization, we can use L1 (Lasso) or L2 (Ridge) regression. We can also combine the two with ElasticNet regularization. L1 adds a linear penalty term to our minimization function (or loss function): $||Y - X\beta||^2 + \alpha|\beta|$. Alpha ($\alpha$) is a hyperparameter we can set. With Ridge regression, we have a squared penalty term: $||Y - X\beta||^2 + \alpha|\beta|^2$. L1 tends to move coefficients to 0 while L2 does not. We can also combine them with ElasticNet and set another hyperparameter that controls the fraction of L1 vs L2. These methods cannot be solved exactly like with ordinary least squares and we must solve them iteratively like we did with logistic regression.

Using `sklearn`, we can easily use regularization:

```
from sklearn.linear_model import LassoCV

l1_lr = LassoCV()
l1_lr.fit(x_train, y_train)
```

Here, we are using the cross-validation implementation of L1 regularization. We could simply import Lasso instead, but we could only try one value for alpha at a time.

Instead, this automatically searches 100 values for alpha for us using cross-validation as we have explained in the previous chapter (see *Figure 11.5*, for example). Recall that we break up our training data into equal parts, then fit the model on part of the data and test on the remainder. We do this *n* times and average the final scores and can compare different settings for alpha this way. We can view the final value of alpha with `l1_lr.alpha_`, which is around 230,000 – that's a large penalty considering the default for the `Lasso` class is 1.0. Then we can see how the coefficients were changed with `l1_lr.coef_`:

```
array([4.27009150e-01, 5.07702347e+02, 0.00000000e+00, 0.00000000e+00,
       8.02080376e+01, 9.60455704e+01, 6.70594638e+01])
```

We can see here that the two coefficients that were negative before have now been regularized down to 0.

If we want to use the other types of regularization (L2 and ElasticNet), we simply import the classes `RidgeCV` and `ElasticNetCV` from `sklearn.linear_model` and fit them in the same way. The coefficients from `RidgeCV` look like this:

```
array([ 4.69964573e-01,  8.26351818e+02, -3.35200764e+03, -4.04117423e+01,
        6.46405518e+01,  9.73549913e+01,  7.17380074e+01])
```

Our coefficients haven't changed that much and are still negative for the two features that had negative coefficients with no regularization. The ElasticNet coefficients turn out to be:

```
array([ 1.28287688,  3.46879826,  0.       ,  0.       ,  27.15263788,
        41.1722103 , 27.02242165])
```

We can see our two coefficients that were negative are now 0, but the other coefficients are quite different from our L1 regularization. To choose the best model to use between the three, we can evaluate scores on the test dataset. First, we will not use the L2 regularization because it contained large negative values for variables we know should have positive coefficients. The R^2 values from the Lasso and ElasticNet models are around 0.73 and 0.4. It's clear that the Lasso model is much better, so we can use that as our best linear regression model so far.

By default, ElasticNet uses a value of 0.5 for the mix between L1 and L2 (this is the `l1_ratio` parameter). We could also try optimizing that hyperparameter like so: `en_lr = ElasticNetCV(l1_ratio=[.1, .5, .7, .9, .95, .99, 1])`. This searches the values in the list along with the 100 default alpha values for an optimum.

If we do this, we find the optimal L1 ratio is 1 (from en_lr.l1_ratio_), meaning L1 regression.

We could also use statsmodels to fit regularized models with the fit_regularized() method for our sm_lr model from before. It is not as easy to use cross-validation with statsmodels, so we could first optimize the alpha and l1_ratio hyperparameters from sklearn, then fit and evaluate the model with statsmodels. Note that the parameter refit should be True to be able to see the summary from statsmodels.

Regression with KNN in sklearn

Almost all models in sklearn have corresponding classification and regression implementations. **KNN** (*k-nearest neighbors*) is one of these models, and we already looked at the classification implementation in the previous chapter. With regression, KNN takes the average target value of the nearest *k* points to make predictions, either with uniform weights (the default with sklearn) or weighted by distance. We can fit and evaluate the R² score of a KNN model like so:

```
from sklearn.neighbors import KNeighborsRegressor

knr = KNeighborsRegressor()
knr.fit(x_train, y_train)
print(knr.score(x_train, y_train))
print(knr.score(x_test, y_test))
```

Again, all sklearn models work in the same fashion – initialize the model class with any parameters (the default for the main hyperparameter, n_neighbors, is 5), then fit it to data, then use the score function to evaluate the performance. Although we won't cover all the other possible regression models here, they can be found in the supervised learning section of the sklearn documentation (https://scikit-learn.org/stable/supervised_learning.html). The R² values from our model on the train and test sets are:

```
0.7169076259605272
0.6053882073906485
```

We can see there is some overfitting since the test score is much lower than the train score. Increasing the number of neighbors helps reduce this overfitting, although the test score does not improve beyond 0.6. Since this is lower than our linear regression model, we will stick with that one versus KNN.

Evaluating regression models

Regression models have their own suite of metrics we can use to evaluate them. We will cover some of the common metrics here:

- R^2
- Adjusted R^2
- Information criteria (we will look at the **Akaike Information Criterion**, **AIC**)
- Mean squared error
- Mean absolute error

These metrics allow us to compare different models and to measure how well the models perform in general.

R^2 or the coefficient of determination

We already saw R^2 in use as the default scoring metric of our `sklearn` models. It is 1 for a perfect model and has lower scores for a less perfect model. The equation for the metric is:

$$R^2 = 1 - \frac{SSR}{SST} = 1 - \frac{\Sigma_i(y_i - \hat{y}_i)^2}{\Sigma_i(y_i - \bar{y})^2}$$

where SSR is the sum of squares of residuals and SST is the total sum of squares. SSR is the difference between actual target values (y_i) and predicted values (y-hat or $\hat{y}$). The SST is the difference between actual values and the average value of the targets. So, by definition, if our predictions are the mean value of the targets, our R^2 score is 0:

```
from sklearn.metrics import r2_score

r2_score(y_train, [y_train.mean()] * y_train.shape[0])
```

This is similar to our "no information rate" from the previous chapter – as a baseline, we can compare our model's score to an R^2 of 0. If our model is particularly bad, we can even get an R^2 value below 0. We can see in the code above that we are importing the `r2_score` function from `sklearn.metrics` - this module holds many other metrics for classification and regression. For the method, we want to give the true values of y first, then the predictions second.

While R^2 is a decent metric, it doesn't take into account overfitting. For that, we can use some other metrics.

Adjusted R²

One way to incorporate a penalty for overfitting is to use the number of predictors (features) to decrease the scoring metric. This is what adjusted R² (R^2_{adj}) does – it adds a penalty for the number of predictors relative to the number of datapoints. We can calculate the adjusted R² manually:

```
r2 = r2_score(y_test, l1_lr.predict(x_test))
n, p = x_test.shape
adj_r2 = 1 - (1 - r2) * (n - 1) / (n - p - 1)
print(r2)
print(adj_r2)
```

Here, we first calculate the R² score using `sklearn` and our Lasso model from earlier. We then get the number of samples (n) and the number of features (p) to use in the adjusted R² equation. Our value for R² is around 0.73 while the adjusted version is 0.726. We don't see a big difference here, but if we have many features (especially relative to our number of datapoints) the adjusted R² value can decrease more.

 We can also see the R² and adjusted R² values output in the summary when we fit a `statsmodels` linear regression, along with many other metrics.

Classically, R² and adjusted R² are used on the training set for linear regression and not the test set. Also, we should ideally be using the mean of the training targets for our SST equation. We can calculate this manually (for example, with numpy as in this Stack Overflow answer: https://stackoverflow.com/a/895063/4549682), but using the built-in `sklearn` function can serve as a quick-and-dirty solution for R2.

A better use of R² and adjusted R² is to compare the performance of linear models on their training datasets. This can be one way to work toward selecting the best model.

Information criteria

Another method for evaluating models is by using information criteria. These have some scoring method and a penalty that increases with the number of parameters (or features). Most, if not all, of the information criteria are better if their value is lower. We will look at the **Akaike Information Criterion (AIC)** here, which is 2 times the log-likelihood plus a penalty term for the number of coefficients (parameters, or features):

$$AIC = n * \log\left(\frac{SSR}{n}\right) + 2k$$

where n is the number of datapoints, SSR is our sum of squares of residuals, and k is the number of features. There is a package in Python that can calculate the AIC as well as some other information criteria such as the BIC (Bayesian information criteria) and Mallow's Cp. This package is only available via `pip` and should be installed with `pip install RegscorePy`. We can then calculate the AIC like so:

```
from RegscorePy.aic import aic

aic(y_train, l1_lr.predict(x_train), x_train.shape[1])
```

We simply import the function from the package's `aic` module, then call it with the true values, predictions, and number of features. Here, we get a value of around 23,500. The value by itself is not of much use, but we can use it to compare models. For example, we can try removing features to find the model with the best AIC score. To do this, we'd need to write our own code, fitting the model and calculating the AIC, and then comparing the results at the end to get the lowest AIC score. This is one instance where the R programming language has an advantage since it already has a function from a library (`stepAIC` from `MASS`) that can do this for us.

The `RegscorePy` package also has `bic` for the BIC. Although there are many other information criteria (for example, many of them are listed here: https://en.wikipedia.org/wiki/Model_selection#Criteria), AIC and BIC are usually sufficient. These are also listed in the results of a `statsmodels` linear regression fit.

Mean squared error

A common way to evaluate regression models is with mean squared error. This has the equation:

$$\frac{1}{n}\sum_i (y_i - \hat{y}_i)^2$$

In other words, we take the difference between each actual value and prediction, square it, then sum those up. Finally, we divide by the number of samples, which gives us the average squared difference between predictions and actual values. We can use this with `sklearn` like so:

```
from sklearn.metrics import mean_squared_error as mse

mse(y_test, l1_lr.predict(x_test))
```

We first import the function from `sklearn` and alias it as `mse` since the function name is long, then we give it the true and predicted values. Our result from the housing price data here is around 1.9 billion, which is hard to interpret. Of course, we can use it to compare with other models. To get a more intuitive result, we can set the squared argument to `False` to get the root-mean-square error, or RMSE. This simply takes the square root of MSE, putting our metric on the same scale as our data. When we do this, our result is around 43,000. This seems decent considering the average home price in the dataset is around 160,000. Another metric that is more easily interpretable than MSE is MAE or mean absolute error.

Mean absolute error

This metric takes the absolute value (converting any negative values to positives) of differences between predictions and actual target values, then divides by the number of samples:

$$\frac{1}{n} \sum_i |y_i - \hat{y}_i|$$

One advantage of this over RMSE or MSE is that it is a little less sensitive to outliers. If we have large outliers in the dataset and the difference between the prediction and actual value is large, squaring this value can heavily influence MSE, but influences MAE less. We use this in exactly the same way as MSE:

```
from sklearn.metrics import mean_absolute_error as mae
```

```
mae(y_test, l1_lr.predict(x_test))
```

Our result here is around 27,000. In this case, using MAE as a metric is probably a better choice than MSE since we do have a skewed dataset with some large outliers.

Linear regression assumptions

When using linear regression, there are several assumptions we should be aware of:

- Linear relationships between features and the target
- Normally distributed data
- No multicollinearity between features
- No autocorrelation of the target
- Homoscedasticity (uniformity of the spread of residual values across the data)

Checking some of these assumptions requires generating some plots. This is another place where R has a small advantage – we can directly plot some of the diagnostic plots from a linear model in R with ease. However, it's not too hard to check these assumptions ourselves, and regardless of using R or Python, we have to go through many of the same steps.

We can check these assumptions in several ways. First, for the linear relationships, we can use Pearson correlation as we did with df.corr() to see if linear relationships exist. We can also simply try the linear model to see if any statistically significant coefficients are found. Another way to check is by simply plotting scatter plots of each feature versus the target. If these methods all agree there are linear relationships between the features and targets, this assumption is met.

One other way to check for linearity of features and the target is with a residuals versus fitted plot. This plots the fitted values on the x-axis and residuals (actual values minus predicted values) on the y-axis. We can create this plot like so:

```
predictions = l1_lr.predict(df.drop('SalePrice', axis=1))
residuals = df['SalePrice'] - predictions
sns.regplot(x=predictions,
            y=residuals,
            lowess=True,
            line_kws={'color': 'red'})
plt.xlabel('fitted values')
plt.ylabel('residuals')
```

First, we get our predictions and residuals, then plot it on a scatter plot with a Lowess line (a locally-fitted linear model). We are using the full dataset here instead of just the train or test set to get a more complete picture of the data. Our plot looks like this:

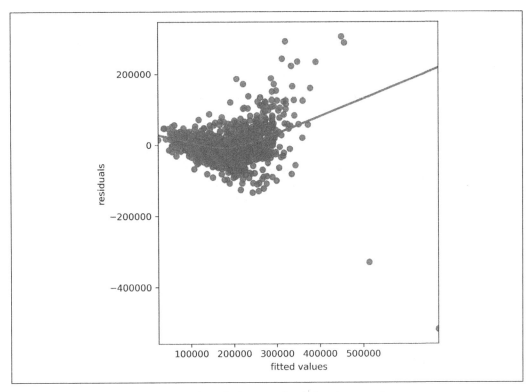

Figure 13.5: A residuals versus fitted plot of our test data

We can see the Lowess line (or Lowess curve) is not very flat, indicating there are some non-linear aspects to our data. This means our linearity assumption is not perfectly captured, and it looks like there are some second-order effects. We could try engineering some features, for example by squaring some of the features, which may fix this issue. We also could simply try a more complex model, like a random forest or another tree-based model. Another issue we see from this plot is the large outliers at the high end of the data. These outliers skew the fit parameters and should probably be excluded from the model.

For our next assumption, we want all our features and target to be normally distributed, or close to it. We can check this by plotting histograms and running statistical tests like the Kolmogorov-Smirnov or Anderson-Darling tests for normality we learned about in *Chapter 9, Statistical Testing for Data Science*. If our distributions aren't exactly normal but are close, we are probably OK. Often the statistical tests for normality are very sensitive and may tell us our distribution is not normal when it is close. However, if our data is obviously very far from a normal distribution, we can transform it to be more normal with the Yeo-Johnson transform we learned about in *Chapter 10, Preparing Data for Machine Learning: Feature Selection, Feature Engineering, and Dimensionality Reduction*.

Multicollinearity is when features are linearly related to one another. A perfectly colinear pair of features will have a Pearson correlation of 1. We can check for this with the Pearson correlation, and if pairs or groups of features have correlations of 1, we only need to keep one of the features. Often if we try to fit a linear regression to data with multicollinearity problems, the function returns an error.

Autocorrelation is when the target follows a temporal pattern. For example, sound waves from a perfectly repeating and uniform sound like a synthesizer follow a repeating pattern and are perfectly autocorrelated. Another example of where autocorrelation can be a problem is stock prices. This only matters for time series data and isn't relevant for our housing dataset. However, we will show how to check this assumption with our data. We can check for autocorrelation with the autocorr function in pandas:

```
for i in range(1, 11):
    print(y_train.autocorr(i))
```

Here, we loop through values 1 through 10 and calculate the Pearson correlation between the target variable and itself spaced by the value of *i* (called the "lag"). We find here that all these values are close to 0, so autocorrelation does not appear to be a problem. An even better way is to use another pandas function:

```
pd.plotting.autocorrelation_plot(y_train)
```

This generates an autocorrelation plot that looks like this:

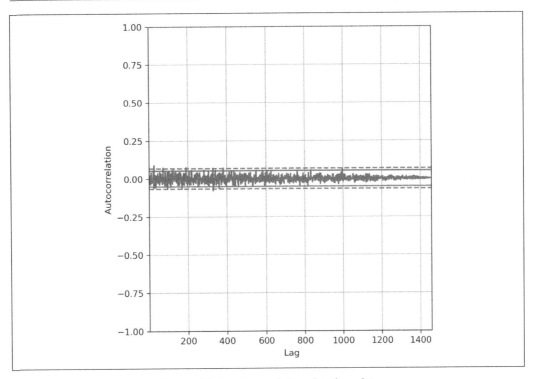

Figure 13.6: An autocorrelation plot of our data

The blue, squiggly line in the middle represents autocorrelation calculations over different lag periods (the x-axis is the lag) and the horizontal lines represent 95% and 99% confidence intervals. If substantial portions of the blue line are outside of the confidence intervals, we likely have autocorrelation present.

Our last assumption is homoscedasticity, which means that the variance of the residuals should be approximately uniform across all values of the target. This word is tricky to pronounce, so it doesn't hurt to look up online how to pronounce it before repeating it to others. We can check this with a scale-location plot (but also from our residuals vs fitted plot). The scale-location plot can be created like this:

```
import numpy as np

standardized_residuals = np.sqrt(residuals / residuals.std())
```

```
sns.regplot(x=predictions,
            y=standardized_residuals,
            lowess=True,
            line_kws={'color': 'red'})
plt.xlabel('predicted values')
plt.ylabel('sqrt(standardized residuals)')
```

First, we create our standardized residuals by dividing by their standard deviation. We then take the square root of the standardized residuals. Next, we plot our predictions on the x-axis and these residuals on the y-axis and fit a Lowess line to it. The plot looks like:

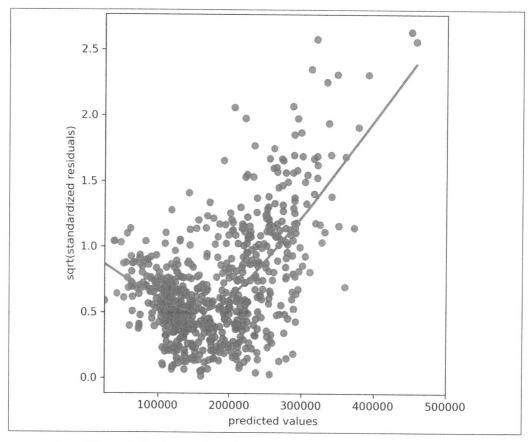

Figure 13.7: A scale-location plot shows the assumption of homoscedasticity has been violated

We can see the standardized residuals become more spread out when the home prices are around 250,000 to 300,000, and are smaller near 100,000, so our assumption is not quite met here.

Although some of our assumptions didn't perfectly hold, the model is still useful as it does better than our baseline of predicting the mean sale value. We can improve the model by removing outliers and doing some feature engineering, or by using a more complex model. For example, we might take the square root of the number of rooms above ground, since there may be diminishing returns to the price with more rooms in the house.

Regression models on big data

We may find ourselves working with data that's too big to fit on our single machine, in which case we need to use big data solutions. These solutions are the same as for logistic regression on the classification side. In fact, many of these use a GLM, or generalized linear model, that can be configured to be logistic or linear regression. Some of our options are:

- Vowpal Wabbit
- H2O
- TensorFlow
- Spark (`pyspark`)
- Dask
- AWS SageMaker's or Google Cloud's Linear Learner

Of course, the solution we choose depends on what we have available and is easiest to use. The cloud solutions like AWS and GCP generally provide easy-to-use services, and we may have to use those for other solutions like Spark or Dask anyway. However, if we have an on-premises cluster with certain software installed and/or specific data privacy concerns, we may not want to use cloud solutions.

Forecasting

Another use of regression is for forecasting. For example, we can forecast future values in a time series like security prices, the weather, sales, or web traffic data. Let's use our daily bitcoin price data from *Chapter 4, Loading and Wrangling Data with Pandas and NumPy* as an example:

```
btc_df = pd.read_csv('data/bitcoin_price.csv')
btc_df['time'] = pd.to_datetime(btc_df['time'], unit='ms')
btc_df.set_index('time', inplace=True)
btc_df = btc_df[['close', 'volume']]
```

We load the data and only keep the closing price and volume. We are also setting the time column as the index after parsing it to a datetime. The units for the time column are milliseconds since the epoch.

To create a target column with future closing price data, we can use a pandas function:

```
btc_df['close_1d_future'] = btc_df['close'].shift(-1)
btc_df.dropna(inplace=True)
```

The shift function moves the data relative to the index. If we move the data back by one timestep relative to the index, it is the closing price one day in the future. We can provide any integer and get the price any day in the future this way. Because this also creates missing values at the end of the dataset, we drop rows with missing values to avoid problems later.

Now we can create our features and targets, as well as a train and test set:

```
features = btc_df.drop('close_1d_future', axis=1)
targets = btc_df['close_1d_future']

train_idx = int(0.75 * btc_df.shape[0])
x_train = features.iloc[:train_idx]
y_train = targets.iloc[:train_idx]
x_test = features.iloc[train_idx:]
y_test = targets.iloc[train_idx:]
```

Here, we first create features by dropping the target column, and create the targets by only selecting the target column. Then we get the index value for the 75th percentile of data. We index the features and targets to keep the first 75% of the data in the training set and then retain 25% of the data in the test set. Since this is a time series dataset, we want to use the latest data as a test set and not randomly mix our data to get the train and test sets.

We can then fit and evaluate a model. Here, we will use the MAE score to evaluate it (to minimize the outliers' effects):

```
from sklearn.model_selection import TimeSeriesSplit

l1_lr = LassoCV(cv=TimeSeriesSplit())
l1_lr.fit(x_train, y_train)
print(mae(y_train, l1_lr.predict(x_train)))
print(mae(y_test, l1_lr.predict(x_test)))
```

We first fit a Lasso regression to the data, which also selects an optimal alpha value from cross-validation. We also provide a time series cross-validator for the `LassoCV` model, which doesn't break up data randomly into train/validation splits but uses the first part of the data as train and the last part of the data as test, and slowly increases the train size (a nice visualization of this can be found here: `https://scikit-learn.org/stable/auto_examples/model_selection/plot_cv_indices.html#sphx-glr-auto-examples-model-selection-plot-cv-indices-py`). Unfortunately, it seems like we still end up with an overfit model, which gives us MAE scores of 86 for train and 221 for test (remember, lower is better for MAE). This is common for forecasting on financial time series data, however. Part of the reason for this is that financial time series are often correlated, which you can see by plotting the autocorrelation plot of our Bitcoin close prices with the `pd.plotting.autocorrelation_plot()` function that we used earlier. We can visualize the data like so:

```
train_dates = btc_df.index[:train_idx]
test_dates = btc_df.index[train_idx:]
train_predictions = l1_lr.predict(x_train)
test_predictions = l1_lr.predict(x_test)
plt.plot_date(train_dates, y_train, fmt='-', color='b')
plt.plot_date(train_dates, train_predictions, fmt='--', color='orange')
plt.plot_date(test_dates, y_test, fmt='-', color='k')
plt.plot_date(test_dates, test_predictions, fmt='--', color='r')
plt.axvline(btc_df.index[train_idx])
plt.yscale('log')
```

This creates a series of dates for the train and test sets, then gets predictions for both train and test. Next, we use `matplotlib`'s `plot_date` function to plot our targets and predictions against the dates. We change the format of the actual data to be a solid line and predictions to be a dashed line and change the colors so train and test as well as actual values and predictions are different. Last, we draw a vertical line at the train/test split and change the y-scale to log. There is a lot of data, so one would need to explore this data interactively to get an idea of where the model is working and where it fails. To do that, we could use the magic command `%matplotlib` or `%matplotlib notebook` in our Jupyter Notebook to make the plots interactive. We would also want to check our assumptions on this data to make sure they hold.

Another nice tool for forecasting is Facebook's Prophet package. This is available in R and Python and can be installed with `conda install -c conda-forge prophet`. First, we need to rearrange our data to be ready for Prophet. We need our dates in a column named `ds`, and our target in a column named `y`:

```
btc_df.reset_index(inplace=True)
btc_df.drop('close_1d_future', axis=1, inplace=True)
btc_df.rename(columns={'close': 'y', 'time': 'ds'}, inplace=True)
```

We don't need the future closing price column anymore, so we dropped it. Next, we can fit our model to the data:

```
from prophet import Prophet

m = Prophet()
m.fit(btc_df)
```

Then we can get a forecast for a year into the future and plot it:

```
future = m.make_future_dataframe(periods=365)
forecast = m.predict(future)
m.plot(forecast)
```

Our plot looks like this:

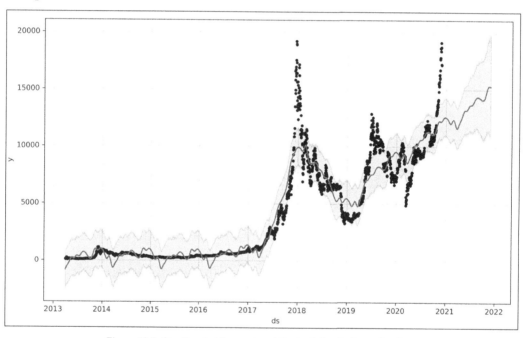

Figure 13.8: Our Prophet forecast on bitcoin daily closing price data

The model consists of a piecewise linear fit along with some season trends that are decomposed using advanced methods. We can examine these components like so:

```
m.plot_components(forecast)
```

Overall, Prophet provides an easy and quick-and-dirty way to do forecasting. However, we can see it doesn't do too well when the data has erratic components like bitcoin price data.

Test your knowledge

Use the full Ames housing dataset in this book's GitHub repository (under `Chapter13\data\housing_data_full.csv`) and improve upon our linear regression model to predict house sale prices. You might try some feature engineering, data cleaning, and feature selection in order to improve your results.

Summary

In this chapter we learned the basics of regression. We mainly covered linear regression, which is one of the easier-to-use models and is easier to interpret. The assumptions for linear regression were discussed, including linear relationships between the features and target, normal distributions of data, no multicollinearity, no autocorrelation of the target, and homoscedasticity (a uniform spread of residuals among target values). We saw how we can use regularization with linear regression to select features with L1 or Lasso regularization, since it will move some coefficients to 0. We also saw how we can try L2 or Ridge regression as well as using a combination of L1 and L2 with ElasticNet.

We saw how other `sklearn` models can be used for regression as well and demonstrated the KNN model for this. Additionally, the `statsmodels` package was used for linear regression to be able to get p-values for the statistical significance of our coefficients. Metrics for evaluating regression models were covered, such as R^2, adjusted R^2, information criteria such as AIC (Akaike Information Criterion) and BIC (Bayesian Information Criterion), MSE (mean squared error), RMSE (root-mean-square error), and MAE (mean absolute error). Recall that MAE is a little better for evaluating datasets with outliers than RMSE or MSE.

Last, we looked at forecasting by properly preparing our data so that our target column has future values and using linear regression to predict the future value of our target. Another way we saw to forecast data was with the Prophet package from Facebook. We saw how forecasting price data for securities or something like bitcoin price is difficult.

In the next chapter, we'll look at ways of optimizing and selecting models by extending what we've already learned in this and the previous chapter.

14

Optimizing Models and Using AutoML

So far, we've looked at a few **machine learning** (**ML**) models for classification and regression: simple linear models (linear regression and logistic regression), *k*-**nearest neighbors** (**KNN**), and Naïve Bayes for classification. As we will see in these next few chapters, there are other models that are commonly used in ML and data science. This chapter will cover how to choose between models and how to optimize models. Specifically, we'll cover:

- Hyperparameter optimization with random, grid, and Bayesian searches
- Using learning curves to optimize the amount of data needed and diagnose ML models
- Optimizing the number of features with recursive feature selection
- Using the `pycaret` AutoML Python package

Let's get started with hyperparameter optimization using a few different search methods.

Hyperparameter optimization with search methods

We've already seen some hyperparameters for the few ML models we've examined so far, for example, the regularization strength hyperparameters for linear and logistic regression, or the value of *k* (for the number of nearest neighbors) in KNN.

Remember that hyperparameters are settings for the models that we choose, while parameters are values the models learn (like the coefficients for linear or logistic regression). Arguments provided to functions in Python and programming are also called parameters as we've seen previously.

We've also seen how there are **cross-validation (CV)** classes for linear and logistic regression in sklearn that allow us to optimize the C or alpha hyperparameter for regularization strength. However, these built-in CV methods only search for one optimum hyperparameter and don't have to worry about multiple hyperparameters at once. When we introduce more than one hyperparameter to optimize, things get more complex.

An example is the KNN algorithm, which makes predictions by averaging the k nearest points to a datapoint. From the sklearn documentation for the regression version of KNN (https://scikit-learn.org/stable/modules/generated/sklearn.neighbors.KNeighborsRegressor.html), we can see there are several hyperparameters we could tune:

- n_neighbors
- weights
- p (the Minkowski distance power parameter)
- Others including algorithm, leaf_size, metric, and metric_params

The Minkowski distance is a general formula for the distance between two points. When p is 2, this is the Euclidean distance (straight line distance); when p is 1, it is the Manhattan or city block distance.

There are a few methods for tuning an ML algorithm with many hyperparameters:

- Random search
- Grid search
- Bayesian search and other advanced search methods

These all take a defined hyperparameter space and search it in different ways. The random search, as the name implies, randomly tries different combinations of hyperparameters. Grid search methodically tries all combinations of hyperparameters we provide. Finally, Bayesian search uses Bayesian statistical principles to more efficiently search a hyperparameter space. There are several other advanced search methods, including the Hyperband, Tree-structured Parzen Estimator (TPE), and the CMA-ES algorithms implemented in the optuna and other Python packages.

We can also modify the random and grid searches with successive halving, as described in the `sklearn` documentation (`https://scikit-learn.org/stable/modules/grid_search.html`).

These search methods use CV, which we covered in *Chapter 11*, *Machine Learning for Classification*, but will review here. For CV, we break up our data into n parts, where a common value for n might be 3 or 5. We can also stratify our data (if we are doing classification) so that the balance of classes is the same between the different parts. Then we train an ML model on all of the parts except one. The dataset that was left out of the training is called the hold-out, validation, or test set, and we evaluate the model's performance on this test set to understand how it performs. Then we do this for all possible combinations of the data. For n-fold CV, we have n combinations. Finally, we average the scores on the test sets to arrive at an overall score. With hyperparameter searches, we do this process for each combination of hyperparameters and choose the combination with the best score. For example, a 3-fold CV strategy is shown in *Figure 14.1*:

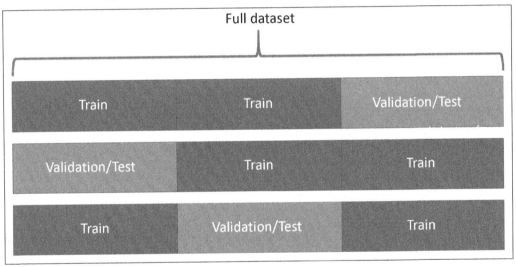

Figure 14.1: An example of 3-fold CV. This is the same as Figure 11.5 from Chapter 11

Let's start with one of the simpler methods: grid search in `sklearn`. First, we will load our data:

```
import pandas as pd

df = pd.read_csv('data/housing_data_sample.csv', index_col='Id')
```

We are using the same data from the previous chapter, which has house sale prices from Ames, Iowa, with numeric features describing the houses (such as year built, number of bedrooms and bathrooms, and so on). This is a regression problem, but the techniques we will cover work just as well for classification. We will only be using the KNN model in our demonstrations, but of course this works for other ML models with hyperparameters as well.

Using grid search

To use grid search, we can use a built-in sklearn class: GridSearchCV. We need to define an ML model and set of hyperparameters first:

```
from sklearn.neighbors import KNeighborsRegressor

knn = KNeighborsRegressor()
hyperparameters = {'n_neighbors': [3, 5, 7],
                   'weights': ['uniform', 'distance'],
                   'p': [1, 2]}
```

We first import the KNN regressor model and initialize it, then we create a dictionary of hyperparameters. Each key in the dictionary is a parameter for the ML model class, and the values are lists of values to try. We can then use the GridSearchCV class to find the optimal combination of hyperparameters:

```
from sklearn.model_selection import GridSearchCV

features = df.drop('SalePrice', axis=1)
targets = df['SalePrice']

gs = GridSearchCV(knn,
                  hyperparameters,
                  scoring='neg_mean_absolute_error',
                  n_jobs=-1)
gs.fit(features, targets)
```

We first import the grid search class, then create our features and targets from our DataFrame. Next, we initialize the grid search class with our KNN model (we could also put the KNeighborsRegressor() class instantiation call there directly), our dictionary of hyperparameters, a scoring metric, and the number of processors to use (-1 for n_jobs specifies to use all available CPUs). Notice we are specifying a custom scoring metric here, which is the negative value of the **mean absolute error** (**MAE**). The default scoring metric for regression models in sklearn is R^2 but using RMSE or MAE can be a little easier to interpret and explain.

Finally, we call the `fit` method on features and targets, which performs CV on the data with each combination of hyperparameters. By default, it uses 5-fold stratified CV (the stratification only matters for classification, and keeps the proportion of different classes the same between train and test sets). We can change the number of CV splits with the `cv` parameter for `GridSearchCV` by providing a number. Grid search tries every possible combination of the hyperparameters we provide to it.

Once our grid search is finished, we can look at the best results:

```
print(gs.best_estimator_)
print(gs.best_params_)
print(gs.best_score_)
```

This shows us the results of the three attributes of the `gs` object on the three lines below:

```
KNeighborsRegressor(n_neighbors=7, p=1, weights='distance')
{'n_neighbors': 7, 'p': 1, 'weights': 'distance'}
-30069.78491711035
```

We can see from the best score (the last line) that the average error between predictions and actual values is around $30k. For regression, we want to use negative values since the grid search here is maximizing the score to find the best model (it also maximizes the score for classification). We can choose from many pre-built scores listed in the documentation (`https://scikit-learn.org/stable/modules/model_evaluation.html#scoring-parameter`) or we can create our own scoring metric using the `make_scorer` function from `sklearn`. In many cases we will be able to use one of the pre-built scoring methods. The `best_params_` attribute gives us a dictionary of hyperparameters for the best model, and the `best_model_` attribute gives us the `sklearn` model we can use to re-train on the full dataset or to make predictions.

Grid search works well if you know a specific set of hyperparameter you want to search. However, it exhaustively searches all possible hyperparameter combinations, which can take a long time for a large dataset or many combinations of hyperparmeters. It does give us a lot of results of scores for different hyperparameters, however. We can examine the sets of hyperparameters and their corresponding CV scores like so:

```
list(zip(gs.cv_results_['params'], gs.cv_results_['mean_test_score']))
```

Which shows that every combination of hyperparameters has been tried:

```
[({'n_neighbors': 3, 'p': 1, 'weights': 'uniform'}, -31795.947260273977),
 ({'n_neighbors': 3, 'p': 1, 'weights': 'distance'}, -31226.346501552915),
 ({'n_neighbors': 3, 'p': 2, 'weights': 'uniform'}, -32975.90890410959),
 ({'n_neighbors': 3, 'p': 2, 'weights': 'distance'}, -32338.55514879399),
 ({'n_neighbors': 5, 'p': 1, 'weights': 'uniform'}, -31175.630547945206),
 ({'n_neighbors': 5, 'p': 1, 'weights': 'distance'}, -30438.96577645269),
 ({'n_neighbors': 5, 'p': 2, 'weights': 'uniform'}, -31986.23561643836),
 ({'n_neighbors': 5, 'p': 2, 'weights': 'distance'}, -31134.3566873946),
 ({'n_neighbors': 7, 'p': 1, 'weights': 'uniform'}, -30935.39412915851),
 ({'n_neighbors': 7, 'p': 1, 'weights': 'distance'}, -30069.78491711035),
 ({'n_neighbors': 7, 'p': 2, 'weights': 'uniform'}, -32122.704011741684),
 ({'n_neighbors': 7, 'p': 2, 'weights': 'distance'}, -31028.74010010045)]
```

We can see the CV scores are not terribly different, so our optimization didn't make a huge difference here. However, if we are using a bigger dataset or a bigger hyperparameter space, random search can speed up the process by trying fewer combinations.

Using random search

The `sklearn` random search for hyperparameters operates like grid search, but we can provide distributions for hyperparameters instead of specific values. For example, we can specify a uniform distribution between 3 and 20 for `n_neighbors`:

```python
from sklearn.model_selection import RandomizedSearchCV
from scipy.stats import randint

hyperparameters = {'n_neighbors': randint(low=3, high=20),
                   'weights': ['uniform', 'distance'],
                   'p': [1, 2]}
rs = RandomizedSearchCV(knn,
                        hyperparameters,
                        scoring='neg_mean_absolute_error',
                        n_jobs=-1,
                        random_state=42)
rs.fit(features, targets)
```

We should use a `scipy` distribution to specify a distribution for hyperparameters where we want to try a range but don't want to specify exact values. For hyperparameters that are integers, we can use `randint`. We can use the `randint`, `uniform`, `loguniform`, or other distributions depending on the hyperparameter we are specifying.

For regularization parameters and some others, such as the gamma hyperparameters for SVMs that we'll learn about in *Chapter 15, Tree-Based Machine Learning Models*, a log uniform distribution can work well. This is because regularization hyperparameters can span orders of magnitude, and a log uniform distribution can search these orders of magnitude efficiently. For example, we might use `scipy.stats.loguniform(1e-4, 1e4)` for C in a logistic regression model. For something with a smaller potential range, like our number for *k* in KNN, a uniform distribution works well (and for an integer hyperparameter, we should use `randint`).

One of the advantages of the random search is we can limit the number of hyperparameter combinations we search with the `n_iter` parameter. Notice that in the above function we didn't set this and left it at the default of 10. We did set the `random_state` parameter so that the results are the same every time we run the above code. In the same way as our grid search, we can get the best model, hyperparameters, and score:

```
print(rs.best_estimator_)
print(rs.best_params_)
print(rs.best_score_)
```

This shows us:

```
KNeighborsRegressor(n_neighbors=13, p=1, weights='distance')
{'n_neighbors': 13, 'p': 1, 'weights': 'distance'}
-29845.646440602075
```

We can see our `n_neighbors` is larger and our MAE is a little better than with our grid search. We can also look at the exact hyperparameters tried like so:

```
list(zip(rs.cv_results_['params'], rs.cv_results_['mean_test_score']))
```

As with the grid search, the results are stored in a dictionary in the `cv_results_` attribute. The hyperparameters and corresponding scores are:

```
[({'n_neighbors': 9, 'p': 2, 'weights': 'uniform'}, -32363.609665144595),
 ({'n_neighbors': 17, 'p': 1, 'weights': 'distance'}, -30055.746440937754),
 ({'n_neighbors': 9, 'p': 2, 'weights': 'uniform'}, -32363.609665144595),
 ({'n_neighbors': 13, 'p': 1, 'weights': 'distance'}, -29845.646440602075),
 ({'n_neighbors': 6, 'p': 2, 'weights': 'distance'}, -30997.193897640995),
 ({'n_neighbors': 5, 'p': 2, 'weights': 'uniform'}, -31986.23561643836),
 ({'n_neighbors': 4, 'p': 2, 'weights': 'distance'}, -31910.191127678332),
 ({'n_neighbors': 8, 'p': 2, 'weights': 'distance'}, -31181.05668402912),
 ({'n_neighbors': 3, 'p': 2, 'weights': 'distance'}, -32338.55514879399),
 ({'n_neighbors': 14, 'p': 1, 'weights': 'uniform'}, -30972.516438356164)]
```

We can see how these are random samples for n_neighbors. The random search takes a random sample from distributions or values provided for hyperparameters. We can also see with a smaller search space some hyperparameter combinations are repeated exactly in some of the trials. Again, this method is advantageous for larger hyperparameter search spaces and larger datasets where a grid search would take too long to run.

> The sklearn package also has a Pipeline class that allows us to chain multiple steps together. This can be used with grid or random search to search hyperparameters as well as other settings for transforms such as scaling. An example of using Pipeline with grid search is in the sklearn documentation: https://scikit-learn.org/stable/tutorial/statistical_inference/putting_together.html.

Another method similar to random search that makes some improvements to random search is Bayesian search.

Using Bayesian search

Bayesian search for hyperparameters searches the hyperparameter space and computes scores similar to the random search. We choose some random points and calculate the scores. However, it then approximates the scoring space in between these known points and uses that to guess which hyperparameters will lead to a better score. One way is to use a Gaussian function to interpolate unknown model scores with combinations of hyperparameters.

To use this method, we need to install a new package, scikit-optimize (skopt), with conda install -c conda-forge scikit-optimize. Unfortunately, some of these extension or helper packages for scikit-learn such as skopt may not be compatible with the latest sklearn version, and we may need to downgrade our sklearn version for skopt to work. This may happen automatically with pip or conda, but at the moment of writing we need to manually downgrade sklearn with conda install -c conda-forge scikit-learn=0.23.2 (if this takes too long with the "solving the environment" step you may want to use pip instead). You may want to check the installation printout from pip or conda to see if sklearn was downgraded. Or, we can check the version of sklearn with import sklearn; sklearn.__version__ in Python. Another way to check the version is with pip freeze or conda list -n env_name (where env_name is the name of your environment you're using) from a terminal. If you are getting an error with the code below, it's worth searching for the error with a search engine and searching GitHub and Stack Overflow for the error to see if it is related to a sklearn versioning issue.

Another option that may be better is to create a separate environment for skopt, such as with `conda create -n skopt python=3.9 -y`, then use that environment for this chapter. Once installed, the `skopt` interface is essentially identical to `sklearn`, and we can use Bayesian optimization instead of a random search like so:

```
from skopt import BayesSearchCV
from skopt.space import Categorical, Integer

hyperparameters = {'n_neighbors': Integer(3, 20),
                   'weights': Categorical(['uniform', 'distance']),
                   'p': Categorical([1, 2])}
bs = BayesSearchCV(knn,
                   hyperparameters,
                   scoring='neg_mean_absolute_error',
                   n_jobs=-1,
                   random_state=42,
                   n_iter=10)
bs.fit(features, targets)
```

First, we import the `BayesSearchCV` class as well as some functions for generating distributions used by `skopt`. We then create our hyperparameter dictionary. We need to use the `skopt.space` search space functions to generate our distributions. Then we create the Bayesian search object in the same way as we did for the random and grid searches and set the number of iterations (`n_iter`) to `10` instead of the default of 100. We then fit our search object to the features and targets, and can examine the best model again:

```
print(bs.best_estimator_)
print(bs.best_params_)
print(bs.best_score_)
```

From this, we see:

```
KNeighborsRegressor(n_neighbors=11, weights='distance')
OrderedDict([('n_neighbors', 11), ('p', 2), ('weights', 'distance')])
-31143.98162060483
```

Our result is not quite as good as the random search in this case, but we didn't search the space very thoroughly. Bayesian search can also be more helpful if we have hyperparameters that span many orders of magnitude, such as regularization hyperparameters.

Other advanced search methods

There are a host of other advanced search methods that can search hyperparameter spaces in a more efficient and intelligent way than random or grid searches. Some of the Python packages that implement these methods are:

- `tune-sklearn`
- `optuna`
- `hyperopt`
- `hpbandster`

These use methods that improve upon random search. In one group of methods, random search is improved by mathematical approximations of the search space, such as the Bayesian search we used, TPE, and CMA-ES. The other group optimizes resource usage, such as using early stopping of training for unpromising hyperparameter combinations. These methods include successive halving, Hyperband, median pruning, and other pruning methods. The resource-optimizing methods require that the ML algorithm can be stopped early or has a warm start option (such as some `sklearn` algorithms). Resource-optimizing methods can work well for neural networks too.

Using learning curves

Another part of model optimization is determining the right amount of data to use. We want to use enough data so that our performance is maximized, but don't want to use too much extra data if it's not going to improve performance, since that would take more resources and longer to train. Using the `yellowbrick` package, we can easily see how our model's performance changes as we increase the amount of data we use:

```
from yellowbrick.model_selection import LearningCurve

lc = LearningCurve(knn, scoring='neg_mean_absolute_error')
lc.fit(features, targets)
lc.show()
```

We simply give the `LearningCurve` class our model, a scoring metric, and possibly other options. By default, it uses 3-fold CV. When we fit and then show the results with `lc.show()`, we get the following:

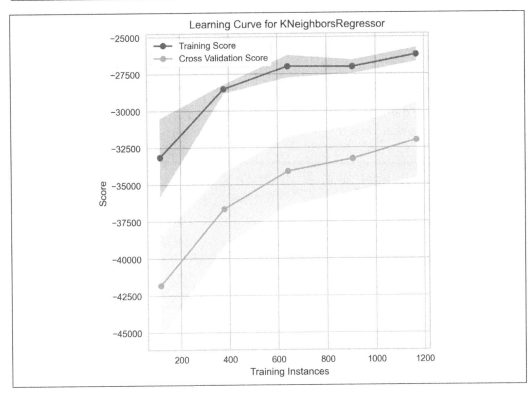

Figure 14.2: The learning curves from our KNN model and house price data

The training score is the average score on the training sets from CV, while the CV score is the average score on the validation sets. We also see the bands, which are the standard deviation of the scores. From our results, it's clear we don't have enough data – our CV score is increasing even when we use the maximum amount of data. For better model performance, we should collect more data until the CV score flattens out.

Optimizing the number of features with ML models

Another way to optimize our models is to use feature selection with the models. To do this, we need models that have a coefficient or feature importance aspect, such as linear regression, logistic regression, or tree-based methods. We can use forward, backward, or recursive feature selection. Both recursive and backward selection start with all features, then remove features that are least important.

However, forward or backward selection (sequential selection) fits several models to select each feature to add or remove, while recursive selection only fits one model for each feature it removes. For example, the first feature from forward selection would be found by fitting a model with each feature separately and taking the model with the best performance. For recursive selection, we fit one model and remove the feature that is least important (indicated by feature importance or feature coefficients). After the process, we can get a Boolean mask to select the specified number of features that gave the best score. We can use recursive feature selection with CV like so:

```
from sklearn.feature_selection import RFECV
from sklearn.linear_model import LinearRegression

lr = LinearRegression()
feature_selector = RFECV(lr, scoring='neg_mean_absolute_error')
feature_selector.fit(features, targets)
```

First, we import the recursive feature selection class (RFECV) and the linear regression model. Then we create our model and feature selection object, using the negative MAE as our metric. Next, we simply fit the feature selection to our features and targets. Then we can get an array of our scores:

```
feature_selector.grid_scores_
```

This returns:

```
array([-44963.06493189, -41860.3132655 , -37319.2626792 , -33319.79319284,
       -28524.60411086, -27607.29672974, -27315.23987193])
```

The results show an array of scores for a number of selected features, starting from 1 and going up to the maximum number of features in our data (7, here). We can see as we remove features our score gets worse, so in this case it's best to keep all features unless we have some other constraint that requires us to remove features (such as training or prediction runtime). If we do find that the score is better without some features, we can select the best features like this:

```
features.iloc[:, feature_selector.support_]
```

There is also a `SequentialFeatureSelector` class that is new in `sklearn` version 0.24 and that behaves similarly with backward feature selection. If we use it with the default forward selection, it adds one feature at a time by trying all features and keeping the one with the best score. Both the recursive CV and sequential methods use 5-fold CV by default.

Using AutoML with PyCaret

So far, we've looked at a few different ML models. However, there are many more, and it can be tedious to try many of them by hand. An easier way to try many models at once is with **automated machine learning**, or **AutoML**.

The no free lunch theorem

In ML, we usually don't know which model will perform best. Take our logistic regression models and Naïve Bayes, and the logistic regression models from *Chapter 11, Machine Learning for Classification,* on classification. We didn't have too many reasons to know which one might perform best before trying them. Of course, we know the Gaussian Naïve Bayes assumes features have a normal distribution, which seemed wrong, so we might guess that model may not work well. We can use assumptions for models to guess which models may or may not work, but beyond that, we should try several different models and compare the results, then choose the best-performing model based on the model evaluation metric we choose.

AutoML solutions

AutoML is an idea that has been around since the 1990s but is just starting to emerge as a widely used technology in the 2020s. Part of this is due to many people making easy-to-use AutoML tools, such as several AutoML packages in Python:

- PyCaret
- H2O
- TPOT
- mljar-supervised
- AutoGluon
- MLBox
- AutoVIML
- NNI (short for Neural Network Intelligence)
- Ludwig
- AutoGL (for graph datasets)
- auto-sklearn (at the time of writing this is in early development and only works on Linux)
- AutoKeras, AdaNet, and Auto-PyTorch (for neural networks)

Most major cloud providers have AutoML solutions as well, and usually these can be done with GUIs, Python APIs, or a combination of the two. Three of the biggest cloud providers, Microsoft's Azure, Amazon's AWS, and Google's GCP, all have AutoML products available. Other major cloud providers, such as Baidu, also have AutoML solutions ready. Many data science GUIs have AutoML tools available as well, including RapidMiner and Weka.

AutoML solutions are still limited – no single AutoML solution tries all available models, and since new models are being developed all the time, this is difficult if not impossible to do. However, it's still a quick way to try several models and pick something better than a default model you might choose. Some of the AutoML solutions will include extensive feature transformation/engineering and selection, while others will not.

Using PyCaret

PyCaret is one of the easiest-to-use Python packages (at the time of writing) for AutoML, although it is relatively new. It can be installed with `conda install -c conda-forge pycaret` (this install may take a long time on "solving the environment" and can be faster with `pip install pycaret` or `mamba install pycaret`) Because PyCaret uses a lot of other ML packages, and the development of a package takes lots of time and effort, it sometimes uses slightly older versions of things like sklearn, scipy, and so on (this is due to compatibility issues). For this reason, it can be helpful to create a separate virtual environment with conda or another method (such as virtualenv) to use PyCaret.

By default, the `pycaret` install uses the minimum requirements. To install all packages for full functionality, we can do `pip install pycaret[full]`, or install the requirements file from here: `https://github.com/pycaret/pycaret/blob/master/requirements-optional.txt`. This can be done by downloading the file and running `pip install -r requirements-optional.txt` or `conda install --file requirements-optional.txt`.

We could also install some of these optional packages manually, such as with `conda install pycaret xgboost catboost -y`. Of the models, `xgboost` and `catboost` are not installed by default. None of the more advanced hyperparameter search packages that pycaret can use, such as scikit-optimize, are installed by default either.

If we want to use a GPU for some ML algorithms with `pycaret` to speed up training, we need to make sure some relevant packages are properly installed. The requirements for this are described in the pycaret documentation: `https://pycaret.readthedocs.io/en/latest/installation.html?highlight=gpu#pycaret-on-gpu`.

For our house price dataset, we can use PyCaret for AutoML like so:

```
from pycaret.regression import setup, compare_models

exp_clf = setup(df, target='SalePrice')
best = compare_models(sort='MAE')
```

First, we import a few functions from PyCaret, then set up our AutoML with the
`setup` function, which takes a DataFrame and a target column string. This will output
a prompt asking to confirm whether the variable types are correct:

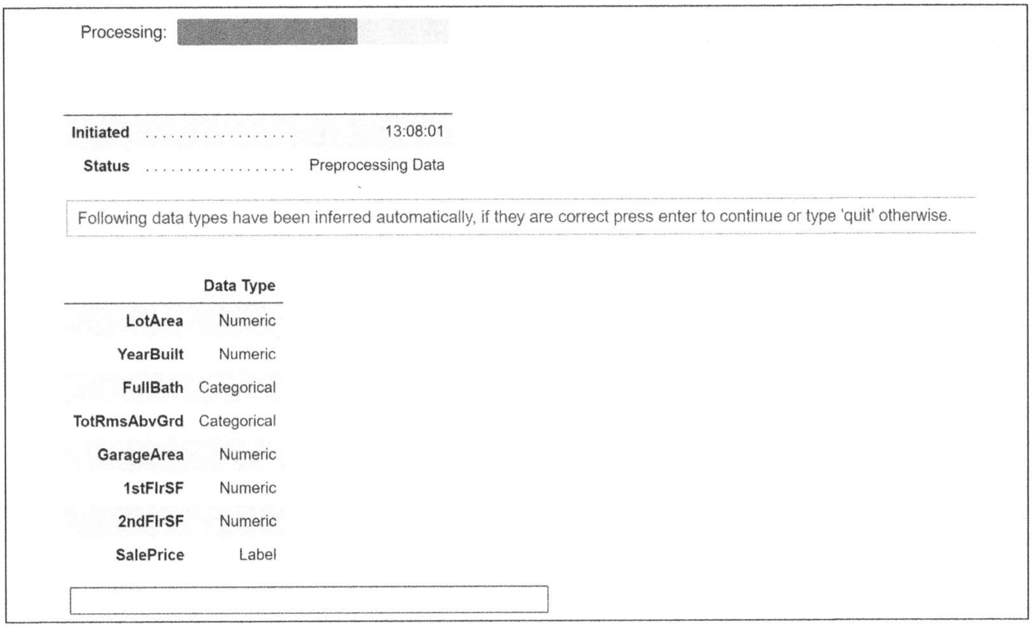

Figure 14.3: The output of the PyCaret setup() function

In our case, we actually want the number of bedrooms and bathrooms to be numeric,
so we can type `quit` in the input prompt and re-run the setup like so:

```
exp_clf = setup(df,
                target='SalePrice',
                numeric_features=['FullBath', 'TotRmsAbvGrd'])
```

Now we have forced those two features to be numeric and can proceed. Note that
there are a huge number of configurations possible with `setup` that can be accessed
through the function parameters, which are described in the documentation.

At the time of writing, the `setup` function of `pycaret` runs some analysis on all data columns and tries to automatically determine several properties of the data. With bigger datasets or data with many features, this can be prohibitively slow. Future releases of PyCaret may improve this, but currently, it's a limitation.

Next, when we run `best = compare_models(sort='MAE')`, `pycaret` tries several ML models with default hyperparameters. As it's running in a Jupyter Notebook or IPython shell, it outputs the results as they become available. The metrics are results from CV. Note that we told PyCaret to sort our results by MAE, as we've been using this metric so far. Our results are the following:

	Model	MAE	MSE	RMSE	R2	RMSLE	MAPE	TT (Sec)
catboost	CatBoost Regressor	22353.7346	1418647627.3685	36051.8438	0.7920	0.1765	0.1309	0.7260
et	Extra Trees Regressor	23329.3219	1441783942.2166	37082.8491	0.7837	0.1860	0.1388	0.0920
gbr	Gradient Boosting Regressor	23470.9520	1403920691.4596	36394.5036	0.7888	0.1839	0.1400	0.0420
rf	Random Forest Regressor	23566.2820	1474049881.5263	37618.4355	0.7771	0.1865	0.1392	0.1280
lightgbm	Light Gradient Boosting Machine	23745.3886	1460994079.8343	37406.6507	0.7785	0.1863	0.1392	0.1010
xgboost	Extreme Gradient Boosting	24041.0336	1414369004.8000	37156.4764	0.7838	0.1902	0.1417	0.3940
br	Bayesian Ridge	27917.6710	2162130678.3645	45052.1027	0.6708	0.2147	0.1609	0.0070
en	Elastic Net	28122.8166	2191205760.0000	45326.6930	0.6664	0.2168	0.1622	0.0050
llar	Lasso Least Angle Regression	28277.0974	2221374815.1595	45602.8589	0.6617	0.2181	0.1632	0.0060
ridge	Ridge Regression	28285.6875	2223337715.2000	45615.3258	0.6614	0.2184	0.1633	0.0070
lasso	Lasso Regression	28286.2037	2223486067.2000	45616.5367	0.6614	0.2184	0.1633	0.0080
lr	Linear Regression	28286.6674	2223548300.8000	45617.1480	0.6614	0.2184	0.1633	0.0080
lar	Least Angle Regression	28286.6725	2223549977.0677	45617.1650	0.6614	0.2184	0.1633	0.0070
dt	Decision Tree Regressor	31129.3049	2267183977.5862	47273.5472	0.6504	0.2515	0.1824	0.0070
huber	Huber Regressor	31270.1470	2505940664.8500	48928.6428	0.6159	0.2343	0.1847	0.0140
ada	AdaBoost Regressor	31745.8409	2017832544.3491	44324.3494	0.6937	0.2446	0.2075	0.0350
knn	K Neighbors Regressor	33974.3541	2735516224.0000	51689.2941	0.5864	0.2513	0.1991	0.0110
omp	Orthogonal Matching Pursuit	44187.6583	4234780237.2675	64456.8225	0.3527	0.3224	0.2670	0.0060
par	Passive Aggressive Regressor	44792.7165	4859497083.9170	66193.0854	0.2468	0.3084	0.2786	0.0080

Figure 14.4: The results of PyCaret AutoML on our house price data

We can see the top model is CatBoost, which is a type of boosted tree-based model. Again, you will need to make sure you've installed the full version of pycaret or installed the packages from requirements.txt or at least catboost and xgboost to access all available models. It looks like tree-based models are all of the top models, such as gradient boosting and random forests. We can see it tries several other models as well. To use our best model to make predictions, we want to use the `predict_model` function from PyCaret:

```
from pycaret.regression import predict_model, save_model, load_model

prediction_df = predict_model(best, features)
```

This will automatically apply any feature transformations that had been done during model selection, such as categorical to numeric conversions. This returns a DataFrame with the same features as the input features DataFrame, but now with a new Label column, which has the predictions. For regression, this simply provides the numeric prediction. For classification (from the pycaret.classification module), it provides the Label column with the category prediction and a Score column with the probability of the predicted label.

Once we have our optimized model, we can save it to a pickle file like so:

```
save_model(best, 'catboost_regressor')
```

This saves our best model to the file catboost_regressor.pkl. We can then load it back with:

```
cb_model = load_model('catboost_regressor')
```

This is useful if it takes a long time to train and optimize our models and we don't want to run the compare_models() repeatedly.

Another useful part of PyCaret is that it can easily tune hyperparameters:

```
from pycaret.regression import tune_model

tuned_knn = tune_model(knn)
```

Here, we use the tune_model function and our KNN model we created earlier to tune the model with a default set of hyperparameters. By printing out the tuned_knn variable, we can see the optimized hyperparameters. Note that we need to run the setup() function from PyCaret before tuning models. We can also supply a custom search space with the custom_grid parameter for the tune_model function, as well as many other parameters to control the process. Another aspect of pycaret hyperparameter tuning is that we can tune models using several different advanced methods, such as the skopt Bayesian search we learned about, or using other packages such as tune-sklearn and optuna.

There are several other classification algorithms we didn't cover in this past few chapters, and many of them are available in `sklearn`. We will cover a few more important ones in the next chapters, but to see more, some ways for listing all the classification algorithms in `sklearn` are described here: `https://stackoverflow.com/questions/41844311/list-of-all-classification-algorithms`. You can also see the entire list of supervised learning algorithms from `sklearn` here: `https://scikit-learn.org/stable/supervised_learning.html`. The list of algorithms contains both classification and regression algorithms, however. A comparison of some of the classifiers on a binary classification task can be found here: `https://scikit-learn.org/stable/auto_examples/classification/plot_classifier_comparison.html`.

PyCaret also has lists of the available models in the documentation, or they can be accessed like so:

```
from pycaret.datasets import get_data
from pycaret.classification import models, setup

data = get_data('credit')
exp = setup(data=data, target='default')

models()
```

The `setup` command must be called before calling `models()` at the time of writing. Additionally, `pycaret` has a lot more functionality described in the documentation. Advanced model ensembling (combining multiple models) is an example.

Now that we've finished up the chapter, you can try practicing these skills on the full house price dataset.

Test your knowledge

Use the full housing dataset from this book's GitHub repository (under `Chapter13/data/housing_data_full.csv`), then use PyCaret and/or another AutoML package to find the best ML model for the data. It may help to first use recursive feature selection to trim down the number of features if it takes too long to run (or sample down the data). Once the optimum model has been found, plot the learning curve of the model to see if we have enough data or should ideally collect more. You should see similar results to what we've seen in this chapter, although if you use the full dataset, you may see the learning curve has flattened out.

Summary

In this chapter, we covered some ways of optimizing ML models and using the PyCaret AutoML package. Some of the model optimizations we looked at were hyperparameters, the amount of data we have (analyzed with learning curves), and the number of features we have with recursive feature selection. Although there are several AutoML packages in Python, we learned about PyCaret since it is quick and easy to use and delivers decent results.

In the next chapter, we will look at an important class of ML models – tree-based models. These include ML models such as decision trees, random forests, LightGBM, CatBoost, and XGBoost.

15

Tree-Based Machine Learning Models

We've seen a few of the simpler machine learning models, and now it's time to examine some more advanced models. In this chapter, we will look at the family of machine learning models that is based on decision trees. These models, especially the boosted models, have won machine learning contests and are used in industry for state-of-the-art ML performance. Here, we'll cover:

- How decision trees work in machine learning
- Random forests in `sklearn` and H2O, which are collections of decision trees
- Feature importances from tree-based methods
- Boosted algorithms, including AdaBoost, XGBoost, LightGBM, and CatBoost

Let's start with the basic decision tree and how it works.

Decision trees

Decision trees are simple algorithms, which split data based on specific values of the data. Let's use our data from the *Test your knowledge* sections in *Chapters 11* and *12*, which is loan data, with a TARGET column that denotes whether someone had trouble paying back a loan (1) or not (0).

First, we'll load the data:

```
import pandas as pd

df = pd.read_csv('data/loan_data_sample.csv', index_col='SK_ID_CURR')
```

If the examples are running slowly on your computer, you might sample down the data using `df.sample()`. There are some string columns that need to be converted to numeric datatypes, since `sklearn` can only handle numeric data:

```
numeric_df = df.copy()
numeric_df['NAME_CONTRACT_TYPE'] = numeric_df['NAME_CONTRACT_TYPE'].map(
    {'Cash loans': 0, 'Revolving loans': 1})
numeric_df['CODE_GENDER'] = numeric_df['CODE_GENDER'].map({'M': 0, 'F': 1})
numeric_df['FLAG_OWN_CAR'] = numeric_df['FLAG_OWN_CAR'].map({'N': 0, 'Y': 1})
numeric_df['FLAG_OWN_REALTY'] = numeric_df['FLAG_OWN_REALTY'].map(
    {'N': 0, 'Y': 1})
numeric_df['NAME_EDUCATION_TYPE'] = \
    numeric_df['NAME_EDUCATION_TYPE'].map({'Lower secondary': 0,
                                           'Secondary / secondary special': 0,
                                           'Incomplete higher': 1,
                                           'Higher education': 2,
                                           'Academic degree': 2})
numeric_df.dropna(inplace=True)
```

We make a copy of the DataFrame so we still have the original version, and convert our string columns to numeric. Most of the columns are binary, so we can convert them to 0s and 1s. The education column has several values, and we turn them into an ordinal variable, which is a categorical category with ordering. We also need to drop missing values since `sklearn` cannot handle them (we could also impute missing values, of course). After this conversion, we can double-check the datatypes are correct with `numeric_df.info()`.

Decision trees work by splitting the data based on specific values from feature columns. For example, we might split our data into two groups based on `AMT_INCOME_TOTAL`, since above a value of around 200,000, the chances of payment difficulty are slightly lower (in other words, the `TARGET` variable is more likely to be 0). Our decision tree split would look like this:

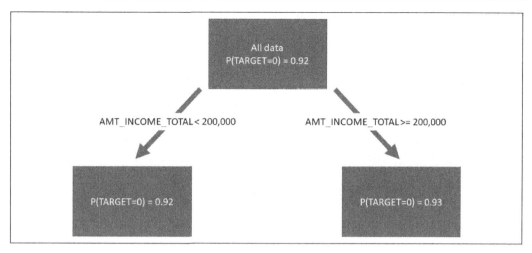

Figure 15.1: A decision tree split on income amount showing probabilities of TARGET=0

We can see that the fraction of samples where TARGET=0 increases by a small amount for high incomes, so we've inched toward gaining some predictive power over the no information rate (the proportion of target values in the overall data) by splitting the data in this way.

Each box in the decision tree shown above is a node. The first node, which is at the top and contains all data, is called the "root" node, like the root of a tree. Once we get to the bottom of the tree, the nodes are called "leaf" nodes. Any nodes in between the root and leaves are internal nodes.

The machine learning aspect comes into play with decision trees from automating splitting decisions. There are several different algorithms for creating decision trees, and some of the top algorithms are C4.5, C5.0, and CART (classification and regression trees). The sklearn package uses a version of CART. With CART, we split the data into binary splits (as shown in *Figure 15.1*) and do so in a greedy manner. For example, we try splitting the data on all features and all values of the features, and then find which one splits the data best. For classification, we measure the best split by the "purity" of the nodes, meaning the split that breaks up the data into unique classes best is used. We can measure this using the Gini criteria or entropy (entropy is also called "information gain"). Both these criteria have a minimum of 0 when the classes in the leaf nodes are pure, and have a maximum value when classes are evenly distributed. For regression, we can use measures such as **mean-square error (MSE)**, **mean-absolute error (MAE)**, or others.

We can compare the value of the Gini criteria, entropy, or regression metrics for the leaf nodes from a split and take the split that minimizes these values. The Gini criteria, which is the default in `sklearn`, has the equation $1 - \sum_j p_j^2$, while entropy is:

$$-\sum_j p_j \log_2 p_j$$

where p_j is the probability of class j. We can see that if a leaf node is pure (for a binary classification problem), our Gini criteria will be 1-1-0=0, since the probability of one class is 1 and the other class is 0. Because of the log operation, entropy is slightly more computationally complex, but also has a slightly higher penalty for severe misclassifications (similar to log loss).

> One difference between C4.5 and CART is that C4.5 doesn't have to end up with binary splits like CART. C4.5 constructs a decision tree, then constructs "rule sets" (strings of if-else statements) which determine how a datapoint is classified. The nodes in the rule sets are pruned to minimize the size of the tree and maximize accuracy.
>
> C5.0 improves upon C4.5, but is only implemented in a package in R.

Before fitting models to the data, let's break it up into train and test sets so we can evaluate the quality of the model:

```
from sklearn.model_selection import train_test_split

features = numeric_df.drop('TARGET', axis=1)
targets = numeric_df['TARGET']

x_train, x_test, y_train, y_test = train_test_split(features,
                                                    targets,
                                                    stratify=targets,
                                                    random_state=42)
```

Next, we can fit and score a decision tree to our data with `sklearn`, which works like any other `sklearn` model:

```
from sklearn.tree import DecisionTreeClassifier

dt = DecisionTreeClassifier()
dt.fit(x_train, y_train)
print(f'Train accuracy: {dt.score(x_train, y_train)}')
print(f'Test accuracy: {dt.score(x_test, y_test)}')
```

The default score method for classification is accuracy, although we could use any of the metrics we learned about in *Chapter 12*, *Evaluating Machine Learning Classification Models and Sampling for Classification*, on classification. Our results look like this:

```
Train accuracy: 0.9835772442407513
Test accuracy: 0.8566890176420806
```

That looks like severe overfitting – the train score is almost 100% accuracy while the test score is much lower. The reason for this is our decision trees are allowed to grow to unlimited depths (or heights, if you want to think of it that way). The tree continues to split the data until each leaf is very pure. While this works great for the training data and we can almost always get near 100% accuracy on the training set this way, it will almost always perform poorly on the test set. We can see how many splits our decision tree has with dt.get_depth(), which turns out to be 50. This means we have 50 splits and 50 layers of nodes after the root node, which is quite a lot. The depth of the tree can be restricted with the max_depth hyperparameter, which we set to 2 here:

```
small_dt = DecisionTreeClassifier(max_depth=2, max_features=None)
small_dt.fit(x_train, y_train)
print(f'Train accuracy: {small_dt.score(x_train, y_train)}')
print(f'Test accuracy: {small_dt.score(x_test, y_test)}')
```

We also set the max_features hyperparameter, which controls how many features are tried at each split. A random subset of features is used at each split, which is the square root of the number of features by default. Setting max_features=None uses all features at every split. There are several other hyperparameters we can set as well: criterion ('gini' or 'entropy') and many others that control how many samples can be in nodes or are required to split a node (such as min_samples_leaf). With classification, we can also set class_weight to control the weights for each class in the Gini criterion or entropy calculations.

Our accuracy on the train and test sets now are both around 91.9%, which is about the same as the no information rate, meaning our model isn't doing better than random chance. This doesn't mean it's completely useless – we might be able to predict certain samples better than random chance and can understand relationships of features to the target from the model. To understand this better, we can plot the tree with an sklearn function:

```
import matplotlib.pyplot as plt
from sklearn.tree import plot_tree

f = plt.figure(figsize=(12, 12))
_ = plot_tree(small_dt, feature_names=features.columns)
```

We use the `plot_tree` function, giving it our small decision tree and feature names as arguments. The result looks like this:

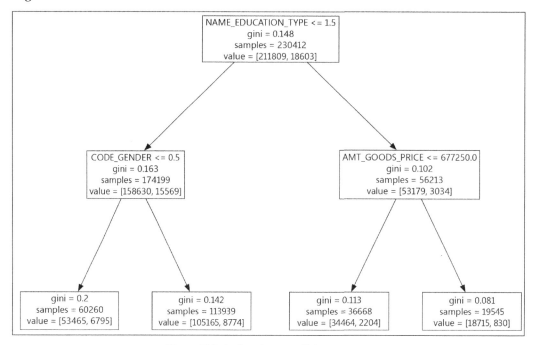

Figure 15.2: A plot of our small decision tree

We can see the education type was found to be the first variable the tree splits on, followed by gender and the price of the goods bought with the loan. The splitting rule is shown at the top of each node, and if the condition is met, the data moves to the right side of the split. We also see the Gini criteria value for each node, the number of samples in the node, and the number of values for each class. From this, we see that education types that are 2 (higher education) with an expensive price of goods for the loan tend to not have trouble with payments (the far-right leaf node, which has mostly `TARGET=0` and the lowest Gini criteria value of all leaf nodes). Recall that lower Gini criteria values mean more pure leaf nodes.

At this point, it also helps to know how the decision tree is making predictions. For classification, we take the majority class for the node as the prediction. For regression, we take the average value of training samples that ended up in each node. For `sklearn` models, there is usually a version that has `Classifier` at the end of the name and one with `Regressor` at the end of the name (as with KNN, decision trees, and more).

A nice feature of `sklearn` decision trees and other tree-based methods is that they can be multi-output or multi-target without any modification – we simply provide a multi-dimensional target array to the algorithm.

Decision trees are easy to explain because we can plot them and see the rules for making splits. However, they are limited in performance (accuracy for classification) due to their simplicity. One method that improves performance is random forests.

Random forests

Random forests build on decision trees. Instead of using a single tree, a forest uses a collection of them (as you may have guessed from the name). Each tree is built with a sample of the data which we get from bootstrapping, or sampling with replacement. We also randomly subset the features at each split, as we saw is possible with `max_features` for the `sklearn` decision trees. Random forests can also be parallelized across processors or computers since we can build each decision tree separately because they are independent of one another. This ML algorithm is called an ensemble method since it uses a collection of models. The combination of bootstrapping and combining several models in an ensemble is called bagging (a portmanteau of bootstrapping and aggregating). There are several implementations of random forests in Python, R, other programming languages, and data science GUIs. Two easy ways to use them in Python are with `sklearn` and the H2O packages.

Random forests with sklearn

Using a random forest in `sklearn` is similar to any other model in `sklearn`, except we have a plethora of hyperparameters. Let's first fit it and only restrict the depth of the trees:

```
from sklearn.ensemble import RandomForestClassifier

rfc = RandomForestClassifier(max_depth=10, n_jobs=-1, random_state=42)
rfc.fit(x_train, y_train)
print(rfc.score(x_train, y_train))
print(rfc.score(x_test, y_test))
```

Here, we set a few other parameters for the classifier class: `n_jobs=-1`, which uses all available CPU cores in parallel, and the `random_state` argument so that results are reproducible. The scores here are about the same as the no information rate – 91.9% accuracy.

To try and improve performance, there are several hyperparameters we can tune:

- The number of trees (`n_estimators`)
- The depth of trees (`max_depth`)
- The number of features considered at each split (`max_features`)

We could also try different settings for `criterion`, samples per leaf (controlled via parameters like `min_samples_split`) and the class weightings (`class_weight`), although most of these other hyperparameters will not usually be as influential as the three in the bullet list above.

The number of trees often falls in the range of 100-500 trees, although it could be outside this range. The depth can typically fall within a range of 5-20, although larger depths can be helpful for more complex problems. The `max_features` hyperparameter can have a big effect on performance and can be searched from 2 or 3 features up to all the available features. By default, it is the square root of the number of features.

We can search some of these hyperparameters with a cross-validation grid search (as we saw in *Chapter 14, Optimizing Models and Using AutoML*) like so:

```python
from sklearn.model_selection import GridSearchCV

x_tr_sample = x_train.sample(1000)
y_tr_sample = y_train.loc[x_tr_sample.index]

params = {'n_estimators': [100, 300, 500],
          'max_depth': [10, 15, 20],
          'max_features': [3, 6, 9],
          'random_state': [42],
          'n_jobs': [-1]}
gs = GridSearchCV(rfc, param_grid=params, n_jobs=-1)
gs.fit(x_tr_sample, y_tr_sample)
print(gs.best_estimator_)
print(gs.best_score_)
```

We are searching some of the typical ranges for the three hyperparameters mentioned above, and also fixing the `random_state` and `n_jobs` arguments. The training data was sampled down to only 1,000 datapoints because this takes a while to run, since we are fitting 135 models with the grid search (using the default of 5 CV splits with 3 unique values of 3 hyperparameters, or 5*3*3*3=135). After the grid search completes, our best hyperparameters and score are the following:

```
RandomForestClassifier(max_depth=10, max_features=3, n_jobs=-1, random_
state=42)
0.9179999999999999
```

We can see we're still not outperforming the no information rate, although we did settle on a different value for the maximum number of features.

The training and hyperparameter search can take a long time with the full dataset or another even bigger dataset, and we have a few options for dealing with it:

- Scale down the data with sampling as we did here
- Wait for the job to complete (although this could take hours or even days)
- Scale up to a more powerful computer (for example, using cloud resources)
- Scale up to a cluster using packages such as Dask
- Use another package or software that can scale using computing clusters

One option for another scalable package that can utilize clusters is H2O, which includes tree-based models such as random forests.

Random forests with H2O

H2O is another ML package in Python besides `sklearn`. It has a few ML algorithms and some nice advantages over `sklearn`. For random forests (and other tree-based methods), it allows us to use missing values and categorical features, unlike `sklearn`. H2O can also scale up on a cluster for big data. The `H2O.ai` company also offers other products, such as their driverless AI, which is a data science and machine learning GUI that offers lots of automation. To use the H2O Python package, we need to install it. An easy way is to use `conda`, which can also install Java. Otherwise, you will need to install Java separately (which is not too hard but can sometimes cause problems due to Java versioning and can be a headache). We can install H2O through `conda` like so: `conda install -c conda-forge h2o-py openjdk -y`. Installing the OpenJDK package installs the Java Development Kit in our conda environment. The H2O documentation also has information on installing and compatible versions of Java if you choose to install with pip: `http://docs.h2o.ai/h2o/latest-stable/h2o-docs/welcome.html`.

Once we have H2O installed, we need to properly import and initialize it. Since H2O uses Java and can scale to a cluster, we must initialize the package after importing it:

```
import h2o
h2o.init()
```

This will take some seconds to run and will print out information on the current H2O instance when finished. Next, we need to prepare our data properly. We don't need to deal with missing values or encode categorical values as numeric, so we can simply use our original DataFrame. However, H2O uses its own data structure, called an H2O Frame.

We can convert our original data to an H2O Frame like this:

```
hf = h2o.H2OFrame(df)
hf['TARGET'] = hf['TARGET'].asfactor()
train, valid = hf.split_frame(ratios=[.8], seed=42)
```

First, we simply use the `h2o.H2OFrame` function to convert our pandas DataFrame to an `H2OFrame`. Then we set the target column as a "factor" datatype, meaning it is a categorical variable. This is necessary so that the random forest will perform categorization and not regression. We could also convert other non-string columns that should be categorical to factors to be more thorough. Lastly, we break up our data into training and validation sets, with 80% of the data going to training. Now we can fit our model to the data and evaluate performance:

```
from h2o.estimators import H2ORandomForestEstimator

drf = H2ORandomForestEstimator(ntrees=100, max_depth=10, mtries=3)
feature_columns = hf.columns
feature_columns.remove('TARGET')
target_column = 'TARGET'
drf.train(x=feature_columns,
          y=target_column,
          training_frame=train,
          validation_frame=valid)

drf
```

We first import the class and initialize it, saving it in the variable `drf`, which stands for "distributed random forest." Since H2O is ready to scale, it will use all CPU cores and resources available, so our random forest is distributed across resources. We set the same three hyperparameters we set for `sklearn`: the number of trees (`ntrees`), the depth of trees (`max_depth`), and the number of features to use at each node split (`mtries`). Although we won't cover it here, H2O has a grid search method similar to `sklearn`, which has examples in the documentation: https://docs.h2o.ai/h2o/ latest-stable/h2o-docs/grid-search.html.

Next, we create a list of our columns that are the features from the columns of the H2OFrame and remove the `TARGET` item from the list. Then we create a variable to store the target value column name (`target_column`). Finally, we train the model with `drf.train`, giving it our feature names, target name, and training and validation `H2OFrames`. This will display a progress bar to show how the fit is progressing (similar to what the `h2o.H2OFrame` function outputs). After it's fit, we can print out the `drf` variable to see the results by simply running it in a separate Jupyter notebook cell.

This shows a large amount of information, including performance on the train and validation sets. It shows a confusion matrix, along with the maximum value of many metrics with optimal thresholds. For example, the max F1 score on the validation set is 0.21 at a threshold of 0.097 – this threshold has been optimized to maximize the F1 score. These values can also be found for the training set through `drf.F1()`, or for arbitrary data with `drf.model_performance(valid).F1()`. We can then get predictions using this threshold like so:

```
predictions = drf.predict(train)
(predictions['p1'] > 0.097).as_data_frame()['p1'].values
```

The first line uses the model to make predictions on the provided H2OFrame, and returns an H2OFrame with three columns: `predict`, `p0`, and `p1`. These are the predictions (using a threshold of 0.5), the probability of class 0, and the probability of class 1. The second line takes our F1-optimized threshold and rounds the predictions for p1 up to 1 if they exceed this threshold. We also convert this to a pandas DataFrame with `as_data_frame()`, then select the p1 column, and convert it to a NumPy array.

If we want to save our model, this is made easy with H2O:

```
save_path = h2o.save_model(model=drf, path='drf', force=True)
drf2 = h2o.load_model(path=save_path)
```

The `save_model` function simply takes our trained model and a path (which creates a folder with that name in our current directory). The `force=True` argument will overwrite the model files if they already exist. The `save_path` variable holds the full path to the model, which we can use to load it into memory with `h2o.load_model`.

Lastly, H2O has a few nice convenience functions for tree models. It has a learning curve plot, which shows a metric on the *y axis* and the number of trees on the *x axis*. This can be used to optimize the number of trees without using grid search. We can plot this with `drf.learning_curve_plot()`. By default, it shows log loss, and in our case, the log loss for the validation set flattens out around 10 trees (so we shouldn't need more than that for optimal performance). Another convenient function it has is plotting variable importance.

Feature importance from tree-based methods

Feature importance, also called variable importance, can be calculated from tree-based methods by summing the reduction in Gini or entropy over all the trees for each variable.

So, if a particular variable is used to split the data and reduces the Gini or entropy value by a large amount, that feature is important for making predictions. This is a nice contrast to using coefficient-based feature importance from logistic or linear regression, because tree-based feature importances are non-linear. There are other ways of calculating feature importance as well, such as permutation feature importance and SHAP (SHapley Additive exPlanations).

Using H2O for feature importance

We can easily get the importances with `drf.varimp()`, or plot them with `drf.varimp_plot(server=True)`. The `server=True` argument uses `matplotlib`, which allows us to do things such as directly saving the figure with `plt.savefig()`. The result looks like this:

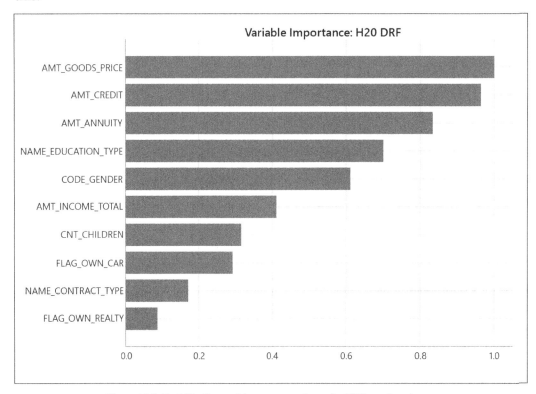

Figure 15.3: Variable (feature) importances from the H2O random forest

From this, we can see there is no single feature that vastly stands above the rest. However, it looks like the top five features have relatively more importance than the rest , and there is a somewhat large drop in importance after the fifth feature (CODE_ GENDER).

 One interesting thing about tree-based feature importances is they can change if we remove other features. Sometimes the changes can be dramatic and features will move drastically in their ranking. For example, try removing the topmost important feature and examining the feature importances again.

Examining feature importances can also easily be done with sklearn models using the yellowbrick package.

Using sklearn random forest feature importances

Thanks to yellowbrick, plotting feature importances with sklearn is easy:

```
from yellowbrick.model_selection import feature_importances

_ = feature_importances(gs.best_estimator_,
                        x_train,
                        y_train,
                        colors=['darkblue'] * features.shape[0])
```

We give the feature_importances function our trained random forest model from our grid search earlier in the chapter, as well as the training data. We then specify that all the colors for the bars should be dark blue, since the default is to use a plethora of colors (which is chartjunk).

Our result looks like the following:

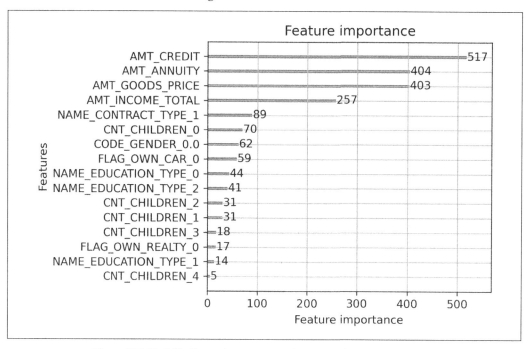

Figure 15.4: Variable (feature) importances from the sklearn random forest
using yellowbrick's plotting function

We can see there are some differences in the feature importances between H2O and
sklearn. Remember that a big difference was that we included the missing values
and categorical columns (such as NAME_EDUCATION_TYPE) as-is with the H2O random
forest, while we pre-processed our data for sklearn to convert everything to numeric
values and removed all missing values.

Random forests are a good model to try and often work well. However, another
class of tree-based models was created that improves upon random forests and often
outperforms them: boosted models.

Boosted trees: AdaBoost, XGboost, LightGBM, and CatBoost

Boosted machine learning models were first introduced around 1989 and have been
shown to perform well. Some of the more common boosting algorithms you will see
are AdaBoost, gradient boosting, XGBoost, LightGBM, and CatBoost.

XGBoost has been used to win several machine learning competitions (for example, on Kaggle), and was initially released in 2014. LightGBM was developed shortly after by Microsoft and released in 2016, while CatBoost was released in 2017. (For a more detailed history of boosting, see this paper: `https://cseweb.ucsd.edu/~yfreund/papers/IntroToBoosting.pdf`.) These boosting algorithms have slightly different algorithms and implementations, and when trying models on a dataset, it doesn't hurt to try as many of them as you can. An easy way to do this is with the PyCaret package we covered in the previous chapter on model optimization and AutoML.

First, let's learn about how boosting works. The idea is to combine several weak learners (for example, a 1-split decision tree called a "stump") to make a strong learner. Weak and strong describe the performance of the ML algorithm, or learner. In general, the steps for boosting are:

1. Fit an initial model to the data (it could be a tree or constant value, such as the mean or mode of the target variable)
2. Calculate the errors of predictions:
    *   For AdaBoost, the errors are used to increase weights of incorrect predictions for the next model
    *   For gradient boosting, we calculate the derivative of the loss function (the gradient, also called pseudo-residuals sometimes)
3. Fit a weak learner to the data:
    *   AdaBoost fits to the weighted data
    *   Gradient boosting fits a model to the derivative of the loss function (the gradient)
4. Linearly add the weak learner to the previous model:
    *   The weak learner is multiplied by a value that minimizes the loss function
    *   We can also scale the weak learner with a "learning rate," which slows down the fitting to the data (this can improve performance, but requires more models)
5. Repeat steps 2-4 above until a specified number of weak learners has been reached

The final model is a linear combination of weak learners which have been weighted to minimize the loss function at each step. Put more simply, we end up with a linear combination of small decision trees which can be used to make our predictions (most boosting algorithms use small decision trees as their weak learner).

When making predictions, we can simply make predictions from the individual weak learners and add them up to get our final prediction (incorporating the multipliers for each weak learner from training, of course).

Gradient boosting is essentially using gradient descent, as we saw with logistic regression. We are finding the errors from our models, and moving the overall model in the direction that is expected to minimize that error.

> The math and process behind gradient boosting is complex and somewhat confusing. Wikipedia has a decent pseudocode explanation: https://en.wikipedia.org/wiki/Gradient_boosting#Algorithm
>
> An even simpler explanation with pseudocode can be found here: https://towardsdatascience.com/boosting-algorithms-explained-d38f56ef3f30

Boosting is similar to a random forest since we use several decision trees, but is an iterative process where each tree depends on the next one. This means it can be harder to parallelize than a random forest, since the random forest trees are all independent. However, boosting often outperforms random forests and are important algorithms to know for getting the best performing ML algorithms. First, let's look at how AdaBoost works.

AdaBoost

With AdaBoost, we can choose what our weak learner is, but usually it is a 1-split decision tree (called a "stump"). The `sklearn` package has classification and regression versions of AdaBoost, and we can use the classifier with our loan payment dataset:

```
from sklearn.ensemble import AdaBoostClassifier

adaboost = AdaBoostClassifier(n_estimators=100,
                              learning_rate=0.5,
                              random_state=42)
adaboost.fit(x_train, y_train)
print(adaboost.score(x_train, y_train))
print(adaboost.score(x_test, y_test))
```

Again, this works the same as all other `sklearn` ML algorithms – create the classifier, fit to the data, then score and make predictions. The two hyperparameters for AdaBoost in `sklearn` are the number of weak learners and the learning rate.

These two interact – the lower the learning rate, the more estimators we will need to arrive at comparable performance. We can also change the base learner from a decision tree stump to another ML algorithm with the `base_estimator` argument. Our train and test scores here are about the same as the no information rate at 0.919.

We can optimize the hyperparameters with the grid search or Bayesian search methods we learned in *Chapter 14, Optimizing Models and Using AutoML*, but we can also use the `pycaret` package to easily search some hyperparameters with cross-validation. We will need to first set up our data (the datatypes should be checked, and confirmed by pressing *Enter*):

```
from pycaret.classification import setup, create_model, tune_model

classification = setup(data=numeric_df, target='TARGET')
```

Then we can create an AdaBoost model and tune it like so:

```
adaboost = create_model('ada', fold=3)
tuned_adaboost, gridsearch = tune_model(adaboost, fold=3, return_tuner=True)
```

We set the `fold` argument to 3 to use 3-fold cross-validation – the default is 10-fold, and this algorithm already takes a long time to fit. In fact, you may want to sample down the data to test this if it takes too long. This searches a default spread of hyperparameters and we can access the hyperparameters and scores from the `gridsearch` variable that was returned because we set `return_tuner=True`.

> We can see the default hyperparameters searched for different models and tuners from the PyCaret source code (for example, in the `pycaret/containers/models/classification.py` file for classification models: `https://github.com/pycaret/pycaret/blob/master/pycaret/containers/models/classification.py`).

We can get the best hyperparameters from our returned model with `tuned_adaboost.get_params()`. In general, the number of trees might range from 50 to 500 and the learning rate might range from 0.001 to 1. At the time of writing, the AdaBoost hyperparameters searched in PyCaret are:

- `n_estimators`: 10-300 in steps of 10
- `learning_rate`: values from 0.0000001 to 0.5
- `algorithm`: SAMME and SAMME.R

The results from the hyperparameter search (if we use the default sklearn grid search) can be found from gridsearch.cv_results_['params'] and gridsearch. cv_results_['mean_test_score'] (for example, you might use zip() to combine and print these out).

Another way to use AdaBoost is directly from sklearn with the AdaBoostClassifier and AdaBoostRegressor classes, along with using a tuner like the sklearn grid search or another package for searching hyperparameters.

AdaBoost can work well for some problems but has been shown to sometimes not work well when the data has too much noise or a specific type of noise. Other boosting algorithms, such as the ones we will cover next, often outperform AdaBoost.

XGBoost

XGBoost stands for "extreme gradient boosting." It makes several improvements upon plain gradient boosting, such as using Newton boosting. Instead of finding the ideal multiplier to scale each weak learner by (which is like a step length in our gradient descent), XGBoost solves the direction and step length in one equation. By contrast, gradient boosting uses something called a line search to find the optimum multiplier (step length) for each weak learner. This means XGBoost can be faster than plain gradient boosting. It also is implemented in several coding languages, meaning it can be deployed in a number of situations. Additionally, it can be used with big data in a few different ways, such as Dask, H2O, Spark, and AWS SageMaker.

XGBoost is implemented in the xgboost library as well as H2O in Python. We will look at using it with pycaret, although it can be used directly from the xgboost library as shown in the documentation: https://xgboost.readthedocs.io/en/latest/python/python_intro.html. Using it with the xgboost package also requires one step of converting our data to a DMatrix datatype from xgboost.

 Using gradient boosting with H2O is very similar to random forests in H2O, with examples in the documentation: https://docs.h2o.ai/h2o/latest-stable/h2o-docs/data-science/gbm.html. The sklearn package also has a GradientBoostingClassifier and regressor, which is plain gradient boosting.

XGBoost with PyCaret

Again, we can use `xgboost` easily through `pycaret`, which, by default, searches the following hyperparameter space:

- `learning_rate`: 0.0000001 to 0.5
- `n_estmators`: 10-300 in steps of 10
- `subsample`: 0.2 to 1
- `max_depth`: 1 to 11 in steps of 1
- `colsample_bytree`: 0.5 to 1
- `min_child_weight`: 1 to 4 in steps of 1
- `reg_alpha`: 0.0000001 to 10
- `reg_lambda`: 0.0000001 to 10
- `scale_pos_weight`: 0 to 50 in steps of 0.1

We can see XGBoost has many more hyperparameters than AdaBoost. This is done using an `sklearn` grid search by default, so it can take a long time. To speed it up, we can use another tuner, like Bayesian search, which searches the following hyperparameter spaces by default in pycaret:

```
tune_distributions = {
    "learning_rate": UniformDistribution(0.000001, 0.5, log=True),
    "n_estimators": IntUniformDistribution(10, 300),
    "subsample": UniformDistribution(0.2, 1),
    "max_depth": IntUniformDistribution(1, 11),
    "colsample_bytree": UniformDistribution(0.5, 1),
    "min_child_weight": IntUniformDistribution(1, 4),
    "reg_alpha": UniformDistribution(0.0000000001, 10, log=True),
    "reg_lambda": UniformDistribution(0.0000000001, 10, log=True),
    "scale_pos_weight": UniformDistribution(1, 50),
}
```

We can see it's the same areas as the grid search. These hyperparameters represent the following:

- `learning_rate`: the scaling factor that multiplies incremental trees in the algorithm
- `n_estmators`: the number of trees in the algorithm
- `subsample`: the fraction of data sampled for each tree
- `max_depth`: the depth of each tree (number of splits)

- `colsample_bytree`: the fraction of features sampled for each tree
- `min_child_weight`: determines if a node should split or not based on the purity of samples in the node
- `reg_alpha`: L1 regularization of weights for each leaf (each leaf of each tree has a weight associated with it in the XGBoost implementation)
- `reg_lambda`: L2 regularization of weights for each leaf
- `scale_pos_weight`: This controls the balance of positive and negative values for a binary classification problem

The `pycaret` search spaces are generally good, although some people use different strategies for tuning XGBoost hyperparameters. Some strategies will fix the number of trees and tune the learning rate, while others fix the learning rate and tune the number of trees. Using `xgboost` with `pycaret` is the same as with AdaBoost, but we will use the scikit-optimize Bayesian search here with 10 iterations (so it completes faster than the grid search from `sklearn`):

```
xgb = create_model('xgboost', fold=3)
best_xgb, tuner = tune_model(xgb,
                            fold=3,
                            search_library='scikit-optimize',
                            return_tuner=True)
```

This will take quite a while to run (xgboost is usually the longest-running model when searching several models using `pycaret`), so you might want to sample down the data or take a break while you let it run.

 If you see an error similar to ValueError: Estimator xgboost not available, you will need to install xgboost with conda or pip. A pip install will include GPU support (for Window and Linux) as long as you have installed CUDA first. An easy way to install CUDA is with `conda install -c anaconda cudatoolkit`.

Once it's finished, we can access the best results from `best_xgb.get_params()`, and the CV results from `tuner.cv_results_['params']` and `tuner.cv_results_['mean_test_score']`.

As with random forests and other tree-based methods, we can get the feature importances. With an `xgboost` model (assuming we are using the `sklearn` API for xgboost as we are here), this can be retrieved from `xgb_model.get_booster().get_score()` or `best_xgb.feature_importances_`, which gives us the feature importance by weight.

This is the number of times a feature is used to split data in all the trees in the model. Other methods for feature importance that can be set with the `importance_type` argument in `get_score` are described in the documentation: `https://xgboost.readthedocs.io/en/latest/python/python_api.html`.

XGBoost with the xgboost package

We can also use the `xgboost` package directly to create and train a model. For this, we first import the package with the alias `xgb` as is the convention in the `xgboost` documentation:

```
import xgboost as xgb
```

Next, we need to convert our data to a `DMatrix` xgboost datatype:

```
dtrain = xgb.DMatrix(x_train, label=y_train)
dtest = xgb.DMatrix(x_test, label=y_test)
```

We give the features as the first argument and the label as the second argument (which we also provide with the keyword label here, although it's not required). Now we can train the model:

```
xgb_model = xgb.train(params={'objective': 'binary:logistic'}, dtrain=dtrain)
```

The first argument is the hyperparameters, set with the `params` keyword. The only thing we must set here is the objective function, which is `'binary:logistic'` for binary classification (by default it's `'req:squarederror'` for regression with a squared error loss function). We can also set other hyperparameters if we wish.

The default hyperparameters can be viewed like so (everything besides `import json` should be on one line):

```
import json

json.loads(xgb_model.save_config())['learner']
['gradient_booster']
['updater']['grow_colmaker']['train_param']
```

Hyperparameter tuning with `xgboost` can be complex. One resource for learning more is the book *XGBoost with Python*, by Jason Brownlee, which covers hyperparameter settings and tuning: `https://machinelearningmastery.com/xgboost-with-python/`.

Once we've trained our `xgboost` model, we can evaluate performance like this:

```
from sklearn.metrics import accuracy_score

train_preds = xgb_model.predict(dtrain)
test_preds = xgb_model.predict(dtest)

print(accuracy_score(y_train, train_preds > 0.5))
print(accuracy_score(y_test, test_preds > 0.5))
```

The predictions from the model are probability predictions, so we need to provide a threshold from which to round predictions up to 1. In this case, we use a value of 0.5, which is the default for other models. Notice that we also need to give a `DMatrix` as our data for the `predict` function.

The XGBoost scikit-learn API

The `xgboost` package also has an `sklearn` API which makes it easy to use `xgboost` in the same way we do with scikit-learn models. This can make it easier to use with `sklearn` pipelines and other tools that depend on a model behaving as others do in `sklearn`. To use this API, we create our model like so:

```
xgb_model = xgb.XGBClassifier()
```

We can provide hyperparameters directly to the class as arguments. Then we can fit it like an `sklearn` model:

```
fit_model = xgb_model.fit(x_train, y_train)
```

This allows us to provide pandas DataFrames or other data structures besides DMatrix datatypes to the `fit` function. Then we can evaluate the model in the same way as other `sklearn` models:

```
fit_model.score(x_train, y_train)
```

This computes the accuracy of the model. Of course, we can do something similar for regression with `xgb.XGBRegressor()`. The `xgboost` documentation also lays out more details on the use of the `xgboost` package, including the `sklearn` API methods we touched on here. As with `sklearn` models, we also have `predict` and `predict_proba` methods with our `xgboost` models in the `sklearn` API style, which can give us predicted values and probabilities, respectively.

Training boosted models on a GPU

One advantage of some of the newer boosting methods and packages is they can be trained and run on GPUs. This significantly speeds up training time, sometimes by a factor of 10. To use a GPU with a boosted model, we only need to supply two extra arguments to the `create_model` function from `pycaret`:

```
xgboost_gpu = create_model('xgboost',
                           fold=3,
                           tree_method='gpu_hist',
                           gpu_id=0)
```

The `tree_method` and `gpu_id` are used to specify GPU training. If you have more than one GPU, you need to determine the correct ID of the GPU you want to use. The 3-fold CV time with the hardware used at the time of writing was about 12s to 14s with the CPU and 6s to 9s with the GPU. The speedup will depend on the specific model and data being used. An explanation of some aspects of this is covered here: `https://stackoverflow.com/a/65667167/4549682`. You can measure the time it takes by using the magic command `%%time` at the beginning of the Jupyter cell where you run this code. Note that sometimes the first time `create_model` is called with `xgboost` and `pycaret`, the runtime can be very long. So, you may want to run it once to get the environment initialized, then run it again to measure the runtime.

> To ensure `xgboost` can use the GPU, it must either be installed with pip or from a different Anaconda package. If using pip, one should also install the CUDA toolkit, such as with `conda install -c anaconda cudatoolkit`. Another way is to install the GPU version directly with `conda install py-xgboost-gpu`. However, the `py-xgboost-gpu` packages are currently (as of the time of writing) at a much lower version number than the `xgboost` package on `pypi.org` (which pip uses). Also see the Jupyter Notebook for this chapter for more information.

An even easier way to use a GPU is to set the `use_gpu` argument to `True` in the `setup()` function with `pycaret`. This will use a GPU for algorithms that support it, which are listed in the documentation: `https://pycaret.readthedocs.io/en/latest/installation.html?highlight=gpu#pycaret-on-gpu`. The other models in PyCaret that can use GPU besides XGBoost at the moment of writing are LightGBM (requires installing a GPU version of `lightgbm`), CatBoost, logistic regression (also with ridge), random forests, KNN classifiers, and SVMs (support vector machines). The non-boosted ML algorithms require another package, cuML, to be installed (which only works on Linux as of the time of writing, although one can use a Docker container to run Linux with cuML).

Note also that there are some other limitations with GPU use in pycaret, such as not being able to use tune-sklearn for optimization with a GPU.

LightGBM

LightGBM is a newer algorithm that includes some improvements compared with XGBoost, although it does not always outperform XGBoost in practice. It creates the decision trees in the ensemble differently using novel techniques (described in the original paper: `https://papers.nips.cc/paper/2017/file/6449f44a102fde848669 bdd9eb6b76fa-Paper.pdf`), which allows it to run faster and use less memory than XGBoost. It also can handle missing values and categorical data natively. It was created by Microsoft and is what Azure's ML GUI uses when a boosted decision tree ML algorithm is chosen (at the moment of writing). There is a `lightgbm` library which can be used in a few different languages, including Python. It's also included with pycaret, and we can tune the model in the same way as the other boosting algorithms:

```
light_gbm = create_model('lightgbm', fold=3)
best_lgbm, tuner = tune_model(light_gbm,
                              fold=3,
                              search_library='scikit-optimize',
                              return_tuner=True)
```

The hyperparameters and spaces searched by pycaret by default are:

- num_leaves: this is the number of leaf nodes allowed per tree; similar to max depth
    - 2 to 256
- learning_rate: a weight each new tree is multiplied by
    - 0.0000001 to 0.5
- n_estimators: number of trees
    - 10 to 300 in steps of 10
- min_split_gain: higher values stop nodes from splitting if the results are not pure enough
    - 0 (all splits are accepted) to 0.9

- reg_alpha: L1 regularization on tree weights as with XGBoost
  - 0.0000001 to 10
- reg_lambda: L2 regularization on leaf weights as with XGBoost
  - 0.0000001 to 10
- feature_fraction: fraction of features selected for each tree
  - 0.4 to 1
- bagging_freq: how often to re-sample the data with bagging (sampling with replacement)
  - 0 to 7
- bagging_fraction: fraction of samples drawn in the bagging process
  - 0.4 to 1
- min_child_samples: similar to min_child_weight in XGBoost, determines if a node should split or not based on the purity and amount of samples in the leaf nodes from a split
  - 1 to 100

Some of these hyperparameters can be used to decrease training time or improve accuracy as described in the documentation: https://lightgbm.readthedocs.io/en/latest/Parameters-Tuning.html.

As we can see, many of the hyperparameters here are similar to XGBoost, with one of the biggest differences being we set the number of leaf nodes instead of the max depth. This has to do with LightGBMs tree-creation method, which uses leaf-based growth rather than depth-based.

LightGBM plotting

The lightgbm package also has some plotting methods (listed in the documentation: https://lightgbm.readthedocs.io/en/latest/Python-API.html#plotting). We will look at plotting the feature importances here:

```
import lightgbm

lightgbm.plot_importance(best_lgbm)
```

We can also get numeric values for these from `best_lgbm.feature_importances_`, which is the same as the `sklearn` interface. Our resulting plot looks like this:

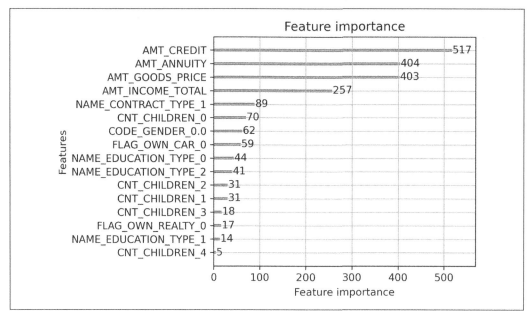

Figure 15.5: Variable (feature) importances from the lightgbm model

We can see the size of the loan (`AMT_CREDIT`) seems to be the most important factor from this model for predicting if someone has loan repayment problems.

Using LightGBM directly

LightGBM has a Python API (described well in the documentation: `https://lightgbm.readthedocs.io/en/latest/Python-API.html`). The style is essentially the same as `sklearn` models. First, we initialize our model, giving it any hyperparameter settings we choose:

```
lgb_model = lightgbm.LGBMClassifier()
```

Then we fit it to data:

```
trained_lgb = lgb_model.fit(x_train, y_train)
```

We can use `score`, `predict`, and `predict_proba` methods in the same way as `sklearn` models to get accuracy (for classification), predicted values, or predicted probabilities.

One note on LightGBM is that we should convert `object` datatypes to `category` in pandas DataFrames if we wish to use categorical features directly (for example, without one-hot encoding them). We can efficiently do this like so:

```
for col in df.select_dtypes(include=['object']):
    df[col] = df[col].astype('category')
```

LightGBM has much more functionality described in its documentation.

CatBoost

One last boosting algorithm we'll cover is CatBoost, which is the newest of the boosting algorithms discussed here. CatBoost is similar to XGBoost, using boosted decision trees, but has some advantages:

- Ostensibly less hyperparameter tuning than XGBoost (simpler to tune)
- Can handle missing data and categorical values natively
- Trains quickly, similar to LightGBM

There is a `catboost` package in Python where we can use the package directly, but we will first show usage through `pycaret`. If using the base `catboost` package, we can also plot some model metrics and show them as the model trains (such as the accuracy as it fits more trees).

To fit our `catboost` model to the data with `pycaret`, it's the same as the other boosting models:

```
catboost_model = create_model('catboost', fold=3)
best_cb, tuner = tune_model(catboost_model,
                        fold=3,
                        search_library='scikit-optimize',
                        return_tuner=True)
```

The results from the tuning end up ever so slightly outperforming the no information rate (accuracy of 0.9196 versus no information rate of 0.9193) – this is not really a significant result, but it is interesting that CatBoost shows a hint of performing better than XGBoost and LightGBM here.

The default hyperparameter search space in `pycaret` for CatBoost is:

- `eta`: the learning rate, or a coefficient that new trees are multiplied by
  - 0.000001 to 0.5
- `depth`: the max depth of the trees
  - 1 to 11
- `n_estimators`: the number of trees in the model
  - 10 to 300
- `random_strength`: the strength of a random Gaussian variable added to the scores of the splits in trees, so that tree splits are not always the best split by score (for example, the Gini coefficient)
  - 0 to 0.8
- `l2_leaf_reg`: L2 regularization of the leaf weights
  - 1 to 200

From this, it looks like CatBoost has fewer hyperparameters than XGBoost or even LightGBM. However, the documentation for classification CatBoosting (`https://catboost.ai/docs/concepts/python-reference_catboostclassifier.html#python-reference_catboostclassifier`) shows that there are a large number of parameters and hyperparameters we can configure.

Using CatBoost natively

To use CatBoost from the Python package, we first import a few classes:

```
from catboost import CatBoostClassifier, Pool
```

We then create our model (we could specify hyperparameters here) and convert our data to the special `Pool` datatype required by CatBoost:

```
cb_model = CatBoostClassifier()
catboost_train_data = Pool(x_train,
                           y_train)
```

Next, we can train the model:

```
cb_model.fit(catboost_train_data)
```

This outputs in real time the value of the metrics (by default, the loss function), the total runtime, and time remaining. We can also visualize the metrics by providing the argument plot=True to fit. Once completed, we can use other methods, such as score, to get the accuracy: cb_model.score(catboost_train_data). We can also use predict and predict_proba on new data with only features (no targets) like this:

```
catboost_test_data = Pool(x_test)
cb_model.predict(catboost_test_data)
```

First, we create a dataset with the catboost Pool class, giving it only our features. Then we simply use the predict method of our model on this data. There are many other methods of catboost models described in the documentation.

Using early stopping with boosting algorithms

When training the XGBoost, LightGBM, and CatBoost models, we can use a practice called early stopping to prevent overfitting. This method is used when fitting the model. We provide a training dataset and a validation set, and our metrics are calculated on both datasets after each new tree is added to the model. If the validation metric does not improve for a specified number of rounds (new trees added), then the model training is stopped and the model iteration with the best validation score is selected. The xgboost, lightgbm, and catboost packages have an argument in their fit or train methods called early_stopping_rounds, which determines the number of trees that can be fit with no validation score improvement before training is stopped. For example, we can use it with catboost like so:

```
import catboost

new_cb = catboost.CatBoostClassifier(**best_cb.get_params())
new_cb.set_params(n_estimators=1000)
new_cb.fit(X=x_train,
           y=y_train,
           eval_set=(x_test, y_test),
           early_stopping_rounds=10,
           plot=True)
```

We are using our parameters from the best CatBoost model we found from model tuning using `pycaret`, and the ** before the dictionary is dictionary unpacking. This expands each dictionary item as an argument to the function or class, so if our dictionary has an element `best_cb.get_params()['n_estimators'] = 100`, (or `{'n_estimators': 10}`) then this would be the same as providing n_estimators=100 in the `CatBoostClassifier` class. We then increase the number of estimators to a large value so we can see early stopping work. Finally, we fit the model to our train set and use the test set as the evaluation set. The `plot=True` argument shows the train and validation scores as it trains. We can see it stops early by examining the number of trees with `new_cb.tree_count_`, which returns 172.

Although early stopping can be used to prevent overfitting, we can also use things like regularization (`l2_leaf_reg` for `catboost`, for example) and cross-validation to prevent and check for overfitting. In fact, using `tune_model` from `pycaret` provides a way to avoid overfitting, since we are optimizing the hyperparameters by using the metric score on a validation set.

There are several books and resources out there for learning XGBoost, such as *Hands-On Gradient Boosting with XGBoost and scikit-learn* by Corey Wade from Packt, or Jason Brownlee's XGBoost book, *XGBoost with Python*. For LightGBM and CatBoost, there are not so many comprehensive resources out there for learning at the moment of writing. Some of the most useful resources for LightGBM and CatBoost are their respective documentation sites. Sometimes looking for a quickstart guide for a package can be helpful as well.

Test your knowledge

Now that we've seen how to use some tree-based and boosting models, try using them on the full set of data for the housing loan dataset we worked on in this chapter. The full dataset has many more features. As always, you may want to perform some data cleaning and preparation before using some of the tree-based ML algorithms, although `pycaret` can auto-clean and prepare data, and `catboost` and `lightgbm` can handle missing values and categorical columns (you need to convert the datatype from `object` to `category` for `lightgbm`, however). Explore the feature importance using the methods we learned in the chapter. Be sure to write a summary of your results.

Summary

We covered a lot of important topics in this chapter, starting with the foundation for tree-based ML models: the decision tree. We saw how trees can automatically determine splits for the data in order to make the best possible predictions, which uses a calculation such as the Gini coefficient or entropy. Next, we saw how these trees can be combined into an ensemble to form a random forest. Remember also that random forests bootstrap data for each decision tree, adding another element to prevent overfitting. Next, we saw how decision trees are used in ML boosting algorithms, such as AdaBoost, gradient boosting, XGBoost, LightGBM, and CatBoost.

These boosted algorithms fit decision trees to the data one step at a time, and each new tree fits to the data with weight added to incorrect predictions (AdaBoost) or fits to the gradient of the loss function (gradient boosting methods) in order to improve the model. We saw how the pycaret package can use the most prominent boosting methods and automatically tune them for us. We also saw that pycaret's hyperparameter search spaces give us an idea of which hyperparameters to search and over what ranges. The advantages of LightGBM and CatBoost were discussed, such as faster training times than XGBoost and the ability to handle missing and categorical values with LightGBM and CatBoost. Lastly, we saw how boosted models can use early stopping to prevent overfitting, although cross-validation and regularization work as well.

Tree-based ML models are extremely important to know in the field of ML and data science but don't always work best for every problem. Another important type of ML algorithm we'll learn next is support vector machines, or SVMs.

16

Support Vector Machine (SVM) Machine Learning Models

The decision tree-based models we covered in the last chapter tend to perform well for many problems. However, depending on our problem, other algorithms may work better. One widely used machine learning algorithm is the **support vector machine** (**SVM**). Like linear and logistic regression, SVMs have been around for a while – since 1963. SVMs can be used for regression and classification, sometimes called **support vector regressors** (**SVRs**) and **support vector classifiers** (**SVCs**). Although SVMs have been around for a while and have become less popular with the rise of other ML algorithms, it's still worth trying SVMs as one of your ML algorithms for supervised learning problems. The basic theory and usage of SVMs will be the focus of this chapter. Specifically, we'll cover:

- The basic idea behind SVMs
- How to use SVMs for classification and regression with `sklearn` and `pycaret`
- How to tune SVM hyperparameters

SVMs have some advantages:

- They work well with a high number of dimensions (many features)
- They are memory-efficient, since they only use a subset of datapoints to classify new ones

- Using kernels to transform data can make them more flexible for higher-dimension and complex feature spaces

However, there are some disadvantages:

- Vanilla SVM implementations do not scale well with increasing features and datapoints (although there are implementations for big data with Spark and other software)
- Probability estimates for class predictions need to be found with cross-validation, which is computationally expensive

Let's begin with the basics of how SVMs work.

How SVMs work

As we mentioned, SVMs can be used for classification and regression, and the implementation differs for each. We'll start with classification.

SVMs for classification

Let's start with a simple example of a dataset for classification, where we have two features on the two axes, and the target is represented by the color and shape. We want to separate the two types of datapoints with different shapes and colors, and we can see how several classification boundary lines could be drawn to separate them. We've currently drawn one potential separation line.

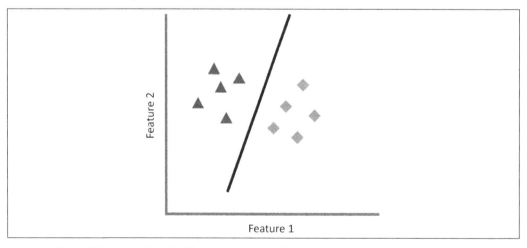

Figure 16.1: A two-class classification example with a hyperplane separating the two classes

SVMs allow us to mathematically find the best separation between groups of data. In the case of two dimensions, this is a line, but with higher dimensions, as we often see, this becomes a hyperplane. The objective of an SVM classifier is to find the optimal hyperplane to separate classes. This hyperplane can be defined similarly to how we defined linear regression, with an equation $w \cdot x + b = 0$, where w is a vector of coefficients, x is a vector of our features, and b is a constant. This hyperplane ends up being mathematically defined by the nearest points. These nearest points define the *support vectors*, from which the name support vector machine is derived. As we move to higher numbers of features beyond two, it becomes a true hyperplane – a surface with several dimensions. Usually, "hyper" is used when we are talking about an arbitrary number of dimensions. Often, it's used to describe more than three dimensions. The exact mathematics of finding the hyperplane is complex and involves optimization, but the short version is that we maximize the distance between the hyperplane and the nearest points of opposite classes. The points nearest to the hyperplane are the support vectors, which are stored in memory after training. This hyperplane is found iteratively through optimization (similar to how we found coefficients for logistic regression with gradient descent or gradient ascent).

You can see illustrations of a hyperplane in 2D in many explanations of SVMs, such as these:

- `https://en.wikipedia.org/wiki/Support-vector_machine`
- `https://towardsdatascience.com/support-vector-machine-simply-explained-fee28eba5496`

This simple way of separating points works for many problems, but not every problem. For example, the classic example of two concentric circles of points cannot be separated linearly in their base feature space, as shown on the left:

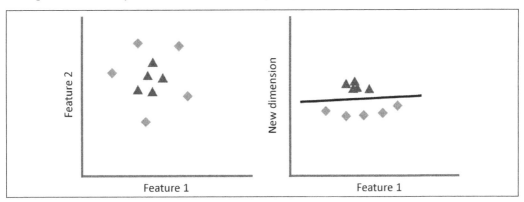

Figure 16.2: Transforming data to make it linearly separable

But as we can see on the right side of *Figure 16.2*, if we transform the data into a new dimension, it can be linearly separated. The new dimension shown here is like taking the square of features 1 and 2 and adding them. Such transformations can be accomplished with the kernel trick. This is a way of essentially transforming data into new and higher dimensions. The mathematics again gets complicated, but we can simply think of it as transforming data into a higher dimension.

 Many articles have been written explaining the kernel trick, such as this one: `https://towardsdatascience.com/the-kernel-trick-c98cdbcaeb3f`. If you want to understand it fully, you will probably need to read several articles and books on the subject.

There are four common kernels we'll see:

- Linear – the first example we saw
- Polynomial – can work for slightly more complex data
- **Radial basis function** (**RBF**) – works for very complex data
- Sigmoid – can work for complex data

In practice, we usually use the linear or RBF kernel. The linear kernel works better for bigger data since it runs a little faster. However, SVM runtimes tend to scale as $n_{features} * n_{samples}^2$ to $n_{features} * n_{samples}^3$ (`https://stats.stackexchange.com/a/88982/120921`), so even a linear kernel can take a long time to run with big data (if we are not using a big data solution such as Spark or `pyspark`).

SVMs for regression

SVMs work a little differently for regression and are called SVRs. Instead of trying to maximize the margin between the hyperplane and points of different classes, SVRs in essence fit a hyperplane to the data. This is similar to how linear regression works, although we are optimizing a different function with SVRs. Essentially, we try to minimize the difference between predictions of datapoints from the hyperplane and actual values.

 The mathematics and concepts behind SVMs are explained in a few different books. One that may be helpful is *Support Vector Machines Succinctly* by Alexandre Kowalczyk, which is free online: `https://www.syncfusion.com/succinctly-free-ebooks/support-vector-machines-succinctly`.

Let's look at using SVMs for classification with `sklearn` and `pycaret`.

Using SVMs

There are many packages we can use for implementing SVMs, but `sklearn` is one of the top Python packages for it. We can also use `pycaret` to easily search the hyperparameter space.

Using SVMs in sklearn

The `sklearn` package has a few different SVC and SVR implementations:

- Linear SVMs (`svm.LinearSVC`, `LinearSVR`, `linear_model.SGDClassifier`, and `SGDRegressor`)
- General SVMs (`svm.SVC` and `SVR`)
- Nu SVMs (`svm.NuSVC` and `NuSVR`)

The linear SVM can be implemented with `svm.LinearSVC` and `svm.SVC`, although the `LinearSVC` implementation is better (because it scales better to large datasets and has more flexibility, as described in the documentation: `https://scikit-learn.org/stable/modules/generated/sklearn.svm.LinearSVC.html`). The SVC implementation allows any kernel to be used, and has pre-made options for using different kernels: polynomial (`poly`), RBF (`rbf`), and sigmoid (`sigmoid`).

The Nu SVMs introduce a hyperparameter, *nu*, which is an upper bound to the number of misclassified points for classification, and a lower bound to the number of support vectors.

Using these is the same as any other `sklearn` supervised learning algorithm – create the model (with any chosen hyperparameters), train it, then use and evaluate it. First, let's load the credit card default data we've used previously and create train and test sets:

```
import pandas as pd
from sklearn.model_selection import train_test_split
from sklearn.preprocessing import StandardScaler

df = pd.read_excel('data/sample - default of credit card clients.xls',
                   skiprows=1,
                   index_col='ID')
target_column = 'default payment next month'
features = df.drop(target_column, axis=1)
targets = df[target_column]
train_x, test_x, train_y, test_y = train_test_split(features,
                                                    targets,
                                                    stratify=targets,
```

```
                                                        random_state=42)
scaler = StandardScaler()
scaled_train_x = scaler.fit_transform(train_x)
scaled_test_x = scaler.transform(test_x)
```

We are loading the data and breaking it into train and test sets, as we've done previously, using `stratify` in `train_test_split` to make sure the balance of binary targets stays the same between the train and test sets. We also prepared some scaled features. For SVMs, there are a few caveats – one is that it is helpful to scale the data. This is due to how the math behind SVMs works (which, again, is complex, and will require deeper/further study to fully understand). One other caveat is that getting probability predictions is not built in, and is not available with `LinearSVC`.

Let's look first at using `LinearSVC` with the default hyperparameters. Almost all of the configuration parameters have to do with the iterative solver for the function, such as `max_iter` (for the maximum number of iterations) and `tol` (which controls when the iteration has stopped, if the optimization has not improved enough after an iteration). The main hyperparameter to tune here is `C`, which is a regularization coefficient. Higher values of `C` mean less regulation (less prevention of overfitting), or a smaller-margin hyperplane (less separation between points and the hyperplane). A good visual explanation of this can be found here: `https://stats.stackexchange.com/a/159051/120921`.

We can fit and score our model like so:

```
from sklearn.svm import LinearSVC

lsvc = LinearSVC()
lsvc.fit(scaled_train_x, train_y)
print(lsvc.score(scaled_train_x, train_y))
print(lsvc.score(scaled_test_x, test_y))
```

This is the same pattern we followed from other `sklearn` models. Our accuracy here is 78.7% on the test set, slightly better than the no information rate of 78.3% (from `targets.value_counts(normalize=True)`). If we instead use the non-scaled data, our accuracy is much lower (around 50%).

We can also implement a linear SVC with a few other methods – using the `linear_model.SGDClassifier` with the default value of `loss='hinge'`, or using the `SVC` or `NuSVC` models with `kernel='linear'`. **SGD** stands for **stochastic gradient descent**, since it is using gradient descent to optimize the model (the hyperplane for our SVC). With the SGD model, we do not have the `C` hyperparameter, though we can fine-tune the gradient descent and L1 and L2 losses used with the model in more detail .

We also have an `alpha` parameter for the L1 and L2 regularization that penalizes bigger values in the w vector from our hyperplane equation.

While `C` penalizes misclassified points, `alpha` penalizes bigger coefficients in w. Both have the same effect of increasing the margin (the distance from the hyperplane to the nearest points) with bigger penalties (small `C` or bigger `alpha` values). For the `SVC` and `NuSVC` models, a different algorithm is used for the linear SVC that does not scale as well with bigger data. However, we can get probability estimates for predictions by setting the `probability=True` parameter:

```
from sklearn.svm import SVC

svc = SVC(probability=True)
svc.fit(scaled_train_x, train_y)
print(svc.score(scaled_train_x, train_y))
print(svc.score(scaled_test_x, test_y))
```

After using probability=True, we can then use the `predict_proba` method of the model (such as `svc.predict_proba(scaled_test_x)`) to predict probabilities of classes. However, these probabilities are estimated from a cross-validation method, so may not always agree with the actual predictions. Interestingly, the different solver used with the SVC model (`libsvm` instead of `liblinear` with `LinearSVC`) seems to perform slightly better than the `LinearSVC` model here, with a test accuracy of 81.8%. We could also try using the `SGDClassifier` and the `NuSVM` models for comparison. The `NuSVM` model works in almost the same way as the SVC model, although it has the `nu` hyperparameter, which should be greater than 0 and less than or equal to 1. The `nu` hyperparameter determines the maximum fraction of misclassified points and the minimum fraction of support vectors.

To use SVMs for regression in `sklearn`, the process is the same, although we don't have the `probability` or `predict_proba` options available and use the SVR-based classes (or `SGDRegressor`) instead of the SVC versions. We also don't have one hyperparameter that we had for classification, `class_weight`, which, if set to `balanced`, inversely weights points occurring to their class frequency. We do have another hyperparameter with SVR, which is `epsilon`. This determines a distance from the hyperplane where wrong predictions are not penalized. A bigger value of `epsilon` means the model will have more bias (less overfitting), while smaller `epsilon` makes the model fit the data more exactly (more variance).

We should optimize our hyperparameters as we do with any ML model to maximize performance. While we can do this manually with grid search, we can also use `pycaret` to make it easier.

Tuning SVMs with pycaret

As with other models, we can easily tune them using `pycaret`. By default, `pycaret` uses the `SGDClassifier` or regressor for a linear SVM and uses `SVC` or `SVR` for an RBF kernel SVM. But we can use `pycaret` to tune any `sklearn` model; so, if want to tune the `LinearSVC` model we already tried, we can do it like so:

```
from pycaret.distributions import UniformDistribution
from pycaret.classification import setup, create_model, tune_model

clf_setup = setup(data=df,
                  target='default payment next month',
                  normalize=True)
lsvc = create_model(LinearSVC())
tuned_lsvc = tune_model(lsvc,
                        search_library='scikit-optimize',
                        custom_grid={"C": UniformDistribution(0, 50)})
```

We import the necessary functions from the `pycaret.classification` module, then set up our `pycaret` space. We leave the defaults for the detected numeric or categorical columns and normalize our features (this normalization uses standardization by default). Then we create our `LinearSVC` model and tune it with Bayesian search in the range 0 to 50. The result is a `C` value of around 2 with an accuracy of about 81% on the 10-fold cross-validation.

To use the default search spaces for the linear SVC and RBF kernel SVC in `pycaret`, we can use `'svm'` or `'rbfsvm'` for our model:

```
lsvc = create_model('svm')
tuned_lsvc = tune_model(lsvc, search_library='scikit-optimize')
```

Here, we search the hyperparameters for the `SGDClassifier` from `sklearn`, including the following hyperparameters with ranges:

- `l1_ratio`: The fraction of L1 and 1-L2 regularization from ElasticNet
    - 0 to 1
- `alpha`: The regularization strength (bigger is stronger)
    - 0 to 1
- `eta0`: The learning rate of gradient descent
    - 0.001 to 0.5
- `penalty`: The L1, L2, or ElasticNet penalties
    - ["elasticnet", "l2", "l1"]

- `fit_intercept`: Adds an intercept term to the hyperplane equation
  - `[True, False]`
- `learning_rate`: The learning rate schedule for gradient descent (how it takes steps in the optimization problem)
  - `["constant", "invscaling", "adaptive", "optimal"]`

The optimal model here was not much different from our `LinearSVC` and had an accuracy of 81.7%. One difference is that `SGDClassifier` runs much faster than `LinearSVC`, however.

`rbfsvm`, which uses `sklearn.svm.SVC` with `kernel='rbf'`, searches the `C` hyperparameter from 0 to 50, and tries using `class_weight='balanced'` and `None`. With `'balanced'`, this will set weights of classes as inversely proportional to their prevalence. `rbfsvm` takes much longer to run than `LinearSVC` or `SGDClassifier` and ends up with an accuracy of 81.6%. In this case, it looks like the best SVC model to use would be `SGDClassifier` (the `svm` model from `pycaret`), since it has similar accuracy to the other models but runs the fastest.

The RBF kernel does have one more hyperparameter, which is gamma. This is set to `auto` with `pycaret`, although we could try tuning it as well. The gamma value affects how the data is transformed into a new dimension, with larger values of gamma tending to cause overfitting and smaller values causing underfitting. A very small value of gamma ends up being like a linear SVM. More details on the RBF hyperparameters are provided in the `sklearn` documentation: `https://scikit-learn.org/stable/auto_examples/svm/plot_rbf_parameters.html`.

Using `pycaret` to optimize SVMs for regression is similar to classification, except we use the `pycaret.regression` module instead. However, the regression models do not have the `class_weight` hyperparameter, but do have an `epsilon` hyperparameter. This `epsilon` hyperparameter determines a distance from the hyperplane where wrong predictions are not penalized, and `pycaret` searches a space of 1-2 for this. There is also not a linear SVM available for SVR by default, although we can create our own `LinearSVR` model and use that.

Test your knowledge

Now that you've seen how SVMs work, try using SVRs to predict the `SalePrice` of home price data we used in *Chapter 14, Optimizing Models and Using AutoML*. This is also available in the `Chapter16\data` folder in the book's GitHub repository. Try comparing this with other models we've learned about so far.

Summary

We've seen how SVMs can be used for both classification and regression and learned a few basics about how they work. For classification, SVMs optimize a hyperplane to separate classes, maximizing the margin between the hyperplane and the datapoints. We can tune the performance with hyperparameters such as C and L1/L2 regularization. For regression, we can use the epsilon hyperparameter to balance the model's bias and variance. Finally, we saw how pycaret can be used to easily tune the SVM models and search hyperparameter spaces.

We've taken a look at several models for classification and regression for supervised learning, which is a major part of machine learning. However, if we don't have target values to predict, we can still use machine learning. In that case, we can use clustering, which helps us uncover patterns in data. In the next chapter, we'll cover some important clustering algorithms and how to use them.

Part V

Text Analysis and Reporting

17

Clustering with Machine Learning

From the last few chapters, we know how to use supervised learning, including using and comparing different models, optimizing hyperparameters, and evaluating models. One of the other major categories of machine learning is clustering. Unlike supervised learning, clustering and unsupervised learning do not require targets or labels for the data. We can still use clustering with labeled data, however, but all inputs are treated as features. Clustering uncovers patterns in data based on the similarity of data points. There are several different methods for performing clustering, but they all rely on distances between data points. In this chapter, we'll learn how to use some of the key clustering methods and will learn how they work, including:

- k-means clustering
- DBSCAN
- Hierarchical clustering

Near the end of the chapter, some of the other models available will be discussed as well as how we can use clustering as part of a semi-supervised learning system. We'll begin with k-means clustering.

Using *k*-means clustering

The k-means clustering method is widespread in data science, in part because it is simple to use and understand.

In this method, we have one primary hyperparameter, k, which determines the number of clusters. The algorithm works like so:

1. Initialize cluster centers: randomly select k points in the feature space as our cluster centroids.

2. Calculate the distance of points to each cluster center with a metric such as Euclidean distance, and then assign points to the nearest cluster.

3. Readjust cluster centers based on average values of points in each cluster.

4. Repeat *steps 2* and *3* until the cluster centers change by a small amount (or not at all).

The initialization of the cluster centers can be done in an intelligent way to speed up convergence – we can initialize cluster centers so that they are far away from each other. The other steps are simple and easy to code by hand, but we can use k-means clustering easily through `sklearn`. Let's revisit our housing price data and see if it clusters into groups. First, we load the data:

```
import pandas as pd

df = pd.read_csv('data/housing_data_sample.csv', index_col='Id')
```

Since clustering algorithms are based on distances, we want to scale our data if the values are not already on the same scale or in the same units. We can do this using `StandardScaler` of `sklearn` and then fit a simple k-means model to the data:

```
from sklearn.preprocessing import StandardScaler
from sklearn.cluster import KMeans

scaler = StandardScaler()
scaled_df = scaler.fit_transform(df)
km = KMeans()
km.fit(scaled_df)
```

By default, this uses eight clusters. However, we don't know the best number of clusters without trying different values and comparing them. For that, we need to use metrics to measure performance.

Clustering metrics

We can use a few different metrics to compare the results of different values for k in k-means clustering (or to compare the results of other clustering algorithms). Here are a few common metrics:

- Within-cluster sum-of-squares (WCSS), also called inertia
- Silhouette score (or silhouette coefficient)
- Calinski Harabasz score (or Calinski Harabasz index)

In general, these methods aim to measure how well our clusters are grouping. The WCSS is simple and calculates the sum of the distance from each point to the center of the cluster. The center of a cluster (the centroid) is the average value of samples in the cluster. A lower WCSS is better, but we typically use an "elbow" plot to pick the ideal value. This method works well for spherical-shaped clusters, but for strange shapes (like ellipsoids) it does not work so well. Another way of describing these spherical cluster shapes is convex, meaning the boundaries of the clusters have a curvature that never bends inward. More information about the WCSS for *k*-means clustering is in the `sklearn` documentation: `https://scikit-learn.org/stable/modules/clustering.html#k-means`.

> Another similar way to measure cluster quality is with the squared Euclidean distance or within cluster variation. This is the sum of squared distances between individual points in a cluster. More information about this can be found in several places, including the *Introduction to Statistical Learning* book: `https://www.statlearning.com/`.

The silhouette score measures a ratio involving the average distance between a single point and all points in the same cluster (*a*) and the average distance between the single point and all points in the next nearest cluster (*b*). This has the equation $ss = \dfrac{b - a}{\max(a, b)}$ for a single point, where the max(*a*,*b*) means we take the larger of the two values, *a* or *b*. To get an average score for a cluster, we can take the average silhouette score over all points in the cluster. This average measures how well each cluster has been formed. We can also average the silhouette score over the entire dataset for a single number to describe how well the entire dataset has clustered. The silhouette score can range from -1 to +1, and we get values for each individual point. We can plot all scores together as well as calculating an average score over all points (for example, as demonstrated here: `https://scikit-learn.org/stable/auto_examples/cluster/plot_kmeans_silhouette_analysis.html`). The values closer to 1 mean better clustering, while 0 is neutral and -1 is poor clustering.

The last metric we'll talk about is the Calinski Harabasz score. This measures a ratio of the separation of cluster centroids to the spread of points in each cluster. Higher values mean tighter and more separated clusters, so we want higher values for this metric. It's a relative metric, so can be used to evaluate different clustering methods on the same data.

More information on this is available in the sklearn documentation: https://
scikit-learn.org/stable/modules/clustering.html#calinski-harabasz-index.

All of these metrics can be used from sklearn, as we will see. There are several
other metrics as well, described in the sklearn documentation: https://scikit-
learn.org/stable/modules/clustering.html#clustering-performance-evaluation.
A few metrics work better for any shape of cluster (not just spherical), although
those metrics require us to know the class labels of each datapoint (such as
the Rand index, mutual information scores, and many others described in the
sklearn documentation). Let's now take a look at using sklearn to optimize the k
hyperparameter for k-means.

Optimizing *k* in *k*-means

We'll first generate an "elbow" plot with the WCSS, or inertia values, to see
which value of k looks best. This value can be found from the model we fit with
km.inertia_. We can loop through a range of values for k and store the inertia values:

```
k_values = list(range(2, 20))
inertias = []

for k in k_values:
    km = KMeans(n_clusters=k)
    km.fit(scaled_df)
    inertias.append(km.inertia_)
```

We create a list of integers from 2 to 19 to use for k, and then loop through the
list and create the k-means model with each value for k. Then we fit this to our
standardized data and store the WCSS value in our inertias list. Next, we can plot
our results, with the values of k on the x axis and the WCSS values on the y axis:

```
import matplotlib.pyplot as plt

plt.plot(k_values, inertias, marker='.')
plt.xticks(k_values)
plt.xlabel('number of clusters')
plt.ylabel('WCSS')
```

This plot looks like the following:

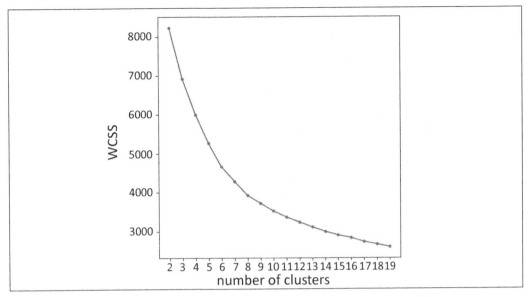

Figure 17.1: An elbow plot of the WCSS values from our *k*-means algorithms

This is called an "elbow" plot because ideally, we will see a kink in the plot where the WCSS or other metric's rate of improvement slows down and the line flattens out quickly. In the case above, there isn't a very clear elbow, suggesting more of a continuous spread of the data. However, we can choose a value of around 8 since it looks like there is a small change in slope there. We can also look at the change in slope for each point (the derivative) by using `np.diff`:

```
import numpy as np

plt.plot(k_values[1:], np.diff(inertias), marker='.')
```

This shows a similar result, that we could pick a value of around 7 to 9. If we want to use the silhouette score and the Calinski Harabasz score, we can use the corresponding functions from `sklearn`:

```
from sklearn.metrics import silhouette_score, calinski_harabasz_score

silhouette_score(scaled_df, km.labels_)
calinski_harabasz_score(scaled_df, km.labels_)
```

Note that we give these methods our data and the cluster labels from our *k*-means algorithm fit (from `km.labels_`). These will be numeric values from 0 to *k*-1.

We can use these other metrics in a loop as well and plot them like we did with the WCSS. Another nice tool for doing all of this automatically is the `yellowbrick` package, which can loop through several values for *k*, plot the results, and automatically choose the best value for *k*:

```
from yellowbrick.cluster.elbow import kelbow_visualizer

kelbow_visualizer(KMeans(), scaled_df, k=(2, 20))
```

By default, this uses distortion, which is the same as the WCSS (with the argument `metric='distortion'`). We can also use `metric='silhouette'` or `metric='calinski_harabasz'` for the other metrics we talked about. Our results look like this:

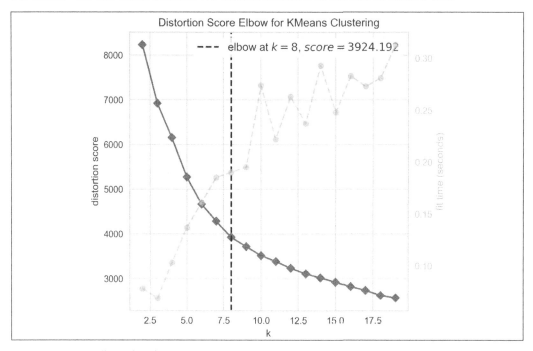

Figure 17.2: An elbow plot of the WCSS (distortion) values from our *k*-means algorithms using yellowbrick

We can see the same elbow was chosen at *k*=8. The plot also displays the time it takes the algorithm to fit to the data, which generally goes up with more clusters (since there are more distances to compute in each iteration).

 The algorithm used by `yellowbrick` to find the best *k*, or elbow, is the kneedle method for the WCSS (described in this paper: https://raghavan.usc.edu//papers/kneedle-simplex11. pdf). For the silhouette and Calinski Harabasz scores, we want the maximum values.

If we try the other metrics such as silhouette score, we will find a different optimum k (3 for silhouette score and 2 for Calinski Harabasz). Ideally, we would want to see some of our metrics agree on a similar number for clusters. For example, the `RbClust` package in R uses 30 different metrics and takes the majority vote as the ideal number of clusters.

Last, let's look at a silhouette plot of our clusters. We'll go with three clusters since this was the ideal score from silhouette score and is the middle of the three values for k we found from our three metrics. We can visualize the silhouette scores for each of the points like so:

```
from yellowbrick.cluster import silhouette_visualizer

viz = silhouette_visualizer(KMeans(3, random_state=42), scaled_df)
```

Notice we are using the `random_state` argument here. There is a small amount of randomness in the k-means algorithm when choosing the initial cluster centers, although it shouldn't affect the final state in any major way. However, the exact labels for the clusters could change, so, setting the random state will ensure the cluster centers are the same every time. Our results look like this:

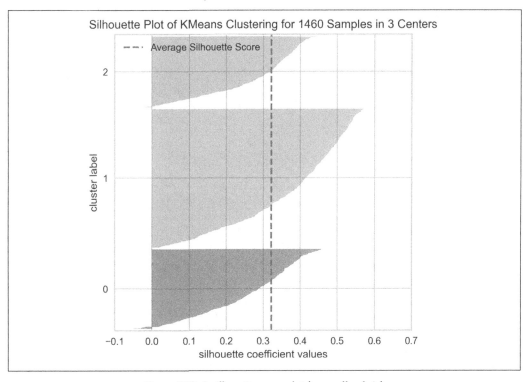

Figure 17.3: A silhouette score plot from yellowbrick

We can see the average score denoted by the dashed line, and the horizontal bars are the silhouette scores of each point. The points with negative scores are on the outskirts of a cluster and close to another cluster, while those with very high scores are close to their cluster center. The ideal silhouette plot would have all points with a high score and a sharp dropoff with a few, if any, points with low scores. Our clustering here looks decent, but not great. We can also see that the size of cluster 1 is much larger than the other two clusters.

 This silhouette plot can also be created with `sklearn` although it is several lines of code instead of the yellowbrick one-liner: `https://scikit-learn.org/stable/auto_examples/cluster/plot_kmeans_silhouette_analysis.html`.

Now that we've chosen our best value for *k*, let's examine the clusters in more detail.

Examining the clusters

We can examine our clusters in a few ways – numerically and visually. Numerically, we can get summary values, such as the average, for each of the clusters. First, let's fit our *k*-means model:

```
km = KMeans(3, random_state=42)
km.fit(scaled_df)
```

Then we can look at the average values for each of the clusters:

```
df_labels = df.copy()
df_labels['label'] = km.labels_

for label in range(3):
    print(f'cluster {label}:')
    print(df_labels[df_labels['label'] == label].mean(), '\n')
```

We first create a copy of our original DataFrame and add the labels to it. Then we loop through each cluster label and print the average value of points in that cluster using DataFrame masking. We also add a newline (`'\n'`) so each group of results is separated by a blank line. The results look like this:

```
cluster 0:
LotArea         11100.957606
YearBuilt        1983.097257
FullBath            2.049875
```

```
TotRmsAbvGrd            7.945137
GarageArea            551.256858
1stFlrSF             1074.279302
2ndFlrSF              921.137157
SalePrice          223219.441397
label                   0.000000
dtype: float64


cluster 1:
LotArea              8717.477889
YearBuilt            1953.158345
FullBath                1.088445
TotRmsAbvGrd            5.596291
GarageArea            357.379458
1stFlrSF              980.592011
2ndFlrSF              181.263909
SalePrice          129434.780314
label                   1.000000
dtype: float64


cluster 2:
LotArea             13385.846369
YearBuilt            1993.477654
FullBath                1.955307
TotRmsAbvGrd            6.723464
GarageArea            611.659218
1stFlrSF             1618.027933
2ndFlrSF               28.399441
SalePrice          234358.013966
label                   2.000000
dtype: float64
```

From this, we can see the first cluster (0) consists of more expensive houses with two stories (or floors). The second cluster (1) are cheaper, older houses. Finally, the last cluster appears to be newer, more expensive houses with a single story (floor).

Another way to examine our data is visualization. One way to do this would be with histograms or other visualization techniques we've learned throughout the book. For example, we could look at histograms of the sale price:

```
import seaborn as sns

sns.histplot(df_labels, x='SalePrice', hue='label', multiple='dodge')
```

This creates histograms for the sale price for each of the three clusters. Looking at certain elements can be helpful, but we can also use 2D and 3D plots to examine the data.

Since each data point has several dimensions, it's helpful to use dimensionality reduction to be able to visualize data well in two or three dimensions. We can use **principal component analysis (PCA)** to do this:

```
from sklearn.decomposition import PCA


pca = PCA(random_state=42)
pca_df = pca.fit_transform(scaled_df)
```

We looked at PCA in *Chapter 10, Preparing Data for Machine Learning: Feature Selection, Feature Engineering, and Dimensionality Reduction*. The idea is that it creates linear combinations of features and creates new features that capture the maximum variance in the dataset. So, the first PCA dimension should capture the most variation, the second has the next most variation in the data, and so on. From `pca.components_`, we can see the relative contributions of each original feature into the PCA components (and we see that the first two PCA dimensions capture a balance of most of the features).

Once we have our PCA transform, we can plot it with the cluster labels:

```
scatter = plt.scatter(pca_df[:, 0],
                      pca_df[:, 1],
                      c=km.labels_,
                      cmap='Dark2',
                      alpha=0.25)
plt.legend(*scatter.legend_elements())
plt.xlabel('PCA dimension 1')
plt.ylabel('PCA dimension 2')
```

We are plotting the first PCA dimension versus the second dimension and using the cluster labels as colors with the argument c=km.labels_. The cmap argument sets the colormap (with more options described in the matplotlib documentation: https://matplotlib.org/stable/tutorials/colors/colormaps.html). We also set the legend for our cluster labels by unpacking the tuple of legend items from our scatter plot with *scatter.legend_elements(). Finally, we give our points 75% transparency with alpha=0.25 so we can see the density of the plots. We might also use something like a hexplot from seaborn to visualize data density in 2D (https://seaborn.pydata.org/generated/seaborn.jointplot.html). Our plot looks like this:

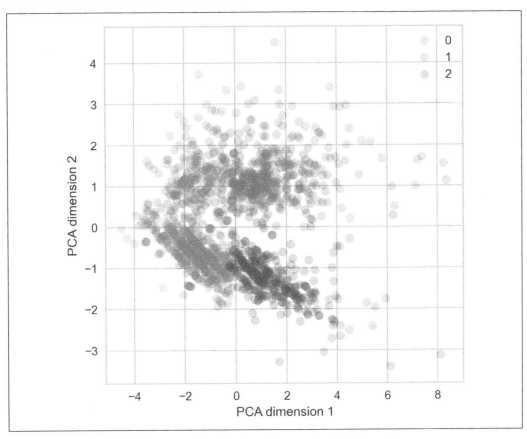

Figure 17.4: A plot of the three clusters using PCA dimensions

We can see the clusters are not perfectly separated and there are some outliers. It even appears from this plot as though we might use four clusters, but remember we optimized *k* using our metrics. Instead of plotting with the PCA dimensions, we could also plot using two dimensions from the original or standardized data to see how the data groups along those dimensions. Or, we could use other dimensionality reduction techniques besides PCA.

Lastly, we can also use `yellowbrick` to easily create a PCA plot similar to the above plot:

```
from yellowbrick.cluster import intercluster_distance

intercluster_distance(km, scaled_df, random_state=42)
```

Instead of showing the raw data points, this shows circles for the cluster centers, with the size of the circle proportional to the number of points:

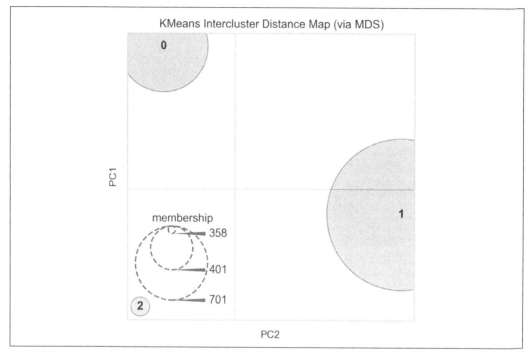

Figure 17.5: A PCA plot of our clusters from yellowbrick

We can see the same relationship of clusters as we had in our original PCA plot, with the sizes of the circles corresponding to the density of points we saw in our first plot as well. However, it's a little easier to read the size of a circle rather than guessing from the density of points.

Now that we've seen k-means, which is one of the canonical methods for clustering, let's look at a few other essential clustering methods.

Hierarchical clustering

Next, we'll examine hierarchical clustering. We already saw this used by pandas-profiling reports in one of the missing value plots. Hierarchical clustering can operate in a bottom-up or top-down approach. The bottom-up approach starts with each point in its own cluster and joins the closest points into clusters based on distance metrics until all points are in one cluster.

The top-down approach starts with all points in one cluster and splits them until all points are in their own cluster.

We can choose a point along these paths that will give us a set of clusters. Let's look at using the sklearn implementation, which uses a bottom-up approach:

```
from sklearn.cluster import AgglomerativeClustering

ac = AgglomerativeClustering(n_clusters=3)
ac.fit(scaled_df)
```

This sklearn class works almost the same as the *k*-means clustering algorithm, with a primary hyperparameter n_clusters. As with *k*-means and other distance-based algorithms, it's usually good to scale our data, so we used scaled_df. We can use the same metrics as before, like distortion (inertia, or WCSS), silhouette score, and Calinski Harabasz. We can use these with yellowbrick again to get the optimal number of clusters:

```
viz = kelbow_visualizer(AgglomerativeClustering(),
                        scaled_df,
                        k=(2, 20),
                        show=False)
```

This produces the following figure:

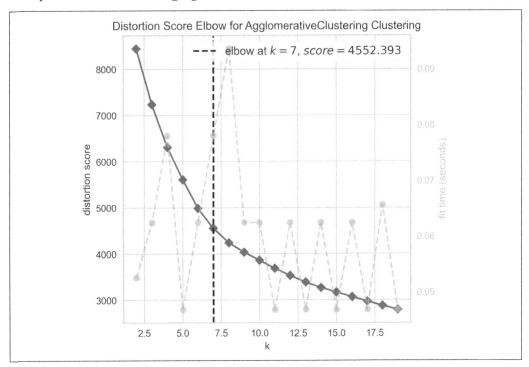

Figure 17.6: An elbow plot using hierarchical clustering using yellowbrick

We can see that the optimal number of clusters is similar to *k*-means using WCSS: 7 here, versus 8 for *k*-means. One big difference is the time to fit is shorter. This is because fewer distances need to be computed due to how the algorithm works.

The hierarchical clustering algorithm works by finding the closest points and joining them together as a cluster. Then it takes a distance metric between each cluster and connects the closest clusters until either the number of clusters has been met or all points have been grouped into a single cluster. To measure distance, we can use a few different methods:

- Single linkage: the distance between the closest points between clusters
- Complete (maximum) linkage: the biggest distance between points in clusters
- Average linkage: the distance between the centroids of clusters (average value of points in the clusters)
- Ward linkage: the sum of squared distances between each point in clusters

The default `linkage` argument or distance methodology with `AggolmerativeClustering` of `sklearn` is Ward (`linkage='ward'`), although it can be any of `ward`, `complete`, `average`, or `single`. Often, there is not a huge difference between using the different linkage methods when working with larger datasets and `ward` works for most applications. However, `average`, `complete`, and `ward` linkage tend to yield more balanced dendrograms compared with other methods according to the ISLR book (`https://www.statlearning.com/`). Using Ward linkage also works well for spherical or convex clusters similar to *k*-means clustering, and using single linkage can capture strange cluster shapes.

 Another place to read about more linkage methods and how to choose which one to use can be found here: `https://stats.stackexchange.com/a/217742/120921`.

One other aspect of hierarchical clustering is the fact that we can plot dendrograms, or tree diagrams. These show how points are joined together to make clusters. The `sklearn` documentation has an example showing how to do this with a custom function (`https://scikit-learn.org/stable/auto_examples/cluster/plot_agglomerative_dendrogram.html`), although we can simply use `scipy`:

```
from scipy.cluster.hierarchy import dendrogram, linkage

dendrogram(linkage(scaled_df), truncate_mode='lastp', p=3)
plt.xlabel('points in cluster')
plt.ylabel('depth')
```

We use the `linkage` function from `scipy` to perform the clustering on our scaled data, and then use the `dendrogram` function to plot it. Using the arguments `truncate_mode='lastp'` and `p=3` specifies that we only want to see three clusters. We can see our following figure:

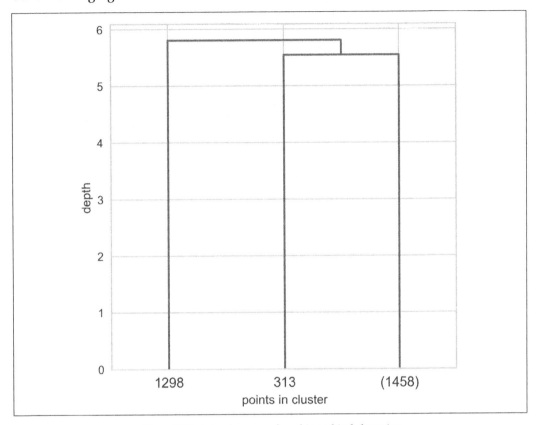

Figure 17.7: A dendrogram of our hierarchical clustering

The y axis in the dendrogram is the distance between points. The horizontal lines show when two clusters, which have a distance corresponding to the y value at the horizontal line, are joined together. We can also see that the number of points in the clusters is similar to what we saw from k-means.

Depending on the linkage method used, hierarchical clustering can work for strangely shaped clusters better than k-means. The `sklearn` documentation has examples showing this (`https://scikit-learn.org/stable/modules/clustering.html#hierarchical-clustering`).

DBSCAN

Another clustering method that can work well for strange cluster shapes is DBSCAN, which stands for Density-Based Spatial Clustering of Applications with Noise. The algorithm is completely different from *k*-means or hierarchical clustering. With DBSCAN, our clusters are composed of core points and non-core points. Core points are all within a distance, epsilon (eps in the sklearn parameters), of at least *n* points in the same cluster (*n* is the min_samples parameter in the sklearn function). Then, any other points within the distance *epsilon* of the core points are also in the cluster. If any points are not within the epsilon distance of any core points, these are outliers. This algorithm assumes we have some dead space between samples, so our clusters must have at least some separation. We can also tune the eps and min_samples hyperparameters to optimize clustering metrics.

The min_samples hyperparameter should generally be between the number of features and two times the number of features, with a higher value for noisier data. A higher number of core points means we need denser groups of points to create clusters. For eps, we can calculate the average distance between points and their min_samples nearest neighbors, plot these values in order, and then find a "knee" or "elbow" in the plot (the point of maximum curvature). We can get the average distances between points and their nearest *n* neighbors with sklearn like this:

```
from sklearn.neighbors import NearestNeighbors

core_points = scaled_df.shape[1] * 2
nn = NearestNeighbors(n_neighbors=core_points + 1)
nn = nn.fit(scaled_df)
distances, neighbors = nn.kneighbors(scaled_df)
average_distances = distances[:, 1:].mean(axis=1)
average_distances.sort()

plt.plot(average_distances)
plt.xlabel('point number')
plt.ylabel(f'average distance to {core_points} neighbors')
```

Our code consists of the following:

- We set our core_points variable to be two times the number of features (the number of columns in our DataFrame) since our dataset is small and probably noisy.

- We calculate the average distance to core_points neighbors with each point. We add 1 because the first nearest neighbor is the point itself with a distance of 0.

- The NearestNeighbors object is fit to the data (overwriting the nn variable with the fitted NearestNeighbors object).
- Distances between neighbors and the indices of the nearest neighbors to each point are extracted with nn.kneighbors.
- We take the average distance to the core_points nearest neighbors (ignoring the first nearest neighbor or self-distance of 0 by indexing with [:, 1:]) and sort this from least to greatest.

Finally, we plot the sorted distances, which look like this:

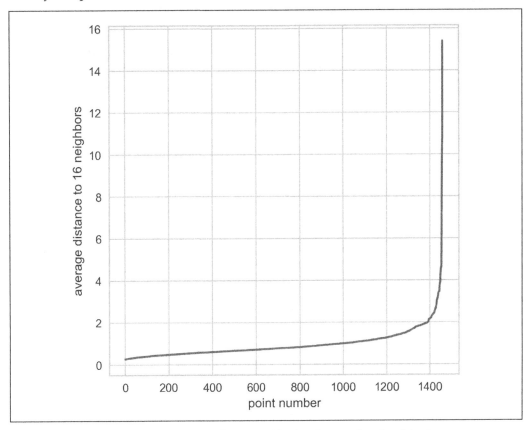

Figure 17.8: The average distance to 16 points from our housing dataset

We can see that the maximum curvature is around index 1400, but we can use a package called kneed to find this automatically (be sure to install the package with conda install -c conda-forge kneed or pip first):

```
from kneed import KneeLocator

kneedle = KneeLocator(range(average_distances.shape[0]),
```

```
                            average_distances,
                            curve="convex",
                            direction="increasing")
    eps = average_distances[kneedle.knee]
```

From this, our index is 1421 and the value for eps is 2.43. We can then put these into DBSCAN and fit the model:

```
from sklearn.cluster import DBSCAN

db = DBSCAN(eps=eps, min_samples=core_points, n_jobs=-1)
db.fit(scaled_df)
```

Note that we are also using n_jobs=-1 here to use all available processors in parallel. We can look at the number of clusters by looking at the unique values in the labels with np.unique(db.labels_). This shows us that we only have one cluster (label 0) and outliers (label -1). If we decrease our eps or core points values, we can get more than a single cluster. However, some metrics, such as the silhouette score, will decrease if we increase the number of clusters. Of course, we could try other methods for optimizing eps and min_samples, such as calculating metrics like WCSS for a variety of hyperparameter values.

We can see that with DBSCAN, we can use it not only for clustering, but also for outlier detection. However, one of the drawbacks of DBSCAN is that it assumes a uniform density of clusters, which is not always true. Several people have made improvements to DBSCAN, such as DMDBSCAN (https://iopscience.iop.org/article/10.1088/1755-1315/31/1/012012/pdf) and many others. One algorithm similar to DBSCAN in sklearn is OPTICS, which uses a more complex method of finding clusters similar to DBSCAN. However, OPTICS does not work better for our small dataset here, at least based on silhouette score.

Other unsupervised methods

We covered some of the basic unsupervised clustering methods here, but there are many more. The sklearn documentation talks about many of the other distance-based clustering methods here: https://scikit-learn.org/stable/modules/clustering.html. Some other algorithms fall under the unsupervised machine learning model category, and many of these are matrix decomposition methods. The other unsupervised methods generally fall into dimensionality reduction techniques and topic modeling.

We saw one of these in *Chapter 10, Preparing Data for Machine Learning: Feature Selection, Feature Engineering, and Dimensionality Reduction*, on feature engineering – PCA, or principal component analysis. PCA can also be used as a preprocessing step for clustering or other unsupervised methods and sometimes improves clustering performance. **SVD (singular value decomposition)** is another dimensionality reduction technique. We can also use t-SNE, which is a more complex dimensionality reduction technique than PCA or SVD.

Similar to t-SNE (but newer and arguably more advanced and generally better) is UMAP, or Uniform Manifold Approximation and Projection. Finally, neural network autoencoders can be used for dimensionality reduction, although the results are often similar to PCA.

Topic modeling techniques include SVD (and variants such as SVD++), **LDA (latent Dirichlet allocation)**, and **LSA (latent semantic analysis, and variants such as PLSA)**. Many of these topic modeling techniques can also be used for recommender systems. These are generally suited for text data, and group documents into different topics where the documents in each topic contain semantically similar text.

We may also find ourselves working with big data that we need to cluster. Some Python packages that can perform some clustering algorithms with big data include Dask, PySpark, and H2O. We can also use cloud solutions such as AWS SageMaker and Google's BigQuery ML.

Test your knowledge

To test your knowledge of the clustering techniques we've learned, try clustering the full housing dataset or a bigger sample of the housing dataset, available in the GitHub repository for this book under `Chapter17/data`. You should be able to use some of the methods we learned (*k*-means, hierarchical clustering, DBSCAN) and be able to optimize the hyperparameters (such as the number of clusters) by using an elbow plot or other metrics, such as the silhouette score.

Summary

As we've seen, unsupervised learning can be a useful technique for uncovering patterns in data without the need for labels or targets. We saw how *k*-means and hierarchical clustering can deliver similar results, and how different metrics such as the within-cluster sum-of-squares (WCSS) and the silhouette score can be used to optimize the number of neighbors for *k*-means and hierarchical clustering. With the WCSS metric, we can use an elbow plot and find the point of maximum curvature on the plot, called the elbow, in order to find the optimal value of n_clusters.

The silhouette plot was demonstrated as another way to evaluate the quality of the clustering fit. We also saw how to create visualizations of clusters and look at summary statistics for clusters to understand what the clustering results mean. Lastly, we looked at how DBSCAN works and one method for deciding on the best eps and `min_samples` hyperparameters that determine how the clusters are formed.

Now that we've learned some supervised and unsupervised learning techniques, in the next chapter, we'll apply these tools and more to a specific type of data that we see quite often as a data source – text.

18
Working with Text

Text is a huge source of data; it's in books, reports, social media, and transcriptions of speech. We can use data science in several different ways with text data to extract useful information and hidden patterns. Much of data science that has to do with text is called **natural language processing**, or **NLP**. This is the process of using computers to extract information or gain an understanding of natural human language. Of course, we need to turn our text into numbers to be able to process it with most machine learning and analytics tools, adding another step to the process. There are also many nuances regarding text analysis that we'll learn about. In this chapter, we'll cover:

- Basic text preprocessing and cleaning, including TFIDF and word vectors
- Text analytics such as word counts and word collocations
- Unsupervised learning for text analysis, including topic modeling
- Supervised learning (classification) with text
- Sentiment analysis

We will see the use of several key Python packages throughout the chapter, including the regular expressions module (re), NLTK, spaCy, `sklearn`, `textblob`, and VADER. Let's begin with some of the basics of text analysis and preprocessing.

Text preprocessing

Before we undertake text analysis, it's often helpful to undertake some common cleaning and preprocessing steps.

This often includes:

- Lowercasing
- Removing punctuation, whitespaces, and numbers
- Removing other specific text patterns (for example, emails)
- Removing stop words
- Stemming or lemmatization

Cleaning and preparing text can improve the performance of ML algorithms as well as make it easier to understand the results of analysis. We'll cover the cleaning and preparation steps we have listed in order.

Basic text cleaning

First, lowercasing is quite easy in Python. We simply take a string variable and use the built-in `.lower()` method. We'll use the book War and Peace by Leo Tolstoy for our text since it's one of the most famous long books. Perhaps we can draw some conclusions about the topics of the book without reading it. The Project Gutenberg website (`https://www.gutenberg.org/`) will be used to retrieve the text with a URL (although a backup is in the GitHub repository for this book). First, be sure to install the gutenberg-cleaner package with `pip install gutenberg-cleaner`, which will help us remove the header and footer from the text. We can then download the text and remove the header and footer like so:

```
from urllib.request import urlopen
from gutenberg_cleaner import simple_cleaner

wnp = urlopen('https://www.gutenberg.org/files/2600/2600-0.txt').\
    read().decode('utf-8')
wnp = simple_cleaner(wnp)
wnp[:100]
```

We are using the `urlopen` technique from *Chapter 7* here, and utilizing the gutenberg-cleaner package to strip the header and footer with the `simple_cleaner()` function. `wnp[:100]` shows us the first 100 characters, from which we can see there is plentiful whitespace (such as the newlines, \r\n) that we'll deal with soon:

```
'\r\n\r\n\r\n\r\nAn Anonymous Volunteer, and David Widger\r\n\r\n\r\n\r\n\r\n\r\
n\r\n\r\nWAR AND PEACE\r\n\r\n\r\n\r\nBy Leo Tolstoy/Tols'
```

If we want to lowercase our text, we can do it like this:

```
wnp = wnp.lower()
```

Lowercasing helps standardize our words for analysis such as word counts and other processing steps. One disadvantage of lowercasing is proper nouns may not be recognized correctly and are not distinguished from regular nouns. Handling entities and proper nouns requires more sophisticated techniques, such as using the spaCy package, which we'll look at later.

Next, we can deal with the excess white space. In most cases, we don't need to worry about excess white space since most methods can handle splitting words with multiple spaces. However, if we want to condense all the whitespaces down to a single whitespace between words, we can do it like so:

```
import re

wnp = re.sub(r'\s+', ' ', wnp).strip()
```

The `re.sub` function takes a pattern, a string to replace the pattern with, and a string to substitute on. We use `\s+` to find one or more occurrences of spaces, then replace them with a single space in the wnp string. Lastly, we use `strip()` to remove whitespace at the beginning and end of the string. Our first hundred characters (`wnp[:100]`) now look like:

```
'an anonymous volunteer, and david widger war and peace by leo tolstoy/
tolstoi contents book one: 180'
```

Using backslashes with regular expressions in Python is a bit confusing. In a Python string, the backslash character can be used in a string literal (a normal string) to escape other characters or in combination with other characters to create a special character. For example, \n is the newline character. Or, if we want to use a backslash in a Python string, we need to "escape" it with another backslash, like "\\" (you can test this with `print("\\")`). With regular expressions, a string that is passed to an `re` function for matching should have the backslashes escaped. For example, if we want the string that is passed to `re.sub` to be `'\s+'`, we should escape the backslash: `'\\s+'`. Another way of doing this is to use a raw string by putting an r just before the string: `r'\s+'`. This means we don't need to escape backslashes. However, confusingly, both of the statements `re.sub('\\s+', ' ', wnp)` and `re.sub('\s+', ' ', wnp)` actually work just fine and accomplish the same thing. It's possible this behavior will change in the future (and sometimes automated continuous integration and development (CI/CD) tools have issues with improper use of regex and backslashes), so it's good to be aware of the proper way to use backslashes with Python regex. More can be read about backslashes in Python regex here: `https://sceweb.sce.uhcl.edu/helm/WEBPAGE-Python/documentation/howto/regex/node8.html`.

The entire guide from A.M. Kuchling (`https://sceweb.sce.uhcl.edu/helm/WEBPAGE-Python/documentation/howto/regex/regex.html`) is also a useful resource for learning regular expressions in Python.

Additionally, the Python documentation is a good resource for Python regex, as well as Google's guide:

- `https://docs.python.org/3/howto/regex.html`
- `https://developers.google.com/edu/python/regular-expressions`

Another common pre-processing step is to remove punctuation. One way to do this is like so:

```
import string

wnp = wnp.translate(str.maketrans('', '', string.punctuation))
```

We use the built-in `string` module to get a string of common punctuation. Then we use the string method `translate` along with `str.maketrans` to replace punctuation with nothing, removing it.

This is similar to using regex or regular expressions (the `re` package), although we are using built-in Python functions here. The `maketrans` function can take up to three arguments and is described in its documentation in more detail. When we provide three arguments, each unique character in the last argument is mapped to `None`, removing these characters from the original string we used with `translate`.

If we wanted to include more characters to remove, such as numbers, we could simply use `string.punctuation + string.digits` as the third argument to `str.maketrans`.

Next, we may need to remove some specific string patterns. An example is email addresses, which have the pattern of a string, the @ symbol, a website, a period, and a domain. The string sections of the email usually only have letters and numbers, so we can use the `\w+` regex string to match one or more characters "that can be a part of any word in any language" (`https://docs.python.org/3/library/re.html`) and numbers and the underscore character. We can again use the `re` module to remove specific patterns like this:

```
wnp = re.sub(r'\w+@\w+\.\w+', '', wnp)
```

The `\w` pattern specifies any alphanumeric character (letters and numbers as well as the underscore character), and the + means match one or more of the proceeding pattern. The `\.` means a literal period. Usually, a period is a wildcard character that matches anything, so we need to "escape" it with the backslash. Put together, this pattern looks for one or more alphanumeric characters, then the @ symbol, another set of alphanumeric characters, a period, and more alphanumeric characters. We then replace this with an empty string, removing any common email addresses.

Our next step is to remove stop words. These are common words that don't have much significance, such as "the", "a", and so on. There are at least three different sources of stop word lists in Python packages: `sklearn`, `nltk`, and `spacy`. We'll use `sklearn` for now since we already have it installed, although the stop words differ slightly between packages. We can first retrieve the stop word list from `sklearn`, then remove these words from our text like this:

```
from sklearn.feature_extraction import _stop_words

non_stopwords = []
for word in wnp.split():
    if word not in _stop_words.ENGLISH_STOP_WORDS:
        non_stopwords.append(word)

cleaned_text = ' '.join(non_stopwords)
```

We loop through each word (split on spaces with `split()`), then add it to the `non_stopwords` list if it's not one of the stop words. When we split the text into words, the individual words are usually called tokens, and the processing of splitting text into tokens is called tokenization. Finally, we join our list of words back together with spaces between the words to get a single string again.

The `_stop_words.ENGLISH_STOP_WORDS` variable is a set. Other stop word lists (like NLTKs) are lists, and it's best to convert them into a set before doing something like the above code example. That's because when we check if a string is in a list of strings, it checks for a match against each element in the list one at a time. If we use a set instead of a list, Python instantly checks if the string we're searching for is in the set, and this is more efficient due to hashing (converting input data into a unique number or alphanumeric combination). Examining the stop word set shows all the words are lowercased and have no punctuation. Depending on if the stop word list has punctuation, you should be careful to remove punctuation before or after you remove stop words.

To use the NLTK stop words, we should install nltk first: `conda install -c conda-forge nltk`. Then we need to download the stop words. From Python, we should run:

```
import nltk
```

```
nltk.download('stopwords')
```

Then we can get a list of stop words like so:

```
nltk.corpus.stopwords.words('english')
```

This NLTK list of stop words has punctuation included with the words.

The text pre-processing steps we just took help to standardize our text and can improve the next pre-processing steps as well as further analysis.

Stemming and Lemmatizing

Our last step is stemming or lemmatizing. Stemming is cutting off the end of a word (the suffix) to get the root. There are a few different algorithms available for this from the NLTK package, which we need to ensure is installed with conda or pip first. We will use the Snowball stemmer, although there are several options to use for a stemmer:

- Porter stemmer: the original stemmer from 1980 and the least aggressive of the stemmers listed here (words are not shortened too much and the resulting stems are usually understandable)

- Snowball (also called Porter2) stemmer: makes some improvements upon the Porter stemmer and is generally considered better than the Porter stemmer (other languages besides English are supported as well)

- Lancaster stemmer: a more aggressive stemmer that may give strange results but can trim words to shorter lengths

- Non-English stemmers, like ISRI (Arabic) and RSLP (Portuguese)

The NLTK documentation also has a good explanation of basic stemming, and we can see the different languages available for the Snowball stemmer: https://www.nltk.org/howto/stem.html.

> The Porter2 stemmer makes some improvements upon the Porter stemmer, some of which are described here:
>
> http://citeseerx.ist.psu.edu/viewdoc/download;jsession id=0A0DD532DC5C20A89C3D3EEA8C9BBC39?doi=10.1.1.300.285 5&rep=rep1&type=pdf

To stem our words, we can do:

```
from nltk.stem import SnowballStemmer

stemmer = SnowballStemmer('english')
stemmed_words = []
for word in cleaned_text.split():
    stemmed_words.append(stemmer.stem(word))

stemmed_text = ' '.join(stemmed_words)
```

We first initialize our stemmer for English, then use a similar loop to our stop words loop above. In fact, we could check for stop words and stem words in the same loop to be more efficient. Let's take a section from the War and Peace book and see how our cleaning and pre-processing steps so far affect it. We'll use the passage:

```
"I knew you would be here," replied Pierre. "I will come to supper
with you. May I?" he added in a low voice so as not to disturb the
vicomte who was continuing his story.
```

Note that curly quotes were included with our punctuation removal using `cleaned_string = cleaned_string.translate(str.maketrans('', '', string.punctuation + '""'))`. Our result after cleaning and stemming is:

```
knew repli pierr come supper ad low voic disturb vicomt continu stori
```

We can see things like "continuing" have been shortened to "continu" and stop words have been removed from our cleaning and pre-processing steps. Clearly, we can see some of the stems of words are difficult to interpret, but this will help us group similar words for analysis such as word counts. The drawback of stemming is words can look a little strange and can be hard to interpret (such as repli instead of reply).

Another option is to use lemmatization instead of stemming. This reduces words to their root in a different way and usually ends up with words being in a more recognizable form. However, lemmatization requires us to know the **part of speech** (**POS**) of a word, such as noun, verb, adjective, and so on. One way to carry out lemmatization is to use the `WordNetLemmatizer` from NLTK. However, this requires us to first do POS tagging, and the NLTK lemmatizer assumes all words are nouns by default (which is not correct and results in incorrect lemmatization). An easier way to perform lemmatization is to use the spaCy package, which we can use for the full suite of cleaning we just described as well.

Preparing text with spaCy

spaCy is an NLP package in Python with a wide range of capabilities. It can clean text, perform lemmatization, extract entities (such as people or places), perform POS tagging, and convert text into vectors (such as word, sentence, or document vectors). We'll look at using spaCy in a simple Python function to clean our text and lemmatize it. First, we need to install `spacy` with `conda` or `pip`. We then need to install a language model, which contains information about the language, such as stopword lists, word vectors, and more. For a simple English model, we can run the following command from the command line: `python -m spacy download en_core_web_sm`. There are many more language models available and described in the spaCy documentation: `https://spacy.io/usage/models`. Then we can use the following code to clean and pre-process our text:

```
import spacy

spacy_en_model = spacy.load('en_core_web_sm', disable=['parser', 'ner'])
spacy_en_model.max_length = 4000000

def clean_text_spacy(text):
    processed_text = spacy_en_model(text)
    lemmas = [w.lemma_ if w.lemma_ != '-PRON-'
                else w.lower_ for w in processed_text
                if w.is_alpha and not w.is_stop]
    return ' '.join(lemmas).lower()

wnp = urlopen('https://www.gutenberg.org/files/2600/2600-0.txt').\
    read().decode('utf-8')
wnp = simple_cleaner(wnp)
lemmatized_text = clean_text_spacy(wnp)
```

First, we import `spacy` and load the small English model. We turn off the parser and named entity recognition (NER) with the `disable` argument in `spacy.load()`. The parser and NER can take a lot of memory and processing power to run, so disabling these parts of the spaCy pipeline speeds up the process significantly. The vectorizer (`tok2vec`) allows us to get word vectors for each word, but also needs extra processing time and memory. For some reason, disabling the vectorizer causes the lemmatization to not work properly, so we leave it enabled. We can see the full list of the pipeline steps that `spacy` uses like this:

```
spacy_en_model = spacy.load('en_core_web_sm')
spacy_en_model.pipe_names
```

This shows us:

```
['tok2vec', 'tagger', 'parser', 'ner', 'attribute_ruler', 'lemmatizer']
```

So, we have kept the vectorizer, tagger, attribute ruler, and lemmatizer steps. These allow us most importantly to lemmatize the words, but the tagger and attribute ruler get the POS tag (providing us with both a simple and complex version of the POS tag). This POS tag is required to properly lemmatize words.

After we've disabled some parts of the pipeline for efficiency, we then increase the max length of our model from the default of 1,000,000 to 4,000,000. Our text is around 3.2 million characters, which exceeds the default max length. Long texts can take a lot of memory and time to run if we are using the parser and NER, but since we disabled them here, it doesn't matter as much.

Next, we get into the function. We first process the text with our language model using `spacy_en_model(text)`. Then we use a list comprehension to go through each token in our processed text. We get the text version of the lemma with `w.lemma_` if it exists, or if the word is a pronoun (represented as `'-PRON-'` by `spacy`), then we use the lowercased version of the word. We also only keep alphanumeric words and words that are not stop words by using `if w.is_alpha and not w.is_stop`. Finally, we join our lemmatized and cleaned words back together into a single string and return it, storing it in the `lemmas` variable.

We use the function by first re-downloading War and Peace and cleaning the header and footer, then using our `clean_text_spacy` function. Again, let's look at the effect on our sample chunk of text:

```
"I knew you would be here," replied Pierre. "I will come to supper
with you. May I?" he added in a low voice so as not to disturb the
vicomte who was continuing his story.
```

After using `spacy` to clean and pre-process it, the lemmatized results are:

```
'know reply pierre come supper add low voice disturb vicomte continue story'
```

For an easy comparison, here are the results of our other cleaning and pre-processing pipeline, which used stemming:

```
knew repli pierr come supper ad low voic disturb vicomt continu stori
```

We can see the words are easier to read and understand in general with lemmatization (such as reply versus repli), and it handled the curly quotes. spaCy also keeps special characters such as letters with accents. In general, this might take slightly longer than stemming because it needs to tag the parts of speech before lemmatizing. However, it generally gives results that are easier to interpret. If we don't have a large amount of text to process or have good computing resources at our disposal, it's better to leave all the pipeline steps enabled instead of disabling NER and the parser as we did here.

Word vectors

As we saw in the `spacy` pipeline, we can get token or word vectors. Sometimes these are called word or text embeddings. These are mappings of words to series of numbers (a vector) that represent the semantic meaning of the word. Several different sets of word vectors have been generated, and many of them are generated with a neural network model that tries to predict nearby words in a huge volume of text like Wikipedia.

A more advanced way to get word embeddings that can distinguish contextual meaning even better are neural network models like BERT or ELMO. However, with BERT and ELMO, we must pass our text through the model to generate the embeddings instead of simply using a lookup dictionary.

We can get word vectors easily in a few ways in Python:

- The Gensim package (`https://radimrehurek.com/gensim/models/word2vec.html`)
- The spaCy package (`https://spacy.io/usage/linguistic-features#vectors-similarity`)
- The fasttext package (`https://github.com/facebookresearch/fastText`)
- Using GloVe, Word2Vec, or other vectors (`http://vectors.nlpl.eu/repository/`)

    - This can be made easier with Python packages such as the word-vectors package

We'll look at using `spacy` since we already have it ready to go. To get word vectors from spaCy we should download a larger model such as the medium or large model (`md` or `lg`), which has the most complete set of word vectors: `python -m spacy download en_core_web_lg`. spaCy uses its own word vectors from its own trained model.

 The way some of the word vector sets are generated are by using skip-gram or **continuous bag-of-words** (**CBOW**) models. There are many resources for learning more about this, for example, here: `https://towardsdatascience.com/nlp-101-word2vec-skip-gram-and-cbow-93512ee24314`

We can load the large `spacy` model and use it on our document:

```
import spacy

spacy_en_model = spacy.load('en_core_web_lg', disable=['parser', 'ner'])
spacy_en_model.max_length = 4000000

processed_text = spacy_en_model(wnp)
```

Again, we disable the parser and NER for speed, and set the max length to 4 million. Then we simply apply the model to our text, and we have vectors available:

```
for word in processed_text[:10]:
    print(word.text, word.vector)
```

Each word has its own vector, which is accessible with the `vector` attribute. We can also get a vector for the entire document with `processed_text.vector`. This takes the average of all word vectors in the document, which can actually work well for applications like classification and topic modeling.

Word vectors are a new technique since the computational power and easily accessible datasets to create them haven't existed for very long. An older technique that has been around and used for a while is TFIDF vectors.

TFIDF vectors

TFIDF stands for **term frequency inverse document frequency** and describes what these vectors are – the term frequency of words (calculated separately for each document) multiplied by the inverse document frequency of words. In other words, the term frequency is simply word counts and the inverse document frequency is 1 divided by the number of documents in which a word is present. With TFIDF, we get a series of numbers for each document in a group of documents we might have. For example, let's look at the 20 newsgroups dataset available in `sklearn`. This is a dataset of internet forum posts on various topics that is often used as a text classification example. A collection of texts or documents like this is often called a corpus. We can load it like so:

```
from sklearn.datasets import fetch_20newsgroups

newsgroups_train = fetch_20newsgroups(remove=('headers', 'footers'))
```

This loads a dictionary into `newsgroups_train`, with the text as a list under the key `'data'`. The `remove` argument here removes the beginning and ends of posts, which usually contain boilerplate words that aren't useful for analysis (and will add clutter/noise our plots and results). Once the data is loaded, we can transform these documents into TFIDF vectors with `sklearn`:

```
from sklearn.feature_extraction.text import TfidfVectorizer

tfidf_vectorizer = TfidfVectorizer()
ng_train_tfidf = tfidf_vectorizer.fit_transform(newsgroups_train['data'])
```

The vectorizer is used similar to scalers we've used before from sklearn, where we initialize the class then use the fit_transform method on our data. This gives us an array with the shape (11314, 130107), which we can see from ng_train_tfidf.shape. Each row is a document (there are 11,314 documents) and each column is a word (so there are around 130,000 unique words in the documents). By default, the equation sklearn uses for TFIDF is:

$$tfidf(t) = tf(t) \times \left(\log \frac{1+n}{1+df(t)} + 1 \right)$$

where *tf(t)* is the term frequency, or number of times a word shows up in a document, and the rest is the **inverse document frequency (IDF)**. The n term is the number of documents in total and *df(t)* is the document frequency of a term, or the number of documents that a term shows up in. This gives us a TFIDF value for each word in each document. These values are also normalized with the Euclidean norm, meaning we divide each value by:

$$\sqrt{v_1^2 + v_2^2 + \cdots + v_n^2}$$

where each v is a TFIDF vector for a document (this is set by the norm= 'l2' argument in the vectorizer class instantiation). The result consists of values that span between 0 and 1, where low values mean the term is not important or rare in the specific document it appears in, and 1 means the term is important or rare in the documents it's in. Generally, TFIDF gives us a measure of which words are most characteristic of each document, with higher values signifying more importance.

The vectorizer has several arguments that can be used to customize behavior. Generally, it's not a bad idea to clean our data before passing it to the vectorizer, but it lowercases text by default (with the argument lowercase=True as default) and can remove stop words if we provide a list to the stop_words argument. We can also use the string 'english' for the stop_words argument to use sklearn's stop word list, although the sklearn documentation recommends against this. Additionally, we can adjust the number of included words with the max_df, min_df, and max_features arguments. If we set the min_df argument to a higher value (its default is 1), this will only include words that appear in at least that many documents. This will trim rare words (for example, typos, slang, or jargon) that likely won't help us in further analysis. It can reduce the size of our TFIDF matrix and can result in faster runtimes for further analysis. The max_df argument works in the same manner but limits the maximum document frequency for terms. The max_features argument causes the vectorizer to only retain the top number of features we specify, ordered by term frequency. One other useful option is to change the n-gram range with the ngram_range parameter. This is a tuple that we can use to set the size of n-grams to be included.

By default, it's (1, 1), meaning we only include unigrams (single words). We could only include bigrams (word pairs, or 2-grams) with (2, 2), or include different n-grams with other combinations (such as 1- and 2-grams with (1, 2)). There are of course some other arguments to the vectorizer we can specify, as described in the documentation.

These TFIDF vectors are returned as a sparse numpy array. This means the values are stored as locations (row and column labels) and the value for any non-zero entries. Since most entries will be zeros with TFIDF matrices, it makes sense to store them as sparse arrays to save memory. We can convert them to dense arrays if needed with the .todense() method.

Let's use our spacy cleaning function on this data to prepare it for further analysis:

```
import pandas as pd
import swifter

ng_train_df = pd.DataFrame({'text': newsgroups_train['data'],
                            'label': newsgroups_train['target']})
ng_train_df['text'] = ng_train_df['text'].swifter.apply(clean_text_spacy)

tfidf_vectorizer = TfidfVectorizer(min_df=10, max_df=0.9)
ng_train_tfidf = tfidf_vectorizer.fit_transform (ng_train_df['text'])
```

First, we convert our data to a pandas DataFrame with the text from each post and the label (which is a forum that it was posted in, such as religion, autos, and so on). Then we apply our spacy cleaning and lemmatization function, using the swifter package to parallelize it. Finally, we use our TFIDF vectorizer with a minimum document frequency of 10 to exclude rare words and a maximum of 0.9 to exclude words that show up too often.

This TFIDF method and averaging the word vectors for a document can be called a **bag-of-words** (BoW) methodology, since we are taking unordered words in our feature extraction. In other words, we are using the words from our data as a multiset (a set, but incorporating the number of counts of each item), but with BoW we are not paying attention to their order or grammar. If we were to use other methods like some neural network models where the order of words matters, it would no longer be using a BoW methodology. Once we have some basic preprocessing done on our text, we can begin to analyze it.

Basic text analysis

The first step in analysis is to explore the data. Common **exploratory data analysis (EDA)** with text includes frequency and TFIDF bar plots as well as plots of word counts. We'll also look at Zipf's law, word collocations, and analyzing the POS tags from our data in this section.

Word frequency plots

A simple way to explore data is with a word frequency or word count plot. There are a few ways to generate this: we could use the CountVectorizer from sklearn, NLTK's FreqDist, pycaret, and more.

Note that at the time of writing, pycaret installs spacy version 2.x.x, while the latest is 3.x.x. One solution is to install pycaret, then reinstall spacy with the latest version with conda install spacy=3.1.2 (using the latest version at the time of reading instead of 3.1.2), although this could potentially cause some problems with pycaret functionality. It may be useful to create a separate conda environment for this chapter to deal with the different versions of packages used here since some of the packages have many dependencies, some of which may conflict. It may even be useful to create separate environments for separate sections of this chapter. Also note that while reinstalling packages it's best to have all Python sessions (such as IPython and Jupyter Notebook sessions) shut down or restarted so that no packages are currently imported and in use in the environment (this can result in a "permission denied" error).

We can plot single words (unigrams or 1-grams), word pairs (bigrams or 2-grams) and word triplets (trigrams or 3-grams) as well as word groups of larger numbers. The pycaret package provides a very easy way to do this. Let's plot the unigram frequencies for the 20 newsgroups data:

```
from pycaret.nlp import setup, plot_model

nlp_setup = setup(newsgroups_train['data'], custom_stopwords=['ax', 'edu',
'com', 'write'])
plot_model(model=None, plot='frequency')
```

We simply use the setup function and provide our list of documents as well as a few other custom stop words that show up in these documents (such as domains from emails), then use plot_model with None for the model.

With 'frequency' as the second argument, we plot unigram frequencies, though there are many other options for plotting such as bigrams, trigrams, and more (described in the documentation: https://pycaret.org/plot-model/). A drawback of pycaret is that it doesn't allow fine-tuning of the cleaning process at the moment of writing, although we can provide pre-cleaned data to it. However, pycaret will still lemmatize words with spacy and perform other cleaning and analysis steps for us even if the data is pre-cleaned. Our resulting word frequency plot from the code above looks like this:

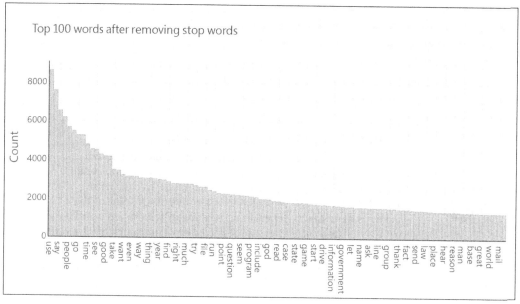

Figure 18.1: A word frequency plot of the 20 newsgroups data.

The plot is generated with plotly, which allows for zoom and mouseovers. In this case, it only shows every other word on the x-axis due to space constraints. We can see some of the top words are short words and seem to be things one might see in online forum posts. We might also want to generate word counts by the different post types, which could be created by converting the newsgroups_train object into a pandas DataFrame, then filtering by the 'target' column.

Generating a frequency plot with NLTK is a little easier and faster. Once our text is pre-processed, we can simply do:

```
from nltk import FreqDist

fd = FreqDist(lemmatized_text.split())
fd.plot(20)
```

The `plot` command will show the top words, and we can limit the number of words with the first argument (otherwise it shows all words). We can also view the top words in a list of tuples with `fd.most_common(20)`. Unigrams are OK to look at, but bi- or trigrams tend to be more informative. To get bigrams from `FreqDist`, we can do:

```
from nltk import bigrams

fd_bg = FreqDist(map(' '.join, bigrams(lemmatized_text.split())))
fd_bg.plot(20)
```

Here, we import the `bigrams` function from `nltk`, then create bigrams from our tokenized (text that has been split on spaces) and lemmatized War and Peace text. Next, we join each of these together with a space using the `map` function, giving it the `join` function as the first argument. Then we plot the top 20 bigrams, which looks like this:

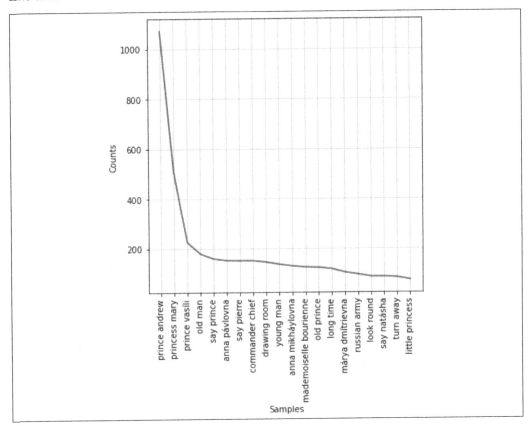

Figure 18.2: A bigram frequency plot of the book War and Peace

We can see the top characters are mentioned quite often, and Pierre appears to be speaking a lot in the book. It seems some common phrases are repeated often as well, such as "long time" and "look round." Remember these are cleaned and lemmatized text, so "look round" may result from "looking round" or something similar.

If we set the `plot` argument of `fd_bg.plot()` to `False`, we can modify the plot before displaying it. The `plot` function returns a `matplotlib.axes` object, and we can modify that to change the style or look of the plot if we wish. We can also use other methods with a little more elbow grease to make nicer-looking plots, such as Python's built-in `Counter` or sklearn's `CountVectorizer` methods.

Similar to looking at results from `CountVectorizer`, we can look at the TFIDF results, plotted with TFIDF ordered from greatest to least:

```
import matplotlib.pyplot as plt
import numpy as np

idx_to_word = {v: k for k, v in tfidf_vectorizer.vocabulary_.items()}

num_words = 20
tfidf_sum = np.asarray(ng_train_tfidf.sum(axis=0)).flatten()
sorted_idx = tfidf_sum.argsort()[::-1]
tfidf_sum = tfidf_sum[sorted_idx]

xticks = range(num_words)
plt.bar(xticks, tfidf_sum[:num_words])
plt.xticks(xticks,
           [idx_to_word[i] for i in sorted_idx[:num_words]],
           rotation=90)
plt.xlabel('word')
plt.ylabel('TFIDF')
```

In the example above, we first create a dictionary mapping the index (column number in the `ng_train_tfidf` numpy array) to each vocabulary item (word, or 1-gram in our case). This requires us to reverse the built-in `vocabulary_` dictionary, which we do using a dictionary comprehension. Then, we get the sum of the TFIDF vectors across each word (the sum of each column, using `axis=0`). This creates a numpy matrix, so we convert it to an array, then flatten it (removing the extraneous singlet dimension, since the shape is (1, 8714)). Next, we get the sorted index of our TFIDF sums from greatest to least with `argsort` and reverse it with `[::-1]`. We index our `tfidf_sum` variable by this, then create a list for our x-axis ticks. We have a variable, `num_words`, that we can use to adjust the number of words we show on the plot. Finally, we can plot it by providing the x-axis tick values and TFIDF sums, and setting the x-axis tick labels with `plt.xticks`. Our result looks like this:

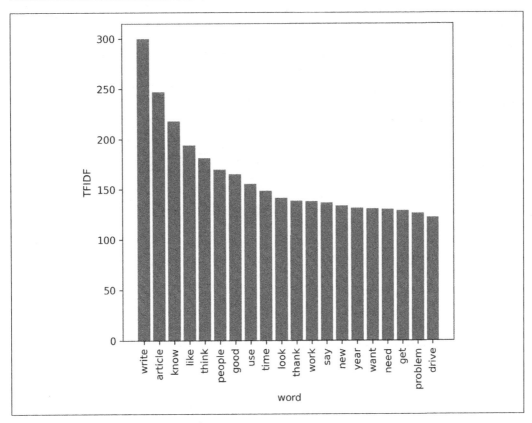

Figure 18.3: A word frequency plot of the 20 newsgroups data

Of course, we can change our TFIDF vectorizer settings to use other n-grams and recreate this plot with larger n-grams, like 2- or 3-grams. One other plot we might be interested in exploring is the distribution of the number of words in each post. We can get this like so:

```
import seaborn as sns

sns.histplot(ng_train_df['text'].apply(lambda x: len(x)))
plt.xscale('log')
```

We simply apply the length function to each of our documents in our DataFrame, then plot a histogram with a log scale on the x-axis. The length of these documents varies widely, so the log axis helps to visualize it more easily. You should find from the plot that the peak of the histogram is around 200 words.

Wordclouds

It is possible to create wordclouds with the `wordcloud` package in Python. Wordclouds are visualizations of word frequencies where the size of the word is proportional to the frequency of the word. However, many people despise wordclouds, and they have even been called "the mullets of the internet" because they can look tacky and are often misused. Wordclouds can be used occasionally as an aesthetic addition to a presentation or web page, but for analysis they are difficult to interpret. It's much better to use a word frequency bar plot as we showed above.

Zipf's law

Interestingly, the word frequency in large texts tends to follow a specific distribution. Not only does it show up in text, but in other situations with ranked order as well, such as the population of cities. You can see some of the situations where this shows up on the Zipf's Law Wikipedia page (`https://en.wikipedia.org/wiki/Zipf%27s_law#Other_data_sets`) as well as this entertaining video (`https://www.youtube.com/watch?v=fCn8zs9120E`). This distribution is called Zipf's law. It says that a word's frequency is inversely proportional to its rank in a frequency table from greatest to least, so that word number k has a frequency of $1/k$. So, the most frequent words in a language or text (highest ranked) have a high frequency, of course, and the less frequent words drop off in frequency in a rapid and logarithmic way. Visualizing this helps – you can take a look at Figure 18.4 to get an idea of what the distribution looks like with our War and Peace text. We can create a Zipf plot of our War and Peace text using a few functions:

```
from sklearn.feature_extraction.text import CountVectorizer

def get_top_grams(docs, n=2):
    v = CountVectorizer(ngram_range=(n, n))
    grams = v.fit_transform(docs)
    gram_sum = np.array(np.sum(grams, axis=0)).flatten()
    gram_dict = {i: v for v, i in v.vocabulary_.items()}
    top_grams = gram_sum.argsort()[::-1]

    return [gram_dict[i] for i in top_grams], gram_sum[top_grams]
```

First, the function we are creating takes in a list of documents and an n-gram value, then performs a process that's similar to what we did with the TFIDF plot. We get n-gram counts with `CountVectorizer`, then get the list of n-grams and their ranked frequencies from greatest to least. We can get this for a few different n-gram values like so:

```
ngrams, ngram_counts = {}, {}
for n in [1, 2, 3]:
    ngrams[n], ngram_counts[n] = get_top_grams([lemmatized_text], n=n)
```

Then we can plot the Zipf plot, which is a little complex:

```
from scipy.stats import zipf

def make_zipf_plot(counts, tokens, a=1.15):
    ranks = np.arange(1, len(counts) + 1)
    indices = np.argsort(-counts)
    normalized_frequencies = counts[indices] / sum(counts)

    f = plt.figure(figsize=(5.5, 5.5))
    plt.loglog(ranks, normalized_frequencies, marker=".")

    plt.loglog(ranks, [z for z in zipf.pmf(ranks, a)])

    plt.title("Zipf Plot")
    plt.xlabel("Word frequency rank")
    plt.ylabel("Word frequency")

    ax = plt.gca()
    ax.set_aspect('equal')   # make the plot square
    plt.grid(True)

    # add text labels
    last_freq = None
    labeled_word_idxs = list(np.logspace(-0.5,
                                    np.log10(len(counts) - 1),
                                    10).astype(int))
    for i in labeled_word_idxs:
        dummy = plt.text(ranks[i],
                        normalized_frequencies[i],
                        " " + tokens[indices[i]],
                        verticalalignment="bottom",
                        horizontalalignment="left")
    plt.show()
```

This function takes in our n-gram counts and the words (tokens) as well as a shape parameter for the Zipf function. It then plots the rank-order frequencies of words along with the Zipf distribution from `scipy`. The Zipf distribution is linear on a log-log scale (log axes for x and y), which is why we use `plt.loglog`. We also normalize our frequencies by dividing them by the sum of word counts in our overall corpus.

This is necessary for the empirical data to line up with the Zipf distribution from `scipy`. The last section of the function adds text labels for some of the words in log space so that they are evenly distributed across the plot. The result looks like this:

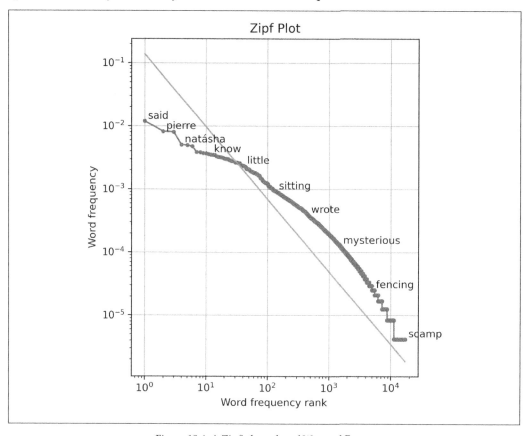

Figure 18.4: A Zipf's law plot of War and Peace

We can see the distribution almost follows the ideal Zipf law line, but deviates somewhat. Words that are top ranked appear less frequently than we'd expect, but the rest of the words appear more frequently than we might expect. This may have to do with the writing style and the fact this text was translated from Russian to English. We also usually don't see a perfect match to the Zipf line from text. The Zipf profile of writing can be used as one of many features to help identify authors (this could be based on the characteristics of the Zipf plot of an author's writings, but we would want to use other measures, such as counts of words with different POS tags). We can also plot bigrams with `make_zipf_plot(ngram_counts[2], ngrams[2], a=1.01)`. Notice that we adjusted the shape parameter for the Zipf distribution here to `1.01` from `1.15` that we used for unigrams. The shape parameter that leads to the best fit can change depending on the author and type of text.

Word collocations

Another interesting way to explore text data is with collocations, which are combinations of words that are statistically unique. One way of measuring a word collocations statistical importance is by the ratio of the co-occurrence of a few words (for example, when two words appear next to each other) to the separate occurrence of each word. This is called **pointwise mutual information**, or **PMI**. If two words in the text mostly show up as bigrams but don't show up much by themselves, that's an interesting word pair. For example, the two words "of the" are very common and don't always appear together. However, the two words "New York" are not very common and tend to appear together. So "New York" would have a high PMI or other collocation statistic value, while "of the" would be a low value. We can extract these collocation values with the NLTK package:

```
from nltk.collocations import BigramAssocMeasures, BigramCollocationFinder

BigramCollocationFinder.from_words(lemmatized_text.split()).\
    nbest(BigramAssocMeasures().pmi, 10)
```

We use the collocation finder from NLTK on our lemmatized and cleaned War and Peace text here, and get the top 10 bigrams by PMI, which returns:

```
[('ab', 'ovo'),
 ('academy', 'jottings'),
 ('achtung', 'nehmen'),
 ('adhere', 'officious'),
 ('adèle', 'tempted'),
 ('agricultural', 'laborers'),
 ('agwee', 'evewything'),
 ('ahahah', 'rrrr'),
 ('alliée', 'sincère'),
 ('alliés', 'détruite')]
```

We can also get the PMI (or other metric) by using the `score_ngrams` method instead, like this:

```
BigramCollocationFinder.from_words(lemmatized_text.split()).\
    score_ngrams(BigramAssocMeasures().pmi)
```

From this, we find the first few hundred bigrams have the same PMI score of around 17.87. So, statistically speaking, there isn't any difference in significance between these first few hundred bigrams. There is also a trigram version of the collocation measures in NLTK that we can use.

Parts of speech

Another way to analyze our text is to look at the POS tags. These are labels given to words to signify their part of speech, such as noun, verb, adjective, and so on. The POS tags allow us to lemmatize text as well as analyze it in different ways, such as counts of different POS tags, the type of writing, and more. We can get POS tags from each word in a spacy-processed text with the pos_ or tag_ attributes. The pos_ attribute is a simple POS tag, while tag_is more granular. We can extract these from our War and Peace text like so:

```
pos_dict = {}
pos_dict['word'] = []
pos_dict['POS'] = []
for word in processed_text:
    if word.is_alpha and not word.is_stop:
        pos_dict['word'].append(word.lower_)
        pos_dict['POS'].append(word.pos_)

wnp_pos_df = pd.DataFrame(pos_dict)
```

First, we create our dictionary with empty lists for our words and parts of speech tags, then loop through each word in the text. If it's alphanumeric and not a stop word, we add the lowercased version to our word list and add the POS tag to the POS list. Then we turn this into a DataFrame. After that, we can look at the top POS tags and top words for each tag:

```
pos_counts = wnp_pos_df.groupby('POS').count().\
                sort_values(by='word', ascending=False).head(10)
pos_counts.columns = ['count']
wnp_pos_df['count'] = 1
wnp_pos_df.groupby(['POS', 'word']).count().\
    sort_values(by='count', ascending=False).head(10)
```

First, we get the top overall POS tags. This usually will be nouns, verbs, and adjectives. We also rename our column to "count" for more clarity. In this case, we have a lot of proper nouns (PROPN, such as names and places), as seen in *Figure 18.5 (a)*. Next, we create a new column, count, with all 1s. Then we group by the POS tag first and the word second, then count the occurrences of these POS-word combinations, which gives us the top words by POS tag. We can see from the results below that there is a lot of dialogue in the book (since the word "said" is the top verb) and the main characters are mentioned quite often (Pierre, Natasha, and Andrew).

(a)	count		(b)		count
POS			**POS**	**word**	
NOUN	92285		**VERB**	said	2839
VERB	72675		**PROPN**	pierre	1963
PROPN	30427			prince	1590
ADJ	29536			natásha	1210
ADV	11077		**NOUN**	man	1172
INTJ	1452		**PROPN**	andrew	1141
SCONJ	942		**NOUN**	time	927
X	479			face	883
ADP	405		**VERB**	went	862
NUM	379			know	846

Figure 18.5: The top POS tags (a) and words by tag (b) from War and Peace

We could also get the top words for each POS tag by filtering the resulting DataFrame from our groupby operation.

The full list of tags can be found in spacy's glossary (using `from spacy.glossary import GLOSSARY`), which is a dictionary. This is also available for viewing from the spacy source code: `https://github.com/explosion/spaCy/blob/master/spacy/glossary.py`

Examples and explanations of the POS tags can be found here:

- `https://universaldependencies.org/docs/u/pos/`
- `https://web.archive.org/web/20190206204307/https://www.clips.uantwerpen.be/pages/mbsp-tags`

POS tags could be used in analysis as part of fingerprinting a writer's style, or simply to understand the subject of a text by looking at nouns.

Unsupervised learning

Another more advanced way to analyze text is with unsupervised learning. We can take the word vectors for each document, or TFIDF vectors, and use them to cluster documents with the clustering techniques we learned in last chapter.

However, this tends to not work well, with the "elbow" in the within cluster sum of squares plot often not clearly appearing, so that we don't have a clear number of clusters. A better way to look at how text groups is with topic modeling.

Topic modeling

There are many algorithms for performing topic modeling:

- Singular value decomposition (SVD), used in latent semantic analysis (LSA) and latent semantic indexing (LSI)
- Probabilistic latent semantic analysis (PLSA)
- Non-negative matrix factorization (NMF)
- Latent dirichlet allocation (LDA)
- Others, such as neural network models (for example, TopicRNN and Top2Vec)

Each of these methods has strengths and weaknesses, although they all attempt the same thing: to find hidden (latent) groupings of words (topics) that commonly appear in groups of documents (the word "latent" means present but hidden). There are several packages in Python for carrying these out:

- sklearn (SVD, LDA, NMF)
- Gensim (LDA)
- Top2Vec
- pycaret
- lda (LDA)
- fasttext

We'll look at using `pycaret` and Top2Vec since they both make topic modeling easy. The results of topic models might be used, for example, to recommend news articles to people or to understand and summarize the content of a large corpus of text.

Topic modeling with pycaret

With `pycaret`, we run our `setup` function as before. Let's use the 20 newsgroups dataset to explore topics talked about in the "space" newsgroup. We can get the label number for each newsgroup with this:

```
list(zip(newsgroups_train['target_names'],
         range(len(newsgroups_train['target_names'])))))
```

Then we can filter our newsgroup DataFrame so we only get the space newsgroup, which is label number 14:

```
space_ng = ng_train_df[ng_train_df['label'] == 14].copy().reset_index()
```

We reset the index so that the `pycaret` function `assign_model` will work properly (it expects an index starting at 0 and increasing incrementally). Again, we need to set up our `pycaret` environment with our data, specifying the column that we will use for our text:

```
from pycaret.nlp import setup, create_model, plot_model, assign_model

space_setup = setup(space_ng, target='text')
```

Then we can create a topic model. There are five topic models available at the time of this writing (listed in the documentation: `https://pycaret.org/nlp/`) but we will use LDA since it is a standard topic modeling technique used by many people. We simply create the model, which uses four topics by default.

```
lda = create_model('lda')
plot_model(lda, 'topic_model')
```

We also plot the model, which uses the pyLDAvis package for visualization. This is an interactive plot and can help us understand the topics that were discovered. Generally, we can look at some of the top words and string together a few words to come up with a summary of each topic. Next, we can get the topics for each text like so:

```
lda_results = assign_model(lda)
```

This returns a DataFrame with the addition of the scores for each topic as well as the dominant topic and its percentage of the total scores for each text.

One way to determine the number of topics we should use is with coherence scores. We can do this with `gensim` for the LDA model from `pycaret`, since it is a `gensim` model. First, we need to import the `CoherenceModel` from `gensim`, instantiate a new instance of it using our model, the LDA model's lookup dictionary for words (`lda.id2word`), and our tokenized text:

```
from gensim.models import CoherenceModel

cm = CoherenceModel(model=lda,
                    texts=lda_results['text'].map(str.split).tolist(),
                    dictionary=lda.id2word)
cm.get_coherence()
```

Then we use the `get_coherence()` method to get the coherence score, where a higher value is better. This measures how similar documents are in a given topic, and there are a few methods for calculating it. We can loop through several values for the number of topics and examine the coherence scores:

```
coherences = []
for num_topics in range(2, 16):
    lda = create_model('lda', num_topics=num_topics)
    lda_results = assign_model(lda)
    cm = CoherenceModel(model=lda,
                        texts=lda_results['text'].map(str.split).tolist(),
                        dictionary=lda.id2word)
    coherences.append(cm.get_coherence())
```

We can plot our coherences like this:

```
plt.plot(range(2, 16), coherences)
plt.xlabel('number of LDA topics')
plt.ylabel('coherence score')
```

Which results in the following plot:

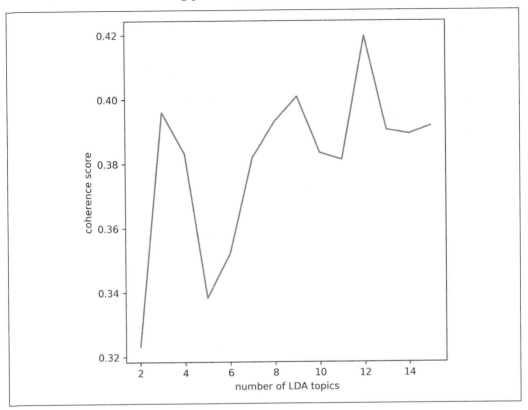

Figure 18.6: The coherence values of LDA models with different numbers of topics, performed on the space newsgroup from the 20 newsgroups dataset

We can see there are local maximums at 3, 9, and 12 topics, with 12 as the global maximum. However, we may want to explore even larger numbers of topics to make sure the coherence scores don't continue to increase. Sometimes metrics for topic models can continue increasing as we increase the number of topics, and it helps to pick a local maximum or "elbow" from plot such as 3 in the coherence plot above.

Topic modeling with Top2Vec

The Top2Vec model was introduced in 2020 and carries out several steps to arrive at a topic model:

- Gets document vectors using neural network methods
- Reduces dimensions with UMAP (an advanced dimensionality reduction technique introduced in 2018)
- Uses HDBSCAN to cluster documents
- Gets word vectors closest to each cluster's centroid (the centroid is taken as the average document vector of documents in each cluster)

This automatically determines the number of clusters since it uses a variation of DBSCAN for clustering, and also carries out several of the necessary steps for us to get to a topic model from raw text. So, we don't even need to pre-process our text when using this model. We need to install the package with `pip install top2vec`, then we can create a model on our raw 20 newsgroups data from the space newsgroup to see how it compares with LDA:

```
from top2vec import Top2Vec

raw_ng_df = pd.DataFrame({'text': newsgroups_train['data'],
                          'label': newsgroups_train['target']})
raw_space_df = raw_ng_df[raw_ng_df['label'] == 14]
model = Top2Vec(documents=raw_space_df['text'].to_list(), workers=8)
```

First, we import the `Top2Vec` function from the package, then create our DataFrame of raw documents, then filter this down to the "space" newsgroup. Next, we give the text from the "space" newsgroup DataFrame (as a list) to the `Top2Vec` function and specify the use of 8 CPU threads with `workers=8`. Usually, the number of threads you use can be at least the same as the number of CPU cores on your machine. Once this completes, we can look at the number of topics with `model.get_topics()[-1].shape[0]`, which shows us 2 here. This is similar to LDA, which is a nice result. We can see the top words in the topics with `topic_words, word_scores, topic_nums = model.get_topics()`. There is a lot more functionality to Top2Vec, which is described in the GitHub readme (`https://github.com/ddangelov/Top2Vec`) and documentation.

Supervised learning

Supervised learning techniques can be used with text as well. We can prepare our text as numeric values and pair each set of features with a target.

The target can be numeric, like a stock price, or categorical, like a budget category for bank transactions. The supervised learning techniques we covered in *Chapter 11, Machine Learning for Classification,* and *Chapter 12, Evaluating Machine Learning Classification Models and Sampling for Classification,* can be used. As an example, we'll look at multi-class classification of the 20 newsgroups dataset.

Classification

Classification is often used with text. For example, bank transactions can be categorized for automatic budgeting. We can also categorize social media posts for a number of purposes, like flagging offensive content. Another example is categorizing emails as spam or not spam. Many machine learning algorithms can be used for this, with some of the highest performing algorithms being neural networks. However, properly using neural networks with text is difficult, and there are entire books dedicated to it (such as *Deep Learning for Natural Language Processing* by Karthiek Reddy Bokka, Shubhangi Hora, Tanuj Jain, and Monicah Wambugu from Packt). We can also use the simpler algorithms we learned before, like logistic regression, Naïve Bayes, and KNN.

Our first step is to prepare our text with cleaning and by converting it to numeric values. We'll use both word vectors and TFIDF vectors and compare the results. Let's begin by converting our 20 newsgroups documents into word vectors using spacy:

```
newsgroups_train = fetch_20newsgroups(remove=('headers', 'footers'))
newsgroups_test = fetch_20newsgroups(subset='test',
                                     remove=('headers', 'footers'))

en_large = spacy.load('en_core_web_lg', disable=['parser', 'ner'])

def get_document_vectors(text):
    processed = en_large(text)
    return processed.vector

ng_train_df = pd.DataFrame({'text': newsgroups_train['data'],
                            'label': newsgroups_train['target']})
ng_train_doc_vectors = pd.DataFrame(
    np.vstack(ng_train_df['text'].
            swifter.apply(get_document_vectors).tolist())
)
ng_test_df = pd.DataFrame({'text': newsgroups_test['data'],
                           'label': newsgroups_test['target']})
ng_test_doc_vectors = pd.DataFrame(
    np.vstack(ng_test_df['text'].
            swifter.apply(get_document_vectors).tolist())
)
```

First, we load the train and test sets from the 20 newsgroups dataset. Then we create a small function to get the document vectors using the large English model from spaCy. Remember this gets the average of all word vectors in each document. Next, we create DataFrames from the newsgroups data using the text from each post and its label (a number, which corresponds to the labels in `newsgroups_train['target_names']`). We then apply the `get_document_vectors` function to our text in parallel with `swifter`. This creates a numpy array for each text. We convert those to a list of numpy arrays and use numpy's `hstack` to turn the list of arrays into a 2D array with shape (`n_documents, 300`). The word vectors have dimensions of 300. Next, we can create a single `pandas` DataFrame with our vectors and labels:

```
ng_train_vector_df = pd.concat([ng_train_df['label'].astype('category'),
                                ng_train_doc_vectors], axis=1)
ng_test_vector_df = pd.concat([ng_test_df['label'].astype('category'),
                               ng_test_doc_vectors], axis=1)
```

We combine our labels from our first DataFrames with our document vectors into one DataFrame for training and one for testing. We also convert the labels to the categorical type (`category`) since they are numeric. This can avoid potential problems that can occur where some algorithms or functions may attempt to perform regression instead of classification with a numeric target.

Next, we can create our TFIDF features:

```
vectorizer = TfidfVectorizer(min_df=10, max_df=0.9)
train_tfidf = vectorizer.fit_transform(newsgroups_train['data'])
test_tfidf = vectorizer.transform(newsgroups_test['data'])

train_tfidf_df = pd.DataFrame(train_tfidf.todense())
test_tfidf_df = pd.DataFrame(test_tfidf.todense())
train_tfidf_df['label'] = pd.Series(newsgroups_train['target']).\
    astype('category')
test_tfidf_df['label'] = pd.Series(newsgroups_test['target']).\
    astype('category')
```

First, we initialize our TFIDF vectorizer with some limitations to decrease the number of words in the vocabulary (using the min and max document frequencies, `min_df` and `max_df`). Then we use it to fit and transform the training data and to transform the test data. This makes sure we use the same vocabulary on the train and test sets, which means we have the same number of features in train and test sets. If there are new words in the test set, they will not be included in our features since they were not in the original vocabulary. This is one disadvantage of TFIDF over word vectors. Another disadvantage is the size of the features.

The shape of the TFIDF training set is (11314, 13269) compared with (11314, 300) for the word vectors. Fewer features that can capture roughly the same information are generally better, and many of the entries in the TFIDF matrix are zeros. Performance-wise (especially for computational runtime), it can be better to go with word or document vectors compared with TFIDF.

Next, we create DataFrames from the TFIDF vectors by converting the sparse numpy arrays to dense ones. Then we add the label column, again converting it to a category datatype. Now we can try out some machine learning. We'll stick with a simple logistic regression model here, although we would want to use the techniques we learned in *Chapter 11, Machine Learning for Classification,* on classification and *Chapter 13, Machine Learning with Regression,* on model optimization to improve our models.

```
from sklearn.linear_model import LogisticRegression

lr = LogisticRegression()
lr.fit(ng_train_vector_df.drop('label', axis=1), ng_train_vector_df['label'])
lr.score(ng_train_vector_df.drop('label', axis=1),
         ng_train_vector_df['label'])
```

We simply fit the logistic regression model to our document vectors and evaluate the accuracy score on the train set, which is around 76%. We can also evaluate the accuracy on the test set, which turns out to be near 69%. This is not bad given the no information rate is about 5% since each class represents around 5% of the data.

Doing the same thing with TFIDF yields around 94% on the training data and 77% on the test set:

```
lr = LogisticRegression()
lr.fit(train_tfidf_df.drop('label', axis=1), train_tfidf_df['label'])
lr.score(train_tfidf_df.drop('label', axis=1), train_tfidf_df['label'])
```

This shows more overfitting, since the training score is much higher than the test score. However, we do see a higher test accuracy than the document vector features. But, it might not be worth using more than 40 times the number of features for this performance gain – we would need to weigh the pros and cons of using more computational power or runtime with higher accuracy. We could also use larger word vectors and optimize the models to come to a more complete conclusion. When evaluating classification performance on text, it can also be helpful to look at precision, recall, and the F1 score, as we saw in *Chapter 12, Evaluating Machine Learning Classification Models and Sampling for Classification.*

Sentiment analysis

One last topic to examine under text analysis is sentiment analysis. This is the measurement of the positive or negative sentiment of text. There are similar analyses that can be done to measure the emotion of text. The way this works is similar to the last section – we create features from our text, then train a classifier to predict either sentiment, emotions, or some other class from a list of labels. With sentiment analysis, we can train a regressor to predict the sentiment if we label our text with values such as -5 ranging to +5, or we can train a classifier to simply predict positive, neutral, or negative.

Another method for determining sentiment of text are rule-based algorithms. These can use lookup dictionaries where words have a sentiment score, and the sentiment score for a text is added up and averaged to get the overall sentiment. Negation rules can be applied, such as the word "not" before another word flips its value.

There are a few packages in Python for determining sentiment:

- NLTK (uses a trained Naïve Bayes classifier)
- Textblob (can also be used through spaCy; uses a lookup dictionary with rules)
- VADER (uses a rule-based system, designed for social media)

Of course, we can also train our own classifier for sentiment based on a variety of free public datasets. There are also several cloud services and APIs that allow us to send text and get back a sentiment score.

 Be careful not to call sentiment analysis "sentimental" analysis. Sentimental means having a nostalgic attachment to something, not the positive or negative sentiment of text.

Sentiment analysis can be used for many things, like gauging customer satisfaction from communications, analyzing public attitude toward public policy, and analyzing public attitude toward other topics being discussed on social media.

Let's use VADER here to estimate the sentiment of each of the 20 newsgroups. The package name is vadersentiment, and it can be installed with pip or conda. Then we can create a function to extract the sentiment and apply it to our newsgroups data:

```
from vaderSentiment.vaderSentiment import SentimentIntensityAnalyzer

vader = SentimentIntensityAnalyzer()

def get_sentiment(text):
    return vader.polarity_scores(text.lower())['compound']

ng_train_df['sentiment_score'] = ng_train_df['text'].\
    swifter.apply(get_sentiment)
```

First, we import the sentiment analyzer from vaderSentiment and initialize it with default settings (no arguments). Then, in our function get_sentiment, we lowercase the text and apply the vaderSentiment polarity_scores function to the text. This applies the lookup dictionary (the lexicon) and the rules, then returns a dictionary with negative, neutral, positive, and compound scores. The compound score is the overall sentiment of the text ranging from -1 (negative) to +1 (positive), which we use here. Then we simply apply this get_sentiment function to the text in our DataFrame. It's important to lowercase the text as we did here, as the text in the lexicon is all lowercase. The vaderSentiment analyzer also handles emojis. The lexicons are easily viewable on the GitHub repository: https://github.com/cjhutto/vaderSentiment/blob/master/vaderSentiment/vader_lexicon.txt. We can see from the lexicon it looks like most words are not lemmatized, so we probably don't want to carry out lemmatization. We also don't need to worry about removing punctuation or stop words, since anything not in the lexicon is ignored by the algorithm.

To view our results, it helps to convert the numbers to actual newsgroup labels in our DataFrame. We can do this by creating a dictionary with numbers as keys and newsgroup labels and values, then replace our numbers in our DataFrame's label column:

```
label_dict = {i: label for i, label in
                enumerate(newsgroups_train['target_names'])}
ng_train_df['label'].replace(label_dict, inplace=True)
```

Now we can view our results by getting the average sentiment score for each category and sorting it from greatest to least:

```
ng_train_df.groupby('label').mean().\
    sort_values(by='sentiment_score', ascending=False)
```

Our results look like the following:

label	sentiment_score
comp.graphics	0.547356
misc.forsale	0.493030
rec.sport.hockey	0.470409
rec.sport.baseball	0.469508
sci.electronics	0.431782
comp.sys.ibm.pc.hardware	0.430881
sci.space	0.424613
soc.religion.christian	0.395767
comp.os.ms-windows.misc	0.394298
comp.sys.mac.hardware	0.377526
comp.windows.x	0.373962
sci.crypt	0.353488
rec.autos	0.338401
rec.motorcycles	0.295666
sci.med	0.183302
talk.religion.misc	0.178544
alt.atheism	0.125859
talk.politics.misc	0.104019
talk.politics.mideast	-0.253308
talk.politics.guns	-0.308504

Figure 18.7: The results of sentiment analysis on the 20 newsgroups

We can see newsgroups related to electronics, sports, and some others have relatively high average sentiments, while the guns and Mideast forums are quite negative. We can examine a few random posts from these to see what makes them so positive or negative by filtering our DataFrame to get very positive or negative posts. We can do this with:

```
ng_train_df[(ng_train_df['label'] == 'talk.politics.guns') &
            (ng_train_df['sentiment_score'] < -0.5)].\
    sample(3, random_state=42)['text'].tolist()
```

to easily look at a few of the posts, and remove.tolist() if we want to see the sentiment scores as well. We can see in the guns forum the words "kill" and "ban" come up frequently, and many of the posts are indeed negative. In the computer graphics forum, many of the posts are questions and use words like "good" and "easy," which result in positive sentiment scores. However, this may be a bit of a misclassification since these words aren't being used to construe positive sentiment (for example, the sentence "Is it good?" comes out as highly sentiment positive). So, when using sentiment analysis, it's a good idea to check some of the positive and negative text examples and check that they make sense.

Lastly, it helps to look at the distributions of the sentiments. We can do this with seaborn:

```
import seaborn as sns

guns_hockey_df = ng_train_df[ng_train_df['label']\
                    .isin(['talk.politics.guns',
                           'rec.sport.hockey'])]
sns.histplot(guns_hockey_df,
                x='sentiment_score',
                hue='label')
```

This plots histograms of the guns and hockey forums. Our results look like this:

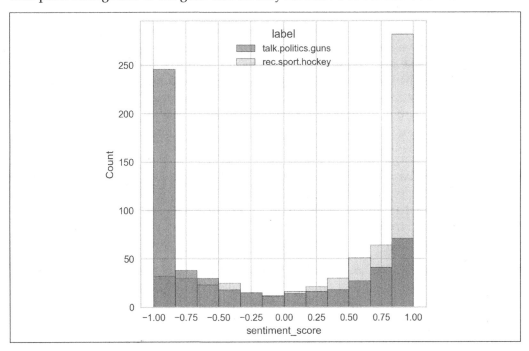

Figure 18.8: Histograms of sentiment scores on the guns and hockey newsgroups

In this case, it seems there are lots of -1 scores for the guns forum and +1 scores for the hockey forum. In the `textblob` package (another package we can use for sentiment analysis, similar to the `vaderSentiment` package), we will often see many neutral posts with a score of 0. Looking at the distribution of sentiments like this can be helpful for understanding the performance of our sentiment analysis.

Test your knowledge

Practice some of what we've learned here on new data. You might collect some social media data using an API, such as from Reddit as we did in chapter 7, and apply some of the basic analysis (word count frequency plots), sentiment analysis, and topic modeling. You might also train your own sentiment or emotion classifier using a public dataset. If you create your own sentiment classifier, you can extract document vectors from the text and use that as features, which might give better results than using TFIDF vectors. However, be careful to use similar training data to the data you will use the classifier on (for example, train the classifier on social media data if that is the application).

Summary

The use of data science techniques with text spans a few different areas, and the broad field of working with language and text with computers is called NLP. We saw first how we can clean text data using Python and the spaCy package by removing things like punctuation, stop words, and numbers. Lowercasing can be used to condense the same words (regardless of capitalization) into the same count for word frequency analysis. We can also use stemming or lemmatizing to reduce words to a stem or root, which further groups similar words for measuring word frequencies. The spaCy package makes cleaning and lemmatizing easy, and this can be done in a few lines of code.

We then saw how basic analytics, such as word frequency plots, POS tags, and word collocations, can be performed to get an understanding of the text. Zipf's law can be used to analyze text as well, to understand a text's characteristic shape parameter from the Zipfian distribution. Although wordclouds can be used, it's best to avoid them since they are not as informative or easy to read as a word frequency plot.

Next, we saw how we can use topic modeling to understand the themes of groups of text. This can be done in several ways, but we looked at the widely used LDA method using the `pycaret` and `gensim` packages, and how to visualize results using `pycaret` with the pyLDAviz package. We also looked at the Top2Vec model, which automatically determines the number of topics for us using advanced word vector, dimensionality reduction, and clustering methods.

We saw how supervised learning can be used with text. First, we need to convert our text to numeric vectors, and we have the options of word count vectors, TFIDF vectors, or document vectors (by taking the average or sum of word vectors in a document). As we saw, the TFIDF and word count vectors are sparse (many 0s are present) and the number of features quickly becomes large as corpus size increases. With word vectors, the feature space can be reduced significantly. These word vectors are usually created with neural network models that try to predict nearby words from a given word, resulting in vectors that capture the context and meaning of words.

Finally, we looked at sentiment analysis and how it can be used in Python. It's often used as a tool on social media data, so one of the Python packages we used (VADER) is geared toward analyzing social media data. We saw how it can capture the sentiment based on keywords in a text, but can also result in inaccurate measurements if the context of words is not what we expect (for example, the word "good" in a question should be neutral but is scored as positive).

We've seen many ways to analyze data over the course of the book. In the next chapter, we'll take a look at automating reports and analysis to increase our productivity.

Part VI

Wrapping Up

19

Data Storytelling and Automated Reporting/ Dashboarding

The skills we've learned so far are important and useful, but often we will need to communicate results to others. Without this communication, the results of our analysis aren't of much use. If the results of our work are more analytic in nature (such as descriptive statistics like standard deviation and histograms), it helps to use data storytelling techniques. Presenting information through a story makes it much more memorable than rattling off a list of statistics. For example, the memory palace technique (where numbers are put into a story) is used by world champion memorizers to remember huge series of arbitrary numbers. Additionally, several people and some studies suggest that emotions are more important than facts in decision making. So, if we are presenting results to a decision maker in our organization, it is usually more effective to tell a story with the data and results rather than simply dump a plethora of numbers on our audience. In the first part of this chapter, *Data Storytelling*, we'll cover some principles of data storytelling and how we can use it.

In the second part of the chapter, we'll look at using automated reporting to generate a data story. This can be done in several ways, including Python packages such as FPDF, Streamlit, Plotly Dash, and others. There are several other tools out there that can be used independently of Python or with Python, but tend to require a subscription or license fee, such as ReportLab, Tableau, Excel, RapidMiner, and other data science GUIs.

Let's get started by learning about data storytelling and how we can make use of it.

Data storytelling

Data storytelling is a good tool to have in your kit as a data scientist. We'll always need to communicate our results to stakeholders, and using a story is a much better way to communicate something than a list of statistics. To create our data story, we need our data, our visualizations, and our narrative. We've already seen how to take data and create visualizations throughout the book, especially in *chapter 5* on EDA and visualization. However, putting together a story and narrative around the data is primarily what's new here.

The steps we'll consider here are:

- Consider your audience and the message you are trying to convey
- Support your message with your findings, and lead up to your central message or insight
- End with some sort of call to action or a recap of your main insight(s)

The first things to consider are our audience and the message we are trying to convey. It's important to consider the technical level of our audience so we know how much we need to explain and how much to simplify our results and visualizations. If we have a more technical audience, like a group of experienced data scientists, we don't need to explain the basics of machine learning. But with executives who may not be ML experts, we probably need to simplify our message somewhat and may need to explain some of the key points of machine learning.

Next, we want to have a central message and insight we want to convey. This central message or insight should also ideally lead to some sort of action. In the example we'll use soon, our dataset will be a credit card default (missing a payment) dataset. We will be conveying which features are most predictive for defaults and if our ML model is ready for deployment. As part of the story, we'll explain what makes the model ready or not ready, such as a lack of data. Our call to action will be a decision from executives and managers on the deployment of our model or authorization for more data collection to improve the model. It's OK to have some other results included, especially if that helps to tell the story, but we want to avoid minor details. For example, we're not going to go over all the approaches that didn't work (such as the ML models that didn't work well) in our data story. However, if a feature engineering step made a big difference in improving the performance of our model, it could be worth including in our story.

In some settings, there isn't necessarily a call to action. One example may be presenting results from a project to peers with the goal of knowledge sharing. In those cases, we can recap our central results at the end of the presentation rather than using a call to action.

Lastly, we need to make visualizations and graphics to tell our story. This should almost completely consist of plots. But, if we have single numbers (for example, an accuracy number or other performance metrics), we can put those in a large, eye-catching fashion, such as using a large font size and making the text bold. However, for a collection of many numbers (such as a time series dataset), it's much better to use visualizations. In the case of a time series dataset, for example, a line chart is often best. If we have a table of data, it's best to put that in the appendix if we must include it, and to only include the relevant important numbers earlier in the presentation. These visualizations and graphics will be used to support and build up to our central message.

With visualizations, the best practices we covered in *Chapter 5, Exploratory Data Analysis and Visualization*, still apply:

- Avoid chart junk
- Use color sensibly
- Present data properly (for example, line charts for time series data)
- Make charts "redundant" in case they are printed in black and white and for the colorblind
- Clearly label axes, datasets, and use a single font size with a sans-serif font
- Tailor your visualizations to the audience

The only best practice that could be partially avoided is the black and white redundancy issue. If we are presenting the data in a PowerPoint presentation and know that colors can be used, for example, we don't have to worry so much about redundancy. However, we should take care to avoid using colorblind-unfriendly colors (such as red and green for line colors in the same plot).

An aspect that can differ with storytelling versus creating general visualizations is that we can use visual techniques to highlight plot areas to draw the audience's attention there. For example, if we want to indicate that a certain point on a scatterplot is the most important, we can make it a different color or change the pattern of it (for example, make it larger and a different shape than other points).

When telling our story, we need a strategy for getting our point and supporting details across. One way that has been devised by Brent Dykes (described in his book *Effective Data Storytelling*) is to use a four-part structure that he calls the Data Storytelling Arc:

1. Setting: Background and hook (and preview of the key insight if needed)
2. Rising insights: Supporting details that lead up to the key insight
3. Key insight: The main finding
4. Solution and next steps: Options and recommendations for action

In the first step, the setting, we provide a background and something to draw the audience in – the hook. This should be something new or interesting that gets the audience's attention, such as a problem with sales or manufacturing numbers, or in our case, a problem with credit card default rates. If the audience is mainly composed of busy executives, we may want to provide a preview or spoiler of the main result of the key insight. This acts as a more potent hook that can draw people in but takes away from any suspense that may be built during the story. You may find some people in management positions tend to not like suspense when data and results are being presented to them. In other settings, such as a conference, the suspense and related storytelling pattern may be more appropriate. If we provide the spoiler to an executive, they may decide they want to hear more or want to skip the rest of the report or presentation. After our setting and hook, we bring any supporting data and visualizations into the picture as necessary. If there was a crucial data cleaning or feature engineering step, or a mini-insight, we could include that here. Next is the key insight, which is our main message. Finally, we wrap up with any options or recommendations for the next steps and actions to take.

Let's look at an example of using data storytelling with the end goal of getting a team of executives to approve the deployment of a machine learning system.

Data storytelling example

For this chapter, we'll use the credit card default dataset we used in earlier chapters and will pretend we're working for the bank that is offering the credit card. Our task is to use machine learning to predict credit card defaults and to help reduce the default rates. The audience, in this case, will be the executives of the bank and our manager, to whom we want to present our results. First, let's load the data:

```
import pandas as pd

df = pd.read_excel('data/default of credit card clients.xls',
                   skiprows=1,
                   index_col='ID')
```

This data has a "default payment next month" column, which is our target with binary values. As usual, we want to familiarize ourselves with the data by doing some EDA (which is easy with pandas-profiling). From this, we notice that the PhiK correlations show strong correlations between late payments in previous months (for example, PAY_0 with the target column). We can create a plot of the PhiK correlations to use in our "rising insights" section:

```
import phik

phik_corr = df.phik_matrix()
sns.heatmap(phik_corr)
```

Next, we can create a bar plot to show the differences between the default and no default groups for the PAY_0 column, since this one is most correlated with the target:

```
import matplotlib.pyplot as plt

plt.ylabel('percent')
sns.barplot(data=df,
            x='PAY_0',
            y='PAY_0',
            hue='default payment next month',
            estimator=lambda x: len(x) / len(df) * 100)
```

Now, we can train a classification model with pycaret:

```
import pycaret.classification as pyclf

setup = pyclf.setup(data=df, target='default payment next month')
best_model = pyclf.compare_models()
tuned_model = pyclf.tune_model(best_model, search_library='scikit-optimize')
```

We first set up our autoML environment with pycaret, using the default settings, which detects the PAY_0 column and several other columns as categorical columns (meaning it one-hot encodes them). In our data story, we don't need to describe this one-hot encoding process since it's not such a crucial detail for our main message. We then tune the model to optimize the hyperparameters to maximize the accuracy. For now, we will stick with reporting accuracy since our audience is not composed of data science experts, but we may actually want to optimize something like the recall of the payment default class (to maximize the number of default payments we detect). Our best model here is a Ridge classifier, although a few others had nearly identical accuracy of around 82%.

Next, we can generate a feature importance plot and a confusion matrix with pycaret:

```
pyclf.evaluate_model(tuned_model)
```

We need to click on the **feature importance** and **confusion matrix** buttons in the resulting output to get the plots. These plots could be used as an appendix or extra information if people have more questions. Now we can put together our story.

As a background and hook, we might talk about how 22% of our customers defaulted in the most recent payment month (which we can see from df['default payment next month'].value_counts(normalize=True)). This is costing the bank and customers money and causing problems. It would be a win-win if we could detect payment defaults early and work with customers to develop a payment plan, or decrease the credit limit of defaulting customers.

If we could come up with some specific numbers on how much money the bank could potentially save by something like looking at the median value of default payments across all customers, that would make a good hook as well. If we have busy executives who want to hear the punchline right away, we can tell them our ML model has an accuracy of 82% and can be tuned to detect more payment defaults if we wish. Assuming our executives want to hear more after seeing the spoiler, we continue.

Next, we build up our story with the "rising insights." We start with the PhiK correlation plot. Note that we also used a bright blue box to highlight the important part of the plot we want to draw the audience's attention to. This could be complimented by a bright blue arrow pointing the box as well.

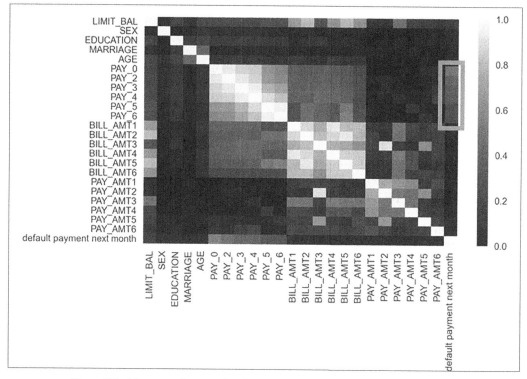

Figure 19.1: A heatmap showing the PhiK correlation of our default payment dataset

Our story with this plot would be something like this: in this plot, brighter colors denote higher correlations – in other words, two variables that change together more strongly have brighter colors in the plot. We can see our target column, "default payment next month," is on the bottom row and far-right column of the plot, and the blue box highlights the area of interest. The PhiK correlations between a default payment are strongest with the PAY_0 column, which is a categorical variable with values of 0 or less than 0 for on-time payments and greater than 0 for the number of months the payment is late.

We can see that as the months get farther from our current month (for example, PAY_1 is 2 months before our current month), the correlation weakens. Looking at this PAY_0 feature, we can see that people with default payments tend to more often have a late payment.

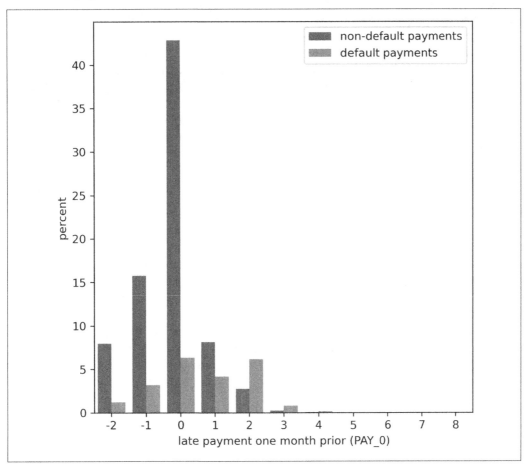

Figure 19.2: A bar plot of the PAY_0 column, separated by the default payment status.
The negative values are other payment methods, such as revolving credit.

The above plot shows that most people are not defaulting, since the total size of the non-defaulting bars is bigger. We can also see that most non-defaults are 0 months late. The -2 and -1 values denote non-late payments via means such as revolving credit. Looking at the default payments, we can see that a higher proportion has late payments, usually by 1 or 2 months. This correlation of previous late payments to a default payment in the current month can be used to predict if someone will default on a payment.

Next, we discuss our main takeaway or result/insight: we use automatic machine learning, or autoML, to find and optimize the best ML model for the problem and achieved an accuracy of 82%. This is good but only slightly better than the 78% fraction of customers who don't default. However, we can tune the model to be more selective and accurate at predicting defaults at the cost of some false positives (where we predict non-defaults as defaults). From our confusion matrix and recall score, we can see we are only identifying about 1/3 of the defaults. We also found from looking at the feature importances that the most recent month's payment status and extremely late payments from previous months tend to strongly relate to the default rate.

We can see how some of the more important features relate to the distribution of defaults in the data with pandas filtering like this:

```
df[df['PAY_5'] == 6]['default payment next month'].
value_counts()
```

Finally, we want to give the solution and next steps: we can use this model to predict payment defaults. Depending on the cost of dealing with the default, we can tune our model to more accurately predict defaults at the cost of more false positive predictions of non-defaults as defaults. So, if we want to simply send out an email to customers providing potential solutions for avoiding a default payment if they are at risk, we can afford more false positives. If someone is going to hand-review the default predictions, then we may want to avoid having too many false positives. Additionally, it will be helpful to work more closely with the data team to gain access to more data, as this should improve the performance of the ML algorithm. We will also need to create a data engineering pipeline to feed into the ML algorithm in deployment.

In this last step, we summarized what we can do going forward and proposed some solutions to deploying our model in production, and the decision is up to management now.

Data storytelling can be a powerful way to convey a message and convince others to take the path you think is best. However, we haven't covered all the details of data storytelling here. We did cover several of the important visualization topics in *Chapter 5* on EDA and visualization, though. Still, it's not a bad idea to read up more on data storytelling. There are at least two good books on the topic worth reading: *Effective Data Storytelling*, by Brent Dykes, and *Storytelling with Data*, by Cole Nussbaumer Knaflic.

The storytelling methodology we covered here is best suited for written reports, presentations, and infographics. Another few useful ways to present data to those who need it are automated reporting and dashboarding.

Automated reporting and dashboarding

When dealing with data that is updated periodically and frequently, it's helpful to use automation tools to generate data reports. This saves us the trouble of constantly re-running a repetitive analysis. There are some different ways to deal with sharing data: reports and dashboarding.

Automated reporting options

Reports will usually consist of something like a PDF or an other document (such as MS Word) or a spreadsheet like MS Excel. We already saw how we can do some work with Excel using pandas, but for more powerful control of Excel, we can use other Python packages as well:

- `xlsxwriter` (easily generates charts; this works well with pandas' `ExcelWriter`)
- `openpyxl` (also allows for charts)

There are also other Excel Python packages. The site `http://www.python-excel.org/` is one place with a list of many of these packages. The `win32com` package can also be used to read and write Excel files on Windows, but its use is not recommended since the documentation for it is lacking. To use Google Sheets through Python, the Google Docs API can be used.

For automated reporting, we have several options. Some solutions use Python as well as non-free licensed software, including ReportLab and Anvil (ReportLab has a freemium model at the time of writing). There are also a few other open source solutions:

- FPDF (writes PDF directly)
- `pdfkit`, `weasyprint`, and `xhtml2pdf` (these convert HTML to PDF)
- PyQt
- `pylatex` (uses LaTeX to create PDFs)
- `rst2pdf`

Similar to Google Sheets, we can use the Google Docs API for Google Docs. For any of these solutions, there is documentation and examples, but the learning curve can be steep for many of them.

One drawback of the PDF or Word document reports is that they are not interactive (but can be printed out if needed). Excel reports can be interactive, but it may not be the best solution for viewing results across different devices such as tablets, phones, and computers. To be able to create multi-platform interactive reports, we can instead use dashboarding.

Automated dashboarding

Dashboarding is used widely in businesses and organizations to monitor results and the status of operations. There are several non-free licensed software options, such as Tableau, Power BI, and many others. These dashboards allow us to easily create interactive plots and combine them into one page or several pages. Then we can share the dashboards easily with others online or by sending them a file. We can also create similar dashboards with open source Python solutions. The advantage of using a licensed solution is that there are often support channels we can call on for help, and they try to make everything as easy as possible to do. The downsides are that it can be expensive and less flexible off the shelf (we can usually combine Python, R, or other languages with dashboarding software such as Tableau, though). With an open source Python dashboarding solution, we can create something for free and it has a lot of flexibility. There are a few different packages for creating dashboards in Python:

- Dash
- Streamlit
- Panel
- Voila

There are other related packages, and the list of dashboard packages on PyViz (https://pyviz.org/dashboarding/) will likely be updated as time goes on. In our case, we will use streamlit to quickly create a simple dashboard with data from our payment default dataset.

 One note about streamlit: it's not the best solution for streaming data at the time of writing – Dash and Voila are better options for streaming data. This is due to the implementation of streamlit and its available code base, which makes certain streaming data operations difficult or impossible.

We need to first install streamlit, which, at the time of writing, works better with pip than conda due to managing package dependencies (pip install streamlit). Then, we can confirm that it's working by opening a terminal and running streamlit hello, which runs a test application. In our dashboard, we are going to include the main points of our data story.

First, we create a .py file we can use, which we will name default_dashboard.py. We can run the app from a terminal or command line with `streamlit run default_dashboard.py` (as long as we are in the correct directory with the file). This will show a web address we can click or copy and paste into our browser to view. In our default_dashboard.py file, we start by importing all the necessary packages (and functions), which totals nine:

```
import phik
import streamlit as st
import pandas as pd
import seaborn as sns
import plotly.express as px
import pycaret.classification as pyclf
import matplotlib.pyplot as plt
from mlxtend.plotting import plot_confusion_matrix
from sklearn.metrics import confusion_matrix
```

Next, we set the page configuration to wide:

```
st.set_page_config(layout="wide")
```

This can also be done from the webpage where we view the app (from the menu button on the upper right). It has the effect of making the dashboard (with multiple plots) easier to view. Then we load our data and fit a LightGBM model to it:

```
df = pd.read_excel('data/default of credit card clients.xls',
                   skiprows=1,
                   index_col='ID').sample(1000)

setup = pyclf.setup(df, target='default payment next month', silent=True)
lgbm = pyclf.create_model('lightgbm')
lgbm, tuner = pyclf.tune_model(lgbm, return_tuner=True)
```

This is similar to what we've seen before, although we are using the `silent=True` argument so that pycaret doesn't ask for confirmation of the data types. We also get the tuner object back from our `tune_model` function using the `return_tuner` argument, which we will use to report our cross-validation accuracy score. We are using a `lightgbm` model because it was one of the top models with a very similar accuracy to the best model, and it has an easily accessible `feature_importances_` attribute we will use soon.

Next, we get the average validation/test set score from our CV and set it as the title of the page:

```
cv_acc = round(tuner.cv_results_['mean_test_score'].mean(), 3)
st.title(f"CV Accuracy is {cv_acc}")
```

This sets the HTML title so that our CV accuracy is displayed as large text at the top of the page.

Now we can calculate the PhiK correlation and create a heatmap of the results, create the same bar chart of counts of the PAY_0 column grouped by default status as we did before, and add these to our app:

```
phik_corr = df.phik_matrix()
correlogram = sns.heatmap(phik_corr)

barchart = px.histogram(df,
                        x='PAY_0',
                        color='default payment next month',
                        barmode='group')
col1, col2 = st.columns(2)
col1.write(correlogram.figure)
col2.write(barchart)
plt.clf()
```

The first few lines are things we've seen before. The `px.histogram` function uses Plotly express to create a histogram of the PAY_0 column, and using the default column as the color creates two sets of bars. Using `barmode='group'` sets the bars next to each other like we had in our earlier plot. Next, we create two columns with streamlit's columns function. Then we use the general-purpose write function from streamlit to add our figures to the columns. For the correlogram or heatmap, we access the `figure` attribute so that the figure shows up (since it is a `matplotlib.axes` object). We can directly drop the Plotly chart in the `write` function, however. Lastly, we use `plt.clf()` to clear the plot area in preparation for the next plots.

The `streamlit,` team uses `beta_` as a prefix for new functions and features, and eventually the `beta_` is removed as the feature becomes mature. For example, the `st.set_page_config` used to be `st.beta_set_page_config`.

Next, we can calculate feature importances:

```
feature_importances = pd.Series(lgbm.feature_importances_,
                        index=pyclf.get_config('X').columns)feat_imp_
plot = feature_importances.nlargest(20).plot(kind='barh')
feat_imp_plot.invert_yaxis()
```

Here, we create a pandas series with our feature importances, and set the index as the column names from our pre-processed data from pycaret. The get_config function allows us to get objects from the setup of our pycaret session, and X is the pre-processed data. Last, we invert the y-axis so that it sorts from greatest to least.

Next, we will create another row for plots (with 2 columns) and add this feature importance plot to the first column:

```
col1, col2 = st.columns(2)
col1.write(feat_imp_plot.figure)
```

Now we can create our confusion matrix and add it to the dashboard:

```
predictions = pyclf.predict_model(lgbm, df)
cm = plot_confusion_matrix(
    confusion_matrix(df['default payment next month'],
    predictions['Label'])
    )
col2.write(cm[1].figure)
```

We get predictions from our model using the pycaret function which pre-processes the data as we need, for example, one-hot encoding categorical variables. Then we create a confusion matrix plot using mlxtend, giving it the result of the sklearn confusion_matrix function with our true values and predictions. The Label column holds the predicted values from our predictions DataFrame. Finally, we add the chart to our dashboard with col2.write.

Now we can run our dashboard with `streamlit run default_dashboard.py`. Our resulting dashboard looks like this:

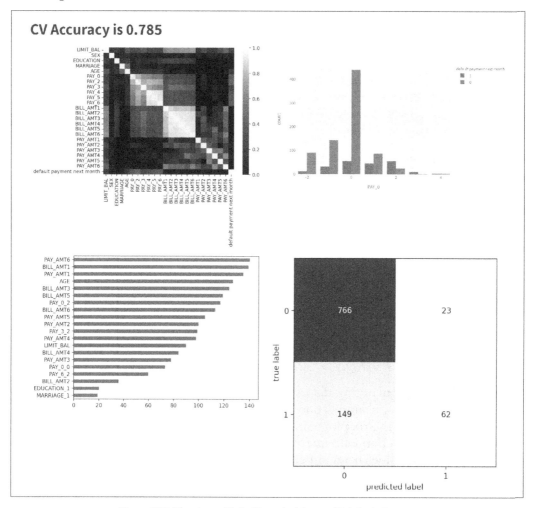

Figure 19.3: The streamlit dashboard of the credit default dataset

We can see we might want to do a little adjusting of the figure shapes and sizes to make it prettier, but it works as a first pass. The `plotly` bar chart on the upper right is the only interactive part of the page, although we can use `plotly` or other interactive packages to make more interactive dashboards.

 Streamlit was originally made for ML engineers to be able to monitor and investigate their ML processes, although it is being increasingly used for data dashboards as well. At the time of writing, there is an active development team constantly improving `streamlit`.

With streamlit, we can also add widgets to a sidebar easily with lines of code like default_choices = st.sidebar.multiselect('Choose default categories:', [0, 1], [0, 1]). This will create a multi-select box with options of 0 and 1 (the second argument) and a default of 0 and 1 (the third argument). When we change the selection, the entire .py file reruns from top to bottom, regenerating the page. There are other widgets we can add such as sliders and more.

When something changes in our selections or sidebar in a streamlit app, it reruns the entire file from top to bottom. However, it can mean we reload our data and rerun long ML training processes. There is a solution that streamlit has for this, which is caching, and is described in more detail in the documentation here: https://docs.streamlit.io/en/stable/caching.html.

Streamlit reruns the file if we change settings or change the source .py file. There is also a **Rerun** button on the app's page, or we can refresh the page to rerun it. However, for other reports or dashboards, we may want to rerun the file at periodic intervals, which we can do in a few different ways.

Scheduling tasks to run automatically

Once we have an automated report or dashboard set up, it can be useful to periodically run the report to get the latest results. This works best for batch applications where we get data updates less frequently. For faster updates, such as streaming data in real time, we would need to use another solution such as the add_rows function of streamlit or another dashboard package such as Dash. There are a few ways to do this:

- Cronjobs (in Mac or Linux)
- Windows Task Scheduler
- Custom Python or other code
- Python packages such as schedule

Cronjobs allow us to use the cron software utility (which uses a crontab file) to periodically run some Linux or Mac command. Windows Task Scheduler works similarly, allowing us to run an executable file or terminal command, but has a GUI instead of the command line interface like cron.

We could also write a custom Python function (or something in almost any other programming language) that runs a loop, waits for a specified amount of time (for example, using time.sleep() with Python), and then runs another Python function or file. However, people have made packages to do this already, such as the schedule Python package, which is easy to use based on examples on the readme of the GitHub repository (https://github.com/dbader/schedule) and in the documentation.

If we use a Python file to periodically run a function or another file, we may also want to add this scheduler file to our startup programs on our computer, which can be done by adding files or shortcuts to the start up folder in Windows, through system preferences in Mac, or configuration files in Linux.

There is a lot more automation we can do with Python, and there are several books on the subject. One is *Automate the Boring Stuff*, by Al Sweigart, along with his other titles on the subject. However, things we've learned in this book can also be leveraged for automation, such as dealing with Excel files and documents, as we learned in *Chapter 6, Data Wrangling Documents and Spreadsheets*.

Test your knowledge

To test your knowledge, use the housing dataset from the GitHub repository for this book (under this chapter's folder, `Chapter19/data`) or another dataset suitable for machine learning. For the housing data, imagine you are working for a real estate company and are trying to segment the data into groups for marketing purposes (you might use clustering for that). Your goal should be to segment customers into sensible groups, where each group could be targeted with specific marketing strategies. Tell a data story with the results of your machine learning work and decide on what your call to action will be (for example, spending more resources to improve and deploy the ML system you started, or using the results straight away). Create a dashboard with `streamlit` (or another Python dashboard package) to display the results of the data story.

Summary

Data storytelling is an important skill for today's world since many jobs use data to drive results. The ability to convince stakeholders to take the action you think is best can be done by telling a good story with your data. Remember that we looked at the four-part data storytelling framework from Brent Dykes: set up the problem (background) and create a hook for the story, then support the story with rising insights, deliver the main message or insight, and finish up with recommendations or potential paths for future steps. Along with a data story, we can also set up a dashboard. This can be done in many ways, but we looked at using the `streamlit` package. We only scratched the surface here – `streamlit` has a lot of flexibility and capabilities we didn't touch on. It's recommended to further explore `streamlit` and other dashboarding solutions to see what else is possible and which dashboarding solution you like best.

We've covered many of the aspects of data science and have acquired some great powers over the course of this book. And as one adage goes, "with great power comes great responsibility." Next up, we'll address this by learning about ethical considerations we should keep in mind while doing data science.

20
Ethics and Privacy

Throughout the book, we have learned several techniques for taking data and turning it into insights. Like any powerful tool, these can be used for good or bad, and can be used in bad ways unintentionally. For example, we could accidentally leak private data through **machine learning** (**ML**) algorithms or data engineering pipelines. Part of being a well-rounded data scientist means we need to understand the ethical considerations of doing data science. Quite often this includes aspects of privacy and bias. We will learn more about these ethical and privacy considerations in this chapter, including:

- Bias in machine learning algorithms
- Data privacy considerations in data preparation and analysis
- How to use *k*-anonymity and *l*-diversity to protect people's data privacy
- Data privacy laws and regulations
- Using data science for the common good

Since we've recently covered machine learning in the book, let's start by looking at how machine learning algorithms can incorporate bias and what we can do about it.

The ethics of machine learning algorithms

Machine learning algorithms are increasingly used in our daily lives, and it's important we consider the ethical side of using these powerful tools.

Bias

A major way in which machine learning algorithms can cause problems has to do with bias. This bias usually shows up as disproportionately affecting a group of people and tends to fall along gender and racial divides. There are many examples to demonstrate this. For gender issues, machine learning algorithms have been seen to maltreat women. Part of this is due to the gender proportions in jobs such as software engineers, data scientists, and other similar jobs – often these have a much higher proportion of men than women overall. To start, most AI assistants such as Siri and Alexa have historically had default female voices that reinforce the stereotype of women being subservient to others (although this is changing). However, that is a design choice rather than an ML issue. Nonetheless, default settings when creating software are important to consider, as many people do not change settings from the defaults. A related issue is how voice recognition often works less well for women and non-white men (`https://hbr.org/2019/05/voice-recognition-still-has-significant-race-and-gender-biases`). This likely started as an issue because primarily white men were developing the first voice recognition systems (such as Ray Kurzweil and his team) and probably simply collected a lot of data on themselves. Since machine learning systems learn patterns from the data they see, it's usually impossible to extrapolate to unseen data that's significantly different.

Another example is facial recognition – in 2017, Apple's face unlock on their iPhones couldn't distinguish between different Chinese people well, or at all (`https://nypost.com/2017/12/21/chinese-users-claim-iphone-x-face-recognition-cant-tell-them-apart/`). Again, this likely comes down to a lack of data on Chinese faces in the ML training set. Similarly, some self-driving car systems are less accurate at detecting dark-skinned people than light-skinned people, with a gap in the accuracy of detection of about 5% (`https://www.vox.com/future-perfect/2019/3/5/18251924/self-driving-car-racial-bias-study-autonomous-vehicle-dark-skin`). To avoid these problems, we should collect a large and diverse training set, being careful to consider all people who will be affected.

In fact, facial recognition software has a host of issues, and these can have real consequences. For example, a man in Michigan was arrested based on grainy security video footage that was processed with facial recognition software (`https://www.nytimes.com/2020/06/24/technology/facial-recognition-arrest.html`). In this case, the authorities put too much trust in the AI system, even though the results of the algorithm were being reviewed by other people.

One last example is the COMPAS system, which has been used by several US court systems. COMPAS predicts the risk of recidivism, or the act of a criminal committing another crime after already being punished for a crime. Analysis by ProPublica (`https://www.propublica.org/article/how-we-analyzed-the-compas-recidivism-algorithm`) found that the system was racially biased, overestimating the risk for black people and underestimating the risk for white people. This was despite the best efforts of COMPAS' creators to remove racial information by removing data on race from the input features. However, the questionnaire collected from criminals and used for COMPAS still incorporated racial information indirectly.

How to decrease ML biases

There are a few ways to combat these biases in ML algorithms:

- Collect more data, especially to balance the dataset
- Create synthetic data, such as using **GANs** (**generative adversarial networks**), SMOTE, or ADASYN
- Use over- or under-sampling techniques such as SMOTE and ADASYN

Data collection is often expensive, so collecting more data can be difficult to accomplish. However, we can target our data collection so as to balance our classes for classification problems, or to increase the amount of data we have for underrepresented groups. An easier way to balance groups in the data is to use SMOTE or other sampling techniques we learned in *Chapter 12*, *Evaluating Machine Learning Classification Models and Sampling for Classification*, for simple classification problems. We can also under-sample data, but generally, it's best to use as much data as we can.

A more advanced way to create more data through synthesis is by using GANs. These are neural networks that generate fake data that follows the distribution of the data they're trained on. An example of using GANs to generate data is `https://thispersondoesnotexist.com/`, which generates a simulated image of a person's face using a GAN. If we have some data on underrepresented groups, we can synthesize more data using GANs. However, it will follow the underlying distribution of our existing data, so we should be sure to have variety in our original dataset.

Carefully evaluating performance and consequences

When using machine learning algorithms, it's important to consider the ramifications of how they will be used. A powerful example is the NSA's ominously named SKYNET program (`https://arstechnica.com/information-technology/2016/02/the-nsas-skynet-program-may-be-killing-thousands-of-innocent-people/`). That project used machine learning (random forests) to predict if someone in Pakistan was a terrorist. Although the system had high accuracy, with a 0.18 false positive rate reported, this still means about 100,000 Pakistanis would incorrectly be flagged as terrorists. If this ML algorithm was being used to order deadly drone strikes in Pakistan, many innocent people could be killed. This situation is an example of the base rate fallacy, in which there are more false positives than true positives with a low number of actual positive cases.

This means both our recall and precision scores would be low and illustrates the importance of choosing the right metric. In the SKYNET case, multiple metrics should be examined (such as recall, precision, Cohen's kappa, and more), especially given the weight of the situation. It's similar to spam classification, where we may have a 99% rate of messages that are not spam, and a classifier with 99% accuracy is no better than random guessing.

The law enforcement facial recognition system described earlier is another example of a high-consequence ML application. Care should be taken to evaluate many metrics and think about which metric would be best to use. Additionally, communication of the end result to the end user should be clear and accurate. For example, the facial recognition system could output the confidence of a match from the classification algorithm, and perhaps some metrics like precision and recall (or false positive rate) would be good to display as well.

Machine learning explainability results could also be added to the dashboard, which could show which parts of the input data were used to arrive at the ML result.

Data privacy

Data privacy is a big part of data science ethics. We may be dealing with healthcare, financial, or other personal data of people. Although we are looking at a screen with numbers on it, it's important to remember that these numbers represent people. A powerful example is the Titanic dataset often used for ML learning materials. This dataset has data on the passengers of the Titanic and is usually used as a classification exercise. The goal of the classification is to classify the survival of a Titanic passenger. When working with the data, it's easy to get lost in the numbers and details of executing the ML algorithm, but we should remember that each datapoint is a person who lived a life just like you or me.

Data privacy can be compromised in many ways:

- Data leaks (for example, being hacked or having data stolen)
- Combining anonymized data from multiple sources to deanonymize people
- Extracting information from ML algorithms
- Profiling
- Publishing results (even aggregated) of small datasets

Privacy breaches and data leaks can expose sensitive data about a person, such as a disease they may have, their web search history, and more. Of course, data leaks via hacking are an obvious way data privacy can be compromised. We should take care to properly secure data, such as protecting it on secure systems with proper authorization (such as multi-factor authentication with strong passwords). Similar to that, data can be stolen from people within an organization. Proper data governance and employee management can help prevent internal data theft.

A more sly way privacy has been breached is by combining public data with supposedly de-identified data. One famous example is when the Massachusetts governor, William Weld, was identified from combining public voting records with a supposedly anonymized health insurance dataset (`https://papers.ssrn.com/sol3/papers.cfm?abstract_id=2076397`). The health insurance dataset had removed **PII** (**personally identifiable information**). However, zip codes, age, gender, and other demographics can be combined to identify someone by combining datasets. This leads to the idea of k-anonymity, where we (essentially) include at least k records that cannot be distinguished from each other. We will revisit k-anonymity and related concepts shortly.

An even more clever way to breach privacy is extracting information from trained and published ML algorithms. A few ways to do this include reconstruction attacks, where we extract some sensitive information about all people in the dataset, and tracing attacks, where we attempt to see if a specific person was present in the dataset (`https://privacytools.seas.harvard.edu/publications/exposed-survey-attacks-private-data`). Determining how privacy can be breached from trained ML models is an active area of research, and more methods will likely be uncovered over time.

Data profiling is related to the three previous data privacy issues. Profiling is when we use personal data (such as web searches or web pages visited) to extract information about a person, such as what products they may be interested in or personal health information. This data can be leaked, combined with public data, or data can be extracted from an ML algorithm used with profiling as described above.

Lastly, publishing data where some subsets of the data are unique can compromise someone's privacy. For example, if only one person has certain attributes in a dataset, such as their zip code and age range, and we publish a table of data with the aggregate statistics of people in a given zip code and the most common medical condition there, that one person may be able to be identified by combining data with public records such as census data. So, it's important to consider how many people we have with unique properties in a given dataset before publishing aggregate results. Again, this relates to *k*-anonymity, which we will cover soon.

Data privacy regulations and laws

To help protect personal privacy, many regulations and laws have been enacted around the world. One of the biggest laws in the EU is the **General Data Protection Regulation (GDPR)**. This gives EU consumers several rights related to their data privacy, such as the right to be informed about data collection being performed on them, the right to request a copy of the data collected on them, rights to rectify and erase data, and a few others.

Importantly, users must give consent before data can be collected on them, such as cookies and IP addresses collected from visiting websites. Additionally, any company that suffers a data breach must notify consumers and their supervisory authority within 72 hours.

The US does not have a nationwide law on data privacy at the time of writing, but a few states have enacted legislation, such as New York's **SHIELD** Act, Virginia's **Consumer Data Protection Act (CDPA)**, the **California Consumer Privacy Act (CCPA)**, and the **California Privacy Rights Act (CPRA)**. The California acts are similar to the GDPR, with rights to erasure and rectification of data, as well as requirements for informing consumers when data is being collected on them.

Other national US laws exist related to specific areas, including:

- The Health Insurance Portability and Accounting Act (HIPAA)
- The Children's Online Privacy Protection Act (COPPA)
- The Graham Leach Bliley Act (GLBA)
- The Fair Credit Reporting Act (FCRA)

Many people have heard of HIPAA, which governs the use of medical record data. COPPA provides rules for companies dealing with children under 13 in the US, such as protecting data privacy and obtaining the consent of the child's parent. The GLBA and FCRA have to do with the financial data privacy of consumers.

There are many other data privacy regulations that have been enacted around the globe, but most (if not all) of them have a few things in common: they are mainly targeted at internet data collection (such as cookies and tracking from websites and phone apps), they apply to the citizens of the governing area, and they are enforced by fines. For example, the California privacy acts should be followed when companies collect data on California citizens. One way this can be determined is with IP location tracking software, although this is not foolproof by any means (for example, if a California resident is traveling). Some of these regulations, such as the California privacy acts, only apply to businesses over a certain size. When working with personal data, it's a good idea to become familiar with the data privacy laws of the area of the customers so that your company isn't fined and to ensure you are following best practices. In 2019, a record-setting fine of 170M USD was imposed on Google and YouTube based on breaking the COPPA laws, so depending on the company and the scale of the problem, the fines can be quite large.

Some other regulations have to do with informed consent when collecting data on people. For example, regulations from a few federal agencies require the informed consent of people being studied (such as pharmaceutical research). There are guidelines as to how the informed consent should be carried out, such as outlining risks and potential benefits of the study to the subjects.

Furthermore, in the US, organizations should have an **institutional review board (IRB)** that reviews and approves studies on human subjects along with the studies' plans for informed consent. This is required for data and knowledge that will be made public, although if data will be kept strictly private within a private organization, it is not required. Similar to the data privacy laws, informed consent and research laws differ from country to country but generally have the same overarching ideas.

k-anonymity, l-diversity, and t-closeness

There are a few methodologies for protecting privacy with data, especially if we are going to be publishing data or sharing it with others. For example, we may need to send data to a service like Amazon Mechanical Turk for data labeling, and we don't want to have a data breach as a result of sending the data there. The first methodology for protecting privacy is *k*-anonymity, which was first introduced in 1998. This says that if we have at least *k* records with identical tuples of **quasi-identifiers (QIs)** then we have *k*-anonymity (where *k* is a positive integer). QIs are **PII** that has been semi-anonymized. For example, age and zip code could make a tuple of quasi-identifiers by converting ages to ranges and removing the last few digits of zip codes.

As an example, let's look at the simple dataset in the GitHub repository for this chapter of the book. This is a mock dataset that has HIV test results of individuals. Let's first load and examine the data:

```
import pandas as pd

df = pd.read_excel('data/HIV_results.xlsx')
```

The data looks like this:

	Name	Age	Zipcode	HIV diagnosis
0	John	24	80401	Positive
1	Bill	27	81033	Negative
2	Sarah	33	80402	Positive
3	Jimmy	31	80221	Negative
4	Martha	44	81034	Negative
5	Sam	47	80211	Negative

Figure 20.1: Our HIV results dataset

We can see there are 3 fields of PII: name, age, and zip code. We also have one field with HIV test results, which is our *sensitive* field. If we are to publish or share this data, the sensitive field is one that we don't want anyone to be able to connect to an individual person.

The process of anonymization starts by removing PII that can't be anonymized (and wouldn't be useful for aggregate statistics anyway) such as removing names and social security numbers:

```
df.drop('Name', axis=1, inplace=True)
```

Next, we can transform the other PII with suppression or generalization. We will bin the ages into groups, which is generalization:

```
df.loc[(df['Age'] >= 20) & (df['Age'] < 30), 'Age'] = 20
df.loc[(df['Age'] >= 30) & (df['Age'] < 40), 'Age'] = 30
df.loc[(df['Age'] >= 40) & (df['Age'] < 50), 'Age'] = 40
df['Age'] = df['Age'].apply(lambda x: str(x) + 's')
```

Here, we round down ages (such as any age in the 20s is replaced with 20), then we convert this to a string and add "s" to the end. Next, we use suppression on the zip code to replace some values with an asterisk:

```
df['Zipcode'] = df['Zipcode'].apply(lambda x: str(x)[:3] + '**')
```

Our data now looks like this:

	Age	Zipcode	HIV diagnosis
0	20s	804**	Positive
1	20s	810**	Negative
2	30s	804**	Positive
3	30s	802**	Negative
4	40s	810**	Negative
5	40s	802**	Negative

Figure 20.2: Our HIV results dataset after generalization and suppression

This process of *k*-anonymization leaves our data in several groups, called equivalence classes. Let's label them and print them out:

```
df['equiv_class'] = [0, 1, 0, 2, 1, 2]
df.sort_values(by='equiv_class')
```

Our equivalence classes are:

	Age	Zipcode	HIV diagnosis	equiv_class
0	20s	804**	Positive	0
2	30s	804**	Positive	0
1	20s	810**	Negative	1
4	40s	810**	Negative	1
3	30s	802**	Negative	2
5	40s	802**	Negative	2

Figure 20.3: Our HIV results dataset after generalization and suppression and with equivalence classes. The data is 2-anonymous.

We can see each equivalence class has two people in it, so our data is 2-anonymous. There is no exact way to determine the ideal value of k for k-anonymity, although there are some methods for trying to estimate it, such as k-Optimize. It should be noted that k-anonymity doesn't work well for high-dimensional datasets.

We can see there are some problems with the dataset and sensitive information could be leaked. For example, if we know John is in his 20s and in the 80401 zip code, we could infer from the released data that John has HIV. This is called a homogeneity attack, where labels in the sensitive class are identical. Since both people in equivalence class 0 are HIV positive, this is possible. We can also use a background knowledge attack to infer the identity of someone in a dataset. For example, if we know there are only a few people of a certain age group in a certain area code (perhaps from census data), we might be able to deduce someone's identity that way.

The k-anonymity method is the oldest privacy method of those we will discuss here and has some problems as we have shown. One improvement on this is l-diversity, which seeks to make sure the sensitive class is at least diverse by a factor of l. This factor of l can simply be the counts of unique class labels. In our example above, we have 1-diversity since the class labels are homogeneous in each equivalence class. If each of our equivalence classes had at least 1 positive and 1 negative HIV result, then we would have 2-diversity. There are ways to measure l-diversity with more advanced math than simply counting the unique classes. However, this can still be an issue for privacy. If we learn a distribution of sensitive classes from the data, we can infer the probability that someone may have a sensitive class label.

An even further improvement upon *l*-diversity is *t*-closeness. This method ensures each equivalence class' distribution of the sensitive class is within a factor of *t* of the distribution of the whole table.

We can measure the distance between distributions in several ways, but the simplest is variational distance. We simply take the difference between unique values in the two distributions. A more advanced method is the **Kullback-Liebler (KL)** distance, which uses entropy and cross-entropy calculations.

 A paper that goes over the calculations and more examples of *k*-anonymity, *l*-diversity, and *t*-closeness can be found here: `https://www.cs.purdue.edu/homes/ninghui/papers/t_closeness_icde07.pdf`.

Unfortunately, there is not a comprehensive Python package that can anonymize data or measure *k*-anonymity, *l*-diversity, and *t*-closeness at the time of writing (pyARXaaS is capable, but uses a non-free API). However, there is an R package, `sdcMicro`. It is possible to run R through Python with the `rpy2` package in Python. There is one Python package that is in early development at the time of writing that can do some basic generalization for *k*-anonymity, called `crowds` (`https://github.com/leo-mazz/crowds`).

Differential privacy

One other method for protecting privacy that has been created is differential privacy. This concerns releasing databases for queries, especially for statistical queries such as means, sums, and machine learning models. The idea is that an attacker could execute a series of queries on a public database and use that to infer sensitive information about a person. Differential privacy adds random noise to the data each time it is queried so that each person in the dataset has roughly the same amount of privacy. The amount of privacy can be tuned with a parameter, epsilon (ε), which increases privacy as ε gets smaller. There are a few Python packages for differential privacy, such as IBM's package for ML (`https://github.com/IBM/differential-privacy-library`) and a wrapper for Google's differential privacy package, PyDP (`https://github.com/OpenMined/PyDP`).

Using data science for the common good

Since data science is a powerful field and often data scientists are highly paid, it's good to give back to the community by using data science for the common good. There are several ways to do this, and it can even be used as a way to break into data science. For example, we can volunteer our skills for non-profit organizations through organizations like DataKind (`https://www.datakind.org/`) and Solve for Good (`https://solveforgood.org/`).

There are also several **data science for social good** (**DSSG**) fellowships throughout the US and Europe, which are often 3-month summer programs where data scientists work on projects that benefit the community. This includes programs at several universities such as Stanford and Carnegie Mellon. Also, data science competitions such as at Kaggle and DrivenData will have some competitions focused on the common good. DrivenData in particular focuses on data science for the common good. Doing a data science project with one of these fellowships or volunteer projects can be a good way to develop your skills and create a portfolio piece for your resume. And if you place highly in a competition (such as in the top 10), you could use that as a portfolio piece.

Other ethical considerations

We covered many of the ethical concerns with data science already, but there are a host of others. Of course, there are common-sense ethics, such as don't steal data or do something purposely malicious. However, other more subtle issues are present as well. In this section, we'll look at:

- The transparency of ML systems
- Cherry-picking information for statistics
- Conflicts of interest
- Web scraping
- Terms of service
- Robot rights for AI

When we create an ML system, it may or may not be in society's best interest to publish the algorithm and supporting work. For example, the facial recognition algorithms used for police may benefit from more transparency and openness, but publishing ML related to law enforcement could enable criminals to game the system.

Another example is the COMPAS system, which is software used by US courts to determine if someone is likely to commit crimes again. On the one hand, being more transparent with the software could help the community point out flaws and bias issues. On the other hand, it could allow criminals to exploit the system for their own benefit. In general, we are seeing a shift towards more open-source software for a variety of reasons, so it seems in many cases making ML and data science software more open-source is better.

Another concern is when calculating statistics, such as summary statistics of health data, we can throw out certain data so that the statistics match our expectations. In general, we want to be very careful about throwing data out when doing analysis, especially if it significantly changes the outcome.

Closely related to cherry-picking is conflicts of interest. If, for example, our research funding depends on obtaining good results, we would be tempted to alter the data in order to show good results. There are multiple examples of people with PhDs losing their PhD and professorship after it was found they falsified or manipulated data (`https://en.wikipedia.org/wiki/List_of_scientific_misconduct_incidents`). Of course, we can also manipulate data to suit a particular narrative we want to tell. This can happen intentionally or even less obviously when cleaning and preparing data. Thinking through our cleaning and preparation steps carefully, and consulting with others, can help avoid problems there.

We discussed some of the ethics of web scraping in *Chapter 7, Web Scraping*. As a reminder, the laws and court rulings around web scraping are still being developed and will likely be constantly evolving. At the moment of writing, the most recent court case with HiQ versus LinkedIn has determined that any public-facing data is OK to scrape. However, this could change in the future, as it used to be different in the early 2000s. When web scraping, we should be careful to not over encumber any servers we are accessing by respecting API limits and not sending too many requests too fast.

The **terms of service (TOS)** of websites constitute another ethical concern. Many websites and services change their terms of service, often to the detriment of the consumer. Although this is legally allowed, it can still be unethical. If we are part of a group or the person deciding on TOS alterations, we should think carefully about the ethical ramifications of our TOS and any changes. One site that is useful for quickly evaluating many websites' TOS is `tosdr.org`.

Lastly, as machine learning, and especially reinforcement learning, becomes more advanced, we may get to a point where we need to consider what rights and responsibilities a robot or AI has. An important and related example is self-driving cars, where not everyone agrees who should be at fault if a self-driving car kills someone. We are already seeing self-driving software contribute to deaths with Tesla's autopilot software, and this issue will become more important over time as self-driving cars develop further and are used more widely.

Self-driving cars closely relate to how ML algorithms are used and how much trust we place in them. For example, if an ML algorithm prevents someone from getting a loan, there isn't a clear and standardized methodology for evaluating the fairness of the decision and if the ML algorithm is ethical. One of the books on this where you can learn more is *Weapons of Math Destruction* by Cathy O'Neil.

Although machine learning tends to have many of the most eye-catching aspects of data science ethics, all steps of the data science process have ethical concerns we should watch out for.

One good summary of these is the DrivenData data science ethics checklist, found here: `https://github.com/drivendataorg/deon#default-checklist`. It covers ethical concerns over the full data science process, from data collection through model deployment.

Test your knowledge

Using the credit card default dataset in this chapter's GitHub `data` folder, generalize and suppress the data so that our *k*-anonymity and *l*-diversity is greater than 1. The sensitive class is the `LIMIT_BAL` column, or the credit limit for each person.

Summary

In this chapter, we examined many of the ethical and privacy concerns for data scientists. These range from accidentally leaking personal information about an individual to who takes the blame when a ML system leads to catastrophic consequences. We started by looking at how ML algorithms can exhibit bias, such as gender and racial bias. Some of the examples we saw were how facial recognition software used by police can cause or augment racial biases in policing, and how voice recognition software usually doesn't work as well for people who weren't in the training dataset. We learned some ways to combat this bias, including sampling techniques like SMOTE, generating synthetic data with GANs, and simply collecting more data.

Next, we saw how privacy can be breached in clever ways by combining so-called anonymized datasets with public data such as census data. We also saw that many laws have been enacted around the globe to protect privacy, and how we should be careful to respect these laws if we are offering a service to citizens of different jurisdictions.

If sharing or publishing data, there are ways to protect the privacy of individuals in the dataset. For publishing aggregations of raw data, the principles of k-anonymity, l-diversity, and t-closeness can be used to reduce the likelihood of an attacker exposing people in the dataset. Each person has a sensitive class (or multiple classes), such as a disease diagnosis. These anonymization methods group people into equivalence groups, where each group has identical quasi-identifiers such as an age range and income range. The minimum number of people in the group defines our value for k, while the level of l can be calculated in a few ways (the simplest being the number of unique class labels for the sensitive class). Lastly, t-closeness ensures the distributions of the sensitive class are within a threshold t of the overall distribution of the sensitive class in the entire data table.

Finally, we wrapped up by learning about some other ethical concerns related to data science, such as our responsibilities as data scientists and using a data science ethical checklist during the data science process.

We've learned a lot about data science throughout the book, but we haven't learned everything. Data science is a wide-ranging field with a plethora of possibilities. To be a serious data scientist, we should stay up-to-date with the latest developments and tools available to us, which we will learn about in the next and final chapter.

21

Staying Up to Date and the Future of Data Science

Throughout the book we've learned about many data science tools and techniques. But, as such a new and dynamic field, data science is constantly changing and evolving. New software packages and libraries are being released every week, libraries like TensorFlow have daily updates, and new statistical methods are being developed all the time. Staying up to date with data science is as important as building a solid data science foundation. In this final chapter, we'll learn ways to stay current on data science developments, as well as discussing topics we didn't have time to cover in this book, including:

- Blogs, newsletters, books, and academic sources to keep an eye on
- Data science competition websites
- Learning platforms
- Cloud services
- Other places to keep an eye on
- Other data science topics we didn't cover
- The future of data science

At the end of the chapter, we'll discuss the future of data science and how staying up to date will help us be ready for data science's future. Let's start with some of the sources for staying current with the latest data science developments.

Blogs, newsletters, books, and academic sources

There are a huge number of websites for staying up to date on data science, and we'll cover some of the top sources at the time of writing. There is such a large number of different sources that it can be overwhelming. Try using a few different sources discussed below until you find the ones you like and stick to a few of them rather than trying to cover too much at once.

Blogs

Data science blogs post a variety of topics, from personal stories to data science tutorials. For example, you can learn how to land your first data science job through blog posts by reading tips from others and their stories. Some of the top general data science multi-author blog sites to keep an eye on are:

- towardsdatascience.com (TDS; hosted through medium.com)
- medium.com
- r-bloggers.com
- kdnuggets.com
- analyticsvidhya.com/blog

These blogs are nice because they cover a variety of data science subjects and include posts (such as tutorials) on Python, R, SQL, and other data science tools. Another category of blogs is learning resource blogs. These are learning platforms that also have blogs:

- datacamp.com/community/blog
- udacity.com/blog
- blog.udemy.com/data-science/

These blogs can be good but tend to also be promotions for their own platforms.

Yet another category is company blogs. New technology that's being developed and pioneered will sometimes first be publicly announced here. Some of these are:

- ai.googleblog.com
- deepmind.com/blog (owned by Google)
- aws.amazon.com/blogs/machine-learning
- ai.facebook.com/blog

The top cloud providers such as Google, Amazon, Baidu, and Azure often have more than one blog, and like the learning platforms, these can also be partly promotions for their own services. The DeepMind blog listed above is particularly interesting because they are one of the world's leaders in developing reinforcement learning and have accomplished impressive feats such as beating the world champion in a game of Go with AIs they created.

Some academic institutions will have data science or related blogs as well (like Berkeley: `https://bids.berkeley.edu/resources/blog-data-science-insights`). As you'd expect, these tend to be more academically focused, posting about studies and education topics more frequently than other more general blogs.

Lastly, data science competition sites have blogs, such as Kaggle (`medium.com/kaggle-blog`) and DrivenData (`drivendata.co/blog.html`). These often feature interviews with competition winners.

There are many more blogs than we covered here, and certainly new blogs will appear over time. It doesn't hurt to take a look at a few of the top blogs listed above and even search for a few more and check them out regularly (weekly or monthly).

Newsletters

An even easier way to stay current than checking blogs is having emails periodically sent to you. Just as there are dozens (maybe even hundreds or thousands) of data science blogs out there, there are several data science and related newsletters. The only newsletter I currently subscribe to is The Batch from deeplearning.ai, although there are surely many other good newsletters out there. For example, a TDS article lists 13 good candidates here: `https://towardsdatascience.com/13-essential-newsletters-for-data-scientists-remastered-f422cb6ea0b0`. It can be helpful to sign up for one or a few data science newsletters so that when you check your email, you'll occasionally get an update of data science news.

Books

As you already know, Packt is an excellent source of data science books that can be used to learn data science and new data science developments, and is found online at `https://www.packtpub.com/`. Of course, there are several other publishers out there that cover data science as well. Amazon's online store can be a good place to find books too. Another place I've found helpful to discover data science books is O'Reilly's product, `learning.oreilly.com`, which has books and other resources from a variety of sources and publishers. With so many data science books, there are several lists of books out there.

In particular, this list of free data science books might be helpful: `https://www.learndatasci.com/free-data-science-books/`. Of particular note are the books *Introduction to Statistical Learning* (**ISLR**) and *The Elements of Statistical Learning* (**ESL**), which have been used by many data science teachers (including myself) and cover many of the principles behind machine learning techniques and statistics. ISLR also provides some examples in the R coding language.

Academic sources

Usually, the most cutting-edge research is published in academic journals. This includes academic journals like the Journal of Machine Learning Research (**JMLR**; `jmlr.org`), NeurIPS (for deep learning, `nips.cc/`), and many more. One place that tends to have lots of data science and related papers is arXiv (`arxiv.org`), which allows authors to "pre-print" their paper on arXiv and officially publish it in an academic journal later. There are other preprint databases like HAL (`hal.archives-ouvertes.fr/`), but arXiv seems to be the top choice for data science and machine learning topics.

A problem with academic journals and arXiv is that the signal to noise can be low. There can be a huge number of publications with minor improvements on previous methodologies, and a few papers that introduce radical new ideas. One way of dealing with this is to use an aggregator. One of the best at the time of writing is Arxiv Sanity Preserver (`arxiv-sanity.com/`), which allows us to sort and filter recent arXiv articles by their popularity and other metrics. In this way, we can see what the top new trends are in machine learning, data science, and deep learning (for example, with the *Top Hype* button). The most popular articles tend to be focused on deep learning at the time of writing. With Arxiv Sanity Preserver, we can create an account and have papers personally recommended to us by a recommendation system (a machine learning-based method).

One other site that can be used to wade through the arXiv ocean is `paperswithcode.com`. This collects academic papers that have corresponding code published on GitHub or another online code repository. Usually this allows us to run the example from the paper or use the new tools that were debuted in the paper. This has a nice advantage over papers posted without code, since translating academic language and complex math into code can be quite difficult.

Data science competition websites

Data science competition websites are great places to get ideas for how to solve data science problems, stay up to date with recent developments, and learn from others.

Perhaps the top data science competition website is `Kaggle.com`, but there are many more such as `drivendata.com`. One aggregator for these competitions is `mlcontests.com`. Since many of the competitions have to do with machine learning, that aggregator is specific to ML. However, some other places offer more general data science and analytics competitions, such as `hackerrank.com/contests`.

Kaggle is its own platform at this point, combining data science competitions, dataset hosting, courses, and a social media-like aspect. By simply scrolling through your newsfeed on Kaggle, you can see some of the cutting-edge data science and ML techniques being used by others. It can also be a place to learn some tricks for coding, although you can also learn bad habits. Many people coding on Kaggle do not use best practices, so be careful not to blindly copy everything others are doing there.

Online learning platforms

Utilizing online learning platforms is a great way to stay up to date and constantly improve your skills. Kaggle, along with everything else it offers, also has a set of free courses they continuously add to. These cover the basics of Python programming through to more advanced topics like neural network tools and techniques. Several other sites can be used to learn data science as well, including:

- DataCamp
- Dataquest
- Udacity
- Udemy
- Manning's liveProject
- Coursera
- `fast.ai`

There are, of course, many other places too. However, those listed above are general (except `fast.ai`) and cover a variety of topics. They each have different methods for delivering content. DataCamp and Dataquest are similar, and their main product is a combination of fill-in-the-blank code with written guides and video presentations. DataCamp is branching out into other methods like more open-ended projects as well. Udacity tends to have larger courses and nano-degrees that combine videos with short quizzes and coding projects. Udemy is a smorgasbord of different courses all created by different people – anyone can create and post their own course. Manning has liveProjects, which are guided but somewhat open-ended projects in data science and other topics. Coursera tends to be more like a university course, with lectures and assignments. `fast.ai` is also a Python package for deep learning, and has courses on neural network theory and usage.

These sites also have corresponding blogs, so utilizing their blogs and course materials can be a good way to learn more data science tools and techniques.

There are other learning platforms and systems as well, such as bootcamps. This includes places like Springboard, Galvanize, and General Assembly. These are much more involved and expensive options in most cases. However, the data science bootcamps will also have corresponding blogs and other resources for learning more data science, and importantly, can plug you into a network that can help with landing a data science or related job.

Cloud services

As we saw earlier in the section on blogs, cloud providers with data science and machine learning offerings will have blogs on data science. Watching the cloud services space and what they are offering for data science and ML can be a good way to keep a close eye on where data science is going. Cloud providers develop new products to make data science and ML easier to do and will also roll out more advanced tools if they can. They usually have conferences, blogs, and other resources for sharing what they are doing. For example, the AWS re:Invent conference is usually published on YouTube and will cover upcoming AWS products and recent advances, including data science products.

Other places to keep an eye on

There are many other places we can monitor for the latest data science developments. This includes social media sites, like YouTube, Twitter, Facebook, LinkedIn, and Reddit. We've also used GitHub throughout the book (and the code and data for the book are published there). GitHub, GitLab, and other online code repositories can also be a good place to see what is being developed in data science.

Some of the data science toolkits can also be a place to look, such as Anaconda's blog and H2O. Lastly, there are local meetups (for example, found through `meetup.com`) for data science, ML, and more related topics in most (if not all) major cities around the globe. Local meetups are also a great way to network and potentially get a job or consulting gig.

Strategies for staying up to date

Everyone will develop their own strategy for staying up to date, and this will depend on your personality and situation in life. For me, I have been teaching and creating course materials frequently since I have worked as a professor for four years at the time of writing.

That has been a good way to stay up to date on data science developments and creating teaching materials (even something like writing a TDS or other blog post) can be a good way to stay current.

I also subscribe to The Batch newsletter from deeplearning.ai, and peruse Kaggle, Twitter, and YouTube when I can. Through working on my own projects and code for teaching and work, I also learn about new data science developments. Occasionally I will visit specific blogs, like Google's blogs and KDnuggets. Students and colleagues will also send me resources to check out. One last method I've used is the Google News app, which suggests news stories based on your interests.

Other data science topics we didn't cover

Although we covered the data science foundation and much of the tools we need for basic data science, we couldn't cover everything. Some of the topics we left uncovered are:

- Recommender systems
- Networks and graph analysis
- Machine learning explainability
- Test-driven development (TDD)
- Reinforcement learning
- Neural networks

Recommender systems were mentioned in the book, and are used to recommend things like products, movies, or articles to people. They can be based on previous preferences of a user or combine data from many users. Packt does have one book on recommender systems in Python, *Hands-On Recommendation Systems with Python* by Rounak Banik. There are also many other resources out there for learning recommendation systems and creating and maintaining recommender systems can be an important job that can take one or several people to accomplish.

Graph analysis encompasses networks, such as social media networks. We can generate features from network systems, such as the connections between nodes and more. Networks make for impressive visualizations. Graph analysis can also be used for things like user tracking and authentication security. Again, there are many places we can learn more about graph theory and network analysis, but one book from Packt on the subject is *Network Science with Python and NetworkX Quick Start Guide* by Edward L. Platt. Machine learning explainability is a newer facet of data science, and stems from the fact that many of the more advanced ML models are "black boxes," meaning we don't know why they do what they do.

For example, an ML model could fail miserably with a certain set of data and it can be hard to figure out why. With the tree-based models we saw, such as random forests and gradient boosting models, understanding the model's behavior becomes complex. This gets even worse with complicated neural network models with millions of parameters learned by the model. There are a few books by Packt on the subject, including books on interpretable machine learning and explainable AI. One book that is available online is *Interpretable Machine Learning* by Christoph Molnar, which covers topics including **Shapley additive explanations (SHAP)** and **local interpretable model-agnostic explanations (LIME)**. SHAP and LIME are ways of explaining individual predictions by a model, and one package in Python for LIME is `lime`.

Another aspect that may be a part of your data science work is test driven development, or TDD. This is a software development process that entails writing tests for the code we write. The idea is to improve the reliability of our software and to make sure we don't break things as we develop and modify our codebase. Depending on your path, this may not be necessary. Some people think data science is moving more toward software engineering, in which case TDD will be important. But in other cases, data science is moving away from software engineering (such as using cloud-based or other GUIs).

Although we discussed **reinforcement learning (RL)** briefly, we didn't cover it in depth. Reinforcement learning is used to create an agent that can operate in an environment with a particular goal, such as a robot trying to navigate a maze. Certain actions can be programmed to provide a reward, and others a loss. One of the more basic RL algorithms is Q-learning, although some of the most advanced methods at the time of writing use neural networks, such as deep Q-learning.

Lastly, neural networks (deep learning) is a topic we didn't cover because it is essentially an entire specialized field. As we saw with arXiv, most of the popular papers there have to do with neural networks. Although some packages make them easy to use (like `fast.ai`), there are a huge number of caveats and specifics that are important when it comes to creating neural networks. For advanced practitioners with complex problems, neural networks can sometimes be the best solution. But as always, it's better to try something simpler first. There are a huge number of resources for learning more about neural networks and deep learning, including several books from Packt and others.

The future of data science

While no one can exactly predict the future, we can observe the current trends and extrapolate from there. We've seen the data science project life cycle and many of the tools throughout the book and have seen some trends. To start, we saw how automation tools are increasing in capability.

For example, we used the `pycaret` Python package to prepare data and execute autoML. There are several other autoML packages and many of them have been created in the past few years as of the time of writing this book. PyCaret and other autoML packages also carry out some automatic data cleaning and preparation, such as feature engineering. Tools for automating data cleaning and preparation should see rapid growth in the near future as well. For some people, this is scary, and people ask if automation will replace data scientists. The answer is no, at least not completely. Just like automation in other industries (like car manufacturing) has not completely replaced human workers, so too will it be in data science for some time. If we get to the point where data science can be nearly or completely automated, these autoML and other data science automation tools are another skill or tool to learn and use as data scientists. The experience of using the latest and best tools and knowledge of how to properly use them will likely be valuable for some time.

Closely related to automation are cloud tools. The major cloud providers are releasing and refining their autoML tools. Other related tools for big data and databases are also being constantly improved. Staying up to date with the latest cloud tools is important since they offer enormous potential and huge productivity gains. These cloud tools and other tools like PyCaret allow for more automated deployment of ML algorithms at scale as well. What used to be a harrowing task of configuring dozens or hundreds of settings and lines of code can now be done in a few lines of code or mouse clicks. Again, this is a tool to leverage as a data scientist and not something to fear.

Another trend likely to continue into the future is open-source software, like the Python packages we used in this book. Even major companies are publishing some of their top tools as open-source, such as Facebook's PyTorch and other Python packages. As data scientists, we can contribute to these open-source projects if we have the time, which contributes to the common good.

We will likely see data science used in more and more places over time as the Internet of Things is expanded and exponentially more data is created. Anywhere there is data, we can use data science. With the massive increase in data, we may see the advent of data markets or marketplaces where proprietary data or models can be purchased or rented. We are already seeing the beginnings of this with some of AWS and Google's cloud data storage solutions where we can pay per access to some data. There are also APIs for machine learning that we can utilize and pay for according to our usage. Again, these are good tools to stay on top of and learn how to use.

Lastly, data science will continue to splinter into specializations. We talked about related fields and specializations in *Chapter 1, Introduction to Data Science*, but even more specializations will arise over time. Currently, data engineering is growing rapidly, but the next specializations may be in data science or machine learning applied to specific fields, such as healthcare, finance, and web services.

Summary

As we've seen in this chapter, there are many ways to stay up to date with data science, such as blogs, data science competition sites, academic papers, social media, and more. It's important to keep up to date with data science and machine learning if you plan on using them, because it is a field that's still undergoing rapid growth. New algorithms and techniques are being created all the time, sometimes powered by new hardware and software developments.

At this point, our journey through this book is complete. However, your journey as a data scientist is just beginning. There is a lot more to learn, but take what you've learned so far and go do something fun and interesting with data science!

packt.com

Subscribe to our online digital library for full access to over 7,000 books and videos, as well as industry leading tools to help you plan your personal development and advance your career. For more information, please visit our website.

Why subscribe?

- Spend less time learning and more time coding with practical eBooks and Videos from over 4,000 industry professionals
- Improve your learning with Skill Plans built especially for you
- Get a free eBook or video every month
- Fully searchable for easy access to vital information
- Copy and paste, print, and bookmark content

At www.packt.com, you can also read a collection of free technical articles, sign up for a range of free newsletters, and receive exclusive discounts and offers on Packt books and eBooks.

Other Books You May Enjoy

If you enjoyed this book, you may be interested in these other books by Packt:

Cleaning Data for Effective Data Science

David Mertz

ISBN: 9781801071291

- Ingest and work with common data formats like JSON, CSV, SQL and NoSQL databases, PDF, and binary serialized data structures
- Understand how and why we use tools such as pandas, SciPy, scikit-learn, Tidyverse, and Bash
- Apply useful rules and heuristics for assessing data quality and detecting bias, like Benford's law and the 68-95-99.7 rule
- Identify and handle unreliable data and outliers, examining z-score and other statistical properties

- Impute sensible values into missing data and use sampling to fix imbalances
- Use dimensionality reduction, quantization, one-hot encoding, and other feature engineering techniques to draw out patterns in your data
- Work carefully with time series data, performing de-trending and interpolation

Pandas 1.x Cookbook, Second Edition

Matthew Harrison

Theodore Petrou

ISBN: 9781839213106

- Master data exploration in pandas through dozens of practice problems
- Group, aggregate, transform, reshape, and filter data
- Merge data from different sources through pandas SQL-like operations
- Create visualizations via pandas hooks to matplotlib and seaborn
- Use pandas, time series functionality to perform powerful analyses
- Import, clean, and prepare real-world datasets for machine learning
- Create workflows for processing big data that doesn't fit in memory

Python Object-Oriented Programming, Fourth Edition

Steven F. Lott

Dusty Phillips

ISBN: 9781801077262

- Implement objects in Python by creating classes and defining methods
- Extend class functionality using inheritance
- Use exceptions to handle unusual situations cleanly
- Understand when to use object-oriented features, and more importantly, when not to use them
- Discover several widely used design patterns and how they are implemented in Python
- Uncover the simplicity of unit and integration testing and understand why they are so important
- Learn to statically type check your dynamic code
- Understand concurrency with asyncio and how it speeds up programs

Packt is searching for authors like you

If you're interested in becoming an author for Packt, please visit authors.packtpub.com and apply today. We have worked with thousands of developers and tech professionals, just like you, to help them share their insight with the global tech community. You can make a general application, apply for a specific hot topic that we are recruiting an author for, or submit your own idea.

Share your thoughts

Now you've finished *Practical Data Science with Python*, we'd love to hear your thoughts! Scan the QR code below to go straight to the Amazon review page for this book and share your feedback or leave a review on the site that you purchased it from.

https://packt.link/r/1801071977

Your review is important to us and the tech community and will help us make sure we're delivering excellent quality content.

Index

A

A/B testing 267-269
  methods 269
academic sources, data science 568
accuracy 357, 358
AdaBoost
  working 442, 443
ADASYN sampling 378
adjusted R² 393
advanced search methods 416
Akaike Information Criterion (AIC) 334, 393
Alexa 550
Anaconda
  installing 26
  used, for installing Python 26
ANOVA 296, 297
  assumptions 272
  used, for testing between several groups 270
Anvil 541
API wrappers
  using 226-230
Application Programming
     Interfaces (APIs) 16, 74
  using, to collect data 223-225
apply function
  using 124
artificial intelligence (AI) 18
AUC score 367, 370
autocorrelation 398
automated dashboarding 541, 542, 546, 547
automated reporting 541
  options 541
automatic machine learning (AutoML) 6
  solutions 419, 420
  using, with PyCaret 419

B

backslash character 494
backslashes, Python regex
  reference link 494
backward selection 283
bagging 433
bag-of-words (BoW) methodology 504
base Python
  files, loading with 72
  files, reading with 72
  files, writing with 72
basic text analysis 505
Bayesian
  versus frequentist 244
Bayesian A/B testing methods
  reference link 269
Bayesian Information Criterion (BIC) 334
Bayesian search
  using 414, 415
Bayes' Theorem 242-244
bell curve 245
Bernoulli distribution 253
BernoulliNB 344
bias 550
bias-variance trade-off 283
big data 17
  regression models 401
binary classification 280
binary cross-entropy 336
binning 311
binomial distribution 253, 254
bitcoin price data
  analyzing 126-128
  wrangling 126-128
blogs, data science 566, 567
books, data science 567

Boolean mask 113
Booleans 54
boosted models 440
  training, on GPU 449
boosting
  reference link 441
  working 441
boosting algorithms
  early stopping, using with 455
Bootstrap sampling 259
boxplot
  creating 135-140
break keyword 52
bs4
  using, to extract data from webpages 220
built-in feature selection 283
built-in JSON module
  using 74-76
built-in Python packages, and modules
  reference link 57
business communication
  skills 15
business intelligence (BI) 16
business understanding
  skills 15

C

C4.5 430
C5.0 430
California Consumer Privacy Act (CCPA) 554
Calinski-Harabasz Index
  reference link 474
Calinski Harabasz score 473
CART (classification and regression
      trees) 429
CatBoost 441, 453
  advantages 453
  using 454, 455
CatBoost, hyperparameters
  reference link 454
catboost package 453
categorical columns
  simplifying 313-315
CategoricalNB 344
category datatype, Pandas' documentation
  reference link 291

cd command 34
central limit theorem 258
chi-squared test 295-297
classes 61
classification 280, 521-523
classification algorithm performance
  evaluating, with metrics 355
classification data
  balancing 375
  sampling 375
classification metrics, sklearn documentation
  reference link 375
classification models, sklearn documentation
  reference link 352
classification report plot
  from yellowbrick 366
classifiers, binary classification task
  reference link 424
CLIs (command-line interfaces) 33
cloud services 570
cloud tools 12-14
clustering
  metrics 472, 473
clustering performance evaluation
  reference link 474
clusters
  examining 478-482
coefficient of determination 392
Cohen's Kappa 359
coin flip example 238, 239
colormap, matplotlib documentation
  reference link 480
command line 33
  basics 34
comma-separated values (CSV) 96
Comment Extraction and Parsing
  reference link 228
competition websites, data science 568, 569
ComplementNB 344
conda 38, 39
  reference link 38
conditional probability 239
conditionals 54
confidence intervals 260
confusion matrix 360-363
Console tab 217
Consumer Data Protection Act (CDPA) 554

with sklearn 385-387
with statsmodels 388, 389
lists 47
  appending 48
  concatenating 47
  indexing 49
  length 48
  methods 47
  repetition 48
  sorting 48
literal period 495
local interpretable model-agnostic
    explanations (LIME) 572
logistic regression 347, 348
  for binary classification 324-326
  statmodels, using for 332-335
  with big data 342, 343
  working 328, 329
logistic regression algorithm 337
logit equation 329, 330
log-loss 336
loops 51-53
lowercasing 492, 493
ls command 35
lxml
  using, to extract data from webpages 218

M

machine learning
  reinforcement learning 281
  supervised learning 280
  types 280
  unsupervised learning 280
machine learning algorithms
  ethics 549
  performance and consequences,
    evaluating 552
machine learning classification
    algorithms 324
  k-nearest neighbors (KNN) 345, 346
  logistic regression 324-326
  Naïve Bayes 343, 344
machine learning engineer 16
machine learning (ML) 16
magic commands, IPython
  reference link 30

Manhattan distance 408
map function
  using 123, 124
markdown guide
  reference link 33
mathematics
  skills 14
math module, Python
  reference link 42
math module, Python 3.9
  reference link 42
Matplotlib
  used, for creating scatter plot 144-146
max_features hyperparameter 431
maximum likelihood estimation 336
mean absolute error (MAE) 395, 410, 429
mean squared error (MSE) 394, 395, 429
metrics, for evaluating classification
    algorithm performance 355
  accuracy 357, 358
  AUC score 367, 370
  Cohen's Kappa 359
  confusion matrix 360-363
  F1 score 364
  optimal cutoff threshold, selecting 370-374
  precision 364
  recall 364, 365
  ROC curve 367-370
  train-validation-test splits 356
Midcontinent Independent System Operator
    (MISO) 192
Minkowski distance 408
  reference link 346
missing value plots
  creating 150, 151
missing values 116-120
  examining 105, 106
ML biases
  decreasing 551
ML models
  number of features, optimizing 417, 418
MLOps 16
model
  computational complexity 352, 353
  predictions, obtaining from 326, 327
  selecting 351
modules 56

synthetic sampling methods 378, 379

T

tasks
  scheduling, to run automatically 547, 548
t-closeness 559
Team Data Science Process (TDSP) 21, 22
  reference link 22
term frequency inverse document frequency
    (TFIDF) 502, 503
terms of service (TOS) 231, 561
text 491
  cleaning, steps 180
  preparing, with spaCy 498-500
  reading, from PDF documents 187-191
  reading, from Word documents 178-180
  words and phrases, analyzing from 183-187
text cleaning 492-495
text preprocessing 491, 492
textract
  installation link 178
TFIDF vectors 502-504
Top2Vec
  reference link 520
topic modeling 516
  with PyCaret 517-519
  with Top2Vec 520
train-validation-test splits 356
Tree-structured Parzen Estimator (TPE) 408
t-test 264
  assumptions 272
  variants 264
tuple 49
two-sample t-tests 267-269
two-sample z-tests 267-269
two-sided t-test 265, 266

U

underfitting 283
undersampling
  reference link 376
uniform distribution 254
univariate statistical selection 283
univariate statistics
  for feature selection 297, 298

univariate statistics feature selection 287
unsupervised learning 280, 515
unsupervised methods 488, 489
urllib
  using, to perform web scraping 206-208

V

variable importance 437
variables 46, 47
variance methods 297
variance thresholding 283-287
vectorization 129
violin plot
  creating 141-143
  reference link 143
virtual environments 39, 40
  creating 37
visualization, best practices
  plots, saving for reports and share 170
  using 161-169
visualization libraries
  in Python 134
Visual Studio 35
Visual Studio Code (VS Code) 35
  Python code, editing 36
voice recognition 550

W

WCSS for k-means clustering, sklearn
  reference link 473
web scraping
  ethics 231
  legality 230-232
  performing, with urllib 206-208
websocket 230
Weibull distribution 256
Word2Vec
  reference link 501
wordclouds 510
word collocations 513
Word documents
  insights, extracting from 180-183
  parsing 178
  processing 178
  text, reading from 178-180

Made in the USA
Middletown, DE
24 November 2021

53312283R00345